Data-Driven Modelling and Predictive Analytics in Business and Finance

Data-driven and AI-aided applications are next-generation technologies that can be used to visualize and realize intelligent transactions in finance, banking, and business. These transactions will be enabled by powerful data-driven solutions, IoT technologies, AI-aided techniques, data analytics, and visualization tools. To implement these solutions, frameworks will be needed to support human control of intelligent computing and modern business systems. The power and consistency of data-driven competencies are a critical challenge, and so is developing explainable AI (XAI) to make data-driven transactions transparent.

Data-Driven Modelling and Predictive Analytics in Business and Finance covers the need for intelligent business solutions and applications. Explaining how business applications use algorithms and models to bring out the desired results, the book covers:

- Data-driven modelling
- Predictive analytics
- Data analytics and visualization tools
- AI-aided applications
- Cybersecurity techniques
- Cloud computing
- IoT-enabled systems for developing smart financial systems.

This book was written for business analysts, financial analysts, scholars, researchers, academics, professionals, and students so they may be able to share and contribute new ideas, methodologies, technologies, approaches, models, frameworks, theories, and practices.

Advances in Computational Collective Intelligence

Edited by
Dr. Subhendu Kumar Pani
Principal, Krupajal Group of Institutions, India

Published

Applications of Machine Learning and Deep Learning on Biological Data
By Faheem Syeed Masoodi, Mohammad Tabrez Quasim, Syed Nisar Hussain Bukhari, Sarvottam Dixit, and Shadab Alam
ISBN: 978-1-032-214375

Artificial Intelligence Techniques in Power Systems Operations and Analysis
By Nagendra Singh, Sitendra Tamrakar, Arvind Mewara, and Sanjeev Kumar Gupta
ISBN: 978-1-032-294865

Technologies for Sustainable Global Higher Education
By Maria José Sousa, Andreia de Bem Machado, and Gertrudes Aparecida Dandolini
ISBN: 978-1-032-262895

Forthcoming

Explainable AI and Cybersecurity
By Mohammad Tabrez Quasim, Abdullah Alharthi, Ali Alqazzaz, Mohammed Mujib Alshahrani, Ali Falh Alshahrani, and Mohammad Ayoub Khan
ISBN: 978-1-032-422213

Machine Learning in Applied Sciences
By M. A. Jabbar, Shankru Guggari, Kingsley Okoye, and Houneida Sakly
ISBN: 978-1-032-251721

Social Media and Crowdsourcing
By Sujoy Chatterjee, Thipendra P Singh, Sunghoon Lim, and Anirban Mukhopadhyay
ISBN: 978-1-032-386874

AI and IoT Technology and Applications for Smart Healthcare
By Alex Khang
ISBN: 978-1-032-684901

Innovations and Applications of Technology in Language Education
By Hung Phu Bui, Raghvendra Kumar, and Nilayam Kamila
ISBN: 978-1-032-560731

Data-Driven Modelling and Predictive Analytics in Business and Finance
By Alex Khang, Rashmi Gujrati, Hayri Uygun, R. K. Tailor, and Sanjaya Singh Gaur
ISBN: 978-1-032-60191-5

Data-Driven Modelling and Predictive Analytics in Business and Finance

Concepts, Designs, Technologies, and Applications

Edited by
Alex Khang, Rashmi Gujrati, Hayri Uygun,
R. K. Tailor, and Sanjaya Singh Gaur

CRC Press
Taylor & Francis Group
Boca Raton London New York

CRC Press is an imprint of the
Taylor & Francis Group, an **informa** business

First edition published 2025
by CRC Press
2385 Executive Center Drive, Suite 320, Boca Raton, FL 33431

and by CRC Press
4 Park Square, Milton Park, Abingdon, Oxon, OX14 4RN

CRC Press is an imprint of Taylor & Francis Group, LLC

ISBN: 9781032601915 (hbk)
ISBN: 9781032600628 (pbk)
ISBN: 9781032618845 (ebk)

DOI: 10.1201/9781032618845

Typeset in Times
by Newgen Publishing UK

Contents

Preface

In today's ever-changing technology edge and unpredictable world, most companies are keen to leverage multi-faceted *Data-driven Modelling and Predictive Analytics in Business and Finance* to deploy and deliver next-generation smart businesses and industrial applications to their clients anywhere, anytime.

All kinds of connected business applications are collectively and/or individually enabled to be intelligent in their operations, offering, and output. Precisely speaking, data-driven and AI-aided applications are being touted as the next-generation technology to visualize and realize a bevy of intelligent transactions in finance and banking business. We are seeing a host of powerful data-driven solutions, IoT technologies, AI-aided techniques, data analytics and visualization tools, libraries, and relevant frameworks aimed at supporting human-controlled capabilities in intelligent computing and modern business systems that are used in the supply chain, agriculture, finance, and banking fields in the real world.

The power and consistency of data-driven competencies are being seen as a critical challenge. Experts and engineers insist on the unambiguous interpretability and explainability of financial system decisions. As people move towards an era of data-driven insights and insights-driven decisions, the aspect of explainable AI-empowered business systems is gaining strong attention from inventors. In this book, we cover the need for business solutions and applications. We then show how business applications uses algorithms and models to bring about the desired results.

This book targets a mixed audience of business analysts, financial analysts, scholars, researchers, academics, professionals, and students from different communities to share and contribute new ideas, methodologies, technologies, approaches, models, frameworks, theories, and practices to resolve the challenging issues associated with the leveraging of combating the six fields of data-driven modelling, predictive analytics, data analytics and visualization tools, AI-aided applications, cybersecurity techniques, cloud computing, and IoT-enabled systems for developing a smart financial systems in the era of Industrial Revolution 4.0.

Happy reading!
Alex Khang

Acknowledgments

The book *Data-driven Modelling and Predictive Analytics in Business and Finance* is based on the design and implementation of topics related to the background of data-driven business modelling and analysis even more transparent, visualization graphs in business scenarios will be introduced in this book. We also will show how a variety of financial technologies can be used towards integrating data fabric solutions and how intelligent business applications can be used to greater effect. Moreover, we will also cover the integration of data-driven business applications to fulfill the goals of trusted AI-aided business solutions.

Planning and designing a book outline to introduce to readers across the globe is the passion and noble goal of the editor. To be able to make ideas a reality and the success of this book, have been the reward due to the efforts, knowledge, skills, expertise, experiences, enthusiasm, collaboration, and trust of the contributors.

To all respected contributors, we really say a big thanks for the high-quality chapters that we received from our human resource managers, talent management leaders, experts, professors, scientists, engineers, scholars, Ph.D. and postgraduate students, educators, and academic colleagues.

To all respected reviewers with whom we have had the opportunity to collaborate and monitor their hard work remotely, we acknowledge their tremendous support and valuable comments, not only for the book but also for future book projects.

We also express our deep gratitude for all the areas of discussion, advice, support, motivation, sharing, collaboration, and inspiration we received from our faculty, contributors, educators, professors, scientists, scholars, engineers, and academic colleagues.

And, last but not least, we are extremely grateful to our publisher CRC Press (Taylor & Francis Group) for their wonderful support in ensuring the timely processing of the manuscript and in making this book available to readers soonest.

Thank you, everyone.

Alex Khang

About the Editors

Alex Khang is a Professor of Information Technology, D.Sc. D.Litt., and a AI and Data scientist, AI and Data Science Research Center, Global Research Institute of Technology and Engineering, North Carolina, United States.

Rashmi Gujrati is a Professor, Campus Director, and Dean of International Affairs at Kamal Gandhi Memorial Ayurvedic College, Nawanshahr, India.

Hayri Uygun holds a Ph.D. from Recep Tayyip Erdogan University, Institute of Social Sciences, Business Administration, Rize, Turkey.

R. K. Tailor is an expert in robotic process automation and robotic accounting and a Senior Associate Professor at the Department of Business Administration, Manipal University, Manipal, India.

Sanjaya Singh Gaur is a Clinical Professor of Marketing at the NYU School of Professional Studies in New York University, New York, United States.

Contributors

Klochko Alla
Department of Public Administration
Interregional Academy of Personnel
  Management
Kyiv, Ukraine

Radhika Baidya
Amity School of Communication
Amity University
Nodia, Uttar Pradesh, India

Dishant Banga
Bridgetree
Fort Mill, South Carolina, USA

Dishant Banga
Bridgetree
Fort Mill, South Carolina, USA

Hemant Bhanawat
School of Commerce
NMIMS Deemed-to-be-University
Chandigarh, India

T. Daniya
Department of Information Technology
GMR Institute of Technology
Rajam, Andra Pradesh, India

Namrata Dhanda
Department of Computer Science and
  Engineering
Amity University Uttar Pradesh
Lucknow Campus, India

Piyush Gupta
Maharana Pratap Govt. PG College
Saiyapurwa, Hardoi, Uttar Pradesh,
  India

E. Gurumoorthi
Department of Information Technology
CMR College of Engineering & Tech
Hyderabad, India

Shaik Himam Saheb
The ICFAI Foundation for Higher
  Education
Hyderabad, India

Semenets-Orlova Inna
Department of Public Administration
PhD (in Politics)
Interregional Academy of Personnel
  Management
Kyiv, Ukraine

Babasaheb Jadhav
D. Y. Patil Vidyapeeth (Deemed to be
  University)
Global Business School & Research
  Centre
Pune, India

Harshita Jadwani
Pranveer Singh Institute of Technology
Kanpur, Uttar Pradesh, India

Luke Jebaraj
Electrical and Electronics Engineering
P.S.R. Engineering College
Sivakasi, Tamil Nadu, India

Cherri Kallimal Aishwarya
The ICFAI Foundation for Higher
  Education
Hyderabad, India

A. Kannagi
School of Computer Science &
  Information Technology
JAIN (Deemed-to-be University)
Bengaluru, Karnataka, India

Amita Kapoor
University of Oxford
Wellington Square, Oxford OX1 2JD,
  United Kingdom

M. P. Karthikeyan
School of Computer Science &
    Information Technology
Jain (Deemed-to-be-University)
Bengaluru, Karnataka, India

Chinnadurai Kathiravan
VIT Business School
Vellore Institute of Technology
Vellore, Tamil Nadu, India

Harpreet Kaur Channi
Department of electrical engineering
Chandigarh University
Gharuan, Mohali, India

R. Kavitha
School of Computer Science &
    Information Technology
Jain (Deemed-to-be-University)
Bengaluru, Karnataka, India

Varun Kesavan
VIT Business School
VIT University
Vellore, Tamil Nadu, India

Alex Khang
Department of AI and Data Science
Global Research Institute of Technology
    and Engineering
North Carolina, United States

Kewal Krishan Sharma
School of Computer Science and
    Applications
IIMT University
Meerut, Uttar Pradesh, India

K. Krishnaveni
Department of Computer Science
Sri S. Ramasamy Naidu Memorial
    College
Sattur, Tamilnadu, India

Bratchykova Kristina
Bratchykova Krystyna—LLC "TPK-
    Center" 2A
Livoberezhniy BC, Kyiv, Ukraine

Ashish Kulkarni
Dr. D. Y. Patil B-School
Tathawade, Pune, Maharashtra, India

Pooja Kulkarni
Vishwakarma University
Kondhwa, Pune, Maharashtra, India

Sagar Kulkarni
MIT World Peace University
Kothrud, Pune, Maharashtra, India

Tarun Kumar Vashishth
School of Computer Science and
    Application
IIMT University Meerut
Uttar Pradesh, India

Bhupendra Kumar
School of Computer Science and
    Application
IIMT University Meerut
Uttar Pradesh, India

Ruhi Lal
Amity School of Communication
Amity University
Nodia, Uttar Pradesh, India

Romanova Lidia
Interregional Academy of Personnel
    Management
Frometivska, Kyiv, Ukraine

Sonam Mittal
Department of IT Madhyanchal
B K Birla Institute of Engineering &
    Technology
Pilani, Rajasthan, India

Shila Mondol
KIIT School of Management
KIIT University
Bhubaneswar, Odisha, India

Arpita Nayak
KIIT School of Management
KIIT University
Patia, Bhubaneswar, Odisha, India

Pushpa Negi
NDIM—New Delhi Institute of
  Management
Tughlakabad Institutional Area
New Delhi, Delhi, India

M. S. Nidhya
Department of Computer
  Science & Information
  Technology
Jain (Deemed-to-be-University)
Bangalore, Karnataka, India

Atmika Patnaik
KIIT School of Management
Kalinga Institute of Industrial
  Technology
Bhubaneswar, Odisha, India

B. C. M. Patnaik
KIIT School of Management
KIIT University
Patia, Bhubaneswar, Odisha,
  India

V. Praba
Department of Computer Science
Sri S. Ramasamy Naidu Memorial
  College
Sattur, Viruthunagar, Tamil Nadu,
  India

Rajasekar Rangasamy
Department of Computer Science and
  Engineering
GITAM Technology
GITAM University
Bengaluru, Karnataka, India

Zehra Raza
Maharana Pratap Govt. PG College
Saiyapurwa
Hardoi, Uttar Pradesh, India

Ravinder Rena
DUT Business School
Durban University of Technology
ML Sultan Campus
Republic of South Africa

Shchokin Rostyslav
President of Interregional Academy of
  Personnel Management
Frometivska
Kyiv, Ukraine

Mykola Rudenko
National Institute of Cardiovascular
  Surgery of the National Academy of
  Medical Sciences
Kyiv, Ukraine

Sithankathan Sakthivel
Nehru Institute of Engineering and
  Technology
Coimbatore, India

Shiney Sam
School of Business and Management
Christ (Deemed to be University)
Bengaluru, Karnataka, India

Ramandeep Sandhu
School of Computer Science and
  Engineering
Lovely Professional University
Phagwara, Punjab, India

Ipseeta Satpathy
Senior KIIT School of Management
Kalinga Institute of Industrial
  Technology (KIIT)
Patia, Bhubaneswar, Odisha, India

Murugesan Selvam
Department of Commerce and Financial
  Studies
Bharathidasan University
Tiruchirappalli, Tamil Nadu, India

Dhanraj Sharma
Department of Financial Administration
Central University of Punjab
Punjab, India

Vikas Sharma
School of Computer Science and
  Application
IIMT University Meerut
Uttar Pradesh, India

Kajal Sharma
Amity School of Communication
Amity University
Noida, Uttar Pradesh, India

Himanshi Shukla
Pranveer Singh Institute of
  Technology
Kanpur, Uttar Pradesh, India

Janaki Singh Rathore
Gitam School of Business
Gitam University
Telangana, India

Nimisha Singh
Symbiosis Centre for Management and
  Human Resource Development
Symbiosis International University
Hinjawadi Rajiv Gandhi Infotech Park
Hinjawadi, Pune, Maharashtra,
  India

Chava Siri Lahari
The ICFAI Foundation for Higher
  Education
Hyderabad, India

Irisappane Soubache
Rajiv Gandhi College of Engineering
  and Technology
Puducherry, India

Sakthi Srinivasan K
VIT Business School
VIT University
Vellore, Tamil Nadu, India

Zakia Tasmin Rahman
Amity School of Communication
Amity University
Nodia, Uttar Pradesh, India

Ruchita Verma
Department of Financial Administration
Central University of Punjab
Punjab, India

Rajat Verma
Pranveer Singh Institute of Technology
Kanpur, Uttar Pradesh, India

Silky Vigg Kushwah
New Delhi Institute of Management
Tughlakabad Institutional Area
New Delhi, Delhi, India

1 Application of Data Technologies and Tools in Business and Finance Sectors

Dishant Banga and Alex Khang

1.1 INTRODUCTION

In today's data-driven world, businesses and organizations are inundated with vast amounts of data from various sources. These data hold the potential to provide valuable insights that can drive informed decision-making and lead to innovation. However, raw data are often complex, unstructured, and overwhelming, making it difficult to derive meaningful information from them. To unlock the true value of data, organizations rely on three essential components: data engineering, data analytics and data visualization. These three interrelated disciplines work together to transform raw data into actionable insights, empowering organizations to make data-driven decisions and gain a competitive advantage (Peddireddy & Banga, 2023).

1.2 RELATED WORK

- Data Engineering: Data engineering forms the foundation of the data lifecycle. It involves the processes and techniques required to design, build and maintain the infrastructure to handle and process large and diverse datasets efficiently. Data engineering focuses on data ingestion, data storage, data processing and data delivery. Data engineering begins with data ingestion, where data are collected from various sources, including databases, sensors, logs, and social media platforms. Data engineers employ techniques such as data extraction, transformation, and loading (ETL) to ingest the data into a central repository for further processing.
- Data Analytics: Data analytics is the process of examining, cleaning, transforming and interpreting data to uncover meaningful patterns, trends and insights. It involves the use of statistical and computational techniques to analyze data and extract valuable information. Data analytics can be categorized into four main types: descriptive analytics, diagnostic analytics, predictive analytics, and prescriptive analytics.

DOI: 10.1201/9781032618845-1

- Data Visualization: Data visualization is the art and science of presenting data in a visual format to facilitate understanding and communication. It involves the use of charts, graphs, maps and interactive dashboards to represent data in a visually compelling and accessible manner. The primary goal of data visualization is to simplify complex data and make them accessible to a broader audience. It complements data analytics by presenting data in a format that is easy to interpret, enabling stakeholders to grasp insights quickly and intuitively.

1.3 IMPACT OF DATA ENGINEERING, DATA ANALYTICS, AND DATA VISUALIZATION

The impact of data engineering, data analytics, and data visualization on organizations cannot be overstated. These interconnected disciplines have revolutionized how data are managed, analyzed, and presented, empowering organizations to make data-driven decisions, gain a competitive edge, and drive innovation.

- Data engineering has provided the foundation for efficient data processing, storage, and integration, enabling organizations to handle large and diverse datasets.
- Data analytics has empowered decision-makers with actionable insights, improved customer understanding, and optimized business processes.
- Data visualization has transformed data communication, making insights accessible and understandable to a broader audience.

As organizations continue to generate massive amounts of data, the seamless integration of data engineering, data analytics, and data visualization will remain essential for harnessing the full potential of data assets. With the continued advancements in technology and the growing importance of data in decision-making, these disciplines will continue to shape the future of data-driven organizations (Khanh & Khang, 2021).

1.4 DATA ENGINEERING

1.4.1 INTRODUCTION TO DATA ENGINEERING

Data engineering is a crucial field that involves the development, deployment and maintenance of systems and processes for collecting, storing, and analyzing data. It plays a fundamental role in enabling organizations to make data-driven decisions and gain insights from large volumes of structured and unstructured data. Data engineering is essential for ensuring data quality, reliability, and scalability in various industries such as finance, healthcare, e-commerce, and more (Khang, 2023).

1.4.2 EVOLUTION OF DATA ENGINEERING

With the ever-increasing volume, velocity, and variety of data being generated over the past few decades, data engineering has evolved significantly. Initially, data engineering focused primarily on batch processing and data warehousing. However, with the advent of big data technologies and real-time analytics, data engineering has transitioned to include technologies like Apache Hadoop, Apache Spark, and cloud-based data platforms. This shift has enabled organizations to access and process data at incredible speeds, enabling them to make decisions in real-time. As a result, data engineering has become a critical component of any organization's data strategy. For instance, many companies now use data engineering techniques to track customer behavior in real-time and dynamically adjust their offerings in response to customer preferences.

1.4.3 ROLE OF THE DATA ENGINEER

It is the responsibility of the data engineer to design, implement and maintain the data infrastructure. Their responsibilities include data ingestion, data transformation, data modeling, and data integration. They work closely with data scientists, analysts, and other stakeholders to understand their requirements and ensure the availability and accessibility of high-quality data for analysis and decision-making. Data engineers also monitor data pipelines and performance, evaluate data tools and technologies, and ensure compliance with data security policies. They are also responsible for troubleshooting data-related issues.

Data engineers are responsible for designing, building, and maintaining data pipelines that are used to capture, store, analyze, and visualize data. They also develop data models and ETL processes to support data-driven decision-making. Additionally, they provide input to data scientists and analysts to ensure that data are being used effectively and efficiently to maximize the value of the data and individual levels helps align efforts toward common objectives.

1.4.4 DATA ENGINEERING PROCESS

The data engineering process is a systematic approach to handle data efficiently. It involves several key stages.

- Data Ingestion: Data engineers collect data from diverse sources, such as databases, APIs, logs, and sensors. They use various techniques to extract and ingest data securely and efficiently.
- Data Storage: Once data are ingested, they need to be stored in appropriate repositories. Data engineers utilize data lakes, data warehouses, or NoSQL databases based on the specific needs and characteristics of the data.
- Data Processing: Data processing involves cleaning, transforming, and aggregating data to make them suitable for analysis and consumption. Data engineers implement data processing pipelines to ensure data are structured and consistent.
- Data Delivery: The final stage involves delivering processed data to end-users, data analysts, and data scientists. Data engineers often utilize APIs, visualization tools, and dashboards for data delivery, facilitating seamless access to insights.

1.4.5   DATA ENGINEERING TOOLS AND TECHNOLOGIES

There are numerous tools and technologies available for data engineers to perform their tasks effectively. Some popular tools include Apache Kafka for real-time data streaming, Apache Airflow for workflow management, Apache Flink for stream processing, and Apache Beam for unified batch and stream processing. Additionally, cloud-based platforms like Amazon Web Services (AWS), Google Cloud Platform (GCP), and Microsoft Azure provide a wide range of services for data engineering. All of these tools and technologies enable data engineers to quickly and effectively build data pipelines and perform data analysis.

For instance, AWS offers serverless computing services like AWS Lambda, which allows data engineers to quickly build data pipelines without the need for managing and provisioning servers. A plethora of tools and technologies support data engineering processes. Some essential ones include:

- Apache Hadoop: A distributed computing framework that enables processing vast datasets across clusters of computers, using the Hadoop Distributed File System (HDFS) and MapReduce.
- Apache Spark: A fast and versatile data processing engine, capable of performing in-memory data processing and supporting batch and real-time data processing.
- Amazon Web Services (AWS) and Google Cloud Platform (GCP): Cloud service providers offering scalable and cost-effective data storage and processing solutions.
- Apache Kafka: A distributed streaming platform that facilitates real-time data streaming and processing.
- Apache Airflow: A workflow management tool used for orchestrating and scheduling complex data workflows.

1.4.6   CHALLENGES IN DATA ENGINEERING

While data engineering offers numerous opportunities, it also presents various challenges. Some common challenges include data integration from heterogeneous sources, ensuring data quality and consistency, handling large-scale data processing, maintaining data privacy and security, and managing evolving data requirements. Data engineers must be equipped with the necessary skills and knowledge to address these challenges effectively. To be successful, data engineers must have a deep understanding of the data engineering process and be able to develop effective solutions. They must also have the skills to work with different technologies and tools, such as databases, programming languages, and analytical tools.

Finally, they must have the ability to manage, organize, and analyze large amounts of data. They must have strong attention to detail and the ability to work with stakeholders from different departments. They must also be able to communicate effectively and collaborate with other members of the team, and also possess excellent problem-solving and decision-making skills, as well as the ability to think strategically and act swiftly. Data engineering faces various challenges that must be addressed to ensure the effectiveness and reliability of data solutions:

- Data Quality: Ensuring data accuracy, consistency, and completeness is critical for making reliable decisions.
- Scalability: Managing large and ever-increasing volumes of data requires scalable infrastructure and processing techniques.
- Real-time Data Processing: Processing data in real-time demands efficient stream processing solutions.
- Data Security and Privacy: Protecting sensitive data and complying with data privacy regulations are essential for data engineering processes.

1.5 DATA ANALYTICS

1.5.1 INTRODUCTION TO DATA ANALYTICS

Data analytics is a systematic and iterative process of examining, interpreting, and deriving meaningful insights from large and diverse datasets. It involves the use of various statistical, mathematical, and computational techniques to analyze data and discover patterns, trends, correlations, and relationships that can inform decision-making and drive business strategies. In today's data-driven world, organizations across industries are leveraging data analytics to gain a competitive edge, optimize operations, enhance customer experiences, and predict future trends. Data analytics has transformed the way businesses operate, enabling them to harness the power of data to make informed and evidence-based decisions.

1.5.2 EVOLUTION OF DATA ANALYTICS

The evolution of data analytics can be traced back to the early days of computing when data processing involved manual methods and simple data summarization techniques. As technology advanced, data analytics evolved from manual calculations to automated data processing.

- Early Data Analysis Techniques: In the 1950s and 1960s, data analysis primarily involved basic statistical methods, such as mean, median, and variance calculations. These methods were performed manually or using early computers.
- Emergence of Business Intelligence (BI): In the 1970s and 1980s, the concept of business intelligence emerged, focusing on the use of data and analytics to support business decision-making. BI tools and data warehouses were developed to store and analyze data, enabling organizations to generate reports and gain insights from historical data.
- The Era of Data Warehousing: In the 1990s, the widespread adoption of data warehousing revolutionized data analytics. Data warehouses allowed

organizations to consolidate and store large volumes of data from various sources, making it easier to perform complex analyses and gain deeper insights.

- Rise of Big Data Analytics: The 21st century brought about the era of big data, where organizations were inundated with massive amounts of data from diverse sources, including social media, sensors, and the Internet of Things (IoT). Big data analytics emerged as a response to the challenges posed by this data deluge.

- Advanced Analytical Techniques: In recent years, advancements in data analytics have been fueled by the development of sophisticated analytical techniques, including machine learning, artificial intelligence, and predictive analytics. These techniques enable organizations to make more accurate predictions and gain deeper insights from their data.

- Self-Service Analytics: Another notable development in data analytics is the rise of self-service analytics tools. These tools empower business users and non-technical professionals to perform data analysis and create visualizations without extensive knowledge of programming or statistics.

1.5.3 ROLE OF A DATA ANALYST

Data analysts play a pivotal role in the data analytics process. They are responsible for gathering, processing, and analyzing data to uncover valuable insights that inform decision-making within an organization.

1.5.4 RESPONSIBILITIES OF A DATA ANALYST

- Data Collection and Preparation: Data analysts collect data from various sources, such as databases, spreadsheets, and external datasets. They clean and preprocess the data to ensure accuracy and consistency, removing duplicates, handling missing values, and transforming the data into a suitable format for analysis.

- Data Analysis and Exploration: Data analysts apply statistical and analytical techniques to explore the data and identify patterns, trends, and relationships. They use tools like Excel, SQL, and statistical software to conduct exploratory data analysis.

- Statistical Analysis: Data analysts perform statistical tests and hypothesis testing to draw meaningful conclusions from data and validate hypotheses. They interpret statistical results and provide insights based on the data analysis.

- Data Interpretation and Insights: Data analysts interpret the results of data analysis and provide actionable insights to inform decision-making. They collaborate with stakeholders to understand business needs and present data-driven recommendations.

- Data Reporting: Data analysts create reports and presentations summarizing the findings of data analysis. These reports provide stakeholders with a comprehensive understanding of the data and their implications.

1.5.5 DATA ANALYSIS PROCESS

The data analysis process is a systematic and iterative approach used by data analysts to extract insights from data. The process typically comprises the following stages:

- Define the Problem and Objectives: The first step of the data analysis process is to clearly define the problem or question to be answered and set specific objectives for the analysis. Understanding the business context and the desired outcomes is essential for a successful analysis.
- Data Collection: Data analysts collect relevant data from various sources, such as databases, spreadsheets, APIs, or external datasets. Data quality and integrity are essential considerations during data collection.
- Data Cleaning and Preprocessing: Data cleaning involves handling missing data, removing duplicates, and resolving data inconsistencies. Preprocessing may include data transformation, normalization, and feature engineering to prepare the data for analysis.
- Exploratory Data Analysis (EDA): In this stage, data analysts perform exploratory data analysis to gain initial insights into the data. They use summary statistics, data visualizations, and charts to identify patterns, trends, and potential outliers.
- Data Analysis Techniques: Data analysts apply appropriate data analysis techniques based on the objectives of the analysis. These techniques may include descriptive statistics, inferential statistics, regression analysis, clustering, or machine learning algorithms.
- Interpretation of Results: Data analysts interpret the results of the data analysis in the context of the problem and objectives. They identify key findings, draw conclusions, and provide actionable insights to stakeholders.
- Data Visualization and Reporting: Data analysts create visualizations, such as charts, graphs, and dashboards, to present the results of the analysis. These visualizations facilitate data communication and make it easier for stakeholders to grasp the insights.
- Validation and Sensitivity Analysis: To ensure the accuracy and reliability of the analysis, data analysts may perform validation checks and sensitivity analysis on the results. They verify the robustness of the findings and explore the impact of different assumptions.
- Communicate Findings: Data analysts communicate the findings and insights to stakeholders through reports, presentations, or interactive dashboards. Effective communication is vital to ensure that the analysis informs decision-making.
- Continuous Improvement: Data analysts reflect on the analysis process and identify areas for improvement. They seek feedback from stakeholders and incorporate lessons learned into future analyses.

1.5.6 DATA ANALYSIS TOOLS AND TECHNOLOGIES

Data analysis requires the use of various tools and technologies to manipulate, analyze, and visualize data efficiently. Data analysts utilize a combination of programming languages, statistical software, and data visualization tools, depending on the complexity of the analysis and their preferences.

- Microsoft Excel is a widely used tool for data analysis and manipulation. It offers basic statistical functions, data visualization capabilities, and pivot tables for data summarization.
- SQL (Structured Query Language) is essential for data analysts working with relational databases. It allows data retrieval, aggregation, and filtering, enabling efficient data analysis.
- R is a powerful programming language and environment for statistical computing and graphics. It offers a wide range of packages for data analysis and visualization.
- Python is a versatile programming language commonly used for data analysis and machine learning. Libraries like Pandas, NumPy, and Matplotlib are popular choices for data manipulation and visualization (McKinney, 2018).
- SPSS (Statistical Package for the Social Sciences) is a statistical software widely used in social sciences and market research for data analysis and reporting.
- SAS (Statistical Analysis System) is another statistical software used for data analysis, reporting, and predictive modeling.
- Jupyter Notebooks provide an interactive environment for data analysis and visualization, allowing data analysts to combine code, text, and visualizations in one document.

1.5.7 CHALLENGES IN DATA ANALYTICS

While data analytics offers immense value, it is not without challenges. Data analysts encounter various obstacles that can hinder the effectiveness of their analyses. Some common challenges in data analytics include:

- Data Quality and Reliability: Data quality issues, such as missing or inconsistent data, can impact the accuracy and reliability of the analysis. Data analysts must invest time in data cleaning and validation.
- Handling Big Data: The volume, variety, and velocity of big data present challenges in data storage, processing, and analysis. Data analysts need to leverage scalable technologies and distributed computing to handle large datasets.
- Choosing the Right Analysis Techniques: Selecting the appropriate data analysis techniques and models is critical for meaningful insights. Data analysts need to consider the data characteristics and the research question to choose the most suitable techniques.
- Interpreting Complex Results: Interpreting results from advanced analytical techniques, such as machine learning algorithms, can be challenging.

Data analysts must ensure that the results are interpreted accurately and communicated effectively.

1.6 DATA VISUALIZATION

1.6.1 INTRODUCTION TO DATA VISUALIZATION

Data visualization is a powerful technique used to present data in a visual format, such as charts, graphs, and maps, to facilitate better understanding, analysis, and communication of complex information. It transforms raw data into compelling visuals, making it easier for decision-makers and stakeholders to interpret and derive insights from the data. Data visualization is an essential part of the data analysis process, helping to identify patterns, trends, and correlations in large datasets that may not be apparent through tabular or textual representations alone. By leveraging the human brain's natural ability to process visual information quickly, data visualization enhances data comprehension and enables more informed decision-making (Khang, Hahanov et al., 2022).

1.6.2 EVOLUTION OF DATA VISUALIZATION

Data visualization has a long history, dating back to prehistoric times when humans used cave paintings and symbols to communicate information. In more recent history, data visualization evolved alongside advancements in technology and data analysis techniques.

- Early Visual Representations: In the 17th century (Costigan-Eaves & Macdonald-Ross, 1990), scholars like William Playfair and John Snow pioneered early forms of data visualization. Playfair introduced statistical graphs, including bar charts and line graphs, while Snow used a map to illustrate the spread of cholera cases in London, effectively demonstrating the power of data visualization in identifying patterns and trends.
- The Rise of Computer-Based Visualization: The advent of computers in the 20th century revolutionized data visualization. Early computer systems allowed researchers and analysts to create simple visualizations using basic plotting tools. However, these early visualizations were limited in their complexity and lacked interactivity.
- Advancements in Interactive Visualization: With the growth of the internet and advancements in software technologies, data visualization evolved to become more interactive and dynamic. Technologies like D3.js (Data-Driven Documents) and other JavaScript libraries enabled the creation of interactive visualizations that respond to user inputs and data changes in real-time.
- Data Visualization in the Big Data Era: In the 21st century, the explosion of big data presented new challenges and opportunities for data visualization. With massive datasets, traditional visualization techniques became insufficient. To address this, visualization tools and techniques evolved to handle large-scale datasets and real-time data streaming.

- Augmented Reality and Virtual Reality Visualization: Recent developments in augmented reality (AR) and virtual reality (VR) have opened up new possibilities for data visualization. AR and VR technologies allow users to immerse themselves in data environments, gaining deeper insights through interactive and immersive experiences.

1.6.3   ROLE OF A DATA VISUALIZATION DEVELOPER

Data visualization developers, also known as data visualization specialists or data visualization designers, play a crucial role in transforming data into insightful and visually appealing visualizations. They bridge the gap between data analysis and effective communication by creating visual representations that convey complex information in a simple and understandable manner.

1.6.4   RESPONSIBILITIES OF A DATA VISUALIZATION DEVELOPER

- Data Analysis and Understanding: Data visualization developers collaborate with data analysts and domain experts to understand the data and the key insights that need to be conveyed through visualizations.
- Choosing Visualization Types: Based on the data and the intended message, data visualization developers select appropriate visualization types, such as bar charts, line charts, pie charts, heatmaps, scatter plots, and more.
- Designing Visualizations: Data visualization developers create visually engaging and informative data visualizations that adhere to best practices in design and readability. They consider factors like color choices, typography, and layout to ensure effective communication.
- Interactive Visualization: Data visualization developers often create interactive visualizations that allow users to explore the data, filter information, and gain deeper insights.
- Usability and Accessibility: They ensure that the visualizations are user-friendly and accessible to a diverse audience, including those with visual impairments.
- Data Integration: Data visualization developers integrate data from various sources to create unified and coherent visualizations that provide a holistic view of the data.
- Optimization for Performance: For large datasets, data visualization developers optimize the visualizations to ensure smooth performance and fast loading times.
- Staying Updated with Tools and Techniques: Data visualization developers stay up-to-date with the latest tools, libraries, and visualization techniques to create innovative and compelling visualizations.

1.6.5   DATA VISUALIZATION PROCESS

The data visualization process involves several stages that data visualization developers follow to create effective and impactful visualizations.

- Understanding Data and Requirements: The process begins with understanding the data and the specific requirements of the visualization. Data visualization developers collaborate with data analysts and stakeholders to gain insights into the data and identify the key messages that need to be conveyed.
- Choosing Visualization Types: Based on the data and the requirements, data visualization developers select appropriate visualization types that best represent the data and facilitate understanding. Different visualization types are suitable for different types of data and insights.
- Data Cleaning and Preparation: Before creating visualizations, data visualization developers clean and preprocess the data to ensure data accuracy and consistency. Data cleaning involves handling missing data, removing outliers, and normalizing data.
- Designing Visualizations: Data visualization developers design visualizations that are visually appealing, informative, and easy to interpret. They consider factors like color choices, fonts, and layout to create compelling visual representations.
- Creating Interactive Visualizations: Interactive visualizations allow users to explore the data and gain deeper insights. Data visualization developers incorporate interactive features such as filtering, zooming, and tooltips to enhance user engagement.

1.6.6   DATA VISUALIZATION TOOLS AND TECHNOLOGIES

Data visualization developers have a wide range of tools and technologies at their disposal to create various types of visualizations. The choice of tools depends on factors such as the complexity of the data, the interactivity required, and the end-user platform. Some popular data visualization tools and technologies include:

- Tableau is a powerful and user-friendly data visualization tool that enables data visualization developers to create interactive dashboards and visualizations without the need for extensive coding.
- D3.js (Data-Driven Documents) is a JavaScript library that provides data visualization developers with full control over visual elements. It is particularly suited for creating custom and interactive visualizations.
- Matplotlib is a popular Python library for creating static, interactive, and animated visualizations. It is widely used in data analysis and scientific research.
- ggplot2 is an R package that allows data visualization developers to create visually appealing and customizable visualizations using a simple grammar of graphics.
- Microsoft Power BI is a business analytics tool that provides interactive visualizations and business intelligence capabilities, making it suitable for data visualization in business contexts.
- Plotly is a web-based data visualization library that supports interactive visualizations in Python, R, and JavaScript.
- Seaborn is a Python library based on Matplotlib that simplifies the creation of informative and aesthetically pleasing statistical visualizations.

- Google Data Studio is a free data visualization tool that allows data visualization developers to create interactive reports and dashboards using data from various sources.

1.6.7 CHALLENGES IN DATA VISUALIZATION

Despite the benefits and advancements in data visualization, data visualization developers face certain challenges that they must address to create effective visualizations.

- Data Complexity: Visualizing complex data, especially big data, can be challenging. Data visualization developers need to find ways to represent complex relationships and patterns in a comprehensible and meaningful manner.
- Choosing the Right Visualization Type: Selecting the appropriate visualization type for the data and the insights can be challenging. Data visualization developers must have a good understanding of the data and the domain to make informed decisions.
- Maintaining Data Accuracy: Data accuracy is crucial for meaningful visualizations. Data visualization developers must ensure that the visualizations accurately represent the underlying data and avoid misinterpretation.
- Color and Design Choices: Effective use of colors and design elements is essential for creating visually appealing visualizations. However, improper color choices or cluttered designs can hinder data comprehension.
- Ensuring Accessibility: Creating visualizations that are accessible to users with visual impairments or other disabilities is a challenge that data visualization developers need to address.
- Interactivity and Responsiveness: While interactivity enhances user engagement, it can also lead to performance issues with large datasets. Data visualization developers must find a balance between interactivity and responsiveness.

CASE STUDY: CUSTOMER SEGMENTATION FOR IMPROVING CUSTOMER RETENTION IN AN E-COMMERCE PLATFORM

Problem statement: An e-commerce platform has been facing challenges in retaining its customers. The platform's management team wants to develop strategies to improve customer retention. To address this issue, a comprehensive data-driven Customer Segmentation approach, incorporating data engineering, data analytics, and data visualization techniques. For the scope of book and exercise publicly available data for e-commerce platform from Kaggle.com has been used to run the analysis, build segmentation, and create visualization.

1.6.8 DATA SOURCING AND PREPARATION

- Data Sources: Various data sources are integrated, including:
- Transactional Data: Customer purchases, order history, and product details.
- Customer data: Demographics, preferences, and past interactions.

- Website data: Clickstream data, page views, and session logs.
- Marketing data: Advertising campaigns, email marketing, and promotional activities.
- Data Warehousing: Data from different sources are transformed, cleaned, and stored in a centralized data warehouse using modern ETL (Extract, Transform, and Load) tools such as Apache Spark or Apache Airflow. This ensures that data are unified and accessible for further analysis. The flow is explained in Figure 1.1.
- Exploratory Data Analysis: To perform the EDA, data processing and cleaning, build segmentation, and other analysis, Python Jupyter notebook tool has been used. The dataset consists of the following variables:
  - Invoice: The unique identifier of each customer invoice.
  - Stock code: The unique identifier of each item in stock.
  - Description: The item purchased by the customer.
  - Quantity: The number of each item purchased by a customer in a single invoice.
  - Invoice date: The purchase date.
  - Unit price: Price of one unit of each item.
  - Customer ID: Unique identifier assigned to each user.
  - Demographics: The country, age, and other customer demographics.

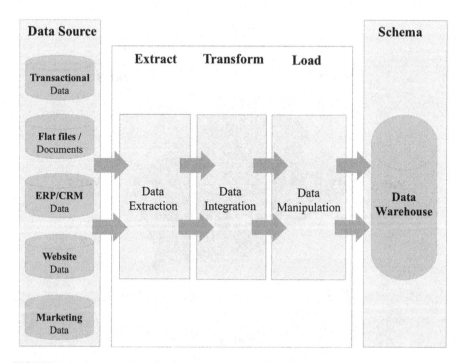

FIGURE 1.1 Data warehousing flow for ETL process using Apache Airflow.

Source: Khang, 2021.

The results consist of the following segments as shown in Figure 1.2. The explanation of segments is as follows:

- Red cluster: high Var 1, Var 3, Var 6, Var 8; mid Var 4, Var 5, Var 7 and low Var 2.
- Purple cluster: high Var 2, Var 3, Var 6, Var 7; mid Var 1, Var 4, Var 5, Var 8.
- Green cluster: high Var 5; mid Var 1, Var 6, Var 7, Var 8 and low Var 2, Var 3, Var 4.
- Visualization: for the exercise the interactive dashboards are created using tools like Tableau. The dashboards display key metrics related to customer such as:
  - Customer segmentation based on demographics and purchase behavior.
  - Visualization of influential factors contributing to customer behavior.

Figure 1.3 is an example of a dashboard which shows the behavior of customers and helps businesses to take and strategize decisions like marketing techniques, etc. This will help the user or business to understand what factors are responsible for influencing customer behavior and purchases such as what products customers are buying more of and the characteristics like demographics and house-o-graphic by segmentation. These dashboards are interactive by using filters. Also, developing customer segmentation dashboards in Tableau is not a one-off effort. To ensure their ongoing relevance and effectiveness, it is crucial to establish best practices for maintaining and updating the dashboards.

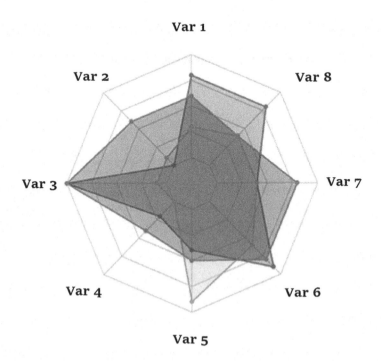

FIGURE 1.2   Spider graph representing clusters using Python Jupyter notebook.

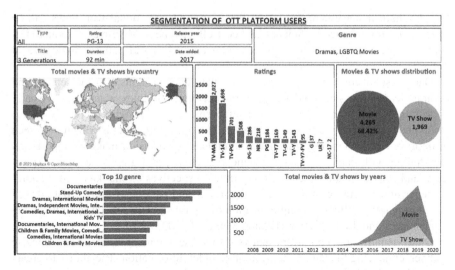

FIGURE 1.3 Customer Segmentation Visualization dashboard using Tableau.

1.7 CONCLUSION

Data engineering plays a pivotal role in establishing a robust foundation for data management. By designing and building scalable data infrastructure and pipelines, data engineering ensures that organizations can efficiently collect, store, and process vast and diverse datasets. The impact of data engineering is evident in the scalability, flexibility, and real-time data processing capabilities it provides. With the help of technologies like Apache Hadoop and Apache Spark, data engineering allows organizations to handle massive datasets and perform distributed computing. Real-time data processing enabled by technologies like Apache Kafka facilitates immediate responses to critical events, enabling organizations to make timely decisions and react to dynamic market conditions (Khang, Abdullayev, et al., 2023).

Data analytics is a transformative force that empowers organizations to uncover valuable insights and patterns hidden within their data. The impact of data analytics can be observed in improved decision-making, customer understanding, process optimization, and risk mitigation. By applying descriptive, diagnostic, predictive, and prescriptive analytics techniques, organizations gain a deeper understanding of historical performance and identify trends. Predictive analytics forecasts future outcomes, while prescriptive analytics offers actionable recommendations to achieve specific goals. Data analytics equips decision-makers with evidence-based insights, enabling them to anticipate challenges, capitalize on opportunities, and stay ahead in a dynamic business landscape.

Customer understanding is significantly enhanced through data analytics, as organizations gain insights into customer behavior, preferences, and needs. Personalized marketing, customer segmentation, and targeted campaigns are made possible through analytics-driven customer insights. In addition, data analytics contributes to process optimization by identifying inefficiencies and bottlenecks.

Supply chain management, resource allocation, and operational workflows can be streamlined for enhanced efficiency and cost-effectiveness. Moreover, data analytics supports risk mitigation efforts by detecting anomalies and patterns indicative of potential risks or fraudulent activities (Khang, Shah et al., 2023).

Data visualization revolutionizes the way data insights are presented and communicated to stakeholders. By transforming complex data into visually appealing representations, data visualization ensures that insights are easily under-stood and accessible to a broader audience. The impact of data visualization is seen in improved understanding, effective communication, decision-making support, and storytelling with data. Interactive dashboards, charts, and graphs facilitate explor-ation and provide stakeholders with multiple perspectives on the data. This enables a deeper understanding of the underlying trends and patterns, fostering data-driven decision-making. Effective communication of data insights is crucial for influencing stakeholders and driving action (Khang, Kali et al., 2023).

Data visualization empowers analysts to present data in a clear and concise manner, enhancing the comprehension of complex information. The ability to create compelling visual narratives enhances engagement and facilitates deeper connections with the data. Data visualization tools support decision-making by allowing users to explore data interactively and assess various scenarios. Decision-makers can analyze data from different angles, leading to more informed choices and strategic planning (Khang, Muthmainnah et al., 2023).

REFERENCES

Costigan-Eaves, P., & Macdonald-Ross, M. (August, 1990). "William Playfair (1759–1823)." *Statistical Science*, 5(3), 318–326. https://doi.org/10.1214/ss/1177012100

Khang, A. (Ed.) (2023). *AI and IoT-Based Technologies for Precision Medicine.* IGI Global Press. ISBN: 9798369308769. https://doi.org/10.4018/979-8-3693-0876-9

Khang, A., Abdullayev, V., Alyar, A. V., Khalilov, M., Murad, B. (2023). AI-Aided Data Analytics Tools and Applications for the Healthcare Sector. In A. Khang (Ed.), *AI and IoT-Based Technologies for Precision Medicine.* IGI Global Press. ISBN: 9798369308769. https://doi.org/10.4018/979-8-3693-0876-9.ch018

Khang, A., Hahanov, V., Abbas, G. L., & Hajimahmud, V. A. (2022). "Cyber-Physical-Social System and İncident Management." In A. Khang, V. Abdullayev, B. Jadhav, G. Morris (Eds.), *AI-Centric Smart City Ecosystems: Technologies, Design and Implementation* (1st Ed.), 2 (15), CRC Press. https://doi.org/10.1201/9781003252542-2

Khang, A., Kali, C. R., Satapathy, S. K., Kumar, A., Ranjan Das, S., & Panda, M. R. (2023). "Enabling the Future of Manufacturing: Integration of Robotics and IoT to Smart Factory Infrastructure in Industry 4.0." In A. Khang, V. Shah, & S. Rani (Eds.), *AI-Based Technologies and Applications in the Era of the Metaverse* (1st Ed.), pp. 25–50. IGI Global Press. https://doi.org/10.4018/978-1-6684-8851-5.ch002

Khang, A., Muthmainnah, M., Seraj, P. M. I., Al Yakin, A., Obaid, A. J., & Panda, M. R. (2023). "AI-Aided Teaching Model for the Education 5.0 Ecosystem." In A. Khang, V. Shah, & S. Rani (Eds.), *AI-Based Technologies and Applications in the Era of the Metaverse* (1st Ed.), pp. 83–104. IGI Global Press. https://doi.org/10.4018/978-1-6684-8851-5.ch004

Khang, A., Shah, V., & Rani, S. (2023). *AI-Based Technologies and Applications in the Era of the Metaverse* (1st Ed.). IGI Global Press. https://doi.org/10.4018/978-1-6684-8851-5

Khanh, H. H., & Khang, A. (2021). The role of artificial intelligence in blockchain applications. In G. Rana (Ed.), *Reinventing Manufacturing and Business Processes through Artificial Intelligence*, 2 (pp. 20–40), CRC Press. https://doi.org/10.1201/9781003145011-2

McKinney, W. (2018). "Python for Data Analysis: Data Wrangling with Pandas, NumPy, and IPython." *O'Reilly Media.* www.ir.juit.ac.in:8080/jspui/bitstream/123456789/6083/1/Python%20for%20Data%20Analysis_%20Data%20Wrangling%20with%20Pandas%2C%20NumPy%2C%20and%20IPython.pdf

Peddireddy, K., & Banga, D. (2023). "Enhancing Customer Experience through Kafka Data Steams for Driven Machine Learning for Complaint Management." *International Journal of Computer Trends and Technology*, 71(3), 7–13. https://ieeexplore.ieee.org/abstract/document/10131800/

2 Data Analytics Tools and Applications for Business and Finance Systems

Cherri Kallimal Aishwarya, Chava Siri Lahari, and Shaik Himam Saheb

2.1 INTRODUCTION

Data analytics is the process of examining large datasets to uncover valuable insights, trends, and patterns that can inform decision-making and drive business growth. It involves the collection, cleaning, processing, and analysis of data to extract meaningful information. To perform data analytics effectively, various tools and applications have been developed to handle the different stages of the analytics workflow. These tools facilitate data manipulation, visualization, statistical analysis, and machine learning (Muthmainnah, Khang et al., 2023).

2.1.1 DATA SCIENCE TOOLS

The commonly used tools and applications in data analytics include the following.

- **Excel**: Microsoft Excel is a widely used tool for data analysis due to its user-friendly interface and familiar spreadsheet format. It offers basic statistical functions, data sorting and filtering, and the ability to create charts and pivot tables.
- **SQL**: Structured Query Language (SQL) is essential for working with databases. SQL allows you to extract, manipulate, and analyze data from relational databases using queries. It is a fundamental skill for data analysts working with structured data.
- **Python**: Python is a versatile programming language commonly used in data analytics. It offers numerous libraries and frameworks for data manipulation (e.g., Pandas), numerical computation (e.g., NumPy), and data visualization (e.g., Matplotlib and Seaborn). Python also has powerful machine learning libraries such as Scikit-learn and TensorFlow.
- **R**: R is a programming language specifically designed for statistical computing and graphics. It provides a wide range of packages and libraries for data manipulation, visualization, and statistical analysis. R is popular among statisticians and data scientists for its extensive statistical capabilities.

 DOI: 10.1201/9781032618845-2

- **Tableau**: Tableau is a powerful data visualization tool that allows users to create interactive and visually appealing dashboards and reports. It simplifies the process of creating charts, graphs, and maps, making it easier to communicate data insights effectively (Chabot et al., 2003).
- **Power BI**: Power BI, developed by Microsoft, is another popular data visualization tool. It enables users to connect to various data sources, transform and model the data, and create interactive visualizations and reports. Power BI offers a user-friendly interface and is widely used for business intelligence purposes.
- **Apache Hadoop**: Hadoop is a framework designed for distributed storage and processing of large datasets. It consists of the Hadoop Distributed File System (HDFS) for data storage and the MapReduce programming model for distributed data processing. Hadoop is commonly used for big data analytics, enabling the processing of massive volumes of data across a cluster of computers (Nandimath et al., 2013).
- **Apache Spark**: Spark is an open-source, cluster computing framework that provides high-speed data processing and analytics. It supports real-time streaming, machine learning, graph processing, and more. Spark offers APIs in various languages, including Java, Scala, and Python, making it versatile for different data processing tasks (Salloum et al., 2016).

These are just a few examples of the many tools and applications available for data analytics. The choice of tools depends on the specific requirements of the analysis, the size of the dataset, and the expertise of the data analysts. It is important to have a good understanding of these tools and their functionalities to perform efficient and insightful data analytics (Pooja et al., 2023).

Data analytics is a critical component of modern business operations and decision-making processes. It involves collecting, processing, and analyzing data to gain valuable insights and make informed decisions. To perform data analytics effectively, various tools and applications are available that facilitate data manipulation, visualization, and analysis. Below are some key conclusions about data analytics tools and applications.

2.1.2 VARIETY OF TOOLS

There is a wide range of tools available for different aspects of data analytics, including data extraction, transformation, loading (ETL), data visualization, statistical analysis, and machine learning. Some popular tools include Python libraries like Pandas, NumPy, and SciPy, as well as programming languages like R and SQL.

2.1.3 OPEN-SOURCE OPTIONS

Many data analytics tools are open-source, which means they are freely available for anyone to use and modify. These tools often have active communities that contribute to their development, offer support, and share resources. Examples of popular open-source tools are Apache Hadoop, Apache Spark, and the R programming language. A review on the benefits of open source software has been provided by Blake and Morse (Blake & Morse, 2016).

- **Integrated Suites**: Several comprehensive data analytics platforms provide end-to-end solutions, combining multiple functionalities within a single environment. These integrated suites offer features like data integration, data preparation, data visualization, advanced analytics, and reporting. Examples include Tableau, Microsoft Power BI, and Google Analytics.
- **Data Visualization:** Visualizing data is crucial for understanding patterns, trends, and relationships within datasets. Data visualization tools help in creating charts, graphs, dashboards, and interactive visual representations of data. Tableau, QlikView, and D3.js are widely used tools for data visualization.
- **Machine Learning and AI**: Machine learning and artificial intelligence (AI) techniques play a significant role in data analytics. Tools and libraries like scikit-learn, TensorFlow, and Keras provide functionalities for building and deploying machine learning models, performing predictive analysis, and implementing advanced algorithms.
- **Cloud-Based Solutions:** Cloud computing has revolutionized data analytics by providing scalable and flexible infrastructure. Cloud-based tools and platforms, such as Amazon Web Services (AWS), Google Cloud Platform (GCP), and Microsoft Azure, offer storage, computing power, and analytical services, enabling organizations to process large datasets efficiently.
- **Data Governance and Security:** With the increasing focus on data privacy and security, data analytics tools and applications are incorporating robust data governance features. These include data encryption, access control, audit trails, and compliance with data protection regulations like GDPR (General Data Protection Regulation) and CCPA (California Consumer Privacy Act).
- **User-Friendly Interfaces:** Many data analytics tools strive to provide user-friendly interfaces and drag-and-drop functionalities to cater to users with

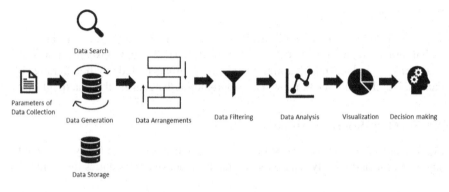

FIGURE 2.1 Stages of data collection to decision-making.

varying technical backgrounds. This accessibility makes it easier for business users and non-technical stakeholders to explore and analyze data independently. The steps involved in the process of decision-making from data collection to decision-making are shown step by step in Figure 2.1.

2.2 IMPORTANCE OF DATA ANALYTICS IN DECISION-MAKING

Due to the following factors, data analytics has become crucial for businesses across all sectors (Monino, 2021; Ghasemaghaei, 2019):

- **Fact-Based Decision-Making:** Organizations can use data analytics to create decisions that are supported by facts rather than assumptions or conjecture. Patterns and trends are revealed through the analysis of historical data, laying the groundwork for well-informed decision-making.
- **Enhanced Operational Efficiency:** Organizations can spot inefficiencies, bottlenecks, and places for improvement by analyzing data. This aids in process improvement, cost cutting, and increased operational effectiveness.
- **Customer Insights and Personalization:** Organizations can comprehend client behavior, preferences, and wants thanks to data analytics. Organizations can modify products or services, personalize marketing campaigns, and provide a better customer experience by analyzing consumer data.
- **Competitive Advantage:** Businesses that use data analytics effectively acquire a competitive advantage. Businesses can proactively change their strategy, remain ahead of the competition, and capture new opportunities by learning about market trends, client demands, and competitors.

2.3 TYPES OF DATA ANALYTICS

Data analytics can be classified into three primary types, each serving a different purpose in extracting insights (Elgendy & Elragal, 2014)

- **Descriptive Analytics:** The goal of descriptive analytics is to provide a thorough knowledge of past occurrences by condensing historical data. Aggregation, data visualization, and summary statistics are some of the methods that can help organizations find patterns, spot trends, and obtain insightful knowledge about what has transpired.
- **Predictive Analytics:** Based on historical data, predictive analytics uses statistical models and machine learning algorithms to produce predictions and projections. Organizations can predict future outcomes, spot potential hazards, and take preventative action by analyzing patterns, correlations, and historical trends.
- **Prescriptive Analytics:** By offering recommendations for activities to improve results, prescriptive analytics goes beyond descriptive and predictive analytics. Prescriptive analytics offers recommendations for the optimal course of action to achieve goals by taking into account various circumstances, restrictions, and objectives. It aids businesses in making data-driven choices and streamlining operations for maximum effectiveness.

2.4 DATA ANALYTICS TOOLS

To effectively perform data analytics, organizations rely on a variety of tools and technologies. Below are three key categories of data analytics tools (Dwivedi et al., 2016).

- **Statistical Software Packages:** Data analysis is frequently performed using statistical software programs like R, Python, and SAS. A variety of statistical operations, data manipulation abilities, and sophisticated analytics algorithms are all provided by these technologies. They enable data scientists and analysts to conduct intricate studies and glean valuable insights from data.
- **Business Intelligence (BI) Tools:** Organizations are able to effectively visualize and understand data thanks to BI solutions like Tableau, Power BI, and QlikView. These solutions provide user-friendly interfaces, engaging visualizations, and powerful reporting features. With the use of BI tools, users may develop intelligent visual representations of data, identify trends, and distribute discoveries throughout the company (Shah & Khang, 2023).
- **Big Data Processing Frameworks:** Specialized solutions like Hadoop, Spark, and Apache Kafka have emerged with the rise of big data. Large-scale data processing, storage, and analysis are handled by these frameworks. They give businesses the ability to handle enormous amounts of structured and unstructured data with efficiency, to extract insights, and to support real-time decision-making.
- **Data Sources and Acquisition:** Data can be obtained from various sources, including databases, application programming interfaces (APIs), and web scraping. Databases store structured data and can be accessed through SQL queries or other data retrieval methods. APIs provide a programmatic way to access data from various services or platforms, allowing real-time data retrieval Using software or programs, web scraping involves gathering data from websites.
- **Data Cleaning and Preprocessing:** Data preparation depends heavily on the data cleaning process. To assure data quality, it requires managing missing values, outliers, and data irregularities. Imputation methods, such as filling in the gaps with the corresponding variable's mean, median, or mode, can be used to deal with missing data. Outliers, which are extreme numbers that dramatically differ from the rest of the data, can be dealt with in a number of ways, including by being eliminated, transformed, or imputed with more appropriate values. By standardizing formats, fixing errors, or deleting problematic information, data inconsistencies can be fixed, including discrepancies like contradictory or incorrect entries.

2.5 EXPLORATORY DATA ANALYSIS (EDA)

EDA is an important step in comprehending data and gaining valuable insights. It entails examining and displaying the data to spot trends, patterns, and connections between different variables. Scattered plots, histograms, and box plots are examples of data visualization techniques that aid in examining the distribution and connections within the data. Mean, median, and standard deviation are examples of summary statistics that offer a succinct summary of the data. The degree and direction of correlations between variables are measured by correlation analysis, which aids in identifying potential dependencies (Nuzzo, 2016).

2.5.1 STATISTICAL ANALYSIS TECHNIQUES

- **Regression Analysis**: To understand how different variables relate to one another, regression models are frequently utilized. While multiple linear regression takes into account several independent variables, simple linear regression examines the association between a dependent variable and one independent variable. Regression models can be used to forecast results and comprehend how various variables affect the target variable. This analysis with an example is discussed by Chatterjee and Hadi (2006).

- **Time Series Analysis**: The main goal of time series analysis is to examine and predict time-dependent data. In order to anticipate the future, it entails looking at patterns, trends, and seasonality in the data. Time series analysis frequently employs methods like moving averages, exponential smoothing, and ARIMA (Autoregressive Integrated Moving Average) models.

- **Clustering and Classification**: To aggregate and categorize data based on similarities or predetermined classifications, clustering and classification algorithms are used. An unsupervised learning approach called K-means clustering divides data points into different clusters according to how similar they are. Contrarily, decision trees are a supervised learning method that builds a model in the shape of a tree to categorize data based on a set of features (Aggarwal & Yu, 1999).

- **Machine Learning and Predictive Analytical Tools**: Machine learning (ML) is a subcategory of artificial intelligence (AI) that concentrates on enabling computers to learn from data and improve without explicit programming. It involves algorithms and models that can automatically learn and make estimates or decisions based on patterns and relationships within the data. Essential topics in machine learning include:
  - **Supervised Learning**: The system learns from labeled training data using input features and related target labels or outcomes. Supervised learning aims to build a predictive model to predict or classify unknown data correctly. Linear regression, decision trees, support vector machines, and neural networks are typical supervised learning techniques.
  - **Unsupervised Learning**: Without any defined target labels or outcomes, the system learns from unlabeled data. Without prior knowledge or direction, it seeks to identify structures, relationships, and patterns within the data. Unsupervised learning frequently employs the techniques of clustering and dimensionality reduction to group-related data points and scales back the size of the dataset.

- **Reinforcement Learning**: This is a method where an agent learns to do subsequent actions in a setting to maximize overall benefits. It involves the agent's interaction with its surroundings and feedback in the form of rewards or punishments determined by the agent's activities. Reinforcement learning algorithms use exploration and exploitation techniques to identify the best action.

Predictive analytics involves predicting future events or results using historical data, statistical modeling, and machine learning methods. To provide insights for forecasting and decision-making, it seeks to elucidate hidden patterns, correlations, and trends in data.

- Create predictive models that can project future results.
- Use data segmentation and clustering to put comparable data points together.
- Carry out anomaly detection to find exceptions or strange data points.
- Use sentiment analysis to examine and comprehend textual material.

Machine learning and predictive analytical tools are powerful technologies transforming several industries by permitting organizations to extract valuable insights from massive amounts of data. The classification of machine learning techniques is shown in Figure 2.2. These techniques have a lot in common and can be utilized as collaboration tools, each enhancing the other. Some similarities include:

- To analyze patterns in data
- To work efficiently, a large data set is needed
- Typically used with the same intended outcome
- Widely used in related fields such as manufacturing, banking, security, supply chains, and even retail
- Utilize historical data to make future predictions

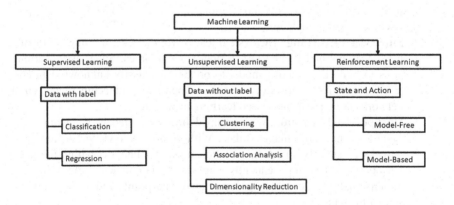

FIGURE 2.2   Classification of machine learning techniques.

Finance, healthcare, marketing, customer relationship management, fraud detection, supply chain optimization, and recommendation systems are just a few industries where machine learning and predictive analytics techniques are used, as shown in Figure 2.2. Organizations can acquire helpful insights, increase decision-making, and improve corporate performance by utilizing these technologies (Arpita et al., 2023).

2.5.2 Big Data Analytics Tools

Big data analytics technologies are made to handle and glean insights from enormous amounts of organized and unstructured data, often known as big data, as shown in Figure 2.3.

With the aid of these technologies, organizations can analyze, examine, and extract relevant information from various data sources to support data-driven decision-making. The following are big data analytics tools and their key features:

- **Apache Hadoop**: Apache Hadoop, an open-source system, offers massive data processing and distributed storage capabilities. There are two main parts to it:
  - **Hadoop Distributed File System (HDFS)**: An open-source distributed file system that allows storing and accessing massive datasets across clusters of inexpensive hardware.
  - **MapReduce**: A computing paradigm for handling massive data sets across distributed clusters. Apache Hive (data warehousing), Apache Pig (data flow scripting), Apache Spark (in-memory data processing), and Apache HBase (NoSQL database) are some of the additional tools and frameworks that are part of the Hadoop ecosystem.

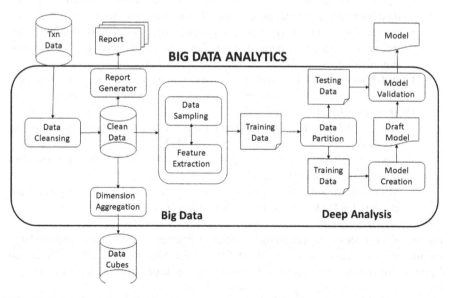

FIGURE 2.3 Big data analytics.

- **Apache Spark**: An open-source, distributed computing platform focusing on large data processing and analytics is called Apache Spark. Compared to conventional MapReduce-based systems, it offers an in-memory computing framework, greatly increasing its speed.
- Support for numerous programming languages (Java, Scala, Python, R), among other features.
  - Interactive shell for data exploration.
  - Spark SQL for SQL-based data manipulation and querying.
  - Scalable machine learning tasks using the MLlib machine learning library.
  - GraphX's ability to process graphs.
- **NoSQL Databases**: Large-scale, unstructured, and semi-structured data may be handled by NoSQL databases, which makes them a popular choice for big data analytics.
- **Apache Cassandra**: A distributed database that is highly scalable and notable for its capacity to handle enormous volumes of data across several nodes.
- **MongoDB**: A database that is focused on documents and offers flexible, schema-free data storage.
- **HBase**: A columnar NoSQL database designed for random read/write access to huge datasets and developed on top of Hadoop HDFS.

2.5.3 DATA VISUALIZATION TOOLS

- **Data Visualization Tools**: are necessary for obtaining insights and effectively communicating findings. A detailed view of big data has been provided by Ali et al. (2016).
  - Tableau, a well-known platform for data visualization and business intelligence, which provides a wide choice of interactive visualizations and dashboards, is one example of a tool that is frequently used.
  - Power BI: A business analytics product from Microsoft that provides interactive reporting, data visualization, and sharing of insights amongst organizations.
- **Cloud-Based Analytics Services**: provide managed services for big data analytics, removing the necessity for setting up and maintaining infrastructure (Manekar et al., 2015).
  - Amazon EMR: their Elastic MapReduce service for running Hadoop and Spark and other big data frameworks on AWS.
  - Google BigQuery: a big dataset-handling, serverless, fully managed data warehouse and analytics platform.
  - Microsoft Azure HDInsight: a service in the cloud that offers managed clusters for Hadoop, Spark, and other big data tools.

The use of these tools and technology enables businesses to process and analyze large amounts of data, generate actionable insights, spot patterns, and make data-driven decisions in a variety of industries, including banking, healthcare, e-commerce, marketing, and social media analysis (Keerthika et al., 2023).

2.5.4 REAL-TIME ANALYTICS TOOLS

Real-time analytics systems are made to handle and analyze data as they are being generated, enabling businesses to get quick answers and move quickly. Real-time decision-making is crucial in today's fast-paced, data-driven environment; thus, these technologies are crucial. The following are real-time analytics tools and their key features (Yadranjiaghdam et al., 2016; Ellis, 2014):

- **Apache Kafka**: Apache Kafka is also a popular real-time analytics tool. It is a distributed event streaming platform that can instantly process fast data streams.
  - Publish-subscribe messaging system for streaming data is one of its essential characteristics.
  - Data processing with a high throughput and low latency.
  - Scalable and fault-tolerant architecture.
  - Integration of other data processing frameworks like Apache Spark or Apache Flink.
- **Apache Flink**: Apache Flink is an open-source framework for stream processing that allows for real-time analyses on ongoing data streams. It offers the following features and supports event-driven architectures:
  - Fault-tolerant stream processing with low latency.
  - Event time processing and windowing support.
  - Guarantees of processing only once.
  - Integration with a range of data sinks and sources.
  - Additionally native support for batch processing.
- **Apache Storm**: An open-source, distributed real-time processing system called Apache Storm handles and analyzes streaming data. It has characteristics such as:
  - Reliable stream processing with guaranteed message processing offering a scalable, fault-tolerant framework.
  - Integration with a range of data sinks and sources.
  - Support for windowing and complicated event processing (CEP) activities.
  - Flexibility via specialized components.
- **Spark Streaming**: Spark streaming is an Apache Spark component that makes it possible to analyze real-time data streams. It allows real-time data intake and processing and connects with the Spark ecosystem.
  - Micro-batch processing model for stream processing is one of its key characteristics.
  - Support for event-time processing and windowed operations.
  - Seamless integration with Spark-based batch processing.
  - Capability to manage batch and streaming workloads.
- **Stream Analytics in Cloud Platforms**: Major cloud providers supply managed stream analytics services that simplify processing and analyzing real-time data. Examples include:
- Amazon Kinesis, an AWS service that is completely managed for ingesting, processing, and analyzing streaming data.

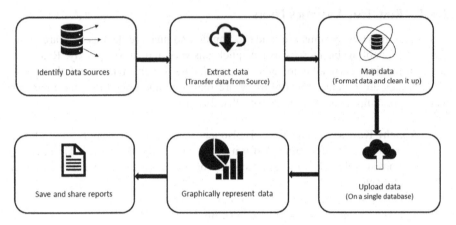

FIGURE 2.4   Stages from data visualization to useful reports.

- Azure Stream Analytics is a real-time analytics service for ingesting, analyzing, and visualizing streaming data provided by Microsoft Azure.
- Google Cloud Dataflow is an exclusively managed service for processing data streams in batches and streams in real-time on the Google Cloud Platform.

With the help of these technologies, organizations can process and analyze data streams in real time, allowing them to make quick decisions, spot abnormalities, keep an eye on events, and react quickly to shifting circumstances. Finance, cybersecurity, e-commerce, the Internet of Things (IoT), telecommunications, and operational intelligence are just a few industries where real-time analytics solutions are used, as shown in Figure 2.4.

2.6   DATA ANALYTICS IN SPECIFIC INDUSTRIES

Data analytics plays a significant role in several industries by empowering businesses to gain insights, make well-informed decisions, and expand their operations. The following are data analytics applications in specific industries:

- **Manufacturing**: The data are a perfect choice for data analytics because they are not only abundant but also complex and difficult to handle. Still, this set of data has not yet been utilized. The focus of attention is now making significant investments in digitization and prophetic analytics tools to become a data-driven decision-making sector. To create meaningful information, businesses use various essential data types, including geographical data, textbooks, graphical data, IoT data, and temporal data, which they ingest and integrate into datasets (Wang et al., 2022).
- **Pharma and Healthcare**: Pharmaceutical companies and the healthcare industry also invest in cutting-edge cloud technology and big data to use analytics to enhance patient care and consumer satisfaction. Wearable trackers and RPM (remote patient monitoring) are only two minor examples

of advancements in the healthcare sector; these technologies also make it easier to determine whether patients are appropriately taking their drugs and adhering to their treatment plans (Khang, Abdullayev, et al., 2023). Physicians can access complete information on their patient's welfare and valuable insights thanks to data gathered and developed over time. It aids doctors in providing better care and reducing waiting times (Mehta & Pandit, 2018).

- **Finance and Banking**: All the "big boys" of the banking and financial markets, including hedge funds, retail trades, and giant banks, have implemented big data technologies to monitor trade analytics used in high-frequency trading, sentiment analysis, pre-trade decision-support analytics, predictive analytics, etc. Enterprise risk management, fraud reduction, KYC (know your customer), risk analysis, and anti-money laundering are a few additional popular fields that significantly rely on data and analytics solutions. Banking and security organizations monitor changes in the financial market using data analytics techniques and solutions. For instance, stock exchanges employ big data analytics, network analytics, and NLP (natural language processing) to track and monitor unethical trading practices in the stock market and apprehend offenders (Hung et al., 2020).

- **Retail and E-Commerce**: Margins and a better customer experience are essential to the retail and wholesale industries' survival. Retailers are employing data analytics to handle the expanding big data to precisely anticipate customer expectations and then deliver those items to beat the fierce competition in the market. Thanks to analytics, they can handle the intense market rivalry and keep one step ahead. They can keep their customers satisfied and encourage them to visit their stores using detailed insights from data analytics solutions (Akter & Wamba, 2016). Retailers use data analytics in practically every facet of their operations, including the following:
  - Customize the consumer experience and improve marketing
  - Improve logistics and supply chain management
  - Control prices to increase sales
  - Benefit from retail data analytics

The technology and tools needed to build a world of big data with both organized and unstructured data sets are provided by data analytics. Utilizing all available data, businesses may utilize these technologies to increase productivity, reduce resource and time waste, and enhance decision-making through the use of data-driven insights. The top industries that have used data analytics at every stage are those mentioned above. To leverage better and more long-lasting results, many more companies are becoming involved and embracing becoming data-driven businesses (Linzbach et al., 2019).

2.7 TEXT ANALYTICS AND SENTIMENT ANALYSIS TOOLS

Many platforms frequently include user-friendly interfaces and allow users to create unique workflows for text analysis.

- **Sentiment Analysis Tools:** Identifying the sentiment or opinion communicated in a text, whether it is favorable, negative, or neutral, is the goal of sentiment analysis, a common text analytics application. There are numerous tools for sentiment analysis that use diverse algorithms and methods. Among the notable tools are the following:
  - **VADER (Valence Aware Dictionary and Sentiment Reasoner):** The popular sentiment analysis program VADER analyzes text sentiment by combining lexical and grammatical heuristics with a pre-trained sentiment lexicon. Because of its proficiency with slang and casual language, it is renowned for processing social media text effectively.
  - **TextBlob:** Python's TextBlob package offers a straightforward and user-friendly interface for carrying out typical NLP operations, such as sentiment analysis. Polarity ratings are provided for text documents using a pre-trained sentiment classifier that has been trained on a sizable dataset.
  - **IBM Watson Natural Language Understanding:** Sentiment analysis is one of a number of potent NLP capabilities provided by IBM Watson. Text can be analyzed and interpreted to extract sentiment, emotions, and other linguistic aspects using its Natural Language Understanding service. It offers customizable models and supports a variety of languages.
  - **Google Cloud Natural Language API:** As part of its portfolio of NLP services, the Google Cloud Natural Language API offers sentiment analysis capabilities. It can classify text as positive, negative, or neutral using machine learning algorithms to determine sentiment. Along with entity recognition, it offers further NLP functions.
- **Topic Modeling Tools:** A method for finding hidden themes or topics in a group of papers is called topic modeling. It aids with the organization and comprehension of massive amounts of text data. Several popular topic modeling instruments are as follows:
  - **Latent Dirichlet Allocation (LDA):** A popular generative probabilistic model for subject modeling is LDA. It is predicated on the idea that documents are a mashup of many themes, with each topic being a distribution of words. LDA implementations are offered by libraries like Gensim and Mallet.
  - **Non-Negative Matrix Factorization (NMF):** Another popular topic modeling method is NMF, which divides a document-term matrix into two smaller matrices that represent the subjects and word distributions for each topic. An implementation of NMF is available in Scikit-Learn.
  - **MALLET:** MALLET (Machine Learning for Language Toolkit) is a Java-based topic modeling toolkit. It provides LDA, NMF, and other algorithm implementations. MALLET offers a variety of tools for text preprocessing and analysis and is renowned for its effectiveness in handling huge datasets.
- **Named Entity Recognition (NER) Tools:** The process of recognizing and categorizing named entities, such as names of individuals, businesses, places, and other specified categories, is known as named entity recognition. NER tools that are frequently utilized include the following:

- **Stanford NER:** A Java library called Stanford NER offers powerful NER capabilities. For text labeling of named entities, conditional random fields (CRF) are used. It offers pre-trained models and supports numerous languages.
- **spaCy:** Popular Python NLP library spaCy features a built-in NER component. It provides a number of other NLP features in addition to high-performance named entity recognition. SpaCy enables users to train unique NER models and supports several languages.
- **OpenNLP:** A library for NLP tasks, such as named entity recognition, is Apache OpenNLP. Users can train models on their particular domain or language using a trainable NER module that is provided by the system.

2.8 CONCLUSION

The discipline of data analytics has completely changed how businesses function and make choices. Businesses can gain a competitive edge and stimulate innovation by utilizing cutting-edge technology and methodologies to mine valuable insights from massive amounts of data. Descriptive, predictive, and prescriptive analytics are just a few of the many approaches and technologies that make up data analytics (Ushaa & Vishal et al., 2023). Organizations may better comprehend the past with the help of descriptive analytics, which offers a historical view of the data. In order to predict future outcomes and trends, predictive analytics makes use of statistical models and machine learning algorithms. By recommending the best courses of action after analyzing the available data, prescriptive analytics goes a step further (Khang, Shah et al., 2023).

Data analytics provides many advantages. It enables businesses to take data-driven decisions, find previously unnoticed patterns and connections, spot growth possibilities, streamline processes, and reduce risks. Businesses may better serve their clients and increase customer satisfaction and loyalty by understanding customer behavior, preferences, and wants (Khang, Kali et al., 2023).

In a variety of fields and sectors, data analytics is also essential. It makes personalized therapy possible, boosts patient outcomes, and improves disease surveillance in the field of healthcare (Khang & Medicine, 2023). It supports risk management, investment strategy optimization, and the detection of fraudulent activity in finance. It facilitates sentiment analysis, customer segmentation, and targeted marketing initiatives (Sampath & Khang, 2023; Namita et al., 2023).

Data analytics has a wide range of uses and is constantly being developed in new fields. Implementing data analytics, however, is not without difficulties. Organizations must resolve problems with data integration, data quality, privacy issues, and skilled staff. To fully utilize the power of analytics, infrastructure, technology, and talent investments are necessary. To further guarantee the privacy and security of people's information, ethical considerations and responsible data practices must be upheld (Saxena et al., 2023).

The future of data analytics looks bright for expansion and innovation. The potential of data analytics will continue to grow with the introduction of new technologies such as artificial intelligence, machine learning, and big data. Embracing data analytics and creating a data-driven culture will put organizations in a good position to handle the complexity of the contemporary business environment and capture new opportunities (Khang, Muthmainnah et al., 2023).

REFERENCES

Aggarwal, C. C., & Yu, P. S. (1999). Data mining techniques for associations, clustering and classification. In *Methodologies for Knowledge Discovery and Data Mining: Third Pacific-Asia Conference, PAKDD-99 Beijing, China, April 26–28*. Proceedings 3 (pp. 13–23). Springer Berlin Heidelberg. https://link.springer.com/chapter/10.1007/3-540-48912-6_4

Akter, S., & Wamba, S. F. (2016). Big data analytics in E-commerce: a systematic review and agenda for future research. Electronic Markets, 26, 173–194. https://link.springer.com/article/10.1007/s12525-016-0219-0

Ali, S. M., Gupta, N., Nayak, G. K., & Lenka, R. K. (2016, December). Big data visualization: Tools and challenges. In *2016 2nd International Conference on Contemporary Computing and Informatics (IC3I)* (pp. 656–660). IEEE. https://ieeexplore.ieee.org/abstract/document/7918044/

Arpita, N., Patnaik, A., Satpathy, I., Patnaik, B. C. M., & Khang, A. (2023). Incorporating Artificial Intelligence (AI) for precision medicine: A narrative analysis. In A. Khang (Ed.), *AI and IoT-Based Technologies for Precision Medicine*. ISBN: 9798369308769. IGI Global Press. https://doi.org/10.4018/979-8-3693-0876-9.ch002

Blake, M. R., & Morse, C. (2016). Keeping your options open: A review of open source and free technologies for instructional use in higher education. *Reference Services Review*, 44(3), 375–389. www.emerald.com/insight/content/doi/10.1108/RSR-05-2016-0033/full/html

Chabot, C., Stolte, C., & Hanrahan, P. (2003). Tableau software. *Tableau Software*, 6. http://tv-prod.s3.amazonaws.com/documents%2F5644-Tableau+History.pdf

Chatterjee, S., & Hadi, A. S. (2006). *Regression Analysis by Example*. John Wiley & Sons. www.google.com/books?hl=en&lr=&id=zyjWBgAAQBAJ&oi=fnd&pg=PP1&dq=Regression+analysis+by+example.+John+Wiley+%26+Sons&ots=O_jF7T4OiX&sig=pf63CCKhWMus6xH5JS8mnDP40zQ

Dwivedi, S., Kasliwal, P., & Soni, S. (2016, March). Comprehensive study of data analytics tools (RapidMiner, Weka, R tool, Knime). In 2016 Symposium on Colossal Data Analysis and Networking (CDAN) (pp. 1–8). IEEE. https://ieeexplore.ieee.org/abstract/document/7570894/

Elgendy, N., & Elragal, A. (2014). Big data analytics: a literature review paper. In Advances in Data Mining. Applications and Theoretical Aspects: 14th Industrial Conference, ICDM 2014, St. Petersburg, Russia, July 16–20, 2014. Proceedings 14 (pp. 214–227). Springer International Publishing. https://bit.ly/3vnIxul

Ellis, B. (2014). *Real-time Analytics: Techniques to Analyze and Visualize Streaming Data*. John Wiley & Sons. https://bit.ly/43GoKTf

Ghasemaghaei, M. (2019). Does data analytics use improve firm decision making quality? The role of knowledge sharing and data analytics competency. *Decision Support Systems*, 120, 14–24. www.sciencedirect.com/science/article/pii/S0167923619300429

Hung, J. L., He, W., & Shen, J. (2020). Big data analytics for supply chain relationship in banking. *Industrial Marketing Management*, 86, 144–153. www.sciencedirect.com/science/article/pii/S0019850118304681

Keerthika, K., Kannan, M., & Khang A. (2023). Medical data analytics: Roles, challenges, and analytical tools. In A. Khang (Ed.), *AI and IoT-Based Technologies for Precision Medicine*. IGI Global Press. ISBN: 9798369308769. https://doi.org/10.4018/979-8-3693-0876-9.ch001

Khang, A., Abdullayev, V., Alyar, A. V., Khalilov, M., Murad, B. (2023). AI-aided data analytics tools and applications for the healthcare sector. In A. Khang (Ed.), *AI and IoT-Based Technologies for Precision Medicine*. IGI Global Press. ISBN: 9798369308769. https://doi.org/10.4018/979-8-3693-0876-9.ch018

Khang, A., Kali, C. R., Satapathy, S. K., Kumar, A., Ranjan Das, S., & Panda, M. R. (2023). Enabling the future of manufacturing: integration of robotics and iot to smart factory infrastructure in industry 4.0. In A. Khang, V. Shah, & S. Rani (Eds.), *AI-Based Technologies and Applications in the Era of the Metaverse* (1st Ed.) (pp. 25–50). IGI Global Press. https://doi.org/10.4018/978-1-6684-8851-5.ch002

Khang A., Muthmainnah M, Prodhan Mahbub Ibna Seraj, Ahmad Al Yakin, Ahmad J. Obaid, Manas Ranjan Panda. "AI-Aided Teaching Model for the Education 5.0 Ecosystem" *AI-Based Technologies and Applications in the Era of the Metaverse*. (1 Ed.) (2023). Page (83–104). IGI Global Press. https://doi.org/10.4018/978-1-6684-8851-5.ch004

Khang, A., Shah V., & Rani S. (2023). *AI-Based Technologies and Applications in the Era of the Metaverse* (1st Ed.). IGI Global Press. https://doi.org/10.4018/978-1-6684-8851-5

Linzbach, P., Inman, J. J., & Nikolova, H. (2019). E-Commerce in a physical store: Which retailing technologies add real value?. *NIM Marketing Intelligence Review*, 11(1), 42–47. www.nim.org/fileadmin/12_NIM_MIR_Issues/MIR_Die_Zukunft_des_Einzelhandels/MIR_Die_Zukunft_des_Einzelhandels_EN/linzbach_ea_vol_11_no_1_eng.pdf

Manekar, A. K., & Pradeepini, G. (2015, December). Cloud based big data analytics a review. *In 2015 International Conference on Computational Intelligence and Communication Networks (CICN)* (pp. 785–788). IEEE. https://ieeexplore.ieee.org/abstract/document/7546203/

Mehta, N., & Pandit, A. (2018). Concurrence of big data analytics and healthcare: A systematic review. International Journal of Medical Informatics, 114, 57–65. www.sciencedirect.com/science/article/pii/S1386505618302466

Monino, J. L. (2021). Data value, big data analytics, and decision-making. Journal of the Knowledge Economy, 12, 256–267. https://link.springer.com/article/10.1007/s13132-016-0396-2

Muthmainnah, M., Khang, A., Mahbub Ibna Seraj, P., Al Yakin, A., Oteir, I., & Alotaibi, A. N. (2023). An innovative teaching model – The Potential of metaverse for english learning. In *AI-Based Technologies and Applications in the Era of the Metaverse* (1st Ed.) (pp. 105–126). IGI Global Press. https://doi.org/10.4018/978-1-6684-8851-5.ch005

Namita, P., Satpathy, I., Chandra Patnaik, B., & Anh, P. T. N. (2023). Application of machine learning for image processing in the healthcare sector. In A. Khang (Ed.), *AI and IoT-Based Technologies for Precision Medicine* (Eds.). IGI Global Press. ISBN: 9798369308769. https://doi.org/10.4018/979-8-3693-0876-9.ch004

Nandimath, J., Banerjee, E., Patil, A., Kakade, P., Vaidya, S., & Chaturvedi, D. (2013, August). Big data analysis using Apache Hadoop. In *2013 IEEE 14th International Conference on Information Reuse & Integration (IRI)* (pp. 700–703). IEEE. https://ieeexplore.ieee.org/abstract/document/6642536/

Nuzzo, R. L. (2016). The box plots alternative for visualizing quantitative data. PM&R, 8(3), 268–272. https://ieeexplore.ieee.org/abstract/document/8528677/

Pooja, K., Jadhav, B., Kulkarni, A., Khang, A., Kulkarni, S. (2023). The role of blockchain technology in metaverse ecosystem. In *AI-Based Technologies and Applications in the*

Era of the Metaverse (1 Ed.) (pp. 228–236). IGI Global Press. https://doi.org/10.4018/ 978-1-6684-8851-5.ch011

Salloum, S., Dautov, R., Chen, 2., Peng, P., & Huang, J. Z. (2016). Big data analytics on Apache Spark. International Journal of Data Science and Analytics, 1, 145–164.

Sampath, B., & Khang, A. (2023). AI-integrated technology for a secure and ethical healthcare ecosystem. In A. Khang (Ed.), *AI and IoT-Based Technologies for Precision Medicine*. IGI Global Press. ISBN: 9798369308769. https://doi.org/10.4018/ 979-8-3693-0876-9.ch003

Saxena, A.C., Ojha, A., Sobti, D., & Khang, A. (2023). Artificial Intelligence (AI) Centric Model in Metaverse Ecosystem. In A. Khang, V. Shah, & S. Rani (Eds.), *AI-Based Technologies and Applications in the Era of the Metaverse* (1st Ed.) (pp. 1–24). IGI Global Press. https://doi.org/10.4018/978-1-6684-8851-5.ch001

Shah, V., & Khang, A. (2023). Metaverse-enabling IoT technology for a futuristic healthcare system. In *AI-Based Technologies and Applications in the Era of the Metaverse* (1 Ed.) (pp. 165–173). IGI Global Press. https://doi.org/10.4018/978-1-6684-8851-5.ch008

Wang, J., Xu, C., Zhang, J., & Zhong, R. (2022). Big data analytics for intelligent manufacturing systems: A review. *Journal of Manufacturing Systems*, 62, 738–752.

Yadranjiaghdam, B., Pool, N., & Tabrizi, N. (2016, December). A survey on real-time big data analytics: Applications and tools. In *2016 International Conference on Computational Science and Computational Intelligence (CSCI)* (pp. 404–409). IEEE.

3 Big Data Tools for Business and Finance Sectors in the Era of Metaverse

Harpreet Kaur Channi and Ramandeep Sandhu

3.1 INTRODUCTION

The metaverse is a revolutionary idea made possible by fast technological improvement. The immersive metaverse merges digital and physical worlds to provide consumers with a smooth and integrated virtual experience. Businesses and financial institutions have many new possibilities in this digital frontier. Big data, a powerful tool that helps organizations make data-driven metaverse choices, is central to this technological revolution. Multiple virtual worlds, augmented reality, and virtual reality experiences make up the metaverse (Khang, Shah et al., 2023). Users may cooperate and interact with digital information and one another in ways never before possible. People, companies, and society may meet, communicate, and trade in a hyper-connected and immersive world. Industry executives should explore the metaverse because it can change corporate operations (Schmitt et al., 2023).

Data growth has accelerated with the metaverse. Data generation has skyrocketed due to the internet, social media, Internet of Things (IoT) devices, and digital platforms. This plethora of data has proven essential in business and finance for analyzing consumer behavior, market trends, risk management, and optimizing operations. Big data has already revolutionized business and finance. It gives companies richer consumer information for personalized experiences and targeted marketing (Saxena et al., 2023).

Data analytics has revolutionized financial services by helping investment businesses make educated judgments, gauge market risks, and find lucrative possibilities. This chapter examines how big data and the metaverse affect business and finance. It covers the tools, technology, and applications that help companies to survive in this new digital world (Wang et al., 2022). The chapter also discusses big data's role in the metaverse, its uses in business and finance, the tools and technologies that enable its implementation, and the ethical issues surrounding data usage in virtual environments. The authors also review successful integration case studies, identify problems, and evaluate future trends and prospects. In conclusion, companies and financial institutions have limitless possibilities for development, innovation, and improved consumer experiences in the metaverse. Embracing big data as an

DOI: 10.1201/9781032618845-3

enabler, organizations may use data-driven insights to manage this changing terrain. Organizations may lead the digital revolution by adopting big data and the metaverse (Nica et al., 2022).

3.2 BIG DATA

The term "big data" was used to describe the increasingly common occurrence of massive, complicated, and varied datasets that conventional data management, processing, and analysis techniques are inadequate for handling. It entails huge amounts of information that can't be stored in a traditional database or processed with conventional software on time. The volume, velocity, and variety of data are sometimes called the "three V's" defining big data. When we talk about "volume," we're referring to the massive amounts of data produced by social media, sensors, transactional systems, and more. How quickly information can be created, gathered, and analyzed in real time or very close to real time is what we mean when we talk about velocity. Data come in many forms, some more organized than others (such as tables and spreadsheets) and others more unstructured (such as text, photos, and videos) (Khang, 2023b).

The potential of big data to provide useful insights, facilitate data-driven decision-making, and unearth important patterns and correlations is enormous. To effectively process, analyze, and gain insights from huge datasets, it is frequently necessary to use specialized technologies and tools, such as distributed computing frameworks like Apache Hadoop and Apache Spark. Information retrieval methods like data mining, machine learning, and predictive analytics are often used to sift through massive datasets in the search for useful insights. Big data is important in many fields, from business to healthcare to finance to transportation and beyond, since it allows for the study of massive datasets that may lead to breakthroughs in these areas (Depari et al., 2022).

The term "big data" has emerged in response to this deluge of information to describe the massive amounts of data (both structured and unstructured) that conventional data-processing tools are ill-equipped to handle. Big data is significant because it can improve decision-making by providing new insights and driving the discovery of previously unknown patterns and connections. The power of big data to revolutionize companies and whole industries is a major factor in the phenomenon's growing importance. Big data allows businesses to understand their consumers better, provide better services, run more efficiently, and find untapped market niches (Sami et al., 2023).

Data-driven choices, enhanced product development, targeted marketing efforts, and the ability to foresee future trends and customer behavior are all made possible by big data analytics. In addition, big data is very useful for scientific study and technological development. It paves the way for academics to examine massive databases, yielding insights that may be used in healthcare, genetics, climate science, and the social sciences. Due to their reliance on large volumes of data for training and advancement, artificial intelligence and machine learning algorithms are likewise propelled by big data. Big data also has important consequences for government and public policy. Governments may use big data analytics to solve social problems, boost public services, revamp city planning, and come to more data-driven policy conclusions (Muthmainnah et al., 2023).

Additionally, it calls for stricter data protection methods and legislation due to significant ethical and privacy issues it presents. Big data's history and relevance stem from the fact that it can transform many facets of modern life, from commerce and science to government and how we live our daily lives. Big data allows us to solve difficult problems and make better choices, enhancing our daily lives and professional endeavors. Several factors, such as technological progress, the expanding digitalization of information, and the increasing need for data-driven insights, have propelled the development of big data. Figure 3.1 provides a high-level overview of big data's history and present state.

- **Data Explosion**: Global data production has increased exponentially with the introduction of the internet, social media platforms, mobile devices, and IoT devices. As a result, innovative methods of collecting, storing, and analyzing massive data volumes are urgently required.
- **Technology Advancements**: Managing big data has been greatly aided by technological advancements in computing power, storage capacity, and networking infrastructure. New technologies like cloud computing, distributed computing frameworks like Hadoop and Spark, and scalable databases have adapted to the difficulties inherent in processing and analyzing large datasets.

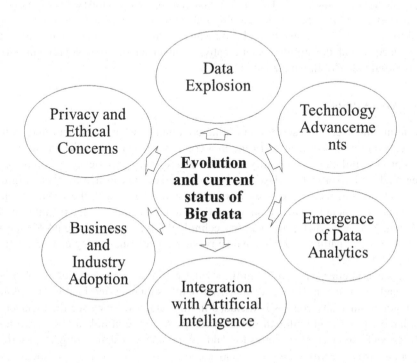

FIGURE 3.1 Evolution and current status of big data.

- **Emergence of Data Analytics**: The promise of big data was gradually recognized as it became more widespread. Data mining, machine learning, and predictive analytics have become popular methods for gleaning useful information from massive databases.
- **Integration with Artificial Intelligence**: The combination of big data with artificial intelligence (AI) and machine learning (ML) has further accelerated the development of the field of big data. The availability of massive datasets facilitates the training and enhancement of artificial intelligence and machine learning models, paving the way for the creation of advanced algorithms capable of real-time data analysis and interpretation.
- **Business and Industry Adoption**: The broad acceptance of big data's benefits results from its acknowledged worth. Companies use big data analytics to learn more about their customers, enhance operations, make better decisions, and spur creative thinking (Lee et al., 2021).
- **Privacy and Ethical Concerns**: Privacy, data security, and ethical issues have all been questioned due to the explosion of big data. The General Data Protection Regulation (GDPR) is one example of the new breed of data security and privacy rules designed to promote ethical data practices.

Growth in data volume, data diversity, and data velocity characterize the present status of big data. The Internet of Things (IoT) and edge computing have switched the spotlight to real-time analytics and streaming data processing. An increasing number of people are concerned with data ethics, data quality, and other aspects of data governance. Big data is generally developing thanks to new tools and an ever-growing need for data-driven insights. It has become an essential aspect of contemporary corporate tactics, with the ability to spur creativity, enhance judgment, and revolutionize fields worldwide (Muthmainnah et al., 2023).

3.3 METAVERSE

The term "metaverse" describes an online community where members may communicate and collaborate in real time in a computer-generated environment. It's a concept of a unified virtual reality universe where every experience is completely integrated with every other. Users in the metaverse often utilize avatars—digital representations of themselves—to move about and interact with the virtual world. The metaverse includes virtual, augmented, mixed, and cutting-edge technology. It aspires to unite and synchronize various technologies for a more coherent VR experience. The social nature of the metaverse is one of its distinguishing characteristics (Pooja et al., 2023).

Users can interact with people in the virtual world via communication, collaboration, and other activities. Everything from online shopping and banking to online gaming and university courses is included in this category. Many see the metaverse as a large, ever-changing digital universe comprising several linked virtual worlds, settings, and experiences. It aspires to build a community by connecting users across disparate virtual reality (VR) apps and games. While the idea of the metaverse originated in science fiction, it has received much more focus and interest in recent years as technological advances bring us closer to realizing this vision (Sihare & Khang, 2023).

Several firms and platforms are aggressively pursuing the creation of the metaverse, which has the potential to revolutionize many different sectors and how we use the internet for things like employment, education, and entertainment. When taken as a whole, the metaverse is an aspirational vision of a vast virtual reality realm where users may freely discover, produce, and interact with digital information and one another in a completely immersive and linked way. As shown in Figure 3.2, the metaverse has several distinguishing characteristics that set it apart from more conventional VR environments (Shah & Khang et al., 2023).

- **Immersion:** The metaverse aims to provide a high level of immersion, transporting users into a virtual environment that feels realistic and fascinating. It leverages virtual, augmented, and mixed-reality technologies to create a sense of presence and immersion for users.
- **Interconnectivity:** The metaverse is characterized by its interconnectivity, allowing users to seamlessly navigate and interact across multiple virtual worlds, platforms, and experiences. It enables users to move between different environments, socialize with others, and access a wide range of digital content and services.
- **Shared Space:** The metaverse is a shared space where users can interact with each other in real time. It fosters social interactions, collaboration, and communication, allowing users to engage with other individuals, form communities, and participate in shared activities.

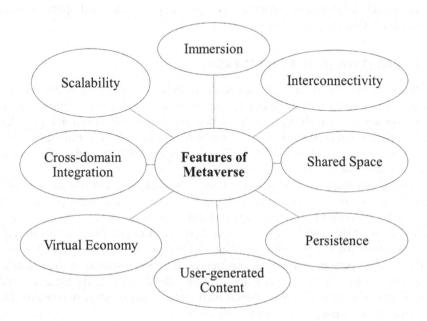

FIGURE 3.2 The features of the metaverse.

- **Persistence:** The metaverse is persistent, meaning it exists and evolves continuously, even when users are not actively present. Digital objects, environments, and interactions persist over time, creating a sense of continuity and a dynamic virtual ecosystem.
- **User-Generated Content:** The metaverse often encourages user-generated content, enabling users to create and contribute digital content, experiences, and environments. Users can design virtual objects, build virtual worlds, and shape the metaverse's landscape, fostering creativity, customization, and personalization.
- **Virtual Economy:** The metaverse may include a virtual economy where users can engage in economic activities, such as buying and selling virtual goods and services. This can involve virtual currencies, digital marketplaces, and even real-world financial transactions within the virtual environment.
- **Cross-Domain Integration:** The metaverse aims to integrate various domains, technologies, and applications, combining elements from gaming, entertainment, social networking, commerce, education, and more. It seeks to break down silos and create a seamless and unified virtual reality experience.
- **Scalability:** The metaverse is designed to scale to accommodate many users and support diverse activities. It can handle simultaneous interactions, communications, and transactions across multiple users and virtual environments without sacrificing performance or user experience.

These characteristics collectively contribute to the vision of the metaverse as a comprehensive, immersive, and interconnected virtual reality space, offering users a dynamic and social digital experience that goes beyond individual applications or experiences (Chauhan et al., 2023).

3.4 BIG DATA IN THE METAVERSE

Utilizing the massive volumes of data produced in the virtual reality world, big data plays a crucial role in the metaverse by improving user experiences, optimizing virtual economies, and enabling data-driven decision-making, as shown in Figure 3.3. User analytics and personalization are two of big data's most important uses in the metaverse (Khang, Shah et al., 2023). Users' activities, choices, and preferences in the metaverse produce much information.

Another essential component of big data in the metaverse is real-time data processing. Users' interactions and activities in the metaverse constantly produce new data, making it a real-time system. Big data technology makes the effective processing and analysis of this continuous stream of real-time data possible. Thanks to real-time data processing, users may get instant responses, make on-the-fly modifications, and have more personalized virtual experiences. It allows instantaneous reactions to user input, making it more natural and engaging. By monitoring the behaviors and preferences of users in real time, virtual environments and events may be tailored to each individual (Khang, Abdullayev et al., 2023).

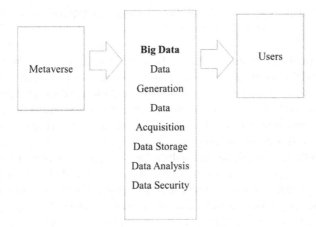

FIGURE 3.3 Big data in the metaverse.

In addition, big data is crucial in the metaverse's content creation and curation processes. Algorithms may provide user-specific content recommendations and suggestions by analyzing user behavior, preferences, and engagement levels. Creators and producers of the content may benefit from big data insights by learning which forms of content are most widely consumed, which forms of engagement are most effective, and how to optimize content distribution best. This data-driven strategy guarantees consumers access to interesting and varied material in the metaverse (Arpita et al., 2023).

Metaverse virtual economies may also benefit from big data's optimization efforts. The metaverse develops its economic structure using digital commodities, including virtual money, digital markets, and digital property. In the digital economy, big data analytics may be used to examine price dynamics, user demand patterns, and market trends. With this knowledge, we can improve the economic environment of the metaverse by adjusting pricing policies, streamlining logistics, and developing virtual assets (Keerthika et al., 2023).

In conclusion, big data in the metaverse allows for enhanced user analytics and customization, continuous data processing, the creation and curation of content, and the enhancement of virtual economies. It will enable the metaverse to create individualized and interesting interactions, respond in real time to user actions, provide rich and varied material, and fine-tune its virtual economies. Using big data, the metaverse may improve user experiences and grow into a dynamic, immersive VR environment (Sampath and Khang, 2023).

3.5 BIG DATA TOOLS FOR THE METAVERSE

Many big data tools and technologies are used in the metaverse to deal with the complexity and scope of the data being created and analyzed in real time. These resources improve the virtual reality industry's capacity for storing, processing, analyzing, and managing data. Some crucial big data resources for the metaverse are shown in Figure 3.4.

- **Distributed File Systems (DFS)**: Both the Apache Hadoop Distributed File System (HDFS) and the Apache Hadoop Compatible File System (HCFS) are widely utilized in the metaverse as distributed file systems. These file systems are designed to store massive volumes of data over several nodes while being scalable and fault-tolerant. They provide dependable and easily accessible data storage across the metaverse.
- **Stream Processing Platforms (SPP)**: Real-time data streams in the metaverse need stream-processing technologies like Apache Kafka and Apache Flink. These systems allow for the real-time processing and analysis of continuous data streams. They make it easier to incorporate data, events, and user interactions in real time into a virtual setting.
- **Data Analytics Frameworks (DAF)**: Data in the metaverse are processed and analyzed using big data analytics frameworks like Apache Spark and Apache Hadoop. These frameworks facilitate the effective analysis of large datasets by providing distributed computing capabilities and parallel processing assistance. They enable many use cases by offering tools for sophisticated analytics in the metaverse, such as batch processing, machine learning, and graph processing.
- **Data Visualization Tools (DVT)**: Tableau and Power BI are two of the data visualization tools used to make sense of data in the metaverse and show them visually. These methods allow for data visualization that would otherwise be

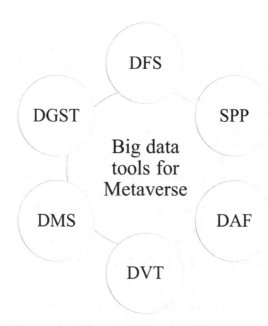

FIGURE 3.4   Big data tools for the metaverse.

difficult to comprehend. Data visualizations enhance usability by making complex datasets more digestible and interactive in a digital environment.

- **Database Management Systems (DMS)**: The metaverse uses database management systems like Apache Cassandra and MongoDB to store and manage structured and unstructured data. These systems provide scalability and adaptability in data storage choices, allowing for more effective data management and retrieval. They enable fast reading and writing, giving users instantaneous VR data access.

- **Data Governance and Security Tools (DGST)**: Data governance and security technologies are crucial in the metaverse because they need to protect users' privacy and their virtual assets. Data access controls, governance principles, and security may be better managed and enforced in a virtual setting with tools like Apache Ranger and Apache Atlas. These systems include authentication, authorization, encryption, and data privacy features to keep users' information secure and the metaverse running smoothly.

With the help of big data tools and technologies, the metaverse can analyze massive quantities of data in real time, extract useful insights, and provide consumers with a truly engaging and immersive virtual reality experience. They are the backbone of the metaverse ecosystem, allowing for streamlined data management, analytics, and protection.

3.6 REAL-TIME DATA PROCESSING AND PREDICTIVE ANALYTICS

Big data technologies' predictive analytics and real-time data-processing capabilities are particularly important in the metaverse (Namita et al., 2023). These features allow the metaverse to process live data streams and make choices based on collected information, resulting in an engaging and unique experience for each user. Big data technology makes real-time data processing and predictive analytics easier for the metaverse, as shown in Figure 3.5.

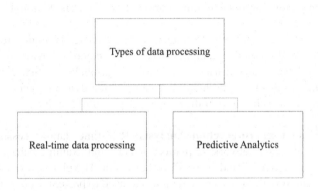

FIGURE 3.5 Types of data processing.

- **Real-Time Data Processing:** In the metaverse, user interactions, events, and activities generate a continuous data stream. Real-time data processing tools, such as Apache Kafka and Apache Flink, are employed to ingest, process, and analyze these data in real time. As users navigate virtual environments, interact with objects, and engage in social interactions, real-time data processing allows the metaverse to respond instantly to user actions. For example, consider a virtual gaming environment where multiple players are engaged in a cooperative mission. Real-time data processing tools can capture and analyze each player's movements, actions, and interactions, enabling collaborative gameplay with minimal latency. This ensures that steps one player takes have immediate consequences for other players, creating an immersive and seamless gaming experience.
- **Predictive Analytics:** Using past data and machine learning algorithms, predictive analytics may foretell how users will act and what they will like in the metaverse. Predictive analytics solutions may analyze user activity, such as clickstream data, content consumption habits, and social network connections, to better understand users and forecast their future moves. Predictive analytics, for instance, may examine a shopper's prior actions in an online store to foretell what they would be interested in buying. A user's browsing experience in an online store may be improved, and the customer's propensity to buy can be increased by using this information to provide informed product suggestions. The metaverse can provide users with highly adaptive and unique encounters with predictive analytics and real-time data processing. Big data technologies constantly monitor users' actions inside the VR environment, which evaluate the data streams to draw conclusions and identify trends. Collecting and using these data may improve the content, virtual environments, and user interactions.

While real-time data processing and predictive analytics in the metaverse have many potential benefits, they pose several obstacles. These include dealing with large amounts of data, ensuring the data are accurate, and controlling the computing complexity involved. Overcoming these obstacles and using the promise of real-time data processing and predictive analytics in the rapidly developing virtual reality ecosystem calls for cutting-edge big data structures and optimization methodologies (Eswaran et al., 2023).

The following case studies illustrate how big data technologies for real-time data processing and predictive analytics may lead to metaverse-wide improvements in dynamic and personalized user experiences, high-quality virtual environments, and secure data exchanges. The metaverse can provide dynamic, personalized, and immersive experiences because of the processing power of big data.

- **Real-Time User Interaction Analysis:** Real-time data-processing systems in a digital social networking platform record and examine behaviors such as "likes," "comments," and "shares" as they occur. The platform's ability to continually analyze these data in real time enables it to present users with real-time contextual suggestions for relevant relationships, material, and events.

- **Real-Time Virtual Environment Optimization:** Through the application of real-time data-processing technologies, virtual environments may be optimized in response to the activities and behaviors of their users in real time. Using information about the player's location, movement, and performance in real time, a virtual reality game's engine may make the game more challenging, add new obstacles, or otherwise adapt the virtual environment to the player's needs (Khang, 2023a).
- **Predictive User Behavior Modeling:** Data from users' previous activities, such as their interactions, preferences, and purchases, may be analyzed by predictive analytics systems to provide future predictions. These models may provide real-time, personalized product suggestions to a user in an e-commerce metaverse based on the user's past purchase history and present browsing activity.
- **Real-Time Personalized Content Delivery:** The metaverse may provide users with highly customized experiences by combining real-time data processing with predictive analytics. For instance, based on a user's interests and the issues that are currently trending, a virtual news platform might recommend certain articles or videos to them.
- **Fraud Detection and Security:** Monitoring user activities, transactions, and interactions inside the metaverse using real-time data-processing technologies may help detect fraudulent activity. These technologies analyze data in real time to keep user data safe and the metaverse secure and utilize predictive models to spot abnormalities, unauthorized access attempts, and fraudulent activity.

When using big data technologies in the metaverse, keeping safety and ethical standards in mind is essential. User privacy, data integrity, and ethical standards must be maintained in the metaverse due to the volume of user data being collected and processed. Security-wise, it is crucial to take strong precautions to protect user information from intrusion, breach, and other cyber dangers. Data encryption during transmission and storage, safe access restrictions, and routine monitoring for suspicious activity all fall under this category. Security mechanisms should also be in place to safeguard virtual assets and forestall their alteration or theft while in the metaverse (Khang & Santosh et al., 2023).

3.7   SECURITY AND ETHICAL GUIDELINES

Using big data technologies in the metaverse requires careful consideration of ethical norms. The collection and use of user data require careful attention to issues of openness and informed permission. Users should be informed of the data being gathered, given a choice over how those data are used, and given the means to exercise that choice. Data anonymization and de-identification procedures should be used to safeguard user identities and guarantee compliance with privacy requirements. Ethical norms should also address data bias, inequality, and justice concerns (Khang & Gadirova et al., 2023).

The metaverse's algorithms and models must be built to reduce discrimination and accommodate users of all identities. The usage of big data technologies should be audited and reviewed often to identify and resolve any ethical problems arising from its deployment. Ethical principles also emphasize the ethical and responsible usage of user-created material in the metaverse. Systems must be in place to deal with accusations of copyright infringement and disputes if user-generated material is used without their permission or without them receiving compensation (Muhammad et al., 2023).

Overall, it is crucial to securely and ethically use big data technologies in the metaverse. The metaverse may establish a secure, trustworthy, and inclusive environment for users by placing a premium on user privacy, data security, and ethical practices, encouraging responsible data use and user involvement (Kamran et al., 2023).

3.8 FUTURE RESEARCH DIRECTION

Virtual reality has much to gain from the implications and future research possibilities for big data technologies in the metaverse. Enhanced individualization, real-time analytics, and agile decision-making are all possible because of big data technologies' ability to gather, analyze, and utilize massive volumes of data in the metaverse. Research into data-driven personalization is a promising area. This necessitates the creation of sophisticated algorithms and models to comprehend metaverse users' tastes, habits, and surroundings. Researchers can improve the engagement and contentment of their users by developing more precise and efficient personalized experiences using big data analytics (Suresh et al., 2023).

Important topics for further study include real-time analytics and decision-making in the metaverse. Quicker and smarter reactions to user interactions and events may be achieved by developing faster and more efficient real-time data-processing methods and investigating innovative methodologies for real-time analytics. This study's findings can potentially improve the realism and interactivity of future VR applications (Durga et al., 2023).

Since user data are collected and processed in the metaverse, privacy and security are paramount. To maintain the safety of user data inside the metaverse, future studies should concentrate on creating effective privacy-preserving strategies, encryption systems, and secure data exchange protocols. We may look at trust models and safe identity management solutions for users to feel safe disclosing information in the virtual world (Lakshmi et al., 2023).

Interoperability and standardization are also worthy of study. It is essential to provide smooth integration and data interchange across the metaverse's many platforms, apps, and virtual worlds. Data sharing, cooperation, and interoperability may be improved by creating standards, protocols, and frameworks, leading to a more cohesive and interconnected metaverse environment. Data-driven personalization, real-time analytics, privacy and security, and interoperability are just a few of the implications and potential research objectives for big data technologies in the metaverse. Keeping these lines of inquiry open will help the metaverse develop, giving consumers a safer, more customized virtual reality experience.

3.9 CASE STUDIES

Due to the novelty of the metaverse idea, there are few concrete examples of how big data tools may be used in the metaverse. However, the use of such technology in parallel worlds would be worth investigating. The following cases illustrate some possible benefits and drawbacks of big data techniques in the virtual world.

- **Virtual Social Networking Platform:** A metaverse-based social media platform may use big data to learn more about its members' habits, passions, and tastes. The platform can deliver appropriate recommendations for new connections, content, and events based on users' current behavior and interests by analyzing the huge volumes of data generated by user behaviors like publishing, commenting, and connecting. This increases participation and helps people feel like they belong in the metaverse.
- **Virtual Reality Gaming:** Using big data tools in virtual reality gaming can potentially enhance the industry. In-game actions and statistics might be recorded in real time for analysis using data analytics and processing. Using these data to dynamically adjust the game difficulty, present new challenges, and adapt the virtual environment in response to player behavior may result in a more engaging and personalized gaming experience.
- **E-Commerce in the Metaverse:** Big data technologies have a great possibility to improve e-commerce in the metaverse. By analyzing user behavior, purchase history, and data on popular things in the present, predictive analytics may be used for personalized product recommendations, targeted promotions, and real-time pricing adjustments. This improves user engagement and conversion rates, allowing for a more tailored consumer experience.
- **Virtual Healthcare:** Virtual healthcare systems in the metaverse have access to big data analytics, biometric monitoring, and activity tracking. These data can be utilized right away for things like remote patient monitoring, anomaly identification, and the development of individualized health suggestions. By identifying patterns in large datasets, big data analytics may also be useful in public health management and research.

These scenarios illustrate potential applications of big data technology in the metaverse. In the metaverse, virtual reality experiences, customization, and decision-making might all benefit from the optimization of big data technology. However, specific applications and results may differ.

3.10 BIG DATA ANALYTICS FOR BUSINESS AND FINANCE

Big data analytics is crucial to business and finance in the metaverse. Companies and financial institutions may employ big data analytics to get useful insights from the metaverse's enormous data volume from user interactions, virtual transactions, and digital engagements. Big data analytics may help businesses personalize marketing and product offers by understanding consumer behavior, preferences, and trends. Big data analytics allows organizations to make data-driven choices, optimize supply chain operations, and forecast market trends, providing a competitive advantage in the dynamic virtual market.

Investment and portfolio management in finance depend on big data analytics. Financial institutions can evaluate risk, find investment possibilities, and make educated choices based on real-time market analysis by analyzing massive volumes of data. Big data analytics helps identify fraud, allowing pre-emptive steps to protect financial transactions and metaverse access.

Real-time data processing and analysis is a major benefit of metaverse big data analytics. This real-time capacity allows companies and financial institutions to quickly adapt to market changes, consumer needs, and new trends, optimizing their plans and remaining nimble in a dynamic virtual world. Big data analytics has great promise but also raises data privacy, security, and ethical issues. Businesses and financial organizations collect massive volumes of consumer data, making data privacy and protection crucial. Companies must balance data-driven personalization with user privacy rights to retain trust and a pleasant metaverse user experience.

In conclusion, companies and financial institutions navigating the metaverse need big data analytics. Organizations may get actionable insights, improve decision-making, and find new virtual possibilities using advanced data analytics tools and technology. Businesses and financial institutions must embrace rigorous data governance practices, enforce ethical standards, and continually innovate in this disruptive age of linked digital realities to fully capitalize on big data analytics in the metaverse.

3.11 CONCLUSION

The metaverse and big data's exponential expansion have transformed corporations and financial institutions. Virtual worlds and huge data creation have enabled unparalleled information harvesting and innovation. Big data technologies provide data-driven decision-making, personalized consumer experiences, and optimization in this dynamic virtual world. Businesses may deepen client relationships by delivering customized goods and services in the metaverse. Big data analytics enables organizations to decipher user behavior, predict market trends, and modify the real-time strategy to stay ahead in the virtual market.

Big data solutions enable financial firms to make data-driven choices and effectively manage portfolios. Analyzing massive data streams allows proactive risk assessment, fraud detection, and discovering profitable possibilities in the ever-changing metaverse financial scene. Big data has limitless possibilities but also ethical issues. Users' trust and sensitive metaverse data must be protected through data privacy and security. Businesses and financial institutions must reconcile data-driven personalization and consumer privacy with responsible data governance (Khang, Kali et al., 2023).

Organizations must invest in cutting-edge technology and talented data experts to maximize big data as the metaverse evolves. This dynamic digital frontier requires creativity, consumer focus, and problem-solving. Businesses and financial institutions that use big data technologies and data-driven insights will lead virtual interactions and digital experiences in the metaverse. Enterprises can traverse this linked digital world and show this exciting new age of business and finance by integrating big data with strategic vision. Big data in the metaverse offers endless prospects, and those who use it may redefine digital success (Khang, Muthmainnah et al., 2023).

REFERENCES

Arpita, N., Patnaik, A., Satpathy, I., Patnaik, B. C. M., & Khang A. (2023). Incorporating Artificial Intelligence (AI) for precision medicine: A narrative analysis. In A. Khang (Ed.), *AI and IoT-Based Technologies for Precision Medicine*. IGI Global Press. ISBN: 9798369308769. https://doi.org/10.4018/979-8-3693-0876-9.ch002

Chauhan, V. S., Chakravorty, J., & Khang A. (2023). Smart cities data indicator-based cyber threats detection using bio-inspired artificial algae algorithm. In *Handbook of Research on AI-Based Technologies and Applications in the Era of the Metaverse* (pp. 436–447). Copyright: © 2023. https://doi.org/10.4018/978-1-6684-8851-5.ch024

Depari, G. S., Shu, E., & Indra, I. (2022). Big data and Metaverse toward business operations in indonesia. *Jurnal Ekonomi*, 11(01), 285–291. http://ejournal.seaninstitute.or.id/index.php/Ekonomi/article/view/246

Durga, P. S. S., Patnaik, B.C.M., Ipseeta, S., & Khang, A. (2023). Revolutionizing agriculture through blockchain: A bibliometric analysis of emerging trends and applications. In *Handbook of Research on AI-Equipped IoT Applications in High-Tech Agriculture* (pp. 295–312). Copyright: © 2023. https://doi.org/10.4018/978-1-6684-9231-4.ch016

Eswaran, U., Khang, A., & Eswaran, V. (Eds.). (2023). Applying machine learning for medical image processing. In A. Khang (Ed.), *AI and IoT-Based Technologies for Precision Medicine*. IGI Global Press. ISBN: 9798369308769. https://doi.org/10.4018/979-8-3693-0876-9.ch009

Kamran, I., Buttar, N. A., Waqas, M. M., Muthmainnah, Omer, M. M., Niaz, Y., & Khang, A. (2023). Robotic innovations in agriculture: maximizing production and sustainability. In A. Khang (Ed.), *Advanced Technologies and AI-Equipped IoT Applications in High-Tech Agriculture* (1st Ed.) (pp. 131–154). IGI Global Press. https://doi.org/10.4018/978-1-6684-9231-4.ch007

Keerthika, K., Kannan, M., & Khang, A. (2023). Medical data analytics: Roles, challenges, and analytical tools. In A. Khang (Ed.), *AI and IoT-Based Technologies for Precision Medicine*. IGI Global Press. ISBN: 9798369308769. https://doi.org/10.4018/979-8-3693-0876-9.ch001

Khang, A. (Ed.) (2023a). *Advanced Technologies and AI-Equipped IoT Applications in High-Tech Agriculture* (1st Ed.). IGI Global Press. https://doi.org/10.4018/978-1-6684-9231-4

Khang, A. (Ed.) (2023b). *AI and IoT-Based Technologies for Precision Medicine*. IGI Global Press. ISBN: 9798369308769. https://doi.org/10.4018/979-8-3693-0876-9

Khang, A., Abdullayev, V., Alyar, A. V., Khalilov, M., & Murad, B. (2023). AI-aided data analytics tools and applications for the healthcare sector. In A. Khang (Ed.). *AI and IoT-Based Technologies for Precision Medicine*. IGI Global Press. ISBN: 9798369308769. https://doi.org/10.4018/979-8-3693-0876-9.ch018

Khang, A., Kali, C. R., Satapathy, S. K., Kumar, A., Ranjan Das, S., & Panda, M. R. (2023). Enabling the future of manufacturing: integration of robotics and iot to smart factory infrastructure in industry 4.0. In A. Khang, V. Shah, & S. Rani (Eds.), *AI-Based Technologies and Applications in the Era of the Metaverse* (1st Ed.) (pp. 25–50). IGI Global Press. https://doi.org/10.4018/978-1-6684-8851-5.ch002

Khang, A., Muthmainnah, M., Seraj, P. M. I., Al Yakin, A., Obaid, A. J., & Panda, M.R. (2023). AI-aided teaching model for the education 5.0 ecosystem. In A. Khang, V. Shah, & S. Rani (Eds.), *AI-Based Technologies and Applications in the Era of the Metaverse* (1st Ed.) (pp. 83–104). IGI Global Press. https://doi.org/10.4018/978-1-6684-8851-5.ch004

Khang, A., Shah, V., & Rani, S. (Eds.) (2023). *AI-Based Technologies and Applications in the Era of the Metaverse* (1 Ed.). IGI Global Press. https://doi.org/10.4018/978-1-6684-8851-5

Lakshmi, H. M., Kumar, G. L. N. V. S., & Khang, A. (2023). Predictive analytics for high-tech agriculture. In A. Khang (Ed.), *Advanced Technologies and AI-Equipped IoT Applications in High-Tech Agriculture* (1st Ed.) (pp. 336–346). IGI Global Press. https://doi.org/10.4018/978-1-6684-9231-4.ch019

Lee, L. H., Braud, T., Zhou, P., Wang, L., Xu, D., Lin, Z., & Hui, P. (2021). *All One Needs to Know About Metaverse: A Complete Survey on Technological Singularity, Virtual Ecosystem, and Research Agenda.* arXiv preprint arXiv:2110.05352.

Muhammad, M. W., Ali, S., Muthmainnah, Rustam, A. R., & Khang, A. (2023). Unmanned aerial vehicles (Uavs) in modern agriculture: advancements and benefits. In A. Khang (Ed.), *Advanced Technologies and AI-Equipped IoT Applications in High-Tech Agriculture* (1st Ed.) (pp. 109–130). IGI Global Press. https://doi.org/10.4018/978-1-6684-9231-4.ch006

Muthmainnah, M., Khang, A., Al Yakin, A., Oteir, I., & Alotaibi, A. N. (2023). An innovative teaching model—The potential of metaverse for english learning. In A. Khang, V. Shah, & S. Rani (Eds.), *AI-Based Technologies and Applications in the Era of the Metaverse* (1st Ed.) (pp. 105–126). IGI Global Press. https://doi.org/10.4018/978-1-6684-8851-5.ch005

Namita, P., Satpathy, I., Chandra Patnaik, B., &Anh, P. T. N. (Eds.) (2023). Application of machine learning for image processing in the healthcare sector. In A. Khang (Ed.), *AI and IoT-Based Technologies for Precision Medicine.* IGI Global Press. ISBN: 9798369308769. https://doi.org/10.4018/979-8-3693-0876-9.ch004

Nica, E., Poliak, M., Popescu, G. H., & Pârvu, I. A. (2022). Decision intelligence and modeling, multisensory customer experiences, and socially interconnected virtual services across the metaverse ecosystem. *Linguistic and Philosophical Investigations,* 21, 137–153. www.ceeol.com/search/article-detail?id=1045819

Pooja, K., Jadhav, B., Kulkarni, A., Khang, A., & Kulkarni, S. (2023). The role of blockchain technology in metaverse ecosystem. In A. Khang, V. Shah, S. Rani (Eds.), *AI-Based Technologies and Applications in the Era of the Metaverse* (1st Ed.) (pp. 228–236). IGI Global Press. https://doi.org/10.4018/978-1-6684-8851-5.ch011

Sami, H., Hammoud, A., Arafeh, M., Wazzeh, M., Arisdakessian, S., Chahoud, M., ... & Guizani, M. (2023). *The Metaverse: Survey, Trends, Novel Pipeline Ecosystem & Future Directions.* arXiv preprint arXiv:2304.09240.

Sampath, B., & Khang, A. (2023). AI-integrated technology for a secure and ethical healthcare ecosystem. In A. Khang (Ed.), *AI and IoT-Based Technologies for Precision Medicine* (Eds.) IGI Global Press. ISBN: 9798369308769. https://doi.org/10.4018/979-8-3693-0876-9.ch003

Saxena, A. C., Ojha, A., Sobti, D., & Khang, A. (2023). Artificial Intelligence (AI) centric model in metaverse ecosystem. In A. Khang, V. Shah, & S. Rani (Eds.), *AI-Based Technologies and Applications in the Era of the Metaverse* (1st Ed.) (pp. 1–24). IGI Global Press. https://doi.org/10.4018/978-1-6684-8851-5.ch001

Schmitt, M. (2023). Big Data Analytics in the Metaverse: Business Value Creation with Artificial Intelligence and Data-Driven Decision Making. Available at SSRN 4385347. https://papers.ssrn.com/sol3/papers.cfm?abstract_id=4385347

Shah, V., & Khang, A. (2023). Metaverse-enabling IoT technology for a futuristic healthcare system. In A. Khang, V. Shah, & S. Rani (Eds.), *AI-Based Technologies and Applications in the Era of the Metaverse* (1st Ed.) (pp. 165–173). IGI Global Press. https://doi.org/ 10.4018/978-1-6684-8851-5.ch008

Sihare, S. R. & Khang, A. (2023). Effects of quantum technology on metaverse. In A. Khang, V. Shah, & S. Rani (Eds.), *AI-Based Technologies and Applications in the Era of the Metaverse* (1st Ed.) (pp. 104–203). IGI Global Press. https://doi.org/10.4018/ 978-1-6684-8851-5.ch009

Suresh, B. C. V., Bala, S., Ganesh, T. K., Kishoor, T. K. & Khang A. (2023). Automatic irrigation system using solar tracking device. In *Handbook of Research on AI-Equipped IoT Applications in High-Tech Agriculture* (pp. 239–256). Copyright: © 2023. https://doi. org/10.4018/978-1-6684-9231-4.ch013

Wang, M., Yu, H., Bell, Z., & Chu, X. (2022). Constructing an Edu-Metaverse ecosystem: A new and innovative framework. IEEE Transactions on Learning Technologies, 15(6), 685–696. https://ieeexplore.ieee.org/abstract/document/9905995/

4 Digital Revolution and Innovation in the Banking and Finance Sectors

Piyush Gupta and Zehra Raza

4.1 INTRODUCTION

The "Indian banking system," which provides new cooperation to aid economic development and social progress in the country, is going through a developing phase currently. Digital technology has made better regulation possible in the system connecting the government directly with the citizen. Moving towards digital banking will shake things up and cause more divisions in the financial services industry. Banks need to make big changes to their business, culture and technology. Most importantly, they should focus on innovation and using data to create new ways to make money and engage with customers. The banking system is totally committed to adapting to our changing financial needs. They are making organizational and structural changes to emerge as a new and mature culture in line with the current trends (Khang, Shah et al., 2023).

Digitalization is all about embracing the digital revolution to transform how businesses operate and how they generate revenue from customer value. It is about recognizing the strong connection between customer satisfaction and bank profitability. Banks are stepping up their work by embracing digitalization, which means they are offering improved customer services. It is about using technology to make banking easier, faster and more convenient for customers. Mobile technology has not only changed our work culture, it has also changed the standards for business (Khang, Kali et al., 2023).

"Digital banking," "mobile banking" and "online banking" are often used interchangeably because they all involve digital applications in some form. These are different terms that refer to various ways of accessing and managing banking services through digital platforms like mobile apps or online portals. Digital transformation has completely changed the game when it comes to banking. It is super flexible, adaptable and secure, making transactions simple for users/customers (Anand, 2023).

With the help of digitalization, customers can ditch cash and make transactions anytime, anywhere. It is about the freedom and flexibility to manage money with

DOI: 10.1201/9781032618845-4

just a few taps on your phone. There is no more the problem of carrying around physical currency. The banking industry of India has indeed seen the introduction of an innovative payment system and the establishment of small finance banks. These modern measures of the RBI are playing a crucial role in restructuring the banking industry.

4.2 REVIEW OF LITERATURE

There are two important issues examined by several academic studies, the first relates to digital transformation in the Indian banking sector and second is challenges as well as opportunities for digital banking in India. For the first issue, Shifa Fathima (2020) explained that the shift to digitalization can indeed help to reduce costs, streamline processes, and automate tasks for the business. Meanwhile, there are some challenges as explained by Anitha (2019) related to e-banking in which the e-banking revolution has had a profound effect on the banking industry, breaking down borders and creating new opportunities (Khang, Chowdhury et al., 2022).

However, developing countries like India face certain challenges in implementing e-banking initiatives. It is important to identify and address these impediments to ensure successful implementation. In one paper some obstacles specific to India's e-banking initiatives were pointed out. Reis et al. (2018) focused on digital transformation, in which they defined the utilization of new digital innovations to drive significant business enhancements and impact every aspect of customers' lives. Vial (2021), based on their framework, highlight digital transformation as a dynamic process. This involves the use of digital technologies that disrupt traditional practices, prompting organizations to respond strategically. These responses aim to modify their value creation strategies while overcoming structural changes and organizational barriers. This process can lead to both positive and negative outcomes. An inductive approach was used in reviewing the literature for their paper. Kraus et al. (2021) described the literature on transformation of digital business.

An analysis of co-occurrence utilizing the software VOS viewer was performed to graphically visualize the literature's node network. The literature on digital transformations offers valuable insights for both the government and private sector. By studying this research, they can better understand and adapt to the disruptive changes brought about by digital transformation. It is crucial to find ways to minimize the negative impacts on society and the environment while harnessing the benefits of this phenomenon. Jagtap (2018) identified in a study that digitalization has converted physical work, transactions and affairs into digital services. Banks have profited in several ways by embracing recently developed technologies. Amudhan et al. (2022) concluded that the results of the digital banking services on rural customers are significant. The primary data were collected through Google forms. The paper concluded that the overall response of customers towards digital banking services is good. Deepa and Barkha (2022) identified the involvement of digitalization in the Indian banking sector.

Digitalization has transfigured the planet into a global village. This inspires investigating the role of current technological development in the Indian banking sector. The Indian banking sector is going through significant innovations caused by this digitalization. Kusuma and College (2020) analyzed the situations and threats within the scope of digitalization of rural banking to obtain a new outlook for that sector. The conclusion of this study was that the digital alterations are making a new image of banking resources all together. The digitalization in banking has begun moving the standard of cash- and paper-based banking to paperless and cashless banking (Khang, Gupta et al., 2023).

Wu and Li (2023) described the World Bank survey data on Chinese enterprises and the use of multi-grid principal component analysis to create a digitalization index at the enterprise level as a comprehensive approach. Digital transformation positively impacts enterprise exports. The findings included that the intensity of enterprise innovation plays a moderating role in the association between digitalization and exports, highlighting the importance of innovation in leveraging the benefits of digitalization. Diener and Špaček (2021) analyzed the main determined barriers to digital transformation in both the private and commercial banking sectors from a managerial way of thinking.

The result also shows a wide-ranging, still young field of research which requires further observation. Vidya and Shailashri (2021) studied several electronic payments systems implemented by the banking sector such as card payments UPI, NEFT, IMPS, and RTGS. Investigation of digital payments was done using ABCD analysis. The benefits and advantages of the digital payment mechanism are more important than its restrictions and drawbacks. It was concluded that digital payments are extremely helpful in the modern scenario. Jeevanandam and Surech Babu (2022) studied numerous digital payment systems implemented by the banking sector, such as card payments IMPS, NEFT, UPI, RTGS, and UPI. Secondary and primary data were used in this paper. Digital payments are performing an essential service in banking as well as the wider economy increasing the country's GDP.

4.2.1 Objectives

- To understand the digital revolution in the Indian banking sector.
- To analyze the evolution of digital payment system in banking services.
- To understand the digital banking new trends in India.

4.2.2 Research Methodology

Descriptive and analytical research designs have been applied to complete the objectives of the study. For the study purposes, statistical tools CAGR (compound average rate of return) and mean have been used and a period of seven years has been taken for this study from FY 2015–16 to FY 2021–22. Data have been accumulated through the secondary sources for this study which were gathered from the RBI websites, research papers, journals, articles, magazines and newspapers, etc.

4.3 EVOLUTION OF DIGITAL BANKING

The current "Global Digital Revolution," on one hand, is contributing a vital role in the effective execution of contactless services in a very short time span, while, on the other hand, it is further establishing new patterns of socio-economic progress. For the purpose of digital banking, a proposal has been made in the Union Budget 2022–2023 to establish 75 digital banks in India. Based on the consumer-friendly concept, all these digital banks will be operated by scheduled banks located in 75 districts of the country. Some of the following digital products are also being continuously developed and expanded.

4.3.1 TELE BANKING

Tele banking refers to a different method of banking where customers can perform transactions over the phone. It allows customers to access their accounts, check balances, transfer funds and even pay bills by simply making a call. Tele banking helps to manage finances without needing to visit a physical bank branch.

4.3.2 AUTOMATED TELLER MACHINE

ATM is short for automated teller machine. An ATM is an electronic machine utilized for financial activities. It facilitates the customer to check their balance, deposit money, withdraw money or even transfer funds. With an ATM card, customers can carry out banking without needing to talk to a human cashier. It is like having a personal banking assistant right at your fingertips, available 24 hours a day, 7 days per week. The first ATM in India was set up by HSBC in Mumbai back in 1987. Since then, ATMs have become a common sight across the country, making banking more accessible and convenient for everyone. Also, it is one way that technology has transformed the way we handle finance.

4.3.3 ARTIFICIAL INTELLIGENCE

Machine learning and artificial intelligence (AI) are revolutionizing the Indian banking system. These technologies are shaping the future of banking services and products. Machine learning and AI are totally changing the work of the banking system in India. Technologies are making a big impact on banking facilities and services. Today, all Indian banks have started using AI-based innovations to provide quick, transparent and secure services to their customers. Artificial intelligence is changing business procedures and customer-facing services in the banking sector in India (Vijai, 2019).

In fact, artificial intelligence technology is providing significant support to banks in the automation of customer services, customer analysis and new customer acquisitions, etc. In today's scenario, AI is playing a crucial role, and is increasingly making banking easier and more efficient. AI technology is doing an amazing job in promoting banking products and managing credit risks. It also helps in reducing fraud, optimizing debt collection strategies, determining customer lifetime value and even using biometric identification.

TABLE 4.1
Government and Private Banks of India with the Support of AI Technology

S. No.	Name of Bank	AI enabled chat-boot
1	State Bank of India	SAI (SBI Intelligent Assistant)
2	Bank of Baroda	ADI (Assisted Digital Interaction)
3	HDFC Bank	EVA
4	Axis Bank	AXAA Voice Bot
5	ICICI Bank	IPal

In India, both government and private banks are using AI technology to operate customer chat-bots. A customer assistance chat-bot is like a virtual assistant that uses AI and machine learning to answer any customer queries. It operates through a business messenger, providing quick and automated responses. Customer chat-bots are being operated by government and private banks in India with the support of AI technology, the main examples of which are described in Table 4.1.

4.3.4 CENTRAL BANK DIGITAL CURRENCY

The e-Rupee is equivalent to a digital category of the Indian Rupee. It is produced by the RBI and it is known as CBDC. The value of an e-Rupee is equivalent to the physical currency and accepted everywhere. CBDC is just like the regular money we use. It is like having an Indian Rupee in digital form. The main objective of the e-Rupee, as stated by the RBI, is to provide a virtual currency for financial transactions. Central Bank Digital Currency makes digital transactions easier and more suitable for customers.

According to the RBI, the e-Rupee functions as a convertible legal tender, which means people can use it for transactions without needing a bank account. India has made incredible progress in digital payments innovation. The country has embraced various digital payment methods, making transactions more convenient and accessible for everyone. Technology has transformed the payment landscape in India. India has enacted a separate law for a payment and settlement system, which has played a pivotal role in ensuring the orderly expansion of the payment ecosystem in the country. It has helped to create a structured and efficient framework for digital payments. The concept of money has indeed evolved over time. It started with commodities like shells and beads then moved to metallic currencies like gold and silver coins. Later, paper currency because the norm, and now we have digital currency, which is changing the way we handle transactions. With the advancements in technology, the digitalization of money is indeed the next milestone in monetary history.

And one exciting development in this area is the emergence of Central Bank Digital Currencies (CBDC). These digital currencies, issued by central banks, have the possibilities to revolutionize the techniques we use to transact and store value. The CBDC is classified into two types, that is Retail (CBDC-R) and Wholesale (CBDC-W). Wholesale CBDC is designed for settling interbank transfers and other wholesale transactions between financial institutions. On the other hand, Retail CBDC is an electronic form of cash that is mainly used for everyday retail transactions. As of July 2022, around 105 countries were considering CBDCs, and 11 countries had already launched their own CBDCs.

4.3.5 NATION FIRST TRANSIT CARD

The National Common Mobility Card (NCMC) is a revolutionary initiative in India that aims to simplify and streamline the payment process for public transportation. SBI has introduced a special card called the "Nation First Transit Card" that customers can use to pay for their metro, bus, water ferry and parking expenses. Instead of carrying multiple cards or cash, customers can use this one card for all commuting needs. It is providing a seamless and convenient experience for digital ticketing and fare payments.

4.4 DIFFERENT PAYMENT SYSTEMS USED IN BANKING SECTOR

Digital payments refer to transferring funds electronically through instructions or orders to a bank. Digital payments are detected under the Payment and Settlement Act. This helps ensure that electronic transactions are secure and regulated. Digital payments surround a wide range of techniques, such as digital wallet, debit card, credit card, direct withdrawals and deposits and online payments.

Technological transactions have become crucial in the banking sector's reform process. They help banks improve efficiency, enhance security and offer more convenient services to customers. Some of the most essential digital payments methods in the present scenario which help to make payments and transfer money digitally include RTGS, IMPS, NEFT, UPI, etc. Volume and value are the segments of the payment system that assist to acknowledge the scale and effect of digital payments in terms of both quantity and value, as shown in Table 4.2.

TABLE 4.2
Volume (in Millions) of Transactions

	Volume in millions						
Year	RTGS	IMPS	NEFT	UPI	BHIM	CR CARD	DR CARD
2016	98.3	220.8	1252.9	0	0	785.7	1173.6
2017	107.9	506.7	1622.1	18	0	1087.1	2399.3
2018	124.4	1009.8	1946.4	915.2	2	1405.2	3343.4
2019	136.6	1752.9	2318.9	5391.5	6.8	1762.6	4414.3
2020	150.7	2579.2	2744.5	12518.6	9.1	2177.3	5061.1
2021	159.2	3278.3	3092.8	22330.7	16.1	1764.1	4014.6
2022	207.8	4662.5	4040.7	45956.1	22.8	2239.9	3938.4
AVRG	140.7	2001.457	2431.186	14521.68	11.36	1603.129	3477.814
CAGR	11%	55%	18%	270%	63%	16%	19%

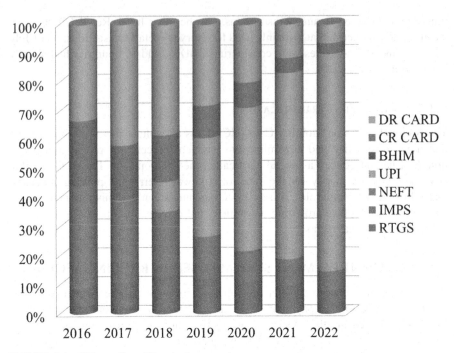

FIGURE 4.1   Volume (in millions) of transactions.

Table 4.2 shows the volume (in millions) of transactions. Volume refers to the total number of transactions or payments processed within a given period. There are some different payments methods such as IMPS, NEFT, BHIM and UPI, which have been analyzed for a period of seven years from 2015–16 to 2021–22 financial years. This indicates the quantity or frequency of payments made through a payment system, as shown in Figure 4.1.

Table 4.3 shows the value (in billions) of the transactions. Value refers to the total monetary worth or amount of transactions processed within a given period.

The value of different payments system recorded robust growth in the previous seven years. The value term represents the total value of payments made through a payment system, as shown in Figure 4.2.

4.5 ANALYSIS OF DIGITAL PAYMENTS SYSTEM

4.5.1 RTGS

RTGS is real time gross settlement. It is a system utilized for transferring funds between banks in India. RTGS makes high-value transactions in real time, which means the money gets transferred instantly and directly from one bank account to another. It is a secure and efficient method to send and accept money electronically. The RBI regulates the RTGS system. They oversee and ensure the functioning and security of RTGS transactions.

TABLE 4.3
Value (in Billions) of the Transactions

Year	Value in billions						
	RTGS	**IMPS**	**NEFT**	**UPI**	**BHIM**	**CR CARD**	**DR CARD**
2016	824578	1622.26	83273.11	0	0	2406.62	1589.27
2017	981903.8	4111.06	120039.7	69.61	0	3283.82	3299.07
2018	1167125	8924.97	172228.5	1098.32	0.78	4589.65	4600.7
2019	1356882	15902.57	227936.1	8769.71	8.15	6034.13	5934.75
2020	1311565	23375.41	229455.8	21317.3	13.03	7308.94	7039.2
2021	1055998	29415	251309.1	41036.58	25.8	6304.14	6613.85
2022	1286575	41710.37	287254.6	84159	61.13	9716.38	7302.13
AVRG	**1140661**	**17865.95**	**195928.1**	**26075.09**	**21.778**	**5663.383**	**5196.996**
CAGR	**7%**	**59%**	**19%**	**226%**	**139%**	**22%**	**24%**

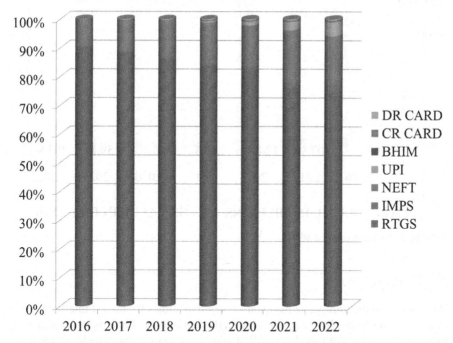

FIGURE 4.2 The total value of payments made through a payment system.

In Table 4.4, the total value of RTGS has shown stable growth at a CAGR of 7% in the seven years from 2016 to 2022. The volume of RTGS has revealed an increase from 98.3 million in the financial year 2015–16 to 207.8 million in 2021–2022. In volume terms, CAGR has recorded a growth of 11% in seven years. It can be concluded that significant growth has been recorded in previous years (Figure 4.3).

TABLE 4.4
Total Value of RTGS

Year	2016	2017	2018	2019	2020	2021	2022	CAGR
Volume in millions	98.3	107.9	124.4	136.6	150.7	159.2	207.8	11%
Value in billions	824,578	981,904	1,167,125	1,356,882	1,311,565	1,055,998	1,286,475	7%

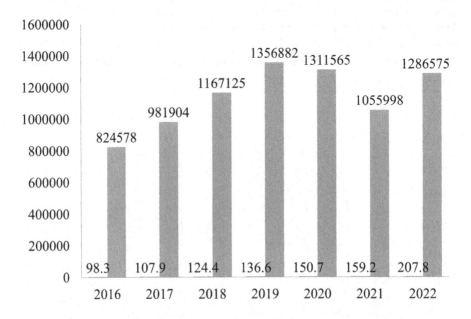

■ RTGS VOLUME IN MILLIONS ■ RTGS VALUE IN BILLIONS

FIGURE 4.3   Total value of RTGS.

4.5.2   IMPS

IMPS refers to the immediate payment system that allows for instant interbank electronic fund transfers. It is a convenient method to transfer funds between different banks in real time. With the help of RBI and NPCI, people can transfer funds from one bank to another using just the bank account number and IFSC code, all through a mobile phone (Figure 4.5).

IMPS value has increase at a CAGR of 59% from 2016 to 2022. The volume (in millions) of IMPS has presented strong growth from 220.8 million in the financial year 2015–16 to 4662.5 million in 2021–22, and the CAGR in volume terms is 55%, as shown in Table 4.5 and Figure 4.4.

TABLE 4.5
The Volume and Value (in Millions and Billions) of IMPS

Year	2016	2017	2018	2019	2020	2021	2022	CAGR
Volume in millions	220.8	506.7	1009.8	1752.9	2579.2	3278.3	4662.5	55%
Value in billions	1622.26	4111.06	8924.97	15,902.57	23,375.4	29,415	41,710.4	59%

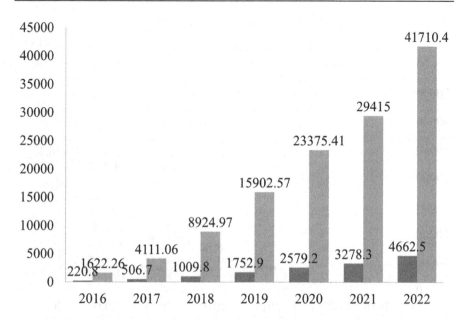

■ IMPS VOLUME IN MILLIONS ■ IMPS VALUE IN BILLIONS

FIGURE 4.4 The average of IMPS in value terms is 17,865.95 million for seven years.

4.5.3 UPI

UPI represents the unified payments interface. In India this is a real-time payment system that permits customers to transfer funds between bank accounts using their mobile phones. UPI allows easy and instant transactions, making it convenient for individuals and businesses to send and receive money digitally. It is regulated by the National Payments Corporation of India (NPCI), ensuring secure and efficient transactions.

As explained in Table 4.6, UPI has recorded tremendous growth in value terms at a CAGR of 270% in the last six years. The volume of UPI has also recorded a great increase from 18 million in FY 2017–18 to 45,956.1 million in FY 2021–22 with a CAGR of 270%.

TABLE 4.6
The Volume and Value (in Millions and Billions) of UPI

Year	2016	2017	2018	2019	2020	2021	2022	CAGR
Volume in millions	0	18	915.2	5391.5	12,518.6	22,330.7	45,956.1	270%
Value in billions	0	69.61	1098.32	8769.71	21,317.3	41,036.6	84,159	226%

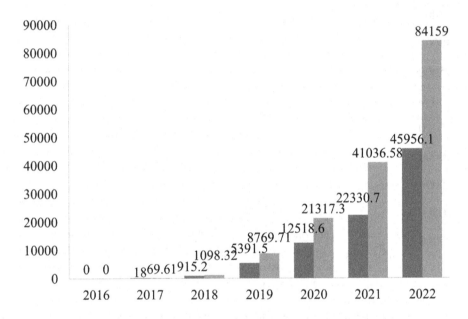

FIGURE 4.5 Total value of IMPS in millions and billions of units.

4.5.4 Debit Cards

Debit cards distributed by the bank are connected to the bank account of the users. Debit cards allow make virtual payments for products and services. Whether shopping online or at a physical store, customers can simply make payments through their debit card. It is like having a digital wallet in your pocket for easy payments. There were over 3.4 billion debit card transactions in the financial year 2023 in India. In the case of debit cards, the money being used to make transactions is already in the bank account. Every time a debit card is used to make transactions the amount is deducted from the bank account.

The increment recorded in value (in billions) for debit cards was from 1589.27 in FY 2015–16 to 7302.13 in FY 2021–2022, as shown in Table 4.7. The CAGR of these seven years in volume terms has recorded a growth of 19% from 1173.6 million in FY 2015–16 to 3938.4 million in 2021–2022 (Figure 4.6).

TABLE 4.7
The Volume and Value (in Millions and Billions) for Debit Cards

Year	2016	2017	2018	2019	2020	2021	2022	CAGR
Volume in millions	1173.6	2399.3	3343.4	4414.3	5061.1	4014.6	3938.4	19%
Value in billions	1589.27	3299.07	4600.7	5934.75	7039.2	6613.85	7302.13	24%

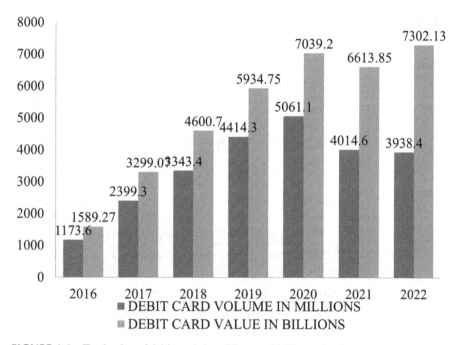

FIGURE 4.6   Total value of debit cards in millions and billions of units.

4.5.5   CREDIT CARDS

A credit card allows the user to borrow money from the bank and use it to make purchases. It is like having a temporary loan that the customer can use for shopping and other expenses. In the case of credit cards the borrower has to pay off the borrowed amount within the given time to avoid extra charges which can be imposed for any delay. In the financial year 2023, people in India made more than 2.9 billion credit card transactions totaling a massive 14 trillion Indian Rupees.

The value of credit cards has shown strong growth at a CAGR of 22% in the seven years from 2016 to 2022. In Table 4.8, the value term shows an increment from 2406.62 billion to 9716.38 billion in seven years. The volume (in millions) has recorded an increase from 785.7 in FY 2016 to 2239.9 in FY 2022, with a CAGR of 16% (Figure 4.7).

TABLE 4.8

The Volume and Value (in Millions and Billions) for Credit Cards

Year	2016	2017	2018	2019	2020	2021	2022	CAGR
Volume in millions	785.7	1087.1	1405.2	1762.6	2177.3	1764.1	2239.9	16%
Value in billions	2406.62	3283.82	4589.65	6034.13	7308.94	6304.14	9716.38	22%

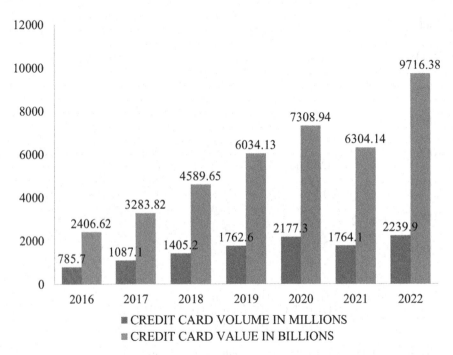

FIGURE 4.7   Total value of credit cards in millions and billions of units.

4.5.6 BHIM

Bharat Interface for Money (BHIM) is a mobile application started by the National Payments Corporation of India (NPIC). It provides a fast, secure and reliable medium to create digital payments using the UPI platform. With the help of BHIM, customers can easily transfer money, pay bills and make online purchases securely and conveniently through their mobile phone. Customers can even send money to banks that do not support UPI by using their IFSC code and MMID.

BHIM usage (in value terms) has shown growth from 0.78 million in FY 2017–2018 to 61.13 million in FY 2021–2022 with a CAGR of 139%, as shown in Table 4.9. Also, in volume terms, growth has been recorded at a CAGR of 63% for the last five years (Figure 4.8).

TABLE 4.9
The Volume and Value (in Millions and Billions) for BHIM

Year	2016	2017	2018	2019	2020	2021	2022	CAGR
Volume in millions	0	0	2	6.8	9.1	16.1	22.8	63%
Value in billions	0	0	0.78	8.15	13.03	25.8	61.13	139%

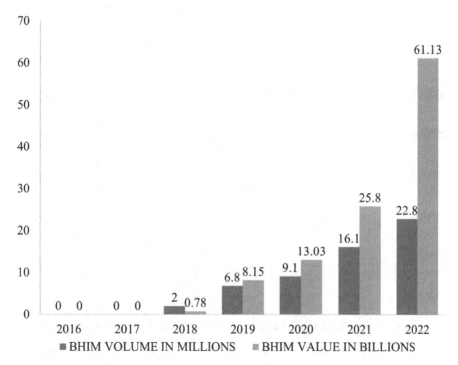

FIGURE 4.8 Total value of BHIM in millions and billions of units.

4.5.7 NEFT

NEFT, which stands for National Electronic Fund Transfer, is a system that allows for online fund transfers between different banks or branches within India. The NEFT payment system has been set up and managed by the RBI. Transactions can be performed 24/7, anytime and anywhere. The amount limit for NEFT transactions varies from bank to bank, and typically ranges from Rs 1 to Rs 10 lakh (Figure 4.9). Table 4.10 shows that the total value of NEFT has recorded a rise from 83,273.1 billion in FY 2015—16 to 287,255 billion in FY 2021–22. And the CAGR for the last seven years has shown a growth of 19%. In volume terms, the NEFT shows an increase from 1252.9 million in FY 2015–16 to 4040.7 million in FY 2021–22, with a CAGR of 18%.

TABLE 4.10
The Volume and Value (in Millions and Billions) for NEFT

Year	2016	2017	2018	2019	2020	2021	2022	CAGR
Volume in millions	1252.9	1622.1	1946.4	2318.9	2744.5	3092.8	4040.7	18%
Value in billions	83273.1	120040	172229	227936.1	229456	251309	287255	19%

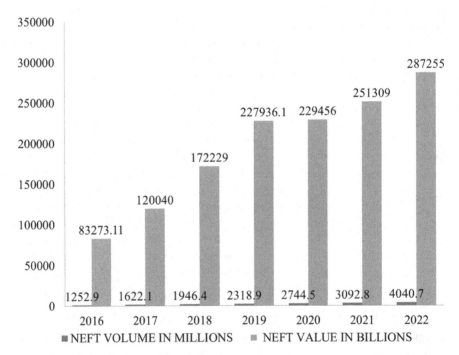

FIGURE 4.9　Total value of NEFT in millions and billions of units.

4.6　CONTRIBUTION OF DIGITAL BANKING IN GDP

GDP, commonly known as gross domestic product, is an estimate of the total value of all the goods and services generated and sold inside a nation during a specific time, generally in a year. It gives an idea of the overall size and health of an economy (Khang, 2023a). Therefore, it is a crucial indicator to understand the economic activity of a country. For purposes of this study, the time period has been taken from 2013–14 to 2021–2022, which is 10 years, to study the growth of GDP and the impact of digital payments on the economy growth of the country, as shown in Table 4.11.

The Reserve Bank of India's Digital Payments Index has shown remarkable growth in digital payments in India during the fiscal year 2022–23. The Index for March

TABLE 4.11

Contribution of Digital Banking to GDP

Year	2013	2014	2015	2016	2017	2018	2019	2020	2021	2022
GDP	6.39	7.41	8	8.26	6.8	6.45	3.87	-5.83	9.05	7

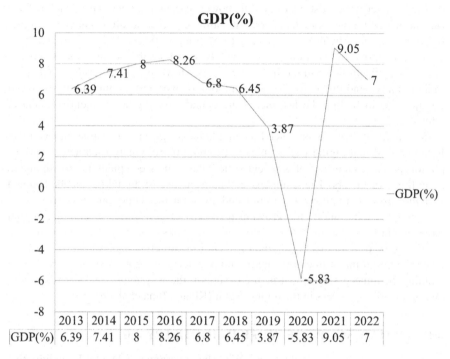

FIGURE 4.10 Contribution of digital banking to GDP.

2023 recorded a value of 395.58, showing impressive growth of 13.24% compared to 377.46 in September 2022. The announcement made on January 31, 2023, highlights the positive momentum and progress in the economy. Globally, the Indian economy is an emerging and fastest growing economy (Sulthana Barvin & Gnanakkan, 2022). During the COVID-19 pandemic, the GDP growth crashed to –5.83% in 2020, which was the worst state of the economy in any year since independence in India. It has indeed had a negative impact on the economy. However, the increased use of financial technology, such as digital modes for buying goods and services and receiving money, has helped offset some of these economic losses. Empirical evidence shows that a higher share of the population using digital modes for payments and making online purchases is a significant and robust determinant of trade in goods and services. By the end of 2022, UPI's total transaction value reached INR 125.95 trillion, showing a remarkable 1.75-fold year-on-year growth. The UPI transaction value accounted for nearly 86% of India's GDP in FY 2022 (Figure 4.10).

4.7 CONCLUSION

In the past, traditional banks primarily focused on accepting deposits from customers and lending those funds to individuals and businesses. Their core banking business revolved around these activities. However, with technological advancements and changing customer demands, banks have expanded their services to include an extensive range of financial products and services (Khang & Rashmi et al., 2024).

The transformation of the banking industry has been driven by technology-led disruption, convergence of services and the power of data analytics. These factors have revolutionized the way that banks operate, allowing them to offer innovative digital solutions and personalized experiences to customers. While digital payments have gained popularity, cash continues to be widely used for various transactions and still holds a significant place in the Indian economy. However, the government's Digital India initiative and the increased use of mobile phones and the internet have played a major role in fueling the fast-increasing demand for digital payments (Khang & AIoCF, 2024).

All payments have experienced a remarkable surge in both value and volume. It can be said that digital payments are becoming more widely used across various platforms. The Indian digital payment system has witnessed epidemic growth due to a multitude of factors. The simplicity and convenience of digital payments, coupled with increased smart phone penetration and favorable regulatory policies, have fueled this growth. Additionally, the growing readiness of consumers to embrace digital payment platforms has played a significant role. Banks have played an important role in driving the development of digital payment infrastructure and system. Banks have taken the initial thrust in embracing digital payments and have been instrumental in building the unnecessary infrastructure to support these systems. Banks are experiencing tremendous success in the digital realm (Khang, Inna et al., 2024).

4.8 FUTURE SCOPE OF WORK IN INDUSTRY 4.0

Digital payments have a bright future. With the government's Digital India initiative and the increasing use of mobile phones and the internet, digital payments will continue to revolutionize the way we transact. In some places, many people still aren't familiar with digital payments. It is important for payment providers to educate people about their platforms and how they can make life easier. They should explain the benefits, such as how it being convenient, safe and fast (Khang, Rani et al., 2023).

By spreading the word and showing how simple it is to use, more people will start using digital payments. Currently, the solutions provided by UPI in India mainly target real-time, low-value, high-volume peer-to-peer payments, as well as e-commerce and m-commerce transactions. They also play a vital role in promoting financial inclusion in developing economies (Rohan, 2019). The digital payments market in India is expected to skyrocket, reaching a whopping $10 trillion by 2026. This tremendous growth reflects the increasing adoption of digital payment methods and the convenience they offer (Khanh & Khang, 2021).

REFERENCES

Amudhan, S., Banerjee, S., Poornima, J. (2022). Impact of Digital Transformation of Banking. *Journal of Positive School Psychology*, *6*(2), 763–771. www.journalppw.com/index. php/jpsp/article/view/1569

Anand, A. (2023). Challenges and Opportunities of E-Commerce in India. *International Journal of Scientific Multidisciplinary Research*, *1*(2), 69–72. https://doi.org/10.55927/ ijsmr.v1i2.3308

Anitha, K. (2019). A Study on Challenges and Opportunities in E-Banking Sector in India. *New Frontiers in Business, Management and Technology*, *7*(3). https://doi.org/10.5281/

Diener, F., & Špaček, M. (2021). Digital Transformation in Banking: A Managerial Perspective on Barriers to Change. *Sustainability (Switzerland)*, *13*(4), 1–26. https://doi.org/ 10.3390/su13042032

Jagtap, D. M. M. V. (2018). The Impact of Digitalisation on Indian Banking Sector. *International Journal of Trend in Scientific Research and Development, Special Issue* (Special Issue-ICDEBI2018), pp. 118–122. https://doi.org/10.31142/ijtsrd18688

Jeevanandam, P., & Surech Babu, P. (2022). Digital Transformation in Banking Sector. *Tierärztliche Praxis*, *42*(6), 30–36. https://go.gale.com/ps/i.do?id=GALE%7CA19 8547956&sid=googleScholar&v=2.1&it=r&linkaccess=abs&issn=09732470&p= AONE&sw=w

Khang, A. (Ed.) (2023). *AI and IoT-Based Technologies for Precision Medicine*. IGI Global Press. ISBN: 9798369308769. https://doi.org/10.4018/979-8-3693-0876-9

Khang, A., & AIoCF (Ed.) (2024). *AI-Oriented Competency Framework for Talent Management in the Digital Economy: Models, Technologies, Applications, and Implementation*. ISBN: 9781032576053. CRC Press. https://doi.org/10.1201/9781003440901

Khang, A., Chowdhury, S., & Sharma, S. (2022). *The Data-Driven Blockchain Ecosystem: Fundamentals, Applications, and Emerging Technologies* (1st Ed.). CRC Press. https://doi.org/10.1201/9781003269281

Khang, A., Gujrati, R., Uygun, H., Tailor, R. K., & Gaur, S. S. (2024). *Data-driven Modelling and Predictive Analytics in Business and Finance* (1st Ed.). ISBN: 9781032600628. CRC Press. https://doi.org/10.1201/9781032600628

Khang, A., Gupta, S. K., Rani, S., & Karras, D. A. (Eds.). (2023). *Smart Cities: IoT Technologies, Big Data Solutions, Cloud Platforms, and Cybersecurity Techniques*. CRC Press. https:// doi.org/10.1201/9781003376064

Khang, A., Inna, S.-O., Alla, K., Rostyslav, S., Rudenko, M., Lidia, R., & Kristina, B. (2024). Management model 6.0 and business recovery strategy of enterprises in the era of digital economy. In *Data-driven Modelling and Predictive Analytics in Business and Finance* (1st Ed.). CRC Press. https://doi.org/10.1201/9781032600628-16

Khang, A., Kali, C. R., Satapathy, S. K., Kumar, A., Ranjan Das, S., & Panda, M. R. (2023). Enabling the future of manufacturing: integration of robotics and iot to smart factory infrastructure in industry 4.0. In *AI-Based Technologies and Applications in the Era of the Metaverse* (1st Ed.) (pp. 25–50). IGI Global Press. https://doi.org/10.4018/ 978-1-6684-8851-5.ch002

Khang, A., Rani, S., Gujrati, R., Uygun, H., & Gupta, S. K. (Eds.) (2023). *Designing Workforce Management Systems for Industry 4.0: Data-Centric and AI-Enabled Approaches*. CRC Press. https://doi.org/10.1201/9781003357070

Khang, A., Shah, V., & Rani, S. (2023). *AI-Based Technologies and Applications in the Era of the Metaverse* (1st Ed.). IGI Global Press. https://doi.org/10.4018/978-1-6684-8851-5

Khanh, H. H., & Khang, A. (2021). The role of artificial intelligence in blockchain applications. In *Reinventing Manufacturing and Business Processes through Artificial Intelligence*, 2 (pp. 20–40). CRC Press. https://doi.org/10.1201/9781003145011-2

Kraus, S., Jones, P., Kailer, N., Weinmann, A., Chaparro-Banegas, N., & Roig-Tierno, N. (2021). Digital Transformation: An Overview of the Current State of the Art of Research. *SAGE Open*, *11*(3). https://doi.org/10.1177/21582440211047576

Kusuma, K. M., & College, P. U. (2020). Digitalization of Banks: An Evidence from India. *International Journal of Research and Analytical Reviews*, *7*(1), 571–579. www.ijrar. org/papers/IJRAR19D1233.pdf

Reis, J., Amorim, M., Melão, N., & Matos, P. (2018). Digital Transformation: A Literature Review and Guidelines for Future Research. *Advances in Intelligent Systems and Computing*, *745* (March), 411–421. https://doi.org/10.1007/978-3-319-77703-0_41

Rohan, S. (2019). Future of Digital Payments. *White Paper, Infosys, January*, 1–8. http://class tap.pbworks.com/f/SkillSoft+-+Blended+Elearning.pdf

Shifa Fathima, J. (2020). Digital Revolution in the Indian Banking Sector. *Shanlax International Journal of Commerce*, *8*(1), 56–64. https://doi.org/10.34293/commerce.v8i1.1619

Sulthana Barvin, M., & Gnanakkan, J. M. (2022). A Study on the Growth and Trend of Indian GDP and its Components. *Journal of Positive School Psychology*, *2022*(6), 6770–6779. http://journalppw.com

Vial, G. (2021). Understanding Digital Transformation. *Managing Digital Transformation*, 13–66. https://doi.org/10.4324/9781003008637-4

Vidya, M., & Shailashri, V. T. (2021). A Study on Evolving Digital Transformation in Indian Banking System. *International Journal of Case Studies in Business, IT, and Education*, *5*(1), 116–130. https://doi.org/10.47992/ijcsbe.2581.6942.0104

Vijai, C. (2019). Artificial Intelligence in Indian Banking Sector: Challenges and Opportunities. *International Journal of Advanced Research*, *7*(4), 1581–1587. https://doi.org/10.21474/ijar01/8987

Wu, S., & Li, Y. (2023). A Study on the Impact of Digital Transformation on Corporate ESG Performance: The Mediating Role of Green Innovation. *Sustainability (Switzerland)*, *15*(8), 854–859. https://doi.org/10.3390/su15086568

5 Impact of AI and Data in Revolutionizing Microfinance in Developing Countries
Improving Outreach and Efficiency

Shila Mondol, Ipseeta Satpathy, B. C. M. Patnaik, Arpita Nayak, Atmika Patnaik, and Alex Khang

5.1 INTRODUCTION

Bangladesh can be considered as the origin of contemporary microfinance (Bangladesh data are used for simulations in this chapter). Bangladesh has a massive market for microfinance services as more than 80% of its 165 million people live on a daily budget of no more than $2, and 85% do not have access to conventional banking services. This demand for microfinance is fulfilled by 685 licensed MFIs, which is greater than in almost any other country.

With such a vast market and so many participants, competition is fierce in the field. BRAC Bank is one of Bangladesh's oldest MFIs and a significant participant in the market. Microfinance is primarily concerned with microcredit. A microcredit is a compact loan that is typically given to those with low income. There is no shortage of attempts in developing countries, but funds to start a business are few. Professor Muhammad Yunus, a Bangladeshi banking pioneer, pioneered microfinance, which has become a critical development tool in underdeveloped nations to alleviate poverty, empower women, and stimulate entrepreneurship.

The provision of financial services to the disadvantaged is known as microfinance. The peculiarity of microfinance is that it stimulates development by bringing commercially excluded individuals into the financial mainstream by fulfilling their financial and non-financial needs. Bangladesh has long been considered the cradle of microfinance, and competition has grown significantly over the last decade. Since its inception, microfinance has expanded as an economic development approach to help low-income persons in rural and urban areas.

DOI: 10.1201/9781032618845-5

Bangladesh has one of the most comprehensive microfinance records. Microfinance in Bangladesh has steadily improved over the years, with the success of Grameen Bank and BRAC pilot programs and testing acting as apparent proof of its long-term usefulness in eliminating poverty and supporting socioeconomic development. Microfinance's notable successes in poverty reduction and socioeconomic progress have piqued the interest of prestigious international commercial financiers and individual investors, as well as organizations such as the World Bank and the United Nations. These organizations see microfinance as an appealing path because of its promising potential in tackling poverty-related issues and encouraging broader socio-economic development.

In Bangladesh, the actual effect of microfinance has been so enormous that Professor Yunus and his colleagues were awarded the Nobel Peace Prize for their pioneering work in poverty eradication through microfinance projects. Microfinance has been practiced in the nation for four decades, with over 700 registered microfinance institutions (MFIs) as of 2014, it served more than 33 million clients, which includes those served by Grameen Bank. These MFIs provide a wide range of both financial and non-financial amenities to their clients, helping to expand the reach and effect of microfinance in Bangladesh (Mia, 2017; Dahal & Fiala, 2020).

The Microcredit Regulatory Authority (MRA), founded under the Microcredit Regulatory Act of 2006, governs microfinance in Bangladesh. As of fiscal year (FY) 2020, there were more than 750 operational MFIs serving 35.6 million individual borrowers. In FY2019, the total amount of microfinance loans outstanding from MFIs was Tk788 billion. Grameen Bank, state-owned commercial banks, and specialized government programs also offer microfinance services in Bangladesh. In 2019, women made up 93% of microfinance borrowers, as shown in Figure 5.1.

Microfinance is a critical component of any economy, and its development is strongly dependent on a country's socioeconomic, macroeconomic, and financial stability. Politicians and academicians must recognize the essential characteristics of a nation where microfinance is a long-term policy solution to poverty reduction.

Bangladesh has a vast population, with many people being neglected or economically disadvantaged by the traditional banking system. Microfinance arose as a way to fill this need and provide financial assistance to those who are unbanked. The Bangladeshi government recognizes the value of microfinance in alleviating poverty and promoting economic growth. They have put in place supporting policies and regulations to foster the expansion of microfinance institutions (MFIs) and to provide a favorable environment for their operations Bangladesh has a widely recognized and well-managed MFI network (Khang, Gadirova et al., 2023). Microfinance institutions such as Grameen Bank, BRAC, and ASA have played an important role in establishing trust among local people (Mia, 2016, 2019).

Bangladesh has a population of 160 million people, which makes it one of the most densely populated countries on the planet. It is an agriculturally oriented country where a fresh wave of recently created technology has impacted it in many areas and given it new momentum. Automation and control technologies are used in a variety of industrial settings. AI, along with IoT, big data, and blockchain, has just lately gained popularity in Bangladesh (Khang, Agriculture et al., 2023).

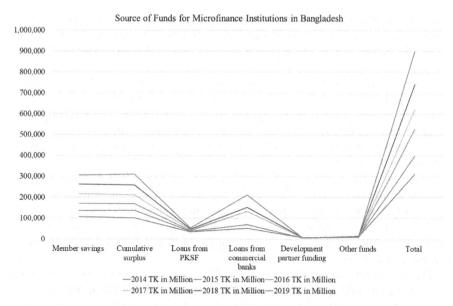

FIGURE 5.1 Source of funds for microfinance institutions in Bangladesh.

Source: Microcredit Regulatory Authority. 2021. Microcredit in Bangladesh June 2019.

Artificial intelligence (AI) is revolutionizing the way financial services are delivered and increasing the effect of MFIs in the microfinance industry. AI technology provides a variety of skills that add to the profitability and efficacy of microfinance operations. AI-powered solutions may automate loan application processing, credit scoring, and risk assessment inside MFIs. AI helps MFIs to manage higher numbers of transactions, streamline operations, and minimize manual labor and processing time by automating these functions. This not only increases efficiency but also allows MFIs to reach out to more consumers and give speedier access to financial services (Chemin, 2008).

According to a study, AI has a positive impact on risk management in microfinance. More accurate risk assessment, fraud detection, and portfolio management are made possible by advanced data analytics and predictive modeling approaches. AI has also aided in the creation of mobile banking systems and digital payment solutions, allowing persons in distant places to gain access to financial services. AI-powered digital solutions have benefited microfinance organizations by automating operations, lowering costs, and improving the client experience (Bhambri, Rani et al., 2022).

Chatbots and virtual assistants powered by AI provide personalized assistance, accurate risk assessment, and broader access to financial services. AI also improves fraud detection by analyzing massive amounts of data, thereby reducing fraudulent activity and safeguarding the interests of microfinance institutions and clients. Overall, AI has had a substantial influence on microfinance organizations and their consumers (Moin & Kraiwanit, 2023).

bKash is a mobile financial service operator in Bangladesh that is using artificial intelligence to revolutionize microfinance. They analyze consumer transaction data and behavior patterns using AI algorithms, allowing them to provide personalized financial services and credit choices to their customers. This has aided in increasing financial inclusion and giving loans to formerly unbanked persons (Yesmin et al., 2019).

Grameenphone, one of Bangladesh's leading mobile network carriers, has incorporated AI-based technologies to improve microfinance services. They use AI algorithms to analyze mobile data and use trends in order to assess potential borrowers' creditworthiness. This has allowed them to provide microloans to small company owners and farmers who would not have been able to secure funding through standard banking channels (Parvez et al., 2015).

Shakti Foundation is a microfinance institution in Bangladesh that uses artificial intelligence to combat fraud. The Shakti Foundation's AI technology detects fraudulent activities by analyzing data from applicants' loan applications. The AI system, for example, may detect borrowers who have applied for several loans from various MFIs or who have submitted fraudulent information on their loan applications (Khang, Santosh et al., 2023).

The AI system developed by the Shakti Foundation has been shown to be quite effective in minimizing fraud. Fraud rates were reduced by 50% in the first year after the system was installed. Shakti Foundation has saved millions of dollars as a result, allowing the organization to lend to additional borrowers. The AI technology assists Shakti Foundation in making more informed financing selections. This is because the algorithm considers more elements than standard credit rating systems (Hossain, 2008).

Grameen Bank, BRAC, and the Association for Social Advancement (ASA) are just a handful of Bangladesh's well-known microfinance institutions (MFIs). Concurrently, numerous smaller MFIs have commenced operations across Bangladesh. As of December 2008, the Microcredit Regulatory Authority (MRA) licensed 402 MFIs, while 4236 MFIs have sought a license. In this study, the authors have highlighted a comparison between India and Bangladesh, with Bangladesh MFIs having a significantly greater number of active clients than Indian MFIs.

Bangladeshi MFIs have had a minuscule increase in clientele. This might be since the notion of microfinance is older in Bangladesh, and hence these institutions have already matured, whilst the client base of Indian MFIs is constantly growing. This information comes from the Centre for Development Finance (CDF), a non-profit organization that collects and analyzes microfinance statistics in Bangladesh. This information was current as of December 2021, with BRAC being Bangladesh's largest microfinance lender, with over 8.5 million clients and a loan portfolio worth $4.3 billion.

Grameen Bank is the second largest lender, with approximately 7.5 million customers and a $3.9 billion loan portfolio. ASA is the third largest lender, with about 5.2 million customers and a $2.7 billion loan portfolio. Bangladesh has around 33 million microfinance consumers and a loan portfolio worth more than $18 billion. This demonstrates that microfinance is a key influence on the Bangladeshi economy, contributing to its growth (Saxena & Sharma, 2021).

5.2 AI: THE NEW METHOD OF PREVENTING FRAUDS IN MICROFINANCE

To defend themselves against the aggravating fraudster, financial institutions want powerful, up-to-date, and customized predictive analytics. Data scientists and sociologists who understand artificial intelligence, machine learning, and methods of statistics are in great demand, and as a result, their availability has lately increased (Rani, Chauhan et al., 2021).

The COVID-19 epidemic has caused significant disruption in the area of digital transactions, and hackers have taken advantage. Fraudulent conduct is becoming not just more sophisticated, but also larger in scope and number. As a result, there is a greater need than ever for effective AI solutions to assist in this battle. GBG's most recent fraud report, which incorporates information from financial institutions (FIs) in key European countries, paints a clear picture of the magnitude of that demand. More than half of those polled want to implement AI technologies to detect unknown fraud incidents.

Almost a third of those polled want to invest in newer AI fraud detection tools such as machine learning and predictive analytics (Awotunde, 2021). Microfinance institutions face a severe threat from fraudulent operations, which jeopardizes their ability to provide financial services to disadvantaged areas. Fraud not only causes significant financial losses, but also erodes faith in the system, hampering microfinance organizations' objective of promoting equitable growth and relieving poverty.

Microfinance institutions must create sophisticated fraud detection systems in order to successfully combat fraud. Early detection and prevention of fraudulent actions are critical in minimizing financial effects and protecting vulnerable clients' assets. According to studies, 58% of AI applications in the financial services sector are especially aimed at countering fraudulent activity. AI employs sophisticated algorithms and data analytics to detect trends, abnormalities, and potentially fraudulent behavior in massive volumes of data (Khang, Abdullayev et al., 2024).

ML algorithms enable AI systems to learn from prior data, adapt to emerging fraud strategies, and detect suspicious activity with amazing precision. According to a McKinsey & Company analysis, machine learning algorithms used in fraud detection have shown a significant increase in accuracy. When it comes to detecting fraudulent operations, several algorithms have reached accuracy rates above 95%. In accordance with a Deloitte analysis, AI-powered fraud detection systems can evaluate activities in immediate detail, detecting fraud within milliseconds, and reducing the financial effect on microfinance institutions and their consumers (Dolgorukov, 2023).

Advanced biometric identification methods, natural language processing for fraud detection in textual data, and the use of blockchain technology to improve data security and transparency are emerging themes in AI-driven fraud detection for microfinance. According to Forecast Markets, between 2023 and 2028, the global market for AI-based methods for identifying and preventing fraud will increase at a compound annual growth rate of 19.1%, reflecting increased acceptance and progress of AI technologies in this sector (Khan & Ashta, 2013).

AI-powered fraud detection systems use algorithms trained to spot trends and abnormalities in data that may suggest fraudulent behavior. One of these systems' primary advantages is their capacity to analyze massive volumes of data in real time. They are skilled in detecting many sorts of fraud, such as card fraud, account take-over (ATO), document counterfeiting, bogus account creation, and others (Khang, Hahanov et al., 2022).

Artificial intelligence uses approaches such as massive data analysis, real-time screening, and advanced digital fraud protection strategies to accomplish this. However, it is critical to understand the most frequent forms of fraud, the methodologies used by AI, and the dangers involved with utilizing AI for fraud detection (Bassey, 2018; Mhlanga, 2020). AI-powered fraud detection systems use trained algorithms to spot trends and abnormalities in data that may suggest fraudulent behavior.

However, it is critical to understand the most frequent forms of fraud, the methodologies used by AI, and the dangers involved with utilizing AI for fraud detection. There are different ways in which AI helps in the prevention of fraud, as illustrated in Figure 5.2 (PM, 2023).

- Big Data—Artificial intelligence-based fraud detection solutions use big data analysis to filter through massive volumes of consumer and transactional data held by financial institutions. These systems can discover patterns and trends linked with fraudulent behavior by analyzing historical data. They employ machine learning algorithms to detect abnormalities and alert users to possibly fraudulent activities or activities.
- Real-Time Screening—AI allows for real-time screening of sensitive data and transactions across multiple accounts and individuals. Instead of depending

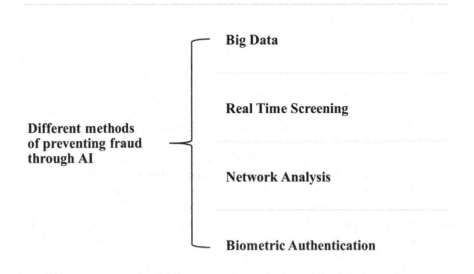

FIGURE 5.2 Methods implemented by AI to detect frauds.

Source: Authors' own compilation.

exclusively on manual checks, AI-powered systems may evaluate incoming data instantaneously and spot questionable activity as it occurs. This functionality enables prompt action to prevent or minimize fraudulent transactions.

- Network Analysis—Artificial intelligence investigates social networks and financial activities through network analysis. AI can detect probable instances of fraud by analyzing the links between persons and their transactional activity. For example, if many accounts are linked to the same source or if there are unexpected links between seemingly unrelated businesses, this might indicate fraudulent behavior.
- Biometric Authentication—Through network analysis, artificial intelligence studies social networks and financial transactions. AI can detect potential cases of fraud by evaluating the connections between people and their transactional activities. For example, if several accounts are linked to the same source, or if there are surprising connections between seemingly unrelated organizations, this might suggest fraudulent activities.

Digital financial services have gained in popularity as mobile technology has become more widely available. The scope of microfinance digitalization has grown considerably in recent years. As a result, as their popularity expands in poor nations, microfinance institutions (MFIs) are on the verge of experiencing a digital transition. The Asia Foundation is collaborating with MFIs from Bangladesh to develop and deploy AI-powered fraud detection solutions. The organization is assisting MFIs with technical help and training on how to utilize AI to avoid fraud.

The organization is also working in Bangladesh to create a standard architecture for AI-powered fraud detection solutions. This framework will aid in ensuring the systems' interoperability and the security of the data they gather. AI has provided the microfinance business with a sophisticated fraud detection and prevention mechanism. Some of the most significant financial scams, such as money laundering, can be avoided by applying machine learning or artificial intelligence. Aside from minimizing fraud, AI can reduce investigative expenses by up to 20% (Karr et al., 2020; Takeda & Ito, 2021).

5.3 THE ROLE OF AI IN MITIGATING RISK IN MICROFINANCE

All financial institution activities, including those of IMFIs, are risky. Risk is something that all financial institutions must deal with; they are unable to prevent it and can only take steps to mitigate it. There are three types of financial risks: quantifiable, immeasurable, and unidentified. Furthermore, the author (Mujeri, 2020) has defined hazards as either systematic or unsystematic.

Externally generated systemic risk cannot be managed or removed; it can only be mitigated. Examples include political factors, the COVID-19 outbreak, market swings, currency rate variations, and changes in other macro situations. Meanwhile, diversification can help to limit unsystematic risk, as outlined by the author's portfolio theory, which encourages not placing all of one's eggs in one basket, but instead spreading them about (Kaicer, 2020; Ganegoda & Evans, 2014).

Profits constitute a portion of the motivation for effective risk-taking in business, and risk-taking is an essential component of financial services in general, and microfinance in especially. Excessive and poorly managed risk, on the other hand, can result in losses, putting microfinance organizations' and depositors' safety at risk. As an outcome, microfinance organizations could fall short of their social and financial goals.

Consequently, proactive risk management is crucial to microfinance institutions' (MFIS) long-term stability. As a result, competent risk management is thought to enable MFIs to capitalize on new possibilities while minimizing threats to their financial survival. As a result, the National Bank of Ethiopia places a high value on the effectiveness of an institution's risk management (Katterbauer & Moschetta, 2022).

A study conducted by BFSI revealed that AI and machine learning can detect and prevent microfinance fraud. This can increase MFI security as well as reduce risk. AI and machine learning can help to automate the tedious task of tracking loan repayments and retrieving payments. MFIs may use this technology to make these operations more efficient and cost-effective.

MFIs' bottom lines have improved as AI and machine learning have been integrated into rural microfinance operations (Mohamed & Elgammal, 2023). They have increased productivity, decreased operating expenses, and enhanced the quality of their loan portfolio. Despite these accomplishments, several difficulties persist, such as poor data quality and a shortage of experienced workers. Certain risks are linked with the creditworthiness of the underlying MFIs in the microfinance business.

The degree of demand for microfinance loans is one of these hazards, as are financial sustainability, liquidity, and operational and governance concerns. Furthermore, credit risk at the MFI level can be impacted by variables such as microfinance borrowers' over-indebtedness, inadequate credit data, and the absence of credit bureaus in some countries. Furthermore, variations in MFI financial reporting might complicate credit risk assessment.

The Asian Development Bank (ADB) takes a comprehensive strategy for managing these risks. Internal ratings issued by participating financial institutions (PFIs) are matched to the scale of international rating organizations. When a PFI lacks an internal rating scale, a more detailed examination is performed to determine the individual MFI credit risk. The evaluation procedure also takes into account the difficulties that certain MFIs have in managing expansion and expanding into new product lines (Lassoued, 2017). The following are the three most critical risk management domains that might benefit from AI adoption:

- Data quality is a risk management industry that could greatly benefit from AML and anti-fraudulent activities provided by AI technologies. By screening operations and external risk factors, financial danger signals may be controlled more efficiently.
- An additional field that could benefit from the efficacy of AI and risk management systems is stress testing. Its primary goal is to develop complicated simulation models based on hypothetical situations in order to assess the company's balance sheet resilience. The financial crisis of 2008 is a textbook example of a poorly controlled portfolio risk driven by a lack of transparency and rules.
- Early-warning mechanisms are also linked to "what if" scenarios, which provide vital information to bankers involved in credit risk management. AI-powered

technology allows for the processing and analysis of real-time financial, behavioral, geographic, industrial, and perceptual data. Early-warning systems can identify even the slightest signs of stress that humans overlook. For example, a proof-of-concept of the early-warning system improved with AI capabilities accurately anticipated default rates, saving €11 million in possible bad loans.

Predictive analytics driven by AI has emerged as a significant risk management tool in the world of MFIs. This method entails using historical data to create predictive models capable of predicting the possibility of loan defaults or delinquencies. The procedure begins with the collection of extensive historical data that include borrower information, loan specifications, repayment histories, credit ratings, and other relevant aspects impacting loan performance.

Following that, the data are pre-processed to resolve missing values, deal with category variables, and standardize numerical characteristics. Following feature selection, important variables are discovered to assure the prediction models' accuracy and importance. AI algorithms are used to build these predictive models, allowing MFIs to proactively detect possible dangers and implement appropriate risk mitigation actions, such as delivering financial education to at-risk borrowers or altering repayment schedules. MFIs may strengthen their risk management methods and promote sustainable lending practices in the microfinance industry by using this research-driven strategy (Hani et al., 2022).

Tala is a fintech firm that makes microloans available to underprivileged groups in emerging economies. They employ AI algorithms to analyze credit risk and establish the creditworthiness of applicants who do not have traditional credit histories. To make financing choices quickly and effectively, Tala analyzes alternative data sources such as cell phone usage trends and behavioral data (Ndung'u, 2022).

5.4 AI COST-SAVING: POINTING MICROFINANCE IN A NEW DIRECTION

Microfinance institutions are essential lenders to low-income borrowers and may thus play an important part in projects to eliminate and/or alleviate poverty and provide economic opportunities in countries around the world. Microfinance as a financial inclusion approach strives to relieve poverty by providing marginalized groups with access to basic financial services. The efficacy of microfinance programs is dependent on adequate cost control. MFIs are often supported by charity or governmental organizations.

In terms of institution size, sustainability, and number of customers served, the microfinance business is highly different to other sectors. Notably, the top 10% of MFIs, composed of about 150 institutions, service over 75% of all microfinance clients and are backed by a diverse range of smaller and more sustainable organizations (Khan et al., 2021). Given the vital role of MFIs in providing credit to underprivileged populations and their reliance on many sources of subsidies, it is critical to obtain a thorough understanding of MFI operations (Caudill et al., 2009).

A study revealed that Accion Mexico reduced transaction and credit assessment costs by 35% by using a group lending approach, allowing them to provide financial services to remote rural communities. As a consequence, over a five-year period, the number of beneficiaries serviced grew by 40%. Also, BRAC, a renowned microfinance institution in Bangladesh, adopted cost-cutting strategies using digital technologies, resulting in a 22% decrease in administrative expenses within three years. This enabled BRAC to devote additional resources to expand its reach, with the goal of reaching over 5 million people by 2022 (Khannam, 2018).

MFIs value cost savings for a variety of reasons. For starters, they can assist MFIs in becoming more financially viable. This is significant because it allows MFIs to continue lending to low-income borrowers while also expanding their reach. Second, cost reductions can assist MFIs in lowering their interest rates. This can assist in making microcredit less expensive for borrowers while also increasing demand for microfinance services.

Third, cost reductions can assist MFIs in improving their effectiveness and efficacy. This can result in improved service delivery and a greater beneficial impact on poverty reduction (Ayoo, 2022). One of the four competitive tactics available to MFIs to improve their performance is cost cutting. The cost leadership approach, differentiation strategy, and focus strategy are the other three tactics. The cost-cutting approach is predicated on the notion that MFIs may gain a competitive advantage by lowering their expenses to below those of their competitors. This may be accomplished through increasing operational efficiency, expanding operations, collaborating with other organizations, and lowering default rates.

The study discovered that cost-cutting strategies were favorably connected with the performance of Kenyan MFIs. MFIs that used a cost-cutting approach were more likely to be financially viable, have lower interest rates, and have a greater number of borrowers (Wanjiku & Deya, 2021). Based on a recent Juniper Research report, chatbots were forecast to decrease banking operational expenses internationally by $7.3 billion by 2023, up from a projected $209 million in 2019.

Rural MFIs in India have begun to use artificial intelligence to automate key operations, such as credit rating and loan application processing. In addition to saving time and money, these methods have increased the overall efficiency of MFIs. According to a survey by Microsave, a non-profit organization that offers technical help to MFIs, the usage of AI in MFIs in Bangladesh has risen by 20% in the last two years. Microfinance firms may improve their operations and cut costs associated with repetitive work by adopting AI technology.

Furthermore, the use of AI systems reduces the occurrence of human mistakes, resulting in increased accuracy in a variety of operations. The integration of AI-based chat software to answer client concerns constantly, 24 hours a day, is an increasingly common application of AI in the microfinance business. This invention successfully overcomes time and space restrictions, as AI-powered chatbots can communicate with clients around the clock and are not constrained by physical office hours.

AI automation helps microfinance firms to manage larger quantities of business processes with more efficiency and accuracy. As a result, many firms achieve significant growth and broaden their reach to bigger markets, maximizing their potential. MFIs in Bangladesh offer financial and human development services to 32 million low-income microenterprises. Savings accounts, loans, and other services are provided. The whole current loan portfolio is worth more than BDT 943 billion, whereas the savings portfolio is worth more than BDT 462 billion.

Cost reductions contribute greatly to the sustainability and efficacy of MFIs. They can achieve heightened financial efficiency and extend their outreach to empower a larger cohort of individuals through enhanced financial inclusion by implementing innovative cost-saving measures such as digitization, group lending methodologies, and robust risk management practices. To ensure the long-term growth and relevance of microfinance in its role in poverty reduction and economic development, policymakers, stakeholders, and practitioners must prioritize the adoption of cost-cutting techniques.

5.5 ENHANCING FINANCIAL EMPOWERMENT: ROLE OF AI IN MOBILE BANKING IN MICROFINANCE INSTITUTIONS

The Microcredit Regulatory Authorities (MRA) reported 805 licensed MFIs functioning in Bangladesh as of June 2018. According to the MRA-MIS database, these MFIs had around 18,000 branches and a staff of 154,000 workers. Notably, the microfinance business in Bangladesh is highly concentrated, with the two largest MFIs, BRAC and ASA, accounting for over half of all MFIs. Likewise, they account for more than half of the sector's total outstanding loans and deposits. Each one serves approximately four million microfinance customers.

Overall, the top 20 MFIs dominate about three-quarters of the market, with the top two controlling more than half of both clients and entire financial portfolios. In order to reap broad and long-term development benefits, Bangladesh's microfinance industry has evolved fast over the years, with substantial shifts from collective limited-scale microcredit enterprises to individual small-scale enterprise operations (Mujeri, 2020). A recent FIS poll of over 1000 American clients (April 2020) confirms this trend, demonstrating that COVID-19 has significantly increased the adoption of digital banking, payments, and commerce. According to the report, nearly 45% of clients have permanently adjusted their banking relationships since the pandemic began.

Within the previous month of the study, around 45% of respondents used mobile payment platforms, and approximately 31% showed a readiness to move to online or mobile banking in the future. Furthermore, in the post-COVID-19 future, 40% of respondents anticipate favoring online purchasing over visiting physical businesses. In recent times, mobile banking has evolved as a new feature of electronic banking.

Mobile banking (M-banking) is the use of wireless devices in banking (cell phones, PDAs, and laptop computers) by clients to browse the Internet and conduct transactions via the Internet at any point in time from any location. The first mobile banking services were delivered using SMS (Short Message Service). With the introduction of the first primitive cellphones with Wireless Applications Protocol (WAP) compatibility, allowing use in 1999, European banks began offering mobile banking services to their customers using this operating system (Ndlovu & Ndlovu, 2013).

Mobile banking enables bank clients to check their account balances and conduct credit card transactions using mobile devices, as well as allowing banks to offer information on the most recent transaction performed by consumers. SMS and WAP-enabled mobile phones are increasingly being utilized for mobile banking. It is described as "a channel through which a customer communicates with a bank through the use of a mobile device, such as a phone or Personal Digital Assistant (PDA)."

Mobile banking overcomes the time and location constraints associated with banking activities such as balance inquiry and fund transfer from one account to another without visiting bank offices. Bangladesh's mobile financial services business is quickly expanding, with at least 17 firms currently on the market. At the end of September 2017, there were 710,026 total agents and about 58.8 million registered consumers, with nearly 21.0 million active accounts under mobile banking.

In 2017, the overall number of transactions was 187.56 crore, with a total value of BDT 3146.62 billion at the end of the same year (Asfaw, 2015). Mobile banking adoption in Bangladesh surged dramatically during the national shutdown, which began on March 26, 2020. Increasing from 80.92 million in January 2020 to 92.57 million in July of the same year, the number of authorized mobile banking clients climbed dramatically. This upward trend has persisted, with the number of registered clients expected to reach 99.34 million by December 2020. Notably, this was a faster pace of increase compared with the previous year (2019).

After June 2020, there was a significant increase in mobile banking enrolments, owing to government and other institutions' measures encouraging the use of mobile banking for payment during the COVID-19 epidemic. As a result of these efforts, the rate of increase in registered mobile banking clients climbed by around 21% from March to December 2020, contrasting with a 16% growth rate during the same period the previous year. These data demonstrate the pandemic's major influence on mobile banking uptake in Bangladesh, where usage and adoption increased significantly throughout the lockdown period, showing a paradigm shift in clients' financial behaviors towards online services.

Bangladesh has achieved significant progress in financial inclusion by providing inexpensive financial services to poor and needy individuals through the adoption of alternate delivery channels such as mobile banking. In 2020, formal financial services will encompass 48% of the adult population, due mostly to the expansion of mobile banking services, increasing from 20% in 2013 before MFS restrictions, as shown in Figure 5.3.

Loan payments, loan expenditures, and savings mobilization have been the three primary areas where m-banking has had the most influence on MFIs so far. Customers who want to use MFIs' mobile banking services must first create an account. This usually entails going to an MFI branch or agent and giving the requisite identity documents. When a consumer registers, their mobile phone is linked to their MFI account, resulting in the creation of a mobile wallet or account for financial activities (Hanouch & Rotman, 2013).

Currently, 15 Bangladesh Bank-approved banks provide MFS services in the country. bKash, Rocket, UCash, and Nagad are significant MFS providers, bKash holds the most market share. According to Bangladesh Bank, the number of agents increased by nearly 83% between December 2015 and October 2020, while the number of registered clients increased by around 203%. During the same time period, the total amount of transactions climbed by about 153%, with a 230% increase in transaction value (Jahan, 2019).

Mobile Banking Customers (In Millions)

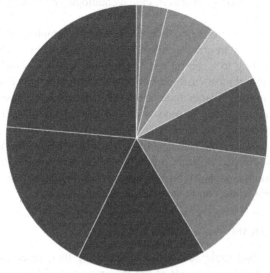

■ 2012 ■ 2013 ■ 2014 ■ 2015 ■ 2016 ■ 2017 ■ 2018 ■ 2019 ■ 2020

FIGURE 5.3 Mobile banking adoption in Bangladesh.

Source: Khang, 2021.

AI-powered chatbots and AI-powered virtual assistants deliver real-time and personalized customer assistance, quickly answering common questions, assisting clients with transaction navigation, and resolving difficulties. This function provides round-the-clock help, resulting in an upgraded and enhanced client experience (Ahmed, 2020). Another aspect where mobile banking plays a significant role in encouraging women entrepreneurs is because banking technology is continuously evolving and can assist women entrepreneurs in gaining access to financial services.

The construction and upkeep of traditional brick-and-mortar banking infrastructure impose significant cost difficulties in the field of microfinance. However, integrating mobile banking is a potential approach for lowering these overhead expenses, making financial services more economically accessible and sustainable for both microfinance organizations and their clients. This integration promotes financial inclusion by expanding services to rural and underserved locations, hence helping low-income individuals and marginalized populations who were previously excluded from traditional banking channels.

Furthermore, mobile banking enables real-time transactions, expediting loan disbursements and repayments and so improving operational efficiency (Nugroho & Chowdhury, 2015; Uddin & Barai, 2022). Globe in the Philippines, Dialogue eZ Cash in Sri Lanka, and CGAP in Brazil, for example, use mobile technology for microfinance. M-Pesa's (a mobile phone-based money transfer, financing, and microfinancing service) success in Kenya, reaching about 40% of the mature population after just two years of operation, can be attributed to the service's popularity. People are gravitating towards mobile technologies on their own, carrying out their own transactions.

Similarly, microfinance organizations have begun to emphasize the adoption of sophisticated technology in order to maximize their proficiency in order to perceive these profits. According to a central bank poll, the new services are reaching many parts of the country, and most customers and agents are cautiously enthusiastic about the usefulness of mobile financial services. Three-quarters of consumers indicated they use this service primarily to send or receive cash, while the remaining quarter stated it is for safekeeping.

Rural customers emphasized the benefits of acquiring money. BRAC Bank, in collaboration with its subsidiary bKash, provides the bKash service. Dutch Bangla Bank also introduced Dutch Bangla Mobile. These two vendors were responsible for over 500,000 new mobile wallets and over 9000 new agents.

5.6   CONCLUSION

MFIs have seen considerable advances in broadening their reach to disadvantaged and marginalized groups as a result of the incorporation of AI technology, helping to increase financial inclusion across the country. MFIs have gained greater insights into client behaviors and preferences thanks to the use of AI-powered algorithms, allowing them to build personalized financial solutions that cater to the particular demands of various customer categories (Khang, Shah et al., 2023).

Furthermore, AI-powered procedures have optimized several parts of microfinance operations, from loan application and approval through distribution and repayment, speeding up the lending process and lowering administrative overheads. AI has decreased lending risks through real-time data processing and decision-making capabilities, resulting in more accurate risk assessment models and sensible credit portfolio management (Khang, Kali et al., 2023). The integration of AI-powered chatbots and customer care software has transformed the way MFIs connect with their clients, allowing them to provide seamless and personalized customer assistance. This has not only increased client trust and loyalty but has also allowed MFIs to serve a larger customer base more effectively (Khang. Muthmainnah et al., 2023).

REFERENCES

Ahmed, M. T., Imtiaz, M. T., & Kauser, A. A. (2020). A comparative study of mobile banking in specific parts of Bangladesh. *International Journal of Science and Business*, 4(6), 129–139. https://bit.ly/3Q5O1kz

Asfaw, H. A. (2015). Financial inclusion through mobile banking: Challenges and prospects. *Research Journal of Finance and Accounting*, 6(5), 98–104. www.academia.edu/download/39808750/17.pdf

Awotunde, J. B., Misra, S., Ayeni, F., Maskeliunas, R., & Damasevicius, R. (2021, December). Artificial Intelligence based system for bank loan fraud prediction. In *International Conference on Hybrid Intelligent Systems* (pp. 463–472). Cham: Springer International Publishing. https://link.springer.com/chapter/10.1007/978-3-030-96305-7_43

Ayoo, C. (2022). Poverty reduction strategies in developing countries. *Rural Development-Education, Sustainability, Multifunctionality*, 19. https://bit.ly/49hi0fK

Bassey, E. B. (2018). Effect of forensic accounting on the management of fraud in microfinance institutions in Cross River State. *Journal of Economics and Finance*, 9(4), 79–89. https://smartlib.umri.ac.id/assets/uploads/files/4738a-j0904017989.pdf

Bhambri, P., Rani, S., Gupta, G., & Khang, A. (2022). *Cloud and Fog Computing Platforms for Internet of Things*. CRC Press. https://doi.org/ 10.1201/9781003213888

Caudill, S. B., Gropper, D. M., & Hartarska, V. (2009). Which microfinance institutions are becoming more cost effective with time? Evidence from a mixture model. *Journal of Money, Credit and Banking*, 41(4), 651–672. https://onlinelibrary.wiley.com/doi/abs/10.1111/J.1538-4616.2009.00226.X

Chemin, M. (2008). The benefits and costs of microfinance: evidence from Bangladesh. *The Journal of Development Studies*, 44(4), 463–484. www.tandfonline.com/doi/abs/10.1080/00220380701846735

Dahal, M., & Fiala, N. (2020). What do we know about the impact of microfinance? The problems of statistical power and precision. *World Development,* 128, 104773. www.econstor.eu/handle/10419/179963

Dolgorukov, D. (2023, June 2). AI empowers microfinance: Revolutionizing Fraud Detection. InsideBIGDATA.https://insidebigdata.com/2023/06/01/ai-empowers-microfinance-revolutionizing-fraud-detection/.

Ganegoda, A., & Evans, J. (2014). A framework to manage the measurable, immeasurable and the unidentifiable financial risk. *Australian Journal of Management*, 39(1), 5–34. https://journals.sagepub.com/doi/abs/10.1177/0312896212461033

Hani, U., Wickramasinghe, A., Kattiyapornpong, U., & Sajib, S. (2022)/ The future of data-driven relationship innovation in the microfinance industry. *Annals of Operations Research*, 1–27. https://link.springer.com/article/10.1007/s10479-022-04943-6

Hanouch, M., & Rotman, S. (2013). Microfinance and mobile banking: Blurring the lines? https://policycommons.net/artifacts/1509764/microfinance-and-mobile-banking/2178170/

Hossain, M. (2008). Satisfaction of Women Beneficiaries on Micro-Credit Program of Shakti Foundation (Doctoral Dissertation Dept. of Agricultural Extension & Information System). http://archive.saulibrary.edu.bd:8080/xmlui/handle/123456789/1710

Jahan, M. T. (2019). A comparative study between premier bank's pmoney and the leading mobile financial service provider bKash. http://dspace.bracu.ac.bd/xmlui/handle/10361/13786

Kaicer, M. (2020). Information Technology performance management by artificial intelligence in microfinance institutions: An overview. *International Journal of Computational Intelligence Studies*, 9(3), 186–189. www.inderscienceonline.com/doi/abs/10.1504/IJCISTUDIES.2020.109599

Karr, J., Loh, K., & Wirjo, A. (2020). Supporting MSME's Digitalization Amid Covid-19. *APEC Policy Support Unit Policy Brief* (35). www.sea-vet.net/images/seb/e-library/doc_file/743/220psusupporting-msmes-digitalization-amid-covid-19.pdf

Katterbauer, K., & Moschetta, P. (2022). A deep learning approach to risk management modeling for Islamic microfinance. *European Journal of Islamic Finance*, 9(2), 35-43. https://ojs.unito.it/index.php/EJIF/article/view/6202

Khan, A. A., Khan, S. U., Fahad, S., Ali, M. A., Khan, A., & Luo, J. (2021). Microfinance and poverty reduction: New evidence from Pakistan. *International Journal of Finance & Economics*, 26(3), 4723–4733. https://onlinelibrary.wiley.com/doi/abs/10.1002/ijfe.2038

Khan, S., & Ashta, A. (2013). Managing multi-faceted risks in microfinance operations. *Strategic Change*, 22(1–2), 1–16. https://bit.ly/3THmg2u

Khang, A. (2021). "Material4Studies." Material of Computer Science, Artificial Intelligence, Data Science, IoT, Blockchain, Cloud, Metaverse, Cybersecurity for Studies. Retrieved from www.researchgate.net/publication/370156102_Material4Studies

Khang, A. (Ed.) (2023). *Advanced Technologies and AI-Equipped IoT Applications in High-Tech Agriculture* (1st Ed.). IGI Global Press. https://doi.org/10.4018/978-1-6684-9231-4

Khang, A., Abdullayev, V., Hahanov, V., & Shah, V. (2024). *Advanced IoT Technologies and Applications in the Industry 4.0 Digital Economy* (1st Ed.). CRC Press. https://doi.org/10.1201/9781003434269

Khang, A., Hahanov, V., Abbas, G. L., & Hajimahmud, V. A. (2022). "Cyber-Physical-Social System and İncident Management." In *AI-Centric Smart City Ecosystems: Technologies, Design and Implementation* (1st Ed.), vol. 2 (p. 15). CRC Press. https://doi.org/10.1201/9781003252542-2

Khang, A., Kali, C. R., Satapathy, S. K., Kumar, A., Ranjan Das, S., & Panda, M. R. (2023). "Enabling the Future of Manufacturing: Integration of Robotics and IOT to Smart Factory Infrastructure in Industry 4.0." In *AI-Based Technologies and Applications in the Era of the Metaverse* (1st Ed.) (pp. 25–50). IGI Global Press. https://doi.org/10.4018/978-1-6684-8851-5.ch002

Khang, A., Muthmainnah, M., Seraj, P. M. I., Al Yakin, A., Obaid, A. J., & Panda, M.R. (2023). "AI-Aided Teaching Model for the Education 5.0 Ecosystem." In *AI-Based Technologies and Applications in the Era of the Metaverse* (1st Ed.) (pp. 83–104). IGI Global Press. https://doi.org/10.4018/978-1-6684-8851-5.ch004

Khang, A., Shah, V., & Rani, S. (2023). *AI-Based Technologies and Applications in the Era of the Metaverse* (1st Ed.). IGI Global Press. https://doi.org/10.4018/978-1-6684-8851-5

Lassoued, N. (2017). What drives credit risk of microfinance institutions? International evidence. *International Journal of Managerial Finance*, 13(5), 541–559. www.emerald.com/insight/content/doi/10.1108/IJMF-03-2017-0042/full/html

Mhlanga, D. (2020). Industry 4.0 in finance: The impact of artificial intelligence (ai) on digital financial inclusion. *International Journal of Financial Studies*, 8(3), 45. www.mdpi.com/2227-7072/8/3/45

Mia, M. A. (2016). Microfinance institutions and legal status: An Overview of the microfinance sector in Bangladesh. *The Journal of Asian Finance, Economics and Business (JAFEB)*, 3(2), 21–31. https://bit.ly/49cWtF3

Mia, M. A. (2017). An overview of the microfinance sector in Bangladesh. *The Journal of Business, Economics, and Environmental Studies*, 7(2), 31–38. https://bit.ly/4awGXFa

Mohamed, T. S., & Elgammal, M. M. (2023). Credit risk in Islamic microfinance institutions: The role of women, groups, and rural borrowers. *Emerging Markets Review*, 54, 100994. www.sciencedirect.com/science/article/pii/S1566014122200111X

Moin, C. M., & Kraiwanit, T. (2023). Digital Improvements to Microfinance in Bangladesh. *International Research E-Journal on Business and Economics*, 8(1), 1–7. www.assumptionjournal.au.edu/index.php/aumitjournal/article/view/7231

Mujeri, M. K. (2020). Digital Transformation of MFIs: A Post Covid-19 Agenda for Bangladesh (No. 63). InM Working Paper. http://inm.org.bd/wp-content/uploads/2020/10/working-pepar-63.pdf

Ndlovu, I., & Ndlovu, M. (2013). Mobile banking the future to rural financial inclusion: Case study of Zimbabwe. *IOSR Journal of Humanities and Social Science*, 9(4), 70–75. https://citeseerx.ist.psu.edu/document?repid=rep1&type=pdf&doi=a559b8f97745e99999760e4df47948ff6b4c50a4

Ndung'u, N. (2022). FinTech in Sub-Saharan Africa. World Institute for Development Economic Research (UNU-WIDER), Working Paper No. wp-2022-101. www.econstor.eu/handle/10419/273899

Nugroho, L., & Chowdhury, S. L. K. (2015). Mobile banking for empowerment muslim women entrepreneur: Evidence from Asia (Indonesia and Bangladesh). *Tazkia Islamic Finance and Business Review*, 9(1). https://tifbr-tazkia.org/index.php/TIFBR/article/view/79

Parvez, J., Islam, A., & Woodard, J. (2015). Mobile Financial Services in Bangladesh. *USAID*, mSTAR and fhi360. www.marketlinks.org/sites/default/files/resource/files/MFSinBangladesh_April2015.pdf

Rani, S., Bhambri, P., Kataria, A., Khang, A., & Sivaraman, A. K. (2023). *Big Data, Cloud Computing and IoT: Tools and Applications* (1st Ed.). Chapman and Hall/CRC. https://doi.org/10.1201/9781003298335

Rani, S., Chauhan, M., Kataria, A., Khang, A. (2021). "IoT Equipped Intelligent Distributed Framework for Smart Healthcare Systems." In *Networking and Internet Architecture*, Computer Science, Cornell University. Vol. 2 (p. 30). https://doi.org/10.48550/arXiv.2110.04997

Saxena, T., & Sharma, N. (2021). Analysis of current trends and emerging issues in microfinance: A comparison of India and Bangladesh. *Pragati: Journal of Indian Economy*, 8(1), 93–115. www.indianjournals.com/ijor.aspx?target=ijor:pjie&volume=8&issue=1&article=006

Takeda, A., & Ito, Y. (2021). A review of FinTech research. *International Journal of Technology Management*, 86(1), 67–88. www.inderscienceonline.com/doi/abs/10.1504/IJTM.2021.115761

Uddin, H., & Barai, M. K. (2022). Will Digital Revolution be Disruptive for the Inclusive Finance in Bangladesh? The Case of the Microfinance Industry. https://catalog.lib.kyushu-u.ac.jp/ja/recordID/6622878/?repository=yes

Wanjiku, M. L., & Deya, J. (2021). Effect of competitive strategies on performance of microfinance institutions in Kenya. *International Journal of Academic Research in Accounting Finance and Management Sciences*, 11(1), 407–422. https://pdfs.semanticscholar.org/1ee3/7ec4076771f5e0028b751131fc37c07210cc.pdf

Yesmin, S., Paul, T.A., & Mohshin Uddin, M. (2019). bKash: Revolutionizing mobile financial services in Bangladesh? *Business and Management Practices in South Asia: A Collection of Case Studies*, 125–148. https://link.springer.com/chapter/10.1007/978-981-13-1399-8_6

6 Digital Payments
The Growth Engine of the Digital Economy

Varun Kesavan and Sakthi Srinivasan K.

6.1 INTRODUCTION

Since demonetization, the potential of electronic payment systems has generated considerable enthusiasm. Its importance has grown over the past several years. Government and business equally have recognized the expanding significance of technology and are maximizing its optimistic outlook. Both the proliferation of new technology and the desire to conduct business on a global scale have contributed to the rise of digital payment methods' popularity. The accelerated development of information communication and technology (ICT) has required both individuals and enterprises to adjust to new realities. In recent years, ICT has had a significant impact on finance and economics in terms of operational costs and organizational efficiency (Slozko & Pelo, 2015). The banking industry has undergone a dramatic transformation as a result of the proliferation of ICT, with more and more transactions taking place digitally and the use of physical currency banknotes decreasing as we move towards a less cash-based payment landscape (Al-Laham et al., 2009).

A contactless transaction facility is one that conducts all transactions digitally. It was not envisaged as a direct replacement for money, but as a superior alternative to monetary exchange and barter (Mukherjee & Roy, 2017). As smartphone usage and internet accessibility increase, digital payment increasingly replaces traditional wallets. In the digital age, the payment system has not accounted for the need for privacy and security. Tokens provide increased security and anonymity for the electronic payment system. Existing payment service providers (PSPs) will act as an intermediary between the customer and the institution, with the latter asserting anonymity, protection against potential fraud, and interoperability across "banks, devices, and service providers" (Rajendran et al., 2017).

Widespread use of mobile payment services is a significant factor in expanding access to the financial system for those without it. After demonetization, the use of mobile payments increased in India (Agarwal et al., 2020). Financial transactions on mobile devices such as smartphones are regarded as secure. The widespread adoption of electronic wallets has been facilitated by the ubiquitous use of devices. A modest business proprietor can accept virtual payments even without point-of-sale terminals. A sizeable population may be attracted to the digital economy with appropriate implementation (Gochhwal, 2017).

DOI: 10.1201/9781032618845-6

6.2   AIM OF THE STUDY

- Examine the growth of electronic transactions in India;
- Investigate the numerous electronic payment methods utilized in India.

6.3   LITERATURE REVIEW

Information communication and technology has revolutionized the banking industry in numerous ways, including telephony, online banking, and electronic money transfers at the point of sale (Abor, 2005). Due in large part to technological advances, we now have a reliable and quick payment method that eliminates the "cash and carry syndrome." The use of physical bank branches for financial transactions has been largely replaced by electronic means. All interactions have been simplified, secured, and accelerated by the economic system. This has increased the popularity of virtual transaction methods over the traditional method of using currency (Oyewole et al., 2013).

As computing capacity increases, so do the digital aspects of individuals' daily existence. Due to increasing demand for immediate gratification, this trend towards digitization has far-reaching effects on people's behaviors, values, and finances. It is impossible to exaggerate the significance of making the financial sector virtual. The electronic transaction is the area where digitization is most evident. Until recently, only cash and cheques were accepted at stores. Nonetheless, the scope of digital innovation in payments has enabled instantaneous payment via smartphone applications or even a wristwatch (Panetta, 2018). Due to the increasing number of internet and smartphone users worldwide (Boro, 2015), banks have a significant opportunity to expand beyond their customary locations.

Electronic payments are defined as "a transaction based on technology in which money is electronically stored, processed, and transacted using digital technologies such as the Internet, mobile devices, and payment cards" (*Payment and settlement systems*, 2007). As opposed to cash, cheques, or plastic cards, virtual payments are made using specialized software, a payment platform, and electronic currency. Money transfer software, the network, and administration are the primary components.

The digital payment ecosystem offers a variety of payment options for purchasing products and services. The advancement of technology has altered human existence in numerous ways. Electronic payment innovations, such as contactless payment, improved security, and real-time payment settlement, etc., are streamlining the payment procedure. E-wallets, mobile banking, and prepaid payment devices have acquired popularity in recent years (Darma & Noviana, 2020).

According to Camenisch et al. (1997), a bank, a client (the payer), and a payee (the recipient) interact through a succession of protocols in the electronic transaction system. The three phases of a transaction are the withdrawal phase, the payment phase, and the deposit phase. When paying in person, these three stages occur in three discrete transactions; when paying online, they occur simultaneously. Banks, users, and beneficiaries must all implement their own unique layers of protection to prevent double spending and fraud. To preserve privacy in the face of prospective government laws, anonymity should be protected (Camenisch et al., 1997). COVID-19 has established incentives for the use of electronic transaction systems (Adhikari et al., 2022).

6.4　DATA AND METHODOLOGY

- The most recent data are derived from research conducted by the RBI, NPCI, and other organizations.
- The data span the years 2017–2018 through 2022–2022.
- The results of the study have been compounded using the technique of CAGR.

6.5　DISCUSSIONS AND FINDINGS OF THE STUDY

6.5.1　Other Electronic Payment Alternatives

6.5.1.1　Debit, Credit, Cash, Travel, and Other Financial Institution Cards

In comparison to other payment methods, financial cards provide consumers with unparalleled security, usability, and administration. The extensive variety of cards, ranging from credit and debit to prepaid, offers a great deal of flexibility. These cards feature a private PIN and a one-time password for secure financial transactions. RuPay, Visa, and MasterCard are examples of well-known card payment systems. Using payment cards, consumers can make in-store, online, catalogue, and telephone purchases. Customers and business proprietors equally can save time and money by utilizing these systems (Rana et al., 2021).

6.5.1.2　USSD (Unstructured Supplementary Service Data)

The *99# payment system utilizes the USSD (Unstructured Supplemental Service Data) protocol (Cashless India, 2023). Mobile banking based on USSD makes it possible to conduct financial transactions from a mobile device without internet access. The objective is to assist the financially disadvantaged in joining the conventional financial system. To make banking accessible to the average citizen, the *99# service was implemented. Customers of participating institutions can use this service by dialing *99#, a "Common number across all Telecom Service Providers (TSPs)," from their mobile phones and traversing an on-screen menu to complete their financial transactions. The *99# service provides access to a variety of banking functions, including account balance inquiries, mini-statements, and interbank remittances. As of 30 November 2016 (source: NPCI), 51 major banks and all GSM service providers offered the *99# service in twelve languages, including Hindi and English. The *99# service is an inventive interoperable direct-to-consumer service that unifies financial institutions and telecommunications service providers (Khang, Gujrati et al., 2024).

6.5.1.3　AEPS (Aadhaar Enabled Payment System)

This payment system uses Aadhaar for authentication ("Cashless India," 2023). You may use the Business Correspondent (BC)/Bank Mitra of any bank to conduct online interoperable financial transactions at point of sale (PoS) or micro-ATM if you have an Aadhaar card.

6.5.1.4   UPI (Unified Payments Interface)

UPI is a platform that combines multiple financial services, such as streamlined money routing and merchant payments, into a single mobile application (from any participating bank). Additionally, it supports "peer to peer" collect requests, which can be planned and paid for at the user's convenience. Each bank is responsible for developing the UPI app for Android, Windows, and iOS.

6.5.1.5   UPI 123PAY

This is described in "Modes of virtual payments I Ministry of electronics and information technology, Government of India" (2022). UPI 123PAY is a quick and secure method for individuals with feature phones to use the UPI (Unified Payments Interface) network to make payments. Utilizing one of the four available technologies, users of feature phones can now conduct a vast array of transactions. Examples include calling an interactive voice response (IVR) number, utilizing applications on feature phones, relying on delayed calls, and making payments using proximity sound (Khang, Misra et al., 2023).

6.5.1.6   UPI LITE

This allows users to store up to INR 2000 in their BHIM-UPI app wallet, reducing the time required to complete a transaction and increasing the likelihood of successful payment processing ("Modes of virtual payments I Ministry of electronics and information technology, Government of India," 2022).

6.5.1.7   BHIM Aadhaar Pay

This enables merchants to accept virtual payments from customers at their physical locations using Aadhaar authentication ("Modes of virtual payments I Ministry of electronics and information technology, Government of India," 2022). Customers of different institutions can make purchases from any BHIM Aadhaar Pay merchant using biometric authentication.

To accomplish this, merchants must equip their Android devices with the BHIM Aadhaar software and a verified biometric scanner, and then connect these devices via a USB port to a micro-ATM/POS (mPOS). The linking of Aadhaar and bank accounts is mandatory for both customers and merchants.

6.5.1.8   Bharat Bill Payment System (BBPS)

The Bharat Bill Payment System (BBPS) is a centralized center that enables users to pay invoices and schedule recurring payments through a variety of convenient channels, such as internet banking, mobile banking, mobile apps, UPI, etc. Users can pay bills for a variety of utilities, including energy and gas, water, telecommunications, digital television, and more.

6.5.1.9   National Electronic Toll Collection (NETC)

FASTag is a simple and convenient digital payment system for toll payments, and the Indian government supports it. Anyone may use this national, interoperable service.

The FASTag device uses radio frequency identification (RFID) technology to facilitate in-vehicle toll payment in real time.

The government or private organizations may issue prepaid electronic vouchers in the form of a QR code or an SMS-based electronic voucher to facilitate the distribution of a particular subsidy or welfare benefit to eligible residents. Beneficiaries can redeem e-RUPI vouchers at participating retailers using an SMS or QR code in lieu of a card, virtual payments app, or internet banking. This contactless e-RUPI is straightforward, safe, and secure, and it safeguards the recipients' privacy by not disclosing their information. The necessary quantity is already included on the voucher, making the entire transaction process using this voucher relatively efficient and reliable (Cashless India, 2003).

Using a mobile wallet is one method to securely tote and access digital funds on the go. You can add funds to your mobile wallet by synchronizing your bank account, credit card, or other online account with the mobile wallet's application. Mobile devices like smartphones, tablets, and wearables have rendered credit cards made of plastic obsolete. Before money can be added to a digital wallet, it must be linked to a bank account.

6.5.1.10   Location of Purchase (POS)

The physical location where transactions occur is known as the point of sale (PoS). A PoS may be as large as a city, shopping facility, or marketplace. The term point of sale refers to the cash terminal at which transactions occur. A currency register may also serve as a point-of-sale terminal.

6.5.2   Transfer of Payments Electronically

6.5.2.1   Internet Banking

"Internet banking," also known as "online banking," "e-banking," and "virtual banking," is an electronic payment system that enables customers of a bank or other financial institution to conduct a variety of financial transactions via the bank's or institution's website.

The Bharat Interface for Money (BHIM) software facilitates making and receiving payments via the Unified Payments Interface (UPI). A user's mobile number, bank account and IFSC code, Aadhaar number, or Virtual Payment Address (VPA) can be used to instantaneously transfer or receive funds between bank accounts. The user can use a QR code scanner and BHIM to make a payment. By selecting "Report problem" in transactions, users can not only view information regarding declined transactions, but also file complaints. On a feature phone, dialing *99# enables users to conduct transactions.

6.5.2.2   National Electronic Funds Transfer

NEFT is one of the many options for transferring money electronically. The NEFT system now allows for direct domestic money transfers. If you have an account at one of the nation's participating institutions, you can electronically transfer funds to any other participating bank. NEFT may be utilized by anyone with a checking or savings account at a branch bank, be it an individual, business, or corporation. Even without a bank account, a customer can still use NEFT to send money by depositing currency at a branch that supports the service. However, these financial transactions cannot exceed Rs. 50,000 in total. Consequently, NEFT can be utilized by individuals without bank accounts. There are currently twelve settlements between 8 a.m. and 7 p.m., Monday through Friday, and six between Saturday morning and early afternoon (Khang, Hajimahmud et al., 2023).

6.5.2.3 Real Time Gross Settlement (RTGS)

This refers to the continuous (real-time) settlement of financial transactions on an order-by-order basis (without aggregating). The term "real moment" refers to the processing of instructions at the time they are received as opposed to a later time, whereas the term "gross settlement" refers to the settlement of individual money transfer instructions (instruction by instruction). Once funds have been deposited into the Reserve Bank of India's designated accounts, they cannot be withdrawn. When interacting with significant quantities of money, RTGS is the preferred method. The minimum quantity that can be transferred via RTGS is Rs. 2 lakh.

6.5.2.4 Electronic Clearing Service (ECS)

Electronic Clearing Service (ECS) Banks, companies, corporations, government agencies, etc. that collect or receive payments for utility bills, insurance premiums, credit card payments, loan repayments, etc. are increasingly turning to the Electronic Clearing Service (ECS) as an alternative to issuing and handling paper instruments in order to better serve their customers (Cashless India, 2003).

6.5.2.5 Instant Payment Service (IMPS)

With Instant payment service or immediate payments service (IMPS), you can electronically send and receive funds between banks at any time, from any location, and even from your mobile phone. In India, the Instant Interbank Funds Transfer (IMPS) system enables instantaneous money transfers between institutions via mobile devices, the internet, and automated teller machines.

6.5.2.6 Mobile Wallet

The term "mobile wallet" refers to a digital wallet that can be stored on a mobile device. The wallet can be linked to a customer's bank account or debit card to secure online transactions. Adding funds to a mobile wallet and then transferring those funds is another frequent use for wallets.

Today, a variety of bank-issued wallets are available. There are notable private companies that have made their mark in the mobile wallet industry. Examples of widely used payment apps include Paytm, Freecharge, Mobikwik, mRupee, Vodafone M-Pesa, Airtel Money, Jio Money, SBI Buddy, Vodafone M-Pesa, Axis Bank Lime, and ICICI Pockets, among others, and prepaid debit cards issued by financial institutions.

6.5.2.7   Bank Prepaid Cards

A bank prepaid card is a debit card issued by a bank that can be loaded in advance and used promptly or at a later date, unlike a traditional debit card, which is linked to a specific bank account and can be used repeatedly. This might or might not impact prepaid debit cards. By accessing the bank's online portal, any customer with a KYC-compliant account can request a prepaid card. Typical applications consist of corporate giveaways, award programs, and one-time donations.

6.5.2.8   Micro-ATMs

Micro-ATMs enable business correspondents (BC) to provide rudimentary banking services to their consumers. These correspondents, who may even be a business proprietor in your immediate area, will function as a "micro-ATM" to process instantaneous financial transactions. Using a biometric authentication device, Aadhaar-linked bank accounts will be able to transfer funds to one another. In essence, business correspondents will serve as the consumers' institutions. Mandatory use of UID (Aadhaar) is required for consumer verification. With the aid of micro-ATMs, withdrawals, deposits, money transfers, and account balance inquiries will all be possible. Your bank account must be linked to Aadhaar in order to use a micro-ATM.

6.6   THE ADVANTAGES OF DIGITAL PAYMENTS

In a country like India, where disparities can be extreme, ensuring financial equality is of paramount importance. The Indian government has pushed for a cashless economy and a digital India in part to increase citizens' accessibility to banking services. Digital payment systems offer numerous benefits.

The convenience they offer customers is a significant advantage of digital payment methods. Online transactions are preferred due to their convenience, speed, and reduced reliance on physical currency. Using cash or a paper cheque increases the risk of fraud, the number of required processes, and the requirement for physical presence. Digital transactions enable instantaneous, worldwide money transfers at the click of a button.

When consumers are confident of the safety, rapidity, and simplicity of digital payment systems, they spend more money online (Virtual payments: Definition and methods – Razorpay payment gateway 2021). This indicates that individuals are becoming increasingly comfortable with online shopping, digital investments, and electronic money transfers. The growth of the money supply and e-commerce both contribute to the expansion of the economy. This results in the daily emergence of new internet enterprises, the majority of which are successful.

Working with physical currency requires time and is inconvenient. Due to the constant risk of larceny, transporting large quantities of currency is inconvenient and hazardous. With virtual payments, it is straightforward to keep digital money secure. Due to UPI, net banking, and mobile wallets, it is now possible to send and receive money using only a mobile phone. In addition, the majority of digital payment gateways provide customers with consistent updates, notifications, and statements for monitoring their finances as shown in Figure 6.1 (see also Figure 6.2).

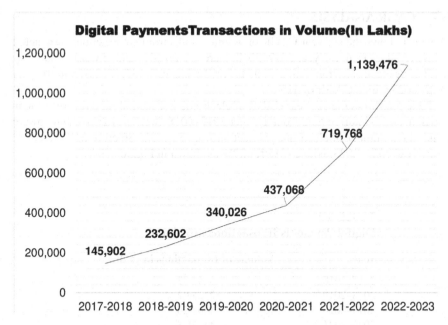

FIGURE 6.1   Electronic transactions in volume (in lakhs).

Source: The authors.

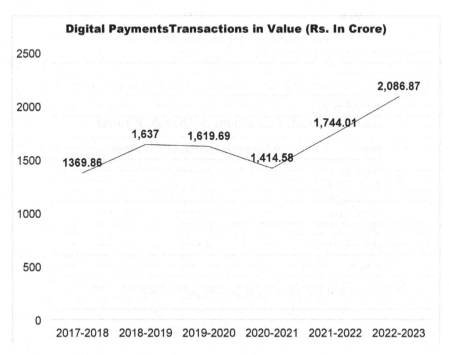

FIGURE 6.2   Electronic transactions in value (Rs. in Crore).

Source: The authors.

6.7   CAGR ANALYSIS

Table 6.1 shows the six-year CAGR of volume of electronic transactions in which it is inferred that, from the year 2017–2018, there is a positive and upward trend in the number of electronic transaction from 145,902 lakhs to 1,139,476 lakhs in the year 2022–2023 with a CAGR of 41%.

Table 6.2 shows the six-year CAGR of electronic transactions in terms of value in which it can be inferred that, from the year 2017–2018 there is a positive and upward trend in the number of electronic transaction from Rs. 1369.86 crore to Rs. 2086.87 in the year 2022–2023, with a CAGR of 7% as shown in Figure 6.3.

TABLE 6.1
Digital Payments Transactions in Volume

Year	Volume of Transactions in Lakhs
2017–2018	145,902
2018–2019	232,602
2019–2020	340,026
2020–2021	437,068
2021–2022	719,768
2022–2023	1,139,476
CAGR	**41%**

Source: RBI data and the CAGR computed by the authors.

TABLE 6.2
Digital Payments Transactions in Value Rs. (Crores)

Year	Value of Transactions Rs. (Crores)
2017–2018	1369.86
2018–2019	1637
2019–2020	1619.69
2020–2021	1414.58
2021–2022	1744.01
2022–2023	2086.87
CAGR	**7%**

Source: RBI data and the CAGR computed by the authors.

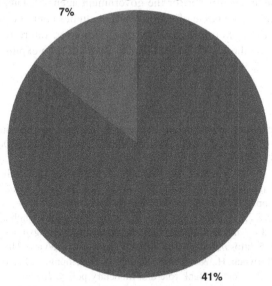

CAGR Analysis of Digital PaymentsTransactions

7%

41%

■ Volume of Transactions In (Lakhs)   ■ Value of Transactions Rs. In (Crores)

FIGURE 6.3   CAGR of electronic transactions.

Source: The authors.

6.8   CONCLUSION

In India, developments in information communication and technology and the expansion of the digital economy have led to a dramatic shift from traditional to contactless transactions in recent years. New technological advancements have caused changes in business models across the globe. Several industries, including the payment and settlements industry, have been disrupted by cutting-edge technologies such as AI, blockchain, machine learning, and cloud computing (Khang, Chowdhury et al., 2022). Despite the challenges posed by rapid technological change, the financial services industry has grown substantially in reality. According to studies conducted in the European Union, China, and other developed nations, it has resulted in a stronger financial system and an increase in consumer confidence (Khang, Shah et al., 2023).

However, an inadequately functioning payment system makes it more difficult for businesses and individuals to swiftly and easily resolve their financial transactions. Few studies have been conducted on the effect of India's technologically driven payment system on the country's financial sector and economy. Current research indicates that the total number of electronic payment transactions and the value of virtual payment transactions have increased by 41% and 7%, respectively, over the past few years (Khang, Muthmainnah et al., 2023).

6.9 FUTURE SCOPE OF WORK

This study will be an eye opener for the government agencies, banks, and financial institutions for the future course of action. Further studies could be carried out combining both primary as well as secondary data, moreover, future researchers could focus upon including those variables which have not yet been explored (Khang, Kali et al., 2023).

REFERENCES

Abor, J. (2005). Technological innovations and banking in Ghana: An evaluation of customers' perceptions. *IFE PsychologIA*, Vol. 13, No. 1, pp. 170–187. Doi: 10.4314/ifep.v13i1.23668

Adhikari, S., Pallavi, D. R., Ghimire, D., Thapa, S., & Sadikshya. (2022). Impact of COVID-19 on digital payment system of India. *Recent Trends in Science and Engineering*, Vol. 2393, No. 1, pp. 020178. Doi: 10.1063/5.0074251

Agarwal, V., Poddar, S., & Karnavat, S. J. (2020). A study on growth of mobile banking in India during covid-19. *PalArch's Journal of Archaeology of Egypt/Egyptology*, Vol. 17, No. 6, pp. 9461–9485. https://mail.palarch.nl/index.php/jae/article/view/2489

Al-Laham, M., Al-Tarwneh, H., & Abdallat, N. (2009). Development of electronic money and its impact on the Central Bank role and monetary policy. *Issues in Informing Science and Information Technology*, Vol. 6, pp. 339–349. Doi: 10.28945/1063

Boro, K. (2015). Prospects and challenges of technological innovation in banking industry of north east India. *The Journal of Internet Banking and Commerce*, Vol. 20, No. 3, pp. 1–6. Doi: 10.4172/1204-5357.1000134

Camenisch, J., Maurer, U., & Stadler, M. (1997). Digital payment systems with passive anonymity-revoking trustees*. *Journal of Computer Security*, Vol. 5, No. 1, pp. 69–89. Doi: 10.3233/jcs-1997-5104

Darma, G. S., & Noviana, I. (2020). Exploring digital marketing strategies during the new normal era in enhancing the use of digital payment. *Jurnal Mantik*, Vol. 4, No. 3, pp. 2257–2262. Doi: 10.35335/mantik.vol4.2020.1084.pp2257-2262

Gochhwal, R. (2017). Unified Payment Interface – An Advancement in Payment Systems. *American Journal of Industrial and Business Management*, Vol. 07, No. 10, pp. 1174–1191. Doi: 10.4236/ajibm.2017.710084

Khang, A., Chowdhury, S., & Sharma S. (2022). *The Data-Driven Blockchain Ecosystem: Fundamentals, Applications, and Emerging Technologies* (1st Ed.). CRC Press. https://doi.org/10.1201/9781003269281

Khang, A., Gujrati, R., Uygun, H., Tailor, R. K., & Gaur, S. S. (2024). *Data-driven Modelling and Predictive Analytics in Business and Finance* (1st Ed.). CRC Press. ISBN: 9781032600628. https://doi.org/10.1201/9781032600628

Khang, A., Hajimahmud, V. A., Gupta, S. K., Babasaheb, J., & Morris, G. (2023). *AI-Centric Modelling and Analytics: Concepts, Designs, Technologies, and Applications* (1st Ed.). CRC Press. https://doi.org/10.1201/9781003400110

Khang, A., Kali, C. R., Satapathy, S. K., Kumar, A., Ranjan Das, S., & Panda, M. R. (2023). Enabling the future of manufacturing: Integration of robotics and IoT to smart factory infrastructure in Industry 4.0. In A. Khang, V. Shah, & S. Rani (Eds.), *AI-Based Technologies and Applications in the Era of the Metaverse* (1st Ed.) (pp. 25–50). IGI Global Press. https://doi.org/10.4018/978-1-6684-8851-5.ch002

Khang, A., Misra, A., Gupta, S. K., & Shah, V. (Eds.) (2023). *AI-aided IoT Technologies and Applications in the Smart Business and Production.* CRC Press. https://doi.org/10.1201/9781003392224

Khang, A., Muthmainnah, M., Seraj, P. M. I., Al Yakin, A., Obaid, A. J., & Panda, M. R. (2023). AI-Aided teaching model for the education 5.0 ecosystem. In A. Khang, V. Shah, & S. Rani (Eds.), *AI-Based Technologies and Applications in the Era of the Metaverse* (1st Ed.) (pp. 83–104). IGI Global Press. https://doi.org/10.4018/978-1-6684-8851-5.ch004

Khang, A., Shah, V., & Rani S. (2023). *AI-Based Technologies and Applications in the Era of the Metaverse* (1st Ed.). IGI Global Press. https://doi.org/10.4018/978-1-6684-8851-5

Mukherjee, M., & Roy, S. (2017). E-Commerce and online payment in the modern era. *International Journal of Advanced Research in Computer Science and Software Engineering,* Vol. 7, No. 5, pp. 1–15. https://bit.ly/49gmhAi

Oyewole, O. S., Gambo, J, Abba, M, & Onuh, M. E. (2013). Electronic payment system and economic growth: a review of transition to cashless economy in Nigeria. *International Journal of Scientific Engineering and Technology,* Vol. 2, No. 9, pp. 913–918. www.indianjournals.com/ijor.aspx?target=ijor:ijset1&volume=2&issue=9&article=023

Panetta, F. (2018). 21st Century cash: Central banking, technological innovation and digital currencies. Do we need central bank digital currency? Overview of Payment Systems in India. *Payment and Settlement Systems* (2007). Reserve Bank of India. www.rbi.org.in/scripts/PaymentSystems_UM.aspx

Rajendran, B., Pandey, A. K., & Bindhumadhava, B. S. (2017). "Secure and privacy preserving digital payment." In 2017 IEEE SmartWorld, Ubiquitous Intelligence & Computing, Advanced & Trusted Computed, Scalable Computing & Communications, Cloud & Big Data Computing, Internet of People and Smart City Innovation (SmartWorld/SCALCOM/UIC/ATC/CBDCom/IOP/SCI), San Francisco, CA, USA, pp. 1–5, doi: 10.1109/UIC-ATC.2017.8397623

Rana, G., Khang, A., Sharma, R., Goel, A. K., & Dubey, A. K. (Eds.) (2021). *Reinventing Manufacturing and Business Processes through Artificial Intelligence.* CRC Press. https://doi.org/10.1201/9781003145011

Slozko, O., & Pelo, A. (2015). Problems and risks of digital technologies introduction into E-payments. *Transformations in Business & Economics,* Vol. 14, No. 1, pp. 225–235. https://bit.ly/3xgx0gR

7 Machine Learning-Based Functionalities for Business Intelligence and Data Analytics Tools

Rajasekar Rangasamy, E. Gurumoorthi, Sonam Mittal, T. Daniya, and M. S. Nidhya

7.1 INTRODUCTION

Any organization's planning and strategy are referred to as business intelligence. There are also many potential additions, including products, technology, and the analysis and presentation of corporate data. A thorough review of business intelligence and analytics tools is provided in this section of the introduction. Businesses are being pushed to increase their inventiveness and performance as a result of depending on outside knowledge and information due to the daily increase in data and information generation (Khang, Kali et al., 2023).

The rapid development of computer intelligence and the emergence of the "big data" concept have increased the importance of business intelligence and analytics for academics and practitioners and as also for the business and finance sectors. Although business intelligence and analytics (BI & A) were initially employed to assist in decision-making processes, they are now frequently utilized to foster organizational learning and opportunities, enhance operational performance, and increase organizational intelligence.

7.1.1 BUSINESS INTELLIGENCE (BI)

Business intelligence (BI) software collects corporate data and presents it in ways that are easy to understand, such as reports, dashboards, charts, and graphs. Business intelligence and analytics, or BIA, is the process of developing tools, methods, processes, and apps for analyzing critical business information to discover fresh details about marketplaces and businesses. These fresh concepts can be applied to maintain a better standard for goods and services, increase operational effectiveness, and strengthen client relationships.

Business intelligence (BI) is defined as "a set of techniques and tools for the acquisition and transformation of raw data into meaningful and useful information for business analysis purposes." Additionally, "data surfacing" is a term that is used more

DOI: 10.1201/9781032618845-7

frequently in relation to BI capability. BI technologies can handle large amounts of structured and occasionally unstructured data to help identify, develop, and otherwise create new strategic business opportunities. BI's goal is to make it simple to understand these enormous volumes of data. Businesses that identify new prospects and put into practice long-term stability and a competitive advantage in the market can be achieved with an insightful plan (Bentley, 2017).

BI technologies offer a historical, real-time, and forecast perspective of organizational activity. Business intelligence systems frequently execute tasks such as reporting, online analytical processing, analytics, predictive and prescriptive analytics, benchmarking, and advanced event processing.

A wide spectrum of business decisions, from tactical to strategic, can be supported by BI. Basic operational decisions frequently involve pricing and product placement. Priorities, goals, and directions are all included in strategic business decisions in the broadest sense. BI functions most effectively in every situation when it integrates information from internal and external sources, such as operational and financial data, as well as market data. A more complete picture may be created when internal and external data are combined, creating "intelligence" that cannot be obtained from any one source of data alone (Khang, Shah et al., 2023).

7.1.2 Business Analytics (BA)

Analytics is the study and dissemination of significant data patterns. Businesses use analytics to raise their performance levels. Among the subjects treated in this literature are software analytics, embedded analytics, learning analytics, and social media analytics. Given the complexity of the subject, the section on analytics provides a thoughtful emphasis.

The discipline of continuously and iteratively analyzing previous business performance is known as business analytics (BA), and it is done to provide knowledge and direct business strategy. Business analytics aims to create fresh insights into how businesses function by using data and statistical techniques. Business intelligence has usually focused on employing a set of indicators that are consistently used to assess past performance and direct business planning, even though business planning also depends on data and statistical approaches.

Explanatory and predictive modeling, as well as fact-based management, is heavily relied on in business analytics to aid in decision-making. A wide spectrum of business decisions, from tactical to strategic, can be supported by BI. Analytics can be used to support fully automated judgments or as data for human decision-making. Business intelligence includes reporting, "alerts," and online analytical processing (OLAP). In other words, queries regarding what happened, how it happened, how many times, where the problem is, and what has to be done can be answered via querying, reporting, OLAP, and alert technologies. The question "Why is this happening?" can be answered using business analytics. What would occur if these trends continued? What will take place next? Things are also addressed, including "What would be best if it happened?"

7.1.3 COMPARISON OF BUSINESS INTELLIGENCE WITH BUSINESS ANALYTICS

Bentley (2017) said that although there are several meanings, business intelligence (BI) and business analytics (BA) are sometimes used synonymously. One definition sets the two in opposition, pointing out that business intelligence is the act of obtaining corporate data primarily through asking, reporting, and online analytical processes, with the goal of learning information. On the other hand, business analytics employs quantitative and statistical methods for explanatory and predictive modeling. Business analytics, reporting, online analytical processing (OLAP), an "alerts" tool, and querying should all be included in a new definition of business intelligence. Business analytics, per this definition, is a branch of business intelligence (BI) that emphasizes statistics, prediction, and optimization over reporting, as shown in Figure 7.1.

7.1.4 BUSINESS

A person who is involved in the manufacturing or offering products or services as a business is sometimes referred to as acting in a manner that is intended to generate profit. The word "business" refers to an ambitious individual, team, or organization that engages in commercial activity. They could be business-related, industrial, or something else.

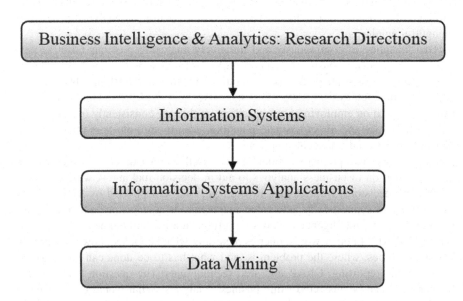

FIGURE 7.1   Research into business intelligence and business analytics.

Source: Khang, 2021.

7.1.5 FINANCE SECTOR

The financial sector, a sector of the economy, consists of companies and institutions that offer financial services to both wholesale and retail customers. There are many different types of corporations in this industry, including banks, financial institutions, insurance providers, and real estate firms.

The financial services industry is made up of banking, investing, taxation, real estate, and insurance, all of which offer various financial services to individuals and businesses. Frequently, the financial markets are used to compare this industry. It offers a venue for trading at a price set by market forces between buyers and sellers.

7.1.6 MACHINE LEARNING

Machine learning is a technique used by artificial intelligence (AI) to teach computers to learn from experience. Machine learning algorithms "learn" data directly, without employing an existing equation as a model. The algorithms adapt to the performance of the samples when more samples are made available for learning, as shown in Figure 7.2.

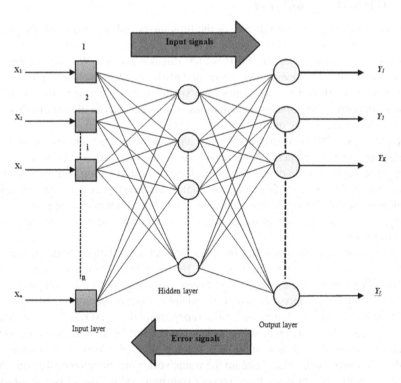

FIGURE 7.2 Block diagram of machine learning.

Source: Khang, 2021.

7.1.7 Machine Learning Functionalities for Business and Finance Sectors

The banking industry uses machine learning most frequently for algorithmic trading, data analytics, process automation, fraud detection, and customer support. Thanks to machine learning, businesses can more successfully manage their marketing and target their advertisements. Spam detection is a wonderful application of machine learning that has been around for a long.

Machine learning algorithms can quickly analyze enormous volumes of financial data by finding patterns and making predictions. For instance, machine learning algorithms can forecast the possibility of a loan default based on a range of variables such as credit scores, income levels, and employment histories.

This chapter consists of five parts. The first section provided the introduction. The drawbacks and limitations of present systems are discussed in the Section 7.2 using a literature review. Section 7.3 explains our new suggested system design. Section 7.4 contains our newly constructed system's overall results and discussion. Section 7.5 provides the chapter's conclusion.

7.2 LITERATURE REVIEW

This literature survey section discusses the limitations and drawbacks of the current systems used in business intelligence and analytical tools in relation to machine learning functionalities for the business and finance sectors. We now understand the fundamentals of business intelligence and analytics. We have seen that it is possible to combine these two disciplines for a single goal in order to manage machine learning initiatives. Significant contributions from numerous academics in this field are included in the debate on the literature survey.

Khatri et al. (2019) proposed compare and contrast factor analysis models for identifying agile developers. A survey-based study was carried out to determine the most significant agile developers with the goal of developing and measuring its prevalence in Indian manufacturing companies and serving as a model for agility developers. Sensitivity to change, relationships with customers and suppliers, adaptability, competency, and responsiveness have all been theorized as the context of agile manufacturing.

Custom software analytics and business intelligence solutions built on machine learning are becoming increasingly popular. However, in practice, such solutions frequently remain at the prototyping stage because of the difficulty and length of time involved in putting in place a deployment and upkeep infrastructure. In order to structure the entire process and increase transparency, using the latest research, we created an end-to-end platform for creating and implementing ML-based business intelligence and software analytics solutions. Prototyping, deployment, and updating are the three iterative cycles that make up the framework's organizational structure. As a result, the platform facilitates these phase's transitions while also covering all other crucial tasks, such as gathering data and retraining already-deployed ML models. We contrast the framework with the real-world ML-based SA/BI solution to test its usefulness (Figalist et al., 2020).

Nazih Omri and Mribah (2022) described a project management paradigm that enables access to it from many data sources and software development tools. We use our technique to analyze project data to improve the following areas: (i) Teamwork, which includes team dashboards and team communication. Additionally, it improves deadlines, status reports, and document sharing. Planning enables the utilization and visibility of the tasks the software has outlined. (ii) In order to show any obstacles that certain team members may be facing without disclosing them, task time tracking will also be required. (iii) Forecasting, which uses behavioral data to anticipate future outcomes and enables the adoption of certain actions. Finally, (iv) documentation, which includes summaries of all pertinent project data including time devoted to activities and graphs that track the project's development. Experimental investigations on the numerous data sets utilized to evaluate our model, as well as the significant models we looked into in the literature, attest to its efficacy in terms of precision, recall, and robustness. Analyses of the outcomes of these research were also provided.

Vashisht et al. (2020) investigates the top platform for business intelligence (BI) solutions, which is Qlik Sense. This is a tool for data visualization and exploration that enables flexible, interactive visualizations and insightful decision-making. It makes use of augmented intelligence to offer timely insights into the organization's data. The information may come from many organizational departments and can be found in various data sources. Self-service BI is based on the idea that it is interactive; particularly useful are business user-driven interfaces to the underlying data when using it for decision-making.

Sarma (2022) provides a succinct overview of the development and function of the data analytics ecosystem. Business analytics provides definitions for words such as data, insight, and action. They discuss how businesses in the digital age need clever analytics. A new area called "intelligent big data analytics," or "intelligent BA," has emerged as a result of recent advancements in AI, big data, and analytics. Intelligent BA also becomes a vital tool for corporations to use when making decisions. There is discussion and illustration of the key components of intelligent BA. Also suggested are additional applications for intelligent BA, along with some of the system implementation difficulties. Finally, several research trajectories for the creation of intelligent BA are discussed (Khang, Hajimahmud et al., 2023).

Early on, BI was only accessible to a small number of strategic users in offline mode, which was primarily used for decision-making. Operational BI, a later iteration of BI, provides data insights to all organizational levels of users for their decision-making, including strategic, tactical, and operational users. Additionally, organizations have started utilizing operational business intelligence (Sarma, 2018) to make low-level decisions for tactical and strategic reasons as well as to ensure effective corporate operations.

Shastry et al. (2022) discussed business analytics (BA) as the process of gathering information from company data by organizing, processing, and analyzing it in order to improve efficiency, productivity, and financial performance. Despite worries that implementing BA functions would result in job losses, machine learning (ML) applications inside BA have flourished recently and have revolutionized the process of business decision-making. It lists the many and distinctive machine learning methods now employed in industry. There are a number of case studies that show how

ML is applied in the commercial world. The topic of open research issues in ML and BA is discussed.

QlikSense, Qlik View, Microsoft PowerBI, Tableau, and Thoughtspot are some of the top BI software packages on the market. These technologies would select the organizational data spread across several data sources, carry out data transformation, and clean up the data. The cleaned data are subsequently shown as a dashboard and report visualization. Tools such as Qlik Sense fall under the category of self-service business intelligence platforms, allowing end users to construct necessary visualizations and reports without enlisting the assistance of the IT department (Gartner_Inc, 2020).

Roth-Dietrich et al. (2023) proposed the Gartner Magic Quadrant BI systems. These technologies have a less clear AI interface and are designed for laypeople with no prior experience in data analysis. Simple problems are better suited for BI systems that can be activated instantly and feature machine learning and high levels of automation, whereas fine-grained settings enable more complicated analyses. It has become evident that there is no BI system that can be used everywhere. Demands for complex control options for ML algorithms go against the wide applicability of those algorithms by many users. The organization must, in general, consider the target user group and their prior experience when selecting the optimal BI solution (Rana, Khang et al., 2021).

Strong evidence supports the use of ANN-based approaches for resolving research issues pertaining to software metrics. Similarly, there are numerous examples where the expected time to finish the job has been seen and ANN is able to predict it. Understanding these facts served as the foundation for developing an ANN-based method for forecasting faults during various stages of the BI project life cycle (Let Machine Learning Boost Your Business Intelligence, 2020).

Gartner assesses each vendor's ability to transform its vision into a distinct market reality that customers are willing to accept. Gartner also evaluates each vendor's performance in doing so. The ability of a vendor to provide an excellent customer experience, which takes into consideration elements such as sales expertise, customer support, product quality, user facilitation, skill accessibility, and ease of upgrade and migration, affects their place on the "ability to execute" axis (Richardson et al., 2020).

Yafooz et al. (2020), with the efficient use of big data, business intelligence, machine learning, and data mining, emphasize the importance of analytics and data management. Additionally, the many methods that may be utilized to extract knowledge and practical information from such data have been analyzed. Many users who are interested in text mining may find this useful as it transforms difficult to interpret data into information that is useful to researchers, analysts, data scientists, and business decision-makers (Khanh & Khang, 2021).

7.3　SYSTEM DESIGN

In this section, we go into more detail about the solution and break down the various elements of the business intelligent management method. We also give a thorough conceptual analysis of the strategy, along with a breakdown of its functional requirements. Here we discuss the system design for business intelligence and analytics (BI & A) tools in relation to machine learning (ML) functionalities in business and finance sectors. Our strategy is a business intelligence tool that addresses management, stands out from the competition, and deals with system outcomes from the past, present, and future while also adjusting to new ones (Khang, Misra et al., 2023).

7.3.1 ARTIFICIAL NEURAL NETWORK (ANN)

Several hundred units or millions of units may make up a layer, depending on how complex the system is. Input, output, and other layers are routinely combined with hidden layers in artificial neural networks. The data that the neural network needs to analyze or learn from come into the input layer from the outside world. These data are then turned into meaningful data for the output layer after traveling through one or more hidden layers (Kubat & Kubat, 2021). An ANN performance is displayed in Figure 7.3.

- Input Layer: As implied by its name, this layer accepts inputs in a variety of programming-provided formats.
- Hidden Layer: The hidden layer lies between the input and output layers. It does all the calculations necessary to find buried features and patterns.
- Output Layer: The output layer is finally used to communicate the output after the input has undergone numerous modifications.

Step 1: method ANN (Input) Make a database for input

Step 2: Input <--- database including all potential variations Prepare ANNS

Step 3: for input = 1 to input's end **do**

Step 4: for 1 to 20 = neuron **do**

Step 5: for recur 1 through 20 **do**

Step 6: Train ANN

Step 7: saving the highest test R^2 for ANN-Storage

Step 8: end for

Step 9: end for

Step 10: ANN-Storage <--- Save the most accurate ANN based on the inputs.

Step 11: end for

Step 12: return ANN-Storage

Step 13: end procedure

FIGURE 7.3 ANN layers and performances.

Source: Khang, 2021.

The weighted sum of inputs used by the artificial neural network additionally includes a bias that is calculated after input. A transfer function serves as the visual representation of this calculation as shown in block code 7.1.

Block code 7.1: Pseudocode for ANN

Step 1: method ANN (Input) Make a database for input

Step 2: Input **<---** database including all potential variations Prepare ANNS

Step 3: for input = 1 to input's end **do**

Step 4: for 1 to 20 = neuron **do**

Step 5: for recur 1 through 20 **do**

Step 6: Train ANN

Step 7: saving the highest test R^2 for ANN-Storage

Step 8: end for

Step 9: end for

Step 10: ANN-Storage **<---** Save the most accurate ANN based on the inputs.

Step 11: end for

Step 12: return ANN-Storage

Step 13: end procedure

7.3.2 MATHEMATICAL MODEL FOR ANN

There are three fundamental elements that are crucial for developing a functional model of the biological neuron. The neuron's connections are first modeled as weights. The weight's value reveals how closely a neuron and an input are coupled. Positive weight values imply excitatory connections, while negative weight values signify inhibitory connections, as shown in Equation (7.1).

$$V_k = \sum_{j=1}^{p} w_{kj} x_j \qquad (7.1)$$

The next two elements simulate how a neuron cell actually functions. This procedure is referred to as a linear combination. Finally, an activation function regulates how strong a neuron's output is. Typically, a range of output values between 0 and 1, or between −1 and 1, is considered acceptable, as shown in Figure 7.4.

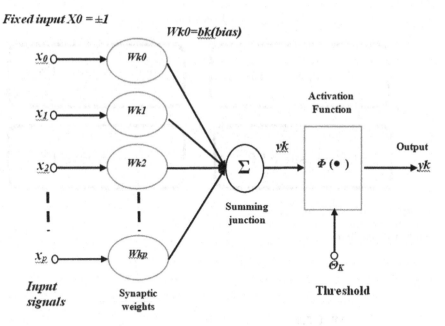

FIGURE 7.4   Mathematical flow of ANN.

Source: Khang, 2021.

7.4   RESULTS AND DISCUSSION

This section discusses the performance of the current system, which has accuracy, sensitivity, specificity, and resolution time ratings as performance parameters. When compared to the current system, the suggested system with the innovative approach to business intelligence and analytics using artificial neural network machine learning will be more effective. Additionally, the accuracy, sensitivity, specificity, and resolution time of this system are improved.

7.4.1   EVALUATION METRICS

A series of error calculations known as evaluation metrics are used to verify the model's accuracy. We frequently employ statistical techniques that calculate margins of error between actual values and predictions. Differently, we evaluated the relevant algorithms for each of our use cases, as shown in Figure 7.5.

A cross-validation technique is used to evaluate the text similarity model. Calculating out-of-sample error is a common practice in machine learning known as cross-validation. For instance, a substantial training batch and a smaller testing sample were created from the data. After training the model on the first batch of data across a number of iterations, we use the test set to confirm that it can make predictions on data that it has never seen before. The number of data points that were anticipated wrongly based on the unknown data is then determined.

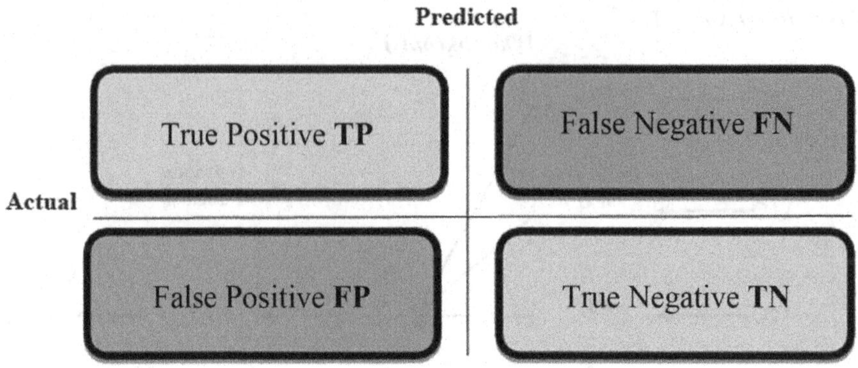

Predicted

FIGURE 7.5   Evaluation metrics.

Source: Khang, 2021.

TABLE 7.1
Accuracy Table

Algorithm	Accuracy (%)
Decision tree	83.04
SVM	84.12
Random forest	91.16
ANN	93.62

7.4.2 Accuracy

According to the accuracy formula, accuracy is defined as the error rate's departure from 100%. To ascertain accuracy, we must first ascertain the error rate. Additionally, by dividing the observed value by the actual value, the error rate is determined as a percentage, as shown in Equation (7.2).

$$\text{Accuracy} = \frac{TP + TN}{TP + TN + FN + FP} \tag{7.2}$$

Table 7.1 and Figure 7.6 show the accuracy of the proposed approach in comparison with the existing approach. It states that the accuracy results of the decision tree, SVM, RF, and ANN are 83.04%, 84.12%, 91.16%, and 93.62%, respectively. In comparison to other current systems, the proposed system's results reveal that it achieves higher accuracy.

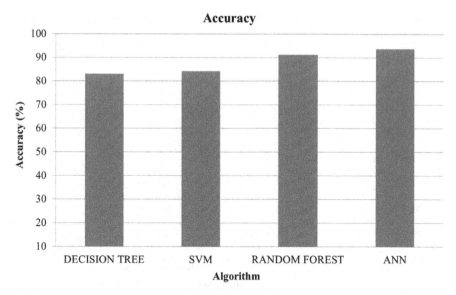

FIGURE 7.6 Accuracy graph.

TABLE 7.2
Sensitivity Table

Algorithm	Sensitivity (%)
DECISION TREE	80.95
SVM	82.35
RANDOM FOREST	90.91
ANN	94.56

7.4.3 SENSITIVITY

The amount of positives divided by the number of precise positive forecasts yields the sensitivity (SN), as shown in Equation 7.3. According to Table 7.2, the results for sensitivity with the proposed and existing systems are shown in Figure 7.7.

$$\text{Sensitivity} = \frac{TP}{TP + FN} \tag{7.3}$$

Table 7.2 and Figure 7.7 provide detailed explanations of the sensitivity of the proposed approach in comparison with existing approaches, showing it offers a much

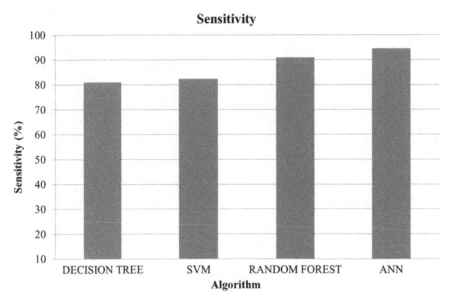

FIGURE 7.7　Sensitivity graph.

TABLE 7.3
Specificity Table

Algorithm	Specificity (%)
Decision tree	85.06
SVM	86.88
Random forest	89.46
ANN	92.01

superior result than the existing systems. The decision tree, SVM, RF, and ANN sensitivity outcomes are given as 80.95%, 82.35%, 90.91%, and 94.56%, respectively.

7.4.4 Specificity

Specificity is a number that indicates the number's value and the number's quantity of information digits, as shown in Equation 7.4.

$$\text{Specificity} = \frac{TP}{TP + FP} \tag{7.4}$$

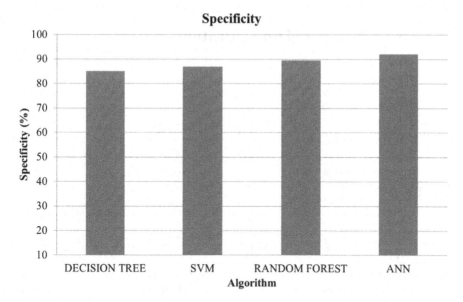

FIGURE 7.8   Specificity graph.

TABLE 7.4
Time Duration Table

Algorithm	Time duration (ms)
Decision tree	8.66
SVM	7.28
Random forest	6.83
ANN	5.34

Table 7.3 and Figure 7.8 provide explanations of the specificity of the proposed approach in comparison with existing approaches, and the indicated results are 85.06%, 86.88%, 89.46%, and 92.01% for the decision tree, SVM, RF, and ANN, respectively.

7.4.5   TIME DURATION

The total time duration is how long something lasts, from the beginning to the end.

Table 7.4 and Figure 7.9 show the time consumption of the proposed system in comparison with existing systems, and the indicated results are 8.66 ms, 7.28 ms, 6.83 ms, and 5.34 ms for the decision tree, SVM, RF, and ANN, respectively.

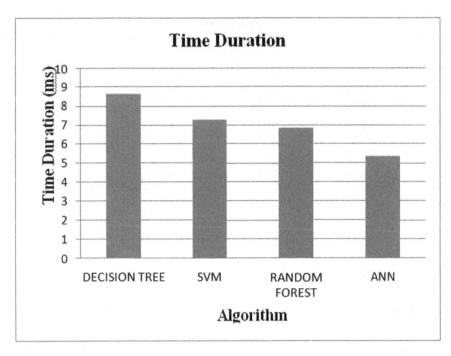

FIGURE 7.9   Time duration graph.

Source: Khang, 2021.

The predictive models used in the application have been described in this section. We were able to investigate several ANN algorithms thanks to the realization of use cases. Then, using ANN, we assessed each of them to determine which was the most accurate.

7.5   CONCLUSION

This chapter aims to evaluate cutting-edge methods and models, and then discuss how they are used in BIA applications. It is a comprehensive study of business intelligence (BI) and business analytical (BA) tools which are discussed clearly in relation to the machine learning functionalities using an artificial neural network. The suggested framework is anticipated to be adaptable to other projects employing different BI technologies, such as PowerBI, Tableau, etc.

The experimental investigation and results analysis demonstrated the viability of our system as well as its performance in relation to various common metrics, such as, the accuracy, sensitivity, specificity, and time consumption parameters, which were performed at 93.62%, 94.56%, 92.01%, and 5.34 milliseconds, respectively. As shown in this chapter, we improved the system and process for business intelligence and analytics tools in relation to the machine learning functionalities in the business and finance sectors. The suggested newly constructed system with machine learning functionalities delivers better efficiency and accuracy. We will also select a few crucial issues for further investigation for future study direction (Khang, Muthmainnah et al., 2023).

REFERENCES

Bentley, D. (2017). "Business Intelligence and Analytics." www.pdfdrive.com/business-intelligence-and-analytics-e56416503.html.

Figalist, I., Elsner, C., Bosch, J., & Olsson, H. H. (2020). "An End-To-End Framework for Productive Use of Machine Learning in Software Analytics and Business Intelligence Solutions." In Product-Focused Software Process Improvement: 21st International Conference, PROFES 2020, Turin, Italy, November 25–27, 2020, Proceedings 21 (pp. 217–233). Springer International Publishing. https://link.springer.com/chapter/10.1007/978-3-030-64148-1_14

Gartner_Inc. (2020)."Magic Quadrant for Analytics and Business Intelligence Platforms." *Gartner.* [Online]. [Accessed: 17 Jan 2020]. Available: www.gartner.com/en/documents/3900992/magic-quadrant-foranalytics-and-business-intelligence-p.

Khang, A. (2021). "Material4Studies." *Material of Computer Science, Artificial Intelligence, Data Science, IoT, Blockchain, Cloud, Metaverse, Cybersecurity for Studies.* Retrieved from www.researchgate.net/publication/370156102_Material4Studies

Khang, A., Hajimahmud, V. A., Gupta, S. K., Babasaheb, J., Morris, G. (2023). *AI-Centric Modelling and Analytics: Concepts, Designs, Technologies, and Applications* (1st Ed.). CRC Press. https://doi.org/10.1201/9781003400110

Khang, A., Kali, C. R., Satapathy, S. K., Kumar, A., Ranjan Das, S., & Panda, M. R. (2023). "Enabling the Future of Manufacturing: Integration of Robotics and IoT to Smart Factory Infrastructure in Industry 4.0." In A. Khang, V. Shah, & S. Rani (Eds.), *AI-Based Technologies and Applications in the Era of the Metaverse* (1st Ed.) (pp. 25–50). IGI Global Press. https://doi.org/10.4018/978-1-6684-8851-5.ch002

Khang, A., Misra, A., Gupta, S. K., & Shah, V. (Eds.). (2023). *AI-aided IoT Technologies and Applications in the Smart Business and Production.* CRC Press. https://doi.org/10.1201/9781003392224

Khang, A., Muthmainnah, M., Seraj, P. M. I., Al Yakin, A., Obaid, A. J., & Panda, M. R. (2023). "AI-Aided Teaching Model for the Education 5.0 Ecosystem." In A. Khang, V. Shah, & S. Rani (Eds.), *AI-Based Technologies and Applications in the Era of the Metaverse* (1st Ed.) (pp. 83–104). IGI Global Press. https://doi.org/10.4018/978-1-6684-8851-5.ch004

Khang, A., Shah, V., & Rani, S. (2023). *AI-Based Technologies and Applications in the Era of the Metaverse* (1st Ed.). IGI Global Press. https://doi.org/10.4018/978-1-6684-8851-5

Khanh, H. H., & Khang A. (2021). The role of artificial intelligence in blockchain applications. In G. Rana, A. Khang, R. Sharma, A. K. Goel & A. K. Dubey (Eds.), *Reinventing Manufacturing and Business Processes through Artificial Intelligence*, Vol. 2 (pp. 20–40). CRC Press. https://doi.org/10.1201/9781003145011-2

Khatri, A., Garg, D., & Dangayach, G. S. (2019). A comparative analysis of factor analysis model for pinpointing agile developers. *International Journal of Agile Systems and Management*, Vol. 12, No. 2, pp. 91–107. www.inderscienceonline.com/doi/abs/10.1504/IJASM.2019.100355

Kubat, M., & Kubat, M. (2021). "Artificial Neural Networks." An *Introduction to Machine Learning*, pp. 117–143. https://link.springer.com/chapter/10.1007/978-3-319-20010-1_5

Let Machine Learning Boost Your Business Intelligence. (2020). "Smarter With Gartner." [Online]. [Accessed: 17 Jan 2020]. Available: www.gartner.com/smarterwithgartner/let-machine-learningboost-your-business-intelligence/.

Nazih Omri, M., & Mribah, W. "Towards an Intelligent Machine Learning-based Business Approach." *International Journal of Intelligent Systems and Applications (IJISA)*, Vol. 14, No. 1, pp. 1–23, 2022. https://doi.org/10.5815/ijisa.2022.01.01.

Rana, G., Khang, A., Sharma, R., Goel, A. K., & Dubey A. K. (Eds.) (2021). *Reinventing Manufacturing and Business Processes through Artificial Intelligence*. CRC Press. https://doi.org/10.1201/9781003145011.

Richardson, J., Sallam, R., Schlegel, K., Kronz, A., & Sun, J. (2020). Magic Quadrant for Analytics and Business Intelligence Platforms. Gartner ID G00386610. https://cedar.princeton.edu/sites/cedar/files/media/gartner_bi_comparison_2018.pdf

Roth-Dietrich, G., Groschel, M., & Reiner, B. (2023). "Comparison of Machine Learning Functionalities of Business Intelligence and Analytics Tools." In G. Roth-Dietrich, M. Gröschel & B. Reiner (Eds.), *Apply Data Science: Introduction, Applications and Projects* (pp. 95–118). Wiesbaden: Springer Fachmedien Wiesbaden.

Sarma A., D. N. (2018). "A Generic Functional Architecture for Operational BI System." *International Journal of Business Intelligence Research*, Vol. 9, pp. 64–77. https://doi.org/10.4018/IJBIR.2018010105.

Sarma A., D. N. (2022). "Intelligent Business Analytics: Need, Functioning, Challenges, and Implications." In Z. Sun & Z. Wu (Eds.), *Handbook of Research on Foundations and Applications of Intelligent Business Analytics* (pp. 21–46). IGI Global. https://doi.org/10.4018/978-1-7998-9016-4.ch002.

Shastry, K. A., Sanjay, H. A., Sushma, V. (2022). "Machine Learning for Business Analytics: Case Studies and Open Research Problems." In M. Alloghani, C. Thron, & S. Subair (Eds), *Artificial Intelligence for Data Science in Theory and Practice. Studies in Computational Intelligence*, Vol. 1006. Springer, Cham. https://doi.org/10.1007/978-3-030-92245-0_1.

Vashisht, V., Kamya, S., & Vashisht, M. (2020, March). "Defect Prediction Framework Using Neural Networks for Business Intelligence Technology Based Projects." In 2020 International Conference on Computer Science, Engineering and Applications (ICCSEA) (pp. 1–5). IEEE. https://ieeexplore.ieee.org/abstract/document/9132944/

Yafooz, W. M., Bakar, Z. B. A., Fahad, S. A., & Mithun, A. M. (2020). "Business Intelligence Through Big Data Analytics, Data Mining and Machine Learning." In *Data Management, Analytics and Innovation: Proceedings of ICDMAI 2019*, Vol. 2 (pp. 217–230). Springer: Singapore. https://link.springer.com/chapter/10.1007/978-981-13-9364-8_17

8 A Study of a Domain-Specific Approach in Business Using Big Data Analytics and Visualization

Babasaheb Jadhav, Pooja Kulkarni,
Ashish Kulkarni, and Sagar Kulkarni

8.1 INTRODUCTION

Decision-making is always a complicated process and generally follows the traditional approach to handling a problem. The way of solving any problem is always to try to resolve it by identifying the problem, generating a possible solution, evaluating alternatives, deciding on a solution, and evaluating the outcomes. Nowadays, this is a proven model that is used in solving various level problems, but if we observe the nature of the problem where required decision-making is repetitive or a bit closer to the problem addressed earlier. Whenever an issue occurs we always search for previous similar issues that have occurred. For example, when the COVID-19 pandemic occurred everything was shut down and humans were closed within their four walls. Medical practitioners or scientists discussing a similar pandemic that occurred 100 years previously and comparing the current situation with those days even predicted that a similar issue may occur 100 years after COVID-19 pandemic.

In short, while making any decision, those involved in decision-making always look for a similar problem that occurred earlier and check for the actions taken at that time and compare the issue with the outcome of the current problem. This simply means that we need to have information-handling technology, tool, and correct information for the probable outcome. In addition, scientists say that this era is an information technology era and information is nothing but raw meaningful data. The proposed structure of this chapter provides useful information for those who can use it to generate outcomes in the form of decisions for certain challenging issues and to help in completing project assignments.

In today's data-driven world data are available everywhere in raw form, and most of data is believed to be accurate, but sometimes it shows the newly discovered places

DOI: 10.1201/9781032618845-8

in our surroundings, sometimes it reminds us to complete a task, we know that while reading this you have seen your cell phone and strikes that google provides this facility to us based on our data, some way google shows recommendation based on our shopping track, in addition, they provide suggestions based on our daily routine recorded through google health app, etc.

Of the total global population, 2.85 billion people have Facebook accounts, and so they know everybody's likes, dislikes, friends, and thoughts. Based on the same business opportunity, Facebook came out with a new organization called Meta. Meta is based on a concept called Metaverse and started a virtual world in which we didn't want to reach physically into board room meetings. All can happen or is possible through our avatars. This is completely based on data that we knowingly or unknowingly share on social platforms. With the help of cases of meta, Metaverse and avatar researchers want to highlight the power of data science based on which the virtual world can be established with the help of big data.

The simplest example of decision-making is playing a game with a computer. If you are playing a chess game with the computer, you know that there are an estimated 10^{111} to 10^{123} positions for a single move, so the computer needs to make a decision, this is not a random decision, it is based on your move. If we take the example of gaming applications in two-player games like chess, checkers, and tic-tac-toe, big data and AI forecasting programs are currently in use. To play video games, a more advanced forecasting program is used. A human-like robot is controlled by an even more advanced forecasting program (Khang, Gujrati et al., 2024).

Allowing an AI program to play video games is the best approach to determine how intelligent it is, rather than utilizing the Turing test. Simulation, shooter, RPG, racing, adventure, strategy, and sports are some of the video game genres. Each category has its own set of goals and rules. We can measure the AI program's intelligence on all cognitive levels by allowing it to play different games.

Some PlayStation 2 games are so difficult that it requires an adult human to complete all the levels. To overcome all the levels in games like Contra, the player must apply pattern methods. By playing the game and watching enemy tendencies, the player can design a variety of ways to win. Other games, such as Zelda for the Nintendo Wii, require the player to solve issues and apply complex logic to progress through each level. The game necessitates that the player comprehends the meaning of words as well as common sense behavior. Throughout the game, the player will interact with several characters who will provide directions on how to complete each level (Khang, Inna et al., 2024).

Playing digital games requires an AI program to have brain power at the human level. There is no artificial intelligence program that can play "all" digital games for all game consoles (NES, Genesis, PlayStation 3, X-box 360, PSP, Wii, and so forth).

Here, with the example of a gaming application, researchers are trying to elaborate on the power of AI as video gaming apps are a more critical example of decision-making where each time the situation is different and which can be solved by forecasting each condition based on data and targeting the possible outcome.

This chapter provides a solution to gaming applications that can provide the solution to any real-time problems during the process of deciding any type of issue in multiple departments of an organization such as marketing, finance, HR, operations, supply chain management as well as day-to-day problems also.

8.2 LITERATURE SURVEY

Farrokhi (2023), in an article titled "AI in strategic marketing decision-making: a research agenda," found that there is little research into applying AI to strategic marketing decision-making. More research is required for the implementation of AI in the field of strategic marketing decisions. To implement this more data are required for the analysis and generation of models for decision-making.

Eriksson (2023), in an article titled "Think with me or think for me?," on the future role of AI in marketing strategy formulation where they were focused on, described how AI can contribute to marketing strategy formulation and strategy creation as a deliberate process.

Liu et al. (2007) described a study in an article titled "AI adoption in business-to-business marketing: toward a conceptual framework." The purpose of this study was to develop a synthesized conceptual framework for AI adoption in the field of business-to-business (B2B) marketing. This paper identifies the drivers of AI adoption as the shortcomings of current marketing activities and the external pressure imposed by informatization. Seven outcomes are identified, namely, efficiency improvements, accuracy improvements, better decision-making, customer relationship improvements, sales increases, cost reductions, and risk reductions. Based on information processing theory and organizational learning theory (OLT), an integrated conceptual framework has been developed to explain the relationship between each construct of AI adoption in B2B marketing.

Sculley et al. (2023) in an article titled "AI on Decision Making" claimed that AI techniques are increasingly extending and enriching decision support through such means as coordinating data delivery, analyzing data trends, providing forecasts, and developing data consistency, providing information to the user in the most appropriate forms, and suggesting courses of action.

Duan (2019) and Phillips and Wren (2023), in an article titled "AI for decision making in the Era of Big Data: evolution, challenges, and research agenda" claimed that the rise of supercomputing power and big data technologies appear to have empowered AI in recent years. This paper aims to identify the challenges associated with the use and impact of revitalized AI-based systems for decision-making and offer a set of research propositions for information systems (IS) researchers.

Farrokhi (2023), in an article titled "Using AI to detect crisis related to events: decision making in B2B by artificial intelligence," claimed that AI could be an important foundation for a competitive advantage in the market for firms. This study examined the role of computer-mediated AI agents in detecting crises related to events in a firm. A crisis threatens organizational performance; therefore, a data-driven strategy will result in efficient and timely reflection, increasing the success of crisis management.

Meyer (2023), in an article titled "From automats to algorithms: the automation of services using AI," aimed to fill this gap by positing a framework that considers the service automation decision as a matter of knowledge management: a choice between human residents and codified knowledge assets. The paper uses information processing theory, which argues that the level of uncertainty in a process should dictate the type of knowledge deployed, as the contingency for the automation choice, and customer interaction uncertainty as the driver of that contingency.

Jiménez (2023), in an article titled "An exploration of the impact of AI and automation for communication professionals," focused on understanding the current and growing impact of AI and automation in the role of communication professionals to identify what skills and training are needed to understand its impacts leading to a recommendation.

8.3   BIG DATA AND DOMAIN-SPECIFIC APPROACH

Data are an integral tool for any organization to align with all the domains in an organization. Data collected from various sources in a specific domain can be used to create patterns for finding solutions to any problem which may predict the future or resolve an on-going issue. We all know that organizations are built to fulfill the needs of customers and make a profit from it. All organizations from NGOs to the academic industry to the automobile to finance require advisors or consultants. The main work of the consultant is to advise the organization to overcome any specific problems and increase the profit or sustainability.

If we refer to big data-centric approaches we mean big data storing, managing, analyzing, and generating results throughout the day by various sources. The main properties of big data are verity, volume, velocity, variability, and complexity, whereas the applications of the data are in business intelligence, security, healthcare, and risk handling (Khang & Medicine, 2023). The data-centric domains are based on real-time data analytics, text analytics, multimedia analytics, spatio-textual analytics, etc. which may have some challenges due to privacy and storage issues. The workflow process of big data analytics to resolve various problems is illustrated in Figure 8.1.

In the era of technology, we have much more information that may not be relevant but looks close to a solution, therefore the tool should segregate the data and provide the right information or close to the required information to solve the problem. Analytical tools should provide visibility of data keeping in mind that although the system has entire data it cannot make any decisions because decision-making is still done by a human. The system needs to be visible in all the incidents and past decisions. The last step is a collaboration of data because the sources and tools that are used are different to retrieve the relevant information (Healthywa, 2023).

The analysis of big data can be used to overcome multiple situations as well as to increase the cash flow of a business. Big data analytics can be used across all the domains of an organization depending on what kind of output the analyst wants. For example, big data which predicts the market value of a product can also be used to forecast the sales of the same product in that area. Big data analytics plays a vital role in the business and finance domains, offering a wide range of applications and benefits.

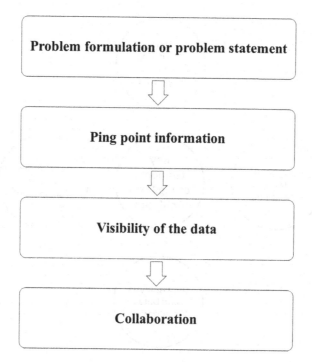

FIGURE 8.1 Key pointers of the workflow process of big data analytics.

Big data helps to reduce risk by analyzing the historical data and patterns that indicate future risk and improve customer service by analyzing customer behavior. It can also be used to run some tasks on autopilot mode such as calculating tax liability and making better and more precise decisions. However, there are some key elements in big data analytics that analyze the data and find insights for the business and finance domains (Figure 8.2) (Khang, Rani et al., 2023).

Below are some examples where big data analytics can be used in the business and finance domains.

- **Fraud Detection**: Big data analytics can be used to identify fraudulent data in transactions, such as money laundering, which can help to protect an organization from financial losses and safeguard the data.
- **Risk Management**: To improve the overall performance of the portfolio as well as investment and return on investment big data plays a vital role.
- **Market Forecasting**: Big data analytics can be used to forecast market situations and market portfolios to reduce the risk of financial losses.
- **Financial Forecasting and Planning**: Big data analytics can be used to forecast the market and to make a financial plan.
- **Cash Flow Management**: Cash flow management is critical for organizations with complex financial measures across different domains/market segments/geographical locations. Big data analytics helps monitor and optimize cash

FIGURE 8.2   Key elements of big data analytics in the finance domain.

flows by analyzing receivables, payables, and financial transactions across various stakeholders.

- **Compliance and Regulatory Reporting**: Big data analytics produces timely and accurate information for compliance with various regulatory authorities across the globe.
- **Asset Management**: Big data analytics helps in optimizing asset allocation, analyzing investment opportunities, and tracking asset performance to maximize returns.
- **Real-Time Financial Insights**: Big data analytics are used to provide real-time financial insights which help to check the current situation and provide information to take subsequent decisions in an organization.

In a nutshell, big data analytics for an organization's financial domain can be used to streamline processes, reduce costs, improve risk management, and stay financially prepared to face any challenging situation (Khang & AIoCF, 2024).

For example, Capital One used big data analytics to make a personalized marketing campaign which ultimately reduced the financial burden on the organization. JPMorgan Chase use big data analytics to manage the risk in the financial portfolio, and all banks mainly use big data tools to carry out fraud analysis. The

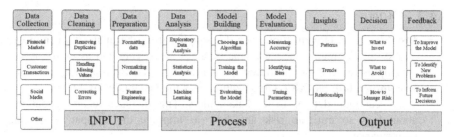

FIGURE 8.3 Steps for big data analytics: business and finance domains.

steps involved in solving the problems of the financial domain through big data are illustrated in Figure 8.3.

8.4 CASE EXAMPLE OF IMPROVED RISK MANAGEMENT

Below it is shown how XYZ Organization uses big data analytics to improve risk management.

8.4.1 INPUT

- **Data Collection**: XYZ Organization collects data from a variety of sources, including financial markets, customer transactions, and social media. These data include information such as customer account balances, trading activity, and social media posts.
- **Data Cleaning**: XYZ Organization cleans the data to remove duplicates, handles missing values, and corrects errors. This ensures that the data are accurate and consistent.
- **Data Preparation**: XYZ Organization prepares the data for analysis by formatting it, normalizing it, and feature engineering. This makes the data easier to analyze and interpret.

8.4.2 PROCESS

- **Data Analysis**: XYZ Organization uses statistical and machine learning techniques to analyze the data. This can be used to identify patterns and trends that may indicate risk. For example, XYZ Organization might use big data analytics to identify customers who are likely to default on their loans.
- **Model Building**: XYZ Organization builds models that can be used to predict risk. These models are trained on historical data and can be used to predict future risks.
- **Model Evaluation**: XYZ Organization evaluates the models to ensure that they are accurate and reliable. This is done by testing the models on historical data and by comparing the results to actual outcomes.

8.4.3 OUTPUT

- **Insights**: XYZ Organization uses the insights from the analysis to improve its risk management practices. This includes identifying and assessing risks, developing risk mitigation strategies, monitoring risks, and reporting on risks.
- **Recommendations**: XYZ Organization uses the insights from the analysis to make recommendations to its stakeholders. This includes recommendations about how to mitigate risk and how to improve the company's overall performance.
- **Decisions**: XYZ Organization uses the insights from the analysis to make decisions about its business. This includes decisions about which risks to mitigate, which strategies to implement, and how to allocate resources.
- **Feedback**: The insights from the analysis are used to improve the models. This is done by incorporating the insights into the models and by retraining the models on the updated data.

The insights from the analysis are also used to identify new risks and to improve the company's overall risk management practices.

8.4.4 CONCLUSION OF CASE

XYZ Organization's use of big data analytics has helped the company to improve risk management in several ways. The company has seen a decrease in financial losses, an improvement in its overall performance, and an increase in stakeholder confidence.

The case study shows how big data analytics can be used to improve risk management in the finance domain. The process begins with data collection and cleaning, followed by data preparation and analysis. The insights from the analysis are then used to build models, make recommendations, and make decisions. The feedback from the process is used to improve the models and the overall risk management practices.

The following are the most common types of visualization used to represent the financial domain data analysis to understand the flow of data and insights about the data.

- **Bar Graph**: Represents the categorical data.
- **Heat Map**: Visualizes the two variable data in different colors.
- **Line Graph**: Shows trends and patterns.
- **Pie Chart**: Compares relative proportions of different categories.
- **Area Chart**: Visualizes the cumulative total, and data over a continuous range.
- **Scatter Plot**: Data points on a two-dimensional coordinate system.
- **Histogram**: Displays continuous data by dividing it into intervals.
- **Box Plot**: Shows the distribution data in quartiles.
- **Bubble Chart**: Visualization of three variables.

8.4.5 DATA VISUALIZATION TOOLS

As per the above example, relevant data can be shown by using heat maps, line charts, and pie charts, and the tools which are used to draw this kind of visualization are as follows:

- **Tableau:** Tableau is a popular data visualization tool that allows users to create interactive and dynamic dashboards, charts, and graphs. Organizations use Tableau to visualize financial performance, market trends, portfolio analysis, and risk metrics, among other financial insights.
- **Power BI:** Microsoft Power BI is a widely used data visualization tool that enables organizations to create interactive reports and dashboards from diverse data sources. It is often integrated with other Microsoft tools, making it a convenient choice for finance teams using Excel and SQL Server.
- **QlikView and Qlik Sense:** QlikView and Qlik Sense are powerful visualization tools that provide organizations with the capability to explore and analyze financial data in real time. They offer interactive visualizations, data discovery, and easy-to-use drag-and-drop features.
- **D3.js:** D3.js is a JavaScript library used for creating customized and interactive data visualizations on the web. It is a popular choice for organizations that require more flexibility and customization in their financial visualizations.
- **SAP Lumira:** SAP Lumira is a data visualization tool that integrates with SAP systems, enabling organizations to create compelling financial visualizations and explore data insights from their SAP databases.
- **Google Data Studio:** Google Data Studio is a free tool that allows organizations to create interactive and shareable dashboards using data from various sources, such as Google Analytics and Google Sheets.
- **MATLAB®:** MATLAB is often used for more advanced financial modeling and data analysis. It also offers visualization capabilities that organizations can control for complex financial analyses.

These visualization tools help organizations in the financial domain to communicate multifaceted financial insights to managers effectively. By transforming big data analytics results into visually appealing and informative charts, graphs, and dashboards, these tools support data-driven decision-making and enhance financial performance across the organization.

8.4.6 BIG DATA ANALYTICS

Big data analytics for the financial domain in an organization can be used to streamline processes, reduce costs, improve risk management, and stay financially sound to face any challenging situations, in addition there are some other areas where the focus is required concerning the financial domain of organization, as described in the table that follows.

Sr. no.	Issue	Solution	Role of big data analytics	Example
1	Regulatory compliance	Establish a robust compliance management framework	Analyzing vast amounts of financial data for regulatory reporting and monitoring	Automating compliance checks and generating accurate regulatory reports
2	Cybersecurity and data privacy	Implement comprehensive cybersecurity measures	Analyzing network logs and user behavior for threat detection	Detecting and responding to potential cyber threats in real time
3	Digital transformation	Develop a clear digital transformation strategy	Utilizing customer behavior data for optimizing experiences	Personalizing product recommendations based on individual preferences
4	Financial inclusion	Design initiatives to promote financial inclusion	Utilizing alternative data sources for assessing credit risk	Building credit scoring models for individuals with limited credit history
5	Customer experience	Foster a customer-centric culture and improve services	Analyzing customer data for segmentation and profiling	Creating targeted marketing campaigns based on customer preferences
6	Data management and analytics	Strengthen data governance and invest in data analytics	Integrating and analyzing diverse financial data	Consolidating transaction records, market data, and customer information
7	Fintech disruption	Embrace collaboration with fintech firms	Evaluating fintech offerings and potential partnerships	Assessing fintech performance and exploring collaboration opportunities
8	Risk management	Implement a comprehensive risk management framework	Developing risk models and stress testing	Predicting credit default risks using historical and real-time data
9	Talent acquisition and retention	Invest in talent development and create a supportive work environment	Utilizing analytics for talent recruitment and retention	Identifying the best-fit candidates based on data-driven assessments
10	Ethical and responsible finance	Integrate ethical practices and sustainability principles	Analyzing data for ESG reporting and analysis	Measuring the organization's environmental and social impacts

Sr. no.	Issue	Solution	Role of big data analytics	Example
11	Budgeting and forecasting	Improve budget planning and forecasting processes	Utilizing data analytics for financial forecasting	Predicting future revenue and budget allocation based on market trends
12	Currency and foreign exchange management	Implement strategies to manage foreign exchange risks	Analyzing data for currency market analysis	Monitoring foreign exchange rate fluctuations and optimizing currency hedging

This table provides a clear presentation of how big data analytics plays a significant role in addressing the various issues faced by the finance industry. It demonstrates how data-driven insights derived from big data analytics contribute to more effective solutions and decision-making across different aspects of the financial domain (Khanh & Khang, 2021).

Decision-making through big data analytics in the finance domain is described in the following table.

Decision-making aspect	Role of big data analytics	Example
Risk assessment	Analyzes vast amounts of financial data, market trends, and economic indicators to identify and assess credit, market, and operational risks	Predicting potential credit defaults by analyzing historical transaction data
Fraud detection	Utilizes advanced algorithms and machine learning to detect fraudulent activities within financial transactions and operations	Identifying unusual patterns in transactions to detect potential fraudulent behavior
Investment strategy	Analyzes market data, historical performance, and economic indicators to inform investment decisions and portfolio optimization	Identifying investment opportunities based on market trends and risk analysis
Financial planning and forecasting	Utilizes historical financial data and economic indicators to forecast future financial performance and plan budgets accordingly	Predicting revenue and expenses to plan budget allocation for the upcoming year
Customer segmentation	Segments customers based on financial behaviors, preferences, and risk profiles to tailor financial products and services	Offering personalized loan products or investment opportunities to different customer segments
Compliance and regulatory reporting	Automates compliance checks and reporting by processing large volumes of financial data and ensuring adherence to regulations	Generating accurate regulatory reports for anti-money laundering (AML) compliance

(continued)

Decision-making aspect	Role of big data analytics	Example
Market analysis	Analyzes market data and customer behavior to identify market trends, customer preferences, and growth opportunities	Identifying emerging markets and customer demand for specific financial products
Fraud prevention	Implements real-time fraud prevention measures by analyzing transaction data and detecting anomalies or suspicious activities	Blocking suspicious transactions in real time to prevent fraudulent activities

Use of big data analytics for financial forecasting and planning response has been developed through ChatGPT.

Big data analytics plays a crucial role in financial forecasting and planning by leveraging vast amounts of data to make accurate predictions and inform strategic decisions. Let's explore a case study example of a financial institution that utilizes big data analytics for financial forecasting, planning, decision-making, and visualization.

8.5   CASE STUDY OF BUDGETING AND PLANNING

8.5.1   Decision-Making Aspect: Financial Forecasting and Planning

- **Role of Big Data Analytics**: The financial institution wants to enhance its budgeting and planning processes to optimize resource allocation, manage risks, and achieve financial goals. They leverage big data analytics to analyze various data sources, including historical financial data, economic indicators, market trends, customer behavior, and external factors that impact the financial industry.
- **Example: Data Collection and Integration**: The financial institution collects and integrates vast volumes of financial data, such as transaction records, customer demographics, and market data, into a centralized data platform.
- **Advanced Analytics for Forecasting**: Big data analytics applies advanced forecasting models, such as time-series analysis and predictive algorithms, to historical financial data to predict future revenue, expenses, and cash flow.
- **Economic Indicators and Market Analysis**: The institution utilizes big data analytics to monitor economic indicators, interest rates, and market trends. This information is used to assess the potential impact on the institution's financial performance.
- **Risk Assessment**: Big data analytics performs risk analysis to identify potential financial risks and market uncertainties. This helps the institution prepare contingency plans and risk management strategies.
- **Scenario Planning**: Using big data analytics, the financial institution conducts scenario planning by simulating various economic conditions and their potential effects on financial outcomes.

8.5.2 DECISION-MAKING ASPECT: VISUALIZATION OF FINANCIAL DATA

- **Role of Big Data Analytics**: To enable effective decision-making, big data analytics facilitates data visualization techniques to present complex financial data in a clear and actionable format. Visualization tools help stakeholders understand trends, patterns, and correlations in financial data, empowering them to make informed decisions.
- **Example: Dashboard Visualization**: Big data analytics creates interactive dashboards that provide real-time updates on financial performance, budget progress, and key performance indicators (KPIs). Executives can access these dashboards to monitor financial health and performance at a glance (Khang, Vugar and Abuzarova et al., 2023).
- **Trend Analysis**: Through data visualization, the financial institution identifies trends and patterns in revenue growth, expense patterns, and customer behavior. Visualizing these trends helps the institution adjust its financial strategies accordingly.
- **What-If Analysis**: Visualization tools enable what-if analysis scenarios, allowing decision-makers to see the potential impact of different financial decisions on the organization's bottom line.
- **Forecast Accuracy Monitoring**: Big data analytics tracks the accuracy of financial forecasts and presents this information visually. Decision-makers can evaluate the effectiveness of forecasting models and make adjustments as needed.
- **Result**: By leveraging big data analytics for financial forecasting, planning, decision-making, and visualization, the financial institution achieves the following outcomes:
  - Accurate financial forecasts and budgeting, leading to improved resource allocation and financial performance.
  - Enhanced risk management strategies to mitigate potential financial risks and uncertainties.
  - Real-time monitoring of financial performance through interactive dashboards, enabling informed decision-making.
  - Better alignment of financial strategies with market trends and economic conditions.

In conclusion, big data analytics plays a transformative role in financial forecasting and planning by providing valuable insights, supporting data-driven decision-making, and presenting complex financial data in an accessible and actionable format. This enables financial institutions to stay competitive, optimize their financial strategies, and achieve their business objectives successfully.

8.5.3 EXPECTED OUTCOMES OF THE STUDY

In today's digitized era running a business successfully is a very difficult task. Organizations ranging from small-scale to large-scale industries face intense competition. In this competitive world, although it is tough, there is always room for innovation and to work in innovative ways (Rani, Bhambri et al., 2023).

Innovation is not possible unless we know what base we need to adopt and upon which platform we need to start with. Big data provides us with the platform to carry out studies and come up with new ways to solve problems and simplify matters. This is the significant importance of big data in the life cycle of the entire organization. Entrepreneurs' primary goals are profit and sustainability in the market, but at the same time, they need to solve many issues faced in day-to-day operations; to solve these problems a hierarchy of people are required at different positions to tackle the various problems encountered.

The organizational hierarchy may be formed for managing things effectively within different domains. Researchers have attempted to form a unique model to solve problems for any domain based on information saved in the form of big data. In addition, researchers have proposed a model that helps the decision-maker to increase their decision-making power and make decisions in favor of stakeholders (Rani, Chauhan et al., 2021).

8.6 CONCLUSION

A technique or methodology for creating human artificial intelligence in machines and computer software is described as an approach to replicate human reasoning, thought, and behavior. This chapter is an excellent attempt to find big data analytics that can store, retrieve, evaluate, assimilate, forecast the future, and modify information in a manner that can be used to solve the complex problems facing an organization concerning any department with a systematic and data-driven approach (Khang, Shah et al., 2023).

Technology or computer systems are not sufficiently developed to make their own decisions, but with the help of human intelligence and big data, we can find and create a pattern that will be helpful to completely or partially solve these problems. As there will be an increase in the amount of data that we gather every day, the decision-making model will help us to make more accurate decisions to solve simple, mediocre, as well as complex problems that we are facing. With meaningful information shared by big data analytics, we can reach the optimal solution and resolve any significant issues or problems (Khang, Kali et al., 2023).

Data are always an integral part of any decision-making, if we provide data to the system and also provide a proper environment in the form of the parameters, the computer system can solve the problem with more integrity and taking into account all the possible consequences. Although humans cannot be kept outside of the decision-making process, human intelligence can provide all possible outcomes and make decisions easier. This is the actual work of the system but, in almost all the domains, problems can be repetitive or related to an earlier problem, in which case big data provides information to all those similar cases making the decision-making easier (Khang & Muthmainnah, 2023).

For example, an employee applies for leave, and his immediate supervisor approves the same but the HR manager does not respond to it, and in between payment cycles are executed without the leave approval of the HR manager (Saxena et al., 2023). The system may deduct the leave day payable amount but the employee has applied for leave as per his available leave records and acknowledged by his immediate supervisor, work or role adjustments are done and he can take the leave. In this case, such types of decisions can be taken by the system with the help of human intelligence and big data, and ask another employee to work extra hours to complete a specific job. Human intelligence and big data systems play a vital role and can provide a solution for the effective management of employees and planning for the completion of work without asking people to stay for longer. In the strategic level decisions such as increasing profitability, sales, turnover, marketing strategy, or competitor's analysis, big data plays a significant role (Khang, Muthmainnah et al., 2023).

REFERENCES

Duan J., J. S. Edwards, Y. K. Dwivedi (2019), "Artificial intelligence for decision making in the era of Big Data – evolution, challenges, and research," *International Journal of Information Management*, Vol. 48. www.sciencedirect.com/science/article/pii/S02684 01219300581

Eriksson T. B., A. Bigi, & M. Bonera. (2023), "Think With Me, or Think for Me? On the Future Role of Artificial Intelligence in Marketing Strategy Formulation," *The TQM Journal*, Vol. 32 No. 4, pp. 795–814. www.emerald.com/insight/content/doi/10.1108/TQM-12-2019-0303/full/html

Farrokhi A., F. Shirazi, N. Hajli, & M. Tajvidi (2023), "Using Artificial Intelligence to Detect Crisis Related to Events: Decision Making in B2B by Artificial Intelligence," *Industrial Marketing Management*, Vol. 91. www.sciencedirect.com/science/article/pii/S00198 50120308464

Healthywa (2023), "www.healthywa.wa.gov.au/Articles/N_R/Problem-solving," [Online].

Jiménez López, E.A. and Ouariachi, T. (2023), "An Exploration of the Impact of Artificial Intelligence (AI) and Automation for Communication Professionals," *Journal of Information, Communication and Ethics in Society*, Vol. 19, No. 2, pp. 249–267. www. emerald.com/insight/content/doi/10.1108/JICES-03-2020-0034/full/html

Khang A. and AIoCF (Eds.) (2024), *AI-Oriented Competency Framework for Talent Management in the Digital Economy: Models, Technologies, Applications, and Implementation* ISBN: 9781032576053. CRC Press. https://doi.org/10.1201/978100 3440901

Khang A., C. R. Kali, S. K. Satapathy, A. Kumar, S. R. Das, & M. R. Panda (2023), "Enabling the Future of Manufacturing: Integration of Robotics and IoT to Smart Factory Infrastructure in Industry 4.0." In In A. Khang, V. Shah, & S. Rani (Eds.), *AI-Based Technologies and Applications in the Era of the Metaverse* (1st Ed.) (pp. 25–50). IGI Global Press. https://doi.org/10.4018/978-1-6684-8851-5.ch002

Khang A., M. Muthmainnah, P. M. I. Seraj, A. Al Yakin, A. J. Obaid, & M. R. Panda. (2023), "AI-Aided Teaching Model for the Education 5.0 Ecosystem." In A. Khang, V. Shah, & S. Rani (Eds.), *AI-Based Technologies and Applications in the Era of the Metaverse* (1st Ed.) (pp. 83–104). IGI Global Press. https://doi.org/10.4018/978-1-6684-8851-5.ch004

Khang A., R. Gujrati, H. Uygun, R. K. Tailor, & S. S. Gaur (2024), *Data-driven Modelling and Predictive Analytics in Business and Finance* (1st Ed.). CRC Press. ISBN: 9781032600628. https://doi.org/10.1201/9781032600628

Khang A., S. Rani, R. Gujrati, H. Uygun, S. K. Gupta (Eds.). (2023), *Designing Workforce Management Systems for Industry 4.0: Data-Centric and AI-Enabled Approaches.* CRC Press. https://doi.org/10.1201/9781003357070

Khang A., S.-O. Inna, K. Alla, S. Rostyslav, M. Rudenko, R. Lidia, & B. Kristina (2024), "Management Model 6.0 and Business Recovery Strategy of Enterprises in the Era of Digital Economy." In A. Khang, R. Gujrati, H. Uygun, R. K. Tailor, & S. S. Gaur (Eds.), *Data-driven Modelling and Predictive Analytics in Business and Finance* (1st Ed.). CRC Press. https://doi.org/10.1201/9781032600628-16

Khang A., V. Shah, & S. Rani (2023), *AI-Based Technologies and Applications in the Era of the Metaverse* (1st Ed.). IGI Global Press. https://doi.org/10.4018/978-1-6684-8851-5

Khanh H. H., & A. Khang (2021), "The Role of Artificial Intelligence in Blockchain Applications," In *Reinventing Manufacturing and Business Processes through Artificial Intelligence*, Vol. 2 (pp. 20–40). CRC Press. https://doi.org/10.1201/9781003145011-2

Liu G., Q. Liu, & W. Zhang (2007), "Model-based testing and validation on artificial intelligence systems," Second International Multi-Symposiums on Computer and Computational Sciences (IMSCCS 2007), Iowa City, IA, USA., DOI: 10.1109/IMSCCS.2007.37

Meyer C., D. Cohen, & S. Nair (2023), "From Automats to Algorithms: The Automation of Services Using Artificial Intelligence," *Journal of Service Management*, Vol. 31, No. 2, pp. 145–161. www.emerald.com/insight/content/doi/10.1108/JOSM-05-2019-0161/full/html

Phillips J. L. & G. Wren (2023), "Artificial Intelligence for Decision Making." *Knowledge-Based Intelligent Information and Engineering Systems.* https://link.springer.com/chapter/10.1007/11893004_69

Rani S., M. Chauhan, A. Kataria, & A. Khang. (2021). "IoT Equipped Intelligent Distributed Framework for Smart Healthcare Systems." In *Networking and Internet Architecture*, Vol. 2 (p. 30). https://doi.org/10.48550/arXiv.2110.04997

Rani, S., P. Bhambri, A. Kataria, A. Khang, & A. K. Sivaraman. (2023). *Big Data, Cloud Computing and IoT: Tools and Applications* (1st Ed.). Chapman and Hall/CRC. https://doi.org/10.1201/9781003298335

Saxena A. C., A. Ojha, D. Sobti, & A. Khang. (2023), "Artificial Intelligence (AI) Centric Model in Metaverse Ecosystem." In A. Khang, V. Shah, & S. Rani (Eds.), *AI-Based Technologies and Applications in the Era of the Metaverse* (1st Ed.) (pp. 1–24). IGI Global Press. https://doi.org/10.4018/978-1-6684-8851-5.ch001

Sculley D., G. Holt, D. Golovin, E. Davydov, T. Phillips, D. Ebner, V. Chaudhary, & M. Young (2023). "Machine Learning: The High-Interest Credit Card of Technical Debt." *Software Engineering for Machine Learning.* http://research.google/pubs/pub43146/

Startuptalk.com (2023). [Online]. Available: https://startuptalky.com/patanjali-ayurved-case-study.

9 Cloud-Based Data Management for Behavior Analytics in Business and Finance Sectors

Tarun Kumar Vashishth, Vikas Sharma,
Bhupendra Kumar, and Kewal Krishan Sharma

9.1 INTRODUCTION

In the dynamic landscape of modern business and finance, harnessing the power of data has become paramount for organizations striving to remain competitive and relevant. The surge in digital interactions, transactions, and engagements has led to an unprecedented influx of data, presenting both opportunities and challenges. Amid this data deluge, customer analytics and personalization have emerged as the cornerstones of effective business strategies (Khang, Shah et al., 2023).

As enterprises seek to understand their customers more profoundly and deliver tailored experiences, the role of cloud-based data management has taken center stage, revolutionizing how data are handled, analyzed, and utilized. The convergence of cloud computing and data analytics has transformed the way businesses and financial institutions approach customer-centric operations. Traditionally, managing and processing extensive datasets required substantial on-premises infrastructure investments, often resulting in inefficiencies, resource limitations, and delayed insights, as shown in Figure 9.1.

Customer analytics has evolved beyond simple demographic profiling, embracing a holistic approach that encompasses transaction histories, online behaviors, social interactions, and even sentiment analysis. This expanded perspective allows organizations to create intricate customer profiles that capture individual preferences, propensities, and needs. The cloud's capability to integrate data from diverse sources in real time empowers businesses to refine their segmentation strategies, identify emerging trends, and predict customer behaviors with unparalleled accuracy.

Personalization, once a luxury, has now become an expectation in the customer experience landscape. Cloud-based data management serves as the backbone of

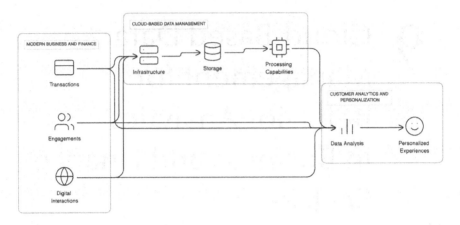

FIGURE 9.1   The emergence of a cloud-based data management system.

personalized interactions by enabling real-time analysis of customer data and subsequent delivery of tailored content, recommendations, and offerings. Machine
learning algorithms operating on the cloud can sift through enormous datasets,
identifying patterns and correlations that drive predictive models for customer
preferences. This translates into personalized product suggestions, targeted
marketing campaigns, and dynamic pricing strategies that resonate with individual
customers on a level previously unattainable. Within the financial sector, cloud-
based data management offers an additional layer of significance. As institutions
grapple with risk assessment, fraud detection, and compliance challenges, the agility
of the cloud proves invaluable. By analyzing vast datasets, financial organizations
can identify anomalies indicative of fraudulent activities, model potential risks,
and streamline regulatory reporting, all within a secure and scalable environment
(Khang, Rani et al., 2022).

However, alongside the benefits come critical considerations. Security and privacy
concerns loom large when handling sensitive customer data on remote servers. Data
integration complexities and vendor selection dilemmas also demand careful navigation. This chapter delves into these intricacies, presenting a comprehensive exploration of cloud-based data management for customer analytics and personalization
in business and finance. By delving into the benefits, challenges, and best practices,
this chapter aims to equip organizations with the knowledge and insights necessary
to leverage cloud technology effectively for a customer-centric future (Khang, Gupta
et al., 2023).

9.2   FOUNDATIONS OF CLOUD-BASED DATA MANAGEMENT

9.2.1   Basic Architecture of Cloud-Based Data Management

The architecture of a cloud-based data management system for customer analytics
and personalization in the business and finance sector typically involves multiple

components and layers to efficiently process and analyze large volumes of data. Here's a high-level overview of such architecture:

- *Data Ingestion Layer:* At the beginning of the pipeline, data from various sources are ingested into the system. These sources can include customer interactions, transactions, website visits, social media, and more. These data are collected and transported to the cloud platform for further processing.
- *Data Storage Layer:* Once the data are ingested, they need to be stored in a scalable and reliable manner. Cloud-based storage solutions like Amazon S3, Google Cloud Storage, or Azure Blob Storage are commonly used for this purpose. The data might be stored in structured databases (e.g., SQL databases), semi-structured formats (e.g., NoSQL databases), or data lakes.
- *Data Processing Layer:* This layer involves processing the raw data to make it usable for analysis. Technologies like Apache Spark, Hadoop, or cloud-based managed services for data processing are utilized to perform tasks such as data cleaning, transformation, enrichment, and aggregation. This step helps prepare the data for advanced analytics.
- *Data Analytics and Machine Learning Layer:* In this layer, data scientists and analysts use various analytics and machine learning techniques to extract valuable insights from the processed data. They might build predictive models, segmentation strategies, churn prediction models, and other algorithms to understand customer behavior, preferences, and trends.
- *Personalization and Recommendations:* The insights gained from the analytics layer are used to create personalized experiences for customers. This can include personalized product recommendations, content recommendations, targeted marketing campaigns, and more. Machine learning models often power these recommendation engines.
- *Real-Time Processing and Streaming:* For certain applications, real-time data processing is crucial. Technologies like Apache Kafka, Amazon Kinesis, or Google Cloud Pub/Sub enable the ingestion and processing of streaming data, allowing businesses to react in real time to customer interactions.
- *Data Visualization and Reporting Layer:* After analysis, the results are visualized for business users. Tools like Tableau, Power BI, or custom dashboards provide interactive visualizations and reports that help decision-makers understand the insights and take informed actions.
- *Security and Compliance Layer:* Given the sensitive nature of financial and customer data, security and compliance are paramount. Encryption, access controls, and compliance with regulations such as GDPR or HIPAA are essential components of the architecture.
- *Scalability and Resource Management:* Cloud platforms offer the advantage of scalability. As data volumes grow, the system can scale up or down based on demand. This elasticity ensures that the system can handle varying workloads efficiently.
- *Data Governance and Management:* Data governance involves defining policies and processes for data quality, metadata management, data lineage,

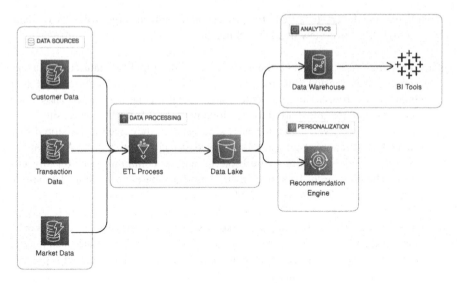

FIGURE 9.2   Architectural diagram of a cloud-based data management model.

and more. This ensures that data remain accurate, consistent, and compliant throughout their lifecycle, as shown in Figure 9.2.

9.2.2 The Role of Cloud-Based Data Management

Cloud-based data management has emerged as a transformative solution that redefines the way businesses and financial institutions handle data for customer analytics and personalization, as shown in Figure 9.3.

- *Scalability and Flexibility:* One of the paramount advantages of cloud-based data management is its elastic scalability. Traditional on-premises data infrastructure often struggles to cope with the fluctuations in data volume and processing requirements that are characteristic of customer analytics and personalization efforts. Cloud platforms, on the other hand, offer the capability to scale resources up or down seamlessly in response to changing demands. Consider a retail business during the holiday season—transaction volumes spike dramatically. With a cloud-based solution, the infrastructure can automatically expand to accommodate the increased workload and then contract when the demand subsides. This agility ensures that businesses can efficiently handle data spikes without over-provisioning resources during quieter periods. In the context of customer analytics, where data inflow might vary based on marketing campaigns or product launches, cloud scalability becomes crucial for maintaining uninterrupted operations.

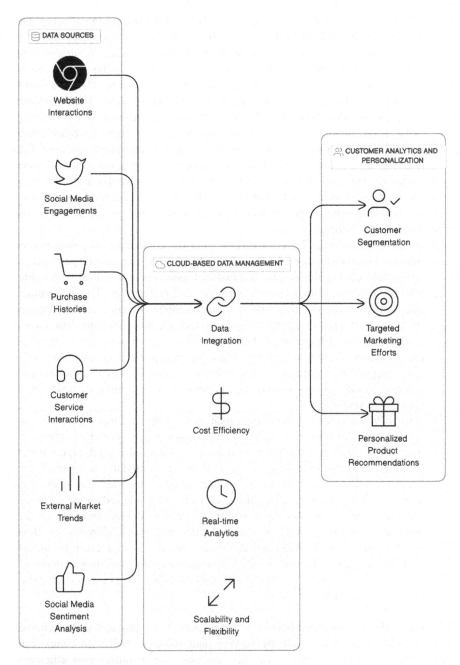

FIGURE 9.3   The role of cloud-based data management.

- *Data Integration:* Cloud-based solutions excel in integrating diverse data sources, both internal and external. In the context of customer analytics and personalization, this is invaluable. Customer data are generated from numerous touchpoints—website interactions, social media engagements, purchase histories, customer service interactions, and more. These data silos often hinder a comprehensive understanding of customers. Cloud platforms facilitate the consolidation of data from these disparate sources. For instance, a financial institution can integrate data from transaction histories, credit scores, external market trends, and social media sentiment analysis. This unified view provides a holistic representation of a customer's financial behavior and preferences, enabling the institution to make more informed decisions. The integration of data also enhances the accuracy and depth of analytical insights, contributing to more effective customer segmentation and targeted marketing efforts.
- *Real-Time Analytics:* Cloud platforms offer the computational power needed for real-time data analysis. In the context of customer analytics and personalization, real-time capabilities are invaluable. Customers now expect interactions that are tailored to their current behaviors and preferences. This necessitates the ability to analyze data and respond promptly. Imagine an e-commerce platform that provides personalized product recommendations based on a customer's recent browsing and purchase history. With real-time analytics on the cloud, the platform can process these data instantaneously and present relevant suggestions before the customer loses interest. The latency between data generation and analysis is minimized, resulting in a more engaging and relevant customer experience.
- *Cost Efficiency:* Cloud-based data management brings forth significant cost advantages. Traditionally, building and maintaining on-premises infrastructure for large-scale data handling required substantial capital expenditures. Moreover, over-provisioning resources to accommodate occasional data spikes resulted in wastage during quieter periods. Cloud services operate on a pay-as-you-go model, where businesses are charged based on the resources they use. This eliminates the need for upfront investments in hardware and software. During periods of increased demand, the scalability of cloud platforms prevents the need to over-invest in resources. As a result, businesses can optimize cost efficiency by aligning expenses with actual usage, making it particularly advantageous for data-intensive activities like customer analytics and personalization.

In essence, the role of cloud-based data management is multifaceted. It addresses the scalability challenges posed by varying data volumes, facilitates comprehensive data integration, empowers real-time analysis, and optimizes cost efficiency. These features collectively enable businesses and financial institutions to harness the power of data for superior customer insights, personalized experiences, and informed decision-making (Khang, Rani et al., 2023).

9.2.3 BENEFITS OF CLOUD-BASED DATA MANAGEMENT

Cloud-based data management offers a multitude of benefits for businesses and financial institutions seeking to enhance customer analytics and personalization strategies, as shown in Figure 9.4.

- *Enhanced Customer Understanding:* Cloud-based data management enables businesses to gain a deeper understanding of their customers by aggregating and analyzing data from various sources. Traditional approaches often involve fragmented data stored in different systems, hindering a comprehensive view of customers. Cloud platforms facilitate the integration of diverse datasets, including transaction histories, website interactions, social media engagements, and customer service interactions. For instance, a retail

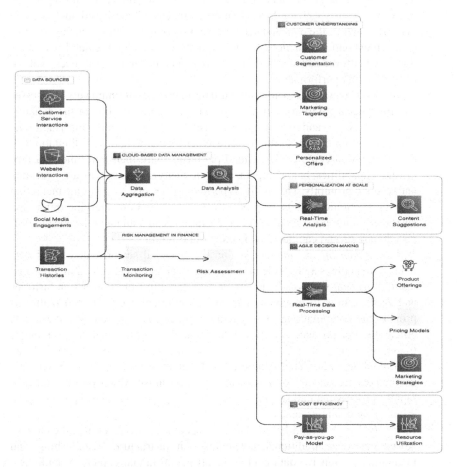

FIGURE 9.4 Key benefits of cloud-based data management.

company can amalgamate purchase history with browsing behavior and social media interactions. This unified dataset paints a comprehensive picture of each customer's preferences, habits, and interests. As a result, businesses can segment their customer base more effectively and target marketing efforts with pinpoint accuracy. This enhanced understanding also empowers the creation of personalized offers and recommendations, increasing the likelihood of customer engagement and conversion.

- *Personalization at Scale:* The true power of cloud-based data management becomes evident in its ability to deliver personalized experiences at scale. Traditional methods struggle to process and analyze massive amounts of data quickly enough to respond to customer behaviors in real time. Cloud platforms, equipped with robust computational resources, allow for the rapid analysis of customer data and the subsequent generation of personalized content and recommendations. Consider a streaming service that tailors content suggestions based on a user's viewing history and preferences. Cloud-based analytics can instantly analyze the data and offer relevant recommendations, enhancing user engagement and satisfaction. As the user base grows, cloud scalability ensures that the platform can continue delivering personalized experiences without compromising performance.

- *Agile Decision-Making:* Cloud-based data management empowers businesses and financial institutions with timely and actionable insights. In the dynamic realms of business and finance, quick decision-making is paramount. Traditional data-processing methods often introduce delays due to hardware limitations or data integration complexities. Cloud platforms, with their real-time data processing capabilities, enable organizations to analyze data as they are generated and respond promptly. This agility is particularly crucial for adapting marketing strategies, pricing models, or product offerings based on emerging trends and customer preferences. As a result, organizations can maintain relevance in fast-paced markets and capitalize on fleeting opportunities.

- *Risk Management in Finance:* Within the financial sector, cloud-based data management plays a vital role in risk assessment and fraud detection. Financial institutions deal with vast amounts of data, ranging from transaction histories and credit scores to market trends and geopolitical events. Cloud platforms provide the computational power required to process and analyze these data efficiently. For instance, a bank can leverage cloud-based analytics to monitor transactions in real time, identifying unusual patterns that might indicate fraudulent activities. The scalability of the cloud ensures that the system can handle peak transaction volumes without compromise. Moreover, the ability to rapidly process data allows institutions to assess and manage risks promptly, minimizing potential losses.

- *Cost Efficiency:* Cloud-based data management introduces significant cost advantages over traditional on-premises infrastructure. Establishing and maintaining extensive data centers involves substantial capital expenditures, along with ongoing operational costs. Cloud services, on the other hand, operate on a pay-as-you-go model. This cost-efficient approach eliminates the need for upfront investments and aligns expenses with actual resource usage. Businesses and financial institutions can avoid over-provisioning resources to accommodate occasional data spikes, as the cloud's scalability adapts to changing demands. This results in optimized resource utilization and reduced operational expenses, enabling organizations to allocate resources more strategically.

9.2.4 CHALLENGES AND CONSIDERATIONS

As promising as cloud-based data management is for customer analytics and personalization, it's important to acknowledge the challenges and considerations that organizations must address to ensure successful implementation. These challenges touch on issues of data security, integration complexity, vendor selection, and latency. Let's delve into each challenge in detail:

- *Data Security and Privacy:* Storing sensitive customer data on cloud platforms introduces concerns about security and compliance. Organizations must ensure that customer data are safeguarded against unauthorized access, breaches, and data leaks. This is especially critical when dealing with personally identifiable information (PII) and financial data in business and finance contexts. To mitigate these risks, organizations need to adopt robust encryption mechanisms to protect data both during transit and while at rest in the cloud. This encryption ensures that even if a breach occurs, the stolen data remain unreadable without the decryption keys. Additionally, access controls must be meticulously configured, granting permissions only to authorized personnel. Compliance with data protection regulations, such as the General Data Protection Regulation (GDPR) and the California Consumer Privacy Act (CCPA), is non-negotiable. Organizations must ensure that data management practices align with these regulations, providing customers with control over their data and their usage.
- *Data Integration Complexity:* Integrating data from various sources is a crucial aspect of effective customer analytics and personalization. However, this integration can be complex, especially when dealing with diverse data formats, structures, and sources. Poor data integration can lead to inaccurate insights and skewed results. To address this challenge, organizations need to establish effective data governance practices. Clear data pipelines must be designed, outlining how data flows from various sources to the cloud. Quality checks should be implemented at each stage to ensure data accuracy and consistency. Data transformation and cleaning processes are essential to standardize the data for analysis. Automated tools for data integration can streamline the process, reducing manual errors and ensuring the reliability of the insights derived from the integrated datasets.
- *Vendor Selection:* Choosing the right cloud service provider is a pivotal decision. The selected provider becomes a custodian of sensitive customer data, making factors like data residency, compliance certifications, and security practices critical.

- Organizations need to assess the provider's compliance with relevant industry standards and regulations. Look for certifications such as ISO 27001 for information security management and SOC 2 for operational controls. The provider's track record in security incidents and data breaches should also be scrutinized. Understanding where and how the data will be stored, as well as the provider's disaster recovery plans, is vital to ensuring data availability and business continuity.
- *Latency Issues:* While cloud platforms offer real-time analytics capabilities, network latency can impact the speed of data retrieval and analysis. Latency refers to the delay between sending a request to the cloud and receiving a response. This delay can undermine the effectiveness of real-time personalization efforts. To mitigate latency, organizations need to optimize data flows and communication between various components of their cloud infrastructure. This might involve employing content delivery networks (CDNs) to cache frequently accessed data closer to the end-user. Additionally, leveraging edge computing—a decentralized computing approach—can bring computation closer to the data source, reducing the time taken for data to travel back and forth.

9.3 LITERATURE REVIEW

Liu et al. (2020) aimed to define the prevailing concepts of financial technologies within the realm of digital banking.

In 2011, Ouf and Nasr proposed leveraging cloud computing as a potential solution to these challenges. They aimed to create a new business intelligence environment that can reduce BI implementation timelines, lower costs compared to traditional on premise BI software, provide testing and upgrade environments, and enhance deployment speed and flexibility for users.

In 2015, Jeknić and Bojan presented process enhancements in marketing automation, lead tracking, and inbound marketing achieved through the utilization of cloud services.

In 2014, Devasena conducted an empirical impact study highlighting the effects of cloud technology adoption on business organizations, including micro, small medium businesses (SMBs), and small medium enterprises (SMEs), and its influence on business development.

In 2020, Chen and Metawa presented the concept of "business-driven value" as an innovative expense management system.

In 2022, Ilyas and Aziz proposed a system with a primary focus on mass personalization, highlighting the distinctive features of cloud computing (CC) and mass customization (MC) strategies compared to other approaches.

In 2019, Al-Kabi and Jirjees presented an abstracted review of big data applications, focusing on its utilization in four key domains: health, education, business and finance, and security and privacy.

In 2021, Janaćković and Leskovac conducted an analysis of cloud computing's application in accounting and finance. The paper emphasizes the characteristics and advantages of cloud-based solutions and their practical use in businesses.

In 2018, Misra and Doneria explored the implementation of cloud-based services in the financial services, intermediaries, and banking industry. Their study utilizes actor-based stakeholder modeling to examine the drivers for adoption, benefits, trade-offs, and challenges in a sector where security has traditionally been a major concern.

In 2022, Jamaludin et al. delved into the applications of big data analytics within the financial services industry, exploring various approaches like text analytics, audio analytics, and predictive analytics. These methods are instrumental in addressing crucial issues such as market forecasting, fraud detection, credit scoring, real-time targeted marketing, and overall customer experience enhancement for financial organizations.

In 2020, Hasan et al. aimed to present an overview of the current financial landscape with respect to big data. Their paper highlights the profound influence of big data on various financial sectors, including financial markets, institutions, internet finance, financial management, internet credit service companies, fraud detection, risk analysis, financial application management, and more (Khang & AIoCF, 2024).

In 2015, Christauskas and Misevičienė explored the latest trends in accounting information systems for small to medium-sized businesses, with a particular focus on cloud computing-based technology, which represents a significant advancement in the realm of information technology.

9.4   BEST PRACTICES

While cloud-based data management offers remarkable advantages, implementing it effectively requires adherence to best practices. These practices guide organizations in maximizing the benefits while minimizing potential challenges (Khang, Rashmi et al., 2024). Let's delve into each best practice in detail.

9.4.1   DATA GOVERNANCE

Establishing robust data governance policies is fundamental to maintaining data accuracy, quality, and compliance. Data governance encompasses the processes, roles, responsibilities, and policies that ensure data are managed consistently and effectively throughout their lifecycle.

Organizations need to define data ownership and accountability, specifying who is responsible for data quality, accuracy, and security. Data classification, tagging, and metadata management should be standardized to facilitate easy data identification and usage. Moreover, organizations must implement data lineage tracking, documenting the data's journey from source to analysis to maintain transparency and account-ability (Khang, Inna et al., 2024).

9.4.2   HYBRID APPROACHES

While cloud platforms offer significant advantages, there might be instances where sensitive or critical data require extra protection. In such cases, adopting a hybrid cloud approach can be beneficial. A hybrid cloud solution involves storing sensitive data on-premises in private data centers and utilizing the cloud for less-sensitive data.

For example, a financial institution might choose to store customer financial records on-premises due to regulatory and compliance concerns, while leveraging

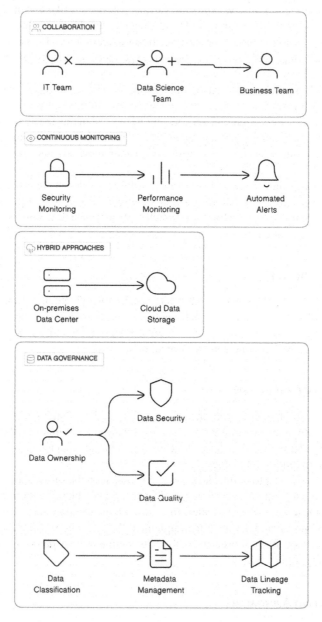

FIGURE 9.5 Best practices for maximizing the benefits while minimizing potential challenges.

the cloud for non-sensitive data like market trends and social media interactions. This approach allows organizations to capitalize on cloud benefits for scalability and analytics while maintaining tighter control over sensitive data.

9.4.3 Continuous Monitoring

Proactive monitoring is crucial to ensure the security, availability, and performance of cloud-based data management systems. Implementing continuous monitoring and alert systems helps detect anomalies, breaches, or performance issues promptly, enabling swift responses to potential threats or disruptions.

Security monitoring involves tracking access logs, user activities, and system behavior to identify unauthorized access attempts or suspicious behavior. Performance monitoring ensures that cloud resources are optimized, preventing bottlenecks or downtime, as shown in Figure 9.5.

9.5 CLOUD-BASED DATA MANAGEMENT IN BUSINESS AND FINANCE

9.5.1 Exploring Cloud Computing and Its Benefits

9.5.1.1 The Essence of Cloud Computing

At its core, cloud computing offers a paradigm shift in how data are stored, processed, and accessed. It involves delivering a suite of computing resources—from storage to processing power—via the internet. This enables businesses and financial institutions to untether themselves from the constraints of physical infrastructure.

9.5.1.2 Benefits for Businesses and Finance

- *Scalability and Flexibility:* Cloud computing delivers an unprecedented level of scalability. As data demands surge, cloud resources can be instantly expanded to accommodate growth. Conversely, during quieter periods, scaling down optimizes costs. This agility empowers businesses to align their operations with market dynamics efficiently.
- *Cost-Efficiency:* Shifting from traditional on-premises data centers to cloud solutions can significantly reduce capital expenditures. The pay-as-you-go model allows organizations to pay only for the resources they consume, obviating the need for upfront investments in hardware and maintenance.
- *Global Accessibility and Collaboration:* Cloud-based data are accessible from any corner of the globe, provided an internet connection exists. This accessibility fosters seamless collaboration among geographically dispersed teams, leading to enhanced productivity and innovation.
- *Rapid Innovation and Deployment:* Cloud platforms provide a treasure trove of cutting-edge tools and technologies. This accelerates innovation by equipping businesses with the resources to swiftly experiment, develop, and deploy new solutions, thus gaining a competitive edge.

- *Data Centralization and Organization:* Cloud-based systems facilitate centralized data storage and management. This organized approach simplifies data retrieval, analysis, and reporting, enhancing decision-making processes in the financial and business sectors.
- *Disaster Recovery and Business Continuity:* Cloud services include robust disaster recovery mechanisms. Data redundancy across multiple data centers ensures that in the event of a local disaster, operations can swiftly transition to alternative locations, minimizing downtime and ensuring business continuity.

9.5.2 CLOUD DATA STORAGE AND SCALABILITY

9.5.2.1 Data Storage Revolution

Traditionally, data storage required substantial physical infrastructure and maintenance. Cloud data storage disrupts this norm by offering virtualized, on-demand storage solutions accessible through the internet. Businesses and financial institutions can now shift their focus from hardware upkeep to strategic data utilization.

9.5.2.2 Unleashing Scalability

- *Seamless Expansion:* Cloud platforms bring the gift of scalability to the forefront. As data volumes surge, organizations can seamlessly scale up storage resources without investing in additional hardware. This ensures data availability while adapting to evolving demands.
- *Cost-Efficiency:* Scalability in the cloud is not only about accommodating growth; it's about cost-effectively matching resources to needs. Scaling down during quieter periods avoids wastage, making it an efficient solution for maintaining operational equilibrium.
- *Bursting Capability:* In scenarios where there's a sudden surge in data usage—such as during financial market volatility—cloud resources can be temporarily boosted to manage the increased workload. This flexibility minimizes disruptions during peak demand.

9.5.2.3 Data Redundancy and Reliability

- *Enhanced Data Protection:* Cloud providers often replicate data across multiple geographical locations0 00. This redundancy minimizes the risk of data loss due to hardware failures, natural disasters, or cyber threats, bolstering data integrity.
- *Reliable Disaster Recovery:* Cloud-based systems often come with robust disaster recovery mechanisms. In the face of unforeseen events, such as system failures or cyberattacks, organizations can quickly restore operations, ensuring business continuity.

9.5.2.4 Agile Decision-Making

Real-Time Access: Cloud-based data storage facilitates real-time access to critical information. This empowers financial institutions to make swift decisions based on up-to-date insights, leading to improved financial analysis and strategic planning.

Collaboration Amplified: Scalable cloud solutions enable teams across different locations to collaborate effectively. Real-time data sharing fosters collaborative decision-making, essential for complex financial transactions and strategic business initiatives.

9.5.3 DATA SECURITY AND PRIVACY CONSIDERATIONS

9.5.3.1 Robust Data Security Measures

Encryption: Encryption serves as a powerful shield for sensitive data. Cloud providers often offer encryption mechanisms for data in transit and at rest. This ensures that even if unauthorized access occurs, the data remain unintelligible.

Multi-Factor Authentication (MFA): MFA adds an extra layer of security by requiring users to provide multiple forms of identification before accessing data. This significantly reduces the risk of unauthorized access, even if passwords are compromised.

Access Control and Authorization: Cloud platforms enable organizations to define and enforce access controls. Only authorized personnel can access specific data, minimizing the risk of data breaches due to unauthorized users.

9.5.3.2 Compliance and Regulation

- *Industry-Specific Regulations:* Businesses and financial institutions operate within stringent regulatory environments (e.g., GDPR, HIPAA). Cloud providers must adhere to these regulations, ensuring that data management practices align with legal requirements.
- *Data Sovereignty:* For organizations operating across different jurisdictions, ensuring compliance with data protection laws becomes complex. Selecting cloud providers with data centers in relevant regions aids in addressing data sovereignty concerns.

9.5.3.3 Vendor Security and Transparency

- *Due Diligence:* Selecting a reputable cloud service provider is crucial. Organizations should conduct thorough assessments of their security protocols, track record, and transparency regarding their data management practices.
- *Contractual Agreements:* Contractual agreements should outline the responsibilities of both the organization and the cloud provider concerning data security. This includes breach notification procedures, data retention policies, and indemnification clauses.

9.5.3.4 Data Privacy

- *Anonymization and Pseudonymization:* Sensitive data can be anonymized or pseudonymized to protect individual identities while maintaining data utility. This is particularly relevant in financial and business scenarios that involve customer data.
- *Consent Management:* In cases where customer data are involved, obtaining clear and informed consent for data usage is imperative. Cloud-based systems can facilitate efficient consent management processes.

9.5.4 CUSTOMER DATA COLLECTION AND SOURCES

In the digital age, customer data have become a goldmine of insights for businesses aiming to enhance customer experiences and tailor their offerings. This section delves into the diverse sources of customer data collection, elucidating the significance of transactional data, behavioral data, and demographic and socio-economic data.

9.5.4.1 Transactional Data

Transactional data encompasses records of customer interactions and transactions. These interactions can involve purchases, subscriptions, payments, and any form of financial engagement with a business. These data reveal valuable insights into customers' purchasing patterns, preferences, and brand loyalty.
Transactional data are primarily derived from:

- Point of Sale (POS) Systems: Retail businesses gather data at the time of purchase, including product details, price, and location.
- Online Transactions: e-Commerce platforms capture data related to products bought, browsing history, and payment methods.
- Financial Institutions: Banks and payment processors possess transactional data related to customers' financial activities.

9.5.4.2 Behavioral Data

Behavioral data encompasses customer actions and interactions across various touch points. These data shed light on how customers engage with a brand, what products they explore, and how they navigate through digital platforms.
Behavioral data are captured through:

- Website Tracking: Analyzing user behavior on websites, including page views, click-through rates, and time spent on pages.
- App Usage: Mobile apps record user interactions, feature usage, and session duration.
- Clickstream Data: Tracking the sequence of clicks and interactions as users navigate digital platforms.

9.5.4.3 Demographic and Socioeconomic Data

Demographic and socioeconomic data involves information about customers' characteristics, such as age, gender, income, education, and location. These data aid in creating customer personas and tailoring marketing strategies.

Demographic and socioeconomic data are collected from:

- Customer Surveys: Surveys and questionnaires provide direct insights into customers' background and preferences.
- Census Data: Publicly available data from governmental sources provide information about population demographics.
- Social Media Profiles: Social media platforms often contain personal information shared by users.

9.6 CHALLENGES AND CONSIDERATIONS

9.6.1 DATA PRIVACY AND SECURITY IN CLOUD-BASED CUSTOMER ANALYTICS

- *Data Breach Vulnerabilities:* Storing sensitive customer data in the cloud can expose businesses to the risk of data breaches. Unauthorized access could lead to customer identity theft, financial fraud, and reputational damage.
- *Compliance and Regulations:* Businesses must adhere to data protection regulations (e.g., GDPR, CCPA) when dealing with customer data. Cloud providers need to offer compliance tools to ensure that data are handled according to legal requirements.
- *Cloud Provider Responsibility:* Businesses entrust cloud providers with their data. Ensuring that the chosen provider has robust security measures, encryption protocols, and strong access controls is essential to maintain data integrity.
- *Data Encryption and Access Controls:* Encrypting data both in transit and at rest is critical to prevent unauthorized access. Effective access controls must be in place to ensure that only authorized personnel can access sensitive customer information.

9.6.2 ETHICAL CONSIDERATIONS IN PERSONALIZATION

- *Invasion of Privacy:* Personalization efforts can sometimes cross ethical boundaries, leading customers to feel that their privacy is being invaded. Businesses must strike a balance between customization and respecting personal boundaries.
- *Transparency and Consent:* Customers should be fully informed about the data being collected and how they will be used for personalization. Obtaining explicit consent is vital, ensuring customers are aware of and comfortable with the personalization efforts.
- *Algorithmic Bias:* Personalization algorithms might inadvertently perpetuate biases present in the data. Businesses must take steps to identify and rectify biases to ensure fair and equitable treatment of all customers.

9.6.3 DATA QUALITY AND INTEGRATION CHALLENGES

- *Data Silos:* Businesses often collect customer data from various sources. Integrating data from different systems and departments can be challenging, leading to fragmented and inconsistent datasets.
- *Data Accuracy and Reliability:* Poor data quality can lead to inaccurate insights. Ensuring that the data collected are accurate, up-to-date, and relevant is essential for making informed decisions.
- *Data Governance:* Implementing effective data governance frameworks is crucial to ensure that data are properly managed, standardized, and accessible across the organization.

9.7 CASE STUDIES: SUCCESSFUL IMPLEMENTATIONS

9.7.1 RETAIL INDUSTRY

- *Amazon: Personalized Shopping Experience* Amazon's recommendation engine is a prime example of successful customer analytics in the retail sector. By analyzing customer behavior, purchase history, and browsing patterns, Amazon suggests products tailored to individual preferences. This personalization has contributed significantly to their high customer retention rates and increased sales.
- *Starbucks: Loyalty Program and Mobile App* Starbucks employs data analytics to enhance customer experience through its mobile app and loyalty program. By tracking purchase history, preferences, and location data, Starbucks delivers personalized offers and rewards, enticing customers to visit more frequently and spend more.

9.7.2 FINANCIAL SERVICES SECTOR

- *JPMorgan Chase: Fraud Detection and Prevention* JPMorgan Chase utilizes advanced analytics to detect and prevent fraudulent activities. By analyzing transactional data in real time, the bank can identify unusual patterns or anomalies that might indicate fraud, ensuring the security of customer accounts.
- *Credit Scoring Companies (e.g., FICO): Risk Assessment:* Financial institutions use credit scoring models to assess the creditworthiness of individuals. These models consider various factors, including payment history, credit utilization, and personal information, to provide accurate risk assessment and determine loan eligibility.

9.7.3 E-COMMERCE PLATFORMS

- *Netflix: Content Recommendation* Netflix employs sophisticated algorithms to analyze customer viewing history and preferences. These data are used to recommend personalized content to subscribers, resulting in increased engagement and longer subscription durations.

- *eBay: Dynamic Pricing Strategy* eBay uses customer analytics to implement a dynamic pricing strategy. By analyzing real-time data on buyer behavior, item popularity, and market trends, eBay adjusts pricing to match demand, optimizing revenue and customer satisfaction.

9.8 FUTURE TRENDS AND IMPLICATIONS

9.8.1 Advances in Cloud-Based Analytics and Machine Learning

- *Enhanced Data Processing:* Cloud-based analytics will continue to evolve, offering even more sophisticated data processing capabilities. This will enable businesses to analyze larger datasets faster, leading to more accurate insights and informed decision-making.
- *Machine Learning Integration:* Cloud platforms will increasingly integrate machine learning capabilities. This will enable businesses to develop predictive models, automate tasks, and uncover complex patterns in customer behavior, allowing for hyper-personalization and improved customer experiences.
- *Real-Time Analytics:* Cloud-based systems will facilitate real-time data analysis, enabling businesses to respond swiftly to changing customer behaviors and market trends. This will be crucial for making timely strategic adjustments.

9.8.2 Evolving Customer Expectations and Personalization

- *Hyper-Personalization:* Customers will expect highly personalized experiences tailored to their unique preferences and needs. Businesses will need to harness customer analytics to create dynamic and individualized interactions at every touchpoint.
- *Ethical and Privacy Concerns:* As personalization deepens, businesses will need to strike a delicate balance between using customer data for customization and respecting privacy concerns. Transparent data usage practices will become a critical part of customer trust-building.
- *Omnichannel Integration:* Future personalization will extend across various channels seamlessly. Customers will anticipate consistent experiences whether interacting with a brand through a website, app, social media, or in-store.

9.8.3 Integration with Emerging Technologies (AI, IoT)

- *AI-Driven Insights:* Artificial intelligence (AI) will play a pivotal role in extracting meaningful insights from customer data. AI algorithms will identify complex patterns and correlations that were previously difficult to detect, offering businesses deeper understanding.
- *IoT-Generated Data:* The Internet of Things (IoT) will generate massive amounts of data from interconnected devices. Integrating IoT data with customer

analytics will provide a holistic view of customer behaviors, preferences, and interactions.

- *Predictive and Proactive Engagement:* AI-powered predictive analytics will enable businesses to anticipate customer needs and preferences, allowing them to engage with customers proactively rather than reactively.

9.9   CONCLUSION

Cloud-based data management has revolutionized customer analytics and personalization in business and finance. It enables organizations to process vast amounts of data, gain deeper customer insights, and deliver tailored experiences at scale (Khang, Kali et al., 2023). While challenges related to security, integration, and latency persist, implementing best practices can mitigate these concerns. As technology advances and cloud services evolve, businesses and financial institutions are poised to refine their customer-centric strategies further, driving innovation and growth in the digital era (Khang, Muthmainnah et al., 2023).

- *Recap of Key Insights:* Throughout this exploration of cloud-based data management and customer analytics, several key insights have emerged. We've examined the significance of various customer data sources, including transactional, behavioral, and demographic data. Challenges such as data privacy, ethical considerations, and data quality have been identified, while successful case studies have showcased real-world implementations. Additionally, we've discussed the future trends involving advances in cloud-based analytics, evolving customer expectations, and integration with emerging technologies.
- *Emphasizing the Importance of Cloud-Based Data Management:* Cloud-based data management has proven to be a transformative force in today's business landscape. By offering scalability, cost-efficiency, and accessibility, the cloud empowers businesses to extract valuable insights from their customer data. This capability is essential for staying competitive, crafting personalized experiences, and making informed strategic decisions.
- *Outlook for the Future of Customer Analytics and Personalization:* The future of customer analytics and personalization is promising and dynamic. As technology continues to evolve, cloud-based analytics will become even more sophisticated, integrating machine learning and AI-driven insights. Businesses will need to align with evolving customer expectations, providing hyper-personalized experiences while maintaining transparency and data privacy. The integration of emerging technologies like AI and IoT will further reshape the landscape, enabling predictive engagement and holistic customer understanding.

In conclusion, cloud-based data management and customer analytics are not only tools for enhancing business operations but also key drivers of customer-centric innovation. By leveraging these capabilities, businesses can forge deeper connections with their customers, fuel growth, and navigate the intricate landscape of data-driven decision-making in the years to come.

9.10   KEY TERMS

- *Artificial Intelligence (AI):* Artificial intelligence (AI) is a technology that enables computers and machines to think and act like humans. It involves creating smart systems that can learn from data, solve problems, and make decisions. AI helps computers recognize images, understand speech, translate languages, and even play games. It is used in many areas, such as self-driving cars, voice assistants like Siri or Alexa, and personalized recommendations on websites. AI is constantly improving and has the potential to revolutionize how we live and work.
- *Internet of Things (IoT):* The Internet of Things (IoT) is a concept that refers to the connection of everyday objects to the internet, allowing them to send and receive data. These objects can include devices like smartphones, thermostats, wearables, home appliances, and even vehicles. The idea behind IoT is to create a network where these objects can communicate with each other, collect and share data, and perform tasks more efficiently.
- *Point of Sale (POS):* POS stands for "point of sale." It refers to the physical or digital location where a transaction occurs between a customer and a business, typically involving the exchange of goods or services for payment.
- *Multi-Factor Authentication (MFA):* This is a security method that requires users to provide multiple forms of identification to access a system, application, or account. This enhances security by adding an extra layer of protection beyond traditional usernames and passwords.
- *Cloud Computing:* Cloud computing is a technology that enables users to access and use computing resources, such as storage, processing power, and applications, over the internet. It eliminates the need for local hardware and allows for flexible and scalable services on demand.

REFERENCES

Al-Kabi, Mohammed N., and Jassim Mohammed Jirjees. "Survey of big data applications: Health, education, business & finance, and security & privacy." *Journal of Information Studies and Technology* 2018, no. 2 (2019): 12. https://doi.org/10.5339/jist.2018.12

Chen, Xuanjun, and Noura Metawa. "Enterprise financial management information system based on cloud computing in big data environment." *Journal of Intelligent & Fuzzy Systems* 39, no. 4 (2020): 5223–5232. https://content.iospress.com/articles/journal-of-intelligent-and-fuzzy-systems/ifs189007

Christauskas, Česlovas, & Misevičienė, Regina. "Services for Implementation of Cloud Technologies for Education." *Society. Integration. Education. Proceedings of the International Scientific Conference* 4(2015): 383–392. https://doi.org/10.17770/sie2015vol4.403

Devasena, C. Lakshmi. "Impact study of cloud computing on business development." *Operations Research and Applications: An International Journal (ORAJ)* 1, no. 1 (2014): 1–7. www.academia.edu/download/38205543/Final_1.pdf

Hasan, Md Morshadul, József Popp, and Judit Oláh. "Current landscape and influence of big data on finance." *Journal of Big Data* 7, no. 1 (2020): 1–17. https://journalofbigdata. springeropen.com/articles/10.1186/s40537-020-00291-z

Ilyas, Ahsan, and Nauman Aziz. "A cloud based customer response management system using the internet of things." *International Journal of Secure and Intelligent* 1, no. 1 (2022): 54–68. https://ijsic.com/index.php/IJS/article/view/1

Jamaludin, Muhamad Akram Arif, Nur Azaliah Abu Bakar, and Saiful Adli Ismail. "A review on the role of big data analytics in the financial services industry." *International Journal of Human and Technology Interaction (IJHaTI)* 6, no. 2 (2022). https://journal.utem. edu.my/index.php/ijhati/article/view/6271

Janaćković, Tanja, and Vlade Jovanovića Leskovac. "The impact of cloud technology on accounting and finance." *PaKSoM* (2021): 169. www.researchgate.net/profile/Vesna-Martin/publication/358288234_Public_Debt_Management_in_Serbia/links/61fbd2df1 1a1090a79ce704a/Public-Debt-Management-in-Serbia.pdf#page=184

Jeknić, Jelena, and Bojan Kraut. "Cloud services and marketing." In 2015 38th International Convention on Information and Communication Technology, Electronics and Microelectronics (MIPRO), pp. 1492–1498. IEEE (2015). DOI: 10.1109/ MIPRO.2015.7160508

Khang, Alex and AIoCF (Eds.), *AI-Oriented Competency Framework for Talent Management in the Digital Economy: Models, Technologies, Applications, and Implementation.* (2024). ISBN: 9781032576053. CRC Press. https://doi.org/10.1201/9781003440901

Khang, Alex, M. Muthmainnah, P. M. I. Seraj, A. Al Yakin, and A. J. Obaid, "AI-Aided Teaching Model for the Education 5.0 Ecosystem." In In A. Khang, V. Shah, & S. Rani (Eds.), Handbook of Research on AI-Based Technologies and Applications in the Era of the Metaverse (pp 83–104). IGI Global Press (2023). https://doi.org/10.4018/ 978-1-6684-8851-5.ch004

Khang, Alex, Rashmi Gujrati, Hayri Uygun, R. K. Tailor, and S. S. Gaur. *Data-driven Modelling and Predictive Analytics in Business and Finance.* ISBN: 9781032600628. (1st Ed.) (2024) CRC Press. https://doi.org/10.1201/9781032600628

Khang, Alex, S. K. Gupta., Sita Rani, and D. A. Karras (Eds.). *Smart Cities: IoT Technologies, Big Data Solutions, Cloud Platforms, and Cybersecurity Techniques* (2023). CRC Press. https://doi.org/10.1201/9781003376064

Khang, Alex, S.-O. Inna, K. Alla, S. Rostyslav, M. Rudenko, R. Lidia, and B. Kristina. "Management Model 6.0 and Business Recovery Strategy of Enterprises in the Era of Digital Economy." In *Data-driven Modelling and Predictive Analytics in Business and Finance* (1st Ed.) (2024). CRC Press. https://doi.org/10.1201/9781032600628-16

Khang, Alex, Sita Rani and A. K. Sivaraman. *AI-Centric Smart City Ecosystems: Technologies, Design and Implementation* (1st Ed.) (2022). CRC Press. https://doi.org/10.1201/ 9781003252542

Khang, Alex, Sita Rani, Rashmi Gujrati, Hayri Uygun, and S. K. Gupta. (Eds.). *Designing Workforce Management Systems for Industry 4.0: Data-Centric and AI-Enabled Approaches* (2023). CRC Press. https://doi.org/10.1201/9781003357070

Khang, Alex, V. Shah, and Sita Rani. *AI-Based Technologies and Applications in the Era of the Metaverse* (1st Ed.) (2023). IGI Global Press. https://doi.org/10.4018/978-1-6684-8851-5

Khang, Alex, C. R. Kali, S. K. Satapathy, A. Kumar, S. R. Das, and M. R. Panda. "Enabling the Future of Manufacturing: Integration of Robotics and IoT to Smart Factory Infrastructure in Industry 4.0." In In A. Khang, V. Shah, & S. Rani (Eds.), *AI-Based Technologies and*

Applications in the Era of the Metaverse (1st Ed.) (2023) (pp. 25–50). IGI Global Press. https://doi.org/10.4018/978-1-6684-8851-5.ch002

Liu, Ying, Anthony Soroka, Liangxiu Han, Jin Jian, and Min Tang. "Cloud-based big data analytics for customer insight-driven design innovation in SMEs." *International Journal of Information Management* 51 (2020): 102034. https://doi.org/10.30525/2256-0742/2020-6-1-92-99

Misra, Subhas C., and Kriti Doneria. "Application of cloud computing in financial services: An agent-oriented modelling approach." *Journal of Modelling in Management* 13, no. 4 (2018): 994–1006. www.emerald.com/insight/content/doi/10.1108/JM2-12-2017-0131/full/html

Ouf, Shimaa, and Mona Nasr. "Business intelligence in the cloud." In 2011 IEEE 3rd International Conference on Communication Software and Networks, pp. 650–655. IEEE, 2011. DOI: 10.1109/ICCSN.2011.6014351

10 Theoretical Analysis and Data Modeling of the Influence of Shadow Banking on Systemic Risk

Hemant Bhanawat and Alex Khang

10.1 INTRODUCTION

The global financial crisis of 2007–2009 witnessed the breakdown of financial stability which was overtaken by panic throughout the entire financial system which resulted in a sharp and long-lasting credit contraction in the entire global economy. From this crisis, it could be learned that the financial strength of financial institutions does not always lead to systemic stability (RBI, 2018). Because of the contagious nature of the impact of the failure of even one big institution in the financial system other institutions are affected, resulting in overall financial instability (Khang & Shah, 2023).

When financial instability becomes widespread, the financial sector enters into a harmful state which aggravates systemic stress leading to a worse economic situation enabling systemic risk (SR). This is the risk imposed due to the inter-linkages and interdependencies in a system, where the failure of a single entity or cluster of entities can cause a cascading failure, which has the potency to bankrupt or bring down the entire system or market. SR is evolved from an institutional set up out of which banks and shadow banks (SBs), also known as non-banking financial companies (NBFCs), are the major contributors (Khang, Kali et al., 2023).

McCulley (2007) introduced the notion of shadow banking as an unregulated financial institution characterized by high leverage without any benefit from a safety net or other official guarantees. The Financial Stability Board (FSB) (2011) defined SB as credit intermediation involving entities and activities outside the regular banking system. It is all financial activities, except traditional banking, which rely on a private or public backstop to operate (Claessens et al., 2014).

SBs are those institutions whose activities include credit intermediation; maturity and liquidity transformation that take place outside the purview of regular banking activities. Their activities are parallel to traditional banks and involved in a huge chain of intermediation activities that are outside the purview of banking regulations, susceptible to run, impacting the financial stability of an economy (Luttrell et al., 2012). They are the major contributors to the SR (FSB, 2011).

DOI: 10.1201/9781032618845-10

Due to the various interlinkages and interdependencies of SB activities with other components of the financial system (FS) a contagion effect is created, consequently spilling the risk over the entire economy leading to instability, which slows down economic activity. As credit intermediations involve activities outside the regular banking activities, SBs raise concerns about economic growth. Over the years, the functioning of the Indian SB sector has gone through various metamorphoses with many interventions by RBI; especially with regard to mandatory certificate of registration, prudential requirements, liquidity risk management, and capital requirements of NBFCs (Khang, Muthmainnah et al., 2023).

Technological advancements and innovations in the financial services etc. have made the working of SBs in the Indian context more complicated, increasing the challenge for regulators (Jhajhria, 2018). Recently, the Indian market has experienced the collapse of Infrastructure Leasing & Financial Services Limited (IL & FS), which was one of the biggest NBFCs. Investors faced losses of around $12.8 bn. and there was a liquidity shortage close to $15.38bn. In the system, Jhajhria (2018) indicates that any financial distress of one NBFC can affect a large group of customers and the entire economy. SB is one of the key components of the financial system. In recent years, the Indian shadow banking system has been receiving increasing attention due to growing credit extension compared to scheduled commercial banks along with NBFC default.

The financial crisis of 2007–9 revealed that SR can build up from SB activities. In this chapter, through a survey of the global literature we try to highlight various activities of SBs, i.e. efficiency and performance, which can contribute to SR, and examine theoretically the various risks associated with their activities at an institutional level that have the potency to build up SR. After this introduction, Section 10.2 provides a brief overview of shadow banks globally and in the Indian context. Section 10.3 presents a literature review on the conceptual framework of shadow banks and systemic risk, the relationships, drivers of systemic risk, and measurement approaches. Section 10.4 discusses the major findings and conclusion (Aakansha, Adhishree et al., 2023).

10.2   BRIEF OVERVIEW OF SHADOW BANKS

Shadow banking was one of the major contributors to the global financial crisis of 2007 which led to distress in the world economy (Lysandrou et al., 2015; Pozsar et al., 2013). As credit intermediation involves activities outside the regular banking system, SB raises significant issues (Ghosh et al., 2012). When a financial firm's capital is low, the re-intermediation of financial services is difficult to pull off. Similarly, when the aggregate capital is low, it is not possible for other financial firms to step into the breach (Acharya et al., 2010).

As the firms are interconnected, the risk produced is not restricted to the firm level but impacts the economy as a whole. And when the size of the SBs increases, along with their linkages with other entities in the financial sector, any shock in the SB system will give rise to SR concern affecting the financial stability of an economy. Before the financial crisis, the SB system was marked by very high growth. Globally, the asset size of SBs increased from $26 trillion in 2002 to $62 trillion in 2007. Immediately after the crisis there was a slight decline in their growth but, in the following years, their assets had increased to $67 trillion in 2011 (FSB 2011).

This size, which was based on an expanded list approach, i.e. MUNFI approach (Monitoring Universe of Non-bank Financial Intermediation), has been revised recently. As per the present narrow-down approach (FSB, 2014), the asset size of SBs was around $45 trillion in 2016. Globally, the total financial assets are $340 trillion, of which the share of NBFIs (non-bank financial intermediaries) is $160 trillion. Presently, SBs represent 13.24% of total financial assets and 28% of the total assets of NBFIs (FSB, 2017). The loans extended by them continue to grow rapidly and the lending activities are found to be greater in emerging economies as compared to advanced countries (Muthmainnah, Yakin et al., 2023).

Further, post crisis it is evident that every year SBs registered a very high growth rate and simultaneously their contribution towards global assets is also increasing. The types of entities that we know as SBs in India are known as non-banking financial companies (NBFCs) (Gandhi, 2014). In India, SBs are not just finance companies but include a wide group of companies. It is a combination of quasi-formal and informal (even illegal, but socially accepted) networks of nidhis, chit funds, moneylenders, gold financing companies, and many others.

In 1988, RBI introduced a new set of regulations for NBFCs where they were classified into three broader groups, i.e., asset financing companies (AFC), non-deposit taking companies, and core investment companies. In 2002, RBI revised the existing regulation of 1998 and reclassified NBFCs as deposit-taking NBFCs and systemically important non-deposit taking finance companies.

In 2006, NBFCs were reclassified as AFCs, loan companies, and investment companies. In 2010, infrastructure finance company was included under the broad classification of NBFC along with infrastructure debt funds, micro financial institutions, and factors (RBI, 2010). The emergence of SBs in India can be traced back to the 1950s (Acharya et al., 2013; Sinha, 2013). During the 1990s, the number of NBFCs grew more than sevenfold from 7603 in 1981, 15,358 in 1985, 24,009 by 1990, and 55,995 in 1995 (Gandhi, 2014; Sinha, 2013).

With total financial assets (TFAs) of Rs. 236.39 trillion (Barbora, 2018) the Indian scheduled commercial bank constitutes 64.5% and the share of NBFC is 11%, which is around Rs. 26 trillion. Out of the latter NBFC-non deposit systemically important (NBFC-ND-SI) accounts for 84.8% (RBI, 2018). The number of NBFC registered under RBI was 9659 as on 31 March 2019, out of which 88 were deposit-taking NBFCs and 263 were NBFC non-deposit systemically important (NBFC-ND-SI) (RBI, 2019). The NBFC sector is almost 15% of the total balance sheet size of scheduled commercial banks (Hede, 2019; RBI, 2018). The consolidated balance sheet of NBFCs grew by 20.6% (Rs. 28.8 trillion) during 2018–19 as against 17.9% (Rs. 24.5 trillion) during 2017–18 (RBI, 2019). The share of NBFCs in total credit extended and had increased from around 9.4% in March 2009 to more than 17% in March 2018 (FSB, 2017; RBI, 2018). At the same time, NBFC is the largest net borrower of funds from the FS, having gross payable of around Rs. 8.446 trillion and receivable of around Rs. 0.723 trillion as on March 2019 (RBI, 2019a).

Although SB plays a complementary role by broadening access to financial services and adds to the economic strength, on the other hand, due to their interconnectedness with the other financial activities and complexity in their operation, the risks emanated from them are spread to the economy as a whole (Sherpa, 2013). Since SB entities do not have access to central funding, deposit insurance, and safety nets they remain vulnerable to shocks giving rise to systemic risk concern. The risks emanating from SB can be broadly classified into five types, namely: (i) liquidity risk; (ii) leverage risk; (iii) regulatory arbitrage risk; (iv) contagion risk; and (v) credit risk (FSB, 2011; Sherpa, 2013; Sinha, 2013). Liquidity risk originates as SBs fund long-term assets with short-term liability (Pooja, Babasaheb et al., 2023).

Risk of asset–liability mismatches leads to liquidity problems. SBs do not have any regulatory restrictions on borrowing which makes them highly leveraged. This increases the stress in the financial economy. Arbitrage risk emanates as regulation of the formal banking system is very strict and much of their activities shift towards less regulated areas of the financial system, that is SBs (Sinha, 2013). Credit risk is the risk of default on a debt that may arise from a borrower failing to make the required payments, which impacts the efficiency of SBs causing distress among large groups of investors.

10.3 REVIEW OF THE LITERATURE

Whereas banks are being well researched, the evidence on the contribution of SBs to financial instability has been only recently emerging. Traditionally, the activities of SBs are considered to be safe and their activities do not impact the economy at large (Pozsar et al., 2013). However, after a financial crisis, it could be realized that other than traditional banks, SR can also arise from SB activities which slows down economic activities. Soon after the global financial crisis (Sihare, Khang et al., 2023), SBs were undertaken on the functions and because of their phenomenal growth they are gaining popularity among researchers. However, globally the academic literature on SBs and their impact on SR are very scant. Academic literature on SR is mostly in the banking sector. Based on the available literature on SBs and SR, a review has been conducted which can be divided into four sections, namely the conceptual framework, drivers of systemic risk, the relationship between SBs and SR, and finally the methodological approaches used in the various studies (Shah, Khang et al., 2023).

10.3.1 CONCEPTUAL FRAMEWORK

To begin with some of the pre-global financial crisis (2007–08) definitions are provided. The International Bank for Settlements described SR as the risk that the failure of a participant to meet its contractual obligations may in turn cause other participants to default, with the chain reaction leading to broader financial difficulties (BIS, 1994).

Similarly, for Kaufman (1996) SR is "the probability that cumulative losses will occur from an event that ignites a series of successive losses along a chain of institutions or markets comprising a system." After the crisis some more definitions emerged. According to Adrian et al. (2009), it is "the risk that institutional distress spreads widely and distorts the supply of credit and capital to the real economy."

Broadly, the European Central Bank (ECB) (2010) characterized it as a risk of financial instability "so widespread that it impairs the functioning of a financial system to the point where economic growth and welfare suffer materially." It is generally acknowledged that SR is the risk of the occurrence of an event that threatens the well-functioning of the system and sometimes to the point of making its operation impossible (Pe et al., 2010). It is viewed to be more damaging than other failures as it impacts the other components of the financial system, leading to system-wide failure.

Alternatively, Betz et al. (2016) defined SR as the propensity of a financial institution being undercapitalized when the financial system is under stress. All these definitions posit that it is a risk at an institutional level that can spill over to the entire economy and can bring down the economic value by the cumulative losses of the participants leading to an adverse effect on the economy (Chauhan et al., 2023).

SR is triggered by SBs, making it one of the potential challenges in creating distress in the economy. The recent banking and financial literature provides several meanings of SB. In the narrow approach, an SB is a system of credit intermediation that involves entities and activities outside the regular banking system and raises the SR concern in particular by maturity and liquidity transformation, leverage, and flawed credit transfer and/or regulatory arbitrage concern. It is a network of specialized financial institutions that channels funding from savers to investors through a range of securitization and secured funding techniques (Pozsar et al., 2010).

They are specialized financial institutions outside the regular banking system involved in credit intermediation activities through a range of techniques that might lead to SR concern due to the maturity liquidity leverage and regulatory arbitrage. The major drivers of shadow banking that emerge from the survey of the previous literature in this field are tight banking regulation, economic growth, innovation, high demand from institutional investors, the search for yield, and the overall development of the financial sector (Claessens et al., 2014; Duca, 2016; Ghosh et al., 2012; Pozsar et al., 2013).

The inclination of financial institutions to avoid taxes, accounting rules, or capital requirements (arbitrage) is also a major driver of shadow banking expansion (Ashcraft et al., 2013) and moreover some specific country-related factors also contribute towards the growth of SBs. The growth of SBs is a major concern due to the opacity and reduced transparency in their operation, which may lead to SR. IMF (2014) suggests that a search for yield, regulatory arbitrage, institutional cash pools, and financial developments contribute to the growth of the shadow banking (Khang & Rashmi et al., 2024).

In the context of emerging economies, the studies reveal that SBs play an important role in financial market inclusion (Hajilee et al., 2017). Their activities help in financial inclusion as they act as a substitute for direct lending for non-urban parts of the economy (Acharya et al., 2013; Du et al., 2016; Acharya et al., 2017). They also provide funds to the sectors which would otherwise have no access to credit and provide investors and banks with a range of tools for liquidity maturity and credit risk management (Ghosh et al., 2012).

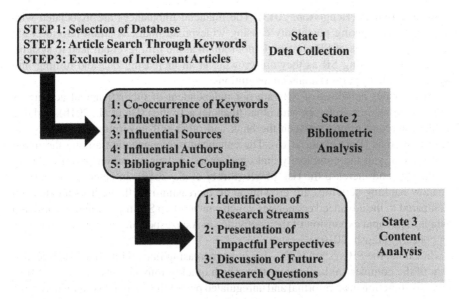

FIGURE 10.1 Workflow of shadow banking used in the present study.

Source: Nath et al., 2021.

SBs play a crucial role in broadening access to financial services, enhancing competition, diversification of the financial sector, and add to economic strength to the extent that they enhance the resilience of the financial system to economic shocks (Sinha, 2013). With the development of SBs in India, they have challenged the traditional banks to improve their services with a range of innovations to improve quality and competence at competitive prices, as shown in Figure 10.1. Apart from that, many unreached areas were first explored by NBFCs before the banks had entered the market which helped in the financial inclusion of the economy (Ashcraft et al., 2015).

10.3.2 Relationship of SBs and SR

Traditionally, SR was only associated with banks. Banks were found to be more fragile and susceptible to runs (Kaufman, 1996). As banks held most of the public deposits, the failure of a bank was not limited to a single banking entity but spread its wings over the entire economy, creating instability as a whole (Lehar, 2005). The greater concentration on interbank connections can lead to systemic risk (Wihlborg, 2018). Shadow banks were considered to be one of the major contributors to SR during the financial crisis of 2008 (FSB, 2011). They played a contagious role during the crisis (Pozsar et al., 2013).

The Financial Stability Board (FSB, 2011) mentioned that the recent financial crisis has shown that the SB system can also become the source of SR due to its interconnectedness with regular banking activities and these risks can spill over to the entire economy. Therefore, it is well understood that financial stability is linked to their activities (Bengtsson, 2013). The financial imbalances are associated with aggressive risk taking potentially causing widespread financial strain (Borio et al., 2009). Any failures of SB entities do not remain at the firm level but lead to system-wide failure causing SR as they are growing at an increasing rate and turning into systematically important financial institutions.

The various activities of SBs are not independent of other financial activity as there are some interlinkages with other financial activities (Du et al., 2016). and due to the interconnections between the bank and other self-governing bodies this can lead to a crisis (Betz et al., 2016). The enhanced interconnection among the financial system, and the complexity and opaqueness in their operation pose regulatory challenges and increase the risk of SR (Strobl et al., 2016). In emerging countries, shadow banking activities are growing at an increasing rate through loan extension compared to the advanced economies which can build up SR impacting the world as a whole. The rapid expansion of their activities in Asia, especially in China, is a matter of concern (Ghosh, 2019).

In China, the SB system is growing at an increasing rate and its size has exceeded that of the commercial banking system which quickly foments risk (Li et al., 2014). The SBs function in an informal and unregulated part of the financial system increasing SR (Du et al., 2016). However, in India, it appears to be the substitute for the bank's direct lending in non-urban areas and plays an important role in financial inclusion.

Most of the liabilities of NBFCs are due to bank lending which flows towards credit enhancement in rural areas. This growing interconnectedness between banks and NBFCs is building up more systemic risk (Acharya et al., 2013). They are prone to various shocks due to the opaqueness in their structure and operation (Barbora, 2018). The interconnectedness between Indian scheduled commercial banks (SCBs) and NBFCs is growing in the form of loans extended by SCBs, and equity holdings of NBFCs in SCBs are an important concern from the perspective of SR (RBI, 2018, 2019).

Indian SBs are fragile and vulnerable, suffering from a severe downturn in asset quality due to a lack of transparency in their operation. They are disorganized in their functions, which also results in regulatory arbitrage and which disrupts their endogeneity which has the capability of enhancing credit in the economy through their wide range of innovative products (Sinha, 2015). The empirical evidence reveals that among the top ten risks coming from institutions in India, four are NBFCs and six are banks. The Industrial Finance Corporation of India Limited (IFCI) transmits the highest risk to all other banks and financial institutions (Ahmad et al., 2019), as shown in Figure 10.2.

10.3.3   DRIVERS OF SYSTEMIC RISK

SBs contribute to SR through various channels. SR can evolve at an institutional (micro) level as well as at a macro-economic (domestic and global economic) level. The performance and efficiency level of a particular institution determine the level of risk built up along with the various macroeconomic factors. In the case of banks, various studies have found different performance- and efficiency-related drivers of SR. Some of those studies have been cited here. Factors of size, loan, high regulatory

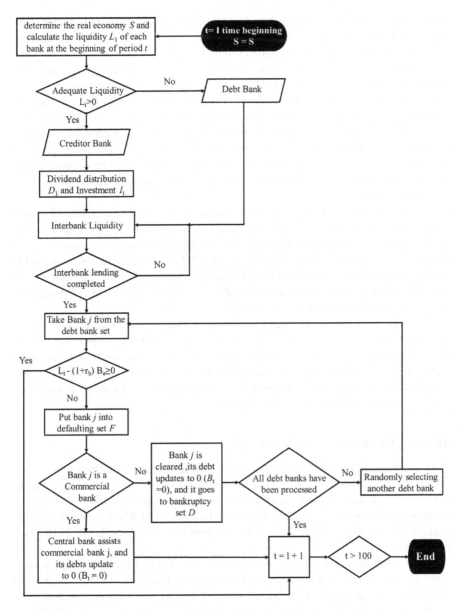

FIGURE 10.2 The dynamic process algorithm of the interbank system.

Source: Hong, 2020.

capital ratio have a positive impact on SR, whereas, non-performing loans, leverage, deposit ratio have an insignificant impact on SR (Kleinow et al., 2015).

Similarly, Weiß et al. (2014) also stated that bank leverage and loan to asset ratio do not build up SR but that quality of portfolio contributes more strongly to the SR.

Apart from size and interconnectedness, leverage also positively impacts the SR (Betz et al., 2016). The author also finds that the securitization activity of a firm determines an institution's systemic risk exposure (Sedunov, 2016).

Credit risk, liquidity risk, maturity transformation risk, and leverage have the potential to pose SR. However, risk taking is one of the inherent qualities of any banking business. But in times of crisis, a firm with higher SR exposure tends to perform poorly compared to firms with low exposure (Sedunov, 2016). Apart from the various risks, the size and pattern of ownership also play an important role in the efficiency of banks (Sarmiento et al., 2017). Though various studies have emphasized that SB activities lead to SR, at the same time those studies also reveal that the SB system supplements and complements the traditional banking system (Gandhi, 2014; Pozsar et al., 2013; Sinha, 2013).

In addition, a lack of efficiency in the banking sector and financial development of an economy play a key role in expanding shadow banking activities (Bose et al., 2012). They are vulnerable to liquidity shocks and are procyclical, raising issues for financial and macro-economic stability (Duca, 2016). Their activities are exposed to similar financial risks as traditional banks but they are not subject to the same degree of oversight and regulations, resulting in enhancement of liquidity risk, arbitrage risk, and procyclicality risk (Ghosh et al., 2012).

The sources of instability linked to SBs have been identified as leverage, moral hazard problem that leads to the origination of loans, and SB exposure to bank runs (Ferrante, 2018). The shadow banking system can raise the systemic risk in the financial markets by reinforcing interconnectedness between financial institutions, even though it has contributed to enhancing the efficiency of the financial markets and improving credit availability in the real sector.

10.3.4 METHODOLOGICAL APPROACH

Most of the studies in the area related to SBs and SR are of a descriptive nature and based on secondary sources of information. In most of the studies relating to measurement of SR, the common variables that were chosen are basically the size, connectedness, timing, leverage, market value of the assets, and return on income (Diallo et al., 2017; Han et al., 2013; Jobst, 2014; Kleinow et al., 2015; Sedunov, 2016; Weiß et al., 2014).

Apart from these variables, asset volatilities, asset correlations, and equity volatility are also used as variables to measure systemic risk (Lehar, 2005). In most of the studies, CoVaR, marginal expected shortfall (MES), and Gragner casuality tests are the most commonly used measurement techniques for assessing the SR (Benoit et al., 2017; Ferreira et al., 2018; Han et al., 2013; Jobst, 2014; Kleinow et al., 2015). Strobl et al. (2016) used the MES technique to measure SR and found that the book capital ratio and price ratio positively influence the SR, whereas loan growth negatively influences the SR.

Apart from CoVar and MES, other techniques that are used to measure SR are SRISK, SIZE, stress test, lower tail dependence, and contingent claim analysis (Jobst, 2014; Kleinow et al., 2015). Apart from analyzing risk there are some studies that are based on the growth of shadow banking and their role in financial inclusion. In most of those studies bank variables and macro-economic variables are chosen but the most commonly used variables are risk-weighted assets, capital adequacy ratio, return on assets (ROA), country GDP growth, leverage, and liquidity (Acharya et al., 2013; Colombo et al., 2016; Diallo et al., 2017; Du et al., 2016; Hajilee et al., 2017).

The measurement techniques that were considered to measure the stability and growth of shadow banking were Z score, SBM super efficiency model, neutral network mode, bank stress test, augmented Dickey Fuller (ADF) test, and Lagrange multiplier (LM). Further, the bank stress test, classical regression analysis, correlation analysis, time series measurement, chi square test, and F test were also used as measurement techniques. Ferrante (2018) used the medium-scale DSGE (dynamic scholastic general equilibrium) model to study the macroeconomic effects on SBs. While performances are examined mostly using accounting ratios, F-test assists in determining the financial performance of selected SBs for study on a random basis (Sinha, 2015).

10.3.5 LITERATURE GAP

The review of the literature indicates that there is a relationship between SR and SB activities. Some studies focused on various ways to measure systemic risk and the various factors that determine SR. However, most of the studies on SB were related to its size and its role in an economy. Very few studies have concentrated on how SB activities lead to SR. Studies on efficiency of SBs are very limited. Further, no concrete works on the SR measurement on SBs were found.

In India, this study articulates that SB activities play an important role in financial inclusion and also supplement and complement the traditional banking system. However, there is no recent study focusing on the relationship between SBs and SR and also the efficiency measurement of NBFCs was not found for India.

10.4 CONCLUSION

From the various empirical studies, it can be understood that SBs are one of the important components in the financial system. Globally, the growing size of SBs and their asset quality is a major concern, as the failure of one institution will have a major setback for other institutions due to increasing interconnections and interdependencies with the other components of the financial system simultaneously impacting the overall economy.

Most of the studies on SBs are concentrated in Europe, the USA, and China, but in India, not many studies have examined the SBs except Acharya et al. (2013) and Ahmad et al. (2019), which gave a deeper insight into the Indian shadow banking system. The study also identifies that there is a growing interconnection between SBs and SCBs, and bank lending forms a significant portion of the NBFC liabilities.

From the different academic literature sources, we can understand that shadow banking activities can build up SR but, empirically the studies on systemic risk assessment on SBs globally and in the Indian context have not been examined. Growing complexities in their activities make them vulnerable, which results in financial instability. The recent IL & FS crisis in India has emphasized the growing development of SR in the Indian financial system (Khang, Rani et al., 2023).

The study also reveals that the growing default on NBFCs is a result of most of the loans turning into NPAs. The range of studies highlighted the possibilities that may lead to SR which can be examined not only by taking into account the banks but also SBs. In India, over the year, shadow banking activities have been growing, which is a major concern, therefore assessing the various factors which have the potency to increase the SR can help in early detection and taking corrective action for the regulators. Performance measurement can be one of the ways which will help us detect the systemic risk exposure of an organization during a crisis, which can help in detecting the early warning indicators, as shown in Figure 10.3.

Simultaneously, the efficiency of banks plays a pivotal role in the growth of SBs. It impacts the risk-taking behavior and its contribution to SR. Empirically, the study of the efficiency and risk assessment of SBs is not examined. Although the RBI has listed NBFCs that are systemically important, to what extent an individual institution contributes towards the total SR has not been studied empirically, as shown in Figure 10.4.

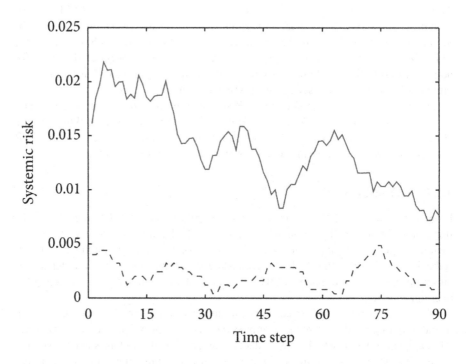

FIGURE 10.3   The impact of the existence of shadow banking.

Source: Hong, 2020.

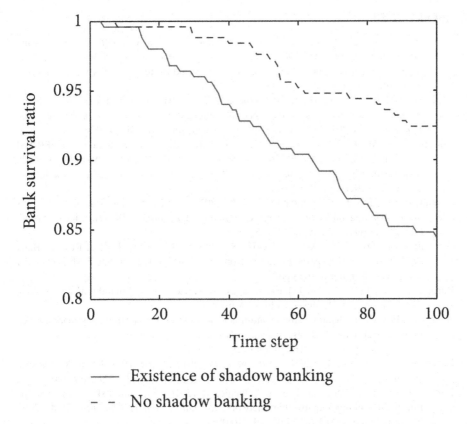

FIGURE 10.4 The impact of the existence of shadow banking on changes in bank survival ratio.

Source: Hong, 2020.

The studies of SBs and SR are of great relevance. SBs are one of the key components of the financial system. The study of SBs in India is very rare. However, the complexity and vulnerability of their functioning is a matter of concern. The shadow banking activities are growing at an increasing rate, which is a matter of concern especially in emerging countries. Therefore, the study of the systemic risk exposure of SBs will help in early detection of the various risks associated with this sector and the various factors which will contribute towards enhancement of the risk (Khang & AIoCF, 2024).

This study will help us understand the various factors that lead to SR, and consequently help policymakers to work on suitable strategies to monitor the activities of shadow banks and undertake preventive and corrective actions to check any economic downturn (Kali & Khang et al., 2024).

REFERENCES

Acharya, V., Brownlees, C., Engle, R., Pedersen, L., & Philippon, T. (2010). How to measure and regulate systemic risk. New York University Leonard N Stern School of Business, 1–18. Retrieved from: https://pages.stern.nyu.edu/~sternfin/vacharya/public_html/measuring_and_regulating_systemic_risk-1.pdf

Acharya, V. V., Khandwala, H., & Sabri Öncü, T. (2013). The growth of a shadow banking system in emerging markets: Evidence from India. *Journal of International Money and Finance*, 39(1), 207–230. https://doi.org/10.1016/j.jimonfin.2013.06.024

Adrian, T., & M. K. Brunnermeier (2009). CoVaR. Paper presented at the CEPR/ESI 13thAnnual Conference on "Financial Supervision in an Uncertain World" on 25–26 September 2009 in Venice. *Staff Report 348, Federal Reserve Bank of New York*. https://doi.org/10.1201/9781003145011

Ahmad, W., Pathak, B., & Bhanumurthy, N. R. (2019). Understanding systemic symptoms of non-banking financial companies. *Economic and Political Weekly*, 54(13), 59–67. https://doi.org/10.1201/9781003145011

Ashcraft, A. B., Adrian, T., Ashcraft, A. B., & Cetorelli, N. (2013). Federal Reserve Bank of New York Staff Reports. Retrieved from: www.newyorkfed.org/medialibrary/media/research/staff_reports/sr638.pdf

Barbora, L. P. (2018, December 11). Financial assets outpace physical in individual portfolios. *Livemint*, pp. 1–4. Retrieved from www.livemint.com

Bengtsson, E. (2013). Shadow banking and financial stability: European money market funds in the global financial crisis. *Journal of International Money and Finance,* 32(1), 579–594. https://doi.org/10.1016/j.jimonfin.2012.05.027

Benoit, S., Colliard, J. E., Hurlin, C., & Pérignon, C. (2017). Where the risks lie: A survey on systemic risk. *Review of Finance*, 21, 109–152. https://doi.org/10.1093/rof/rfw026

Betz, F., Hautsch, N., Peltonen, T. A., & Schienle, M. (2016). Systemic risk spillovers in the European banking and sovereign network. *Journal of Financial Stability*, 25(4), 206–224. https://doi.org/10.1016/j.jfs.2015.10.006

BIS. (1994). 64th Annual Report, *Bank for International Settlements*. Retrieved from www.bis.org/publ/ar67f02.pdf

Borio, C., & Drehmann, M. (2009). Assessing the risk of banking crises. *BIS Quarterly Review* (March), 29–46. Retrieved from www.bis.org/publ/qtrpdf/r_qt0903e.pdf

Bose, N., Capasso, S., & Wurm, M. A. (2012). The impact of banking development on the size of shadow economies. *Journal of Economic Studies*, 39(6), 620–638. https://doi.org/10.1108/01443581211274584

Chauhan, V. S., Chakravorty, J., & Khang, A. (2023). "Smart Cities Data Indicator-Based Cyber Threats Detection Using Bio-Inspired Artificial Algae Algorithm." In *Handbook of Research on AI-Based Technologies and Applications in the Era of the Metaverse.* Copyright: © 2023 I (pp. 436–447). https://doi.org/10.4018/978-1-6684-8851-5.ch024

Claessens, S., & Ratnovski, L. (2014). What is shadow banking? *IMF Working Papers*, 14(25). https://doi.org/10.5089/9781475597349.001

Colombo, E., Onnis, L., & Tirelli, P. (2016). Shadow economies at times of banking crises: *Empirics and theory. Journal of Banking and Finance*, 62(1), 180–190. https://doi.org/10.1016/j.jbankfin.2014.09.017

Diallo, B., & Al-Mansour, A. (2017). Shadow banking, insurance and financial sector stability. *Research in International Business and Finance*, 42(December), 224–232. https://doi.org/10.1016/j.ribaf.2017.04.024

Du, J., Li, C., & Wang, Y. (2016). A comparative study of shadow banking activities of non-financial firms in transition economies. *China Economic Review*, 46(5), 35–49. https://doi.org/10.1016/j.chieco.2016.09.001

Duca, J. V. (2016). How capital regulation and other factors drive the role of shadow banking in funding short-term business credit. *Journal of Banking and Finance*, 69(8), S10–S24. https://doi.org/10.1016/j.jbankfin.2015.06.016

Ferrante, F. (2018). A model of endogenous loan quality and the collapse of the shadow banking system. *American Economic Journal: Macroeconomics*,10(4),152–201. https://doi.org/10.1257/mac.20160118

Ferreira, H., Mendonça, D., & Bernardo, R. (2018). Effect of banking and macroeconomic variables on systemic risk: An application of Δ COVAR for an emerging economy. *North American Journal of Economics and Finance*, 43(1),141–157. https://doi.org/10.1016/j.najef.2017.10.011

FSB F. S. (2011). Shadow Banking: Strengthening Oversight and Regulation. Retrieved from: www.fsb.org/2012/11/r_121118/

FSB F. S. (2014). Global Shadow Banking Monitoring Report 2014. *Financial Stability Board* (October), 1–53. Retrieved from www.fsb.org/wpcontent/ uploads/r_141030. pdf

FSB F. S. (2017). Global Shadow Banking Monitoring Report 2017. Retrieved from www.fsb. org/wp-content/uploads/r_141030.pdf

Gandhi, R. (2014). Danger Posed by Shadow Banking Systems to the Global. Danger Posed by Shadow Banking Systems to the Global Financial System: The Indian Case. *In Address at the Indian Council for Research on International Economic Relations Conference on Governance and Development: Views from G20 Countries. Mumbai* (Vol. 21). (August), 25–32. Retrieved from www.bis.org/review/r140827b.pdf

Ghosh, C. P. C. (2019, March). Is shadow banking a serious threat in emerging markets? OPINION-The Hindu BusinessLine, pp. 1–4. Retrieved from www.thehindubusinessl ine.com/opinion/columns/c-p-chandrasekhar/is-shadow-bankinga-serious-threat-in-emerging-markets/article25656071.ece

Ghosh, S., Mazo, I. G. Del, & İnci Ötker-Robe. (2012). Chasing the Shadows: How Significant Is Shadow Banking in Emerging Markets? The World Bank, *Economic Premise*, 88(ic), 1–7. https://doi.org/10.2139/ssrn.1686004

Hajilee, M., Stringer, D. Y., & Metghalchi, M. (2017). New evidence from emerging economies. *Quarterly Review of Economics and Finance*, 66(4), 149–158. https://doi.org/10.1016/j.qref.2017.07.015

Han, J., & Jaemin, L. (2013). Measures of systemic risk and financial fragility in Korea. *Annals of Finance*, 9(4), 757–786. https://doi.org/10.1007/s10436-012-0218-x

Hede, S. (2019). Profile of the NBFC Sector based on RBI's study. Retrieved from www.care ratings.com

Hong, F., & Pan, H. (2020). The effect of shadow banking on the systemic risk in a dynamic complex interbank network system. Complexity, 2020, Article ID 3951892, 10 pages. https://doi.org/10.1155/2020/3951892

Jhajhria, H. (2018). Building the NBFC of the future-A scalable and profitable model PWC. Retrieved from www.pwc.in

Jobst, A. A. (2014). Systemic risk in the insurance sector: A review of current assessment approaches, In Courbage C. (Eds.), *The Geneva Papers. Palgrave Macmillan, London*, 39(3), 440–470. https://doi.org/10.1057/gpp.2013.7

Kantawala, A. S. (2001). Financial performance of non-banking finance companies in India. *Indian Economic Journal*, 49(1), 86–92. https://journals.sagepub.com/doi/pdf/10.1177/0019466220010109

Kaufman, G. G. (1996). Bank failures, systemic risk, and bank regulation. *Cato Journal*, 16, 17–45. https://heinonline.org/hol-cgi-bin/get_pdf.cgi?handle=hein.journals/cato j16&section=5

Khang A., and AIoCF. (Eds.). (2024). *AI-Oriented Competency Framework for Talent Management in the Digital Economy: Models, Technologies, Applications, and Implementation.* ISBN: 9781032576053. CRC Press. https://doi.org/10.1201/978100 3440901

Khang A., and AIoCF. (Eds.) (2024). Future directions and challenges in designing workforce management systems for industry 4. In *AI-Oriented Competency Framework for Talent Management in the Digital Economy: Models, Technologies, Applications, and Implementation.* ISBN: 9781032576053. CRC Press. https://doi.org/10.1201/978100 3440901-1

Khang, A., Kali, C. R., Satapathy, S. R., Kumar, A., Das, R. S., & Panda, M. R. (2023). Enabling the future of manufacturing: integration of robotics and IoT to smart factory infrastructure in industry 4.0. In *AI-Based Technologies and Applications in the Era of the Metaverse* (1st Ed.) (2023) (pp. 25–50). IGI Global Press. https://doi.org/10.4018/ 978-1-6684-8851-5.ch002

Khang, A., Muthmainnah, M., Seraj, P. M. I., Al Yakin, A., Obaid, A. J., & Panda, M. R. (2023). AI-aided teaching model for the education 5.0 ecosystem. In A. Khang, V. Shah, & S. Rani (Eds.), *AI-Based Technologies and Applications in the Era of the Metaverse* (1st Ed.) (pp. 83–104). IGI Global Press. https://doi.org/10.4018/978-1-6684-8851-5.ch004

Khang, A., Rani, S., Gujrati, R., Uygun, H., & Gupta S. K. (Eds.) (2023). *Designing Workforce Management Systems for Industry 4.0: Data-Centric and AI-Enabled Approaches.* CRC Press. https://doi.org/10.1201/9781003357070

Khang, A., Shah, V., & Rani, S. (2023). *AI-Based Technologies and Applications in the Era of the Metaverse.* (1st Ed.). IGI Global Press. https://doi.org/10.4018/978-1-6684-8851-5

Khang, A., Muthmainnah, M., Seraj, P. M. I., Al Yakin, A., Obaid, A. J., & Panda, M. R. (2023). An innovative teaching model – the potential of metaverse for English learning. In A. Khang, V. Shah, & S. Rani (Eds.), *AI-Based Technologies and Applications in the Era of the Metaverse* (1st Ed.) (pp. 105–126). IGI Global Press. https://doi.org/10.4018/ 978-1-6684-8851-5.ch005

Kleinow, J., Nell, T., & Kleinow, J. (2015). Determinants of systemically important banks: the case of Europe. *Journal of Financial Economic Policy*, 7(4), 446–476. https://doi.org/ 10.1108/JFEP-07-2015-0042

Lehar, A. (2005). Measuring systemic risk: A risk management approach. *Journal of Banking and Finance*, 29(10), 2577–2603. https://doi.org/10.1016/j.jbankfin.2004.09.007

Li, J., Hsu, S., & Qin, Y. (2014). Shadow banking in China: *Institutional risks. China Economic Review*, 31(4), 119–129. https://doi.org/10.1016/j.chieco.2014.08.003

Luttrell, D., Rosenblum, H., & Thies, J. (2012). Understanding the risks inherent in shadow banking: A primer and practical lessons learned. *Federal Reserve Bank of Dallas* (18), 47. Retrieved from https://ideas.repec.org/a/fip/feddst/y2012inovn18.html

Lysandrou, P., & Nesvetailova, A. (2015). The role of shadow banking entities in the financial crisis: A disaggregated view. *Review of International Political Economy*, 22(2), 257–279. https://doi.org/10.1080/09692290.2014.896269

McCulley, P. (2007). Teton Reflections, PIMCO Global Central Bank Focus, No. 2. https://doi.org/10.1201/9781003145011

Nath & Chowdhury (2021) From Financial Innovation – SpringerOpen, accessed 22 March 2023, https://jfin-swufe.springeropen.com/articles/10.1186/s40854-021-00286-6

Pe, O., Dey, G., Embriz, F. A., & Lo, F. (2010). Systemic risk, financial contagion and financial fragility. Journal of Economic Dynamics & Control, 34(11), 2358–2374. https://doi.org/ 10.1016/j.jedc.2010.06.004

Pooja, K., Jadhav, B., Kulkarni, A., Khang, A., & Kulkarni, S. (2023). "The Role of Blockchain Technology in Metaverse Ecosystem." In A. Khang, V. Shah, & S. Rani (Eds.), *AI-Based*

Technologies and Applications in the Era of the Metaverse (1st Ed.) (pp. 228–236). IGI Global Press. https://doi.org/10.4018/978-1-6684-8851-5.ch011

Pozsar, Z., Adrian, T., Ashcraft, A., & Boesky, H. (2013). Shadow banking. FRBNY *Economic Policy Review*, 1–16. https://link.springer.com/chapter/10.1057/9781137553799_29

RBI. (2010). Report on Trend and Progress of Banking In India 2009-10 Reserve Bank Of India. Retrieved from https://rbidocs.rbi.org.in/rdocs/Publications/PDFs

RBI. (2018). Report on Trend and Progress of Banking in India 2017-18 (Vol. 36). Retrieved from https://rbidocs.rbi.org.in/rdocs/Publications/PDFs

RBI. (2019a). *Financial Stability Report*. Retrieved from www.snb.ch/en/iabout/pub/oecpub/id/pub_oecpub_stabrep

RBI. (2019b). RBI Bulletin. RBI Bulletin, LXXIII NUM (7), 1–108. Retrieved from https://bulletin.rbi.org.in/

Sarmiento, M., & Galán, J. E. (2017). The influence of risk-taking on bank efficiency: Evidence from Colombia. *Emerging Market Review*, 32(4), 52–73. https://doi.org/10.1016/j.ememar.2017.05.007

Saxena, A. C., Ojha, A., Sobti, D., & Khang, A. (2023). "Artificial Intelligence (AI) Centric Model in Metaverse Ecosystem." In A. Khang, V. Shah, & S. Rani (Eds.), *AI-Based Technologies and Applications in the Era of the Metaverse* (1st Ed.) (pp. 1–24). IGI Global Press. https://doi.org/10.4018/978-1-6684-8851-5.ch001

Sedunov, J. (2016). What is the systemic risk exposure of financial institutions? *Journal of Financial Stability*, 24(3), 71–87. https://doi.org/10.1016/j.jfs.2016.04.005

Shah, V., & Khang, A. (2023). "Metaverse-Enabling IoT Technology for a Futuristic Healthcare System." In A. Khang, V. Shah, & S. Rani (Eds.), *AI-Based Technologies and Applications in the Era of the Metaverse* (1st Ed.) (pp. 165–173). IGI Global Press. https://doi.org/10.4018/978-1-6684-8851-5.ch008

Sherpa, D. (2013). Shadow banking in India and China: Causes and consequences. *Economic and Political Weekly*, 48(43), 113–122. www.jstor.org/stable/23528847

Sihare, S. R. & Khang, A. (2023). "Effects of Quantum Technology on Metaverse," In A. Khang, V. Shah, & S. Rani (Eds.), *AI-Based Technologies and Applications in the Era of the Metaverse* (1st Ed.) (pp. 104–203). IGI Global Press. https://doi.org/10.4018/978-1-6684-8851-5.ch009

Sinha, A. (2013). Regulation of shadow banking – issues and challenges. *BIS Central Banker Speeches*. https://doi.org/10.1201/9781003145011

Sinha, A. (2015). Non-Banking Financial Institutions of India- Their Onset, Growth and Performance of Selected NBFCs. *The Institute of Company Secretaries of India*. Retrieved from: www.icsi.edu/media/portals/86/manorama/DBIMS%20Journal%20.pdf

Strobl, S., & Strobl, S. (2016). Stand-alone vs systemic risk-taking of financial institutions. *Journal of Risk Finance*, 17(4), 374–389. https://doi.org/10.1108/JRF-05-2016-0064

Vishwanathan N.S. (2018). RBI Bulletin January 2018. In RBI Bulletin. Retrieved from https://bulletin.rbi.org.in/

Weiß, G. N. F., Bostandzic, D., & Neumann, S. (2014). What factors drive systemic risk during international financial crises? *Journal of Banking and Finance*, 41(4), 78–96. https://doi.org/10.1016/j.jbankfin.2014.01.001

Wihlborg, C. (2018). Systemic risk and the organization of the financial system: overview. *Journal of Financial Economic Policy*, 10(2), 202–212. https://doi.org/10.1108/JFEP-02-20180021

11 The Potential of a Fintech-Driven Model in Enabling Financial Inclusion

Muhammed Basid Amnas, Murugesan Selvam, and Chinnadurai Kathiravan

11.1 INTRODUCTION

Access to finance, investment, and development of the financial sector have been the major policy objective of the government of India. This has been realized over the past few years, with the help of fintech and the digitalization policy of the government (Datta & Singh, 2019). Today, the importance of digital finance and financial inclusion towards poverty reduction and economic growth is attracting the attention of policymakers because digital money works better for the growth of individuals, businesses, governments, and the economy (Senyo & Osabutey, 2020).

According to Rangarajan, financial inclusion is defined as the process of ensuring timely access to financial services and fulfilling credit needs, particularly for vulnerable groups such as weaker sections of society and low-income groups, at an affordable cost (Reserve Bank of India [RBI], 2019a). It is also worth recalling that the United Nations Sustainable Development Goals (UNSDGs) subsume financial inclusion as the key to achieving sustainable development globally, by improving the standard of living of the poor and disadvantaged sections of society (Raj & Upadhyay, 2020). To achieve the objectives of financial inclusion in a systematic and timely manner, the National Strategy for Financial Inclusion (2019–24) was prepared by the Reserve Bank of India. Under this strategy, fintech is considered one of the important tools for the successful adoption of financial inclusion (Makina, 2019).

The term "fintech" is a combination of the words, "finance" and "technology." Fintech is broadly defined as the technology-enabled innovation in financial services, that could result in new business models, applications, processes, or products with an associated material effect on the provision of financial services (International Monetary Fund [IMF], 2020). Fintech is using software, applications, and digital platforms, to deliver financial services to consumers and businesses, simply and easily (Morgan & Long, 2020).

DOI: 10.1201/9781032618845-11

A few of the latest fintech options used by individuals include crowdfunding, digital payment systems, peer-to-peer (P2P), electronic wallets, Robo-advisor, and InsurTech (Wang & Guan, 2017). Fintech firms play an important role in extending financial inclusion in India, by reducing costs and improving the access to financial services for people in low-income, rural, and other disadvantaged sectors. Nowadays, commercial banks and fintech companies work together to discover a simpler and faster method of financial services that could reduce unnecessary costs (Khurana, 2018).

The Indian government has already adopted several financial inclusion strategies through fintech and one such strategy is to improve the payment system, by introducing Immediate Payments Service (IMPS), Unified Payments Interface (UPI), Bharat Money Interface (BHIM), Barat Bill Pay System (BBPS), and Aadhaar Enabled Payment System (AEPS). Thus, the face of the Indian financial system is changing with fintech (Raj & Upadhyay, 2020). India, a developing country, welcomes fintech's opportunities to boost economic growth and financial inclusion (Kandpal & Mehrotra, 2019). RegTech and SupTech are emerging new technologies that would help to improve efficiency through automation, introducing new skills, and facilitating workflow (Barruetabeña, 2020).

New technologies transform the provision of financial services and therefore, it is important to understand the implications of these developments in economic growth, especially financial inclusion (Romero & Ahamed, 2020). The relevance of fintech and financial inclusion towards poverty reduction and economic growth has been attracting the attention of policymakers. The latest reports show the significant growth of the fintech industry in India. This is the best time to use the potential of fintech, to provide prompt financial services for the poor and disadvantaged sections of society, at a minimal cost.

The remainder of this chapter is structured as follows. Section 11.2 presents the growth of fintech and its impact on financial services. Section 11.3 presents the government initiatives to promote fintech and financial inclusion in India. Section 11.4 describes the key challenges to the fintech sector in India. Section 11.5 points out the future direction for the fintech sector. Finally, Section 11.6 presents the conclusion of the chapter (Khang, Shah et al., 2023).

11.2   GROWTH OF FINTECH AND ITS INFLUENCE ON FINANCIAL SERVICES

According to the EY Global Fintech Adoption Index (2019), fintech services continued to rise sharply, from 16% in 2015, the year in which the first FinTech Adoption Index was published, to 33% in 2017 and later to 64% in 2019. Awareness of fintech was satisfactory even among non-adopters. For example, 96% of consumers knew at least one available fintech service, to transfer money and pay. Fintech is an industry that has evolved beyond its first stages, to deliver much of customer expectations. Fintech has gripped the world, by entering the mainstream in every market. Emerging markets are leading the way in both China and India, and the adoption rate in India was at

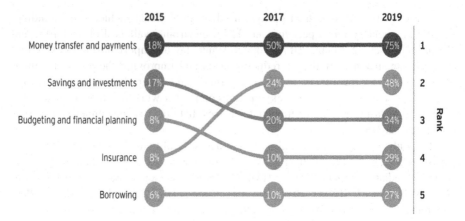

FIGURE 11.1　Fintech categories ranked by adoption rate from 2015 to 2019.

Source: EY Global Fintech Adoption Index 2019.

87%, followed by Russia and South Africa, both with 82% adoption rates. Among the developed countries, the Netherlands, the UK, and Ireland lead in adoption. It is clear from Figure 11.1 that people mostly use fintech for money transfers and payments and it is least used for borrowing (Rana et al., 2021).

　　PwC's (PricewaterhouseCoopers) Global Fintech Report 2019 found that consumers are ready to accept digital financial services. The question is no longer whether fintech will change financial services, but which firms will use it effectively and emerge as leaders. The report predicts that the winning companies would be those that would find a better way to use fintech to provide financial services. The PwC study found that 47% of TMT (technology, multimedia, and telecommunication) and 48% of FS (financial service) organizations, incorporated fintech completely into their performance model. Besides, 44% of TMT and 37% of FS organizations have incorporated emerging technologies into the products and services they sell. Many TMT companies applied for FS licenses and FS organizations are ready to call themselves technology companies (Khanh & Khang et al., 2021).

　　The IMF report (2020) "The Promise of Fintech: Financial Inclusion in the Post Covid-19 Eras" clearly shows that digital finance has been increasing financial inclusion and leading to higher GDP growth. The report found that digital financial inclusion could play a key role in reducing the economic and social impact of the ongoing COVID-19 disaster. Expanding access to finance, for low-income households and small businesses, could also support inclusive recovery. The IMF's digital financial inclusion index reveals that digital financial inclusion has increased significantly in recent years and in some countries, digital financial inclusion is a game-changer. Besides, fintech plays a role in closing the gender gaps in financial inclusion across different regions. Gender gaps are lower in fintech-driven financial inclusion compared to traditional financial systems.

　　According to a report by Deloitte (2017), entitled "FinTech in India – Ready for Breakout," fintech firms could reshape financial services in India as they could create unique and innovative risk assessment models. By using big data, machine learning, and other data to underwrite the credit and develop credit scores for customers with a limited credit history, access to financial services and financial inclusion in India could be improved.

11.3 GOVERNMENT INITIATIVES TO PROMOTE FINTECH AND FINANCIAL INCLUSION IN INDIA

11.3.1 NATIONAL STRATEGY FOR FINANCIAL INCLUSION (NSFI)

The National Strategy for Financial Inclusion (NSFI) (2019–2024) sets out the vision and objectives of the financial inclusion strategies in India to expand and sustain the national financial inclusion process, through a comprehensive engagement process, involving all stakeholders in the financial sector. The strategy aims to provide access to formal financial services and promote financial literacy and consumer protection. The National Strategy for Financial Inclusion (2019–2024) was prepared by the RBI, under the auspices of the Financial Inclusion Advisory Committee and the strategy was based on inputs and recommendations from the government of India, other financial sector regulators, the Securities Exchange Board of India (SEBI), Insurance Regulatory and Development Authority of India (IRDAI), and the Pension Fund Regulatory and Development Authority of India (PFRDA). Figure 11.2 shows the Strategic Pillars of the National Strategy for Financial Inclusion (Khang, Rani

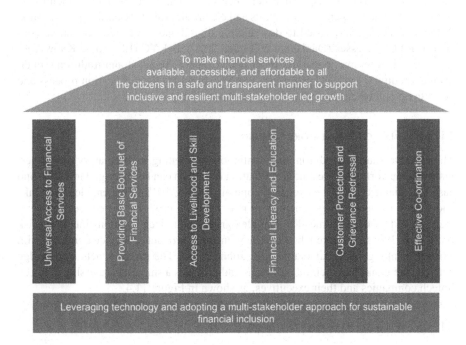

FIGURE 11.2   Strategic pillars of the National Strategy for Financial Inclusion.

Source: National Strategy for Financial Inclusion 2019–2024.

et al., 2023). The NSFI aims to make financial services available, accessible, and affordable to all citizens, securely and transparently, to promote sustainable growth. The strategic objectives of the policy include universal access to financial services, by providing a basic bouquet of financial services such as Access to Livelihood and Skill Development, Financial Literacy and Education, Customer Protection and Grievance Redressal, and Effective Coordination.

11.3.2   HIGH-LEVEL COMMITTEE ON DEEPENING OF DIGITAL PAYMENTS

The Reserve Bank of India is committed to promoting and deepening financial inclusion in India. To promote digital payments and improve financial inclusion through digitization, the RBI established a High-Level Committee on Deepening Digital Payments, under the Chairmanship of Shri. Nandan Nilekani, in January 2019. The committee reviewed the current state of digital payments in financial transactions, identifying best practices, recommending ways to strengthen the safety and security of digital payments, increasing confidence in digital financial services, and proposing a medium-term strategy to deepen digital payments.

11.3.3   E-KYC

Aadhaar KYC is a paperless process of Know Your Customer (KYC), through which the identity and address of the registrant are verified electronically through Aadhaar Authentication. The widespread acceptance of Aadhaar, the biometric identity in India, has helped to open bank accounts and electronic wallets (Bhardwaj & Kaushik, 2018). E-KYC is a term used to describe the digital and electronic and online concept of KYC processes (Danisman & Tarazi, 2020). E-KYC (Electronic Know Your Customer) is a remote, paperless process that reduces the cost and traditional management required for KYC processes. E-KYC simplifies the verification process and helps to open financial accounts faster, as shown in Figure 11.3.

11.3.4   FINTECH REGULATORY SANDBOX

The Reserve Bank of India is also continuously aligning its regulatory and supervisory frameworks. As a result, the evolution of fintech can be leveraged to widen and ease financial access by the excluded population (Das, 2019). This enables the banks and fintech players to experiment with new financial products or services, within a well-defined space and time. The complex growth of fintech solutions increased risk levels also. It has to ensure whether a new financial product or service complies with existing banking standards (Jagtiani & John, 2018). The sandbox acts as a bridge between the banks and their new systems and provides a smooth partnership between fintech companies and their executives, as shown in Figure 11.4.

11.3.5   UNIFIED PAYMENTS INTERFACE (UPI)

The Unified Payment Interface is one of the important steps in achieving a cashless economy (Bhardwaj & Kaushik, 2018). The UPI model allows everyone to use a

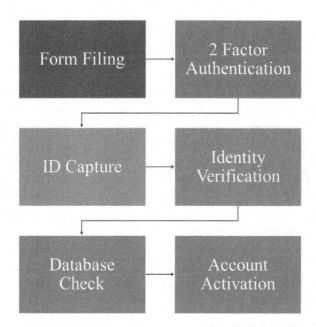

FIGURE 11.3 E-KYC process.

FIGURE 11.4 Regulatory sandbox lifecycle process.

smartphone as a tool for making financial transactions (Figure 11.5). The UPI ID and pin are enough to send and receive money. One can make transactions faster with the help of UPI now. UPI is an initiative taken by the National Payments Corporation of India (NPCI), the Reserve Bank of India (RBI), and the Indian Banks Association (IBA). Nowadays, one need not have an account number, IFSC code, account type, bank name, etc., to pay money. Instead, one can transfer the money by knowing only the Aadhaar number and mobile phone number registered with a bank account, or UPI ID (Khang & AIoCF, 2024).

11.3.6 OTHER INITIATIVES

There are many other initiatives that include the following:

- The other initiatives include Immediate Payments Service (IMPS), Unified Payments Interface (UPI), Bharat Interface for Money (BHIM), Bharat Bill Pay System (BBPS), and Aadhaar-enabled Payment System (AePS).

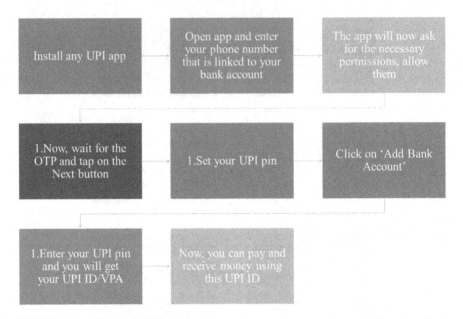

FIGURE 11.5   How does UPI work.

- Direct Benefit Transfer (DBT), under Government schemes, to Aadhaar-linked Bank Accounts.
- The Reserve Bank of India has also licensed several firms to use peer-to-peer (P2P) platforms that have the potential to improve access to finance, for individuals and SMEs.
- The Trade Receivables Discounting System (TReDs) is a new financing system where technology is used to discount bills and invoices.

11.4   KEY CHALLENGES TO THE FINTECH SECTOR IN INDIA

The following are the main challenges to the fintech sector in India.

11.4.1   CYBER SECURITY AND DATA PROTECTION

Indian fintech companies had increased in number and established interfaces with banks and other information sources such as the UID database. Interfaces between systems could present cyber vulnerabilities and data security issues (Bongomin & Ntayi, 2020). The issues of data privacy and customer protection are the major concerns in the present situation. Fintech companies will not be able to access sensitive financial information about customers but may be able to collect more information about their customers (Ozili, 2018). The strong security mechanisms and procedures to address these concerns are an important part of the fintech sector.

11.4.2 Gain Trust in Fintech Products

Mutual trust is always an important factor in the financial services industry. Indian consumers are known to have a conservative mindset and they are more comfortable with physical transactions, including spending (Kandpal & Mehrotra, 2019). However, the percentage of people who want an online transaction has increased recently. The unbanked and underbanked sectors have limited information on banking services. Therefore, it is a challenge to build trust and accept the services offered by fintech companies (Demir et al., 2020). Changing the way consumers perceive and receive financial services is critical to the broad acceptance of the fintech industry (Barruetabeña, 2020). It is equally challenging to educate the target audience on the appropriateness of access to financial services through fintech.

11.4.3 Regulatory Measures to Improve Quality of Fintech Products

Legal clarity will strengthen the finance industry over time to gain customer trust, and thus attract more capital investment (Lim et al., 2019). Fintech companies are required to undergo more scrutiny from regulators. Many interventions such as the Bharat Bill Payment System (BBPS), Payments Bank licenses, Unified Payment Interface (UPI), etc., by the government, have increased the growth of the fintech sector. A major challenge for the regulator is to create an environment that promotes creativity in respect of customer protection, data security, and privacy (Stewart & Jürjens, 2018).

11.4.4 Development of Financial Infrastructure and Utilities

A new fintech business requires data and infrastructure. The government has to create a financial environment that promotes technological innovation, without compromising the data security of the individuals concerned (Wang & Guan, 2017). The government, in the recent past, has taken major steps to expand digital infrastructures, such as Immediate Payments Service (IMPS), Unified Payments Interface (UPI), Bharat Money Interface (BHIM), Barat Bill Pay System (BBPS), and Aadhaar Enabled Payment System (AEPS). It is expected that the government will continue this digital infrastructure development, without compromising on security, for extending financial inclusion to underbanked segments effectively (Beck et al., 2018).

11.5 THE WAY FORWARD

11.5.1 Cooperation between Commercial Banks and Fintech Companies

The ability of commercial banks and financial institutions, to work with fintech could be a major competitive advantage in the years to come (Khurana, 2018). Hence the Reserve Bank of India should encourage commercial banks to establish cooperation with fintech companies as this is necessary for speeding up the financial inclusion process. The PwC 2019 Global Fintech Survey clearly emphasizes that in the pace of technological development, financial institutions cannot ignore fintech companies. Fintech could help commercial banks and financial institutions to reduce costs, improve their performance and customer retention, and generate revenue (Shah & Khang, 2023).

11.5.2 PROTECTION OF PERSONAL DATA

Fintech companies collect a lot of data from their customers and use the same for marketing and analysis of their creditworthiness. Therefore, to address concerns regarding the protection of personal data and digital privacy in India, the Personal Data Protection Bill 2019 was introduced in the Indian Parliament and referred to the Joint Committee of Parliament for consultation with various stakeholders. The successful implementation of this law would lead to a new dawn of privacy in India, ensuring greater performance of fintech companies, and improving financial inclusion throughout India (Bansal, 2014).

11.5.3 FOCUS ON RURAL POPULATION

According to India FinTech Report 2019, fintech firms need to improve the quality of life of underbanked communities and individuals, especially in rural and semi-urban India. As per the World Bank Report (2018), 65% of the population in India is still from rural areas and many of these people are not aware of the formal financial system. The digitalization of financial services is one of the best ways to reach the poorest people located in remote areas of India at a minimal cost.

11.5.4 FINTECH ADOPTION IN SME SECTOR

Small and medium enterprises (SMEs) are an important part of the Indian economy. Fintech could create tailored financial products, as per the needs of SME businesses (Bongomin & Ntayi, 2020). Indeed, the majority of Indian retailers are part of the digital world. Recently, the number of firms accepting digital payments has been increasing due to the digital policy of the Indian government. It is believed that fintech could bring an innovative business model to the SME sector which would increase the efficiency and effectiveness of small businesses in India (Datta & Singh, 2019).

11.5.5 GENDER GAP IN FINANCIAL INCLUSION

Financial inclusion and empowerment of women could have a significant social and economic impact. The World Bank Global Findex 2017 report found that men are more financially included than women. Therefore, as recommended by the High-Level Committee on Deepening Digital Payments, gender data need to be collected to know the gender gap and finally remove it. In this regard, fintech could empower women by designing financial products and services exclusively for women, and for this purpose, an arrangement must be made for deploying them with mobile phones and the internet (Radcliffe & Voorhies 2012). This would increase their access to such products and services. Fintech needs to use the appropriate research methods to gather the necessary data for this purpose (Senyo &

Osabutey, 2020). In the long run, such efforts would reduce or remove the gender gap in financial inclusion.

11.5.6   DESIGNING TAILORED FINANCIAL PRODUCTS

In India, enhancing access to financial services through Fintech is essential. Therefore, designing tailored financial products to address the specific needs of people who were financially excluded is essential to achieve the goal of financial inclusion (Datta & Singh, 2019). As stated earlier, fintech can improve financial services, such as payment, credit, insurance, and pensions, by introducing digital features or creating functional efficiency to bring more access to customer experiences (Lacasse et al., 2016). In practice, the players often collect better data for developing more options for further product improvement. It is easier to develop financial products for different customer groups based on their needs with the help of fintech. It could also attract financially excluded people to the formal financial system (Sihare et al., 2023).

11.5.7   DIGITAL FINANCIAL LITERACY

The efforts of India to expand access to formal financial systems through digital payments could gain momentum only with increased digital knowledge among the public (Raj & Upadhyay, 2020). The digital culture spreads rapidly through digital payments, online shopping, etc. This is the perfect time for India to accelerate digital literacy campaigns, as shown in Figure 11.6.

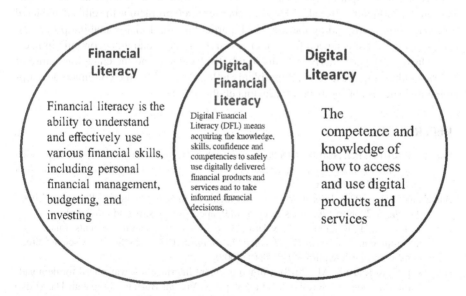

FIGURE 11.6   Digital financial literacy.

11.6 CONCLUSION

Incorporating the Internet of Things (IoT) as a crucial element, Industry 4.0 has transformed various sectors by enabling a variety of smart devices to connect and communicate with each other. This technology has increased productivity, efficiency, and safety in numerous industries. Smart factories, which are highly automated and networked industrial facilities, are made possible by IoT technology and are indispensable in Industry 4.0. In smart factories, IoT devices monitor and enhance manufacturing processes, anticipate maintenance requirements, and improve product quality. Additionally, logistics, inventory, and supply chain management processes are made more efficient through the use of IoT technology (Khang. Kali et al., 2023).

Gaining insights into consumer behavior, market trends, and manufacturing methods by gathering and analyzing massive amounts of data from interconnected devices is one of the primary advantages of the IoT in Industry 4.0 (Pooja et al., 2023). These data can be utilized by businesses to make better decisions and operate their operations more efficiently. However, implementing IoT in Industry 4.0 also comes with challenges, including the need for robust cybersecurity measures to protect sensitive data, the high cost of implementation, and the potential for job displacement due to increased automation (Khang et al., 2023).

11.7 FUTURE SCOPE OF WORK IN INDUSTRY 4.0

While Industry 4.0 presents exciting opportunities for growth and innovation, there are still research problems that need to be addressed to fully realize it's potential. One such problem is the lack of standardization in IoT devices and data analytics, which can result in compatibility issues and hinder seamless integration across various systems (Muthmainnah et al., 2023). Another research problem is the ethical and legal considerations surrounding the use of AI, particularly in decision-making processes. Additionally, there is a need for further research on the social and economic impacts of Industry 4.0, particularly in terms of job displacement and the changing nature of work. Addressing these research problems will be crucial for the continued development and success of Industry 4.0 (Saxena et al., 2023).

REFERENCES

Bansal, S. (2014). Perspective of technology in achieving financial inclusion in rural India. *Procedia Economics and Finance,* 11, 472–480. www.sciencedirect.com/science/arti cle/pii/S2212567114002135

Barruetabeña, E. (2020). Impact of new technologies on financial inclusion. *Banco de Espana Article,* 5, 20. https://papers.ssrn.com/sol3/papers.cfm?abstract_id=3678000

Beck, T., Pamuk, H., Ramrattan, R., & Uras, B. R. (2018). Payment instruments, finance and development. *Journal of Development Economics,* 133, 162–186. www.sciencedirect. com/science/article/pii/S0304387818300075

Bhardwaj, S., & Kaushik, M. (2018). Unified payment interface – A way ahead for demonetization in India. In Suresh Chandra Satapathy, Vikrant Bhateja, Swagatam Das (Eds.) *Smart Computing and Informatics* (pp. 273–280). Springer, Singapore. https://link.sprin ger.com/chapter/10.1007/978-981-10-5547-8_29

Bongomin, G. O. C., & Ntayi, J. M. (2020). Mobile money adoption and usage and financial inclusion: mediating effect of digital consumer protection. *Digital Policy, Regulation and Governance*, 22(3). www.emerald.com/insight/content/doi/10.1108/DPRG-01-2019-0005

Bongomin, G. O. C., Mpeera Ntayi, J., & Munene, J. C. (2017). Institutional framing and financial inclusion: Testing the mediating effect of financial literacy using SEM bootstrap approach. *International Journal of Social Economics*, 44(12), 1727–1744. www.emerald.com/insight/content/doi/10.1108/IJSE-02-2015-0032/full/html

Danisman, G. O., & Tarazi, A. (2020). Financial inclusion and bank stability: evidence from Europe. *The European Journal of Finance*, 26(18), 1842–1855. www.tandfonline.com/doi/abs/10.1080/1351847X.2020.1782958

Das, S. (2019). Opportunities and challenges of FinTech. *Keynote Address Delivered at NITI.* https://papers.ssrn.com/sol3/papers.cfm?abstract_id=3591018

Datta, S. K., & Singh, K. (2019). Variation and determinants of financial inclusion and their association with human development: A cross-country analysis. *IIMB Management Review*, 31(4), 336–349. www.sciencedirect.com/science/article/pii/S0970389616301574

Deloitte (2017). FinTech in India – Ready for Breakout. Available at: www2.deloitte.com/in/en/pages/financial-services/articles/fintech-india-ready-for-breakout.html

Demir, A., Pesqué-Cela, V., Altunbas, Y., & Murinde, V. (2020). Fintech, financial inclusion and income inequality: A quantile regression approach. *The European Journal of Finance*, 1–22. www.tandfonline.com/doi/abs/10.1080/1351847X.2020.1772335

Gutiérrez-Romero, R., & Ahamed, M. (2021). COVID-19 response needs to broaden financial inclusion to curb the rise in poverty. *World Development,* 138, 105229. www.sciencedirect.com/science/article/pii/S0305750X20303569

International Monetary Fund (IMF). (2020). The Promise of Fintech; Financial Inclusion in the Post COVID-19 Era. Available at: https://bit.ly/3U0bINv

Jagtiani, J., & John, K. (2018). Fintech: The impact on consumers and regulatory responses. www.sciencedirect.com/science/article/pii/S0148619518302765

Kandpal, V., & Mehrotra, R. (2019). Financial inclusion: The role of Fintech and digital financial services in India. *Indian Journal of Economics & Business*, 19(1), 85–93. https://papers.ssrn.com/sol3/papers.cfm?abstract_id=3485038

Kathiravan, C., Selvam, M., Maniam, B., & Dharani, M. (2021). Effect of weather on stock market: A literature review and research agenda. *Cogent Economics & Finance*, 9(1), 1971353. www.tandfonline.com/doi/abs/10.1080/23322039.2021.1971353

Kathiravan, C., Selvam, M., Maniam, B., Dana, L. P., & Babu, M. (2023). The effects of crude oil price surprises on national income: Evidence from India. *Energies*, 16(3), 1148. www.mdpi.com/1996-1073/16/3/1148

Kathiravan, C., Selvam, M., Maniam, B., Venkateswar, S., & Sigo, M. O. (2021). Does temperature influence the carbon index? Evidences from India. *Journal of Public Affairs*, 21(1), e2117. https://onlinelibrary.wiley.com/doi/abs/10.1002/pa.2117

Khang, A. & AIoCF. (Eds.) (2024). *AI-Oriented Competency Framework for Talent Management in the Digital Economy: Models, Technologies, Applications, and Implementation*. CRC Press. ISBN: 9781032576053. https://doi.org/10.1201/9781003440901

Khang, A., Gujrati, R., Uygun, H., Tailor, R. K., & Gaur S. S. (2024). *Data-driven Modelling and Predictive Analytics in Business and Finance* (1st Ed.). CRC Press. ISBN: 9781032600628. https://doi.org/10.1201/9781032600628

Khang, A., Inna, S.-O., Alla, K., Rostyslav, S., Rudenko, M., Lidia, R., Kristina, B. (2024). Management model 6.0 and business recovery strategy of enterprises in the era of digital economy. In *Data-driven Modelling and Predictive Analytics in Business and Finance* (1st Ed.). CRC Press. https://doi.org/10.1201/9781032600628-16

Khang, A., Kali, C. R., Satapathy, S. K., Kumar, A., Ranjan Das, S., & Panda, M. R. (2023). Enabling the future of manufacturing: Integration of robotics and IoT to smart factory infrastructure in Industry 4.0. In A. Khang, V. Shah, & S. Rani (Eds.), *AI-Based Technologies and Applications in the Era of the Metaverse* (1st Ed.) (pp. 25–50). IGI Global Press. https://doi.org/10.4018/978-1-6684-8851-5.ch002

Khang, A., Muthmainnah, M., Seraj, P. M. I., Al Yakin, A., Obaid, A. J., & Panda, M. R. (2023). AI-Aided teaching model for the education 5.0 ecosystem. In A. Khang, V. Shah, & S. Rani (Eds.), *AI-Based Technologies and Applications in the Era of the Metaverse* (1st Ed.) (pp. 83–104). IGI Global Press. https://doi.org/10.4018/978-1-6684-8851-5.ch004

Khang, A., Rani S., Gujrati R., Uygun H., & Gupta S. K. (Eds.) (2023). *Designing Workforce Management Systems for Industry 4.0: Data-Centric and AI-Enabled Approaches.* CRC Press. https://doi.org/10.1201/9781003357070

Khang, A., Shah V., & Rani S. (2023). *AI-Based Technologies and Applications in the Era of the Metaverse* (1st Ed.). IGI Global Press. https://doi.org/10.4018/978-1-6684-8851-5

Khanh, H. H., & Khang A. (2021). The role of artificial intelligence in blockchain applications. In *Reinventing Manufacturing and Business Processes through Artificial Intelligence*, 2 (pp. 20–40). CRC Press. https://doi.org/10.1201/9781003145011-2

Khurana, N. (2018). A study of impact of financial technology on banking sector in India. *International Journal in Management & Social Science*, 6(8), 73–82. https://bit.ly/4aAioXT

Lacasse, R. M., Lambert, B. A., Roy, N., Sylvain, J., & Nadeau, F. (2016). A digital tsunami: FinTech and crowdfunding. In *International Scientific Conference on Digital Intelligence* (pp. 1–5). http://fintechlab.ca/wp-content/uploads/2016/11/Digital-Tsunami-Site-Web.pdf

Lim, S. H., Kim, D. J., Hur, Y., & Park, K. (2019). An empirical study of the impacts of perceived security and knowledge on continuous intention to use mobile fintech payment services. *International Journal of Human–Computer Interaction*, 35(10), 886–898. https://scholar.kyobobook.co.kr/article/detail/4010028480025

Makina, D. (2019). The potential of FinTech in enabling financial inclusion. In *Extending Financial Inclusion in Africa* (pp. 299–318). Academic Press. www.sciencedirect.com/science/article/pii/B9780128141649000141

MEDICI (2019). India FinTech Report. Available at: https://mediciinnercircle.com/wp-content/uploads/2019/03/FintegrateReport_ExecutiveSummary_Final.pdf

Morgan, P. J., & Long, T. Q. (2020). Financial literacy, financial inclusion, and savings behavior in Laos. *Journal of Asian Economics,* 68, 101197. www.sciencedirect.com/science/article/pii/S1049007820300415

Muthmainnah, M., Khang, A., Seraj, P. M. I., Al Yakin, A., Oteir, I., Alotaibi, A. N. (2023). An innovative teaching model – The potential of metaverse for English Learning. In A. Khang, V. Shah, & S. Rani (Eds.), *AI-Based Technologies and Applications in the Era of the Metaverse* (1st Ed.) (pp. 105–126). IGI Global Press. https://doi.org/10.4018/978-1-6684-8851-5.ch005

Ozili, P. K. (2018). Impact of digital finance on financial inclusion and stability. *Borsa Istanbul Review,* 18(4), 329–340. www.sciencedirect.com/science/article/pii/S2214845017301503

Pooja, K., Jadhav, B., Kulkarni, A., Khang, A., & Kulkarni, S. (2023). The role of blockchain technology in metaverse ecosystem. In A. Khang, V. Shah, & S. Rani (Eds.), *AI-Based Technologies and Applications in the Era of the Metaverse* (1st Ed.) (pp. 228–236). IGI Global Press. https://doi.org/10.4018/978-1-6684-8851-5.ch011

PwC (2019). Global Fintech Survey. Available at: www.pwc.com/gx/en/industries/financial-services/assets/pwc-global-fintech-report-2019.pdf

Radcliffe, D., & Voorhies, R. (2012). A Digital Pathway to Financial Inclusion. Available at SSRN 2186926. https://papers.ssrn.com/sol3/papers.cfm?abstract_id=2186926

Raj, B., & Upadhyay, V. (2020). Role of FinTech in Accelerating Financial Inclusion in India. In 3rd International Conference on Economics and Finance Organised by the Nepal Rastra Bank at Kathmandu, Nepal during February (pp. 28–29). https://papers.ssrn.com/sol3/papers.cfm?abstract_id=3591018

Rana, G., Khang, A., Sharma, R., Goel, A. K., & Dubey, A. K. (Eds.) (2021). *Reinventing Manufacturing and Business Processes through Artificial Intelligence.* CRC Press. https://doi.org/10.1201/9781003145011

Reserve Bank of India (RBI). (2018). Report of the Working Group on FinTech and Digital Banking. Available at: www.rbi.org.in/Scripts/PublicationReportDetails.aspx?UrlPage=&ID=892

Reserve Bank of India (RBI). (2019a). National Strategy for Financial Inclusion: 2019:2024. Available at: www.rbi.org.in/Scripts/PublicationReportDetails.aspx?UrlPage=&ID=115 4

Reserve Bank of India (RBI). (2019b). Press Release by RBI on Setting up of High-Level Committee on Deepening of Digital Payments. Available at: www.rbi.org.in/Scripts/BS_PressReleaseDisplay.aspx?prid=45949

Saxena, A. C., Ojha, A., Sobti, D., & Khang, A. (2023). Artificial Intelligence (AI) centric model in metaverse ecosystem. In A. Khang, V. Shah, & S. Rani (Eds.), *AI-Based Technologies and Applications in the Era of the Metaverse* (1st Ed.) (pp. 1–24). IGI Global Press. https://doi.org/10.4018/978-1-6684-8851-5.ch001

Senyo, P. K., & Osabutey, E. L. (2020). Unearthing antecedents to financial inclusion through FinTech innovations. *Technovation,* 98, 102155. www.sciencedirect.com/science/article/pii/S0166497220300365

Senyo, P. K., Liu, K., & Effah, J. (2019). Digital business ecosystem: Literature review and a framework for future research. *International Journal of Information Management,* 47, 52–64. www.sciencedirect.com/science/article/pii/S0268401218305991

Shah, V., & Khang A. (2023). Metaverse-enabling iot technology for a futuristic healthcare system. In A. Khang, V. Shah, & S. Rani (Eds.), *AI-Based Technologies and Applications in the Era of the Metaverse* (1st Ed.) (pp. 165–173). IGI Global Press. https://doi.org/10.4018/978-1-6684-8851-5.ch008

Stewart, H., & Jürjens, J. (2018). Data security and consumer trust in FinTech innovation in Germany. *Information & Computer Security.* www.emerald.com/insight/content/doi/10.1108/ICS-06-2017-0039/full/html?fullSc=1

Vidyakala, K. (2018). A conceptual study on strategies adopted by RBI for financial inclusion in India. *Journal of Emerging Technologies and Innovative Research.* https://papers.ssrn.com/sol3/papers.cfm?abstract_id=3615525

Wang, L., & Guan, J. (2017). Financial inclusion: Measurement, spatial effects and influencing factors. *Applied Economics*, 49(18), 1751–1762. www.tandfonline.com/doi/abs/10.1080/00036846.2016.1226488

World Bank. (2017). The Global Findex Database. Available at: https://globalfinde11.worldbank.org/

World Bank. (2018). The World Bank Annual Report 2018. Available at: http://documents.worldbank.org/curated/en/630671538158537244/The-World-Bank-Annual-Report-2018

12 Predicting the Impact of Exchange Rate Volatility on Sectoral Indices

Silky Vigg Kushwah and Pushpa Negi

12.1 INTRODUCTION

Financial liberalization policies in developing countries have been linked to significant fluctuations in exchange rates (Elkhuizen et al., 2017). In fact, these policies, aimed at opening up financial markets, have introduced a greater degree of flexibility into exchange rates, resulting in a notable increase in their volatility. As a consequence, developing nations have had to grapple with increased exchange rate risks and interest rate risks, as observed by Brown (2009). The volatility in exchange rates has created a challenging environment for economic planning and financial stability in these countries. Also, fluctuations in exchange rates could potentially have adverse impacts on import and export activities. According to Becker and Greenberg (2012), changes in exchange rates have a lesser impact on export flows in financially developing economies. Conversely, in highly financially developed countries, import flows are more sensitive to fluctuations in exchange rates. Combes et al. (2011) argue that adopting more flexible exchange rates can help minimize these fluctuations and recommend that countries with underdeveloped and less stable financial markets consider implementing more flexible exchange rate policies during economic shocks.

Exchange rate volatility has a significant influence on various economic indicators and financial markets. Numerous studies have investigated the relationship between real exchange rates and different economic variables, including productivity differentials, foreign aid, real interest rates, current accounts, and international payments (Ibhagui, 2019; Meese & Rogofp, 1988; Lane & Milesi-Ferretti (2002). The relationship between exchange rates and stock price volatility is also crucial to examine because it impacts the overall health of the economy, the performance of financial markets, and the financial stability of nations (Khang, Vugar and Abuzarova et al., 2023). Similarly, the volatility of stock prices can have an effect on investor confidence, which can have repercussions for financial markets and the economy as a whole (Khang & Medicine, 2023). Numerous studies have been conducted to examine the impact of exchange rate volatility on stock prices volatility (Bahmani-Oskooee

DOI: 10.1201/9781032618845-12

& Sohrabian, 1992; Bollerslev, 1990; Nieh & Lee, 2001; Yang & Doong, 2004). Furthermore, excessive volatility in currency rates and stock prices can lead to financial crises and enhance systemic risk (Hussain et al., 2023).

This study is aimed at assessing the impact of exchange rate volatility on NIFTY sectoral indices, including Pharma, Auto, Metal, Energy, IT, and Financial Services. The selection of Pharma, Auto, Metal, Energy, IT, and Financial Services sectors for the study was due to their crucial roles in the Indian economy and their varied susceptibilities to exchange rate fluctuations. These sectors collectively represent diverse facets of India's economic landscape, with unique sensitivities to currency movements. Studying them enables a comprehensive understanding of how different industries respond to exchange rate shifts, informing both policy decisions and investment strategies in a nation where these sectors significantly contribute to economic growth, employment, and international trade. These research objectives are significant for several reasons. Firstly, they provide investors and market participants with a comprehensive understanding of how fluctuations in exchange rates can influence the performance of specific sectors within the Indian economy. This knowledge is crucial for making informed investment decisions and managing portfolio risks effectively. Secondly, by analyzing the historical data and patterns of these sectoral indices in response to exchange rate movements, the study can identify trends and links that are valuable for traders, investors, and asset managers (Khang, Misra et al., 2023).

Further, another objective of this study is to identify and compare variations in the responses of the selected sectoral indices to exchange rate volatility. This objective is of paramount significance due to the importance of these sectors in terms of investment, policy implications, market representation, global linkages, and their diverse risk profiles. Conducting a comprehensive analysis of how exchange rate movements affect sectoral indices is particularly relevant because it identifies that various sectors within the Indian economy may display unique sensitivities to exchange rate fluctuations (Shah & Khang, 2024).

Understanding these variations can be invaluable for investors looking to diversify their portfolios. For instance, if the study reveals that the Pharma sector is less affected by exchange rate volatility compared to the Auto sector, investors can make more precise decisions about their asset allocation and risk management strategies. Therefore this study seeks to provide policy insights based on the findings of the research. Businesses operating within these sectors can also benefit from a deeper understanding of how exchange rate volatility can affect their revenues and costs (Chauhan et al., 2023).

Hence, each research objective in this study carries its own set of implications. These objectives contribute to a more comprehensive understanding of the complex relationship between exchange rate volatility and NIFTY sectoral indices, thereby offering valuable insights for investors, policymakers, and businesses operating within these sectors. The subsequent sections of the chapter are organized as follows. In Section 12.2, there is an extensive exploration of the existing literature. Section 12.3 delves deeply into the research design and methodology, encompassing topics such as the computation of logarithmic returns, the application of the Jarque Bera (JB) test, the execution of the Augmented Dickey-Fuller (ADF) unit root test, and the utilization of the GARCH (1, 1) model. Section 12.4 provides an exhaustive presentation and analysis of the research findings and ensuing discussions. Finally, Section 12.5, serving as the conclusion, delivers a comprehensive recapitulation of the conclusions reached in the study.

12.2 LITERATURE REVIEW

Extensive research has investigated the impact of exchange rate volatility on stock prices across various contexts and nations. Investigations by Lawal et al. (2016) in Nigeria revealed that both exchange rate and oil price fluctuations wielded substantial influence on stock market turbulence. Mwambuli et al. (2016) explored the interplay of volatility between stock prices and exchange rates, discovering indicative evidence of volatility spillovers, underscoring the interconnectedness of these domains in emerging economies.

Further insights from Xiong and Han (2015) exposed asymmetric volatility spillover effects within financial markets, including exchange rates and the stock market, signifying that shocks in one realm could profoundly influence the volatility of the other. This body of literature collectively underscores that exchange rate volatility can wield a substantial impact on stock prices, albeit with variable dynamics dependent on the specific country or region under examination. Policymakers and investors should take these findings into account when shaping policies and investment strategies.

The correlation between interest rates and stock prices has undergone extensive scrutiny, encompassing both developed and developing countries. Granger et al. (2000) concentrated their research on developing nations in East Asia, empirically investigating this relationship and uncovering how changes in exchange rates can impact stock prices in these regions. Khang, Gujrati et al. (2024) identified interest rates as a determinant of stock prices, particularly noting a direct association between interest rates and Vietnam's stock market.

He et al. (2023) proposed that the global financial crisis of 2007–2009 played a pivotal role in linking domestic stock markets with foreign exchange markets. Their findings indicated a negative link between exchange rates and the domestic stock market in emerging countries but a positive one in developed countries, both across the entire dataset and during the crisis period. This suggests that exchange rate fluctuations hold valuable information for predicting stock returns in these markets. Erdoğan et al. (2020) explored volatility spillovers in three emerging countries, observing evidence of such spillovers from the Islamic stock market to the foreign exchange market, primarily in Turkey. Their time-varying analysis revealed the presence of volatility spillovers in at least one direction between exchange rates and the Islamic stock market at specific time intervals.

Mahalakshmi et al. (2022) delved into return and volatility spillover effects between the Indian rupee and the US dollar, along with stock index volatility in neighboring Asian nations. They found that when the rupee depreciates against the US dollar, foreign institutional investors tend to withdraw their portfolio investments from other Asian markets and channel them into the Indian stock market. Conversely, if the rupee appreciates, they may divest their investments to secure profits.

Numerous studies have delved into the impact of exchange rates on stock prices, with a focus on both short-term Granger causality and potential long-term relationships between these variables. Phoong et al. (2023) conducted research on predictive causality between stock prices and exchange rates in Malaysia, Singapore, China, and the US. Their findings from Gregory and Hansen cointegration and Granger causality tests unveiled unidirectional Granger causality relations in Malaysia, the US, and Singapore. Interestingly, even when two markets exhibited the same unidirectional Granger causality relation, the signs of causal effects differed. Moreover, the study identified cointegration between stock prices and exchange rates in the US and Singapore.

Ajala et al. (2021) applied linear Granger causality tests, revealing that stock prices are Granger caused by oil prices and exchange rates, while oil prices are Granger caused by stock prices and exchange rates. Sucuahi (2023) employed the Augmented Dickey-Fuller (ADF) test for stationarity and Johansen Cointegration, along with Granger Causality tests, to investigate long-term and short-term relationships among six sectoral indices. Their results indicated a lack of long-run relationships but a short-run relationship in both directions among the sectoral indices.

Nagayasu (2000) explored the influence of benchmark stock and sectoral indices on Thailand and the Philippines' exchange rates using Vector Autoregression and Granger causality. Their findings suggested that benchmark stock did not significantly impact exchange rates, nor did exchange rates affect benchmark stock. Lastly, Palamalai and Kalaivani (2015) assessed the weak-form efficiency of the Bombay Stock Exchange (BSE) using various statistical methods, including autocorrelation.

Apart from examining short-term Granger causality and enduring associations between exchange rates and stock prices, numerous research have been explored diverse volatility models. Krishnan and Dagar (2022), for instance, harnessed the GARCH model to gauge volatility and scrutinize the influence of exchange rates on the stock market. Their GARCH model findings disclosed dissimilarities in conditional variance dynamics, revealing lower volatility for Nifty volume but heightened volatility for SSE and DJI stock volumes traded. Similarly, Hung (2022) employed a bivariate GARCH-BEKK framework, coupled with constant and dynamic conditional correlation models, to dissect the dynamic ties and volatility spillover effects linking exchange rates and stock returns.

Meanwhile, Bhargava and Konku (2023) explored volatility spillover from exchange rate fluctuations across various markets to the US stock market's volatility, deploying an array of GARCH models, including EGARCH and TGARCH. Rai and Garg (2022) investigated the COVID-19 pandemic's ramifications on dynamic correlations and volatility transmission between stock prices and exchange rates in BRIICS economies, revealing significant negative dynamic correlations and volatility transmission channels in most of these economies, offering vital insights into pandemic-induced challenges within interconnected financial markets.

12.3 RESEARCH METHODOLOGY

This study examines the dynamics of exchange rate fluctuations and its interconnection with the volatility of some of the most crucial stock market indices of the

National Stock Exchange (NSE) in India. The present study investigates the impact of volatility of the exchange rate, namely INR/USD, on the six major sectorial indices of NSE, including Nifty Pharma, Nifty Auto, Nifty Metal, Nifty Energy, Nifty IT, and Nifty Financial Services.

Secondary data in the form of prices of seven time series including exchange rate and six sectorial indices have been collected for the period from the financial years 2016–17 to 2021–22. Time series of exchange rate have been collected from the official website of the RBI, i.e. www.rbi.org.in, and time series of six sectorial indices have been collected from the official website of the NSE, i.e. www.nseindia.com. Descriptive statistics have been applied to explore the basic characteristics of all the time series used in the study. Daily log returns of all seven time series, namely INR/US, Nifty Pharma, Nifty Auto, Nifty Metal, Nifty Energy, Nifty IT, and Nifty Financial Services, have been calculated using equation (12.1):

$$R_t = \log\left(\frac{P_t}{P_{t-1}}\right) \tag{12.1}$$

Where, R_t refers to the daily returns during the period t, P_t denotes the closing price at the time t, while, P_{t-1} indicates the closing price during the preceding day. As it's a time series data, the Jarque Bera test has been applied to check the normality in the collected data (Nathani and Kushwah, 2022; Bhatia and Kushwah, 2023). The main objective of the study, to analyze the impact of exchange rate volatility on the volatility of sectorial indices has been tested using the GARCH model.

Some researchers prefer to apply the ARIMA model over the GARCH model. However, the former is restricted to a mean equation due to which the conditional variance cannot be identified. This limitation has been overcome by using the GARCH model which adopts a lagged conditional variance ((Nathani and Kushwah, 2022). Equation (12.2) depicts the mean equation for developing the GARCH (1, 1) model:

$$B_y = D_1 + D_2 * Z + \epsilon_1 \tag{12.2}$$

Where, B_y refers to the returns of the dependent variable, D_1 is the constant term, D_2 is the coefficient of the independent variable Z, while the error term is denoted by ϵ_1. Equation (12.3) shows the variance equation used to apply the GARCH (1, 1) model:

$$U_t = D_3 + D_4 * U_{t-1} + D_5 * \epsilon_{2,t-1} \tag{12.3}$$

Where, U_t is the residual term calculated from Equation (12.2) and is referred to as the return volatility of the dependent variable, U_{t-1} indicates the GARCH term and is the volatility in return of the preceding day, and finally $\epsilon_{2,t-1}$ indicates the ARCH term implying the previous day returns and the main factor causing volatility in present returns. The six equations were formed to analyze the interrelationship between the volatility of each sectorial indices and primarily the exchange rate volatility and secondarily with other sectorial indices volatility.

GARCH (1,1) Auto = C(1) + C(2)*RESID(-1)^2 + C(3)*GARCH(-1) + C(4)*LOG_CURRENCY + C(5)*LOG_ENERGY + C(6)*LOG_FINANCIAL_ SERVICE + C(7)*LOG_IT + C(8)*LOG_METAL + C(9)*LOG_PHARMA

GARCH (1,1) Energy = C(1) + C(2)*RESID(-1)^2 + C(3)*GARCH(-1) + C(4) *LOG_CURRENCY + C(5)*LOG_AUTO + C(6)*LOG_FINANCIAL_SERVICE + C(7)*LOG_IT + C(8)*LOG_METAL + C(9)*LOG_PHARMA

GARCH (1,1) Financial Services = C(1) + C(2)*RESID(-1)^2 + C(3)*GARCH(- 1) + C(4) *LOG_CURRENCY + C(5)*LOG_AUTO + C(6)*LOG_ENERGY + C(7)*LOG_IT + C(8)*LOG_METAL + C(9)*LOG_PHARMA

GARCH (1,1) IT = C(1) + C(2)*RESID(-1)^2 + C(3)*GARCH(-1) + C(4) *LOG_ CURRENCY + C(5)*LOG_ENERGY + C(6)*LOG_FINANCIAL_SERVICE + C(7)*LOG_IT + C(8)*LOG_ METAL + C(9)*LOG_PHARMA

GARCH (1,1) Metal = C(1) + C(2)*RESID(-1)^2 + C(3)*GARCH(-1) + C(4)*LOG_CURRENCY+ C(5)*LOG_AUTO + (6)*LOG _ENERGY + C(7)*LOG_ FINANCIAL_SERVICE + C(8)*LOG_IT + C(9)* LOG_PHARMA

GARCH (1,1) Pharma = C(1) + C(2)*RESID(-1)^2 + C(3)*GARCH(-1) + C(4)*LOG_CURRENCY + C(5)*LOG_ENERGY + C(6)*LOG_FINANCIAL_ SERVICE + C(7)*LOG_AUTO + C(8)*LOG_IT + C(9)*LOG_METAL

12.4   RESULTS AND DISCUSSIONS

12.4.1   DESCRIPTIVE STATISTICS

The initial step in our analysis involved conducting the Jarque-Bera (JB) test to measure the normality of the dataset (Kushwah and Garg, 2020). Table 12.1 presents a comprehensive set of descriptive statistics for both exchange rates and various sectoral indices, including Pharma, Auto, Metal, Energy, IT, and Financial Services. For the analysis, we calculated the log returns of exchange rate and other indices to calculate a range of key statistical measures. These statistics encompassed essential parameters such as mean, median, maximum, minimum values, standard deviation, skewness, and kurtosis.

Notably, we observed that the mean returns for both exchange rates and sectoral indices were positive, indicating an overall tendency toward positive returns within the dataset. Additionally, we determined variations in standard deviations across the indices; Nifty Metal and Nifty Auto exhibited relatively lower standard deviations

TABLE 12.1
Jarque Bera (JB) Test Results

Pattern name	t-Statistics	p Value
Exchange Rate	–42.127	0.0000
NIFTY Auto	–32.063	0.0000
NIFTY Energy	–33.637	0.0000
NIFTY Financial Services	–13.643	0.0000
NIFTY IT	–33.980	0.0000
NIFTY Metal	–33.699	0.0000
NIFTY Pharma	–34.128	0.0000

compared to other indices, while Nifty IT and Nifty Energy displayed the highest standard deviations. The skewness values for all exchange rate returns fell within the acceptable range of +1 to –1, indicating a balanced distribution of data. Similarly, with the exception of Nifty Energy, the kurtosis values for all countries remained within the acceptable range of –3 to +3, although Nifty Energy displayed a slightly higher kurtosis value of 3.72, suggesting a more peaked distribution.

In addition, the table includes the Jarque-Bera test statistics, which are typically positive; however, in this instance, they deviated significantly from zero. This deviation implies that the sample data, encompassing exchange rates and various sectoral indices like Pharma, Auto, Metal, Energy, IT, and Financial Services, do not adhere to a normal distribution pattern. This inference is supported by the p-values obtained from the Jarque-Bera test, all of which were less than 0.01 for exchange rates and the mentioned sectoral indices. These low p-values led to the rejection of the null hypothesis, which posits that the data follow a normal distribution. In conclusion, our analysis indicates that the data for exchange rates and the selected sectoral indices, including Pharma, Auto, Metal, Energy, IT, and Financial Services, do not conform to a normal distribution pattern as shown in Table 12.1.

12.4.2   Unit Root Test

Before investigating the impact of exchange rate volatility on NIFTY sectoral indices, which include Pharma, Auto, Metal, Energy, IT, and Financial Services, we conducted an initial examination of the time series data using the Augmented Dickey-Fuller (ADF) unit root test to calculate stationarity. Initially, each univariate series exhibited non-stationarity. It is worth noting that the presence of a unit root in exchange rate and other sectorial indices returns is a well-established phenomenon in the literature, documented in various contexts such as Asian markets (Siddiqui and Kushwah, 2022; Bhatia and Kushwah, 2023). Consequently, in line with existing research, our study also employed a unit root test, which confirmed the presence of unit roots in all series, aligning with the null unit root hypothesis for the exchange rates of all series, as shown in Table 12.2.

Thus, both the NIFTY sectoral indices and the exchange rates series exhibited non-stationarity at the level, signifying that these variables were integrated at order 1,

TABLE 12.2
Augmented Dickey-Fuller (ADF) Test Results (after First Difference)

	Exchange Rate	NIFTY Auto	NIFTY Energy	NIFTY Financial Services	NIFTY IT	NIFTY Metal	NIFTY Pharma
Mean	70.83	9469.78	16065.75	12840.61	18793.25	3509.04	10353.05
Median	71.58	9994.42	15179.98	11707.55	15583.3	3261	9497.85
Maximum	77.57	12061.8	25989.3	19651.1	39370.7	6571.85	14812.4
Minimum	63.26	4517.75	6850.5	8298.5	9943.7	1496.45	6432.3
Std. Dev.	3.92	1681.87	3414.25	2833.51	8035.756	1156.26	2150.48
Skewness	−0.53	−0.56	1.19	0.63	1.1	0.77	0.63
Kurtosis	1.99	2.38	3.72	2.16	2.93	2.74	2.06
Jarque-Bera	109.49	84.67	320.67	118.99	247.75	125.77	127.35
Probability	0	0	0	0	0	0	0

denoted as I (1). To address this issue, we proceeded to take first differences of the logarithms of the time series, rendering them stationary. As a result, the associated variables could now be characterized as I (1) integrated, enabling us to make further analysis as shown in Table 12.3.

12.4.3 GARCH (1, 1) MODEL RESULTS

12.4.3.1 Impact on Auto Sector Indices

The p-value for the residual term (RESID $(-1)^2$) is 2.541, indicating that we cannot reject the null hypothesis in Table 12.3. This implies that there is no observed ARCH effect on the Auto sector indices, specifically in terms of how yesterday's returns influence today's returns. Similarly, the GARCH effect, denoted by the term GARCH (-1), is not present because its p-value is 4.3093, which exceeds the 0.05 significance threshold. Hence, we can conclude with 95% confidence that yesterday's volatility does not significantly impact today's volatility in the Auto sector. If we look at the other independent variables like exchange rate, Pharma, Metal, Energy, IT, and Financial Services, their p-values are all greater than 0.05. This indicates that these variables do not significantly affect the volatility of the Auto sector. Therefore, our analysis suggests that neither internal shocks nor external independent variables have a substantial impact on Auto sector indices' volatility.

12.4.3.2 Impact on Energy Sector Indices

The p-value for the residual term is 3.688, indicating that we cannot reject the null hypothesis in Table 12.3. This suggests the absence of an ARCH effect on Energy sector indices, denoted by the term RESID $(-1)^2$. This absence implies that yesterday's returns have no significant impact on today's returns in this sector. However, there is a GARCH effect present in the Auto sector, denoted by the term GARCH (-1), as the p-value is less than 0.05. Therefore, with 95% confidence, we can conclude that yesterday's volatility will influence today's volatility in the Auto

TABLE 12.3
Results of the GARCH (1,1) Model

	Variable	Coefficient	Std. Error	z-Statistics	Probability
GARCH (1,1) Auto	C	2.49E-07	6.54E-08	3.809992	0.0001
= GARCH = C(1) + C(2)*RESID(-1)^2 +	RESID(-1)^2	0.319	0.043	7.316	2.541
C(3)*GARCH(-1) + C(4)	GARCH(-1)	0.576	0.0295	19.547	4.3093
*LOG_CURRENCY + C(5)*LOG_ENERGY	LOG_CURRENCY	−0.0014	0.0003	−4.4372	9.1106
+ C(6)*LOG_FINANCIAL_SERVICE +	LOG_ENERGY	−6.002	0.0001	−0.044	0.964
C(7)*LOG_IT + C(8)*LOG_METAL +	LOG_FINANCIAL_SERVICE	−0.000	0.0001	−0.902	0.367
C(9)*LOG_PHARMA	LOG_IT	−0.000	5.7194	−8.633	5.9605
	LOG_METAL	−0.0001	8.7595	−1.6076	0.1079
	LOG_PHARMA	−0.0003	7.8543	−4.6660	3.0701
GARCH (1,1) Energy = C(1) + C(2)*RESID	C	1.503	2.933	5.124	2.982
(-1)^2 + C(3)*GARCH(-1) + C(4) *LOG_	RESID(-1)^2	0.078	0.013	5.897	3.688
CURRENCY + C(5)*LOG_AUTO +	GARCH(-1)	0.877	0.016	53.442	0
C(6)*LOG_FINANCIAL_SERVICE +	LOG_CURRENCY	0.000	0.000	0.943	0.345
C(7)*LOG_IT + C(8)*LOG_METAL +	LOG_AUTO	0.000	8.537	1.301	0.192
C(9)*LOG_PHARMA	LOG_FINANCIAL_SERVICE	0.000	0.000	2.766	0.005
	LOG_IT	5.451	7.945	0.686	0.492
	LOG_METAL	5.718	5.839	0.979	0.327
	LOG_PHARMA	0.000	9.905	3.076	0.002
GARCH (1,1) Financial Services = C(1)	C	1.380	2.344	5.887	3.923
+ C(2)* RESID(-1)^2 + C(3) *GARCH(-1)	RESID(-1)^2	0.105	0.017	6.101	1.049
+ C(4) *LOG_CURRENCY + C(5)*LOG_	GARCH(-1)	0.855	0.019	43.436	0
AUTO + C(6)*LOG_ENERGY + C(7) *LOG_	LOG_CURRENCY	4.819	0.000	0.200	0.841
IT + C(8)*LOG_METAL + C(9)*LOG_	LOG_AUTO	6.103	6.289	0.970	0.331
PHARMA	LOG_ENERGY	0.000	7.632	2.420	0.015
	LOG_IT	0.000	6.846	3.802	0.000
	LOG_METAL	2.023	6.126	0.330	0.741
	LOG_PHARMA	0.000	6.836	3.576	0.000

GARCH (1,1) IT = C(1) + C(2)*RESID(-1)^2 + C(3) *GARCH(-1) + C(4) *LOG_CURRENCY + C(5)*LOG_ENERGY + C(6)*LOG_FINANCIAL_SERVICE + C(7)* LOG_IT + C(8)*LOG_ METAL + C(9)* LOG_PHARMA

C	1.114	2.447	4.552	5.292
RESID(-1)^2	0.067	0.011	6.086	1.153
GARCH(-1)	0.897	0.016	56.015	0
LOG_CURRENCY	2.955	0.000	0.122	0.902
LOG_ENERGY	8.888	7.779	1.142	0.253
LOG_FINANCIAL_SERVICE	3.356	6.821	0.492	0.622
LOG_IT	5.780	4.107	1.407	0.159
LOG_METAL	0.000	6.199	2.859	0.004
LOG_PHARMA	0.000	7.201	1.809	0.070

GARCH (1,1) Metal = C(1) + C(2)*RESID(-1)^2 + C(3)*GARCH(-1) + C(4) *LOG_CURRENCY+ C(5) *LOG_AUTO + (6)*LOG_ENERGY + C(7) *LOG_FINANCIAL_SERVICE + C(8)*LOG_IT + C(9)* LOG_PHARMA

C	1.735	4.728	3.670	0.000
RESID(-1)^2	0.040	0.009	4.251	2.120
GARCH(-1)	0.935	0.013	70.828	0
LOG_CURRENCY	0.000	0.000	0.549	0.582
LOG_AUTO	0.000	0.000	0.905	0.365
LOG_ENERGY	0.000	0.000	2.131	0.033
LOG_FINANCIAL_SERVICE	0.000	0.000	1.785	0.074
LOG_IT	0.000	0.000	0.820	0.412
LOG_PHARMA	0.000	0.000	2.372	0.017

GARCH (1,1) Pharma = C(1) + C(2)*RESID(-1)^2 + C(3)*GARCH(-1) + C(4) *LOG_CURRENCY + C(5)*LOG_ENERGY + C(6)*LOG_FINANCIAL_SERVICE + C(7)*LOG_AUTO + C(8)*LOG_IT + C(9)*LOG_METAL

C	2.578	5.099	5.056	4.268
RESID(-1)^2	0.075	0.014	5.213	1.855
GARCH(-1)	0.853	0.022	38.706	0
LOG_CURRENCY	0.000	0.000	0.442	0.657
LOG_ENERGY	0.000	0.000	1.280	0.200
LOG_FINANCIAL_SERVICE	5.245	9.454	0.554	0.578
LOG_AUTO	0.000	0.000	4.336	1.445
LOG_IT	6.787	9.936	0.683	0.494
LOG_METAL	4.562	7.496	0.608	0.542

sector. When examining other independent variables such as exchange rate, Auto, Metal, and IT, we find that they do not significantly affect the volatility of Energy sectors, as all their p-values exceed 0.05. Conversely, Pharma and Financial Services sector indices do impact the volatility of Energy Sectors.

12.4.3.3 Impact on Financial Services Sector Indices

The p-value for the residual term is 1.049, leading us to not reject the null hypothesis in Table 12.3. This indicates no ARCH effect on Financial Services sector indices, represented by the term RESID(−1)^2. Therefore, yesterday's returns do not have a substantial impact on today's returns in this sector. However, there is a GARCH effect in the Auto sector, denoted by GARCH(−1), as the p-value is less than 0.05, suggesting that yesterday's volatility will affect today's volatility with 95% confidence. When considering other independent variables, such as exchange rate, Auto, Metal, all show p-values greater than 0.05, indicating no significant influence on the volatility of Financial Services sectors. In contrast, Pharma, IT, and Energy sector indices do impact the volatility of Financial Services Sectors.

12.4.3.4 Impact on IT Sector Indices

The p-value for the residual term is 1.153, leading to the non-rejection of the null hypothesis in Table 12.3. This suggests no ARCH effect on IT sector indices, indicated by RESID (−1)^2, implying that yesterday's returns have no significant impact on today's returns in this sector. However, there is a GARCH effect in the Auto sector, denoted by GARCH (-1), as the p-value is less than 0.05, meaning that yesterday's volatility will affect today's volatility with 95% confidence. Examining other independent variables, including exchange rate, Energy, Pharma, Auto, and Financial Services, all exhibit p-values greater than 0.05, indicating no significant impact on the volatility of IT sectors. Nevertheless, Metal sector indices do impact the volatility of IT Sectors.

12.4.3.5 Impact On Metal Sector Indices

The p-value for the residual term is 2.120, leading to the non-rejection of the null hypothesis in Table 12.3. This suggests no ARCH effect on Metal sector indices, denoted by RESID (−1)^2, indicating that yesterday's returns do not significantly influence today's returns in this sector. However, a GARCH effect is present in the Auto sector, denoted by GARCH(-1), as the p-value is less than 0.05, suggesting that yesterday's volatility will affect today's volatility with 95% confidence. When considering other independent variables, including exchange rate, IT, Auto, and Financial Services, all show p-values greater than 0.05, indicating no significant impact on the volatility of Metal sectors. On the other hand, Energy and Pharma sector indices do impact the volatility of Metal sectors (Khang, Hajimahmud et al., 2023).

12.4.3.6 Impact On Pharma Sector Indices

The p-value for the residual term is 1.855, leading to the non-rejection of the null hypothesis in Table 12.3. This implies the absence of an ARCH effect on Pharma sector indices, represented by the term RESID (−1)^2, suggesting that yesterday's returns have no significant impact on today's returns in this sector. However, there is a GARCH effect in the Auto sector, denoted by GARCH (-1), as the p-value is less than 0.05, meaning that yesterday's volatility will affect today's volatility with 95% confidence. Examining other independent variables, including exchange rate, IT, Auto, Metal, Energy, and Financial Services, all exhibit p-values greater than 0.05, indicating no significant impact on the volatility of Pharma sectors.

12.4.3.7 Impact Of Exchange rate on Stock Indices

Based on the outcomes derived from the GARCH $(1,1)$ model, as illustrated in Table 12.3, it is evident that the volatility of Pharma, Metal, Auto, Energy, IT, and Financial Services sector indices during the study period remains unaffected by fluctuations in exchange rates. This observation aligns with previous research findings, such as those of Smyth and Nandha (2003), which established the absence of a long-term relationship between these variables across Pakistan, India, Bangladesh, and Sri Lanka, despite recognizing unidirectional causality between exchange rates and stock prices in India and Sri Lanka.

Similarly, studies by Muller and Verschoor (2006), Andries et al. (2014), Suhaibu et al. (2017), and Chebbi and Ammer (2021) have also concurred, highlighting the absence of a substantial connection between exchange rate fluctuations and stock returns. Conversely, research by Takeshi (2008) found no discernible link between stock returns and exchange rates. Notably, Pan et al. (2007) identified bidirectional causality between exchange rates and stock prices in the case of Hong Kong predating the 1997 Asian crisis, and unidirectional causality in Japan, Malaysia, and Thailand, with Korea and Singapore exhibiting a unidirectional relationship from stock prices to exchange rates. Additionally, Agrawal (2010) observed a lack of correlation between these two variables within the Indian economy, using daily data spanning from October 2007 to May 2009, emphasizing the presence of a unidirectional relationship running from stock returns to exchange rates, consistent with Takeshi (2008).

The limited impact of exchange rate volatility on Indian sectorial indices can be attributed to a range of factors. Firstly, many companies operating within these sectors have adopted prudent hedging practices to shield themselves from the adverse effects of exchange rate fluctuations. Secondly, the diversity of revenue sources among Indian companies plays a crucial role. Several firms within these sectors generate revenue from both domestic and international markets. This diversity acts as a natural hedge, as gains in one currency can offset losses in another, reducing the overall sensitivity of these companies to exchange rate movements. Additionally, certain sectors, like the automotive and pharmaceutical industries, predominantly cater to the domestic market. As a result, their performance is mainly influenced by domestic factors and demand, making them less susceptible to exchange rate volatility (Khang, Shah et al., 2023).

Ultimately, these sectors may be more strongly influenced by factors other than exchange rates, such as economic conditions, domestic market, industry-specific dynamics, regulatory changes, or global trade policy. Subsequently, a comprehensive understanding of the dynamics at play is essential to explain why exchange rate volatility appears to have a limited effect on Indian sectorial indices during the specified study period.

12.5 CONCLUSION

This study is an attempt to find the complex relationship between exchange rate volatility and NIFTY sectoral indices in India. Financial liberalization policies in developing nations have led to increased exchange rate fluctuations, introducing greater risks and challenges in economic planning and financial stability. The impact of exchange rate fluctuations on various economic factors and financial markets, including stock prices, is a topic of immense importance. This study focuses on six key sectors, namely, Pharma, Auto, Metal, Energy, IT, and Financial Services, each playing crucial roles in India's economy and displaying unique susceptibilities to currency movements (Khang, Kali et al., 2023).

The valuable understandings into how these sectors respond to exchange rate volatility, providing investors, market participants, and policy-makers with a comprehensive understanding of the dynamics at play, has also been extracted from this research. We have found that the sectors exhibit varying degrees of sensitivity to exchange rate fluctuations, with potential implications for investment strategies and risk management. This research contributes to the broader understanding of the intricate relationship between exchange rates and sectoral performance in India, offering direction for investment decisions and policy formulation. Businesses within these sectors can also benefit from this knowledge to better navigate the challenges posed by exchange rate volatility, ultimately contributing to more informed and resilient economic practices (Khang, Muthmainnah et al., 2023).

Additionally, the results underscore the nuanced nature of the connection between exchange rates and sectorial indices in India. While exchange rate fluctuations do not seem to significantly impact the volatility of Pharma, Metal, Auto, Energy, IT, and Financial Services sectors, it is critical to recognize that the nonappearance of a direct relationship does not imply that these sectors are immune to external economic influences (Sihare & Khang et al., 2023).

Various other factors, both domestic and international, can exert significant effects on their performance. In addition, the findings underline the importance of sector-specific analysis. Different sectors may respond differently to exchange rate volatility due to their unique characteristics, market dynamics, and exposure to international trade. Understanding these variations is essential for investors, policymakers, and businesses operating within these sectors to make informed decisions and manage risks effectively (Muthmainnah, Khang et al., 2023).

In the broader context, this study contributes to the body of knowledge on the relationship between exchange rates and sectorial indices, offering comprehensions that can inform investment strategies, risk management practices, and economic policies. It highlights the complexity of the global financial landscape, where various economic variables interact in intricate ways, ultimately shaping the performance of different sectors within an economy (Pooja et al., 2023).

REFERENCES

Agrawal, G., Srivastav, A. K., & Srivastava, A. (2010). A study of exchange rates movement and stock market volatility. *International Journal of Business and Management*, 5(12). https://doi.org/10.5539/ijbm.v5n12p62

Ajala, K., Sakanko, M. A., & Adeniji, S. O. (2021). The asymmetric effect of oil price on the exchange rate and stock price in Nigeria. *International Journal of Energy Economics and Policy*, 11(4), 202–208. www.zbw.eu/econis-archiv/bitstream/11159/7769/1/17717 67227_0.pdf

Andries, A. M., Ihnatov, I., & Tiwari, A. K. (2014). Analyzing time–frequency relationship between interest rate, stock price and exchange rate through continuous wavelet. *Economic Modelling*, 41, 227–238. https://doi.org/10.1016/j.econmod.2014.05.013

Bahmani-Oskooee, M., & Sohrabian, A. (1992). Stock prices and the effective exchange rate of the dollar. *Applied Economics*, 24(4), 459–464. www.tandfonline.com/doi/abs/10.1080/00036849200000020

Becker, B., Chen, J., & Greenberg, D. (2012). Financial development, fixed costs, and international trade. *Review of Corporate Finance Studies*, 2(1), 1–28. https://doi.org/10.1093/rcfs/cfs005

Bhargava, V., & Konku, D. (2023). Impact of exchange rate fluctuations on US stock market returns. *Managerial Finance*. www.emerald.com/insight/content/doi/10.1108/MF-08-2022-0387/full/html

Bhatia, P., & Kushwah, S. V. (2023). Diversification potential among the n-10 countries: an empirical investigation. *International Journal of Accounting & Business Finance*, 9(1), 145–166. http://repo.lib.jfn.ac.lk/ujrr/handle/123456789/9602

Bollerslev, T. (1990). Modelling the coherence in short-run nominal exchange rates: a multivariate generalized ARCH model. *Review of Economics and Statistics*, 498–505. www.jstor.org/stable/2109358

Brown, G. M. (2009). International evidence on financial derivatives usage. *Financial Management*, 38(1), 185–206. https://doi.org/10.1111/j.1755-05312.2009.01033.x

Chauhan, V. S., Chakravorty, J., & Khang A. (2023). Smart cities data indicator-based cyber threats detection using bio-inspired artificial algae algorithm. In *Handbook of Research on AI-Based Technologies and Applications in the Era of the Metaverse* (pp. 436–447). Copyright: © 2023. https://doi.org/10.4018/978-1-6684-8851-5.ch024

Chebbi, K., & Ammer, M. A. (2021). The covid-19 pandemic and stock liquidity: evidence from s&p 500. *Quarterly Review of Economics and Finance,* 81, 134–142. https://doi.org/10.1016/j.qref.2021.05.008

Combes, J. L., & Ebeke, C. (2011). Remittances and household consumption instability in developing countries. *World Development*, 39(7), 1076–1089. www.sciencedirect.com/science/article/pii/S0305750X10002287

Elkhuizen, L., Hermes, N., Jacobs, J., & Meesters, A. (2017). Financial development, financial liberalization and social capital. *Applied Economics*, 50(11), 1268–1288. https://doi.org/10.1080/00036846.2017.1358446

Erdoğan, S., Gedikli, A., & Çevik, E. İ. (2020). Volatility spillover effects between Islamic stock markets and exchange rates: evidence from three emerging countries. *Borsa Istanbul Review*, 20(4), 322–333. www.sciencedirect.com/science/article/pii/S22148 45020300260

Granger, C. W., Huangb, B. N., & Yang, C. W. (2000). A bivariate causality between stock prices and exchange rates: evidence from recent Asianflu☆. *Quarterly Review of Economics and Finance*, 40(3), 337–354. www.sciencedirect.com/science/article/pii/S1062976900000429

He, X., Gokmenoglu, K. K., Kirikkaleli, D., & Rizvi, S. K. A. (2023). Comovement of foreign exchange rate returns and stock market returns in an emerging market: Evidence from the wavelet coherence approach. *International Journal of Finance & Economics*, 28(2), 1994–2005. https://onlinelibrary.wiley.com/doi/abs/10.1002/ijfe.2522

Hung, N. T. (2022). Spillover effects between stock prices and exchange rates for the Central and Eastern European Countries. *Global Business Review*, 23(2), 259–286. https://doi.org/10.1177/0972150919869772

Hussain, M., Bashir, U., & Rehman, R. U. (2023). Exchange rate and stock prices volatility connectedness and spillover during pandemic induced-crises: evidence from BRICS Countries. *Asia-Pacific Financial Markets*, 1–21.

Ibhagui, O. (2019). The transfer problem surfaces in sub-saharan africa: net foreign assets, financial liberalization and real exchange rates. *Review of Economic Analysis*, 11(3), 325–381. https://doi.org/10.15353/rea.v11i3.1687

Khang, A., Gujrati, R., Uygun, H., Tailor, R. K., & Gaur S. S. (2024) *Data-driven Modelling and Predictive Analytics in Business and Finance* (1st Ed.). ISBN: 9781032600628. CRC Press. https://doi.org/10.1201/9781032600628

Khang, A., Hajimahmud, V. A., Gupta, S. K., Babasaheb, J., & Morris, G. (2023). *AI-Centric Modelling and Analytics: Concepts, Designs, Technologies, and Applications* (1st Ed.). CRC Press. https://doi.org/10.1201/9781003400110

Khang, A., Kali, C. R., Satapathy, S. K., Kumar, A., Ranjan Das, S., & Panda, M. R. (2023). "Enabling the Future of Manufacturing: Integration of Robotics and IoT to Smart Factory Infrastructure in Industry 4.0." In A. Khang, V. Shah, & S. Rani (Eds.), *AI-Based Technologies and Applications in the Era of the Metaverse* (1st Ed.), pp. 25–50. IGI Global Press. https://doi.org/10.4018/978-1-6684-8851-5.ch002

Khang, A., Misra, A., Gupta, S. K., & Shah V. (Eds.) (2023). *AI-aided IoT Technologies and Applications in the Smart Business and Production*. CRC Press. https://doi.org/10.1201/9781003392224

Khang, A., Muthmainnah, M., Seraj, P. M. I., Al Yakin, A., Obaid, A. J., & Panda, M. R. (2023). "AI-Aided Teaching Model for the Education 5.0 Ecosystem." In A. Khang, V. Shah, & S. Rani (Eds.), *AI-Based Technologies and Applications in the Era of the Metaverse* (1st Ed.), pp. 83–104. IGI Global Press. https://doi.org/10.4018/978-1-6684-8851-5.ch004

Khang, A., Shah, V., & Rani, S. (2023). *AI-Based Technologies and Applications in the Era of the Metaverse* (1st Ed.). IGI Global Press. https://doi.org/10.4018/978-1-6684-8851-5

Krishnan, D., & Dagar, V. (2022). Exchange rate and stock markets during trade conflicts in the USA, China, and India. *Global Journal of Emerging Market Economies*, 14(2), 185–203. https://doi.org/10.1177/09749101221082724

Kushwah, S. V., & Garg, M. (2020). The determinants of foreign direct investment: a VECM approach. *International Journal of Accounting & Business Finance*, 6(2), 55–70. http://192.248.56.27:8080/jspui/handle/123456789/4554

Lane, P. R., & Milesi-Ferretti, G. M. (2002). External wealth, the trade balance, and the real exchange rate. *European Economic Review*, 46(6), 1049–1071. www.sciencedirect.com/science/article/pii/S0014292102001605

Lawal, A., Somoye, R., & Babajide, A. (2016). Impact of oil price shocks and exchange rate volatility on stock market behavior in nigeria. *Binus Business Review*, 7(2), 171. https://doi.org/10.21512/bbr.v7i2.1453

Mahalakshmi, S., Thiyagarajan, S., Vasudevan, G.K., & Naresh, G. (2022). Return and volatility spillover effects between rupee–dollar exchange rate and Asian Stock Indices. *Journal of Emerging Market Finance*, 21, 428–450. https://journals.sagepub.com/doi/abs/10.1177/09726527221100467

Meese, R., & Rogofp, K. (1988). Was it real? The exchange rate-interest differential relation over the modern floating-rate period. *Journal of Finance*, 43(4), 933–948. www.nber. org/papers/w1732

Muller, A., & Verschoor, W. F. C. (2006). European foreign exchange risk exposure. *European Financial Management*, 12(2), 195–220. https://doi.org/10.1111/j.1354-7798.2006.00316.x

Muthmainnah, M., Khang, A., Mahbub Ibna Seraj, P., Al Yakin, A., Oteir, I., & Alotaibi, A. N. (2023). An innovative teaching model – The Potential of metaverse for english learning. In *AI-Based Technologies and Applications in the Era of the Metaverse* (1st Ed.) (pp. 105–126). IGI Global Press. https://doi.org/10.4018/978-1-6684-8851-5.ch005

Mwambuli, E., Xianzhi, Z., & Kisava, Z. (2016). Volatility spillover effects between stock prices and exchange rates in emerging economies: evidence from turkey. *Business and Economic Research*, 6(2), 343. https://doi.org/10.5296/ber.v6i2.10245

Nagayasu, J. (2000). Currency crisis and contagion: evidence from exchange rates and sectoral stock indices of the Philippines and Thailand. IMF Working Paper, 1–26. https://doi.org/ 10.5089/9781451845822.001

Nathani, N., & Kushwah, S. V. (2022). Volatility study in some of the emerging stock markets: a GARCH approach. *World Review of Science, Technology and Sustainable Development*, 18(3–4), 364–378. www.inderscienceonline.com/doi/abs/10.1504/WRS TSD.2022.123781

Nieh, C. C., & Lee, C. F. (2001). Dynamic relationship between stock prices and exchange rates for G-7 countries. *Quarterly Review of Economics and Finance*, 41(4), 477–490. www.sciencedirect.com/science/article/pii/S1062976901000850

Palamalai, S., & Kalaivani, M. (2015). Are Indian stock markets weak-form efficient? Evidence from NSE and BSE sectoral indices. *IUP Journal of Financial Risk Management*, 12(4), 7–34. https://bit.ly/3TyAl2e

Pan, M., Fok, R. C., & Liu, Y. W. (2007). Dynamic linkages between exchange rates and stock prices: evidence from East Asian markets. *International Review of Economics & Finance*, 16(4), 503–520. https://doi.org/10.1016/j.iref.2005.09.003

Phoong, S. Y., Lim, C. Z., & Phoong, S. W. (2023). A Granger causality analysis between stock prices and exchange rates: evidence from four countries. *International Journal of Computing Science and Mathematics*, 17 (3), 284–294. www.inderscienceonline.com/ doi/pdf/10.1504/ IJCSM.2023.131452

Pooja, K., Jadhav, B., Kulkarni, A., Khang, A., & Kulkarni, S. (2023). The role of blockchain technology in metaverse ecosystem. In *AI-Based Technologies and Applications in the Era of the Metaverse* (1 Ed.) (pp. 228–236). IGI Global Press. https://doi.org/10.4018/ 978-1-6684-8851-5.ch011

Rai, K., & Garg, B. (2022). Dynamic correlations and volatility spillovers between stock price and exchange rate in BRIICS economies: evidence from the COVID-19 outbreak period. *Applied Economics Letters*, 29(8), 738–745. www.tandfonline.com/doi/abs/10.1080/ 13504851.2021.1884835

Shah, V., & Khang, A. (2023). Metaverse-enabling IoT technology for a futuristic healthcare system. In *AI-Based Technologies and Applications in the Era of the Metaverse* (1 Ed.) (pp. 165–173). IGI Global Press. https://doi.org/10.4018/978-1-6684-8851-5.ch008

Siddiqui, A. A., & Kushwah, S. V. (2022). Oil prices and equity returns: analysis of oil exporting economies. *BANK PARIKRAMA*, 47(3 & 4), 137. http://zarss-bibm.s3.amazonaws.com/ bibm_org/publications/publication_attachment/Oh64TCLxRD9ueMvfUoUC2x9Ad 3YRhBD3QbRTzXuQ.pdf#page=138

Sihare, S. R., & Khang, A. (2023). Effects of quantum technology on metaverse. In A. Khang, V. Shah, & S. Rani (Eds.), *AI-Based Technologies and Applications in the Era of the Metaverse* (1st Ed.) (pp. 104–203). IGI Global Press. https://doi.org/10.4018/978-1-6684-8851-5.ch009

Smyth, R., & Nandha, M. S. (2003). Bivariate causality between exchange rates and stock prices in south asia. *Applied Economics Letters*, 10(11), 699–704. https://doi.org/10.1080/1350485032000133282

Sucuahi, W. (2023). Predicting long-run and short-run movement of sectoral index: evidence from Philippine stock market. *International Journal of Financial Research*, *14*(2). https://papers.ssrn.com/sol3/papers.cfm?abstract_id=4389048

Suhaibu, I., Harvey, S. K., & Amidu, M. (2017). The impact of monetary policy on stock market performance: evidence from twelve (12) african countries. *Research in International Business and Finance, 42*, 1372–1382. https://doi.org/10.1016/j.ribaf.2017.07.075

Takeshi, I. (2008). The causal relationship in mean and variance between stock returns and foreign institutional investment in India. *Journal of Applied Economic Research*, 9, 321–351. https://journals.sagepub.com/doi/abs/10.1177/097380100900300401

Xiong, Z., & Han, L. (2015). Volatility spillover effect between financial markets: evidence since the reform of the rmb exchange rate mechanism. *Financial Innovation,* 1(1). https://doi.org/10.1186/s40854-015-0009-2

Yang, S. Y., & Doong, S. C. (2004). Price and volatility spillovers between stock prices and exchange rates: empirical evidence from the G-7 countries. *International Journal of Business and Economics*, 3(2), 139. https://ijbe.fcu.edu.tw/assets/ijbe/past_issue/No.03-2/pdf/vol_3-2-4.pdf

13 Digital Competency Assessment and Data-Driven Performance Management for Start-Ups

Radhika Baidya, Ruhi Lal, and Ravinder Rena

13.1 INTRODUCTION

Digital competencies refer to the skills, knowledge, and attitudes necessary to effectively navigate and utilize digital technologies in the workplace (Alzahrani & Yu, 2018). As technology continues to advance and become increasingly prevalent in business operations, it is important for start-ups to assess their digital competencies to ensure they have the necessary skills to remain competitive and successful (Barseghian, 2019).

One way to assess digital competencies in a start-up is through a digital competencies assessment. This type of assessment evaluates an individual's or team's ability to use digital tools and technologies to achieve business objectives (Bengtsson & Lakemond, 2017). The assessment can be used to identify strengths and weaknesses in digital competencies and to develop strategies for improvement (Ertmer & Ottenbreit-Leftwich, 2013).

Performance management is another important aspect of start-up success. Performance management involves setting clear goals, monitoring progress, providing feedback, and evaluating performance (Zahra & George, 2002). Effective performance management can help start-ups improve productivity, increase employee engagement, and achieve business objectives (Wang, Xu, & Wang, 2014).

Digital competencies and performance management are closely related in the start-up environment (Watson & Watson, 2017). Strong digital competencies can lead to improved performance management by providing the tools and technologies necessary to effectively monitor progress and achieve goals (Wechtler & Kastner, 2018). Effective performance management, in turn, can help to identify areas where digital competencies can be improved to better support business objectives (Khang, Gujarti et al., 2024), as shown in Figure 13.1.

DOI: 10.1201/9781032618845-13

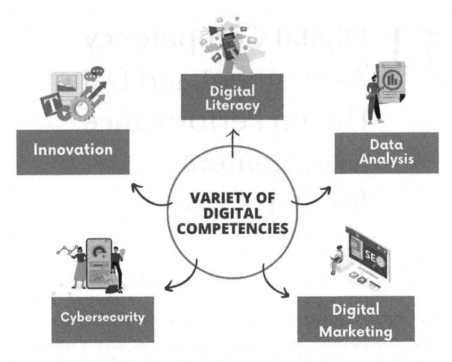

FIGURE 13.1   Variety of digital competencies.

- Digital literacy: The ability to use digital tools and technologies to communicate, collaborate, and complete tasks (Zott & Amit, 2013).
- Data analysis: The ability to collect, analyze, and interpret data to make informed business decisions (Zupic & Čater, 2015).
- Digital marketing: The ability to use digital channels to promote products or services and reach target audiences (Zott & Amit, 2013).
- Cybersecurity: The ability to protect digital assets and data from cyber threats (Zwilling, 2014).
- Innovation: The ability to identify and implement new digital technologies to improve business processes and outcomes (Zupic & Čater, 2015).

Effective performance management in start-ups should focus on setting clear goals, providing regular feedback, and evaluating performance based on objective criteria. It is important to recognize and reward high-performing employees while also providing support and guidance to those who may be struggling (Alzahrani & Yu, 2018).

Assessing digital competencies and implementing effective performance management strategies are both essential for start-up success in the digital age (Vuorikari et al., 2016). By identifying areas where digital competencies can be improved and implementing strategies for effective performance management, start-ups can achieve their business objectives and remain competitive in an ever-changing digital landscape (Khang, Semenets et al., 2024).

13.2 BACKGROUND OF RESEARCH

Digital competencies are essential in modern workplaces due to the increasing importance of digital technologies (Barseghian, 2019). Proficient digital skills are required for employees to effectively utilize these technologies.

Organizations, including start-ups, recognize the importance of assessing digital skills for long-term competitiveness and achievement. Digital competencies can be evaluated through methods like online assessments, simulations, and role-playing exercises.

Effective performance management is vital for the success of start-ups. Performance management systems now rely on digital tools to track progress, offer feedback, and assess performance based on objective criteria (Vuorikari et al., 2016).

Research is examining how start-ups adapt to the changing digital landscape through digital competency assessment and performance management. Start-ups with strong digital skills and effective performance management are more likely to succeed in the current digital age (Wang, Xu, & Wang, 2014).

The study of evaluating digital skills and performance management in start-ups is expanding because of the increasing importance of digital technologies in the workplace and the need for organizations to adapt to the changing digital landscape (Warschauer & Matuchniak, 2010). Continuous research and development of innovative tools and methodologies are essential for the competitiveness and success of organizations in the digital era (Watson & Watson, 2017)

13.2.1 Historical Overview of Research

Assessment of digital competencies and performance management has emerged as a result of the increasing importance of digital technologies in the workplace (Bargh & McKenna, 2004). The rise of digital tools and technologies has necessitated proficient personnel capable of utilizing them to achieve organizational objectives (Chai, Koh, & Tsai, 2010).

Digital competencies assessment and performance management rely on conventional competency-based practices (Bargh & McKenna, 2004). Digital technologies have revolutionized the assessment of digital competencies and performance management in the current era (Ertmer, Ottenbreit-Leftwich, & York, 2006).

Digital literacy is a concept that has existed since the beginning of computing (Livingstone & Helsper, 2007). Proficiency in digital literacy became essential for professional achievement only with the ubiquitous use of the internet and mobile technology (Bargh & McKenna, 2004). The complexity of digital technologies has resulted in the need for new competencies, such as data analysis, digital marketing, and cybersecurity, which are essential for success in the digital age (Chai, Koh, & Tsai, 2010).

Digital technologies have influenced the evolution of performance management in the workplace (Martin, 2006). Traditional performance management practices assessed employee performance using subjective criteria, such as personal opinions and observations (Alzahrani & Yu, 2018). Digital tools and data have made performance management more objective and data-driven (Eshet-Alkalai & Amichai-Hamburger, 2004).

Digital tools can assess competencies and performance in organizations (Friesen & Lowe, 2012). Digital competency assessments evaluate the proficiency of individuals or teams in utilizing digital tools and technologies to accomplish business goals (Ferrari, 2012). This may involve online assessments, simulations, and role-playing exercises. Digital tools, such as data analytics, can be utilized in performance management systems to objectively monitor progress, provide feedback, and evaluate performance (Friesen & Clifford, 2009).

Digital competencies are increasingly important in the workplace, leading to the development of assessment and management strategies (Kiili & Lainema, 2008). Evaluating digital skills and utilizing performance management tactics can aid companies in meeting their goals and staying competitive in the digital era (Ertmer, Ottenbreit-Leftwich, & York, 2006).

13.2.2 RESEARCH QUESTIONS

Some possible research questions for the research on digital competitiveness assessment of start-ups and performance management could include:

- What are the key digital competencies required for start-ups to succeed in the current business environment?
- How do these competencies vary across different industries and sectors?
- What are the key performance indicators (KPIs) that can be used to assess the digital competitiveness and performance of start-ups?
- How do start-ups perform on the digital competitiveness, and what are the factors that contribute to their success or failure on these KPIs?
- What are the key success factors for start-ups in terms of digital competitiveness and performance, and how do these factors vary across different stages of the start-up lifecycle?
- What are the best practices for improving digital competitiveness and performance in start-ups, and how can these practices be integrated into existing performance management processes?
- What are the challenges and opportunities associated with adopting digital technologies and competencies in start-ups, and how can these be effectively managed and addressed?
- What are the implications of digital competitiveness and performance for talent acquisition and management in start-ups, and how can start-ups attract and retain the talent needed to succeed in the digital age?

13.2.3 OBJECTIVES OF THE STUDY

- To identify the digital competencies that are critical for start-ups to succeed in the current business environment.
- Developing a framework for assessing the digital competitiveness of start-ups.
- To identify key performance indicators to assess digital competitiveness and performance of start-ups.
- Developing recommendations for start-ups and their managers to improve their digital competitiveness and performance.

13.2.4 Significance of the Research

Assessing digital competencies and managing performance in start-ups is a significant topic for various reasons, as described below.

Digital-savvy start-ups with efficient performance management strategies are better equipped to compete in the digital era by utilizing digital technologies to meet business goals (Rovai & Barnum, 2003). Digital competency assessments can pinpoint areas for employee training and development, improving job performance and career opportunities (Van Deursen & Van Dijk, 2010). Performance management can enhance productivity and efficiency in start-ups through goal setting, progress monitoring, feedback provision, and performance evaluation (Vanderlinde, van Braak, & Dexter, 2017). Performance management can identify high-performing employees and provide growth opportunities, increasing job satisfaction and reducing turnover (Vekiri, 2008). Assessing digital competencies and managing performance in start-ups is important for adapting to the digital landscape, improving efficiency, and staying competitive (Verheul, Wennekers, Audretsch, & Thurik, 2002).

13.3 REVIEW OF LITERATURE

13.3.1 Digital Competencies for Start-ups

Digital competencies are the necessary skills, knowledge, and abilities needed to effectively use digital technologies in professional settings. Digital competencies are crucial in various industries, including IT, marketing, finance, and customer service, for success in the current digital era (Bengtsson & Lakemond, 2017).

Digital competencies usually include basic digital literacy skills, such as being skilled in using common digital tools like email, word processing, and web browsing. Data analysis involves using digital tools such as statistical software, spreadsheets, and data visualization tools to examine data (Alzahrani & Yu, 2018). Digital marketing employs online channels, including social media, email, and online advertising, to promote products and services (Raza, Standing, Jiang, & Standing, 2020). Cybersecurity protects digital resources and information from cyber threats using effective measures (Di Pietro, Di Virgilio, & Bartolo, 2020). Cloud computing encompasses cloud-based storage, computing, and applications. Programming employs languages and tools for software development and evaluation. UX design develops digital products and interfaces that are user-friendly (DeWitt et al., 2019).

Digital competencies can be evaluated through online assessments, simulations, and role-playing exercises. Assessing digital competencies can aid in identifying employee training and development requirements for organizations (Ertmer et al., 2012).

Digital competencies can be divided into several categories, including technical competencies, information management competencies, communication competencies, and digital citizenship competencies (Ferraz, Ferreira, & Cruz-Jesus, 2018).

- Technical Competencies: Technical capabilities refer to the proficiency in utilizing digital tools and technology. Skill proficiency is crucial (Fraillon, Schulz, & Ainley, 2013). Technical skill pertains to proficiency in utilizing software, programming languages, and hardware systems. Technical skills encompass proficiency in SQL and Tableau for data analysis, and capability in Photoshop and Adobe Premiere for digital media (Vanderlinde, van Braak, & Dexter, 2014). Proficient in Microsoft Office, including Excel, Word, and PowerPoint, Python, or Java proficiency is required. Proficiency in diagnosing and resolving hardware issues pertaining to computers, printers, and servers is needed (Fraillon et al., 2013).

- Information Management Competencies: Competencies relate to information management skills (DeWitt et al., 2019). Mastery of these skills is crucial for efficient digital information management and utilization. Information management competencies comprise data handling, analysis, and presentation (Ertmer et al., 2012). Data analysis is part of information management. Information management competencies are exemplified below. Data analysis is crucial for informed decision-making in the workplace (Garcia & Romero, 2017). Proficiency in MySQL or Oracle database management is also needed, and also proficiency in data visualization tools like PowerBI and D3.js (Punie, Cabrera, & Redecker, 2017). Digital literacy encompasses the utilization of technology, such as search engines and applications, to locate and evaluate information (Crompton & Burke, 2018).

- Communication Competencies: Competencies in communication are essential for successful digital communication. "Communication capabilities" is a commonly used term. Communication competence requires mastery of oral, written, and digital media (Eynon & Geniets, 2016). Here are some examples of communication skills. The proficiency in (concise and persuasive) digital communication is crucial, including emails and reports. Proficiency in Adobe Creative Suite is necessary for digital media production (Ferraz, Ferreira, & Cruz-Jesus, 2018). Social media proficiency plays a vital role for business communication and marketing. Proficiency in email, instant messaging, and video conferencing constitutes electronic communication skills are needed (Ertmer & Ottenbreit-Leftwich, 2013).

- Digital Citizenship Competencies: Digital citizenship competencies are essential for responsible and ethical digital platform interaction (Redecker & Punie, 2017). This term refers to individuals' essential competencies. Skills can be classified as basic or advanced (Fraillon, Schulz, & Ainley, 2013). Digital citizenship includes online safety and security, digital ethics, and community building skills. Identifying and addressing online harassment and cyberbullying is a component of digital citizenship (Hinojo-Lucena, Romero-Rodríguez, & Fernández-Martínez, 2019). Other examples are familiarity with digital copyright and intellectual property rights, proficiency in building and sustaining online communities and networks, and capability in recognizing and resolving online harassment and cyberbullying (Eynon & Geniets, 2016).

Digital competencies are essential for success in the digital age (Vaast & Kaganer, 2013). Employers seek employees with strong digital competencies who can effectively navigate and utilize digital technologies to achieve business objectives

TABLE 13.1
Types of Digital Competencies

Technical competencies	• Proficiency in Microsoft Office applications such as Excel, Word, and PowerPoint • Ability to use digital media tools such as Photoshop or Adobe Premiere • Knowledge of programming languages such as Python or Java • Proficiency in data analysis tools such as SQL or Tableau • Ability to operate and troubleshoot hardware systems such as computers, printers, and servers
Information management competencies	• Ability to collect and analyze data to inform business decisions • Proficiency in data visualization tools such as PowerBI or D3.js • Knowledge of database management systems such as MySQL or Oracle • Ability to use search engines and other digital tools to find and evaluate information
Communication competencies	• Ability to communicate effectively through email, instant messaging, and video conferencing • Knowledge of social media platforms and how to use them effectively for business communication and marketing • Ability to write clear and effective emails, reports, and other digital communications • Knowledge of digital media production tools such as Adobe Creative Suite
Digital citizenship competencies	• Knowledge of cybersecurity threats and how to protect digital assets and data • Ability to identify and respond to online harassment and cyberbullying • Understanding of digital copyright and intellectual property rights • Ability to build and maintain positive online communities and networks

Source: Authors' compilation based on review of the literature.

(Crompton & Burke, 2018). By developing and enhancing digital competencies, individuals can improve their job performance, career prospects, and overall digital literacy (Table 13.1) (Garcia & Romero, 2017).

13.3.2 Digital Competency Assessment Tools

Digital competency assessment tools are designed to evaluate an individual's proficiency in digital technologies and related competencies (Ertmer & Ottenbreit-Leftwich, 2013). These tools can be used by employers, educators, or individuals to identify areas where further training and development may be needed. Some commonly used digital competency assessment tools include:

• LinkedIn Skill Assessments: LinkedIn provides skill exams for users to showcase their digital proficiency. LinkedIn's skill assessments are accessible on the homepage under the "Skill Assessments" tab (Grover & Pérez-Sanagustín,

2018). These exams assess proficiency in Adobe Creative Suite, Microsoft Excel, and programming languages such as Python and JavaScript. LinkedIn can display results as proof of an individual's expertise in a specific area, viewable by prospective employers (Hargittai & Hsieh, 2013).

- Google Digital Garage: Google Digital Garage is an e-learning platform that teaches digital skills and competencies (Janssen & Stoyanov, 2012a, b). The programs are accessible on any internet-connected computer. The software is readily accessible (Rovai & Barnum, 2003). Assessment activities can demonstrate individuals' comprehension of concepts such as data analysis, social media marketing, and search engine optimization upon course completion (Koh & Kim, 2004). The course titles encompass these concepts. Possible academic and shorter rewrite: Potential discussion topics comprise SEO, SMM, and data analysis. Online tutorials are available (Kozma & McGhee, 2000).

- Digital Competence Framework for Citizens (DigComp): The European Commission developed the DigComp framework for evaluating individuals' digital competencies. This was done to comply with the Digital Single Market participation requirements (Guàrdia, Sangrà, & Koskinen, 2019). The framework includes 21 abilities grouped into information and data literacy, communication and collaboration, digital content creation, safety, and problem-solving (Thibaut et al., 2017). DigComp assesses digital competence for individuals in business and education. Individual results can be benchmarked (Gutiérrez-Santiuste, Roblin, Román-González, & Olmos-Migueláñez, 2019).

- The International Computer Driving License (ICDL): The ICDL certifies proficiency in digital skills. The digital skills assessment was standardized in the curriculum (Tsai & Tsai, 2010). ICDL· certification can be obtained online (Leijen & Valtna, 2018). This talent group includes computer skills such as word processing, spreadsheet management, database administration, presentation software usage, and computer operation (Turel, Liu, & Yuan, 2020). This software's user-friendly platform enables businesses to assess individuals' digital skills (Grover & Pérez-Sanagustín, 2018).

- Skillsoft Digital Skills Assessments: Skillsoft assesses individuals' competency in various digital skill domains, including cloud computing, cybersecurity, digital marketing, and data analytics, using a variety of digital skill assessments (Barseghian, 2019). Skillsoft can evaluate digital skills proficiency. The exams assess knowledge in cloud computing, cybersecurity, data analytics, and digital marketing (Renko, Shrader, & Simon, 2012). Employers administer tests to pinpoint skill deficiencies in employees and collaborate with them to enhance those competencies (Guàrdia, Sangrà, & Koskinen, 2019). Companies can offer targeted training to enhance employees' career prospects within the company (Renko, Shrader, & Simon, 2012).

Digital competency assessment tools can be valuable for individuals and employers seeking to evaluate and develop digital competencies (Li & Tsai, 2019). By identifying areas where further training and development may be needed, individuals can enhance their job performance and career prospects, while employers can

TABLE 13.2
Digital Competency Assessment Tools

S. No	Assessment Tool	Description
1	LinkedIn Skill Assessments	LinkedIn provides skill assessments to showcase digital competencies. The assessments evaluate proficiency in Microsoft Excel, Adobe Creative Suite, and coding languages like Python and JavaScript. LinkedIn profiles can exhibit an individual's competencies to potential employers through displayed results
2	Google Digital Garage	Google Digital Garage provides online courses on digital skills and competencies. Assessments can be taken after courses to exhibit proficiency in data analysis, social media marketing, and search engine optimization
3	Digital Competence Framework for Citizens (DigComp)	DigComp is a framework created by the European Commission to evaluate the digital competencies of citizens. The framework includes 21 competencies divided into five domains: information and data literacy, communication and collaboration, digital content creation, safety, and problem-solving. DigComp evaluates digital competencies and benefits educators and employers
4	The International Computer Driving License (ICDL)	The ICDL is a certification program that evaluates digital competencies, such as computer use, word processing, spreadsheets, databases, and presentation software. The program has international recognition and employers can use it to assess digital skills
5	Skillsoft Digital Skills Assessments	Skillsoft provides digital skills assessments to evaluate proficiency in cloud computing, cybersecurity, digital marketing, and data analytics. Employers can use these assessments to pinpoint skills gaps and offer specific training and development options

Source: Authors' compilation based on review of the literature.

ensure that their workforce has the digital skills needed to remain competitive in the digital age (Table 13.2) (Gutiérrez-Santiuste, Roblin, Román-González, & Olmos-Miguéláñez, 2019).

13.3.3 DIRECT AND INDIRECT ASSESSMENT TOOLS FOR MAPPING DIGITAL COMPETENCIES

Tools that are considered to be direct assessment tools are those that test certain abilities and skills directly. They often include some kind of test, examination, or assessment in which the student is required to show the digital skills they have acquired (Redecker & Punie, 2017). Direct evaluation tools for digital abilities include something like the following examples:

- Simulation-based assessments: These tests simulate real-world scenarios and assess students' readiness for them. It is now feasible to evaluate learners' digital skills in suitable contexts (Lindell & Fransson, 2008).
- Performance-based assessments: Students must complete digital projects or assignments to pass tests and demonstrate their knowledge and expertise (Punie, Cabrera, & Redecker, 2017). These activities can be accomplished through various methods, including website or application development and software program creation (Liu, Guo, & Lee, 2016).
- Project-based assessments: Active participation in digital project creation is a prerequisite for receiving assessment credit (Raza, Standing, Jiang, & Standing, 2020). This category encompasses projects such as creating e-learning courses, formulating social media plans, and implementing digital marketing initiatives. Additional projects could fit within this category (Martens, 2017).
- Certifications: Formal certifications are one method that a person may show their expertise in digital technologies to a potential employer. Certifications in this category include those bestowed by Microsoft, Adobe, and Google, to name a few examples (Opazo-Basáez & Bresciani, 2020).
- On the other hand, indirect assessment tools evaluate digital competences in an indirect manner by taking into consideration the learners' attitudes, behaviors, and self-perceptions. Some examples of indirect evaluation techniques for digital skills include the following.
- Self-assessment tools: Typically, students complete a questionnaire or survey to assess their digital abilities and competencies. These tools assess the learner's digital proficiency level in an objective and quantitative manner (Pai & Wang, 2019).
- Peer assessment tools: Through the use of these technologies, students assess the level of digital ability and expertise possessed by their fellow students. This method is able to provide a more objective evaluation of digital abilities due to the fact that it is based on the observation of digital skills by peers (Pereira, Morgado, Lencastre, & Oliveira, 2018).
- Reflective journals: Students utilize diaries for reflecting on their digital experiences and competencies. This is a component of the digital diaries' assignment. The journals aim to enhance students' digital competences (Pinto, Morgado, & Santos, 2020).
- 360-degree feedback: This is a complete feedback process that involves gathering information on an individual's digital abilities from a variety of sources, such as the individual's own self-assessment, the feedback from peers, and the feedback from supervisors. There may also be some room for other kinds of comments and suggestions (Prange, Schröder, & Schäfer, 2018).

Both direct and indirect assessment tools can be useful for mapping digital competencies, depending on the specific objectives of the assessment and the nature of the competencies being measured (Table 13.3).

TABLE 13.3
Direct/indirect Assessment Tools

Direct assessment tools	Indirect assessment tools
• **Simulation-based assessments:** These assessments are designed to simulate real-world scenarios to evaluate learners' ability to apply their digital skills in practical situations	• **Self-assessment tools:** These tools usually take the form of a questionnaire or survey that asks learners to rate their digital skills and competencies. These tools provide a subjective measure of learners' perceived digital competence
• **Performance-based assessments:** These **assessments** require learners to perform specific digital tasks or assignments, such as creating a website, developing an app or programming a software application	• **Peer assessment tools:** These tools involve learners evaluating their peers' digital skills and competencies. This method can provide a more objective measure of digital skills, as it is based on peer observation
• **Project-based assessments:** These assessments require learners to work on digital projects, such as designing and implementing a digital marketing campaign, developing a social media strategy, or creating an e-learning course	• **Reflective journals:** These journals require learners to reflect on their digital experiences and skills development, and provide insights into their digital competencies
• **Certifications:** These are formal certifications that demonstrate an individual's digital competencies, such as those offered by Microsoft, Adobe, or Google	• **360-Degree Feedback:** This is a comprehensive feedback process that involves gathering feedback on an individual's digital competencies from multiple sources, including peers, supervisors, and self-assessment

Source: Authors' compilation based on review of the literature.

13.3.4 THEORETICAL FOUNDATIONS AND FRAMEWORK

The theoretical foundations and framework for a research study on the assessment of digital competency of start-ups and performance management can draw upon various theories and frameworks related to digital competencies, performance management, and organizational behavior, as shown in Figure 13.2.

Some key theories on which the study is based are the foundations of this research, as shown in Figure 13.3.

- Digital Competency Theories: Resource-Based View (RBV): This theory emphasizes the importance of unique resources and capabilities, including digital competencies, in achieving competitive advantage. It suggests that start-ups with superior digital competencies are better positioned to outperform competitors.
- Dynamic Capability Theory: This theory focuses on an organization's ability to adapt and respond to changing environments. It highlights the importance of

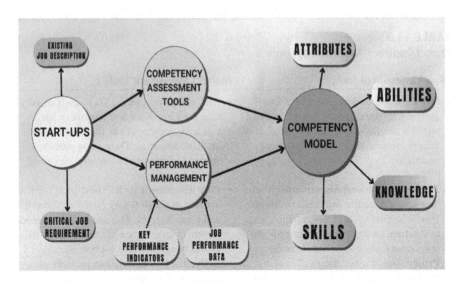

FIGURE 13.2   Conceptual framework.

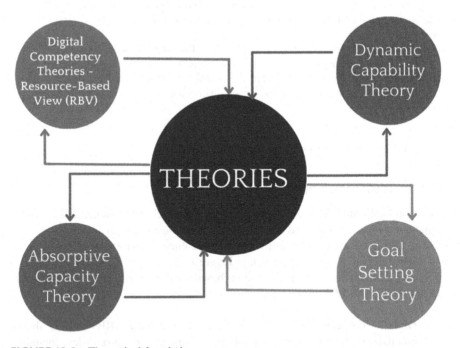

FIGURE 13.3   Theoretical foundations.

digital competencies as dynamic capabilities that enable start-ups to effectively navigate the digital landscape.

- Absorptive Capacity Theory: This theory explores how organizations acquire, assimilate, and exploit knowledge. In the context of digital competencies, it

TABLE 13.4
The Key Constructs, Variables, and Relationships between Digital Competencies and Performance Outcomes

Theories	Independent	Dependent
Digital Competency Theories: Resource-Based View (RBV)	• Unique resources • Capabilities	• Digital Competencies
Dynamic Capability Theory	• Organizational Capabilities	• Digital Competencies
Absorptive Capacity Theory	• Digital Competencies • Skills	• Performance
Goal Setting Theory	• Specific Challenging Goals • Digital Competency Goals	• Performance

Source: Theoretical foundation and framework.

emphasizes the start-up's ability to absorb and leverage digital knowledge and skills to enhance performance.
• Goal Setting Theory: This theory suggests that setting specific, challenging goals can motivate individuals and teams to perform better. It can be applied to performance management in start-ups by setting specific digital competency goals and monitoring progress.

It is important to critically review and integrate relevant theories, frameworks, and models. In this study the framework is outlined with the key constructs, variables, and relationships between digital competencies and performance outcomes, as shown in Table 13.4.

The study also considered the contextual factors that may influence the relationship, such as industry dynamics, organizational culture, and start-up characteristics for a better outcome of the research, as shown in Figure 13.4.

13.4   RESEARCH METHODOLOGY

For the purpose of generating new measures of digital competences and performance management, this study employs the approach of reviewing the relevant previous research. It requires completing a thorough search and study of all existing research studies, academic papers, and any other sources that are relevant in order to discover any gaps, strengths, and shortcomings in the present knowledge and practice of digital skills and performance management. The research highlighted important ideas that are significant to the creation of new measures of digital competences and performance management. These key concepts were recognized as being relevant by the study.

A review of the literature was used as a research methodology that involved gathering and analyzing existing literature relevant to a particular research question. The method allowed the researchers to identify existing knowledge and research gaps in their field

THEORATICAL FRAMEWORK

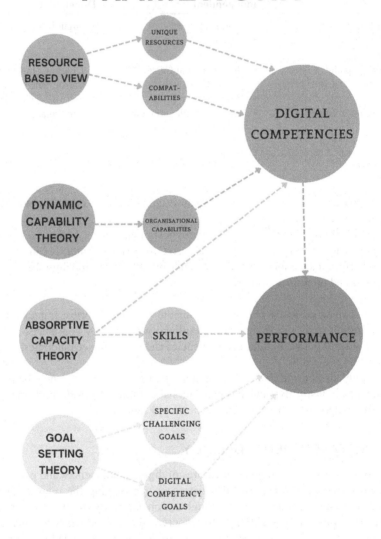

FIGURE 13.4 Theoretical framework.

of study. By examining previous studies, researchers determined areas that require further investigation or where new contributions can be made, researchers established a theoretical framework for their study. By examining existing theories, models, and concepts, researchers build a foundation for their own research and position it within the context of prior knowledge. This helped researchers make informed decisions about the most appropriate methods to use in their own research. By applying a literature review as a method, researchers refined their research questions and objectives. By analyzing existing literature, researchers identified gaps or limitations in current knowledge, which shaped their research focus and objectives. The literature reviews provide researchers with evidence and support for their research study. By referencing and citing relevant studies, researchers can strengthen the credibility of their work and demonstrate the need for and significance of their research. To synthesize and summarize findings from multiple studies, analyzing and comparing results across various sources, researchers identified patterns, discrepancies, or emerging trends.

Researchers ensured that their research is original and contributes something new to the field. It helped them avoid duplicating previous studies and provides a basis for building on existing knowledge. Literature review as a method of research assisted the researchers in interpreting their own data and findings. By referencing relevant studies, researchers compared and contrasted their results with prior research, which provided context and insights during the data analysis process.

By conducting a thorough literature review, researchers demonstrated their commitment to rigor and validity. It showcased their familiarity with prior research, theoretical foundations, and methodologies, thereby strengthening the credibility of their own study. The study provided insights into the practical implications and applications of their research findings. By examining how previous research study has been applied in practice, researchers can identify potential implications for policymakers, practitioners, or other stakeholders, as shown in Figure 13.5.

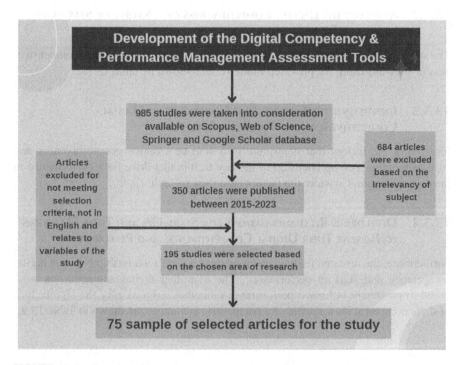

FIGURE 13.5 Samples of inclusion/exclusion.

13.5 FINDINGS AND ANALYSIS

The aim was to identify the digital competencies that are critical for start-ups to succeed in the current business environment. Start-ups need a variety of digital competencies to succeed in the current business environment. These skills provide individuals the ability to use technology, navigate the digital world, and take advantage of new opportunities. The following are some essential digital skills for start-ups. Start-ups must comprehend the best practices for online marketing their goods and services. This involves proficiency with digital advertising, social media marketing, email marketing, content marketing, and search engine optimization (SEO) as shown in Table 13.5.

While these competencies are critical, it is important to note that the specific needs may vary depending on the nature of the start-up and its industry. Continuous learning, keeping up with industry trends, and staying updated on emerging technologies are crucial for start-ups to remain competitive in the digital era.

13.5.1 DEVELOPING A FRAMEWORK FOR ASSESSING THE DIGITAL COMPETITIVENESS OF START-UPS

Evaluating the digital efficacy of start-ups necessitates a comprehensive framework that considers a variety of factors and indicators. The following framework can be used to evaluate the digital competitiveness of start-ups as shown in Table 13.6.

13.5.2 ASSESSING THE DIGITAL COMPETITIVENESS OF A SAMPLE OF START-UPS USING THE FRAMEWORK

The steps in the following framework can be used to evaluate the digital competitiveness of start-ups using the provided framework as shown in Table 13.7.

13.5.3 IDENTIFYING THE FACTORS THAT CONTRIBUTE TO DIGITAL COMPETITIVENESS AND SUCCESS IN START-UPS

Identifying the factors that contribute to a start-up's digital competitiveness and success requires a comprehension of the key factors that drive their performance in the digital domain. Consider the factors described in Table 13.8.

13.5.4 DEVELOPING RECOMMENDATIONS FOR START-UPS AND THEIR MANAGERS TO IMPROVE THEIR DIGITAL COMPETITIVENESS AND PERFORMANCE

Furthermore, the research findings demonstrated a clear relationship between digital competency and start-up performance. The identified digital competencies were found to positively influence performance outcomes, emphasizing the significance of these competencies for achieving competitive advantage, as shown in Table 13.9.

TABLE 13.5
The Digital Competencies for Start-Ups

S. No.	Various Digital Competencies	
1.	Data analytics	To learn more about their consumers, markets, and operations, start-ups should be able to gather, analyze, and understand data. They can optimize their tactics and make educated decisions thanks to their data analytics prowess
2.	User Experience (UX) Design	It's essential for start-ups to offer a seamless and simple user experience. UX design skills are useful for developing user-friendly user interfaces and improving client interactions on numerous digital platforms
3	Agile Development	Start-ups frequently work in frantic, dynamic environments. They can quickly adapt, iterate, and produce high-quality software solutions thanks to their proficiency in agile development approaches
4	Cybersecurity	Due to the growing number of online dangers, start-ups must prioritize cybersecurity in order to safeguard their data, systems, and client information. Understanding best practices, putting them into practice, and keeping up with potential vulnerabilities are all essential cybersecurity competencies
5	E-commerce	In the age of digital transactions and online shopping, start-ups need e-commerce skills to create and run online storefronts, payment gateways, inventory control systems, and fulfilment procedures
6	Cloud computing	For start-ups, utilizing cloud platforms offers scalability, flexibility, and cost-efficiency. Businesses can develop and manage apps, store and analyze data, and access numerous cloud-based services thanks to their cloud computing competencies
7	Mobile app development	With the extensive usage of smartphones, start-ups may find it necessary to develop a mobile app. They can produce compelling and user-friendly mobile experiences thanks to their proficiency in mobile app development
8	Collaborate digitally with clients, partners, and remote teams	Start-ups frequently collaborate digitally with clients, partners, and remote teams. Digital collaboration skills and platforms enable effective project management, cross-cultural teamwork, and communication
9	Innovation and adaptability	Digital competences are not restricted to certain tools or technology; they also include innovation and adaptability. To stay ahead in the rapidly changing digital landscape, start-ups must promote a culture of creativity, continual learning, and adaptation

TABLE 13.6
Framework for Assessing the Digital Competitiveness of Start-Ups

S. No.	Framework for Assessing the Digital Competitiveness of Start-Ups	
1.	Presence and visibility in the market	Assess the website, social media presence, and search engine rankings of the start-up. Evaluate the quality of their online content, branding consistency, and audience engagement
2	Effectiveness of digital marketing	Analyze their digital marketing strategies, campaigns, and ability to reach and engage their target audience. Consider metrics such as website traffic, social media followers, conversion rates, and feedback from customers
3.	Scalability	Evaluate the start-up's technological infrastructure, including their capacity to scale their operations, manage increased user traffic, and adapt to changing conditions
4.	Assess data collection, storage, and analytic capabilities	Effectively leverage data insights to enhance their products or services and drive decision-making
5	User experience and innovation	Assess the user interface (UI), website/app navigation, and overall user experience of the start-up. Think about usability, intuitiveness, responsiveness, and accessibility
6	Innovation culture	Evaluate the start-up's dedication to innovation, its capacity to introduce new features, products, or services, and its adaptability to market trends and emerging technologies
7	Digital skills and talent	Evaluate the start-up's internal digital competencies, such as digital marketing, data analytics, UX design, and software development expertise the team
8	Digital trends and technologies	Assess the start-up's investment in continuous skill development and learning opportunities for its employees in order to remain current with digital trends and technologies
9	Security measures	Cybersecurity and privacy: Assess the cybersecurity protocols of the start-up, including data encryption, access controls, and vulnerability assessments. Consider their proactive approach to identifying and mitigating potential security hazards
10	Privacy compliance	Evaluate their adherence to data protection regulations and privacy best practices, such as GDPR or CCPA Collaboration and alliances: Evaluate the start-up's participation in industry networks, partnerships, and collaborations with other organizations and start-ups. Consider their capacity to capitalize on external knowledge, resources, and market opportunities
11	Performance measurements	Define and monitor pertinent key performance indicators (KPIs) for measuring the digital competitiveness of the start-up. This may include metrics such as customer acquisition cost, lifetime customer value, conversion rates, customer satisfaction, and user engagement

TABLE 13.6 (Continued)
Framework for Assessing the Digital Competitiveness of Start-Ups

S. No.	Framework for Assessing the Digital Competitiveness of Start-Ups	
12	Competitive evaluation	Benchmarking: Compare the digital competitiveness of the start-up to that of its industry rivals. Identify their distinct value proposition and areas where they excel or underperform

TABLE 13.7
Steps to Evaluate the Digital Competitiveness of Start-Ups Using the Framework

S. No.	Steps to evaluate the digital competitiveness of start-ups using the provided framework	
1	Determine the start-ups	Choose an evaluation sample of start-ups. Ensure that they represent a variety of industries, sizes, and development stages
2	Collect data	Collect pertinent information regarding each start-up based on the criteria of the framework. This may involve conducting investigation, analyzing their online presence, and collecting information from a variety of sources
3	Assess market visibility and presence	Evaluate their online presence, including their website quality, social media engagement, search engine rankings, and digital marketing efficiency. Assign ratings or rankings based on predefined criteria
4	Evaluate technological infrastructure	Evaluate the organization's technological capabilities, scalability, and data management procedures. Consider their capacity to manage increased user traffic, their adaptability to changing demands, and their utilization of data insights
5	Analyze user experience and innovation	Assess the user experience design of the start-ups, including the intuitiveness of their website or app, responsiveness, and overall user satisfaction. Evaluate their commitment to innovation, the introduction of new features, and market adaptability
6	Assess digital skills and talent	Evaluate the start-up's team's expertise in digital competencies, including digital marketing, data analytics, UX design, and software development. Consider the organization's investment in opportunities for talent development and learning
7	Assess cybersecurity and privacy measures	Evaluate the start-ups' cybersecurity protocols, which should include data encryption, access controls, and vulnerability assessments. Assess their compliance with data protection regulations and best practices for privacy

(continued)

TABLE 13.7 (Continued)
Steps to Evaluate the Digital Competitiveness of Start-Ups Using the Framework

S. No.	Steps to evaluate the digital competitiveness of start-ups using the provided framework	
8	Evaluate collaboration and partnerships	Evaluate their participation in industry networks, collaborations, and partnerships. Consider their capacity to capitalize on external knowledge, resources, and market opportunities
9	Performance metrics analysis	Use the defined KPIs to evaluate the efficacy of each start-up in key areas. Comparing their customer acquisition cost, customer lifetime value, conversion rates, customer satisfaction, and user engagement will help you to determine which company is the best
10	Performance analyses of the start-ups	Analyze the start-ups in comparison to their competitors in terms of digital competitiveness. Determine the areas in which they outperform or languish behind the competition and assess their unique value proposition
11	Restate and report	Compile the results of each start-up's assessment and present them in a comprehensive report. Include suggestions for enhancement areas and strategies to increase their digital competitiveness

TABLE 13.8
The Factors That Contribute to Digital Competitiveness and Success in Start-Ups

S. No.	Identifying the factors that contribute to digital competitiveness and success in start-ups	
1	Value proposition	Start-ups must have a distinct and compelling value proposition that sets them apart from competitors. Their digital offerings should address customer pain points, provide distinctive benefits, and provide value in a manner that resonates with their target audience
2	Targeting and market research	Conducting extensive market research assists new businesses in understanding their target audience, their preferences, and the competitive landscape. Start-ups can maximize the impact of their offerings and marketing strategies by identifying and targeting the appropriate market segment with their digital solutions
3	Digital strategy and planning	Developing a solid digital strategy is essential for start-ups in order to set distinct objectives, define the actions required to achieve them, and allocate resources efficiently. This strategy should incorporate all facets of the business, such as product development, marketing, customer experience, and technology infrastructure

TABLE 13.8 (Continued)
The Factors That Contribute to Digital Competitiveness and Success in Start-Ups

S. No.	Identifying the factors that contribute to digital competitiveness and success in start-ups	
4	User-Centric Design	Start-ups that priorities user-centric design produce digital solutions that are intuitive, user-friendly, and in line with consumer requirements. They invest in gaining an understanding of user behavior, undertake usability testing, and refine their designs based on user feedback, resulting in increased customer satisfaction and loyalty
5	Agility and adaptability	Start-ups operating in the digital landscape must be agile and responsive to changes in technology, market trends, and consumer preferences. Their ability to rapidly pivot, experiment, and iterate their digital strategies enables them to remain competitive and capitalize on emergent opportunities
6	Technology infrastructure	A robust technology infrastructure is essential for start-ups to support their digital operations. This consists of dependable hosting, scalable cloud services, comprehensive cybersecurity measures, and integration capabilities to ensure data integrity and seamless operation
7	Data-driven decision-making	Start-ups that utilize data analytics proficiently can acquire valuable insights into customer behavior, market trends, and business performance. By using data to drive decision-making, businesses can optimize their digital strategies, identify growth opportunities, and strengthen their competitive edge
8	Digital marketing and customer acquisition	Start-ups must create effective digital marketing strategies in order to attract, engage, and convert customers. This includes utilizing a variety of channels, such as search engine optimization (SEO), social media marketing, content marketing, and paid advertising, to increase brand awareness and consumer acquisition
9	Consumer experience and engagement	Providing a seamless and personalized consumer experience across digital touchpoints is crucial for a start-up's success. By focusing on customer satisfaction, engagement, and retention, new businesses can develop a loyal customer base and generate positive word-of-mouth
10	Continuous learning and innovation	Successful digital start-ups encourage a culture of continuous learning and innovation. They invest in employee development, encourage experimentation, embrace emergent technologies, and keep abreast of industry trends in order to promote digital competitiveness

TABLE 13.9

The List of Recommendations to Enhance the Digital Competitiveness and Performance of Start-Ups and Their Managers

S. No.	Recommendations to enhance the digital competitiveness and performance of start-ups and their managers	
1	Construct a digital strategy	Start-ups should develop a digital strategy that correlates with their overarching business objectives. The strategy should include a detailed road map, executable plans, and quantifiable goals for leveraging digital technologies and channels to fuel growth and competitiveness
2	Spend money on digital talent	Hire and cultivate a team with diverse digital skills, including digital marketing, data analytics, UX design, and software development expertise. Continuously invest in their training and development to keep them abreast of emerging technologies and trends
3	Prioritize user-centric design	Prioritize user-centric design in order to create seamless and intuitive digital experiences for your customers. Conduct user research, collect feedback, and iterate designs in accordance with user insights. Ensure that the digital products and interfaces are user-friendly, visually alluring, and mobile-optimized
4	Utilize data analytics	Utilize data analytics to acquire insight into customer behavior, market trends, and operational efficiency. Implement tools and procedures to efficiently collect, analyze, and interpret data. Utilize data-driven decision-making to optimize marketing strategies, enhance products/services, and uncover new growth opportunities.
5	Develop a comprehensive digital marketing strategy	Develop a comprehensive digital marketing strategy that includes search engine optimization (SEO), social media marketing, content marketing, and email marketing. Utilize data analytics to improve campaign performance by refining targeting, personalizing messaging, and optimizing campaign performance. Continuously monitor and assess results in order to make data-driven enhancements
6	Adopt innovative technologies	Keep abreast of emerging technologies pertinent to the start-up's industry and investigate opportunities for their incorporation. Consider adopting artificial intelligence (AI), machine learning, blockchain, or Internet of Things (IoT) solutions to improve operations, enhance consumer experiences, or promote innovation, for instance
7	Foster an innovation culture	Promote and sustain an innovative culture within the start-up. Create opportunities for workers to share their ideas, experiment, and take calculated risks. Establish processes for evaluating and implementing innovative business concepts

TABLE 13.9 (Continued)
The Factors That Contribute to Digital Competitiveness and Success in Start-Ups

S. No.	Recommendations to enhance the digital competitiveness and performance of start-ups and their managers	
8	Develop strategic alliances	Utilize the expertise, resources, and networks of complementary start-ups, established businesses, and industry experts through collaboration. Strategic alliances can facilitate access to new markets, technologies, and growth opportunities
9	Increase cybersecurity efforts	Prioritize cybersecurity to safeguard the digital assets, sensitive data, and consumer information of the start-up. Implement comprehensive security protocols, update software and systems on a regular basis, and educate employees on best practices for mitigating potential risks
10	Continuously monitor the digital landscape	Continuously monitor the digital landscape, industry trends, and competitors in order to identify emerging opportunities and threats. Assess the efficacy of digital strategies on a regular basis and modify your tactics accordingly. Maintain agility and adaptability as market dynamics and customer preferences evolve

13.6 CONCLUSION

In conclusion, this research study on the assessment of the digital competency of start-ups and performance management has shed light on the critical role of digital competencies in driving start-up success. Through a comprehensive analysis of digital competencies and their impact on performance, several key findings have emerged.

- Firstly, the assessment of digital competencies revealed specific areas where start-ups exhibited strengths and weaknesses. These findings provide valuable insights into the competencies that are crucial for start-up success in the digital landscape.
- Secondly, the study highlighted the implications of digital competency assessment for performance management in start-ups. Integrating digital competencies into performance management practices, such as goal setting, measurement, feedback, and employee development, can significantly enhance overall performance.

Based on these insights, practical recommendations have been provided for start-ups and managers to improve digital competencies and enhance performance management strategies. By leveraging these recommendations, start-ups can strengthen their digital capabilities and position themselves for sustainable growth in the digital era.

It is important to acknowledge the limitations of this study, such as the sample size and potential biases, which may affect the generalizability of the findings. Future research should consider expanding the scope and incorporating additional factors to further explore the complex dynamics between digital competencies and start-up performance.

Overall, this research study contributes to the existing body of knowledge by providing valuable insights into the assessment of digital competencies in start-ups and their implications for performance management. By embracing and cultivating digital competencies, start-ups can navigate the digital landscape more effectively and achieve long-term success.

13.7   LIMITATIONS

While conducting research on the assessment of digital competency of start-ups and performance management, several limitations should be acknowledged:

- The study may have been limited by a relatively small sample size or a specific focus on a particular industry or geographic region. This could affect the generalizability of the findings to a broader population of start-ups.
- The data collected for the assessment of digital competencies and performance management have relied on a review of literature and not first-hand data.
- Assessing digital competencies can be subjective, as it often relies on self-assessment or the perceptions of individuals within the start-up. Different evaluators may have different interpretations of digital competencies, leading to potential inconsistencies in the assessment process.
- The research study may have been conducted within a limited timeframe, which could have constrained the depth and breadth of data collection and analysis. Longitudinal studies over an extended period may provide a more comprehensive understanding of the relationship between digital competency and performance.
- The study might not have fully accounted for external factors and contextual dynamics that can influence digital competencies and performance management in start-ups. Factors such as industry-specific challenges, market conditions, and technological advancements could impact the findings.
- Identifying and quantifying the specific digital competencies relevant to start-up performance management can be challenging. Developing robust measurement instruments and defining clear indicators of digital competency could be an area of limitation.
- Establishing a causal relationship between digital competencies and performance can be incomplete. The study may have faced challenges in determining whether digital competencies directly drive performance or if high-performing start-ups naturally develop strong digital competencies.
- The rapid pace of technological advancements means that the digital landscape is constantly evolving. The findings of the study may become outdated relatively quickly as new technologies and digital competencies emerge (Khang, Rani et al., 2023).

Acknowledging these limitations is important as it ensures transparency and provides opportunities for future research to address these gaps. Despite these limitations, the research study provides valuable insights into the assessment of digital competencies and performance management in start-ups, contributing to the existing body of knowledge in the field (Khang & AIoCF, 2024).

13.8 RECOMMENDATIONS AND SUGGESTIONS

Based on the research study on the assessment of digital competency of start-ups and performance management, the following recommendations and suggestions can be made to help start-ups improve their digital competencies and enhance performance management:

- Conduct a Comprehensive Digital Competency Assessment: Start-ups should regularly assess their digital competencies using a structured framework or assessment tool. This will help identify strengths and weaknesses and provide a baseline for improvement.
- Align Digital Competencies with Organizational Goals: Start-ups should ensure that their digital competencies align with their overall business objectives. By identifying specific digital competencies that directly contribute to their strategic goals, start-ups can focus their efforts on developing those competencies.
- Invest in Continuous Learning and Development: Start-ups should prioritize learning and development initiatives to enhance digital competencies among employees. This can include training programs, workshops, mentoring, and access to external resources to keep up with the evolving digital landscape.
- Foster a Culture of Innovation and Experimentation: Start-ups should create an environment that encourages innovation and experimentation with digital technologies. This can be achieved by promoting a culture that embraces failure as a learning opportunity, allowing employees to explore new digital tools and approaches.
- Establish Clear Performance Metrics: Start-ups should define clear performance metrics that align with their digital competencies and overall business objectives. This includes both quantitative and qualitative measures to assess the impact of digital competencies on performance outcomes.
- Provide Ongoing Feedback and Coaching: Start-ups should implement regular feedback mechanisms and coaching sessions to support employees' development of digital competencies. Managers should provide constructive feedback and guidance to help employees improve their skills and bridge any competency gaps.
- Foster Collaboration and Cross-Functional Teams: Start-ups should encourage collaboration and create cross-functional teams that bring together individuals with diverse digital competencies. This promotes knowledge sharing, cross-pollination of ideas, and the ability to leverage different strengths to drive overall performance.
- Stay Updated on Technological Advancements: Start-ups should stay informed about emerging technologies and industry trends relevant to their digital competencies. This can be achieved through industry events, conferences, online resources, and networking with experts in the field.

- Embrace Agile and Adaptive Strategies: Start-ups should adopt agile and adaptive strategies to respond quickly to changing market demands and technological advancements. This includes the ability to pivot, experiment, and iterate based on feedback and insights gained through digital competencies.
- Continuously evaluate and evolve: Start-ups should regularly evaluate their digital competencies and performance management strategies to identify areas for improvement. They should be open to adapting and evolving their approaches based on new learnings, market conditions, and emerging best practices.

By implementing these recommendations, start-ups can strengthen their digital competencies, optimize performance management practices, and position themselves for success in the digital era. It is essential for start-up leaders and managers to prioritize continuous improvement and foster a culture that values and nurtures digital competencies as a key driver of organizational performance (Khang, Shah et al., 2023).

13.9   FUTURE SCOPE OF WORK

The research study on the assessment of digital competency of start-ups and performance management opens up several avenues for future research. Here are some potential areas for further investigation:

- Longitudinal Study: Conducting a longitudinal study that follows start-ups over an extended period can provide deeper insights into the long-term effects of digital competencies on performance. Examining the trajectory of digital competency development and its impact on start-up success can uncover valuable patterns and trends (Muthmainnah, Khang et al., 2023).
- Comparative Analysis: Comparing start-ups across different industries, sizes, or geographic regions can help identify variations in digital competencies and performance management practices. This comparative analysis can uncover industry-specific challenges, best practices, and factors that influence the relationship between digital competencies and performance.
- Qualitative Research: Complementing quantitative assessments with qualitative research methods, such as interviews or case studies, can provide richer insights into the nuances of digital competency development and its impact on performance management. Qualitative research can capture in-depth experiences, challenges, and success stories of start-ups in relation to their digital competencies.
- Multi-Level Analysis: Exploring the impact of digital competencies and performance management practices at different levels of the organization, such as individual, team, and organizational levels, can offer a more comprehensive understanding. This analysis can shed light on how digital competencies are interconnected and how they influence performance outcomes at various organizational levels.

- External Factors and Ecosystem Analysis: Investigating the influence of external factors, such as the start-up ecosystem, government policies, industry dynamics, and technological advancements, can provide a broader perspective on the assessment of digital competencies and performance management. Understanding how the external environment shapes digital competencies and performance can help start-ups adapt and thrive.
- Impact of Digital Competencies on Innovation and Disruption: Exploring the relationship between digital competencies, innovation capabilities, and disruptive potential can be an interesting avenue for future research. Understanding how digital competencies enable start-ups to innovate, disrupt traditional industries, and create new business models can provide valuable insights.
- Contextual Factors and Contingency Analysis: Investigating contextual factors, such as organizational culture, leadership styles, and resource availability, and their interaction with digital competencies and performance management can deepen our understanding of their relationship. Contingency analysis can identify the conditions under which certain digital competencies have a more significant impact on performance (Khang, Shah et al., 2023).
- Multi-Dimensional Performance Measurement: Extending the performance measurement framework to include multiple dimensions, such as financial performance, customer satisfaction, employee engagement, and innovation outcomes, can provide a holistic view of the impact of digital competencies on various aspects of start-up performance.
- Cross-Cultural Studies: Examining the role of cultural factors in the development and utilization of digital competencies can be an interesting area for cross-cultural research. Comparing start-ups across different cultural contexts can uncover unique challenges, enablers, and strategies for developing and leveraging digital competencies (Khang, Kali et al., 2023).
- Impact of Digital Competencies on Business Resilience and Sustainability: Investigating how digital competencies contribute to start-up resilience and long-term sustainability can be an important area of research. Understanding how digital competencies help start-ups navigate disruptions, adapt to changing market conditions, and sustain competitive advantage can provide valuable insights for building resilient organizations (Khang, Muthmainnah et al., 2023).

REFERENCES

Alzahrani, A., & Yu, S (2018). Digital competence development in higher education: A systematic review of literature. *International Journal of Information and Education Technology*, 8(1), 30–34. https://link.springer.com/article/10.1007/s11423-019-09718-8

Bargh, J. A., & McKenna, K. Y (2004). The Internet and social life. *Annual Review of Psychology*, 55, 573–590. www.annualreviews.org/doi/abs/10.1146/annurev.psych.55.090902.141922

Barseghian, T (2019). The role of digital literacy in empowering youth as active citizens. *Information, Communication & Society*, 22(14), 2099–2115. https://doi.org/10.1201/9781032600628

Bengtsson, L., & Lakemond, N (2017). Digital competence in small and medium-sized enterprises: A typology of digital practices. *International Journal of Innovation Management*, 21(06), 1750053. https://doi.org/10.1201/9781032600628

Chai, C. S., Koh, J. H. L., & Tsai, C. C (2010). Facilitating preservice teachers' development of technological, pedagogical, and content knowledge (TPACK). *Educational Technology & Society*, 13(4), 63–73. www.jstor.org/stable/pdf/jeductechsoci.13.4.63.pdf

Crompton, H., & Burke, D (2018). The use of mobile learning in PK-12 education: A systematic review. *Computers & Education*, 123, 75–85. www.sciencedirect.com/science/article/pii/S0360131517300660

DeWitt, D., Alias, N., Siraj, S., Abdullah, M. R., & Siraj, S (2019). Digital competence for teaching and learning in higher education: A systematic review of conceptual frameworks. *Computers & Education*, 137, 1–22. www.sciencedirect.com/science/article/pii/S0360131521000890

Di Pietro, G., Di Virgilio, F., & Bartolo, M. G (2020). Digital competence in education: Exploring teachers' self-efficacy, attitudes, and training needs. *Computers & Education*, 144, 103701. https://dl.acm.org/doi/abs/10.1145/3230977.3230993

Ertmer, P. A., & Ottenbreit-Leftwich, A. T (2013). Removing obstacles to the pedagogical changes required by Jonassen's vision of authentic technology-enabled learning. *Computers & Education*, 64, 175–182. www.sciencedirect.com/science/article/pii/S0360131512002308

Ertmer, P. A., Ottenbreit-Leftwich, A. T., & York, C. S (2006). Exemplary technology-using teachers: Perceptions of factors influencing success. *Journal of Computing in Teacher Education*, 23(2), 55–61. www.tandfonline.com/doi/abs/10.1080/10402454.2006.10784561

Ertmer, P. A., Ottenbreit-Leftwich, A. T., Sadik, O., Sendurur, E., & Sendurur, P (2012). Teacher beliefs and technology integration practices: A critical relationship. *Computers & Education*, 59(2), 423–435. www.sciencedirect.com/science/article/pii/S0742051X1200131X

Eshet-Alkalai, Y., & Amichai-Hamburger, Y (2004). Experiments in digital literacy. *CyberPsychology & Behavior*, 7(4), 421–429. www.liebertpub.com/doi/abs/10.1089/cpb.2004.7.421

Eynon, R., & Geniets, A (2016). Introduction to the special issue: Learning, social media and social networks: The digital native debate revisited. *Learning, Media and Technology*, 41(3), 381–393. www.tandfonline.com/doi/abs/10.1080/17439884.2015.1064954

Ferrari, A (2012). Digital competence in practice: An analysis of frameworks. *Joint Research Centre, European Commission*. www.ifap.ru/library/book522.pdf

Ferraz, D., Ferreira, M. J., & Cruz-Jesus, F (2018). Digital competence assessment instruments for teachers: A systematic review. *Computers & Education*, 123, 74–92. www.sciencedirect.com/science/article/pii/S0360131521000890

Fraillon, J., Ainley, J., Schulz, W., Friedman, T., & Duckworth, D (2013). International computer and information literacy study: Assessment framework. Springer. https://eric.ed.gov/?id=ED545260

Fraillon, J., Ainley, J., Schulz, W., Friedman, T., & Gebhardt, E (2014). Preparing for life in a digital age: The IEA International Computer and Information Literacy Study International Report. Springer. https://library.oapen.org/bitstream/handle/20.500.12657/28001/1001996.pdf

Fraillon, J., Schulz, W., & Ainley, J (2013). International computer and information literacy study framework. *IEA International Computer and Information Literacy Study (ICILS) Assessment Framework*. https://eric.ed.gov/?id=ED545260

Friesen, N., & Clifford, P (2009). Digital natives with a cause? A knowledge survey of a student generation. *Canadian Journal of Learning and Technology/La Revue Canadienne de l'apprentissage et de la technologies*, 35(2), 6. www.learntechlib. org/p/42755/

Friesen, N., & Lowe, S (2012). The questionable promise of social media for education: Connective learning and the commercial imperative. *Journal of Computer Assisted Learning*, 28(3), 183–194. https://onlinelibrary.wiley.com/doi/abs/10.1111/ j.1365-2729.2011.00426.x

Garcia, E., & Romero, C (2017). Evaluation framework for digital competence in higher education: The case of digital skills assessment at Universidad Carlos III de Madrid. *Computers in Human Behavior,* 76, 567–576. www.mdpi.com/2304-6775/8/4/47

Grover, S., & Pérez-Sanagustín, M (2018). Digital competence development in higher education: An international perspective. *Internet and Higher Education,* 37, 13–24. www.tand fonline.com/doi/abs/10.1080/21532974.2019.1646169

Guàrdia, L., Sangrà, A., & Koskinen, T (2019). Research trends in digital competence development in higher education. *Computers in Human Behavior,* 95, 137–149. www.scienc edirect.com/science/article/pii/S0747563217301590

Gutiérrez-Santiuste, E., Roblin, N. P., Román-González, M., & Olmos-Migueláñez, S (2019). Digital competence in initial teacher education: An analysis of the perception and self-efficacy of pre-service teachers. *British Journal of Educational Technology*, 50(3), 1130–1146. www.cell.com/heliyon/pdf/S2405-8440(23)06746-4.pdf

Hargittai, E., & Hsieh, Y. P (2013). Digital inequality. *Social Science Computer Review*, 31(3), 307–325. https://journals.sagepub.com/doi/abs/10.1177/089443930302 1002002

Hinojo-Lucena, F. J., Romero-Rodríguez, J. M., & Fernández-Martínez, E (2019). Digital competence in the 21st century: An analysis of scientific production. *Comunicar*, 27(60), 39–49. https://rio.upo.es/xmlui/handle/10433/10497

Janssen, J., & Stoyanov, S (2012b). Empowering digital citizens in schools: A multi-level analysis of the relationship between digital citizenship education and digital competences. *Technology, Pedagogy and Education*, 21(2), 225–239. https://bit.ly/ 49hCSDC

Janssen, J., & Stoyanov, S (Eds.) (2012a). Digital skills for learning. University Press Antwerp. www.sciencedirect.com/science/article/pii/S0167494322000760

Khang, A., and AIoCF (Eds.). (2024), AI-Oriented Competency Framework for Talent Management in the Digital Economy: Models, Technologies, Applications, and Implementation. CRC Press. ISBN: 9781032576053. https://doi.org/10.1201/978100 3440901

Khang, A., Gujrati, R., Uygun, H., Tailor, R. K., & Gaur S. S (2024) *Data-driven Modelling and Predictive Analytics in Business and Finance* (1st Ed.). CRC Press. ISBN: 9781032600628. https://doi.org/10.1201/9781032600628

Khang, A., Inna, S-O., Alla, K., Rostyslav, S., Rudenko, M., Lidia, R., & Kristina, B (2024). "Management model 6.0 and business recovery strategy of enterprises in the era of digital economy." In *Data-driven Modelling and Predictive Analytics in Business and Finance* (1st Ed.).CRC Press. https://doi.org/10.1201/9781032600628-16

Khang, A., Kali, C. R., Satapathy, S. K., Kumar, A., Ranjan Das, S., & Panda, M. R (2023). "Enabling the Future of Manufacturing: Integration of Robotics and IoT to Smart Factory Infrastructure in Industry 4.0." In A. Khang, V. Shah, & S. Rani (Eds.), *AI-Based Technologies and Applications in the Era of the Metaverse* (1st Ed.), pp. 25–50. IGI Global Press. https://doi.org/10.4018/978-1-6684-8851-5.ch002

Khang, A., Muthmainnah, M., Seraj, P. M. I., Al Yakin, A., Obaid, A. J., & Panda, M. R (2023). "AI-Aided Teaching Model for the Education 5.0 Ecosystem." In A. Khang, V. Shah, & S. Rani (Eds.), *AI-Based Technologies and Applications in the Era of the Metaverse* (1st Ed.), pp. 83–104. IGI Global Press. https://doi.org/10.4018/978-1-6684-8851-5.ch004

Khang, A., Rani, S., Gujrati, R., Uygun, H., & Gupta, S. K. (Eds.) (2023). *Designing Workforce Management Systems for Industry 4.0: data-centric and AI-enabled approaches.* CRC Press. https://doi.org/10.1201/9781003357070

Khang, A., Shah, V., & Rani, S (2023). *AI-Based Technologies and Applications in the Era of the Metaverse* (1st Ed.). IGI Global Press. https://doi.org/10.4018/978-1-6684-8851-5

Kiili, C., & Lainema, T (2008). Foundation for measuring engagement in educational games. *Journal of Interactive Learning Research*, 19(3), 469–488. www.learntechlib.org/p/24197/

Koh, J. H. L., & Kim, Y (2004). Knowledge sharing in virtual communities: An e-business perspective. *Expert Systems with Applications*, 26(2), 155–166. www.sciencedirect.com/science/article/pii/S0957417403001167

Kozma, R. B., & McGhee, R (2000). Using online tools to support problem-based learning. *Journal of Technology and Teacher Education*, 8(4), 333–350. www.learntechlib.org/p/8040/

Leijen, Ä., & Valtna, K (2018). Factors influencing teachers' digital competence and readiness for educational innovation: A systematic review. *Educational Technology Research and Development*, 66(6), 1535–1563. www.sciencedirect.com/science/article/pii/S0360131521000890

Li, K., & Tsai, C (2019). A systematic review of digital competence frameworks: A focus on digital literacy, information literacy, and media literacy. *Educational Research Review*, 27, 1–13. www.tandfonline.com/doi/abs/10.1080/2331186X.2018.1519143

Lindell, C., & Fransson, G (2008). Development and evaluation of an instrument for measuring digital competence in higher education. *Journal of Educational Multimedia and Hypermedia*, 17(4), 449–470. https://journals.sagepub.com/doi/abs/10.1177/0735633115620432

Liu, Y., Guo, F., & Lee, M. K. O (2016). The impact of social media on knowledge sharing: An empirical examination. *International Journal of Information Management*, 36(6), 761–772. www.emerald.com/insight/content/doi/10.1108/AJIM-02-2015-0018/full/html

Livingstone, S., & Helsper, E (2007). Gradations in digital inclusion: Children, young people and the digital divide. *New Media & Society*, 9(4), 671–696. https://journals.sagepub.com/doi/abs/10.1177/1461444807080335

Martens, R. L (2017). Competence assessment in education: Research, models and instruments. Springer. https://link.springer.com/content/pdf/10.1007/978-3-319-50030-0.pdf

Martin, A (2006). Digital competence: A conceptual framework for teaching and learning. *Australian Journal of Educational Technology*, 22(2), 128–150. https://ajet.org.au/index.php/AJET/article/view/6622

Muthmainnah, M., Khang, A., Mahbub Ibna Seraj, P., Al Yakin, A., Oteir, I., & Alotaibi, A. N (2023). An innovative teaching model—The Potential of metaverse for english learning. In *AI-Based Technologies and Applications in the Era of the Metaverse* (1st Ed.) (pp. 105–126). IGI Global Press. https://doi.org/10.4018/978-1-6684-8851-5.ch005

Opazo-Basáez, M., & Bresciani, S (2020). A typology of digital transformation initiatives in startups. *Technological Forecasting and Social Change*, 157, 120080. www.sciencedirect.com/science/article/pii/S0040162518311156

Pai, J. C., & Wang, S. Y (2019). Unlocking the knowledge-sharing conundrum in digital startups: An exploratory study of internal knowledge-sharing mechanisms. *Technological*

Forecasting and Social Change, 144, 473–484. https://pubsonline.informs.org/doi/abs/10.1287/orsc.13.2.179.536

Pereira, A., Morgado, L., Lencastre, J. A., & Oliveira, L (2018). Digital competences in higher education: From theory to practice. *Telematics and Informatics,* 35(1), 128–144. www.sciencedirect.com/science/article/pii/S0736585317303246

Pinto, M., Morgado, L., & Santos, C (2020). A systematic literature review on digital competences in higher education. *International Journal of Educational Technology in Higher Education,* 17(1), 1–29. https://educationaltechnologyjournal.springeropen.com/articles/10.1186/s41239-021-00312-8

Prange, C., Schröder, A., & Schäfer, L (2018). Digital competences in entrepreneurial contexts: Lessons from an explorative study. *Journal of Small Business and Entrepreneurship,* 30(2), 153–172. www.emerald.com/insight/content/doi/10.1108/JSBED-10-2020-0359/full/html

Punie, Y., Cabrera, M., & Redecker, C (2017). Assessment of key competences in school education: A conceptual framework in the context of the Common European Framework of Reference (CEFR) and DigComp. *European Commission, Joint Research Centre.* www.scitepress.org/Papers/2019/76790/76790.pdf

Raza, S. A., Standing, C., Jiang, N., & Standing, S (2020). The impact of digital entrepreneurship on knowledge-based resources and innovation in start-ups. *Technological Forecasting and Social Change,* 153, 119923. www.sciencedirect.com/science/article/pii/S0040162516300567

Redecker, C., & Punie, Y (2017). European Framework for the Digital Competence of Educators: DigCompEdu. *Joint Research Centre, Institute for Prospective Technological Studies, European Commission.* https://policycommons.net/artifacts/2163302/european-framework-for-the-digital-competence-of-educators/2918998/

Renko, M., Shrader, R. C., & Simon, M (2012). Perceptions of entrepreneurial passion and employee performance: An exploratory analysis. *Journal of Small Business Management,* 50(3), 366–389. www.tandfonline.com/doi/abs/10.1080/08276331.2018.1551460

Rovai, A. P., & Barnum, K. T (2003). On-line course effectiveness: An analysis of student interactions and perceptions of learning. *Journal of Distance Education,* 18(1), 57–73. www.ijede.ca/index.php/jde/article/view/121

Thibaut, P., Ceulemans, M., Dejonckheere, P., Spruyt, B., & De Schutter, S (2017). The role of educational level in the relationship between digital skills, diverse information experiences, and online participation. *Computers in Human Behavior,* 68, 532–541. https://doi.org/10.1201/9781032600628

Tsai, M. J., & Tsai, C. C (2010). Junior high school students' Internet usage and self-efficacy: A re-examination of the gender gap. *Computers & Education,* 54(4), 1182–1192. www.sciencedirect.com/science/article/pii/S0360131509003169

Turel, O., Liu, Y., & Yuan, Y (2020). A dynamic framework for assessing the benefits and drawbacks of digital technologies in startups. *Technological Forecasting and Social Change,* 158, 120174. www.sciencedirect.com/science/article/pii/S0040162512002934

Vaast, E., & Kaganer, E (2013). Social media affordances and governance in the workplace: An examination of organizational policies. *Journal of Computer-Mediated Communication,* 19(1), 78–101. https://academic.oup.com/jcmc/article-abstract/19/1/78/4067520

van Deursen, A. J., & van Dijk, J. A (2010). Internet skills performance tests: Are people ready for eHealth? *Journal of Medical Internet Research,* 12(2), e22. www.jmir.org/2011/2/e35/v13i2e35

Vanderlinde, R., van Braak, J., & Dexter, S (2014). School-level predictors for the use of ICT in primary education: Evidence from Flanders. *Journal of Computer Assisted*

Learning, 30(6), 518–532. https://onlinelibrary.wiley.com/doi/abs/10.1111/j.1365-2729.2008.00285.x

Vanderlinde, R., van Braak, J., & Dexter, S (2017). The digital competence framework for Belgian secondary education: Exploring the link with educational innovation. *Computers & Education,* 109, 40–58. www.sciencedirect.com/science/article/pii/S036013151 2002801

Vekiri, I (2008). Socioeconomic differences in elementary students' ICT beliefs and out-of-school experiences. *Journal of Computer Assisted Learning,* 24(3), 201–210. www.sciencedirect.com/science/article/pii/S0360131509002723

Verheul, I., Wennekers, S., Audretsch, D. B., & Thurik, R (2002). An eclectic theory of entrepreneurship: Policies, institutions and culture. In *Innovation, entrepreneurship, and technological change* (pp. 19–56). Springer. https://ideas.repec.org/p/eim/papers/h200 012.html

Vuorikari, R., Punie, Y., Carretero, S., & Van den Brande, G (2016). DigComp 2.0: The Digital Competence Framework for Citizens. Update Phase 1: The Conceptual Reference Model. *European Commission, Joint Research Centre, Institute for Prospective Technological Studies.* www.acrmalta.com/wp-content/uploads/2017/04/DigCompConsumersfinalp ublicationJRC103155.pdf

Wang, H., Xu, C., & Wang, L (2014). The effect of entrepreneurial networking on firms' performance in China's transition economy. *Journal of Small Business Management,* 52(3), 366-389. www.tandfonline.com/doi/abs/10.1111/j.1540-627X.2007.00235.x

Warschauer, M., & Matuchniak, T (2010). New technology and digital worlds: Analyzing evidence of equity in access, use, and outcomes. *Review of Research in Education,* 34(1), 179–225. https://journals.sagepub.com/doi/abs/10.3102/0091732X09349791

Watson, C. E., & Watson, G (2017). Measuring digital literacy: Evaluating learning outcomes in digital literacy courses. *TechTrends,* 61(3), 269–275. https://jurnal.unimed.ac.id/2012/index.php/geo/article/view/31234

Wechtler, H., & Kastner, G (2018). Entrepreneurs' digital competences and performance: The impact of openness to experience, proactivity, and visionary leadership. *Journal of Business Economics,* 88(3), 379–413. www.sciencedirect.com/science/article/pii/S014829632 3001054

Zahra, S. A., & George, G (2002). Absorptive capacity: A review, reconceptualization, and extension. *Academy of Management Review,* 27(2), 185–203. https://go.gale.com/ps/i.do?id=GALE%7CA366235650&sid=googleScholar&v=2.1&it=r&linkaccess= abs&issn=19804865&p=AONE&sw=w

Zott, C., & Amit, R (2013). The business model: Recent developments and future research. *Journal of Management,* 39(4), 1207–1246. https://journals.sagepub.com/doi/abs/10.1177/0149206311406265

Zupic, I., & Čater, T (2015). Bibliometric methods in management and organization. *Organizational Research Methods,* 18(3), 429–472. https://journals.sagepub.com/doi/abs/10.1177/1094428114562629

Zwilling, M (2014). *Startup leadership: How savvy entrepreneurs turn their ideas into successful enterprises.* John Wiley & Sons. https://go.gale.com/ps/i.do?id=GALE%7CA373370593&sid=googleScholar&v=2.1&it=r&linkaccess=abs&issn=00067385&p=LitRC&sw=w

14 Blockchain Technologies and Applications for Business and Finance Systems

Luke Jebaraj, Sithankathan Sakthivel, and Irisappane Soubache

14.1 INTRODUCTION

Blockchain technology was originally initiated by Satoshi Nakamoto, who defined it as a distributed, decentralized and application-oriented, digital public ledger, based on cryptology (Xu et al., 2019). A centralized architecture is required to check a variety of transactions and applications, in a decentralized operating manner, with the equivalent level of confidence (Christidis and Devetsikiotis, 2016). The basics of blockchain technology such as its importance, architecture, characteristics, components and working, are described in this section.

14.1.1 IMPORTANCE OF BLOCKCHAIN TECHNOLOGY

All business-orientated activities depend upon speedy sharing of information between various sub-sectors of the network. Blockchain plays a crucial role in this domain of sharing such information in a swift manner and storing it on an unalterable ledger clearly. This information can be accessed only by authorized members of the system (Khang, Gujrati et al., 2024). A blockchain network is capable of tracking orders, accounts, production, payments and other important requirements in a faster way. It can help in tracing and verifying multi-step transactions on demand. The speedy processing of data transfer, reduction in acquiescence cost and security of transactions are also the hallmarks of this technology (Khanh & Khang, 2021).

14.1.2 ARCHITECTURE OF BLOCKCHAIN

A blockchain is a digitally open, financial record, with official transactions. The design of blockchain is based on a decentralized network, comprising numerous computers called nodes. The position of each node, as an administrator of the network, is blended willingly in the network. Blockchain architecture does not have centralized information and is protected against hacking. It supports an increasing

DOI: 10.1201/9781032618845-14

list of prearranged records, identified as blocks, and each of them keeps a timestamp connected with the preceding block (Khang, Chowdhury et al., 2022).

14.1.3 Working Steps of Blockchain

This is a digitally dispersed public record of all information (transactions) across a P2P (peer to peer system). Contributors to this technology can verify the transactions, without going through the centralized certifying authority. The working of blockchain is a multistep process; these steps are depicted in Figure 14.1.

Step 1: Facilitates Easier Transaction
Generally, the transaction will be completed by means of a blockchain. Initially, the exchange of information, through the blockchain, is encrypted twice by the main (public and private) encryption algorithms (Khang, Semenets et al., 2024).

Step 2: Verification of a Transaction
A verification message will be received, after the information encryption. It is executed on all the nodes engaged with the network of the blockchain. It is essential to ensure and confirm every significant parameter associated with the transaction by the nodes connected with the blockchain network.

Step 3: New Block Configuration
All the verified transactions are queued in a mempool together, to generate a fresh block for storing.

Step 4: Proof-of-Network
Proof-of-network is a consensus, decentralized system, used to confirm the transactions and attach fresh blocks to the blockchain securely.

Step 5: Add New Block
A fresh block is added to the blockchain after it has received its sole hash value and verification provided by the proof-of-network.

Step 6: Complete Transaction
If a block is successfully added, then the transaction will be complete and stored securely in the blockchain.

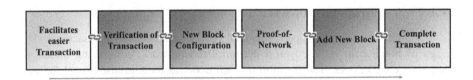

FIGURE 14.1 Working steps of blockchain.

Source: Khang, 2021.

14.1.4 COMPONENTS OF BLOCKCHAIN

The core parts in blockchain structural design are called node, transaction, consensus, block, chain and miner. There are numerous other components in a blockchain to perform successful transactions. The roles of every constituent are portrayed as follows.

Ledger: This is a present and preceding condition data storage record, kept by every node in the system.

Wallet: This is a secret and secured storing part of the user's credentials.

Peer Network: In this network, each node is linked to every other node, to share the resources with each other, without the participation of third-party servers.

Smart Contract: This is coding lines stored in blockchain ledgers. It can perform mechanically when the decided stipulations and states are met.

Membership: This component of the blockchain is employed for approving, validating and handling individuality on a blockchain.

Events: This makes notifications on a system that consist of smart agreements, implementation of transaction, activation of payment and some other imperative processes. It depends on the internal processing of the association.

System Management: This helps to make, modify, supervise and organize the components of blockchain.

System Integration: This incorporates blockchain with some exterior applications in a bidirectional manner.

14.1.5 CHARACTERISTICS OF BLOCKCHAIN

The characteristics of blockchain can be classified as functional and embryonic. Functional characteristics are very significant and obligatory for appropriate function. Embryonic characteristics are the outcome of the functional characteristics as shown in Figure 14.2.

14.1.5.1 Functional Characteristics

Decentralized Network: In this network, all the nodes are deemed as peers. These nodes have been allocated consent and function, determined by the application. It abolishes the requirement for a server for verification and eradicates the hindrance of a single point failure in the centralized system.

Distributed Record: A shared distributed record is a duplicated ledger, used to record transactions, kept by the contributing nodes. The data structure of the record is blockchain. It allows only the authorized contributors to access, examine and check the transaction condition in its lifecycle.

Consensus: this is a type of validation process, to change transaction, by agreement between members, to alter its position from one state to another. The main chain consists of only consensus-achieved blocks. Orphaned blocks are those blocks where transactions moved away from the main chain. The procedure of consensus depends upon the structural design of the blockchain application.

Finality (Immutable): The property of immutable implies that the data cannot be modified after being encrypted into the block and included in the blockchain.

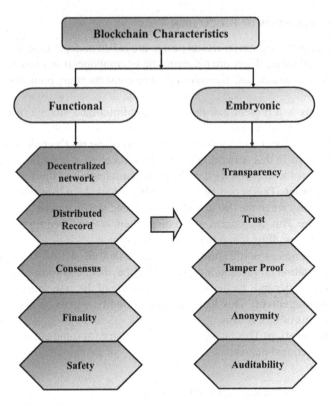

FIGURE 14.2 Blockchain characteristics.

Source: Khang, 2021.

In other words, after getting the members' consensus, the block can only be written.

Safety (Security): It is not easy to hack because the output value is generated in a permanent fashion and irrespective of the length of the input data. The level of complexity prevents hacking, increases in the components that go into block generation creates complexity. Additionally, immutability ensures information security.

14.1.5.2 Embryonic Characteristics

Transparency: The peer-to-peer network arrangement makes it easy for parity in the middle of the nodes. During the transaction process, members can monitor the condition of a transaction and check any minor modifications in this arrangement. Peers experience shared duplicated records and thus blockchain enables complete transparency for any transactions.

Trust: This technology is a peer-to-peer structure, which accepts only consensus-based transactions and prevents any third-party transactions.

Tamper-Proof: The authenticated data, stored in a block, cannot be delayed or modified. Any attempt to modify them would render the hash pointer of the next block invalid.

Anonymity: The identification of members and their transactions are extremely important and they should remain anonymous. This confidentiality of information ensures every transaction is secure.

Auditability: The read-only blocks in a blockchain perform as an archive and the timestamp confirms the sequence. Thus the system enables easy attribution and auditability.

14.2 TYPES OF BLOCKCHAIN TECHNOLOGY

Based on the accommodation for all types of users, there are four types of blockchain technologies.

14.2.1 PUBLIC BLOCKCHAIN

Public blockchain is generally known as being non-authorized, non-control and open to access, present and previous records, by public clients. Transaction verification can also be performed by public members, using the open source code, without altering the valid transaction on the system. Every computer linked to the system holds a replica of other blocks or nodes in this system. Litecoin (LTC), Bitcoin (BTC) and Ethereum (ETH) are examples of public blockchain technology.

14.2.1.1 Advantages
1. The size of the network is bigger, with open access and the distribution is recorded in a superior and protected way.
2. The possibility of fraudulent activities is eliminated due to the secured algorithms used in this network. Hence the contributors need not be anxious about the other nodes which are available in the network.
3. Every transaction can be done in this platform in a protected way, without disclosing the contributor's name or identity.
4. Every participant has a ledger copy to perform in this network.

14.2.1.2 Disadvantages
1. The transaction process is at a slow pace due to the huge size and the node verification procedure, taking more time.
2. Energy utilization demands proof-of-network and hence a high-quality hardware configuration is necessary in the system.
3. Due to the nonattendance of a central authority, problems are encountered by the system.

14.2.2 PRIVATE BLOCKCHAIN

Private blockchain is generally known as an authorized, restricted and closed network, controlled by a solitary entity, to access present and preceding records. It is a small-scale network, performed by only a few authenticated members who are permitted to contribute within any organization or corporation. Transaction verification can also be done by similar authenticated users only and hence access to certain information from third parties can be prohibited. Corda, Multichain and Hyperleger projects are examples of private blockchain technology (Tailor, Ranu et al., 2022).

14.2.2.1 Advantages

1. The degree of privacy of this network is greater and it suits businesses.
2. The network size can be physically determined and it is easy to change the scalability.
3. The node verification and rate of transaction take less time due to its smaller size.
4. The overall performance is better due to the restricted and authenticated access.

14.2.2.2 Disadvantages

1. The entire network can be jeopardized when all the nodes go into offline mode.
2. The risk of manipulation is possible due to the restricted node number and the network being more susceptible.
3. Due to the centralization, unprofessional conduct, executed by organizations, is possible.

14.2.3 HYBRID BLOCKCHAIN

The grouping of hybrid blockchain is of both public and private blockchain elements. It allows setting up non-consent- as well as consent-based systems and allows them to control the specific, accessed data amassed in the blockchain, and data are open in public. The information of client access for transactions is permissible through a smart contract. Confidential information is kept within the network but it is still provable. It is not possible to modify the transactions even if a personal body employs the hybrid blockchain. Dragonchain is an example of hybrid blockchain technology.

14.2.3.1 Advantages

1. It works in a closed bionetwork and is free from exterior hackers because of almost 51% of users being denied access to the system.
2. It authorizes intermediary communication but protects privacy.
3. This architecture maintains safety, honesty and lucidity as it is extremely customizable.
4. It provides speedy transactions, with least computational cost.

14.2.3.2 Disadvantages

1. There are no inducements for contributors of this network, owing to its closed bionetwork.
2. Somebody can conceal information from the contributor, resulting in a lack of transparency.

14.2.4 CONSORTIUM BLOCKCHAIN

The federated or consortium blockchain is a decentralized network that facilitates collaboration between multiple members of an organization and eliminates the risk of hacking. It is a ground-breaking method and the process of consensus is managed by prearranged nodes. The transactions are initiated, received and authenticated by an authenticator node. R3 and Energy Web Foundation (EWF) are examples of consortium blockchain technology.

14.2.4.1 Advantages

1. It is a high-speed process managed by only a few contributors, to make confirmation faster.
2. The information about verification cannot be identified by outsiders, however any certified contributor to this blockchain can access and hence it keeps privacy intact.
3. It is possible to decentralize at every stage, by taking part in multiple organization authorities.

14.2.4.2 Disadvantages

1. Possibility of hacking is high due to corrupt organizations who conceal information from the contributors.
2. Lack of suppleness due to the vision of interest defers from the contributed organizations to approve the protocol.

14.3 APPLICATIONS OF BLOCKCHAIN TECHNOLOGY

The salient applications of blockchain are related to various domains such as finance (Gad et al., 2022), cloud computing (Habib et al., 2022), Internet of Things (Uddin et al., 2021), big data management (Rani, Bhambri et al., 2023), industry (Javaid et al., 2021), education (Alammary et al., 2019), healthcare (Haleem et al., 2021), e-commerce (Treiblmaier and Sillaber, 2021), e-government service (Lykidis et al., 2021), real estate (Sarri et al., 2022), power and energy (Sawa, 2019), transportation (Astarita et al., 2020), wireless networks (Rathod et al., 2022), agriculture (Xiong et al., 2020), aviation (Yadav et al., 2022) and forensic science and investigation (FSI) (Akinbi et al., 2022), as shown in Figure 14.3.

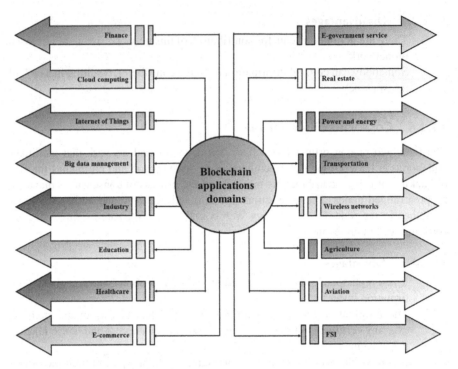

FIGURE 14.3   The application domains.

Source: Khang, 2021.

14.3.1   FINANCE

The key applications of blockchain technology employed by various financial domains such as banking services, cryptocurrency, payments, auditing, asset management and ledger maintenance are tabulated in Table 14.1.

14.3.2   CLOUD COMPUTING

The salient applications of blockchain technology employed by various cloud computing area versions such as security for various platforms, fog cloud integration, smart provenance, and knowledge sharing and users privacy are tabulated in Table 14.2.

14.3.3   INTERNET OF THINGS

The principal applications of blockchain technology employed by various IoT domain adaptations such as healthcare and security architecture, security and validation of transactions, privacy, network protocol, storage, service, identification and access control are tabularized in Table 14.3.

TABLE 14.1

Key Applications of Blockchain Technology Related to Finance

S. No.	Application	Description	References
1	Credit score calculation	The credit score was calculated through non-conventional criteria. So as to evaluate the creditworthiness of a person, lenders are allowed to utilize unassailable records of monetary transactions	Guo and Liang, 2016
2	General banking services	Evaluate the competence of the Bitcoin network in terms of operational efficiency, economic efficiency and service efficiency in the general banking services	Cocco et al., 2017
3	Identity management	Consumers can build their individual tamper-proof secure identity in a digital manner by utilizing this technology. It is a protected way by making their user ID and password based on blockchain for logging in to the online accounting	Joseph et al., 2017
4	Cryptocurrency	A new real time "SMERCOIN"-based inducement system plan integrated with the ideas of cryptocurrency and prioritization to electric vehicle charging system users through monetary and non-monetary renewable energy-based flat rate system	Zhang et al., 2018
5	Digital payments	Introduced a digital payment process mechanism via three phases such as bill generation, payment execution and payment record sharing vehicle to grid (V2G) networks	Gao et al., 2018
6	Digital asset management	The encrypted digital distributed ledger was used in this process to avoid the necessity of immediate verification of transaction from the payment authorities and banks	Halilbegovic et al., 2019
7	Auditing process	All the financial-related data are easily accessed during the auditing process and will help to decrease the time of auditing	Bürer et al, 2019
8	International payments	The international payment facility is possible in the quickest way from any location via electronic gadgets with no charges for the transaction through banking or credit cards	Zhou et al., 2020
9	Fraud prevention	Protect the stored transaction particulars, contracts and financial procedures against fraudulent activities using cryptographic algorithms	Liu et al., 2021

(continued)

TABLE 14.1 (Continued)
Key Applications of Blockchain Technology Related to Finance

S. No.	Application	Description	References
10	Tokenization	The tangible assets are represented as tokens stored on blockchain in a protected way to avoid the possibility of fraud and theft. The asset marketplace, data on the assets and registry of the land are also standardized and secured by blockchain technology	Sanka et al., 2021
11	Financial ledger maintenance	The transfer of property of ownership and exact financial ledger maintenance are mainly projected. Financial data analysis and distribution are the imperative things in ledger management	Krichen et al., 2022

TABLE 14.2
Key Applications of Blockchain Technology Connected to Cloud Computing

S. No.	Application	Description	References
1	Cyber security enhancement	The enhancement of cyber security is proposed to reduce the delay in operation and threat detection using parallel cloud computation for larger corporate networks	Yu et al., 2017
2	Information security	Construct a firewall to make active information security applied to intelligent campuses	Bhuyan et al., 2022
3	Fog bus	Establish a fog bus mechanism to make possible IoT fog–cloud integration	Lakhan et al., 2022
4	Smart provenance	Introduce data provenance management for amassing, confirming and organizing the data source with smart contract to construe the data trials	Jyoti and Chauhan, 2022
5	Knowledge sharing	Knowledge sharing about the redesigning operation of an injection mold in a secured way through cloud-based platform	Nguyen and Prentice, 2022
6	Security of records	Security for electronic health records against unlawful alteration to minimize the time of computation	Li et al., 2022
7	Privacy of users	Privacy protection for users while purchasing at network and cloud services integrated with consensus accounting to avoid provincial data uploading to cloud server	Xiong et al., 2022

14.3.4 Big Data Management

The key applications of blockchain technology employed by various big data management such as personal data management, security, data set trading, data storage and sharing, fog computing, key word search and task scheduling are given in Table 14.4.

TABLE 14.3

Major Applications of Blockchain Technology Associated with the Internet of Things

S. No.	Application	Description	References
1	e-Healthcare architecture	A remote patient monitoring architecture is proposed with two levels. Solution of data streaming and storage was provided in the lower level and healthcare control unit structure is managed at an upper level to handle huge numbers of patient	Uddin et al., 2018
2	Transaction security	An IoT-based structure was devised for intra- and inter-organizational transactions through an internal certification authority for registration procedure in a secured manner	Biswas et al., 2018
3	Privacy	A powerful digital signature system is provided to protect the user's responsive data from privacy leakage for the purpose of verification and safe running of privacy preferences	Cha et al., 2018
4	Network protocol	A contractual routing protocol is implemented for the IoT using the Ethereum blockchain platform with four performance metrics: routing overhead, throughput, and packet delivery ratio and route acquisition latency	Ramezan and Leung, 2018
5	Secure storage	The customer's data can be processed through the servers through homomorphic computation, called a BeeKeeper system, by drawing outside computing resources to link it	Zhou et al., 2018
6	Consumer service	A reputable software agent model is proposed for customer feedback services in the distributed IoT network platform	Fortino et al., 2019
7	Forensic evidence collection	A new software-based forensic structural design is used to collect the proof and helps to enhance the analysis by specialists from the forensic department. This entire architecture is designed with LHS (Linear Homomorphic Signature) algorithm	Pourvahab and Ekbatanifard, 2019

(continued)

TABLE 14.3 (Continued)
Major Applications of Blockchain Technology Associated with the Internet of Things

S. No.	Application	Description	References
8	Security architecture	Decentralized security attack detection technique named "BlockSecIoTNet" is focused by using SDN (software defined networking), EC (edge computing) and FG (fog computing) methods	Rathore et al., 2019
9	Identification technology	The magnetic field strength sequence-based fingerprint system is implemented to indoor magnetic positioning used real-world datasets	Chen et al., 2019
10	Access control	Role assignment and preparing an access control list is possible in a speedy manner through an attribute-based access control scheme. Devices engaged in this technique are portrayed by a set of predefined traits and issued by accredited authorities	Ding et al., 2019
11	Transaction validation	Authenticate the decentralized transactions by means of a context-aware corroboration method and the transaction is legalized by a miner with the precedence of service for a dispersed and protected IoT network	Hosen et al., 2020

14.3.5 INDUSTRY

The key applications of blockchain technology employed by various industrial domain versions such as digital directory, manufacturing data, automotive, industrial finance, product, information, purchasing, supervision and management are given in Table 14.5.

14.3.6 EDUCATION

The main applications of blockchain technology employed by various educational field adaptations such as collaborative and lifelong learning, coordination, competition and copyright management, credits and grading, digital guardianship, e-learning, verification of student's record, examination evaluation and review are displayed in Table 14.6.

14.3.7 HEALTHCARE

The principal applications of blockchain technology employed by various healthcare domains such as data management, safety and monitoring of patients including senior

TABLE 14.4

Key Applications of Blockchain Technology Connected to Big Data Management

S. No.	Application	Description	References
1	Personal data management	Consumers can manage their own sensitive data through an individual decentralized data management system associated with an automatic access control manager	Zyskind et al., 2015
2	Security	Checking the sign of user and information authentication integrated with a universal unique identifier is performed by using a digital signature to prevent IP cheating	Jung and Jang, 2017
3	Dataset trading	Peer and consensus mechanism-based distributed anonymous dataset platform integrated with hyperledger fabric to perform data transfer, receiver and transaction verification	Kiyomoto et al., 2017
4	Data storage	A keyword search service-based distributed and secured data storage was initiated to upload the encrypted form of client's data using cryptographic methods	Do and Ng, 2017
5	Fog computing	Sharing the transaction process by means of fog computers enabled by blockchain with comparing to preceding fog and cloud computing system in a secured way using P2P networks or centralized database	Jeong et al., 2018
6	Data sharing	A blockchain-based distribution model is used to make sure the secured circulation of data reserves integrating with smart contract	Yang et al., 2018
7	Key word search	A key word search method called "searchchain" is used to facilitate the unaware search over restricted keyword privacy in the dispersed storage	Jiang et al., 2020
8	Task scheduling	Hybrid dragonfly optimization with β-hill climbing technique-based big data intelligent task scheduling to IoT cloud computing application is projected	Abualigah et al., 2021

citizens, maintenance, sharing and evaluation of health records are tabularized in Table 14.7.

14.3.8 E-Commerce

The key applications of blockchain technology employed by various e-commerce domain adaptations such as crop trading, consumer business model cross-border transactions, mechanism of trading, selection of sales mode and decision-making are tabularized in Table 14.8.

TABLE 14.5

Main Applications of Blockchain Technology Related to Industry

S. No.	Application	Description	References
1	Digital directory	Private and public peer-to-peer transactions for industrial usage are archived in a digital decentralized directory with unique digital signature per transaction	Xu et al., 2018
2	Manufacturing data protection	Industrial data protection technique to avoid unwanted viewing and data transmission through a public network	Lu, 2019
3	Automotive	The purchased data and other imperative data for the automotive industry can be digitally stored	Fraga-Lamas and Fernandez-Carames, 2019
4	System integration	The security for IoT structure is offered by CTN (Communicating Things Network) and every activity and information is evidenced at diverse locations	Rathee et al., 2019
5	Industrial finance	Credit condition for customer, restructured credit system for financial management are implemented through blockchain to help to enhance the efficiency of cross-border transactions and payments	Zhang et al., 2020
6	Product and assembly identification	The information relating to components, assemblies and products is collected through blockchain environment at every level to help to decrease disturbances and prompt costs	Issaoui et al., 2020
7	Information and security	The information regarding production of goods, shipping and other quantities is securely stored and avoids the possibility of cyber-attacks	Bouachir et al., 2020
8	Digital purchasing	The incorporated information system is implemented by a digital purchasing process with financial data tracking for both traditional and blockchain purchasing scenarios	Martins et al., 2020
9	Supervision	Every investment, donations and other funding processes of associated agencies of individual campaigns is incessantly supervised while minimizing the probability of fraud	Haleem and Javaid, 2020
10	Proper management	Information about the products is essential for appropriate marketing and management with a secured digital author ID for performing financial transfers to avoid hacking	Dietrich et al., 2021

TABLE 14.6
Main Applications of Blockchain Technology Related to Education

S. No.	Application	Description	References
1	Collaborative learning environment	The learning environment named ULE (Ubiquitous Learning Environment) is integrated with IoT devices for exchanging information between them in a blockchain-based cloud platform	Bdiwi et al., 2018
2	Learning objects coordination	A group of learning objects called UBLO (Unified Bank of Learning Objects) is used under EEE (Electronic Educational Environment) for functioning in a network via an educational community to develop the academic courses and hypothetical foundations	Sychov and Chirtsov, 2018
3	Competitions management	Focused on the present standards and rivalry of trustworthiness in digital education and an evaluation model is created and designed for skill competition evaluation through the e-business sandbox	Wu and Li, 2018
4	Credits and grading	A new credit platform for higher education named "EduCTX" is implemented in higher education institutions for the purpose of education grading and crediting of students and other possible stakeholders	Turkanovic et al., 2018
5	Digital guardianship consent	The digital signature of consent is used to process the multiple types of forms handled by an educational institution received from parents or guardians through hyperledger fabric and composer	Gilda and Mehrotra, 2018
6	Copyright management	A new learning system named CHiLO (Creative Higher Education with Learning Object) to utilize e-books with free from copyright issues by means of paying virtual currency	Hori et al., 2018
7	e-Learning	A new e-learning conceptual model is designed and examined with an ISO quality model	Zhong et al., 2018
8	Lifelong learning	There is a learner-centered bionetwork built for a lifelong learning progress with evolving teaching, official approval and e-portfolio etc.	Mikroyannidis et al., 2018
9	Records verification	Digitalized educational records and certificates of students and scholars in schools, colleges and universities are maintained in a secured way and cannot be altered or accessed by unauthorized contributors	Han et al., 2018

(continued)

TABLE 14.6 (Continued)
Main Applications of Blockchain Technology Related to Education

S. No.	Application	Description	References
10	Competencies and learning outcomes	This is an artificial intelligence-based knowledge-intensive method to analyze the impacts of growth in graduate lines of work by securing the student's credentials and potential impacts of educational institutions	Williams, 2018
11	Students' professional ability evaluation	This is a combined system structure and assessment model to examine the educational performance and attainments of students in various categories of institutions that are evaluated by a clustering algorithm	Zhao et al., 2019
12	Examination review	Academic examination papers are examined, reviewed and assessed by an automatic excellence assurance mechanism called "dAppER" to enhance the quality and standard	Mitchell et al., 2019

14.3.9 E-GOVERNMENT SERVICE

The major applications of blockchain technology employed by various e-government services such as contracting, e-voting, verification, human resource management and public, e-delivery and land asset services are projected in Table 14.9.

14.3.10 REAL ESTATE

The key applications of blockchain technology employed by various real estate domain adaptations such as land record management, registration of assets, transactions of real estate transactions, tokenization and land administration are tabulated in Table 14.10.

14.3.11 POWER AND ENERGY

The principal applications of blockchain technology employed by various power and energy domains such as battery flexibility, charging of electric vehicles, optimization of reactive power, renewable energy consumption, energy trading, micro grids, smart grids, energy market and power flow optimization are displayed in Table 14.11.

TABLE 14.7

Main Applications of Blockchain Technology Connected to Healthcare

S. No.	Application	Description	References
1	Data management	The data management for health care is designed by "lightweight" terminology and avoids forking to handle the transactions by using HBCM (Head Blockchain Manager) to handle the transactions	Ismail et al., 2019
2	Patient safety	A human activity recognition system is framed to watch remotely located patients affected by sickness, mental activities and disabilities from the video frames in a secured manner. A multi-level and category of recognition are performed with ECOC (Error Correcting Output Code) framework by means of a supporting vector machine	Islam et al., 2019
3	Health record keeping	Maintain the health records of patients such as blood tests, diagnoses, disease summary and treatment, etc., by collecting clinical samples from patients through an interconnected hospital cloud system called tele-medical laboratory set up	Celesti et al., 2020
4	e-Records evaluation	Two approaches named TOPOSIS (Technique for Order of Preference by Similarity to Ideal Solution) and Fuzzy-based ANP (Analytic Network Process) are implemented to analyze and evaluate the electronic health records through blockchain	Zarour et al., 2020
5	Sharing information	Critical information about health is shared and monitored while reducing unnecessary expenses in an efficient way	Agbo and Mahmoud, 2020
6	Patient monitoring	The health data are collected from patients based on IoT sensory data integrated "IoBHealth" frame work in a secured way	Ray et al., 2020
7	Telehealth and telemedicine	The information and communication technology named Telehealth is used to monitor and manage the sickness of remote patients through an enhanced self-care process. Also, identifying the disease and medical treatment process for remote patients was enabled by telemedicine service	Ahmad et al., 2020
8	Sharing of e-records	A new "BinDaas" (Blockchain-Based Deep Learning as-a-Service) framework is implemented to share electronic health records in the midst of multiple users of health care through lattices-based cryptography	Bhattacharya et al., 2021
9	Health monitoring for the elderly	Three-tier IoT edge architecture is framed to monitor elderly people at a distant location and keep the medical history of senior people in an effective way	Ejaz et al., 2021

TABLE 14.8
Chief Applications of Blockchain Technology Related to e-Commerce

S. No.	Application	Description	References
1	Crop trading	A mobile-based android application is initiated for cultivators to sell or purchase harvest products in the nearest markets under the different stages of marketing through the GPS system	Bhende et al., 2018
2	Business model between consumers	The prescribed business process between customers is established in a way of maintaining the record regarding the information of consumers, list of sales products and reviews and ratings of the products. The feedback option is also available to appraise the product which gives better assurance and trustworthiness of the manufactured goods	Shorman et al., 2019
3	Cross-border transactions	The security of user's information about cross-border e-commerce is ensured initially. The transmission efficiency and recognition between both parties sharing the data is verified by a cross-domain acquisition contract to prevent illegal users and data stealing	Hongmei, 2021
4	Trading mechanism	A trading mechanism is executed to swap the individual loyalty points of customers to match both sides of an exchange mechanically under a hyperledger fabric platform	Tu et al., 2022
5	Sales mode selection	Interaction between the selection of sales mode and strategy of service effort is scrutinized in front of a show rooming effect initially, with thought of online and offline operating costs	Wang and Chaolu, 2022
6	Decision-making	Analyze and study of the risk aversion of sellers and capital constraints through a decision-making model	Song et al., 2022

14.3.12 TRANSPORTATION

The chief applications of blockchain technology for different transportation domain adaptations such as intelligent transportation, automotive security, key management, forensic application, communication and security of vehicles and trust management are tabulated in Table 14.12.

14.3.13 WIRELESS NETWORKS

The main applications of blockchain technology for various wireless network domain adaptations such as radio spectrum management, active spectrum access, cellular networks, distributed spectrum enforcement, drone surveillance and

TABLE 14.9

Foremost Applications of Blockchain Technology Associated with e-Government Service

S. No.	Application	Description	References
1	Contracting	The e-governing system is enhanced by adopting the blockchain-based DAO (Decentralized Autonomous Organization) framework for government contracting and takes the US policy of SBO (Small Business Organization) as a case study	Diallo et al., 2018
2	e-Voting	An Ethereum network-based wallet is used to test the model e-voting system with the rigidity language. Also, people can be permitted to use the e-voting system using the android application, if they do not have an Ethereum wallet	Yavuz et al., 2018
3	Authentication	A blockchain consensus-based trust relocating model is used for transfer and trust enrichment for manifold PKI (Public Key Infrastructure) systems in place of traditional trusted third parties for improved effectiveness, security and unified authentication	Chen et al., 2019
4	Public service	An interoperable framework is designed to activate a variety of unified, sustainable citizen services in the state organizations of Bahrain	Ghanem and Alsoufi, 2019
5	e-Delivery services	The registered multi-party e-delivery system model is initiated to curtail or take away the involvement of TTP (trusted third parties) and contract with the fair swap problem	Payeras-Capella et al., 2019
6	Human resources management	The application processes for vacancy positions of various postings are published as smart contracts of blockchain. Reviewing and appraising processes are also prized for their accurate contribution	Neiheiser et al., 2019
7	Land property services	Analysis of land asset services using a blockchain-based government bionetwork through a hyperledger fabric platform in a protected manner	Alketbi et al., 2020

communication, ad-hoc networks and edge caching technology are projected in Table 14.13.

14.3.14 AGRICULTURE

The principal applications of blockchain technology for a variety of agriculture field adaptations such as food supply chain, farming, smart agriculture, supply chain

TABLE 14.10

Main Applications of Blockchain Technology Associated with Real Estate

S. No.	Application	Description	References
1	Digital tokenization	The ownership of the assets can be moved from one party to another by means of digital tokens without any mediators	Garcia-Teruel and Simon-Moreno, 2016
2	Land records management	Management of land records and maintenance, land survey, land registration and settlement processes are performed by the blockchain environment to avoid general and key issues	Thakur et al., 2020
3	Property registration system	Design of a land and property registration system enabled by blockchain-based smart contract platform for selling, buying and access of land records by contributors	Ali et al., 2020
4	Real estate transactions	Online real estate transactions are performed to buy or sell any type of immovable assets through a smart contract, enabled between the consumer and vendor, when the deal is accepted by both sides	Ahmad et al., 2021
5	Land administration	The land administration procedure is implemented via a smart contact and develops the proof of concept for exact land dealings of within the pertinent authorities	Bennett et al., 2021

TABLE 14.11

Key Applications of Blockchain Technology Linked to Power and Energy

S. No.	Application	Description	References
1	**Battery flexibility**	Capability of battery storage for consumers through peer-to-peer trading was focused on under diverse distributed energy system patterns. Also analyzes the role of batteries between a variety of levels of consumer premises and central battery distribution community	Lüth et al., 2018
2	**Electric vehicles charging system**	A secured charging system for electric vehicles is devised with secured mutual verification using BAN (Burrows-Abadi-Needham) logic and an official confirmation of security by means of the Automated Validation of Internet Security Protocols and Applications (AVISPA) simulation tool	Kim et al., 2019

TABLE 14.11 (Continued)
Key Applications of Blockchain Technology Linked to Power and Energy

S. No.	Application	Description	References
3	Reactive power optimization	A blockchain-based reactive power price management is implemented through SBDE (Self Balanced Differential Evolution algorithm) to optimize the reactive power, active power loss and price management	Danalakshmi et al., 2020
4	Renewable energy consumption	Differentiate the performance of electric vehicle drivers through PRA (Prioritization Ranking Algorithm) and initiate the process of an electric vehicle incentive system to make best use of renewable energy utilization and guiding capability enhancement in a secured way	Chen and Zhang, 2020
5	Energy trading	A consensus model named CRSM (Consensus Resource Slicing Model) is framed for comprehensive energy trading situations and optimizes the protocol of consistency in the process of consensus to decrease the intricacy of communication	Hu and Shen, 2020
6	Combined market operation	Devised a cross chain-based mechanism for combined operation of joint dispersed photovoltaic power generation and carbon markets enabled by "mainchain" and "sidechain" through a blockchain environment	He and Luo, 2020
7	Multi-micro grid system trading	A peer-to-peer distributed trading technique under multi-micro grid overcrowding management is framed for dynamic distribution networks integrated with a cost-based self-directed demand response load	Liu and Junjie, 2020
8	Payment system for electric vehicles charging	Payment system for charging of electric vehicles is designed and consumers can put up for sale their surplus electricity via smart contracts to the charging stations	Khan and Byun, 2021
9	Energy flexibility market	Peer-to-peer dispersed energy flexibility trading platform for professional consumers focused in terms of modulation of load relating to the standard energy profiles	Antal et al., 2021
10	Distributed network power flow	Performed power flow optimization of a distributed power network using Distributed Consensus-based Alternating Direction Method of Multiplier (DCADMM) algorithm with coupled BESS (Battery Energy Storage Systems) and mixed integer constraints for a dynamic day beyond strategy of power dispatch	Shah and King, 2021

(continued)

TABLE 14.11 (Continued)
Key Applications of Blockchain Technology Linked to Power and Energy

S. No.	Application	Description	References
11	Power flow	Carried out OPF (Optimal Power Flow) to enable the different nodes of power grid integrated with the consensus dispersed algorithm in blockchain environment and tested with three benchmark systems like New England 39-bus, IEEE 57-bus and 118-bus networks	Foti et al., 2021
12	Smart grid	A smart grid transactions management incorporated with blockchain-based smart contracts is focused and interfaced between the consumers and the network using a mobile application	Agung and Handayani, 2022

TABLE 14.12
Main Applications of Blockchain Technology Connected to Transportation

S. No.	Application	Description	References
1	Intelligent transportation	An ITS (Intelligent Transportation Systems) bionetwork-familiarized seven-layer theoretical model is studied for PTMS (Parallel Transportation Management Systems) in the blockchain platform	Yuan and Wang, 2016
2	Automotive security and privacy	A protected and dispersed smart vehicle bionetwork is focused in a privacy-defended way through OBM (Overlay Block Manager) nodes to keep away from the middle broker	Dorri et al., 2017
3	Secured key management	Construct a safe key management by collecting the information about the departure of vehicles in a heterogeneous network. Additionally, it is designed towards reducing the time of key transfer during handover of vehicles using an active collection period of transaction	Lei et al., 2017
4	Forensics applications of connected vehicles	A forensic vehicular investigation frame work named "Block4Forensic" integrated with VPKI (Vehicular Public Key Infrastructure) is initiated to congregate the information about the maintenance centers, drivers, car manufacturers and law enforcement in case of incident.	Cebe et al., 2018
5	Smart vehicle communication	An effectual message network named "CreditCoin" is attempted for conveying the anonymous announcements to users in a confidential situation	Li et al., 2018

TABLE 14.12 (Continued)
Main Applications of Blockchain Technology Connected to Transportation

S. No.	Application	Description	References
6	Security for electric vehicles	The enhanced protection of security is focused for electric vehicles through hybrid CEC (Cloud and Edge Computing) under a blockchain platform	Liu et al., 2018
7	Trust management	A Bayesian interface mode is framed for vehicles to authenticate the messages obtained from the adjacent vehicle through a dispersed trust management scheme	Yang et al., 2019

TABLE 14.13
Chief Applications of Blockchain Technology Related to Wireless Networks

S. No.	Application	Description	References
1	Radio spectrum management	Focused active radio spectrum distribution applications in four major sharing categories of spectrum including cooperative primary and secondary sharing, primary non-cooperative primary and secondary sharing, etc.	Weiss et al., 2019
2	Dynamic spectrum access	Follow and authenticate the certified frequency band usage by means of a digital token system named "spectral token" based on DSA (Dynamic Spectrum Access) platform through smart contract	Ariyarathna et al., 2019
3	Cellular networks	A cost-based incentive mechanism is executed wherein primary MNO (Mobile Network Operator) rents its personal spectrum to a secondary UAV (Unmanned Aerial Vehicles) system with monetary exchange as of the UAV operators	Qiu et al., 2019
4	Distributed spectrum enforcement	A dispersed consensus mechanism platform named "SenseChain" is leveraged to spot fake sensors using a dispersed irregularity finding system	Careem and Dutta, 2019
5	Drone surveillance	The drones are interrelated wireless networks under a blockchain environment for improved communication and control. The drone-finding process is rooted in the WiFi statistical fingerprint	Bisio et al., 2019
6	Ad-hoc networks	A framework is established to put together on-demand confirmation, forwarding strategy and IKCB (Interest Key Content Binding) to find disillusioned content competently	Lei et al., 2019

(continued)

TABLE 14.13 (Continued)
Chief Applications of Blockchain Technology Related to Wireless Networks

S. No.	Application	Description	References
7	Edge caching technology	A two-hop edge caching construction is designed to enhance the cache competence under 6G cellular wireless networks and also the probability of content caching and rate of idleness are equally optimized	Sun et al., 2021
8	Drone communication	5G-enabled drone communication architecture is initiated to reduce privacy breaks under a blockchain platform	Wu et al., 2021

TABLE 14.14
Major Applications of Blockchain Technology Linked to Agriculture

S. No.	Application	Description	References
1	Agricultural food	The traceability of food supply chain system is built and integrated with RFID (Radio Frequency IDentification) to ensure the confidential information of food safety by sharing and relocating the valid data for processing, manufacturing, allocation, storing and selling	Tian, 2016
2	Greenhouse farming	Agriculture farming is developed via greenhouse technology rooted in IoT (Internet of Things) devices to provide protected communication	Patil et al., 2017
3	Smart agriculture	A smart agriculture bionetwork for food traceability is framed to track and observe food production, farming, transporting of farming goods, selling and stocking with IoT-based LPWAN (Low Power Wide Area Network)	Lin et al., 2018
4	Supply chain management	A decentralized traceability system named "AgriBlockIoT" is designed for food supply chain management from production side to consumption side through hyperledger and ethereum platform	Caro et al., 2018
5	Grain quality assurance	The quality guarantee for grain is carried out using BGEBN (Brazilian Grain Exporters Business Network)-based blockchain to collect data from authenticated quality guarantee processes	Lucena et al., 2018
6	Food safety with market efficiency	By increasing the business revenue and food safety, a digital system is implemented to minimize the changeable costs and maximize the competitiveness and efficiency of the organization	Sgroi, 2022

management, grain quality assurance and food safety with market efficiency are tabularized in Table 14.14.

14.3.15 AVIATION

The chief applications of blockchain technology employed by various aviation field adaptations such as supply chain management, air traffic and inventory management, maintenance of aircraft ledgers and industry are tabulated in Table 14.15.

14.3.16 FORENSIC SCIENCE AND INVESTIGATION

The chief applications of blockchain technology for various forensic science and investigation domain adaptations such as digital forensic investigation and evidence,

---

TABLE 14.15
Most Important Applications of Blockchain Technology Associated with Aviation

S. No.	Application	Description	References
1	Supply chain management	A transparent aircraft parts supply chain management system is focused on reducing the threat of black market accessibility of aircraft parts	Madhwal and Panfilov, 2017
2	Air traffic management	Improvement of security for responsive aeronautical data sharing over air traffic management amongst collaborators with well-matched SWIM (System Wide Information Management) standards through a blockchain platform	Clementi et al., 2019
3	Aviation industry	The interactions and level-based services are emphasized among the constituents of aviation structures that are initiated and framed through a blockchain environment	Ahmad et al., 2020
4	Records maintenance	A model is designed to uphold the aircraft parameters and records to monitor the process for the lifetime of an airplane in a sequence of interconnected blocks through a python programming base	Andrei et al., 2021
5	Inventory management	The superiority and traceability data of the aircraft parts associated with reducing error maintenance and effective decision-making inventory control are enhanced through Hyperledger Fabric system based ASPM (Aircraft Spare Parts inventory Management)	Ho et al., 2021

TABLE 14.16

Principal Applications of Blockchain Technology Related to Forensic Science and Investigation

S. No.	Application	Description	References
1	Digital forensics investigation	Social system-based IoT is implemented with a blockchain-based forensic platform named "IoTFC" (IoT Forensic Chain), to maintain coordination between the investigators and accuracy of evidence	Li et al., 2019
2	Digital evidence	To maintain a record of a sequence of safekeeping for digital evidence through BIFF (blockchain-based IoT forensics framework) platform against cyber-attacks	Le et al., 2019
3	Forensic proof	The collection and preservation of forensic evidences and data in a digital mode through an IoT-based blockchain environment	Brotsis et al., 2019
4	Evidence submission and retrieval	A digital evidence framework is projected to maintain and store the evidence and related data in a confidence platform using PBFT (Practical Byzantine Fault Tolerance) mechanism. The recovery and submission process of evidence is carried out with multi-signature methods	Tian et al., 2019
5	Electronic evidence generation	The generation of electronic evidence is performed under a consortium blockchain platform through the procedure of evidence compilation, protection and assessment with nodes of judicial bodies	Chen et al., 2020
6	Lawful evidence management	The privacy of jurors and witnesses in evidence collection is performed through "LEChain" (Lawful Evidence Chain) platform for court trials	Li et al., 2021

forensic proof, submission and retrieval of evidence, generation of evidence in electronic mode and evidence management are tabulated in Table 14.16.

14.3.17 ADDITIONAL APPLICATIONS

The applications of blockchain technology are also available for some other supplementary domain adaptations such as crowd funding platforms (Zhu and Zhou, 2016), philanthropy and humanitarian sector (Larios-Hernández, 2017), military employability (Sudhan and Nene, 2017), grid computing (Gattermayer and Tvrdik, 2017), dynamics for social sharing improvement (Pazaitis et al., 2017), emission trading plans (Fu et al., 2018), dispersed e-voting schemes (Hsiao et al., 2018), railways (Naser, 2018), supply chain management (Dujak and Sajter, 2018), logistics (Tijan et al., 2019), hotel management (Flecha-Barrio et al., 2020), space industry (Ibrahim et al., 2021), beverages labeling (Gayialis et al., 2021), movie rating systems (Saveetha and Maragatham, 2021), marketing (Stallone et al., 2021), insurance sector (Shetty et al., 2022), sports (Du and Gu, 2022), shipping (Kapnissis et al., 2022), smart villages (Kaur and Parashar, 2022), climatic weather telecommunication system (Quasim et al., 2022), intelligent robots (Huo and Pan, 2022), IoT-based musical things (Turchet and Ngo, 2022) and fishery and aquaculture (Zondervan et al., 2023).

14.4 CONCLUSION

This chapter has elucidated various applications of blockchain technology, integrated with diverse versions and variants. These versions and variants have been devised to manipulate various aspects and constraints in a customized manner. The extensibility of the blockchain technology-based solutions has been substantiated to be better than the other notable computer-generated methods, including effort and handling. As the application of blockchain increases, it could be employed in several other domains (Khang, Shah et al., 2023).

In this chapter, various blockchain technology-based applications such as finance, cloud computing, Internet of Things, big data management, industry, education, healthcare, e-commerce, e-government services, real estate, power and energy, transportation, wireless networks, agriculture, aviation, forensic science and investigation and more are presented, based on earlier research. Blockchain technology and its different adaptations are also explained (Khang, Kali et al., 2023; Khang, Muthmainnah et al., 2023).

REFERENCES

Abualigah, L., Diabat, A., Abd Elaziz, M., "Intelligent workflow scheduling for big data applications in IoT cloud computing environments", *Cluster Computing*, vol. 24, pp. 2957–2976, 2021. https://link.springer.com/article/10.1007/s10586-021-03291-7

Agbo, C.C., Mahmoud, Q.H., "Blockchain in healthcare: opportunities, challenges, and possible solutions", *International Journal of Healthcare Information Systems and Informatics*, vol. 15, no. 3, pp. 82–97, 2020. www.igi-global.com/article/blockchain-in-healthcare/251847

Agung, A.K.G., Handayani, R., "Blockchain for smart grid", *Journal of King Saud University – Computer and Information Sciences*, vol. 34, no. 3, pp. 666–675, 2022. www.sciencedirect.com/science/article/pii/S1319157819309000

Ahmad, I., Alqarni, M.A., Almazroi, A.A., Alam, L., "Real estate management via a decentralized blockchain platform", *Computers, Materials & Continua*, vol. 66, no.2, pp.1813–1822, 2021. www.academia.edu/download/72410329/pdf.pdf

Ahmad, R.W., Jayaraman, K.S.R. Hasan, H.R., Yaqoob, I., Omar, M., "The role of blockchain technology in aviation industry", *IEEE Aerospace and Electronic Systems Magazine*, vol. 36, no.3, pp. 4–15, 2020. https://ieeexplore.ieee.org/abstract/document/9374036/

Ahmad, R.W., Salah, K., Jayaraman, R., Yaqoob, I., Ellahham, S., Omar, M., "The role of blockchain technology in telehealth and telemedicine", *International Journal of Medical Informatics*, vol. 148, pp. 1–10, 2020. www.sciencedirect.com/science/article/pii/S1386505621000253

Akinbi, A., MacDermott, A., Ismael, A.M., "A systematic literature review of blockchain-based Internet of Things (IoT) forensic investigation process models", *Forensic Science International: Digital Investigation*, vol. 42–43, pp. 1–11, 2022. www.sciencedirect.com/science/article/pii/S2666281722001512

Alammary, A., Alhazmi, S., Almasri, M., Gillani, S., "Blockchain-based applications in education: a systematic review", *Applied Sciences*, vol. 9, pp.1–18, 2019. www.mdpi.com/2076-3417/9/12/2400

Ali, T., Nadeem, A., Alzahrani, A., Jan, S., "Transparent and trusted property registration system on permissioned blockchain". *International Conference on Advances in the Emerging Computing Technologies (AECT)*, pp. 1–6, 2020. https://ieeexplore.ieee.org/abstract/document/9194222/

Alketbi, A., Nasir, Q., Abu Talib, M., "Novel blockchain reference model for government services: Dubai government case study", *International Journal of System Assurance Engineering and Management*, vol. 11, pp. 1170–1191, 2020. https://link.springer.com/article/10.1007/s13198-020-00971-2

Andrei, A.G., Balasa, R., Costea, M.I., Semenescu, A., "Building a blockchain for aviation maintenance records". *International Conference on Applied Sciences (ICAS)*, vol. 1781, no. 1, pp. 1–12, 2021. https://iopscience.iop.org/article/10.1088/1742-6596/1781/1/012067/meta

Antal, C., Cioara, T., Antal, M., Mihailescu, V., Mitrea, D., Anghel, I., Salomie, I., Raveduto, G., Bertoncini, M., Croce, V., Bragatto, T., Career, F., Bellesini, F., "Blockchain based decentralized local energy flexibility market", *Energy Reports*, vol. 7, 5269–5288, 2021. www.sciencedirect.com/science/article/pii/S2352484721007204

Ariyarathna, T., Harankahadeniya, P., Isthikar, S., Pathirana, N., Bandara, H.D., Madanayake, A., "Dynamic spectrum access via smart contracts on blockchain", *IEEE Wireless Communications and Networking Conference (WCNC)*, pp. 1–6, 2019. https://ieeexplore.ieee.org/abstract/document/8885750/

Astarita, V., Giofrè, V.P., Mirabelli, G., Solina, V., "A review of blockchain-based systems in transportation", *Information*, vol. 11, pp. 1–24, 2020. www.mdpi.com/2078-2489/11/1/21

Bdiwi, R., De Runz, C., Faiz, S., Cherif, A.A., "A Blockchain based decentralized platform for ubiquitous learning environment". *IEEE 18th International Conference on Advanced Learning Technologies (ICALT)*, pp. 90–92, 2018. https://ieeexplore.ieee.org/abstract/document/8433463/

Bennett, R.M., Pickering, M., Kara, A.K., "Hybrid approaches for smart contracts in land administration: lessons from three blockchain proofs-of-concept", *Land*, vol. 10, no.2, pp. 1–22, 2021. www.mdpi.com/2073-445X/10/2/220?ref=blog.chromaway.com

Bhattacharya, P., Tanwar, S., Bodke, U., Tyagi, S., Kumar, N., "Bindaas: blockchainbased deep-learning as-a-service in healthcare 4.0 applications", *IEEE Transactions on Network Science and Engineering*, vol. 8, no.2, pp. 1242–1255, 2021. https://ieeexplore.ieee.org/abstract/document/8943171/

Bhende, M., Avatade, M.S., Patil, S., Mishra, P., Prasad, P., Shewalkar, S., "Digital market: E-commerce application for farmers", *Fourth International Conference on Computing Communication Control and Automation (ICCUBEA)*, pp. 1–7, 2018. https://ieeexplore.ieee.org/abstract/document/8697615/

Bhuyan, M., Kashihara, S., Fall, D., Taenaka, Y., Kadobayashi, Y., "A survey on blockchain, SDN and NFV for the smart-home security", *Internet Things*, vol.20, pp. 2022, 100588. https://doi.org/10.1016/j.iot.2022.100588.

Bisio, I., Garibotto, C., Lavadetto, F., Sciarrone, A., Zappatore, S., "Blind detection: advanced techniques for WiFi-based drone surveillance", *IEEE Transactions on Vehicular*

Technology, vol. 68, no. 1, pp. 938–46, 2019. https://ieeexplore.ieee.org/abstract/docum ent/8556480/

Biswas, S., Sharif, K., Li, F., Naur, B., Wang, Y., "A scalable blockchain framework for secure transactions in IoT", *IEEE Internet of Things Journal*, vol. 6, no.3, pp. 4650–4659, 2018. https://ieeexplore.ieee.org/abstract/document/8481466/

Bouachir, O., Aloqaily, M., Tseng, L., Boukerchi,A., "Blockchain and fog computing for cyber physical systems: the case of smart industry", *Computer,* vol. 53, no. 9, pp. 36–45, 2020. https://ieeexplore.ieee.org/abstract/document/9187468/

Brotsis, S., Kolokotronis, N., Limniotis, K., Shiaeles, S., Kavallieros, D., Bellini, E., Pavue, C., "Blockchain solutions for forensic evidence preservation in IoT environments", *IEEE Conference on Network Softwarization*, pp. 1–5, 2019. https://ieeexplore.ieee.org/abstr act/document/8806675/

Bürer, M.J., De lapparent, M., Pallotta, V., Capezzali, M., Carpita, M., "Use cases for Blockchain in the Energy Industry Opportunities of emerging business models and related risks", *Computers & Industrial Engineering*, vol. 137, pp. 1–9, 2019. www.sciencedirect.com/ science/article/pii/S0360835219304607

Careem, M.A.A., Dutta, A., "Sensechain: Blockchain based reputation system for distributed spectrum enforcement", *IEEE International Symposium on Dynamic Spectrum Access Networks (DySPAN)*, pp. 1–10, 2019. https://ieeexplore.ieee.org/abstract/document/ 8935812/

Caro, M. P., Ali, M. S., Vecchio, M., and Giaffreda, R., "Blockchain-based traceability in agri-food supply chain management: a practical implementation", *IoT Vertical and Topical Summit on Agriculture*, pp. 1–4, 2018. https://ieeexplore.ieee.org/abstract/document/ 8373021/

Cebe, M., Erdin, E., Akkaya, K., Aksu, H., Uluagac, S., "Block4forensic: An integrated light-weight blockchain framework for forensics applications of connected vehicles", *IEEE Communications. Magazine*, vol. 56, pp. 50–57, 2018. https://ieeexplore.ieee.org/abstr act/document/8493118/

Celesti, A., Ruggeri, A., Fazio, M., Galletta, A., Villari, M., Romano, A., "Blockchain based healthcare workflow for tele medical laboratory in federated hospital IoT clouds", *Sensors*, vol. 20, pp. 1–12, 2020. www.mdpi.com/1424-8220/20/9/2590

Cha, S. Chen, J., Su, C., Yeh, K., "A blockchain connected gateway for BLE-based devices in the Internet of Things", *IEEE Access*, vol. 6, pp. 24639–24649, 2018. https://ieeexplore. ieee.org/abstract/document/8274964/

Chen, 14., Zhang, T., "Blockchain-based electric vehicle incentive system for renewable energy consumption", *IEEE Transactions on Circuits and Systems II Express Briefs*, vol. 68, no.1, pp. 396–400, 2020. https://ieeexplore.ieee.org/abstract/document/9097307/

Chen, S., Zhao, C., Huang, L., Yuan, J., Liu, M., "Study and implementation on the application of blockchain in electronic evidence generation", *Forensic Science International: Digital Investigation*, vol. 35, pp. 1–16, 2020. www.sciencedirect.com/science/article/pii/ S2666281720300573

Chen, Y., Dong, G., Bai, J., Hao, Y., Li, F.; Peng, H., "Trust enhancement scheme for cross domain authentication of PKI system", *International Conference on Cyber-Enabled Distributed Computing and Knowledge Discovery (CyberC)*, pp. 103–110, 2019. https:// ieeexplore.ieee.org/abstract/document/8945998/

Chen, Y., Zhou, M., Zheng, Z., "Learning sequence-based fingerprint for magnetic indoor positioning system", *IEEE Access*, vol. 7, pp. 163231–163244, 2019. https://ieeexplore. ieee.org/abstract/document/8895736/

Christidis, K., Devetsikiotis, M., "Blockchains and smart contracts for the internet of things", *IEEE Access*, vol. 4, pp. 2292–2303, 2016. https://ieeexplore.ieee.org/abstract/docum ent/7467408/

Clementi, M.D., Larrieu, N., Lochin, E., Kaafar, M.A., Asghar, H., "When air traffic management meets Blockchain technology: a Blockchain-based concept for securing the sharing of flight data", *IEEE/AIAA 38th Digital Avionics Systems Conference (DASC)*, pp. 1–10, 2019. https://ieeexplore.ieee.org/abstract/document/9081622/

Cocco, L., Pinna, A., Marchesi, M., "Banking on blockchain: Costs savings thanks to the blockchain technology", *Future Internet*, vol. 9, no.3, pp.1–20, 2017. www.mdpi.com/ 1999-5903/9/3/25

Danalakshmi, D., Gopi, R., Hariharasudan, A., Otola, I., Bilan, Y., "Reactive power optimization and price management in microgrid enabled with Blockchain", *Energies*, vol. 13, pp. 6179–6198, 2020. www.mdpi.com/1996-1073/13/23/6179

Diallo, N., Shi, W., Xu, L., Gao, Z., Chen, L., Lu, Y., Shah, N., Carranco, L., Le, T.C., Surez, A., Turner, G.., "EGov-DAO: A better government using blockchain based decentralized autonomous organization", *International Conference on e-Democracy and e-Government (ICEDEG)*, pp. 166–171, 2018. www.inderscienceonline.com/doi/ abs/10.1504/IJEG.2022.123251

Dietrich, F., Ge, Y., Turgut, A., Louw, L., D. Palm, D., "Review and analysis of blockchain projects in supply chain management", *Procedia Computer Science*, vol. 180, pp. 724–733, 2021. www.sciencedirect.com/science/article/pii/S1877050921003446

Ding, S., Cao, J., Li, C., Fan, K., Li, H., "A Novel attribute based access control scheme using Blockchain for IoT", *IEEE Access*, vol. 7, pp. 38431–38441, 2019. https://ieeexplore. ieee.org/abstract/document/8668769/

Do, H.G., and Ng, W.K., "Blockchain-based system for secure data storage with private keyword search", *IEEE World Congress on Services*, pp. 90–93, 2017. https://ieeexplore. ieee.org/abstract/document/8036727/

Dorri, A., Steger, M., Kanhere, S., Jurdak, R., "BlockChain: A distributed solution to automotive security and privacy", *IEEE Communications Magazine*, vol. 55, pp. 119–125, 2017. https://ieeexplore.ieee.org/abstract/document/8198814/

Du, Y., Gu, F., "Application of sports industry blockchain technology under the background of big data", *Wireless Communications and Mobile Computing*, vol. 2022, pp. 1–11, 2022. https://doi.org/10.1155/2022/9655589.

Dujak, D., Sajter, D., "Blockchain applications in supply chain", *SMART Supply Network, EcoProduction*, pp. 21–46, Springer, 2018. https://doi.org/10.1007/978-3-319-91668-2_2.

Ejaz, M., Kumar, T., Kovacevic, I., Ylianttila, M., Harjula, E., "Health-BlockEdge: blockchain-edge framework for reliable low-latency digital healthcare applications", *Sensors*, vol. 21, no.7, pp. 1–22, 2021. www.mdpi.com/1424-8220/21/7/2502

Flecha-Barrio, M.D., Palomo, J., Figueroa-Domecq, C., Segovia-Perez, M., "Blockchain Implementation in Hotel Management", *Information and Communication Technologies in Tourism*, Springer, pp. 255–266, 2020. https://doi.org/10.1007/978-3-030-36737-4_21

Fortino, G., Messina, F., Rosaci, D., Sarne, G.M.L., "Using blockchain in a reputation-based model for grouping agents in the internet of things", *IEEE Transactions on Engineering Management*, vol. 67, no.4, pp. 1231–1243, 2019. https://ieeexplore.ieee.org/abstract/ document/8736824/

Foti, M., Mavromatis. C., Vavalis, M., "Decentralized blockchain-based consensus for optimal power flow solutions", *Applied Energy*, vol. 283, 2021. https://doi.org/10.1016/j.apene rgy.2020.116100.

Fraga-Lamas, P., Fernandez-Carames, T.M., "A review on blockchain technologies for an advanced and cyber-resilient automotive industry", *IEEE Access*, vol. 7, pp. 17578–17598, 2019. https://ieeexplore.ieee.org/abstract/document/8626103/

Fu, B., Shu, Z., Liu, 14., "Blockchain enhanced emission trading framework in fashion apparel manufacturing industry", *Sustainability*, vol. 10, no.4, pp. 1–19, 2018. www.mdpi.com/2071-1050/10/4/1105

Gad, A.G., Mosa, D.T., Abualigah, L., Abohany, A.A., "Emerging Trends in Blockchain Technology and Applications: A Review and Outlook", *Journal of King Saud University – Computer and Information Sciences*, vol.34, pp. 6719–6742, 2022. www.sciencedirect.com/science/article/pii/S1319157822000891

Gao, F., Zhu, L., Shen, M., Sharif, K., Wan, Z., Ren, K., "A blockchain-based privacy-preserving payment mechanism for vehicle-to-grid networks", *IEEE Network*, vol. 32, no.6, pp.184–192, 2018. https://ieeexplore.ieee.org/abstract/document/8338177/

Garcia-Teruel, R.M., Simon-Moreno, H., "The digital tokenization of property rights. A comparative perspective", *Computer Law & Security Review*, vol. 41, pp.1–16, 2016. 100. www.sciencedirect.com/science/article/pii/S0267364921000169

Gattermayer, J., Tvrdik, P., "Blockchain-based multi-level scoring system for p2p clusters", *International Conference on Parallel Processing Workshops (ICPPW)*, pp. 301–308, 2017. https://ieeexplore.ieee.org/abstract/document/8026098/

Gayialis, S.P., Kechagias, E.P., Konstantakopoulos, G.D., Papadopoulos, G.A., Tatsiopoulos, I.P., "An approach for creating a blockchain platform for labeling and tracing wines and spirits", *IFIP International Conference on Advances in Production Management Systems*, vol. 633, pp. 81–89, 2021. https://link.springer.com/chapter/10.1007/978-3-030-85910-7_9

Ghanem, M.E., Alsoufi, A., "Interoperable Framework to Enhance Citizen Services in the Kingdom of Bahrain", *International Conference on Innovation and Intelligence for Informatics, Computing, and Technologies (3ICT)*, pp. 1–4, 2019. https://ieeexplore.ieee.org/abstract/document/8910330/

Gilda, S., Mehrotra, M., "Blockchain for Student Data Privacy and Consent". *International Conference on Computer Communication and Informatics (ICCCI)*, pp. 1–5, 2018. https://ieeexplore.ieee.org/abstract/document/8441445/

Guo, Y., Liang, C., "Blockchain application and outlook in the banking industry", *Financial Innovation*, vol. 2, no.1, pp. 1–12, 2016. https://link.springer.com/article/10.1186/s40854-016-0034-9

Habib, G., Sharma, S., Ibrahim, S., Ahmad, I., Qureshi, S., Ishfaq, M., "Blockchain technology: benefits, challenges, applications, and integration of blockchain technology with cloud computing", *Future Internet*, vol.14, pp.1–22, 2022. www.mdpi.com/1999-5903/14/11/341

Haleem, A., Javaid, M., "Industry 4.0 and its applications in dentistry", *Indian Journal of Dental Research*, vol. 31, no. 5, pp. 824–825, 2020. www.ijdr.in/article.asp?issn=0970-9290;year=2020;volume=31;issue=5;spage=824;epage=825;aulast=

Haleem, A., Javaid, M., Singh, R.P., Suman, R., Rab, S., "Blockchain technology applications in healthcare: An overview", *International Journal of Intelligent Networks*, vol. 2, pp. 130–139, 2021. www.sciencedirect.com/science/article/pii/S266660302100021X

Halilbegovic, S., Arapovic, A., Celebic, N., Atovic, T., "Exploratory analysis of blockchain application in trade finance", *European Journal of Economic Studies*, vol.8, no.2, pp. 110–119, 2019. https://bit.ly/3TWOtDL

Han, M., Li, Z., He, J.S., Wu, D., Xie, Y., Baba, A., "A novel blockchain-based education records verification solution", *Annual SIG Conference on Information Technology Education*, pp. 178–183, 2018. https://dl.acm.org/doi/abs/10.1145/3241815.3241870

He, H., Luo, Z., "Joint operation mechanism of distributed photovoltaic power generation market and carbon market based on cross-chain trading technology", *IEEE Access*, vol. 8, pp. 66116–66130, 2020. https://ieeexplore.ieee.org/abstract/document/9056463/

Ho, G.T.S., Tang, Y.M., Tsang, K.Y., Tang, V., Chau, K.Y., "A blockchain-based system to enhance aircraft parts traceability and trackability for inventory management", *Expert Systems with Applications*, vol. 179, pp.1–15, 2021. www.sciencedirect.com/science/article/pii/S095741742100542X

Hongmei, Z., "A cross-border e-commerce approach based on blockchain technology", *Mobile Information Systems*, vol. 2021, pp. 1–10, 2021. www.hindawi.com/journals/misy/2021/2006082/

Hori, M., Ono, S., Miyashita, K., Kobayashi, S., Miyahara, H., Kita, T., Yamada, T., Yamaji, K., "Learning system based on decentralized learning model using blockchain and SNS", *International Conference on Computer Supported Education*, pp. 183–190, 2018. https://bit.ly/3VH0C1a

Hosen, A.S.M.S., Singh, S., Sharma, P.K., Ghosh, U., Wang, J., "Blockchain-based transaction validation protocol for a secure distributed IoT network", *IEEE Access*, vol. 8, pp. 117266–117277, 2020. https://ieeexplore.ieee.org/abstract/document/9123403/

Hsiao, J.H., Tso, R., Chen, C.M., Wu, M.E., "Decentralized E-voting systems based on the blockchain technology", *Lecture Notes in Electrical Engineering*, vol. 474, pp. 305–309, 2018. https://link.springer.com/chapter/10.1007/978-981-10-7605-3_50

Hu, M., Shen, T., "CRSM: An effective blockchain consensus resource slicing model for real-time distributed energy trading", *IEEE Access*, vol. 8, pp. 206876–206887, 2020. https://ieeexplore.ieee.org/abstract/document/9257446/

Huo, J., Pan, B., "Study the path planning of intelligent robots and the application of blockchain technology", *Energy Reports*, vol. 8, pp. 5235–5245, 2022. www.sciencedirect.com/science/article/pii/S2352484722007594

Ibrahim, H., Shouman, M.A., El-Fishawy, N.A., Ahmed, A., "Literature review of blockchain technology in space industry: challenges and applications", *International Conference on Electronic Engineering (ICEEM)*, pp. 1–8, 2021. https://ieeexplore.ieee.org/abstract/document/9480642/

Islam, N., Faheem, Y., Din, I.U., Talha, M., Guizani, M., Khalil, M., "A blockchain-based fog computing framework for activity recognition as an application to e- Healthcare services", *Future Generation Computer Systems*, vol. 100, pp. 569–578, 2019. www.sciencedirect.com/science/article/pii/S0167739X19309860

Ismail, L., Material, H., Zeadally, S., "Lightweight blockchain for healthcare", *IEEE Access*, vol. 7, pp.149935–149951, 2019. https://ieeexplore.ieee.org/abstract/document/8869754/

Issaoui, Y., Khiat, A., Bahnasse, A., Quajji, H., "Smart logistics: blockchain trends and applications", *Journal of Ubiquitous Systems & Pervasive Networks*, vol. 12, no. 2, pp. 9–15, 2020. https://iasks.org/articles/juspn-v12-i2-pp-09-15.pdf

Javaid, M., Haleem, A., Singh, R.P. Khan, S., Suman, R., "Blockchain technology applications for Industry 4.0: A literature-based review", *Blockchain: Research and Applications*, vol. 2, no. 4, pp. 1–11, 2021. www.sciencedirect.com/science/article/pii/S2096720921000221

Jeong, J.W., Kim, B.Y., Jang, J.W., "Security and device control method for fog computer using blockchain". *IEEE International Conference on Information Science and System*, pp. 234–238, 2018. https://dl.acm.org/doi/abs/10.1145/3209914.3209917

Jiang, P., Guo, F., Liang, K., Lai, J., Wen, Q., "Searchain: Blockchain-based private keyword search in decentralized storage", *Future Generation Computer Systems*, vol. 107, pp. 781–792, 2020. www.sciencedirect.com/science/article/pii/S0167739X17318630

Joseph, M.W., Augustine Jr., F.K., Giberson, W., "Blockchain Technology Adoption Status and Strategies", *Journal of International Technology and Information Management*, vol. 26, no. 2, pp. 65–93, 2017. https://scholarworks.lib.csusb.edu/jitim/vol26/iss2/4/

Jung, M.Y., Jang, J.W., "Data management and searching system and method to provide increased security for IoT platform", *IEEE International conference on information and communication technology convergence*, pp. 873–878, 2017. https://ieeexplore.ieee.org/abstract/document/8190803/

Jyoti, A., Chauhan, R., "A blockchain and smart contract-based data provenance collection and storing in cloud environment", *Wireless Networks*, vol. 28, pp. 1541–1562, 2022. https://link.springer.com/article/10.1007/s11276-022-02924-y

Kapnissis, G., Vaggelas, G.K., Leligou, H.C., Panos, A., Doumi, M., "Blockchain adoption from the Shipping industry: An empirical study", *Maritime Transport Research*, vol. 3, pp. 1–13, 2022.

Kaur, P., Parashar, A., "Systematic Literature Review of Blockchain Technology for mart Villages", *Archives of Computational Methods in Engineering*, vol. 29, pp. 2417–2468, 2022. www.sciencedirect.com/science/article/pii/S2666822X22000090

Khan, P.W., Byun, Y.C., "Blockchain-based peer-to-peer energy trading and charging payment system for electric vehicles", *Sustainability*, vol. 13, pp. 1–16, 2021. www.mdpi.com/2071-1050/13/14/7962

Khang A. (2021). "Material4Studies," *Material of Computer Science, Artificial Intelligence, Data Science, IoT, Blockchain, Cloud, Metaverse, Cybersecurity for Studies*. Retrieved from www.researchgate.net/publication/370156102_Material4Studies

Khang, A., Chowdhury, S., & Sharma, S., *The Data-Driven Blockchain Ecosystem: Fundamentals, Applications, and Emerging Technologies* (1st Ed.) 2022. CRC Press. https://doi.org/10.1201/9781003269281

Khang, A., Gujrati, R., Uygun, H., Tailor, R.K., Gaur S.S., *Data-driven Modelling and Predictive Analytics in Business and Finance* (1st Ed.), 2024. CRC Press. ISBN: 9781032600628. https://doi.org/10.1201/9781032600628

Khang, A., Inna, S-O., Alla, K., Rostyslav, S., Rudenko, M., Lidia, R., Kristina, B "Management model 6.0 and business recovery strategy of enterprises in the era of digital economy". In *Data-driven Modelling and Predictive Analytics in Business and Finance* (1st Ed.), 2024. CRC Press. https://doi.org/10.1201/9781032600628-16

Khang, A., Kali, C.R., Satapathy, S.K., Kumar, A., Ranjan Das, S., Panda, M.R., "Enabling the Future of Manufacturing: Integration of Robotics and IoT to Smart Factory Infrastructure in Industry 4.0". In A. Khang, V. Shah, & S. Rani (Eds.), *AI-Based Technologies and Applications in the Era of the Metaverse* (1st Ed.), pp. 25–50, 2023. IGI Global Press. https://doi.org/10.4018/978-1-6684-8851-5.ch002

Khang, A., Muthmainnah, M., Mahbub Ibna Seraj, P., Al Yakin, A., Obaid, A.J., & Panda, M.R., "AI-Aided Teaching Model for the Education 5.0 Ecosystem" *AI-Based Technologies and Applications in the Era of the Metaverse* (1st Ed.), pp. 83–104, 2023. IGI Global Press. https://doi.org/10.4018/978-1-6684-8851-5.ch004

Khang, A., Shah, V., & Rani S., *AI-Based Technologies and Applications in the Era of the Metaverse* (1st Ed.), 2023. IGI Global Press. https://doi.org/10.4018/978-1-6684-8851-5

Khanh H.H., Khang A., "The Role of Artificial Intelligence in Blockchain Applications", *Reinventing Manufacturing and Business Processes through Artificial Intelligence*, vol. 2 no. 20–40, 2021. CRC Press. https://doi.org/10.1201/9781003145011-2

Kim, M., Park, K., Yu, S., Lee, J., Park, Y., Lee, S., Chung, B., "A secure charging system for electric vehicles based on Blockchain", *Sensors*, vol. 19, no. 13, pp. 1–22, 2019. www.mdpi.com/1424-8220/19/13/3028

Kiyomoto, S., Rahman, M.S., Basu, A., "On blockchain-based anonymized dataset distribution platform", *IEEE International Conference on Software Engineering Research, Management and Applications*, pp. 85–92, 2017. https://ieeexplore.ieee.org/abstract/document/7965711/

Krichen, M., Ammi, M., Mihoub, A., Almutiq, M., "Blockchain for Modern Applications: A Survey". *Sensors*, vol. 22, pp. 1–27, 2022. www.mdpi.com/1424-8220/22/14/5274

Lakhan, A., Mohammed, M.A., Elhoseny, M., Alshehri, M.D., Abdulkareem, K.H., "Blockchain multi-objective optimization approach-enabled secure and cost-efficient scheduling for the Internet of Medical Things (IoMT) in fog-cloud system", *Soft Computing*, vol. 26, pp. 6429–6442, 2022. https://link.springer.com/article/10.1007/s00500-022-07167-9

Larios-Hernández, G.J., "Blockchain entrepreneurship opportunity in the practices of the unbanked", *Business. Horizons*, vol. 60, no. 6, pp.865–874, 2017. www.sciencedirect.com/science/article/pii/S0007681317301209

Le, D.P., Meng, H., Su, L., Yeo, S.L., Thing, V., "BIFF: A blockchain-based IoT forensics framework with identity privacy", *IEEE Region 10 Annual International Conference (TENCON)*, pp. 1–6, 2019. https://ieeexplore.ieee.org/abstract/document/8650434/

Lei, A., Cruickshank, H., Cao, Y., Asuquo, P., Ogah, C.P., Sun, Z., "Blockchain-based dynamic key management for heterogeneous intelligent transportation systems", *IEEE Internet Things Journal*, vol. 4, pp. 1832–1843, 2017. https://ieeexplore.ieee.org/abstract/document/8010820/

Lei, K., Zhang, Q., Lou, J., Bai, B., Xu, K., "Securing ICN-Based UAV Ad Hoc Networks with Blockchain", *IEEE Communications Magazine*, vol. 57, no. 6, pp. 26–32, 2019. https://ieeexplore.ieee.org/abstract/document/8740789/

Li, L., Liu, J., Cheng, L., Qiu, S., Wang, W., Zhang, 14., Zhang, Z., "CreditCoin: A privacy-preserving blockchain-based incentive announcement network for communications of smart vehicles", *IEEE Transactions on Intelligent Transportation Systems*, vol. 19, pp. 2204–2220, 2018. https://ieeexplore.ieee.org/abstract/document/8267113/

Li, M., Lal, C., Conti, M., Hu, D., "LEChain A blockchain-based lawful evidence management scheme for digital forensics", *Future Generation Computer Systems*, vol. 115, pp. 1–15, 2021. www.sciencedirect.com/science/article/pii/S0167739X1933167X

Li, S., Qin, T., Min, G., "Blockchain-based digital forensics investigation framework in the internet of things and social systems", *IEEE Transactions on Computational Social Systems*, vol. 6, no. 6, pp. 1433–1441, 2019. https://ieeexplore.ieee.org/abstract/document/8777292/

Li, S., Zhang, Y., Xu, C., Cheng, N., Liu, Z., Du, Y., Shen, 14., "HealthFort: A cloud-based e-health system with conditional forward transparency and secure provenance via Blockchain", *IEEE Transactions on Mobile Computing*, pp.1–18, 2022. https://doi.org/10.1109/TMC.2022.3199048.

Lin, J., Shen, Z., Zhang, A., and Chai, Y., "Blockchain and IoT based food traceability for smart agriculture", *International Conference on Crowd Science and Engineering*, pp. 1–6, 2018. https://dl.acm.org/doi/abs/10.1145/3265689.3265692

Liu, H., Junjie, L., "Distributed day-ahead peer-to-peer trading for multi-microgrid systems in active distribution networks", *IEEE Access*, vol. 8, pp. 66961–66976, 2020. https://ieeexplore.ieee.org/abstract/document/9049140/

Liu, H., Zhang, Y., Yang, T., "Blockchain-enabled security in electric vehicles cloud and edge computing", *IEEE Network*, vol. 32, no. 3, pp. 78–83, 2018. https://ieeexplore.ieee.org/abstract/document/8370882/

Liu, L., Li, Y., Jiang, T., "Optimal strategies for financing a three-level supply chain through blockchain platform finance", *International Journal of Production Research*, pp.1–18, 2021. Available on line: https://doi.org/10.1080/00207543.2021.2001601.

Lu, Y., "The blockchain: state-of-the-art and research challenges", *Journal of Industrial Information Integration*, vol. 15, pp. 80–90, 2019. www.sciencedirect.com/science/article/pii/S2452414X19300019

Lucena, P., Binotto, A.P.D., Momo, F.D.S., Kim, H., "A case study for grain quality assurance tracking based on a blockchain business network", *arXiv preprint*: https://arxiv.org/abs/1803.07877, 2018.

Lüth, A., Zepter, J.M., Del granado, P.C., Egging, R., "Local electricity market designs for peer-to-peer trading: the role of battery flexibility", *Applied Energy*, vol. 229, pp. 1233–1243, 2018. www.sciencedirect.com/science/article/pii/S0306261918311590

Lykidis, I., Drosatos, G., Rantos, K., "The Use of Blockchain Technology in e-Government Services", *Computers*, vol. 10, pp. 1–17, 2021. www.mdpi.com/2073-431X/10/12/168

Madhwal, Y., Panfilov, P.B., "Industrial case: Blockchain on aircraft's parts supply chain management", *Workshop on Smart Manufacturing*, vol. 6, pp.1–6, 2017. https://aisel.aisnet.org/sigbd2017/6/

Martins, G.J.D.U., Reis, J.Z., Petroni, B.C.A., Gonçalves, R.F., Andrlić, B. "Evaluating a Blockchain-based supply chain purchasing process through Simulation", *IFIP International Conference on Advances in Production Management Systems,* vol. 591, pp. 325–332, 2020. https://doi.org/10.1007/978-3-030-57993-7_37.

Mikroyannidis, A., Domingue, J., Bachler, M., Quick, K., "A learner-centred approach for lifelong learning powered by the blockchain", *EdMedia: World Conference on Educational Media and Technology*, pp. 1388–1393, 2018. www.learntechlib.org/p/184356/

Mitchell, I., Hara, S., Sheri, M., "dAppER: Decentralised Application for Examination Review", *IEEE 12th International Conference on Global Security, Safety and Sustainability (ICGS3)*, pp. 1–14, 2019. https://ieeexplore.ieee.org/abstract/document/8688143/

Naser, F., "Review: The potential use of blockchain technology in railway applications: an introduction of a mobility and speech recognition prototype", *IEEE International Conference on Big Data*, pp. 4516–4524, 2018. https://ieeexplore.ieee.org/abstract/document/8622234/

Neiheiser, R., Inacio, G., Rech, L., Fraga, J., "HRM smart contracts on the blockchain", *IEEE Symposium on Computers and Communications (ISCC)*, pp. 1–6, 2019. https://ieeexplore.ieee.org/abstract/document/8969692/

Nguyen, T.M., Prentice, C., "Reverse relationship between reward, knowledge sharing and performance", *Knowledge Management Research Practice*, vol.20, pp. 516–527, 2022. www.tandfonline.com/doi/abs/10.1080/14778238.2020.1821588

Patil, A.S., Tama, B.A., Park, Y., and Rhee, K.H., "A framework for blockchain based secure smart green house farming", *International Conference on Computer Science and its Applications*, pp. 1162–1167, 2017. https://link.springer.com/chapter/10.1007/978-981-10-7605-3_185

Payeras-Capella, M.M, Mut-Puigserver, M., Cabot-Nadal, M.A., "Blockchain-based system for multiparty electronic registered delivery services", *IEEE Access*, vol. 7, pp. 95825–95843, 2019. https://ieeexplore.ieee.org/abstract/document/8764454/

Pazaitis, A., De Filippi, P., Kostakis, V., "Blockchain and value systems in the sharing economy: The illustrative case of backfeed", *Technological Forecasting & Social Change*, vol. 125, pp. 105–115, 2017. www.sciencedirect.com/science/article/pii/S0040162517307084

Pourvahab, M., Ekbatanifard, G., "An efficient forensics architecture in softwaredefined networking-IoT using blockchain technology", *IEEE Access*, vol. 7, pp. 99573–99588, 2019. https://ieeexplore.ieee.org/abstract/document/8768376/

Qiu, J., Grace, D., Ding, G., Yao, J., Wu, Q., "Blockchain-based secure spectrum trading for unmanned-aerial-vehicle-assisted cellular networks: An operator's perspective", *IEEE Internet Things Journal*, vol. 7, no. 1, pp. 451–466, 2019. https://ieeexplore.ieee.org/abstract/document/8851203/

Quasim, M.T., Sulaiman, A., Shaikh, A., Younus, M., "Blockchain in churn prediction based telecommunication system on climatic weather application", *Sustainable Computing: Informatics and Systems*, vol. 35, 2022, Article ID: 100705. www.sciencedirect.com/science/article/pii/S2210537922000452

Ramezan, G., Leung, C., "A Blockchain-Based Contractual Routing Protocol for the Internet of Things Using Smart Contracts", *Wireless Communications and Mobile Computing*, vol. 2018, pp. 1–14, 2018. www.hindawi.com/journals/wcmc/2018/4029591/abs/

Rani, S., Bhambri, P., Kataria, A., Khang, A., Sivaraman, A.K., *Big data, cloud computing and iot: tools and applications* (1st Ed.) (2023). Chapman and Hall/CRC. https://doi.org/10.1201/9781003298335

Rathee, G., Sharma, A., Kumar, R., Iqbal, R., "A secure communicating things network framework for industrial IoT using blockchain technology", *Ad Hoc Networks*, vol. 94, pp. 1–15, 2019. www.sciencedirect.com/science/article/pii/S1570870519302902

Rathod, T., Jadav, N.K., Alshehri, M.D., Tanwar, S., Sharma, R., Felseghi, R.A., Raboaca, M.S., "Blockchain for future wireless networks: A decade survey", *Sensors*, vol. 22, no. 11, pp.1–36, 2022. www.mdpi.com/1424-8220/22/11/4182

Rathore, S., Kwon, B.W., Park, J.H., "Blockseciotnet, Blockchain-based decentralized security architecture for IoT network", *Journal of Network and Computer Applications*, vol. 143, pp. 167–177, 2019. www.sciencedirect.com/science/article/pii/S1084804519302243

Ray, P.P., Dash, D., Salah, K., Kumar,N., "Blockchain for IoT-based healthcare: background, consensus, platforms, and use cases", *IEEE Systems Journal*, vol. 15, no.1, pp.85–94, 2020. https://ieeexplore.ieee.org/abstract/document/8964444/

Sanka, A.I., Irfan, M., Huang, I., Cheung, R.C.C., "A survey of breakthrough in blockchain technology: Adoptions, applications, challenges and future research", *Computer Communications*, vol.169, pp.179–201, 2021. www.sciencedirect.com/science/article/pii/S0140366421000268

Saveetha, D., Maragatham, G., "Movie rating system based on blockchain", *2021 International Conference on Computer Communication and Informatics (ICCCI)*, pp. 1–3, 2021. https://ieeexplore.ieee.org/abstract/document/9402381/

Sawa, T., "Blockchain technology outline and its application to field of power and energy system", *Electrical Engineering Japan*, vol. 206, no. 2, pp. 11–15, 2019. https://onlinelibrary.wiley.com/doi/abs/10.1002/eej.23167

Sgroi, F., "The role of blockchain for food safety and market efficiency", *Journal of Agriculture and Food Research*, vol. 9, pp. 1–6, 2022. www.sciencedirect.com/science/article/pii/S266615432200059X

Shah, C., King, J., "Distributed ADMM using private blockchain for power flow optimization in distribution network with coupled and mixed-integer constraints", *IEEE Access*, vol.9, pp. 46560–46572, 2021. https://ieeexplore.ieee.org/abstract/document/9381210/

Shetty, A., Shetty, A.D., Pai, R.Y., Rao, R.R., Bhandary, R., Shetty, J., Nayak, S., Keerthi Dinesh, T., Dsouza, K.J., "Block chain application in insurance services: a systematic review of the evidence", *SAGE Open*, vol. 12, no. 1, pp. 1–15, 2022. https://journals.sagepub.com/doi/abs/10.1177/21582440221079877

Shorman, S., Allaymoun, M., Hamid, O., "Developing the e-Commerce model a consumer to consumer using blockchain network technique", *International Journal of Managing Information Technology*, vol. 11, no. 2, pp. 55–64, 2019. https://papers.ssrn.com/sol3/papers.cfm?abstract_id=3407739

Song, Y., Liu, J., Zhang, W. Li. J., "Blockchain's role in e-commerce seller's' decision-making on information disclosure under competition", *Annals of Operations Research*, pp. 1–40, 2022. https://doi.org/10.1007/s10479-021-04276-w.

Stallone, V., Wetzels, M., Klaas, M., "Applications of Blockchain Technology in marketing – A systematic review of marketing technology companies", *Blockchain: Research and Applications*, vol. 2, pp. 1–9, 2021. www.sciencedirect.com/science/article/pii/S20967 2092100018X

Sudhan, A., Nene, M.J., "Employability of blockchain technology in defense applications", *International Conference on Intelligent Sustainable Systems (ICISS)*, pp. 630–637, 2017. https://ieeexplore.ieee.org/abstract/document/8389247/

Sun, W., Li, S., Zhang, Y., "Edge caching in blockchain empowered 6G", *China Communications*, vol.18, no.1, pp. 1–17, 2021. https://ieeexplore.ieee.org/abstract/document/8726067/

Sychov, S., Chirtsov, A., "Towards developing the unified bank of learning objects for electronic educational environment and its protection". *Workshop on PhD Software Engineering Education: Challenges, Trends, and Programs*, pp. 1–6, 2018. https://ceur-ws.org/Vol-2256/SWEPHD18_paper_09.pdf

Tailor, R.K., Pareek, R., Khang, A., "Robot Process Automation in Blockchain", In: Khang A., Chowdhury, S., & Sharma S. (Eds.). *The Data-Driven Blockchain Ecosystem: Fundamentals, Applications, and Emerging Technologies* (1st Ed.), vol. 8 no 13, pp. 149–164, 2022. CRC Press. https://doi.org/10.1201/9781003269281-8

Thakur, V., Doja, M.N., Dwivedi, Y.K., Ahmad, T., Khadanga, G., "Land records on Blockchain for implementation of Land Titling in India", *International Journal of Information Management*, vol. 52, pp. 1–9, 2020. www.sciencedirect.com/science/article/pii/S02684 01219303329

Tian, F., "An agri-food supply chain traceability system for China based on RFID & blockchain technology", *International conference on service systems and service management (ICSSSM)*, 1–6, 2016. https://ieeexplore.ieee.org/abstract/document/7538424/

Tian, Z., Li, M., Qiu, M., Sun, Y., Su, S., "Block-DEF: A secure digital evidence framework using blockchain", *Information Sciences*, vol. 491, pp. 151–165, 2019. www.sciencedir ect.com/science/article/pii/S002002551930297X

Tijan, T., Aksentijević, S., Ivanić, K., M. Jardas, M., "Blockchain technology implementation in logistics", *Sustainability*, vol. 11, no. 4, pp. 1–13, 2019. www.mdpi.com/2071-1050/11/4/1185

Treiblmaier, H., Sillaber, C., "The impact of blockchain on e-commerce: A framework for salient research topics", *Electronic Commerce Research and Applications*, vol. 48, pp. 1–14, 2021. www.sciencedirect.com/science/article/pii/S1567422321000260

Tu, S.F., Hsu, C.S. Wu, Y.T., "A loyalty system incorporated with Blockchain and Call auction", *Journal of Theoretical and Applied Electronic Commerce Research*, vo. 17, no.3, pp. 1107–1123, 2022. www.mdpi.com/0718-1876/17/3/56

Turchet, L., Ngo, C.N., "Blockchain-based Internet of Musical Things", *Blockchain: Research and Applications*, vol. 3, pp. 1–10, 2022. www.sciencedirect.com/science/article/pii/S2096720922000240

Turkanovic, M., Hölbl, M., Košic, K., Hericko, M., Kamišalic, A., "EduCTX: A blockchain-based higher education credit platform", *IEEE Access*, vol.6, pp. 5112–5127, 2018. https://ieeexplore.ieee.org/abstract/document/8247166/

Uddin, M.A., Stranieri, A., Gondal, A.I., Balasubramanian, V., "Continuous patient monitoring with a patient centric agent: a block architecture", *IEEE Access,* vol. 6, pp. 32700–32726, 2018. https://ieeexplore.ieee.org/abstract/document/8383967/

Uddin, M.A., Stranieri, A., Gondal, I., Balasubramanian, V., "A survey on the adoption of blockchain in IoT: challenges and solutions", *Blockchain: Research and Applications*, vol. 2, no. 2, pp. 1–49, 2021. www.sciencedirect.com/science/article/pii/S209672092 1000014

Wang, 14., Chaolu, T., "The impact of offline service effort strategy on sales mode selection in an e-commerce supply chain with showrooming effect". *Journal of Theoretical and Applied Electronic Commerce Research*, vol. 17, no. 3, pp. 893–908, 2022. www.mdpi.com/0718-1876/17/3/46

Weiss, M.B., Werbach, K., Sicker, D.C., Bastidas, C.E.C., "On the application of blockchains to spectrum management", *IEEE Transactions on Cognitive Communications and Networking*, vol. 5, no. 2, pp. 193–205, 2019. https://ieeexplore.ieee.org/abstract/document/8703084/

Williams, P., "Does competency-based education with blockchain signal a new mission for universities"? *Journal of Higher Education Policy and Management*, vol. 41, no. 1, pp.104–117, 2018. www.tandfonline.com/doi/abs/10.1080/1360080X.2018.1520491

Wu, B., Li, Y., "Design of evaluation system for digital education operational skill competition based on blockchain". *IEEE 15th International Conference on e-Business Engineering (ICEBE)*, pp. 102–109, 2018. https://ieeexplore.ieee.org/abstract/document/8592636/

Wu, Y., Dai, H.N., Wang, H., Choo, K.K.R., "Blockchain-based privacy preservation for 5G-enabled drone communications", *IEEE Network*, vol. 35, no. 1, pp. 50–56, 2021. https://ieeexplore.ieee.org/abstract/document/9354922/

Xiong, H., Chen, M., Wu, C., Zhao, Y., Yi, W., "Research on progress of blockchain consensus algorithm: a review on recent progress of blockchain consensus algorithms", *Future Internet*, vol. 14, no. 2, pp. 1–24, 2022. www.mdpi.com/1999-5903/14/2/47

Xiong, H., Dalhaus, T., Wang, P., Huang, J., "Blockchain technology for agriculture: applications and rationale", *Frontiers in Blockchain*, vol. 3, pp.1–7, 2020. www.frontiersin.org/articles/10.3389/fbloc.2020.00007/full

Xu, L.D., Xu, E.L., Li, L., "Industry 4.0: state of the art and future trends", *International Journal of Production Research*, vol. 56, no. 8, pp.2941–2962, 2018. www.tandfonline.com/doi/abs/10.1080/00207543.2018.1444806

Xu, M., Chen, 14., Kou, G., "A systematic review of blockchain", *Financial Innovation*, vol. 5, no. 1, pp. 1–14, 2019. https://link.springer.com/article/10.1186/s40854-019-0147-z

Yadav, J.K., Verma, D.C., Jangirala, S., Srivastava, S.K., Aman, M.N., "Blockchain for aviation industry: Applications and used cases", In: S.Fong,, N. Dey, A.Joshi (eds) ICT Analysis and Applications, *Lecture Notes in Networks and Systems*, vol. 314, pp.475–486, 2022. https://doi.org/10.1007/978-981-16-5655-2_46.

Yang, C., Chen, 14., Xiang, Y., "Blockchain-based publicly verifiable data deletion scheme for cloud storage", *Journal of Network and Computer Applications*, vol. 103, pp. 185–193, 2018. www.sciencedirect.com/science/article/pii/S1084804517303910

Yang, Z., Yang, K., Lei, L., Zheng, K., Leung, V.C.M., "Blockchain-based decentralized trust management in vehicular networks", *IEEE Internet Things Journal*, vol. 6, no. 2, pp. 1495–1505, 2019. https://ieeexplore.ieee.org/abstract/document/8358773/

Yavuz, E., Koc, A.K., Cabuk, U.C., Dalkilic, G., "Towards secure e-voting using ethereum blockchain", *IEEE 6th International Symposium on Digital Forensic and Security (ISDFS)*, pp. 1–7, 2018. https://ieeexplore.ieee.org/abstract/document/8355340/

Yu, W., Liang, F., He, 14., Hatcher, W.G., Lu, C., Lin, J., Yang, 14., "A survey on the edge computing for the internet of things", *IEEE Access*, vol. 6, pp. 6900–6919, 2017. https://iee explore.ieee.org/abstract/document/8123913/

Yuan, Y., Wang, F.Y., "Towards blockchain-based intelligent transportation systems", IEEE *International Conference on Intelligent Transportation Systems (ITSC)*, pp. 1–6, 2016. https://ieeexplore.ieee.org/abstract/document/7795984/

Zarour, M., Ansari, M.T., Alenezi, M., Sarkar, A.K., Faizan, M., Agrawal, A., Kumar, R., Khan, R.A., "Evaluating the impact of blockchain models for secure and trustworthy electronic healthcare records", *IEEE Access*, vol. 8, pp. 157959–157973, 2020.

Zhang, L., Xie, Y.P., Zheng,Y., Xue, W., Zheng, 14., Xu, 14., "The challenges and countermeasures of blockchain in finance and economics", *Systems Research and Behavioral Science*, vol. 37, no. 4, pp. 691–698, 2020. https://onlinelibrary.wiley.com/doi/abs/10.1002/sres.2710

Zhang, T., Pota, H., Chu, C.C., Gadh, R., "Real-time renewable energy incentive system for electric vehicles using prioritization and cryptocurrency", *Applied Energy*, vol. 226, pp. 582–594, 2018. www.sciencedirect.com/science/article/pii/S0306261918308912

Zhao,W., Liu, K., Ma, K., "Design of student capability evaluation system merging blockchain technology", *Journal of Physics: Conference Series*, vol. 1168, no. 3, pp. 1–7, 2019. https://iopscience.iop.org/article/10.1088/1742-6596/1168/3/032123/meta

Zhong, J., Xie, H., Zou, D., Chui, D.K., "A blockchain model for word-learning systems", *International Conference on Behavioral, Economic, and Socio-Cultural Computing (BESC)*, pp. 130–131, 2018. https://ieeexplore.ieee.org/abstract/document/8697299/

Zhou, L., Wang, L., Sun, Y., Lv, P., "BeeKeeper: A blockchainbased IoT system with secure storage and homomorphic computation", *IEEE Access*, vol. 6, pp. 43472–43488, 2018. https://ieeexplore.ieee.org/abstract/document/8386749/

Zhou, Z., Li, R., Cao, Y., Zheng, L., and Xiao, H., "Dynamic performance evaluation of block chain technologies", *IEEE Access*, vol. 8, pp. 217762–217772, 2020. https://ieeexplore. ieee.org/abstract/document/9622659/

Zhu, Z., Zhou, Z.Z., "Analysis and outlook of applications of blockchain technology to equity crowdfunding in china", *Financial innovation*, vol.2, no. 1, pp. 1–11, 2016. https://jfin-swufe.springeropen.com/articles/10.1186/s40854-016-0044-7

Zondervan, F.T., Ngoc, P.T.A., Roskam, J.K., "Use cases and future prospects of blockchain applications in global fishery and aquaculture value chains", *Aquaculture*, Vol. 565, pp. 1–11, 2023. www.sciencedirect.com/science/article/pii/S0044848622012765

Zyskind, G., Nathan, O., Pentland, A.S., "Decentralizing privacy: Using blockchain to protect personal data", *IEEE Security and Privacy Workshops*, pp.180–184, 2015. https://doi.org/10.1109/SPW.2015.27

15 Analysing the Reaction for M&A of Rivals in an Emerging Market Economy

Ruchita Verma, Dhanraj Sharma, and Janaki Singh Rathore

15.1 INTRODUCTION

While merger deals are prevalent paths to inorganic growth in most industries, especially energy, pharmaceuticals, high technology, and telecommunications, the financial sector sees the largest number of transactions, in terms of value. Since 1985, the banking industry has accounted for 16.3% of global mergers and acquisitions (M&A) value ($5072 billion). Recently, in many emerging market economies, supervisory authorities have resorted to implementing industry-wide structural and regulatory changes with the hope of creating stronger and larger banks capable of competing globally while avoiding future economic crises. Mergers are expected to improve asset quality, scale and scope, as well as cost efficiency and profitability. The literature on banking mergers is vast but not exhaustive. Although the most significant sources of synergy for merging companies are market power and efficiency, few studies have attempted to assess how competitors (rivals) perceive them.

Research focuses strongly on developed countries, particularly the USA and Europe, while studies in emerging markets are rare. India is a good example, having a highly regulated financial industry and recent experience of substantial financial reforms (Elango et al., 2019). The consolidation programme aimed to improve Indian banks' efficiency, manage and reclaim bad loans, and build international banks. Analysis of M&As and the implementation of India's public-sector consolidation policy could provide valuable insight into the success or failure of the restructuring process, as well as recommendations for future growth opportunities in the Indian banking industry and other emerging economies' financial industries.

Based on the extensive review of M&A studies and the recent changes in the Indian banking industry, this study seeks to answer the following research question: How do emerging market stock markets value the competitive and contagion effects of bank M&As? The study collected empirical data from the Indian banking industry (2006–2019) to investigate whether and to what extent market concentration and efficiency

DOI: 10.1201/9781032618845-15

are priced in the changes in shareholders' wealth of rival banks. Unlike previous studies that only selected close/related rivals based on size, market capitalization, etc., the current study considers the biggest feasible sample of rival banks for inclusion in the sample. The findings are, thus, comparable to other banking studies with overlapping study periods or sample units (Al-Khasawneh & Essaddam, 2012).

The research on effects of M&As is vast and difficult to organize. However, the literature clearly identifies two primary facets: financial performance and shareholder value. Businesses and non-profits alike use performance measurement techniques for planning and control strategies (Burgstaller, 2020; Mihaiu et al., 2021). It usually involves comparing financial statements to benchmarks such as prior, historical, forecasted, or budgeted performance, industry average or leader, and direct competitors. Financial performance review is crucial in a competitive economy, especially one characterized by inorganic development processes like M&As.

Statistics-based efficiency measurement has emerged as the most superior method for assessing an organization's performance (Castro & Galán, 2019; Du & Sim, 2015; Sufian et al., 2007). The multiple efficiency metrics (Staub et al., 2010; Wanke et al., 2017) offer a true picture of an organization's ability to use internal resources to develop revenue-generating products or services. The industry's environment will change as firms merge. Any corporation's first concern, as with any change in the status quo, is its shareholders.

Corporate and industry stakeholders react to M&As based on expected future earnings. It is possible that the market will react negatively (favourably) to a proposed merger, causing stock price swings and poor (positive) returns for shareholders. In this way, the first announcement of a merger can impact the wealth of shareholders while also expressing the market's expectations and perceptions of future performance and subsequent creation (Chaudary & Mirza, 2017; Khan & Zia, 2019) or destruction (Rahman et al., 2018) of shareholder value. Market structure (Evren et al., 2021; Olivero et al., 2011; Short and Ho, 2020) and competitiveness (Liu et al., 2017; Zhang et al., 2020) are key criteria to measure, analyse or control in industry-specific studies. Market concentration is the degree of dominating market power held by a few of the largest companies. To improve a firm's performance in a more concentrated market, Porter (1980) proposes organic or inorganic growth strategies.

M&As allow merging companies to grow inorganically, increasing their chances of synergistic efficiency and market power. The likelihood of synergy formation depends on whether the merger is domestic (all parties from the same geographic area) or cross-border (at least one participant belongs to a different geographical territory than the others) (Chaudary & Mirza, 2017; Vanwalleghem et al., 2020). Domestic M&As in the financial services industry have expanded over the previous decade, drawing both criticism and praise from academics and practitioners. Consolidation is done to create global financial giants, or 'national champions'. Domestic M&As, especially in regulated areas like banking, can be problematic since they increase concentration as the local market shrinks. Concentration harms consumers due to unequal market power distribution among banks and increased likelihood of service price increases. Policymakers must therefore balance the need for national champions with consumer protection.

A synergy effect occurs when the merged business provides more value than the combined businesses working individually (Chatterjee, 1986). It is possible to achieve scale and scope economies through operational synergies that improve cost (Golden & Yang, 2019; Oke et al., 2017) and revenue (Klimek, 2014). Market power, buyer power or productive efficiency theories/hypotheses suggest financial synergies. Agency issues (Jensen, 1986) or innate inefficiencies of managers (inefficient management hypothesis) create merger losses. Shareholders expect management, as agents, to prioritize their interests. This isn't always the case. Often, the management's self-serving practices reduce any shareholder benefits, causing owner–manager agency conflict. As a result, top-level managers tend to overestimate their contribution to the firm's value creation (self-attribution bias) and disregard shareholder interests. M&As result in larger organizations, increasing the expected value of the CEO-brand and its associated remuneration. The management Hubris theory predicts gains only for targets (Carletti et al., 2021; Fatemi et al., 2017). Therefore, the acquirer would lose all profits made by the target, leaving them with a net loss. Acquiring a target with hubris results in a far higher payment than what market conditions warrant.

External stakeholders (such as rivals, customers, suppliers, etc.) have been studied very little. Customers and suppliers (Bernile & Lyandres, 2018; Cicero et al., 2021; Fee & Thomas, 2004; Shahrur, 2005) may not be from the same industry, but they are frequently recipients of the merger's antecedents and consequences. The literature on market pricing by rivals examines intra-industry informational spillovers (Schipper, 1990) on the stock market in response to an announcement of a M&A deal.

Competitive or contagion are two possible effects (Burns & Liebenberg, 2011; Lang & Stulz, 1992). Several theories (mentioned in the previous paragraph) can help identify the sources of these consequences. The contagion effect occurs when rivals experience the same market reaction (movement in value) as the merging firms. Because merging firms and their rivals share the same industry, changes in the industry are expected to impact both firms' shareholder values. A competitive effect occurs when the market reaction to a merger is the opposite of that of rival firms. In response to a merger announcement, one company's shareholders react negatively (favourably), while rivals' shareholders react positively (unfavourably). The average effect of an M&A announcement on rivals is determined by which effect dominates (Khang & Agriculture et al., 2023).

An examination of prior M&A research revealed a significant gap. These findings highlight the importance of M&A research in an emerging market like India. Little research has been done on how industry competitors (rivals) view market concentration and efficiency. The majority of research excludes banking and other regulated industries. Most studies that focus on similar objectives as the present research work only look at pre-crisis and crisis periods (Bernile & Lyandres, 2018; Clougherty & Duso, 2011; Filson et al., 2015; Gaur et al., 2013). Because of the GFC's impact on competitive conditions, these findings may not be applicable post-crisis. Finally, developed countries, especially the US and Europe, dominate M&A research. There are few studies in developing countries like India (Elango et al., 2019; Ranju & Mallikarjunappa, 2019), and a worldwide low emphasis on financial or regulated industries (Hankir et al., 2011; Otchere & Ip, 2006; Tsangarakis et al., 2013; Khang & Medicine, 2023).

15.2 DATA AND METHODOLOGY

15.2.1 SAMPLE, EMPIRICAL STRATEGY AND MODEL

This study sampled all eligible bank-to-bank mergers during 2006–2019. Hence, a comparison of the banking industry's performance before and after the GFC of 2007–2009 is also possible. The current study uses secondary data from the NSE and RBI websites. The full universe of Indian public and private sector banks (working concurrently with the merging banks) is considered for the selection of rivals/non-merging banks for each M&A deal. The final sample consists of 433 rivals corresponding to 16 announced mergers.

Cross-sectional OLS regression examines rival banks' pricing of efficiency gains and increased market concentration from impending mergers. During the study period, CARs are estimated using event study methodology. The main variables of interest are merger efficiency and market concentration. Other independent and control variables are also regressed on rivals' CARs.

The study uses DEA (Charnes et al. 1978) to estimate merger efficiency. Every bank in the study received a cost, allocative, and scale efficiency score (Farell, 1957). The scores are computed using a VRS model and an input-oriented technique (input minimization). The intermediation approach (Berger & Humphrey, 1994; Sealey & Lindley, 1977) is used to define the DEA parameters.

Market concentration is calculated using concentration ratios (CRn) and Hirschman Herfindahl indices (HHI). Unlike the former, which measures the role of the largest market players (n), the latter includes all market participants, with greater weightage given to the larger firms. For large-scale bank M&As, this HHI attribute is particularly useful in assessing efficiency and synergy (Amel et al., 2004; Igan et al., 2021). Market shares (MS) of each individual bank in the industry are calculated for each measure of bank size:

$$CR_n = \frac{\left(\sum_{i=1}^{n} MS\right) * 100}{Size} \tag{15.1}$$

$$HHI = \sum_{i=1}^{m} MS_i^2 \tag{15.2}$$

where MS_i is the market share of bank i, and m is the total number of banks in the market. In Equations (15.1) (15.2): CR_n is the concentration ratio of the largest n firms in the market and $Size$ refers to 'Total Assets/Deposits/Total Loans' of all banks in the market. In the present study, CR5 is calculated corresponding to $n = 5$.

In the regression model given below, the dependent variable is rivals' CARs. On the right-hand side are the principal variables of interest and other independent variables as shown in Equation (15.3).

$$
\begin{aligned}
CAR_R = \alpha + \left(\beta_1 * Concentration\right) + \left(\beta_2 * In\ Merger\ Efficiency_M\right) \\
+ (\beta_3 * In\ Rival\ Efficiency_R) + (\beta_4 * In\ Relative\ Efficiency) \\
+ (\beta_5 * In\ Size) + (\beta_6 * EXP\_ACQ_A) + (\beta_7 * LIST\_TAR_T) + e \quad (15.3)
\end{aligned}
$$

An extension to this basic model is obtained by adding the four control variables as shown in Equation (15.4):

$$
\begin{aligned}
CAR_R = \alpha + \left(\beta_1 * Concentration\right) + \left(\beta_2 * In\ Merger\ Efficiency_M\right) \\
+ (\beta_3 * In\ Rival\ Efficiency_R) + (\beta_4 * In\ Relative\ Efficiency) \\
+ (\beta_5 * In\ Size) + (\beta_6 * EXP\_ACQ_A) + (\beta_7 * LIST_T) \\
+ (\beta_8 * Rival\ Characteristics_R) + (\beta_9 * Merger\ Characteristics_M) \\
+ (\beta_{10} * Market\ shares of\ Merging\ Banks_M) + (\beta_{11} * CRISIS + \in \quad (15.4)
\end{aligned}
$$

15.2.2 VARIABLES

Based on previous research on mergers (Fee & Thomas, 2004; Song & Walkling, 2000), dividends, and bankruptcy (Lang & Stulz, 1992), this study uses stock prices (forward-looking) to assess impact. The present study uses changes in shareholders' wealth on merger announcement as the dependent variable, to represent M&As' impact on the rival banks.

During the study period, each rival bank's abnormal returns (ARs) are estimated using the standard event study methodology (Binder, 1998). From −30 to −230 trading days before the event (day '0': M&A announcement date), these returns are estimated using the market model (Brenner, 1979) parameters. First, the OLS regression framework is used to calculate expected returns for each bank over the estimation period (200 days), as given in Equation (15.6). Then the ARs are calculated using the formula in Equation (15.6):

$$
ER_{it} = a_i + b_i R_{mt} + \varepsilon_{it} \quad (15.5)
$$

$$
AR_{it} = ER_{it} - (a_i + b_i R_{mt}) \quad (15.6)
$$

where ER_{it} is the equity return of bank i at time t, R_{mt} is the return of the Nifty 50 market index (portfolio market returns) at time t, and ε_{it} is the error term. Also, AR_{it} is the abnormal returns of bank i at time t. For drawing inferences about the impact of M&A announcement, CARs for each rival bank are calculated for three event windows, relative to the event day as shown in Equation (15.7):

$$CAR_{t1t2} = \sum_{t=t1}^{t2} AR_t \qquad (15.7)$$

where, $t1$ and $t2$ are the first and last days, respectively, of the window for which CAR is being calculated. The first window is Post_2 (two days after the M&A announcement), which is supposed to capture the market's reaction. Additional dependent variable specifications are used to test the robustness of regression results. The Pre_10 event window of [–10, 0] attempts to capture any market leakage before the M&A is announced, while the symmetric Sym_20 window of [–20,20] should cover the largest short-term window relative to the event day and show the net ARs accrued to the merging banks' rivals.

Market concentration indices measure the top firms' dominance. The SCP hypothesis encourages firms to grow organically or inorganically in a more concentrated market. Because horizontal mergers benefit merging banks, their rivals' shareholders are expected to react negatively (Elango et al., 2019; Ranju & Mallikarjunappa, 2019). While the collusion/market power theory predicts a positive impact on rivals' returns, the productive efficiency theory predicts a negative impact (Eckbo, 1983; Fee & Thomas, 2004; Shahrur, 2005). In the present study, concentration is measured by the CR5 and three values of HHI. The HHI indices are based on total assets (HHI_A), loans (HHI_L), and deposits (HHI_TD) of all banks.

Merger efficiency consists of the individual and combined efficiencies of the merging banks. High-efficiency banks' shareholders prefer acquisitions of less efficient targets because efficient banks can better withstand integration costs and challenges (Aggarwal et al., 2006; Al-Khasawneh & Essaddam, 2012; Leledakis & Pyrgiotakis, 2019). Less efficient targets allow acquirer banks to improve post-merger (productive efficiency hypothesis). Rivals' reactions to merger announcements may also be negatively impacted by merging banks' efficiency (competitive effects of M&As).

According to contrasting results, non-merging firms either expect to benefit from improved industry efficiency standards or perceive it as an increased likelihood of being targeted in future M&As (signalling hypothesis). In the present study, three measures of efficiency are computed for both, acquirers and targets: 1 = cost efficiency, 2 = allocative efficiency, 3 = scale efficiency. EFF1, EFF2, and EFF3 are proxies for the pre-announcement average efficiency scores of the merging banks. Thus, merger efficiency is measured by a total of nine DEA scores under three categories: acquirer efficiency (EFF_ACQ_1, EFF_ACQ_2, EFF_ACQ_3), target efficiency (EFF_TAR_1, EFF_TAR_2, EFF_TAR_3), and relative efficiency (EFF1, EFF2 and EFF3)

Rival efficiency measures a bank's ability to withstand, survive, and compete against those peers that implement inorganic growth methods. Shareholders expect a strong and efficient bank to effectively deliver future earnings (Clougherty &

Duso, 2011). The three measures of rival efficiency used are cost efficiency (EFF_RV_1), allocative efficiency (EFF_RV_2), and scale efficiency (EFF_RV_3)

In an M&A context, relative efficiency compares a bank's efficiency (here, rival) to that of its peers (here, merging banks). This variable could be either positively or negatively related to the stock market reaction (Clougherty & Duso, 2011). If the merging banks (pre-merger) are equally efficient as the rival bank, the latter should lag due to synergistic gains to the merged unit. Rivals' growth, however, can be organic without M&A costs or post-merger integration issues. In the present study, relative efficiency scores EFF_Rel_1, EFF_Rel_2, and EFF_Rel_3 measure the merging banks' cost efficiency, allocative efficiency, and scale efficiency, respectively, in relation to the rival bank.

Size has been found to positively impact bank profitability and stability. The government and regulators also shelter the too-big-to-fail banks from insolvency. Size of acquirer implies ability to absorb merger premiums and post-merger integration shocks (Elango et al., 2019; Song et al., 2021). The relationship between merging banks' size and stock market reaction is ambiguous (Aggarwal et al., 2006; Al-Khasawneh & Essaddam, 2012; Chronopoulos et al., 2013; Leledakis & Pyrgiotakis, 2019; Li & Singal, 2021). Any good news for the merging banks' shareholders should be bad news for rivals. This section also has limited research. Size matters in evaluating rival M&A returns (Clougherty & Duso, 2009; Uhlenbruck et al., 2017). Palepu (1986) claimed that bank size affects signalling, but organic growth is difficult for smaller banks. The current regression model measures the size-effect of the acquirer, target, and rival banks.

According to previous research, if the acquiring bank in a proposed merger deal has recently been involved in similar deals, it gives the bank the necessary experience in handling merger woes (Aggarwal et al., 2006; Chronopoulos et al., 2013; Song et al., 2021; Wu & Reuer, 2021). Some studies found this acquirer experience to benefit to their shareholders, while others found it disadvantageous (agency issues).

Target status refers to a target bank's stock being traded freely on a stock exchange, thus being subject to the same regulations as all other publicly traded companies. There is evidence that the listing effect harms acquirers' shareholders (Faccio et al., 2006; Nguyen et al., 2017; Zámborský et al., 2021). Thus, it should benefit rivals' shareholders. A set of four control variables (identified through extensive literature review) is added to the main regression model.

Rival characteristics include a bank's merger experience, industry sector (Wu & Reuer, 2021), and deposit-to-asset ratio (Aggarwal et al., 2006). Merger characteristics control for the acquirer bank's age (Wu & Reuer, 2021), the merging banks' relatedness (Li & Singal, 2021; Song et al., 2021; Zámborský et al., 2021), and a merger identifier MA (Akhigbe et al., 2000; Wu & Reuer, 2021). Market shares of merging banks estimates the merged unit's reasonably minimum market share post-merger. Due to extreme pessimism and lack of general demand, stock markets crash during a crisis. Even though GFC had only a minor impact on the Indian stock market, it must be recognized in any financial research conducted on that period (Igan et al., 2021; Leledakis & Pyrgiotakis, 2019).

15.3   EMPIRICAL RESULTS

15.3.1   DESCRIPTIVE STATISTICS

Table 15.1 shows descriptive statistics for the dependent variable (Panel A), and the independent and control variables (Panels B and C, respectively). In Panel A, the standard deviations are high, and the mean and median are not equal. Before running the regression models, the data are thus winsorized (at 1% and 99% levels) and standardized.

First, the market is low-level concentrated, and the targets have higher costs but are less efficient allocatively. Also, they operate on a more efficient scale of operations than the acquirers. Second, the pre-merger synergies are comparable to those of rival banks. The three rival efficiency measures show that these banks were 48% less cost efficient and 22% less allocatively efficient than the benchmark efficient banks at the time of merger announcement. Third, the merged entity could become 20% more cost efficient than its competitors.

Allocative efficiency variation is negligible and scale efficiency is marginally inferior as a result of mergers. Fourth, acquirers are 71% larger than targets, but a few large acquirers or small targets are skewing the distribution and inflating the mean. Finally, the two dummy variables of acquirer experience and target status indicate that at least half of the rival banks are first-time acquirers and correspond to NSE-listed targets at the time of the merger announcement. Panel C shows the basic regression model with various control variable combinations.

15.3.2   RESULTS OF CROSS-SECTIONAL REGRESSION ANALYSIS

Table 15.2 (Part A), Table 15.3 (Part B), and Table 15.4 (Part C) show 16 regression frameworks, where the dependent variable is the rivals' CARs of the main specification: Post_2. Each framework shows a different combination of the variables to incorporate all their representations, while avoiding the problem of multicollinearity ($r > 0.7$) among the independent variables.

The regression frameworks can only explain about 10% of the variance in rivals' CARs on M&A announcements. This is in line with recent studies (Bernile & Lyandres, 2018; Clougherty & Duso, 2009; Fee & Thomas, 2004; Leledakis & Pyrgiotakis, 2019; Molyneux & Zhou, 2020). Overall, the results appear robust, with stable coefficients and signs of independent variable measurements. The F-values show that the estimated regression coefficients are jointly significant at the 1% and 5% levels.

First, results of rivals' CARs are regressed on industry concentration measures. All seem to have a negative and significant effect on the dependent variable. Thus, in a low-concentration market (as in all years studied), rival bank's shareholders see increasing concentration as a threat to fair competition. Second, the nine merger efficiency metrics are examined. Only three have a significant correlation with the dependent variable.

CARs are positively correlated with acquirers' cost efficiency and significantly different from zero by 5%. There is also a positive correlation between target scale

TABLE 15.1
Descriptive Statistics

Panel A: Dependent Variable			
Variable	**Mean**	**Median**	**S.D.**
Post_2	−0.004	−0.002	0.030
Pre_10	0.012	0.009	0.135
Sym_20	0.017	−0.013	0.278

Panel B: Independent Variables				
Variable		**Mean**	**Median**	**S.D.**
Concentration	HHI_TA	667.94	653.08	78.79
	HHI_L	665.10	643.71	70.26
	HHI_TD	633.80	615.93	85.76
	CR5	43.63	43.96	2.20
Merger Efficiency	EFF_ACQ_1	0.656	0.633	0.183
	EFF_ACQ_2	0.844	0.823	0.118
	EFF_ACQ_3	0.889	0.863	0.075
	EFF_TAR_1	0.429	0.406	0.154
	EFF_TAR_2	0.685	0.664	0.111
	EFF_TAR_3	0.918	0.981	0.114
	EFF1	0.564	0.498	0.147
	EFF2	0.771	0.768	0.087
	EFF3	0.902	0.920	0.066
Rival Efficiency	EFF_RV_1	0.512	0.485	0.162
	EFF_RV_2	0.786	0.784	0.121
	EFF_RV_3	0.959	0.991	0.061
Relative Efficiency	EFF_Rel_1	1.200	1.107	0.456
	EFF_Rel_2	1.005	0.980	0.197
	EFF_Rel_3	0.945	0.937	0.100
Size_ (in1000 Cr.)	SIZE_RV	309.77	73.51	978.13
	SIZE_ACQ	1831.00	251.39	5277.44
	SIZE_TAR	720.92	18.48	2490.14
	SIZE_ACQ_TAR	0.29	0.08	0.51
	SIZE_RV_ACQ	1.14	0.29	2.19
Acquirer Experience	EXP_ACQ	0.47	0	0.50
Target Status	LIST_TAR	0.55	1	0.50

Panel C: Control Variables				
Variable		**Mean**	**Median**	**S.D.**
Rival Characteristics	EXP_RV	0.20	0	0.40
	SECTOR	0.51	1	0.50
	DEPOSITS	10.25	8.52	12.48
Merger Characteristics	AGE_ACQ	48.31	52	35.31
	RELATED	0.14	0	0.35
	MA	7.07	7	3.67
Market Shares of Merging	MS_TA	9.13	6.06	8.37
Banks_ (in%)	MS_L	9.44	5.69	8.98
	MS_TD	9.24	4.81	9.74
Crisis_Period	CRISIS	0.23	0	0.42

Source: Author's own calculations.

TABLE 15.2
Results of Regression Analysis Part A: Dependent Variable Post_2

Panel A

Variables	(1)	(2)	(3)	(4)	(5)
Intercept	6.88**(2.22)	4.28***(3.90)	9.70***(2.91)	7.60**(2.46)	8.12**(2.51)
HHI_TA	-0.95*(-1.91)	-0.09***(-3.00)	-1.45**(-2.68)	-1.12*(-2.36)	-1.18**(-2.35)
CR5					
EFF_ACQ_1	0.76**(2.16)				
EFF_TAR_1		0.14(0.78)		0.83**(2.20)	0.31(1.61)
EFF1			-0.07(-0.35)		
EFF_RV_1	-0.24(-0.55)	0.24(0.72)		-0.37(-0.86)	0.23(0.77)
EFF_ReL1	-0.83**(-2.08)	-0.23(-0.79)	0.49***(2.98)	-0.87**(-2.16)	-0.43(-1.42)
SIZE_RV	-0.11**(-2.56)				
SIZE_ACQ		-0.01(-0.42)			
SIZE_TAR			0.01(-0.14)		
SIZE_ACQ_TAR				0.02(0.41)	
SIZE_RV_ACQ					-0.03(-0.73)
EXP_ACQ	-0.30***(-3.11)	-0.37***(-3.53)	-0.33***(-3.32)	-0.29***(-3.04)	
LIST_TAR	0.26**(2.27)	0.31***(2.86)	0.35***(2.84)	0.18(1.24)	
Adj. R-squared	0.096	0.092	0.084	0.095	0.041
F-value	7.554***	7.241***	7.610***	7.445***	4.712***

TABLE 15.3
Results of Regression Analysis Part B: Dependent Variable Post_2

				Panel B		
Variables	(6)	(7)	(8)	(9)	(10)	(11)
Intercept	7.91**(2.64)	4.64(1.93)	8.72***(2.80)	5.09**(2.14)	8.17***(2.69)	5.67**(2.17)
HHI_L	−1.16**(−2.53)	−0.72(−1.94)	−1.28***(−2.69)	−0.79**(−2.15)	−1.20**(−2.58)	−0.84**(−2.09)
HHI_TD						
EFF_ACQ_2	0.39(1.28)					
EFF_ACQ_3		0.70(1.15)				
EFF_TAR_2			0.37(1.21)			
EFF_TAR_3				0.93***(3.00)		
EFF2					0.27(0.74)	
EFF3						2.27***(3.39)
EFF_RV_2	0.71**(2.09)		0.68*(1.99)		0.70**(2.04)	
EFF_RV_3		−1.99***(−3.12)		−1.73***(−2.83)		
EFF_Rel_2		−0.23(−0.76)		−0.55*(−1.97)		−0.46*(−1.69)
EFF_Rel_3	1.98***(3.99)		1.79***(3.55)		1.95***(3.90)	
Adj. R-squared	0.051	0.019	0.051	0.033	0.049	0.029
F-value	6.794***	3.136**	6.763***	4.642***	6.528***	5.368***

TABLE 15.4
Results of Regression Analysis Part C: Dependent Variable Post_2

Panel C

Variables	(12)	(13)	(14)	(15)	(16)
Intercept	1.58***(3.61)	8.95***(2.67)	0.39***(2.84)	0.36**(2.65)	0.33**(2.36)
Concentration		-1.36**(-2.57)			
Merger Efficiency	1.52***(4.09)	0.88*(1.71)	1.57***(4.01)	1.61***(4.11)	1.40***(3.69)
Rival Efficiency	-1.40**(-2.31)		-0.93(-1.56)	-0.93(-1.54)	-0.94(-1.56)
Relative Efficiency	-0.58***(-3.55)		-0.35**(-2.40)	-0.37**(-2.54)	-0.38***(-2.66)
Size	-0.10**(-2.55)				
EXP_ACQ	-0.46***(-3.84)	-0.40***(-3.89)	-0.24**(-2.51)	-0.23**(-2.22)	-0.28***(-2.88)
LIST_TAR	0.43***(4.30)	0.44***(3.32)	0.33***(3.48)	0.34***(3.56)	0.36***(3.58)
EXP_RV		0.19*(1.94)			
SECTOR	0.10(1.05)				
DEPOSITS		0.01(0.19)			
AGE_ACQ	-0.01*(-1.96)				
RELATED				0.13(1.05)	
MA		-0.01(-0.34)			
CRISIS					0.08(0.60)
MS_TA			-0.02***(-2.87)		
MS_L				-0.02***(-3.01)	
MS_TD					-0.02***(-3.34)
Adj. R-squared	0.105	0.078	0.090	0.092	0.094
F-value	7.379***	6.256***	8.105***	7.252***	7.401***

Source: Author's own calculations.

Note: _***, **, and * indicate significance at 1%, 5%, and 10% levels, respectively, and t-statistics are given in parentheses. Results are robust to heteroscedasticity using White-adjusted standard errors. Number of observations is 433 in each framework.

efficiency and average scale efficiency of the merging banks, which is significant at 1%. Therefore, rivals expect already scale-efficient banks (with limited potential to improve efficiency) to suffer during post-merger integration due to size expansion. Also, the market anticipates benefiting from increased intra-industry contagion of efficient banks. The results for rival efficiency are significant in frameworks (6)–(11).

Comparative allocative efficiency is related to CARs positively, while scale efficiency is negatively related. To put it simply, the more efficient a competitor's allocation, the higher its abnormal returns on M&A announcements. That way, they can compete with the bigger and better-capitalized merged banks for market share. This news is not well received by rivals with high scale efficiency (see Table 15.1).

For example, as observed by Otchere & Ip (2006), banks that already operate efficiently do not respond positively to the increased likelihood of participating in a merger transaction. Then we compare the merged banks' relative efficiency to their rivals. A negative relationship between relative cost efficiency and competitors' CARs is found. A stronger rival is perceived positively by the market in M&A announcements. When the merged bank is expected to be more efficient than the rival bank, the rival's abnormal returns fall. Post-merger synergies would be less likely to be realized if the merged bank already operated efficiently.

The current results show a positive impact of relative scale efficiency on rivals' CARs at a significance level of 1%. Next, considering the size effect on merger announcement ARs: According to the research, only the size of a rival bank matters. An increase in bank size reduces the abnormal returns to shareholders. As a result, industry M&As do not add value to large rival banks. Possibly, the market perceives mergers as harmful to acquirers' shareholders. Large rival banks may become acquirers in future deals as the frequency of expansionary M&As increases in the industry.

To account for acquirer experience and target status, the current model includes two dummy variables. For experienced acquirers and targets listed on the NSE, the dummy coefficients are found to be significant, as expected (Pessanha et al., 2016). Results show that CARs to rivals are higher when acquirers have no prior merger experience than when acquirers have prior acquisition experience. Rivals benefit from listed targets because they earn substantially more than unlisted targets (Khang, Semenets et al., 2024).

All variables, independent and control, are included in Panel C's regression frameworks (12)–(16). Control variables are regressed along with the significant proxies of independent variables (in Panels A and B). EXP RV and AGE ACQ show only 10% significance. Thus, market perception can be said to favourably perceive the rivals which have previous experience in M&A transactions and when the corresponding acquirer is a relatively newer bank (approximately less than 52 years since being established). Considering the cumulative market shares of merging banks, the effect is negative and significant at the 1% level, across the three measures. Thus, a decline in rivals' CARs occurs as a result of a merger. The news of an impending merger does not sit well with rivals' investors.

Aside from the main specification of the dependent variable, two additional specifications[1] are used to investigate rivals' CARs: Pre_10 (10 days before the event) and Sym_20 (20 days before and after the event). For Pre 10, almost all independent variable coefficients have the same sign and significance as the main specification results. Concentration has only a minor impact, while DEPOSITS effect has grown. Several variables show interesting results when the dependent variable is Sym_20. Except for target status, all independent variables become insignificant. Only relative efficiency is significant at 5% significant. Market share of merging banks still have a big impact on CARs. Variables unrelated to the merger announcement have a greater impact here. CARs during crises are higher than non-crises. But the proof is weak here (Khang, Gujrati et al., 2024).

15.4 CONCLUSION

According to the findings of regression analysis, while market concentration influenced rival reactions negatively (competitive effect), cost efficiency and scale efficiency of acquirers and targets positively influenced rival reactions (contagion effect). In a low-concentration market, rival bank shareholders viewed increased concentration as harmful to fair competition. Regarding merger efficiency, rivals expected already scale-efficient banks to suffer during post-merger integration from a further expansion in size.

Another explanation is that the market anticipated benefiting from intra-industry contagion from a larger number of efficient banks. The higher a rival's allocative efficiency, the higher its abnormal returns on M&A announcements in the industry. These strong banks were expected to outlast the merged banks, which would be larger and hold larger market shares. However, highly efficient rivals reacted negatively. This finding supports the signalling and acquisition probability hypotheses, where efficient banks do not react positively to increased future probability of participating in a merger transaction.

The findings on relative efficiency support the market's positive perception of stronger rivals in M&A announcements. When the merged bank is expected to be more efficient than the rival bank, the rival's abnormal returns fall. Alternatively, if the merging banks already operate at a high level of efficiency, post-merger synergies will be limited. Thus, the news of the impending merger did not go down well with the rivals' shareholders.

The results conclude that efficiency concerns rather than collusion aspirations drive average horizontal M&A in Indian banking. In contrast to Eckbo (1983), Bernile and Lyandres (2018), Fee and Thomas (2004), and Shahrur (2005), this evidence agrees with Elango et al. (2019) and Ranju and Mallikarjunappa (2019). The results are inconsistent because none of these studies focused on the banking industry. This reinforces the need and significance of the present study (Khang, Shah et al., 2023).

There are inherent shortcomings in each analysis technique as well as secondary data acquired in this study. A few other factors also limit the findings. Because of the small number of M&As in India, random selection was not an option. This constraint is common to studies of mergers in oligopolistic/regulated industries in a single country setting. Finally, the current study excludes the impact of mergers on commercial banks' customers and suppliers. An analysis of these groups would help assess the overall impact of M&As on external stakeholders (Khang, Kali et al., 2023).

The present study has multiple practical implications. The findings may aid future bank consolidation and restructuring efforts. M&As have been shown to irk rivals. Recent research suggests rivals' reactions vary depending on internal and external factors. This study supported the results in the context of Indian banking. The analysis could help policymakers (government and RBI) estimate future M&A implications on bank performance and investor perception. The results may help or hinder future banking consolidation efforts. Investors' reactions to M&As reflect their faith in the industry's organic growth. Less attention is paid to theoretical assumptions and predictions relating to external stakeholders in M&A transactions. This study is also relevant for stock market investors. Lessons learned may help investors sell or buy banking stocks (Khang, Muthmainnah et al., 2023).

NOTE

1   Tabular results are not provided in the manuscript for the sake of brevity. These can be provided by the author on request.

REFERENCES

Aggarwal, R., Akhigbe, A. & McNulty, J. E. (2006) 'Are differences in acquiring bank profit efficiency priced in financial markets?', *Journal of Financial Services Research,* Vol. 30, pp. 265–286. https://link.springer.com/article/10.1007/s10693-006-0419-4

Akhigbe, A., Borde, S. F. & Whyte, A. M. (2000) 'The source of gains to targets and their industry rivals: evidence based on terminated merger proposals', *Financial Management,* Vol. 29 No. 4, pp. 101–118. www.jstor.org/stable/3666370

Al-Khasawneh, J. A. & Essaddam, N. (2012) 'Market reaction to the merger announcements of US banks: A non-parametric X-efficiency framework', *Global Finance Journal,* Vol. 23 No. 3, pp. 167–183. www.sciencedirect.com/science/article/pii/S104402831 2000348

Amel, D., Barnes, C., Panetta, F. & Salleo, C. (2004) 'Consolidation and efficiency in the financial sector: A review of the international evidence', *Journal of Banking & Finance,* Vol. 28 No. 10, pp. 2493–2519. www.sciencedirect.com/science/article/pii/S037842660 3002759

Berger, A. N. & Humphrey, D. B. (1994) *Bank scale economies, mergers, concentration, and efficiency: The US experience.,* Wharton Financial Institutions Centre. www.academia. edu/download/71985900/Bank_Scale_Economies_Mergers_Concentrati20211009- 4579-171t9k1.pdf

Bernile, G. & Lyandres, E. (2018) 'The effects of horizontal merger operating efficiencies on rivals, customers, and suppliers', *Review of Finance,* Vol. 23 No. 1, pp. 1–44. https:// academic.oup.com/rof/article-abstract/23/1/117/5018712

Binder, J. (1998) 'The event study methodology since 1969', *Review of Quantitative Finance and Accounting,* Vol. 11, pp. 111–137. https://link.springer.com/article/10.1023/ A:1008295500105

Brenner, M. (1979) 'The sensitivity of the efficient market hypothesis to alternative specifications of the market model', *Journal of Finance,* Vol. 34 No. 4, pp. 915–929. www.jstor.org/stable/2327056

Burgstaller, J. (2020) 'Retail-bank efficiency: Nonstandard goals and environmental determinants', *Annals of Public and Cooperative Economics,* Vol. 91 No. 2, pp. 269–301. https://doi.org/10.1201/9781032600628

Burns, N. & Liebenberg, I. (2011) 'US takeovers in foreign markets: Do they impact emerging and developed markets differently?', *Journal of Corporate Finance,* Vol. 17 No. 4, pp. 1028–1046. www.sciencedirect.com/science/article/pii/S0929119911000551

Carletti, E., Ongena, S., Siedlarek, J. P. & Spagnolo, G. (2021) 'The impacts of stricter merger legislation on bank mergers and acquisitions: Too-Big-To-Fail and competition', *Journal of Financial Intermediation,* Vol. 46, p. 100859. www.sciencedirect.com/science/article/pii/S1042957320300139

Castro, C. & Galán, J. E. (2019) 'Drivers of productivity in the Spanish Banking sector: Recent evidence', *Journal of Financial Services Research,* Vol. 55, pp. 115–141. https://link.springer.com/article/10.1007/s10693-019-00312-w

Charnes, A., Cooper, W. & Rhodes, E. (1978) 'Measuring the efficiency of decision making units', *European Journal of Operational Research,* Vol. 2 No. 6, pp. 429–444. www.sciencedirect.com/science/article/pii/0377221778901388

Chatterjee, S. (1986) 'Types of synergy and economic value: The impact of acquisitions on merging and rival firms', *Strategic Management Journal,* Vol. 7 No. 2, pp. 119–139. https://onlinelibrary.wiley.com/doi/abs/10.1002/smj.4250070203

Chaudary, S. & Mirza, N. (2017) 'Domestic and cross-border returns to bidders in acquisitions into the E.U', *Economic Research-Ekonomska Istraživanja,* Vol. 30 No. 1, pp. 1021–1032. https://hrcak.srce.hr/file/269211

Chronopoulos, D. K., Girardone, C. & Nankervis, J. C. (2013) 'How do stock markets in the US and Europe price efficiency gains from bank M&As?', *Journal of Financial Services Research,* Vol. 43, pp. 243–263. https://link.springer.com/article/10.1007/s10 693-012-0132-4

Cicero, D. C., Shen, M. & Shenoy, J. (2021) *Corporate M&As and labor market concentration: Efficiency gains or power grabs?.* [Online] https://papers.ssrn.com/sol3/papers. cfm?abstract_id=3990297

Clougherty, J. & Duso, T. (2009) 'The impact of horizontal mergers on rivals: gains to being left outside a merger', *Journal of Management Studies,* Vol. 46 No. 8, pp. 1365–1395. https://onlinelibrary.wiley.com/doi/abs/10.1111/j.1467-6486.2009.00852.x

Clougherty, J. A. & Duso, T. (2011) 'Using rival effects to identify synergies and improve merger typologies', *Strategic Organization,* Vol. 9 No. 4, pp. 310–335. https://journals. sagepub.com/doi/abs/10.1177/1476127011421536

Du, K. & Sim, N. (2015) 'Mergers, acquisitions, and bank efficiency: Cross-country evidence from emerging markets', *Research in International Business and Finance,* Vol. 36, pp. 499–510. www.sciencedirect.com/science/article/pii/S0275531915300441

Eckbo, B. E. (1983) 'Horizontal mergers, collusion, and stockholder wealth', *Journal of financial Economics,* Vol. 11 No. 1–4, pp. 241–273. www.sciencedirect.com/science/article/pii/0304405X83900132

Elango, B., Dhandapani, K. & Giachetti, C. (2019) 'Impact of institutional reforms and industry structural factors on market returns of emerging market rivals during acquisitions by foreign firms', *International Business Review,* Vol. 28 No. 5, p. 101493. www.sciencedirect.com/science/article/pii/S0969593117300720

Evren, A., Tuna, E., Ustaoglu, E. & Sahin, B. (2021) 'Some dominance indices to determine market concentration', *Journal of Applied Statistics*, Vol. 48 No. 13–15, pp. 2755–2775. www.tandfonline.com/doi/abs/10.1080/02664763.2021.1963421

Faccio, M., McConnell, J. J. & Stolin, D. (2006) 'Returns to acquirers of listed and unlisted targets', *Journal of Financial and Quantitative Analysis*, Vol. 41 No. 1, pp. 197–220. www.cambridge.org/core/journals/journal-of-financial-and-quantitative-analysis/arti cle/returns-to-acquirers-of-listed-and-unlisted-targets/F0F24CCC092297C03D33A 7CDA7963295

Farell, P. (1957) 'DEA in production center: An input-output mode', *Journal of Econometrics*, Vol. 3, pp. 23–49. https://ieeexplore.ieee.org/abstract/document/6301411/

Fatemi, A. M., Fooladi, I. & Garehkoolchian, N. (2017) 'Gains from mergers and acquisitions in Japan', *Global Finance Journal*, Vol. 32, pp. 166–178. https://link.springer.com/cont ent/pdf/10.1007/978-1-4757-2799-9.pdf

Fee, C. E. & Thomas, S. (2004) 'Sources of gains in horizontal mergers: evidence from customer, supplier, and rival firms', *Journal of Financial Economics*, Vol. 74 No. 3, pp. 423–460. www.sciencedirect.com/science/article/pii/S0304405X04000765

Filson, D., Olfati, S. & Radoniqi, F. (2015) 'Evaluating mergers in the presence of dynamic competition using impacts on rivals', *Journal of Law & Economics*, Vol. 58 No. 4, pp. 915–934. www.journals.uchicago.edu/doi/abs/10.1086/684299

Gaur, A. S., Malhotra, S. & Zhu, P. (2013) 'Acquisition announcements and stock market valuations of acquiring firms' rivals: a test of the growth probability hypothesis in China', *Strategic Management Journal*, Vol. 34 No. 2, pp. 215–232. https://onlinelibr ary.wiley.com/doi/abs/10.1002/smj.2009

Golden, L. L. & Yang, C. C. (2019) 'Efficiency analysis of health insurers' scale of operations and group affiliation with a perspective toward health insurers' mergers and acquisitions effects', *North American Actuarial Journal*, Vol. 23 No. 4, pp. 626–645. www.tandfonl ine.com/doi/abs/10.1080/10920277.2019.1626252

Hankir, Y., Rauch, C. & Umber, M. P. (2011) 'Bank M&A: A market power story?', *Journal of Banking & Finance*, Vol. 35, pp. 2341–2354. www.sciencedirect.com/science/article/ pii/S0378426611000513

Igan, D., Peria, M. S. M., Pierri, N. & Presbitero, A. F. (2021) 'When they go low, we go high? Measuring bank market power in a low-for-long environment', *IMF Working Papers*, May. https://papers.ssrn.com/sol3/papers.cfm?abstract_id=4026327

Jensen, M. C. (1986) 'Agency costs of free cash flow, corporate finance, and takeovers', *American Economic Review*, Vol. 76 No. 2, pp. 323–329. www.jstor.org/stable/ 1818789

Khan, A. A. & Zia, A. (2019) 'Market volatility of banking stock return vis-à-vis banks merger: An application of GARCH model', *Management Science Letters*, Vol. 9 No. 5, pp. 629–638. http://m.growingscience.com/beta/msl/3093-market-volatility-of-bank ing-stock-return-vis-vis-banks-merger-an-application-of-garch-model.html

Khang, A. (2023a) *Advanced Technologies and AI-Equipped IoT Applications in High-Tech Agriculture* (1st Ed.). IGI Global Press. https://doi.org/10.4018/978-1-6684-9231-4

Khang, A. (2023b) *AI and IoT-Based Technologies for Precision Medicine*. IGI Global Press. ISBN: 9798369308769. https://doi.org/10.4018/979-8-3693-0876-9

Khang, A., Gujrati, R., Uygun, H., Tailor, R. K., & Gaur S. S (2024) *Data-driven Modelling and Predictive Analytics in Business and Finance* (1st Ed.). CRC Press. ISBN: 9781032600628. https://doi.org/10.1201/9781032600628

Khang, A., Inna, S-O., Alla, K., Rostyslav, S., Rudenko, M., Lidia, R., & Kristina, B (2024) 'Management model 6.0 and business recovery strategy of enterprises in the era of digital economy'. In *Data-driven Modelling and Predictive Analytics in Business and Finance* (1st Ed.).CRC Press. https://doi.org/10.1201/9781032600628-16

Khang, A., Kali, C. R., Satapathy, S. K., Kumar, A., Ranjan Das, S., Panda, M. R. (2023) 'Enabling the Future of Manufacturing: Integration of Robotics and IoT to Smart Factory Infrastructure in Industry 4.0'. In A. Khang, V. Shah, & S. Rani (Eds.), *AI-Based Technologies and Applications in the Era of the Metaverse* (1st Ed.), pp. 25–50. IGI Global Press. https://doi.org/10.4018/978-1-6684-8851-5.ch002

Khang, A., Muthmainnah, M., Mahbub Ibna Seraj, P., Al Yakin, A., Obaid, A. J., & Panda, M. R. (2023) 'AI-Aided Teaching Model for the Education 5.0 Ecosystem', *AI-Based Technologies and Applications in the Era of the Metaverse* (1st Ed.). pp. 83–104. IGI Global Press. https://doi.org/10.4018/978-1-6684-8851-5.ch004

Khang, A., Shah, V., & Rani S. (2023) *AI-Based Technologies and Applications in the Era of the Metaverse* (1st Ed.). IGI Global Press. https://doi.org/10.4018/978-1-6684-8851-5

Klimek, A. (2014) 'Results of cross-border mergers and acquisitions by multinational corporations from emerging countries', *Eastern European Economics,* Vol. 52 No. 4, pp. 92–104. www.tandfonline.com/doi/abs/10.2753/EEE0012-8775520404

Lang, L. H. P. & Stulz, R. M. (1992) 'Contagion and competitive intra-industry effects of bankruptcy announcements: An empirical analysis', *Journal of Financial Economics,* Vol. 32 No. 1, pp. 45–60. www.sciencedirect.com/science/article/pii/0304405X9290024R

Leledakis, G. N. & Pyrgiotakis, E. G. (2019) *Market concentration and bank M&As: Evidence from the European sovereign debt crisis,* MPRA. https://mpra.ub.uni-muenchen.de/id/eprint/95739

Li, Y. & Singal, M. (2021) 'Deal characteristics and M&A performance: How do hospitality firms fare?', *International Journal of Hospitality Management,* Vol. 96, p. 102974. www.sciencedirect.com/science/article/pii/S0278431921000906

Liu, Y.-C., Chen, H.-J. & Su, M.-C. (2017) 'Product market competition, type of mergers, and post-merger performance in Taiwan', *Pacific-Basin Finance Journal,* Vol. 46(Part B), pp. 292–308. www.sciencedirect.com/science/article/pii/S0927538X17301270

Mihaiu, D. M. et al. (2021) 'The Impact of Mergers and Acquisitions and Sustainability on Company Performance in the Pharmaceutical Sector', *Sustainability,* Vol. 13 No. 12, p. 6525. www.mdpi.com/2071-1050/13/12/6525

Molyneux, P. & Zhou, T. M. (2020) 'Banking market reaction to auctions of failed banks', *International Journal of Finance & Economics,* pp. 1–17. https://onlinelibrary.wiley.com/doi/abs/10.1002/ijfe.2166

Nguyen, P., Rahman, N. & Zhao, R. (2017) 'Returns to acquirers of listed and unlisted targets: an empirical study of Australian bidders', *Studies in Economics and Finance,* Vol. 34 No. 1, pp. 24–48. https://bit.ly/4awrIvZ

Oke, D. M., Ogbuji, I. A. & Bokana, K. G. (2017) 'Deposit money banks' efficiency in three years after, during and before the 2004–2005 consolidation in Nigeria: the puzzle on size', *Banks and Bank Systems,* Vol. 12 No. 3, p. 193. https://bit.ly/3THFB3A

Olivero, M. P., Li, Y. & Jeon, B. N. (2011) 'Consolidation in banking and the lending channel of monetary transmission: Evidence from Asia and Latin America', *Journal of International Money and Finance,* Vol. 30 No. 6, pp. 1034–1054. www.sciencedirect.com/science/article/pii/S0261560611000829

Otchere, I. & Ip, E. (2006) 'Intra-industry effects of completed and cancelled cross border acquisitions in Australia: A test of the acquisition probability hypothesis', *Pacific-Basin Finance Journal,* Vol. 14, pp. 209–230. www.sciencedirect.com/science/article/pii/S0927538X0500051X

Pessanha, G. R. G. et al. (2016) 'Mergers and acquisitions and market volatility of Brazilian banking stocks: An application of GARCH models', *Latin American Business Review,*

Vol. 17 No. 4, pp. 333–357. www.tandfonline.com/doi/abs/10.1080/10978
526.2016.1232596

Porter, M. E. (1980) *Competitive strategy: Techniques for analyzing industries and companies.*
New York: Free Press. https://search.proquest.com/openview/b61daad357d02fe93bb51
9a74cd987e2/1?pq-origsite=gscholar&cbl=46967

Rahman, Z., Ali, A. & Jebran, K. (2018) 'The effects of mergers and acquisitions on stock price
behavior in banking sector of Pakistan', *Journal of Finance and Data Science,* Vol. 4 No.
1, pp. 44–54. www.sciencedirect.com/science/article/pii/S2405918817300557

Ranju, P. K. & Mallikarjunappa, T. (2019) 'Spillover effect of M&A announcements on
acquiring firms' rivals: Evidence from India', *Global Business Review,* Vol. 20 No. 3,
pp. 692–707. https://journals.sagepub.com/doi/abs/10.1177/0972150919837080

Schipper, K. (1990) 'Information transfer', *Accounting Horizons,* Vol. 4 No. 4, pp. 97. https://
search.proquest.com/openview/3c82d617573971c9c80275819edd4169/1?pq-origsite=
gscholar&cbl=3330

Sealey, C. W. & Lindley, J. T. (1977) 'Inputs, outputs, and a theory of production and cost at
depository financial institutions', *Journal of Finance,* Vol. 32 No. 4, pp. 1251–1266.
https://onlinelibrary.wiley.com/doi/abs/10.1111/j.1540-6261.1977.tb03324.x

Shahrur, H. (2005) 'Industry structure and horizontal takeovers: Analysis of wealth effects on
rivals, suppliers, and corporate customers', *Journal of Financial Economics,* Vol. 76, pp.
61–98. www.sciencedirect.com/science/article/pii/S0304405X04001345

Short, M. N. & Ho, V. (2020) 'Weighing the effects of vertical integration versus market concentration on hospital quality', *Medical Care Research and Review,* Vol. 77 No. 6, pp.
538–548. https://journals.sagepub.com/doi/abs/10.1177/1077558719828938

Song, S., Zeng, Y. & Zhou, B. (2021) 'Information asymmetry, cross-listing, and post-M&A
performance', *Journal of Business Research,* Vol. 122, pp. 447–457. www.sciencedirect.
com/science/article/pii/S0148296320305452

Staub, R. B., Souza, G. D. S. e. & Tabak, B. M. (2010) 'Evolution of bank efficiency in
Brazil: A DEA approach', *European Journal of Operational Research,* Vol. 202 No. 1,
pp. 204–2013. www.sciencedirect.com/science/article/pii/S0377221709002951

Sufian, F., Majid, A., Zulkhibri, M. & Haron, R. (2007) *Efficiency and bank merger in
Singapore: A joint estimation of non-parametric, parametric and financial ratios analysis.* https://mpra.ub.uni-muenchen.de/id/eprint/12129

Tsangarakis, N. V., Tsirigotakis, H. K. & Tsiritakis, E. D. (2013) 'Shareholders wealth
effects and intra-industry signals from European financial institution consolidation
announcements', *Applied Financial Economics,* Vol. 23 No. 23, pp. 1765–1782. www.
tandfonline.com/doi/abs/10.1080/09603107.2013.848027

Uhlenbruck, K. et al. (2017) 'Rivals' reactions to mergers and acquisitions', *Strategic
Organization,* Vol. 15 No. 1, pp. 40–66. https://journals.sagepub.com/doi/abs/10.1177/
1476127016630526

Vanwalleghem, D., Yildirim, C. & Mukanya, A. (2020) 'Leveraging local knowledge or global
advantage: Cross border bank mergers and acquisitions in Africa', *Emerging Markets
Review,* Vol. 42, p. 100656. www.sciencedirect.com/science/article/pii/S156601411
9300391

Wanke, P., Maredza, A. & Gupta, R. (2017) 'Merger and acquisitions in South African
banking: A network DEA model', *Research in International Business and Finance,*
Vol. 41, pp. 362–376. www.sciencedirect.com/science/article/pii/S027553191
6303312

Wu, C. W. & Reuer, J. J. (2021) 'Acquirers' reception of signals in M&A markets: Effects of acquirer experiences on target selection', *Journal of Management Studies*, Vol. 58 No. 5, pp. 1237–1266. https://onlinelibrary.wiley.com/doi/abs/10.1111/joms.12637

Zámborský, P., Yan, Z. J., Sbaï, E. & Larsen, M. (2021) 'Cross-border M&A motives and home country institutions: role of regulatory quality and dynamics in the Asia-Pacific region', *Journal of Risk and Financial Management*, Vol. 14 No. 10, p. 468. www.mdpi.com/1911-8074/14/10/468

Zhang, Q. et al. (2020) 'Impact of high-speed rail on market concentration and Lerner index in China's airline market', *Journal of Air Transport Management*, Vol. 83, p. 101755. www.sciencedirect.com/science/article/pii/S0969699718304344

16 Management Model 6.0 and SWOT Analysis for the Market Share of Product in the Global Market

Alex Khang, Semenets-Orlova Inna, Klochko Alla, Shchokin Rostyslav, Mykola Rudenko, Romanova Lidia, and Bratchykova Kristina

16.1 INTRODUCTION

In order to maintain the competitiveness of organizations, it is necessary to improve their business processes with the help of the most relevant modern resources. A key feature of the digital economy is the implementation of basic communications between subjects of economic activity through the introduction of digital technologies in the working environment. The introduction of digital technologies is accompanied by serious organizational transformations that lead to a radical transformation of business principles at the level of individual companies and entire industries. Most studies on this topic pay attention to the technological aspect of this phenomenon.

At the same time, the problems of methods and tools for managing the digital transformation of organizations remain much less researched. A huge potential for economy development is contained in the application of methodologies and means of project management of digital transformation. There is a need to identify the specific characteristics of the organization's digital transformation management, artificial intelligence (AI) technologies, and to identify the project management tools that most contribute to ensuring comprehensive alignment between technological changes and strategic goals. Another key characteristic is hybridity, aimed at combining flexibility and stability in management, technical and social development of the organization, and innovative and regular management (Khang, Gujarati et al., 2024).

16.2 LITERATURE REVIEW

The high level of variability of the external environment, rapid development of the digital economy and severe market competition require organizations to optimize

DOI: 10.1201/9781032618845-16

and effectively build management processes, as well as focus on improving competitiveness mechanisms. As modern scientists and economists emphasize in their research, long-term market leadership due to innovation, adaptation, and creation of new opportunities are the characteristics of organizations in the age of digital transformation of Society 5.0 (Saldanha, 2019).

Digital transformation involves not only introduction of technologies but also changes in management, use of new approaches, and promotion of innovations. This dictates the need for the development of an effective and efficient organization management system. Understanding the regularities of transformations, information technology regulators, managers can foresee changes as a result of digitalization, which will lead to better assessment of the digital economy. Thus, measuring the influence of the digital economy is essential to assess overall economic growth in the post-COVID-19 pandemic period (Avotra et al., 2021; Yingfei et al., 2021).

The future of the organization depends on those who work to accelerate innovation (Denning, 2019). Miller et al. (2001) point out that it is just innovation which is an important feature of the digital economy rather than technology. A correct strategic vision and creative imagination of the organization manager help to achieve sustainability and build new partnerships.

The functional component of innovations to ensure effective implementation of management processes has several aspects. In the context of digitization, it is possible to distinguish transformational managerial functions that are implemented through such types of management activity as management of using information technologies (virtual reality); high adaptability to changes; a high decision speed; and real-time data acquisition and processing. All this requires a high level of self-organization and self-development of managers for effective interaction with personnel of various levels.

16.3 MATERIALS AND METHODS

The following methods were used in the work to solve the set of tasks: scientific abstraction, analysis and synthesis, functional and systemic analysis, induction and deduction; analogies, quantitative and qualitative comparisons. A special mention should be made of the functions of the innovation process in the organization management system, which focus on tasks of ensuring intra-system transformation. In our opinion, the main functions of innovations in management activity should include:

- Intellectualization of activities (introduction of intellectual achievements of mankind, results of new information technologies into managerial activity);
- Satisfaction of needs of each member of the organization and the team in general; and expansion of possibilities for structuring management processes.

Through these functions, the integrity of innovative changes in the organization management system is ensured in the context of the needs of Society 5.0. This makes it possible to distinguish the innovative features of management activities of organization managers.

- First, management activity belongs to the class of professional activity carried out under special conditions; is of a heterochronic, sociotechnical nature, which constantly complexifies; and contains a variety of complex types of specific activity included in hierarchical relationships.
- Second, it is important to note the creative nature of management activity due to the dominance of unusual situations; the pronounced prognostic nature of the tasks in hand; the need to make responsible decisions in challenging situations; and the variety of managerial functions—planning, control, correction, adaptation, emotional identification, consolidation, etc.
- Third, management activity imposes very strict requirements on individual professional qualities of a given actor and his/her professional competence due to the dual nature of its definition (it means both activities of a manager who acts under certain circumstances and personalized joint activities), which necessitates the need for support in the optimal operating mode of control systems, ensuring functional relationships among its components; at the same time, people holding certain professional positions in the organization's structure and enter into certain sociopsychological relations are the most important among these components of the system.
- Fourth, management activity is characterized by its high information saturation, the need to receive and process information, generate new information in the form of a managerial decision, and retransmit this information to other people, personal participation of the manager in implementation of the managerial solution of professional tasks he/she devised him/herself, which provides for a dual process of incitement to action.
- Fifth, managerial activity is accompanied by severe mental stress and other negative mental states, has a high psychological value due to personal responsibility for the activity results along with a chronic time shortage, and constant risk that can cause occupational stress, fatigability, the manager's health deterioration, and so on (Khang, 2023).
- Sixth, management activity requires constantly changing the management paradigm, using innovative management technologies along with traditional ones (Semenets-Orlova et al., 2021; Semenets-Orlova et al., 2020).

If we consider the combination of "manager—digitalization," then, in our opinion, it is necessary to improve management, enhance the quality of personnel potential, and afterwards—implement digital management.

16.4 FEATURES OF THE DEVELOPMENT OF MANAGEMENT MODEL 6.0

Although Industry 4.0 is part of digitalization, digital transformation goes way beyond Industry 4.0. As organizations invest heavily in their digital transformation, cooperation and collective innovation make all the difference. The Global Risks Report 2022 by World Economic Forum shows that growth prospects are expected to be 2.3% weaker in 2024, although this figure does not take into account the impact of ongoing international geopolitical uncertainty, conflicts, and unrest. However, with a correct approach, organizations using digital technologies can help reduce this impact (The Global Risks Report, 2022).

The main goals of digitalization are to develop innovations focused on development of Society 5.0 and ensure free flow of data and capital. The industrial revolution includes the process of automation, robotization, use of artificial intelligence, and implementation of modern digital technologies in sectors of the digital economy (Khang, Vugar et al., 2023).

To successfully introduce innovations in the United States economy, development of information technologies, which act as a driver of labor productivity growth, and, as a result, of reduction in input intensity of manufactured products, is of paramount importance. Enhancement of the intellectual development effectiveness is only possible subject to the availability of an innovation-driven development management system with a single ideology for all participants in the process, a regulated mechanism, a clear structure, and a formalized process. Developed countries support the digitalization process throughout their territory, as the results of research in this field show that, on average, intensified implementation of digital technologies in a given country leads to 1% gross domestic product (GDP) growth (Khang & AIoCF, 2024).

Digital transformation helps to improve business development, in the long run increasing business stability and resilience to dramatic changes of digital technologies. Thus, the purpose of the chapter is to outline the key factors determining the specifics of management development in the context of economy digitalization (Khang, Rani et al., 2023).

16.4.1 ARTIFICIAL INTELLIGENCE-POWERED MANAGEMENT MODEL

Data show that if an organization does not implement digital technologies, then there is an increase in its profit by 9%, and if it uses digital technologies, by 26% (Capgemini Consulting, 2017). To increase profit greater than 26%, Prof. Dr. Alex Khang has proposed a new introduction of management model 6.0 based on Industry 4.0, artificial intelligence (AI)-powered platforms, and Society 5.0 concepts led to significant changes in the process of managing organizations as described below.

- First, digital technologies allowed organization members to exchange views asynchronously, which increased the speed of communications, effectiveness, and performance of managers;
- Second, the role of managers has changed; there is no rigid hierarchy; flexible management of the organization is introduced with the help of digital tools, which allows management.
- Third, with the advent of digital transformation, the time frame of managing organizations has changed; managers pay more attention to strategic tasks than to processing work.
- The fourth point concerns the digitization of work processes, which allows obtaining additional data necessary for monitoring and quantifying the work at hand.

- Fifth, teams have become more decentralized; digital platforms have made it possible to implement a remote work format, which is particularly relevant in the context of territorial remoteness and unfavorable situations.
- And sixth, operations have used cutting-edge technologies, fostered and applied the AI-powered platforms that can support the decision-making faster and accuracy, which is particularly relevant in the high precision of high-tech areas.

In order for transformational changes in the organization to be successful, he suggests six levels of management model 6.0 for planning implementation of key changes as shown in Figure 16.1.

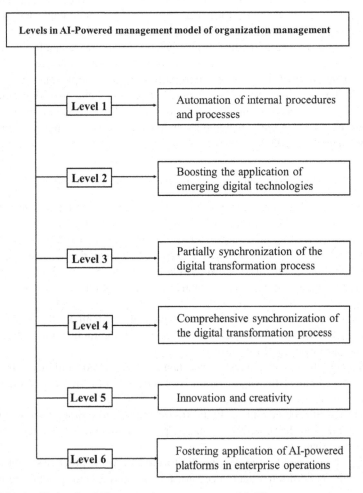

FIGURE 16.1   Six levels of AI-powered management model 6.0.

- Level 1 (automation of internal processes) of the model provides for automation of manual tasks (digitization) and data collection, which will later be used to start transformation.
- At level 2, the use of modern technologies begins to create new management models at the organizational level of transformational changes.
- Partial synchronization of transformation occurs at level 3, where there occurs combination of old and new technologies and processes. At this stage, formation of an innovation-oriented and flexible organizational culture takes place.
- At level 4, complete transformation takes place, during which the ability to adapt to changes develops.
- At level 5, which can be described as innovation and flexibility, digital opportunities are created that allow to constantly change (transform) the organizational culture using continuous innovation, which, in turn, will maintain the leadership position of the organization in the market despite the existing risks and threats.
- And at level 6, which can be added as add-in intelligent components, these AI-based applications are created that allow quick decision-making for the organizational business, increasing productivity despite the labor crisis and potential risks.

It is important for the manager to take responsibility for preparing, monitoring, and taking measures for transformation purposes. The organization manager's knowledge of modern technologies and their capabilities, the ability to make managerial decisions in order to introduce transformational changes, and his knowledge of how to use devised innovative solutions become key competencies required in Society 5.0. Management model 6.0 with the use of digital technologies and AI-powered platforms will makes it possible to increase resource efficiency, shorten the implementation timeframe, ensure achievement of intended results, subject to transparency, reasonableness, and timeliness of the decisions made, and increase the level of interaction of all process participants.

16.4.2 SCIENCE-DRIVEN GROWTH BUSINESS MODEL

Science-driven growth of the economy requires well-timed development of a methodology for institutional innovation designing based on adaptation of the economic system to the basic institutional characteristics (level of technological development, principles of the global division of labor), adaptation of the institutional mechanism for ensuring national security as an expression of the level of protection of national interests to the main trends in the innovation sector, and active transformation of the institutional matrix in order to preserve competitiveness (global economic identity) of the state on the back of innovations.

The goals of such designing should be achieved through the following managerial and analytical mechanisms: identification of industries with highest (current and prospective) priority and localization of competencies (innovation potential, level of technological excellence, human resources, AI platforms, and sectoral opportunities), their efficient and effective use; creation of a set of organizational advantages (a unique concept or model of development, special configuration of processes, inimitable innovation-oriented culture, innovation ecosystem).

In order to enhance performance of the sphere of intellectual property, and improve the image and investment attractiveness of the economy, a methodology for managing development of the intellectual innovation sector is suggested providing for phased and systemic assessment of the opportunities and targets of the proactive stance of the country regarding the creation of initiatives and standards of interaction in the sphere of intellectual property, depending on the level of infrastructural support. In order to determine the strategic vector of the economy's intellectual development and ensure an exponential increase in innovations, an organizational mechanism for assessing the effectiveness of economic incentives for the development of intellectual development targets by aggregate factors (level of intellectual and patent activity, level of government support for intellectual activities and provision of the industry with national researchers) was developed.

The mechanism presented is based on an integrated assessment system, includes a model of base concepts that characterize various aspects of development of intellectual property objects, allows to assess patentability of the intellectual property sphere by segments (inventions, marks for goods and services, utility models, industrial designs), evaluate financial support, appraise favorableness of the legal and political environment and the competitive landscape, and comprehensively describe the status of development of the intellectual property sphere.

The effectiveness of digitalization changes can be improved with approaches and tools that enable management and coordination among all parts of the organization. Therefore, we believe that using such an approach, which is supported by appropriate mechanisms, will contribute to more successful management at the 2nd and 3rd levels of the model as shown in Figure 16.1 and digital transformation will be much more successful. Successful digital transformation is ensured not only by technology, but also by effective management that encourages changes and innovation. It is necessary to introduce methods, processes, and tools in the organization that would ensure effective and flexible management.

16.4.3 Digital-Driven Management Model

Hernández et al. (2017) note that investment by organizations in information technologies is a propensity for innovation. If organizations have potential for a deep understanding of digital innovation, then this will lead to sustainability (Khin, 2019). Saleem et al. (2020) proved the positive impact of digital solutions on social, economic, managerial, organizational, strategic, and transformational development of organizations.

Bag et al. note that digitalization of the economy is a central factor for achieving a sustainable and competitive economy as a whole (Bag et al., 2021). It is the digital economy that requires revision of the organization management mechanisms and transition to more flexible and adaptive management mechanisms (The Global Risks Report, 2022; Oliinyk et al., 2021).

Linkov et al. (2018) distinguish three strategies for managing the digital economy, which include laissez-faire, precautionary strategy, and stewardship, and allow reducing digitalization risks, while at the same time supporting innovation. Adaptive management makes it possible to regulate introduction of new technologies and balance the merits and risks of digital activities.

Research shows that adaptive management is able enough to cope with the contemporary challenges of the digital economy (Ganin et al., 2020; Koval et al., 2021). The digital economy has a positive impact on social reforms, a sustainable digital economy, and social governance mechanisms. This indicates that the digital economy prosperity strengthens a sustainable digital economy and plays a vital role in the development of a strong social governance mechanism (Saldanha, 2019).

16.4.4 TECHNOLOGY-DRIVEN BUSINESS RECOVERY STRATEGY

During the COVID-19 period, people had one topic on their lips: when would the COVID-19 pandemic end and the recovery of normal life after the pandemic begin. And one of the most urgent issues is the rebuilding normal social activity as before the pandemic. There have been 1,127,152 deaths in 103,436,829 confirmed cases (from 3 January 2020 to 7:50 pm CEST, 4 October 2023) in the United States (WHO – COVID-19, 2023). Thus, according to preliminary data from the WHO, as of 4 October 2023, the economic toll of the COVID-19 pandemic in the US had direct losses to the economy amounting to US$14 trillion (USA Economy COVID-19, 2023), corresponding to the economy contracting by 19.2% during the COVID-19 pandemic recession (Lucia, 2021).

Overall, from 2020 to 2023, the cumulative net economic output of the United States will amount to about $103 trillion, without the pandemic, the total of GDP over those four years would have been $117 trillion—nearly 14% higher in inflation-adjusted 2020 dollars, according to our analysis (USA Economy COVID-19, 2023). The question is how to recover the business as quickly as possible? These are the tasks set out in the Business Recovery Plan in the United States, taking into account global trends and the green industry as well as the US's competitive position, to build back better.

For such a restoration, a modern building material is needed, which is sandwich panels. Therefore, the problem of development of enterprises in the market of sandwich panels and its marketing strategy in the context of the restoration of business is quite relevant. The object of the case study is Global TPK Product Company (United States), which produces high-quality sandwich panels. The purpose of this chapter is to study the directions of the formation of the company's marketing strategy in the period of the economy's recovery which is presented in Section 16.5.

16.4.5 BEHAVIORAL-DRIVEN MARKETING STRATEGY

In the literature, marketing strategy is defined as a tool for achieving business goals and objectives through the use of a sustainable competitive advantage in the market and provides for policies and rules for ensuring the direction of the company's marketing activities. It is with the help of a marketing strategy that companies can increase their competitive advantage (Sari et al., 2020). Porter defines three strategies of competitive advantage: cost leadership, differentiation, and specialization.

At the present stage of economic development, the role of marketing strategy is growing and it is defined as a construct that lies at the conceptual center of the strategic marketing sphere and occupies a central place in marketing practice. Marketing strategy includes the processes of developing and implementing a strategy for the desired goals of the firm for the future period of time and the means of achieving them: selection of target markets and customers, determination of the necessary value propositions, as well as the design and implementation of integrated marketing programs for the development, delivery, and communication of the value proposition.

Strategic planning at the level of a business unit includes eight stages: mission of the business unit, analysis of the external and internal environment—Strengths, Weaknesses, Opportunities, and Threats (SWOT) analysis, goal setting, strategy, programs, program implementation, feedback, and control. It is proposed to study resources and opportunities such as narcissistic personality disorder (NPD) and customer relationship management (CRM), and when determining its effectiveness—customer thinking, behavioral results, and economic results. Environmental factors affect the marketing strategy and the relationship with internal components. Thus, marketing strategy is not limited to competitive advantages. On the other hand, the marketing environment is an important factor for the formation of a marketing strategy by an enterprise and its transformation in the case of its changes. Therefore, it is very important to carry out SWOT analysis as a method of evaluating a business portfolio (Taherdoost et al., 2021).

With regard to construction enterprises, Chinese researchers believe that the performance of construction SMEs critically depends on three key components: competitive marketing strategy, relationship marketing, and business environment, and they confirmed the importance of differentiating marketing, innovation, and relationship system to achieve their performance. Moreover, relationships are given a very important role (Shigang et al., 2020). The quality of customer experience (QCQ) has become an important component of the business marketing strategy (Raisa et al., 2016). At industrial enterprises, relationship marketing is determined as a key strategic resource, therefore, in modern conditions there is a transition to strategic partnerships and the formation of marketing partnership networks that include the enterprise, consumers, suppliers, and intermediaries (Romanova et al., 2017). A modern tool for forming a relationship marketing strategy is digital marketing (Zinchenko et al., 2021).

Thus, the problem of the marketing strategy of enterprises, and in particular, construction enterprises, is sufficiently studied in the literature. However, the directions of formation of the marketing strategy of enterprises in the period of recovery of the economy, and especially those engaged in the production of sandwich panels, are not sufficiently studied.

16.5 CASE STUDY—GLOBAL TPK PRODUCT COMPANY (TPK)

16.5.1 ANALYTICS METHODOLOGY

This study uses theoretical research methods: analysis and generalization. The practical part includes statistical methods of analysis, SWOT (Strengths, Weaknesses, Opportunities, and Threats) analysis, BKG matrix, marketplace analysis, and research of personal data obtained through a CRM system, during a survey using Google services (Google Forms). We interviewed 36 clients of the company using Google surveys. Questions in the questionnaire included:

1. What sandwich panels were the most popular among customers in 2019?
2. Do customers have a binding to the company, brand?
3. What are the main competitors named during negotiations?
   a) price;
   b) availability of a "ready-made solution" for the client;
   c) competencies of the seller (product knowledge, ability to persuade, friendly relations);
   d) quality of sandwich panels;
   e) timely delivery.
4. What is a quality sandwich panel in the customer's understanding?

16.5.2 ANALYTICS RESULTS

The construction market around the world is developing rapidly and construction services occupy a significant share of GDP. Thus, in 2021, according to international market research experts, the global construction market was estimated at US$7.28 trillion and by 2030 it will reach US$14.41 trillion, with an average annual growth rate of 7.3% in 2022–2030 (GCM, 2022). Growing investments, renewable energy capacity, urbanization, and digitalization will contribute to the market's prospective growth until 2030 (CM, 2022). The main strategies for the development of the construction market include the use of autonomous construction vehicles, the introduction of green building technologies, the use of digital technologies to improve construction safety, and the use of advanced building materials (GCMOS, 2022).

Autonomous construction vehicles are automated vehicles equipped with sensors, cameras, and GPS. Green building involves the use of sustainable building materials and construction processes to create energy-efficient buildings with minimal environmental impact (CM, 2022). Such building materials include sandwich panels, the use of which allows achieving sustainable development goals due to their properties.

Based on the above, it is clear that the demand for sandwich panels is growing. Thus, according to international experts, the global sandwich panel market is expected to grow. Thus, while in 2022 it was estimated at US$16.08 billion, by 2031, it will be worth US$28.8 billion. This growth is driven by the increasing demand for rapid construction services in various industries, residential and commercial construction, and infrastructure. The growing preference for polyurethane-filled panels is due to their low cost and durability. This segment dominated the market in 2021, and this trend is projected to continue until 2030 (SPM, 2022).

A similar trend can be observed in the European sandwich panel market, which according to experts, is projected to grow by 5.2% on average between 2023 and 2028 due to increased investment in residential and industrial construction projects in the region. The development of the European sandwich panel market will be driven by environmentally friendly structures with an advanced core consisting of rigid polyurethane foam, polystyrene foam, and mineral wool to improve their quality standards (Europe Report, 2023).

16.5.3 DATA SIMULATION

The United States is experiencing an increase in the volume of construction products produced. Thus, in 2019, the market volume amounted to US$181,697.9 million, in 2020 it was US$202,080.8, and in 2021 it reached US$258,073.6 million. However, if we compare the indices of construction products, we can see their decline in 2020 due to the COVID-19 pandemic, as shown in Table 16.1. The same trend can be observed with the volume of capital investment in construction, which in the United States in these years amounted to 62,346,613, 37,980,503 and 51,832,667 million US$, respectively.

According to the data sample in Table 16.1, to meet the demand for housing during the period of the economy's recovery, it is proposed to build cottages and high-rise buildings using sandwich panels. TPK has developed a technology for the construction of one-story houses in 7 days from sandwich panels with a service life of 50 years. The sandwich panel market in United States is developing rapidly. The market volume for the period 2015–2020 increased by 2.4 times, and from 2019 to 2020 by 1.3 times, with a tendency to increase the volume of its own production. There are about 30 companies operating in the market and their capacities are shown in Figure 16.2.

TABLE 16.1
Sample of Indices of Construction Products in United States (%)

Name	2019 to 2018	2020 to 2019	2021 to 2020
Construction	120.0	105.6	106.8
Buildings	116.3	93.7	110.0
Residential	104.8	83.5	119.2
Non-residential	130.3	100.3	105.1
Engineering structures	123.3	115.6	104.6

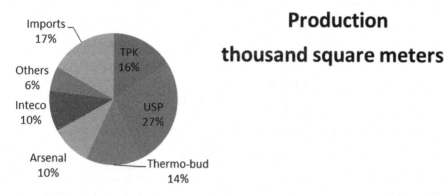

Production

thousand square meters

FIGURE 16.2   List of 30 companies and TPK operating in the market.

Source: Research by TPK Company.

16.5.4 SWOT ANALYSIS

In 2018–2020, there was a tendency to redistribute the sandwich panel market by the type of their fillers: a decrease in mineral wool (MB) panels from 46% to 28% and an increase in the share of panels with polyurethane (PPY) foam insulation from 54% to 72%, as shown in Figure 16.3. Such panels are used, in particular, in the agricultural sector, which is currently being actively built in United States (Table 16.2) (Khang et al., 2023a; Khang, Santosh et al., 2023).

From the SWOT analysis matrix, the following conclusions can be drawn: the firm's strongest advantages are product quality, reputation, and market leadership. However, the company's biggest disadvantage is its high price. Another significant disadvantage is the high maintenance costs. These two indicators significantly reduce the company's competitiveness, but a marketing strategy to strengthen customer relations regarding the benefits of product quality will offset these weaknesses. Among the favorable opportunities, the most likely are:

- Active work with designers and inclusion of TPK Company's products in projects to eliminate competitors at the initial stage of construction;
- Development of new products;
- Regulation of the sandwich panel market by regulatory documents.

An important part of marketing in business is the business portfolio management function. Let's analyze the market position of TPK Company using the Boston Consulting Group (BCG) matrix. The company has four strategic business units: sandwich panels with mineral wool insulation, polyurethane foam insulation, metal products (corrugated board, metal tiles), and resale of accessories and components for installation.

Taking into account the market positions of the company's strategic business units and the prospects of its sales markets, the following strategic decisions can be proposed:

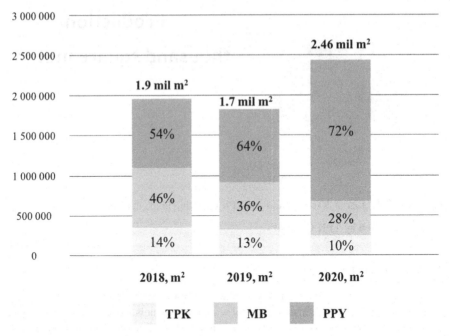

FIGURE 16.3   Sandwich panels market in United States in 2018–2020, m².

Source: Research by TPK Company.

- To support and develop the new product "Polyurethane (PU) foam sandwich panels" in order to increase its market share—the "BUILD" strategy;
- Maintain the existing market positions of the strategic business units "Components"—the "HOLD" strategy;
- Reducing investment and marketing attention to the strategic business unit "Sandwich panels made of mineral wool"—the "harvesting" strategy;
- Excluding the Metal Products strategic business unit from the company's business portfolio, which is, accordingly, an unpromising "dog"—the elimination strategy.

The marketing strategy for entering the foreign market is as follows. The company's favorable strengths and capabilities make it expedient to enter foreign markets with sandwich panels, thereby reducing the threats of an aggressive internal environment. TPK Company has every reason to do so. This is facilitated by the implementation of Regulation in European Union (EU) No 305/2011 of the European Parliament and of the Council establishing harmonized conditions for the provision of construction products on the market. In addition to organizational measures, it is necessary to introduce Building Information Modeling (BIM) technology based on the use of intelligent 3D models, which helps architecture and engineering (A&E) professionals to plan, design, construct, and operate buildings and infrastructure more efficiently.

TABLE 16.2

Matrix of SWOT Analysis of TPK Company

Strengths	Weaknesses
1. Modern production technology using own high-tech equipment at the European level	1. High production costs
2. Wide range of products	2. Lack of systematic promotion of the company in the market
3. TPK brand—experience and reputation of a reliable partner in the United States market	3. Insufficient implementation of digital marketing in the company
4. An impressive portfolio of facilities	3. High price
5. Support of the client from the development of the most effective solution in terms of design, operation, and price at the design stage and until the end of installation work	4. Lack of working capital makes it impossible to reduce the purchase price, ensure the efficiency of supply and production
6. Availability of a sales network throughout the United States	
7. Availability of qualified engineering service	**Threats**
8. Implementation of a quality control system for manufactured products	1. Instability in the country due to the COVID-19 pandemic, in particular, lack of funds to invest in the construction of facilities
9. Availability of proven and reliable suppliers of raw materials	2. Increased aggressive actions by importers
	3. Aggressive price war by competitors
Opportunities	
1. Projected market growth due to the Business Recovery Plan of the United States	
2. Working with designers and architects	
3. Development in the segment of residential and own construction	
4. Introduction of new products to complement existing products of own production	
5. Work on the culture of product consumption— participation in the development of regulatory documents and standards of the construction industry, its development	
6. Introduction of import quotas	

Source: Developed by the authors.

Analysis of the company's customer base. To better understand the sales structure and our customers, we analyzed the customer base using a CRM system for the period from 2017 to 2020. In 2020, the first 6 months of the analyzed period, it is reasonable to predict a twofold increase in the customer base, as shown in Figure 16.4. The analysis revealed a drop in the customer base.

As for customer loyalty, 70% of customers are not loyal and have worked with the company once, and only 10% of customers who have been working for more than 3 years can be described as loyal. Most customers bought once, in small orders for

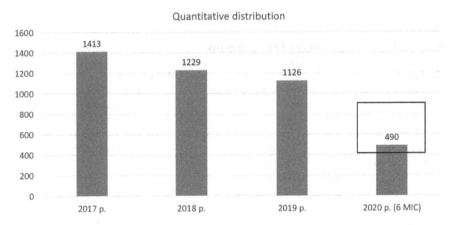

FIGURE 16.4 Quantitative distribution of the company's customers in 2017–2020.

residential and private construction. According to the data in the company's CRM system, the company needs to build long-term partnerships with 67% of its customers. And they don't have them, because only 10% of them are loyal customers.

16.5.5 Customer Satisfaction Monitoring Through Surveys

When analyzing the data obtained, it was found that customers have virtually no attachment to a specific company or brand, and the main competitors are ESC and USS (United States Steel Corporation) companies. The price of sandwich panels is important, but not the main selection criterion. Customers do not understand the "engineering service" and "turnkey solutions" service, so this service does not influence the client's choice. The company's reputation and meeting deadlines are among the main factors of influence. The concept of quality is vague for customers, and its main physical dimension is "high-quality lock" and "European raw materials." Everything else is secondary because it affects the speed of installation work on the site (Khang & Shah et al., 2023).

The company has done a lot of work on the use of digital technologies in product promotion. In particular, the company's main website in 2021 became an effective tool for lead generation, and the number of customer requests through the website increased almost twofold. The research has shown that Internet marketing requires constant monitoring and analysis of effectiveness. Outsourcing this activity is not effective due to the impossibility of perfect control (Khang, Kali et al., 2023).

The conducted research has confirmed the feasibility of the conclusions about the need to change approaches to defining a marketing strategy due to changes in the environment. The analysis of the market environment has shown that the main product competitor for TPK is PU foam sandwich panels and requires changes in the assortment and adjustment of the marketing strategy. However, despite the fall in demand for mineral wool panels, they should be kept in the product range because of their possible use in certain areas of construction where they are indispensable.

This approach requires refinement of the analysis methods (Khang, Muthmainnah et al., 2023).

According to the study, the main marketing strategy for competitive advantage is differentiation. However, the change in competitive strategy alone does not solve the problem of TPK's market share decline. This requires research of the customer base using a CRM system and surveys. It has been established that the company's system of interaction with clients needs to be thoroughly improved. The task is to create a high-quality customer experience, intensify communication interaction, and establish genuine partnerships with customers. As for digital marketing, the work of the relevant specialists on outsourcing has not paid off. Therefore, the conclusion was made that it is advisable to have specialists in the company's marketing department promote and advertise products on the Internet—Chief Executive Officer (CEO) specialists, social media marketing (SMM) specialists, content managers, creative designers. The results of the research will be correct in the case of positive developments after the end of the COVID-19 pandemic period. However, the construction industry may face a number of problems after the COVID-19 pandemic period and therefore it needs to change quickly and be ready to accept them (Aakansha & Adhishree et al., 2023).

16.6 CONCLUSION

A conceptual model for implementing strategic macro projects has been developed based on taking into account global innovation trends, their impact on knowledge creation and absorption, as well as on the management quality level, which will determine the long-term competitiveness and sustainability of organizations and the national economic system in general. The development of a system of intellectual innovation-driven growth takes into account interaction capital generation and innovation policy optimization based on selection of the most effective forms of joint innovative activities. The developed organizational mechanism for assessing the effectiveness of economic incentives to intellectual development will allow competently and efficiently developing and implementing managerial decisions regarding the formation and commercialization of the intellectual activity results at all levels of management (Muthmainnah, Yakin et al., 2023).

In our opinion, successful digital transformation requires effective management, a new attitude towards employees, enhanced innovativeness and flexibility, greater cooperation, and greater readiness for constant changes on the part of not only managers but also all employees, which requires the possession of new digital competencies. We believe that, in addition to modern management approaches, readiness and opportunities for continuous acquisition of new digital competencies will be key digital transformation success factors in the future (Pooja & Babasaheb et al., 2023).

The conducted research has shown that sandwich panels are building materials that meet the requirements of environmental friendliness and energy efficiency (Shyam & Khang et al., 2023). Around the world, including in the United States, there is a tendency to decrease the demand for sandwich panels with mineral wool, which should be taken into account when forming the marketing strategy of the business (Chauhan et al., 2023). The definition of the marketing strategy of competitive advantages should be complemented by a powerful analysis of the customer base, since it showed the need to form a marketing partner system and Customer Experience Quotient (CXQ) at the enterprise. It is also proposed to expand the scope of digital marketing, and to supplement the marketing strategy of differentiation with an export strategy (Shah & Khang et al., 2023).

REFERENCES

Avotra AARN, Chengang Y, Sandra Marcelline TR, Asad A, Yingfei Y. (2021) Examining the impact of e-government on corporate social responsibility performance: the mediating effect of mandatory corporate social responsibility policy, corruption, and information and communication technologies development during the COVID era. *Front Psychol.* 12:4221. doi: 10.3389/fpsyd.2021.737100

Bag S, Yadav G, Dhamija P, Kataria KK. (2021) Key resources for industry 4.0 adoption and its effect on sustainable production and circular economy: an empirical study. *J Clean Prod.* 281:125233.doi: 10.1016/j.jclepro.2020.125233

Capgemini Consulting, MIT Sloan School of Management. "The Digital Advantage: How digital leaders outperform their peers in every industry. Transform to the power of digital". URL: www.capgemini.com/wp-content/uploads/2017/07/The_Digital_Advantage__ How_Digital_Leaders_Outperform_their_Peers_in_Every_Industry.pdf

Chauhan VS, Chakravorty J, Khang A. (2023) "Smart cities data indicator-based cyber threats detection using bio-inspired artificial algae algorithm,"In: Handbook of Research on AI-Based Technologies and Applications in the Era of the Metaverse".Copyright: © 2023 | 436–447. https://doi.org/10.4018/978-1-6684-8851-5.ch024

CM (2022) Construction Market 2022. www.thebusinessresearchcompany.com/report/const ruction-market

Denning, S. (2019). Post-bureaucratic management goes global. *Strategy & Leadership*, 47(2), 19–24.

Europe Report (2023). Europe Sandwich Panels Market Report and Forecast 2023-2028. www. researchandmarkets.com/reports/5713673/europe-sandwich-panels-market-report-and-forecast

Ganin AA, Quach P, Panwar M, Collier ZA, Keisler JM, Marchese D., et al. (2020) Multi criteria decision framework for cybersecurity risk assessment and management. *Risk Anal.* 40:183–99. doi: 10.1111/risa.12891

GCM (2022). GlobalConstructionMarketReport 2022: IndustrytoReach $14.41 Trillionby 2030 ataCAGRof 7.3% URL https://finance.yahoo.com/news/global-construction-mar ket-report-2022-081800388.html

GCMOS (2022). Global Construction Market Opportunities and Strategies Report 2022: Use of autonomous construction vehicles, green construction projects, digital technologies are improving construction safety www.globenewswire.com/en/news-release/2022/08/ 04/2492427/28124/en/Global-Construction-Market-Opportunities-and-Strategies-Rep ort-2022-Use-Of-Auton]

Hernández HG, Cardona DA, Del Rio JL. (2017) Strategic direction: Projection of technological innovation and administrative management in small enterprises. Direccionamiento estratégico: Proyección de la innovation technological y gestation administrativa en las pequeñas empresas. *Informacion Tecnologica,* 28(5):15–22. DOI: 10_4067S0718-07642017000500003.pdf

Khang A. (2021) Material4Studies. *Material of Computer Science, Artificial Intelligence, Data Science, IoT, Blockchain, Cloud, Metaverse, Cybersecurity for Studies.* Retrieved from www.researchgate.net/publication/370156102_Material4Studies

Khang A. (2023) Advanced technologies and AI-equipped IoT applications in high-tech agriculture (1st Ed.). IGI Global Press. https://doi.org/10.4018/978-1-6684-9231-4

Khang A, AI, IoT-Based Technologies for Precision Medicine. (Eds.) (2023) ISBN: 9798369308769. IGI Global Press. https://doi.org/10.4018/979-8-3693-0876-9

Khang A. AIoCF (Eds.) (2024) AI-oriented competency framework for talent management in the digital economy: Models, technologies, applications, and implementation. ISBN: 9781032576053. CRC Press. https://doi.org/10.1201/9781003440901

Khang A, Abdullayev V, Alyar AV, Khalilov M, Murad B. (2023) AI-aided data analytics tools and applications for the healthcare sector. In A. Khang (Ed.), *AI and IoT-Based Technologies for Precision Medicine.* IGI Global Press. ISBN: 9798369308769. https://doi.org/10.4018/979-8-3693-0876-9.ch018

Khang A, Gujrati R, Uygun H, Tailor RK, Gaur SS (2024) *Data-driven Modelling and Predictive Analytics in Business and Finance* (1st Ed.). CRC Press. ISBN: 9781032600628. https://doi.org/10.1201/9781032600628

Khang A, Kali CR, Satapathy SK, Kumar A, Ranjan Das S, Panda MR. (2023). "Enabling the Future of Manufacturing: Integration of Robotics and IoT to Smart Factory Infrastructure in Industry 4.0." In A. Khang, V. Shah, & S. Rani (Eds.), *AI-Based Technologies and Applications in the Era of the Metaverse* (1st Ed.), pp. 25–50. IGI Global Press. https://doi.org/10.4018/978-1-6684-8851-5.ch002

Khang A, Kali CR, Panda S, Kiran Sree P, Kumar Panda S. (2023a). "Revolutionizing Agriculture: Exploring Advanced Technologies for Plant Protection in the Agriculture Sector,"In: *Handbook of Research on AI-Equipped IoT Applications in High-Tech Agriculture.* Copyright: ©. pp. 1–22. https://doi.org/10.4018/978-1-6684-9231-4.ch001

Khang A, Muthmainnah M, Mahbub Ibna Seraj P, Al Yakin A, Obaid AJ, Panda MR. (2023). "AI-Aided Teaching Model for the Education 5.0 Ecosystem" *AI-Based Technologies and Applications in the Era of the Metaverse* (1st Ed.), pp. 83–104. IGI Global Press. https://doi.org/10.4018/978-1-6684-8851-5.ch004

Khang A, Rani S, Gujrati R, Uygun H, Gupta SK. (Eds.) (2023). *Designing workforce management systems for industry 4.0: Data-centric and AI-enabled approaches.* CRC Press. https://doi.org/10.1201/9781003357070

Khang A, Shah V, Rani S. (2023). *AI-Based Technologies and Applications in the Era of the Metaverse* (1st Ed.). IGI Global Press. https://doi.org/10.4018/978-1-6684-8851-5

Khin S, Ho TCF. (2019) Digital technology, digital capability and organizational performance: a mediating role of digital innovation. *Int J Innov Sci.*11:177–95. doi: 10.1108/IJIS-08-2018-0083

Koval V, Mikhno I, Udovychenko I, Gordiichuk Y, Kalina I. (2021) Sustainable natural resource management to ensure strategic environmental development. *TEM Journal*, 10(3):1022–1030. DOI:10.18421/TEM103-03.

Linkov I, Trump BD, Poinsatte-Jones K, Florin M-V. (2018) Governance strategies for a sustainable digital world. *Sustainability*, 10:440.doi: 10.3390/su10020440

Miller P, Wilsdon J. (2001) Digital futures – an agenda for a sustainable digital economy. *Corp Environ Strateg.* 8:275–80. doi: 10.1016/S1066-7938(01)00116-6

Morgan NA, Whitler KA, Feng H, Chari S. (2018) Received: Research in marketing strategy 14 January 2018 /Accepted: 20 July 2018 # Academy of Marketing Science https://doi.org/10.1007/s11747-018-0598-1

Muthmainnah M, Khang A, Mahbub Ibna Seraj P, Al Yakin A, Oteir I, Alotaibi AN. (2023) An innovative teaching model – The Potential of metaverse for english learning. In *AI-Based Technologies and Applications in the Era of the Metaverse* (1st Ed.) (pp. 105–126). IGI Global Press. https://doi.org/10.4018/978-1-6684-8851-5.ch005

Mutikani L. (July 29, 2021) U.S. economy contracted 19.2% during COVID-19 pandemic recession.   www.reuters.com/business/us-economy-contracted-192-during-covid-19-pandemic-recession-2021-07-29/

Oliinyk O, Bilan Y, Mishchuk H, Akimov O, Vasa L. (2021) The impact of migration of highly skilled workers on the country's competitiveness and economic growth. *Montenegrin Journal of Economics*, 17(3):7–19. doi:10.14254/1800-5845/2021.17-3.1

Pooja K, Jadhav B, Kulkarni A, Khang A, Kulkarni S. (2023) "The Role of Blockchain Technology in Metaverse Ecosystem," *AI-Based Technologies and Applications in the Era of the Metaverse* (1st Ed.). pp. 228–236. IGI Global Press. https://doi.org/10.4018/978-1-6684-8851-5.ch011

Raisa M, Musab R, Mudac M, Ayub A. (2016) *Reconceptualisation of Customer Experience Quality (CXQ) Measurement Scale Malaysia*. 2212–5671. doi: 10.1016/S2212-5671(16)30128

Romanova L. (2017) Theoretical and practical aspects of development of marketing management on industrial enterprises. Economics and management. *Austrian Journal of Humanities and Social Sciences*, 3–4. DOI: http://dx.doi.org/10.20534/AJH-17-3.4-158-169

Saldanha T. (2019) *Why digital transformations fail: the surprising disciplines of how to take off and stay ahead*. Oakland, CA: Berrett-Koehler Publishers, str. 21–31. https://bit.ly/3xapkMY

Saleem F, Salim N, Altalhi AH, Ullah Z, AL-Ghamdi AAL-M, Khan, ZM, (2020) Assessing the effects of information and communication technologies on organizational development: business values perspectives. *Information Technology for Development*, 26(1):54–88. DOI: 10.1080/02681102.2017.1335279.

Sari Y та Gultom, Angga W, (2020) Marketing Strategy in Effort to Increase Competitive Advantage in Small and Medium Enterprises. Copyright©2020. JIMFE Jurnal Ilmiah Manajemen Fakultas Ekonomi) Universitas Pakuan https://doi.org/10.34203/jimfe.v6i2.2390.

Saxena AC, Ojha A, Sobti D, Khang A, (2023) Artificial Intelligence (AI) Centric Model in Metaverse Ecosystem*AI-Based Technologies and Applications in the Era of the Metaverse* (1st Ed.) (pp. 1–24). IGI Global Press. https://doi.org/10.4018/978-1-6684-8851-5.ch001

Semenets-Orlova I, Klochko A, Tolubyak V, Sebalo L,. Rudina M, (2020) Functional and role-playing positions in modern management teams: an educational institution case study. *Problems and Perspectives in Management*. 18(3):129–140. doi: 10.21511/ppm.18(3).2020.11.

Semenets-Orlova I, Kushnir V, Rodchenko L, Chernenko I, Druz O, Rudenko M, (2023) Organizational Development and Educational Changes Management in Public Sector. *International Journal of Professional Business Review*, 8(4): e01699. https://doi.org/10.

Semenets-Orlova I, Teslenko V, Dakal A, Zadorozhnyi V, Marusina O, Klochko A. (2021) Distance learning technologies and innovations in education for sustainable development. *Studies of Applied Economics. Special Issue Innovation in the Economy and Society of the Digital Age*, 39(5). https://ojs.ual.es/ojs/index.php/eea/article/view/5065

Shah V, Khang A, (2023) "Metaverse-Enabling IoT Technology for a Futuristic Healthcare System," *AI-Based Technologies and Applications in the Era of the Metaverse* (1st Ed.). 165–173. IGI Global Press. https://doi.org/10.4018/978-1-6684-8851-5.ch008

Shyam RS, Khang A, (2023) "Effects of Quantum Technology on Metaverse," *AI-Based Technologies and Applications in the Era of the Metaverse* (1st Ed.) . 104–203. IGI Global Press. https://doi.org/10.4018/978-1-6684-8851-5.ch009

SPM (2022) Sandwich Panels Market 2022 I Industry Share, Size, Growth www.transparenc ymarketresearch.com/sandwich-panels-market.html

Taherdoost H, Madanchian M, (2021) HAL Id: Determination of Business Strategies Using SWOT Analysis; Planning and Managing the Organizational Resources to Enhance Growth and Profitability Hamed Management and public policy, 3(1): c.19–22. ff10.30564/mmpp.v3i1.2748ff.ffhal-03741850f;https://hal.science/hal-03741850/ document

The Global Risks Report (2022) 17th Edition, is published by the World Economic Forum. chrome-extension://efaidnbmnnnibpcajpcglclefindmkaj/https://www3.weforum.org/ docs/WEF_The_Global_Risks_Report_2022.pdf

USA Economy COVID-19 (2023) COVID-19's Total Cost to the U.S. Economy Will Reach $14 Trillion by End of 2023, https://healthpolicy.usc.edu/article/covid-19s-total-cost-to-the-economy-in-us-will-reach-14-trillion-by-end-of-2023-new-research/

WHO—COVID-19 (2023) In United States of America, from 3 January 2020 to 7:50pm CEST, 4 October 2023. Last updated: 7:50pm CEST, 4 October 2023. https://covid19.who.int/ region/amro/country/us

Yan S, Chew DAS (2020, February) An investigation of marketing strategy, business environment and performance of construction SMEs in China. *International Journal of Accounting, Auditing and Taxation,* 7(2): 001–010. ISSN: 2756–3634. Available at www.internationalscholarsjournals.org

Yingfei Y, Mengze Z, Zeyu L, Ki-Hyung B, Avotra AARN, Nawaz A. (2021) Greenlogistics performance and infrastructure on service trade and environment-measuring firm's performance and service quality. *J King Saud Univ.* 34:101683. doi: 10.1016/ j.jksus.2021.1016839

Zinchenko T, Derzhak N. (2021) Digital Marketing as a Direction for Improving Communication Interactions with Consumers. DOI: https://doi.org/10.33216/ 1998-7927-2021-270-6-115-120

17 Human-Centered and Design-Thinking Approaches for Predictive Analytics

Nimisha Singh and Amita Kapoor

17.1 INTRODUCTION

Data-centric decision-making has been cited as contributing to a firm's potential and success (Rana et al., 2022), with 89% of firms attributing success in a volatile market to the adoption of BA solutions (Delen & Zolbanin, 2018). At the same time, unintended consequences of data analytics can hinder business value (Zuboff, 2015). The predictive analytics lifecycle has three major stages: design, develop, and deploy. Based on decision-makers' understanding of the problem or opportunity to address, data are collected and models are designed which are then deployed and maintained.

To make predictions better, it is imperative to understand the issues that may be associated with each of the stages. For example, data quality plays a vital role in effective utilization of technology (Rana et al., 2022), bringing the focus on a firm's management in acquisition of quality data (Sharma et al., 2014). Inconsistent, incorrect, poorly defined data or data not relevant to bringing business value (Xu et al., 2020) used for business analytics provide inappropriate solutions (Harlow, 2018). In a broad sense, the quality of output for any business analytics solution will depend on the data quality and diverse set of data. Poor data quality, lack of governance, and inefficient training of employees were found to contribute to suboptimal decision-making (Rana et al., 2022).

In the case of predictive analytics, which aims to predict the future or unknown events, the problems associated with data will provide suboptimal results. In this chapter, we first identify the biases that predictive analytics may be prone to and their impact. As a solution, we propose the employment of design thinking, a human-centered approach, to frame pertinent questions. This approach guides optimal data collection and model development processes, ultimately mitigating the influence of biases and enhancing the reliability of predictive analytics (Khang & Rashmi et al., 2024).

DOI: 10.1201/9781032618845-17

17.2 DATA-DRIVEN DECISION-MAKING

In recent years, recommender systems have become increasingly prevalent in many aspects of our lives. From online shopping to social media, these systems play a key role in helping us find the products, services, and content that we are looking for. However, these systems are not perfect. In particular, they can often suffer from a variety of biases that can lead to recommendations that may not be suitable for the problem at hand (Khang, Semenets et al., 2024).

For example, a recommender system may inadvertently favor certain groups of users over others. This can result in unusable recommendations for some users and can even lead to discriminatory behavior. Therefore, it is essential to address the potential for unfairness in recommender systems. Fortunately, there has been recent progress in this area, and there are now a number of methods that can help to mitigate the problem. With continued research, there is the potential for recommender systems to be made more fair and inclusive for all users. Recommender systems are multi-stake platforms, with three stakeholders: consumers, the supplier, and the platform:

- Consumers are the users of the platform. They come for suggestions. They use the platform because they might be searching for something or having difficulty in deciding, say, what to buy. They anticipate that the platform will provide a fair and objective suggestion.
- Suppliers or providers are on the other side of the recommender system. They provide the service and, in return, gain some utility from the consumers.
- Finally, there is the platform itself. It brings consumers and providers together and makes some benefit from it.

Therefore, when we talk of fairness in recommender systems, we also need to clarify which type of fairness we are talking about. In general, we talk of two types of fairness, that is, provider fairness and consumer fairness:

- Provider fairness is concerned with the items that are being ranked or recommended. Here, the notion of fairness is that similar items or groups of items should be ranked or recommended in a similar way. As an example, consider two articles about the same subject. If one is ranked higher because it has more views, this would be unfair because it is giving more weight to popularity instead of quality. To do this, the algorithm could look at other factors, such as recency, number of shares, and number of likes, to get a more accurate idea of quality. By taking these factors into account, the algorithm would be fairer to both articles.
- Consumer fairness has a focus on the users who receive or use the data or service. A fair recommendation algorithm, in this case, would ensure that users or groups of users receive the same recommendations or rankings. Continuing with the example of the recommender system suggesting articles, if two readers have the same educational background and interest, the algorithm should recommend the same/similar articles to them, without considering sensitive attributes such as gender or age.

The recommendation system so designed to predict what the consumers would prefer makes use of the available data which in certain cases leads to answering the wrong question. What organizations need is identifying the decision that needs to be made and identifying the data needed to make that decision.

Data-driven decision-making such as the use of predictive analytics implies that the availability of data and insights drawn from it will help make the right decisions. The generation of huge sets of data has made organizations data-rich but insight-poor. The paradoxical thinking arises from the fact that incumbent organizations with a huge set of data would have made the right moves from the insights gained from the data. Today, companies have access to data both structured and unstructured from multiple sources, but experience disappointing results as their data analytics initiatives do not provide actionable insights (Langhe & Puntoni, 2021). Thus, companies are investing in data analytics to extract value from available data, but that doesn't necessarily mean that these initiatives are answering the right questions. This brings the focus to understanding the problem or opportunity to be addressed by framing the right question.

Part of the problem is that data-driven decision-making uses the data that are available and start from the known, whereas, making the prediction requires an understanding about the unknown, identifying the data to be used for the need, and taking a decision-driven data analytics approach. Langhe and Puntoni (2021) suggest to gather enough information to decide and explore the unknowns and identify data blindspots. The historical data optimize the knowns but may not model the future events. Data are important, but we should be careful about making inferences, and especially causal inferences. Often the data-driven approach relied on models as predictors of the future and failed due to a flawed assumption that the future will resemble the past. A decision-driven approach leans heavily on abductive and inductive reasoning. It relies on trusted, often competing judgment backed by evidence (often different perspectives on the same data to create a picture of what it means), and bet on best opportunities to reveal more information.

17.3   PREDICTIVE ANALYTICS LIFE CYCLE

Predictive analytics is a multifaceted domain that draws from statistical, computational, and business intelligence techniques to forecast future events (Kumar & Garg, 2018). By leveraging both historical and current data, predictive analytics doesn't merely dissect past patterns but strives to project the trajectory of future occurrences. The aim is to facilitate data-driven decisions, optimize processes, and anticipate potential future scenarios.

To ensure the efficacy of predictive analytics in real-world applications, it is vital to comprehend its structured lifecycle. Predictive analytics has primarily four phases: discover, design, develop, and deploy, which can be dissected into several integral stages.

17.3.1 Discover Stage

Problem Understanding: The initial step necessitates the comprehensive understanding and delineation of the specific issues or queries that predictive analytics is envisioned to resolve. Engaging in meaningful dialogue with pertinent stakeholders is imperative to elucidate objectives and expectations. This phase culminates in the unambiguous articulation of goals and the establishment of metrics for success.

Preliminary Data Assessment: Subsequently, an inaugural exploration of the available data is conducted to assess its pertinence, accessibility, and quality. This crucial phase aims to identify prospective challenges and prerequisites for adept data processing, thereby cultivating profound insights into data-related demands and obstacles.

17.3.2 Design Stage

Data Collection: The crux of predictive analytics lies in its data. As the starting point, it involves amassing relevant data from diverse sources—ranging from traditional databases and logs to more modern streams such as IoT devices and social media. The granularity, volume, and velocity of data can greatly influence the subsequent stages.

Data Preparation: Raw data often come with irregularities. This stage involves meticulous cleaning, normalization, and transformation of data to convert them into a structured and usable format. Activities might encompass outlier detection, handling of missing values, and the creation of derived attributes, ensuring the data's integrity and relevance.

17.3.3 Develop Stage

Data Analysis: Armed with processed data, the next step is its deep analysis. Through techniques such as correlation analysis, trend spotting, and clustering, insights regarding underlying patterns and relationships are unearthed.

Model Building: Based on analytical insights, predictive models are sculpted. These models, ranging from simple linear regression to intricate deep learning algorithms, serve as the core mechanism for making future predictions. The model's complexity is often tailored according to the data's nature and the specific challenges posed by the business problem.

Model Validation: A model's real-world viability hinges on its accuracy and generalization. Hence, before a full-fledged deployment, it undergoes rigorous validation, often using a separate dataset (test data) to gauge its predictive accuracy and avoid overfitting.

17.3.4 Deploy Stage

Model Deployment: Post-validation, the predictive model is transitioned into a live environment. Here, it starts its primary function of generating predictions on real-time data. The deployment infrastructure can vary ranging from centralized servers to decentralized cloud platforms.

Model Monitoring and Updating: The dynamic nature of data means that even the best models might lose their predictive prowess over time. Regular audits and performance metrics ensure the model's continued relevance. Based on feedback loops, models might undergo fine-tuning, retraining, or even complete overhauls to maintain their effectiveness.

Predictive models are devised to identify patterns from historical data to predict the behavioral outcomes in the current context. With a changing business environment and uncertainty, certain patterns may not exist in the past data. That means the algorithm will not be able to detect or form a pattern, even though human analysts may be aware that such patterns are likely to manifest at some point in time. To bridge this gap between reality and the available evidence, synthetic data points can be used to train the model (Nikolenko, 2021).

Even after following a structured approach, predictive models are also prone to bias which may get introduced at any step in the lifecycle. This bias can eventually hamper the decision-making by providing predictions that may be inaccurate, unfair, or even unethical. We build on Ntoutsi et al.'s (2019) three broad categories of work to follow for ensuring that the models provide better predictions.

- Understanding bias—understand how the societal biases enter our sociotechnical systems;
- Mitigating bias—tackle bias at different stages of predictive analytics, i.e. design, development and deployment of the model;
- Accounting for bias—with an understanding about the bias and how it can be mitigated, identify the measures to proactively account for bias.

17.4 TYPES AND SOURCES OF BIASES

Individuals rely on their judgments and heuristics for making decisions. According to Rana, Khang et al. (2021), the human mind is both intuitive and logical and handles decisions with automatic and involuntary cognitive activity. While this allows complex tasks to be accomplished, it can also be a source of cognitive biases when intuition gets influenced by other factors. For example, cost, time pressure, and tendency to use the same data that have been used for human decision-making may deter the team from collecting other types of data.

Since predictive analytics is used to predict behavioral outcomes based on the historical data, the model will reinforce past biases (Baer & Kamalnath, 2017). An attempt to mitigate or overcome biases associated with statistical decision-making, such as predictive analytics, may not work if the data scientists and model developers themselves are subject to these biases. Humans have a limited mental capacity, which makes it difficult for them to capture and process all the complexities and this makes project teams susceptible to cognitive bias, i.e. a discrepancy between an individual's judgment and reality (Virine & Trumper, 2008). People can focus only on a few things when they think consciously.

Predictive analytics is not immune to bias. This bias may not always be due to the specific intents but it may get introduced as an unintentional oversight. The first step in making the system produce the intended outcomes is the identification of potential biases. The sources of bias can be any stage of the predictive analytics lifecycle such as the data collection, processing, model design, evaluation, and deployment of the model. These biases may creep through the input data, decision-making of the team developing and deploying the model, and validating the results, i.e. output for a specific user group or specific domain. The bias in input data and the bias in the decision-making for the computation model can be addressed even before the project starts. Assessing outcome bias requires domain knowledge and evaluation metrics. To address this issue we first need to understand the type of biases and how these biases can be addressed to achieve the intended outcome.

Predictive analytics uses pattern recognition models using historical data to predict outcomes for new observations. Humans tend to give importance to their personal experiences, causing anchoring bias. The tendency to over-emphasize one factor or piece of information while ignoring other factors leads to focusing illusion. Also, when faced with decisions people tend to take mental shortcuts to make familiar assumptions, called availability bias. While these assumptions may have worked in the past, they may not work in new situations. Non-random selection of individuals, groups, or data for data analysis induces selection bias.

Confirmation bias arises with individuals selectively gather and rely on evidence that confirms their existing beliefs. Humans also tend to be conservative in decision-making processes, causing loss aversion bias. As some groups may be underrepresented or unrepresented, the causal inferences may not be accurate for the target population. Table 17.1 describes some of the cognitive biases team members may be prone to when making judgments and their impacts on predictive analytics life stages.

TABLE 17.1
Cognitive Biases and Their Impact on Predictive Analytics

Cognitive bias	Description	Consequences for analytics
Projection bias	Project past into future	Impedes development of ideas and their assessment
Anchoring bias	Give importance to personal experiences	Problem with idea generation and testing
Focusing illusion	Overemphasizing particular elements	Impacts hypotheses generation and testing
Selection bias	Non-random selection	Underrepresentation or misrepresentation of certain groups or information
Loss aversion bias	Tendency to be conservative in decision-making	May miss out on new and improved solutions
Hypothesis confirmation bias	Select evidence to support own beliefs	Impacts model selection
Availability bias	Go with familiar assumptions	Impacts model selection

The onus to eliminate bias or protect from the negative impact it may have, lies with both the data scientists and the users. Users need to be aware of the shortcomings of the algorithms. The data scientists need to identify sample data used for developing the model in a way that the biases are minimized. This study predominantly centers on the biases in model development, emphasizing strategies for building models that substantially reduce or eliminate biases. The overarching goal is to navigate the uncharted territories of data and modeling, framing pertinent questions to be addressed by the models, and ensuring the systematic eradication of biases. For mitigating the biases, we focus our attention on two issues: (1) minimize bias associated with data and (2) minimize bias associated with developing the model.

17.5 MITIGATION STRATEGIES FOR DIFFERENT STAGES OF MODEL DEVELOPMENT

As bias can get introduced at any stage in the predictive analytics lifecycle, it is important that efforts are aimed at identifying the sources of bias at each of these stages and accordingly devising a strategy to mitigate or eliminate the bias. These models draw conclusions from the data, hence any error or misrepresentation in data will propagate the same as output. There are implicit biases that humans are not aware of and hence, unintentionally transfer to the algorithms.

The quality and diversity of data play a crucial role in the model. During data collection and preprocessing, it needs to be checked for fair representation from all groups, the characteristics, distribution, inconsistencies, and errors.

Emphasizing bias mitigation techniques during model development addresses bias and error minimization, underscoring the ethical imperative of equal representation across diverse demographic groups and preventing the amplification of societal biases. Such a focus enhances the transparency and accountability of the algorithm which empowers stakeholders by demystifying the processes and promoting responsibility for model outcomes.

17.6 CHOICE OF ALGORITHMS

The decision regarding the selection of a suitable algorithm significantly shapes the model development lifecycle. Distinct algorithms manifest unique strengths and vulnerabilities, with certain algorithms demonstrating enhanced resilience to bias compared to others. To mitigate bias within predictive analytics models, selecting an algorithm with inherently low sensitivity to bias, such as linear regression, proves beneficial. This strategy, embracing simplicity, offers a shield against the bias amplified by more intricate algorithms, including deep learning models.

In addition to choosing inherently unbiased algorithms, employing algorithms specifically crafted to counteract bias further bolsters the fairness of predictive models. Such algorithms are meticulously designed to fortify model predictions against bias, contributing to the equitable treatment of diverse groups. One such notable algorithm is the Equalized Odds algorithm, a post-processing tool that adjusts model predictions to equalize false-positive and false-negative rates across disparate groups, fostering fairness in critical decisions such as bail and loan approvals (Khang, Muthmainnah et al., 2023).

Moreover, the Adversarial Debiasing algorithm, a pre-processing tool, excels in eradicating sensitive features from data, concurrently maintaining the model's predictive efficacy (Zhang, Lemoine, & Mitchell, 2018). This algorithm plays a pivotal role in diminishing bias within decisions related to hiring and promotions, fortifying organizational commitment to fairness and equality. Additionally, resources like Fairlearn, a Python toolkit, further augment the arsenal of tools available for bias mitigation, offering diverse algorithms for both pre-processing and post-processing (Fairlearn: A toolkit for assessing and improving fairness in AI, n.d.), enhancing the robustness of machine learning models against bias.

In the classification task, adding a prejudice removal regularizer to the loss function enhances the model fairness while maintaining accuracy. On the other hand, Zafar et al. (2017) addressed fairness against disparate treatment and impact by introducing decision boundary covariance, helping in maximizing fairness under accuracy constraints, achieving a balance between the p-rule and accuracy. For regression tasks, Berk et al. (2017) developed a framework, incorporating a λ-weighted fairness loss term, to achieve both individual and group fairness. This approach penalizes the model every time it treats inputs from different groups differently, ensuring fairness at the expense of potential accuracy loss.

In clustering tasks, fairness penalties have been articulated through mathematical expressions involving demographic proportions and the marginal probability. In the domain of reinforcement learning, fairness constraints have been applied to the multi-armed bandit-based resource allocation. Claure et al. (2020) enforced fairness constraints in their algorithm to ensure equitable resource allocation, promoting trust among individuals without compromising performance.

In recommendation systems, fairness is seen through two lenses: provider and consumer fairness. Ensuring fairness in recommendation systems involves considering various factors, such as the number of items from different groups appearing in the top k places of the ranking. Celis et al. (2017) proposed an approach where upper and lower bounds are set to achieve fairness in ranking, contributing to a more unbiased recommendation system.

One approach to achieving fairness in recommendation systems is to treat them as classification algorithms, with recommendation being a class. In line with the methodology delineated earlier, a prejudice removal regularizer term was integrated into the objective function. A four-layer neural network classifier was constructed and subjected to training on the Adult dataset[1] (https://archive.ics.uci.edu/dataset/2/adult), employing the revised objective function.

Figure 17.1 delineates both the Calder's and Verwer's 2Naïve Bayes (CV2NB) score and the accuracy of the classifier. It is observable that an augmentation in η (the fairness parameter) is concomitant with an enhancement in the CV2NB score, signaling an elevation in fairness. This upsurge in the fairness parameter unequivocally imposes fairness, albeit at the expense of accuracy. This inverse correlation necessitates the establishment of an equilibrium between fairness and accuracy. Furthermore, a classifier encompassing the prejudice removal regularizer is marked by a superior CV2NB score of 0.16, in comparison to its counterpart devoid of the

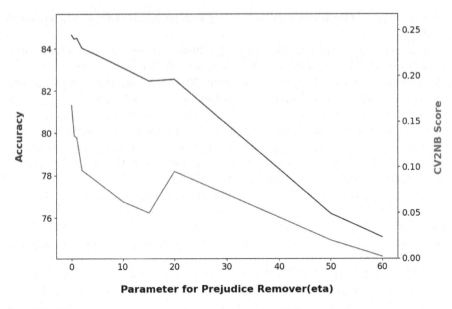

FIGURE 17.1 Calder's and Verwer's 2Naïve Bayes (CV2NB).

regularizer. This empirical evidence robustly substantiates the assertion that the integration of the regularizer contributes substantially to the generation of a more equitable model.

Another way is to treat recommendation systems as a ranking problem; here, the recommendation is a ranked list. In ranking problems, items are ranked in an order that is most valuable to the customer or provider. In a ranking maximization problem, the task is to assign each item a position such that the total value is maximized. To ensure fairness, Celis et al. (2017) added constraints in the form of upper and lower bounds on the number of objects that are allowed to appear in the top position of the ranking.

In the exploration of fairness in ranking, the research conducted by Celis et al. (2017) underscores the paramount role of constraints in shaping equitable rankings. By utilizing constraints, specifically upper and lower bounds, the researchers offered a clear and concise example to elucidate the tangible impact of such parameters on ranking outcomes. In this illustration, they particularly spotlight the scenario of constrained ranking maximization, examining the results that transpire when only the upper-bound constraint is in effect, as shown in Figure 17.2.

Figure 17.3a presents an instance of the optimal unconstrained ranking. Despite the imposed upper-bound constraint at a specified position, D in this case, a violation is evident as three men are ranked as opposed to the allowable limit of two. Contrastingly, Figure 17.3b exemplifies the optimal constrained ranking, wherein the upper-bound constraint at position D is seamlessly adhered to, leading to a scenario where all the outlined constraints are satisfactorily fulfilled, ensuring a balanced and equitable ranking system.

A	97	93	89	81	73	72	64	62
B	94	90	86	79	71	69	61	60
C	90	86	82	75	68	66	59	57
D	78	74	71	65	58	57	51	49
E	74	71	68	62	56	55	48	47
F	71	68	65	59	53	52	46	45

FIGURE 17.2 An example value matrix; values corresponding to unconstrained ranking are in gray and values corresponding to constrained ranking are in orange.

Source: Adapted from Figure 17.1 in Celis et al. (2017).

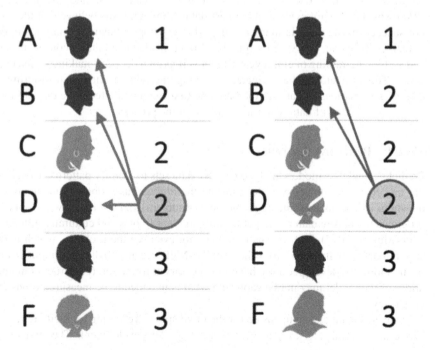

FIGURE 17.3 (a) Optimal unconstrained ranking; (b) optimal constrained ranking.

It is paramount to acknowledge that no single algorithm emerges as a panacea for bias mitigation across all predictive analytics models. The optimal algorithm selection hinges on the intricate interplay of the specific dataset and the underlying business problem at hand. An informed awareness of the multifaceted algorithms available for bias mitigation empowers stakeholders to make judicious decisions, steering predictive analytics models towards fairness, equity, and robustness against bias, reinforcing ethical and just outcomes in diverse predictive scenarios.

17.7 HUMAN-CENTERED APPROACH TO PREDICTIVE ANALYTICS

Studies have suggested taking a sociotechnical approach to solve organizational problems. Building predictive analytics models entails the technical components, data about human behavior, social and strategic outlook, and relationship between individuals (Akbarighatar et al., 2023). The technical component of the model is a human-created tool to meet the predefined goals (Sarker et al., 2019). Even for the technical component, the emphasis here is more towards the human-centered approach as the developed model is a human-created tool using data about human behavior to meet the predefined goals of the organization set by the senior management. The social component in the predictive analytics refers to actors in the social setting, their relationships and interactions, and the overall social environment. For example, a recommender system predicts what a user may be interested in by analyzing users' past behavior and other users who have made similar decisions.

The issue with data-driven predictive modeling is not about the insights or future predictions that it provides. The real issue is what data to use and also the future unknowns that are not evident in the past data. Although firms believe that they will not succeed in the volatile market if they do not adopt a business analytics option (Delen & Zolbanin, 2018), poor quality of data, inadequate data, inconsistent data, and inefficient training of employees trigger suboptimal decision-making (Rana et al., 2022). This problem can be navigated by asking the right questions and fostering the emerging scenarios. As data are the base and first step in the predictive modeling life cycle, poor quality of data will affect the rest of the process.

17.7.1 PREDICTIVE ANALYTICS

Predictive analytics models analyze massive data sets to identify patterns. To develop the model, programmers need to translate the ambiguous problem statements into questions that focus on some target variable (Raub, 2018). Developers who create the programs to analyze data rarely get training to identify bias and culturally influenced data (Mundy, 2017). That means they may not even see the problem, which makes it impossible for them to avoid the pitfalls (Miller et al., 2018). The input feature of the model so developed may have unnecessary information (construct contamination) or the model may not be capturing what is intended to be measured (construct deficiency).

A diverse team can compensate for the blind spots, preventing implicit prejudices. There are several decisions to be taken for model development. The first one is defining and clarifying the objective, i.e. what is the model trying to predict and why? What could be the potential benefits and risks of these predictions? With these clear goals, the scope and criteria can be validated for developing the model. There are certain statistical approaches that have been used to develop the model in such a way as to mitigate the biases (Khang, Kali et al., 2023).

For example, for classification tasks, adding a prejudice removal regularizer, ensures fairness. However, it affects the accuracy of the prediction. Another technique, minimizing the covariance decision boundary protects the decrease in accuracy. Similarly, statistical measures have been devised for regression tasks, clustering tasks, reinforcement learning tasks, and recommendation tasks. These statistical measures also need decision-making about choosing the criteria and the evaluation metric which again may be prone to human bias.

17.7.2 DESIGN THINKING

The human-centered approach puts people at the heart of the process to address the problem. The approach is anchored in understanding the needs with empathy for the users. Design thinking is a user-centric way of approaching a design (in this case predictive models) by understanding the wants, needs, and pain points of the users for whom the system is being designed. As we propose decision-driven analytics and start from the unknown, a design-thinking approach is deemed fit for human-centered predictive analytics.

Design thinking, a managerial discourse from the design research that seeks to understand how professional designers think and work, evolved as design methods (Asimov, 1962), problem-solving methods (Gordon, 2006), and science of design portrayed from the perspective of different disciplines and research interests. In practice and thought processes, design thinking aims to bring design principles and methods to management by using the designer's sensibility and methods to match people's needs with what is technologically feasible and what a viable business strategy can convert into customer value and market opportunity. Involving stakeholders in the decision-making process creates a better environment (Melles, Howard & Thompson-Whiteside, 2012) that enables managers to develop new ideas when faced with opposing alternatives.

Design thinking has been conceptualized in different ways and phases (Plattner Meinel & Weinberg, 2009; Stanford d.school). One of the popular approaches to design thinking was developed at Stanford University in 1980s in the d.school which has been used in the field of products and services and tangible or intangible matters (Table 17.2).

The studies on design thinking have cited three main methods: needfinding, brainstorming, and prototyping, which are executed in a non-linear, iterative way to develop ideas from insights gained. Needfinding takes a user-focused approach to determine requirements for a novel concept, problem, or opportunity taking a user-focused approach (Patnaik & Becker, 1999). Needfinding draws on existing capabilities (Verganti, 2008) to develop deep user insight through empathy and immersion in the user's context (Leonard & Rayport, 1997).

TABLE 17.2
Design-thinking Models

Stage	IDEO	Stanford Design School	Darden Business School
Needfinding	Discovery and interpretation	Empathize and define	What is?
Idea generation	Ideation	Ideation	What if?
Prototype and testing	Experimentation and evolution	Prototyping and experimentation	What wows? What works?

Sources:
- IDEO 2018. https://designthinkingforeducators.com/
- Stanford Design School 2018 https://dschool.stanford.edu/resources/
- Darden Business School, Design at Darden 2018 https://designatdarden.org/

Brainstorming takes inputs from multiple disciplines and applies techniques to search for solutions which may not have been possible through individual ideation (Seidel & Fixson, 2012). Needfinding and brainstorming for solutions are followed by prototyping that develops the novel idea into a preliminary model. The prototyping process enables evaluation and opens potential for further ideation. Prototyping or building to think at an early stage is not validation for the idea, rather it is used to simulate imagination (Hargadon & Sutton, 1997).

Being user-centric, design thinking converts user insights into viable business outcomes. The expected outcome from DT is a "more desirable solution," creative alternatives, emotionally satisfying and meaningful experiences, a collective approach to problems (Hobday, Boddington, & Grantham, 2012). By imbibing abductive thinking, i.e. dealing with conflicting constraints, it improves collaboration and motivation through empathy, and supports knowledge sharing through prototyping. Various researches have suggested remedies for cognitive bias. In this study we explore how design thinking can contribute towards reducing cognitive bias associated with different stages of the predictive analytics (Khang, Shah et al., 2023).

17.8 DESIGN-THINKING APPROACH FOR PREDICTIVE ANALYTICS

Design thinking is a user-centered approach to frame problems and discover solutions through intensive collaboration to understand user needs and principal problems (Lugmayr, Stockleben, Zou, Anzenhofer, & Jalonen, 2014). As the concept of design thinking is contextual depending on an organization's needs and the sources of knowledge and practices adopted (Carlgren, Ruth, & Elmquist, 2016), we look at the specific problems outlined in the previous sections and explore how a design-thinking approach can mitigate these issues. We do so by categorizing the cognitive biases under two categories: the predisposition of the decision-maker towards a particular thing and the decision-maker's capability to make judgments. This is followed by

TABLE 17.3
Biases, Remedies, and Design-thinking Methods

Bias	Remedies	Design thinking method
Category 1 bias (projection bias, anchoring bias, focusing illusion, selection bias)	Make teams diverse	Needfinding tools, ideation tools, experimentation
	Collect data from diverse set of stakeholders and sources	Needfinding tools
	Improve ability to imagine different scenarios	Needfinding tools
Category 2 bias (loss aversion bias, hypotheses confirmation bias, availability bias)	Expose decision-makers to different perspectives	Needfinding tools
	Explore and work with multiple options	Needfinding tools, ideation tools
	Help decision-makers to be better at evaluations	Ideation tools, prototyping, and testing

mapping the two categories of biases with the design-thinking methods: needfinding, idea generation, and prototyping and testing (Eswaran, Khang et al., 2023).

Category 1 bias relates to an individual's inclination towards a particular thing because of the world view they have formed with their past experiences, personal preferences, or perspectives. By collecting data from diverse sources, diverse stakeholders which are central to the needfinding stage of design thinking, will help in understanding the viewpoint of others and imagine what others may be experiencing. Taking into consideration the perspective and viewpoint of others reduces their reliance on their own perspectives. In summary, design thinking with its various tools helps decision-makers in broadening their perspectives so that their past experiences and personal preferences do not interfere with stages of predictive analytics life cycle (Namita, Satpathy et al., 2023).

Category 2 bias reflects the decision-maker's capability to explore and test different alternatives. Prototyping surfaces the unarticulated assumptions, making them better at hypothesis testing and thus addressing the loss aversion, confirmation, and availability bias. Through prototyping and testing, they can see and experience multiple predictions of future and their possible outcomes, mitigating the loss aversion and attachment to first solution. With an emphasis on prototyping and testing, design thinking exposes the decision-makers to detailed assumptions and creates vivid experiences which get refined through an iterative feedback loop. Through this process, decision-makers are able to test different hypotheses and assumptions for designing and developing the model. Testing these models and improvising through feedback gives a better prediction of the future (Table 17.3) (Boopathi and Khang, 2023).

17.9 DISCUSSION AND LIMITATIONS

Through identification of potential biases and mitigation strategies using the design-thinking process and tools has been suggested for better prediction of future behavior.

However, there are certain limitations to using the design-thinking approach. Even with a diverse team, there is a potential for group think which will eventually enhance the bias rather than reduce it. Similarly, brainstorming techniques need reflection and evaluation, in the absence of which the accuracy of the outcomes will be affected (Khang, 2023).

The needfinding stage and brainstorming produce a lot of information which may affect decision-making. There are over a hundred cognitive biases. Only a few biases have been considered, which the authors felt were more relevant for predictive analytics. Grounding design-thinking research with cognitive biases has provided potential for rigorously assessing whether the approach will bring the proposed outcomes or will increase the unanticipated negative outcomes (Khang, Vugar, & Abuzarova et al., 2023).

17.10   CONCLUSION

With businesses' heavy reliance on analytics to guide their decision-making, predictive analytics has become a popular tool which uses different statistical techniques, AI. and ML to predict future behavior by identifying patterns (Keerthika et al., 2023). This chapter has identified different cognitive biases that have the potential to negatively affect the stages of predictive analytics lifecycle. Taking a human-centered approach, specifically design-thinking tools, mitigation strategies have been suggested (Nayak and Atmika et al., 2023).

NOTE

1   The "Adult" dataset, also known as the "Adult Income" dataset, is a popular dataset used in machine learning for binary classification tasks to predict whether a person makes over $50K a year based on various features like age, education, marital status, and occupation.

REFERENCES

Akbarighatar, P., Pappas, I., & Vassilakopoulou, P. (2023). A sociotechnical perspective for responsible AI maturity models: Findings from a mixed-method literature review. *International Journal of Information Management Data Insights*, *3*(2), 100193.

Baer, T., & Kamalnath, V. (2017). *Controlling machine-learning algorithms and their biases*. McKinsey Insights. www.mckinsey.de/~/media/McKinsey/Business%20Functions/ Risk/Our%20Insights/Controlling%20machine%20learning%20algorithms%20 and%20their%20biases/Controlling-machine-learning-algorithms-and-their-biases.pdf

Boopathi, S.,, & Khang A. (Eds.) (2023). "AI-Integrated Technology for a Secure and Ethical Healthcare Ecosystem, *"AI and IoT-Based Technologies for Precision Medicine"*. IGI Global Press. ISBN: 9798369308769. https://doi.org/10.4018/979-8-3693-0876-9.ch003

Carlgren, L., Rauth, I., & Elmquist, M. (2016) Framing design thinking: the concept in idea and enhancement. *Creativity and Innovation Management*, *25*(1), 38–57. https://online library.wiley.com/doi/abs/10.1111/caim.12153

Celis-Morales, C. et al. (2017) Dietary fat and total energy intake modifies the association of genetic profile risk score on obesity: evidence from 48 170 UK Biobank participants. *International Journal of Obesity*, 41, 1761–1768. doi:10.1038/ijo.2017.169

Claure H., Chen Y., Modi J., Jung M., & Nikolaidis S. (2020). Multi-Armed Bandits with Fairness Constraints for Distributing Resources to Human Teammates. In *ACM/IEEE International Conference on Human-Robot Interaction* March 2020, 299–308. https://doi.org/10.1145/3319502.3374806

Delen, D., & Zolbanin, H. M. (2018). The analytics paradigm in business research. *Journal of Business Research*, *90*, 186–195. www.sciencedirect.com/science/article/pii/S01482 96318302480

Eswaran, U., Khang A., & Eswaran, V., (Eds.) (2023) Applying Machine Learning for Medical Image Processing, *"AI and IoT-Based Technologies for Precision Medicine"*. IGI Global Press. ISBN: 9798369308769. https://doi.org/10.4018/979-8-3693-0876-9.ch009

Fairlearn: A toolkit for assessing and improving fairness in AI. (n.d.). Retrieved from https://fairlearn.github.io/

Hargadon, A., & Sutton, R. I. (1997). Technology brokering and innovation in a product development firm. *Administrative Science Quarterly*, 716–749. www.jstor.org/stable/2393655

Harlow, H. (2018). Developing a knowledge management strategy for data analytics and intellectual capital. *Meditari Accountancy Research*, *26*(3), 400–419. www.emerald.com/insight/content/doi/10.1108/MEDAR-09-2017-0217/full/html

Hobday, M., Boddington, A., & Grantham, A. (2012) Policies for design and policies for innovation: Contrasting perspectives and remaining challenges. *Technovation*, *32*(5), 272–281. www.sciencedirect.com/science/article/pii/S0166497211001696

Keerthika K., Kannan M., & Khang A., (Eds.) (2023) Medical Data Analytics: Roles, Challenges, and Analytical Tools, *"AI and IoT-Based Technologies for Precision Medicine"*. IGI Global Press. ISBN: 9798369308769. https://doi.org/10.4018/979-8-3693-0876-9.ch001

Khang, A., (Ed.) (2023) AI and IoT-Based Technologies for Precision Medicine. IGI Global Press. ISBN: 9798369308769. https://doi.org/10.4018/979-8-3693-0876-9

Khang A, Abdullayev V, Alyar AV, Khalilov M, Murad B. (2023) AI-aided data analytics tools and applications for the healthcare sector. In A. Khang (Ed.), *AI and IoT-Based Technologies for Precision Medicine*. IGI Global Press. ISBN: 9798369308769. https://doi.org/10.4018/979-8-3693-0876-9.ch018

Khang, A., Gujrati, R., Uygun, H., Tailor, R. K., Gaur, S. S. (2024) *Data-driven Modelling and Predictive Analytics in Business and Finance* (1st Ed.). CRC Press. ISBN: 9781032600628. https://doi.org/10.1201/9781032600628

Khang, A., Inna, S-O., Alla, K., Rostyslav, S., Rudenko, M., Lidia, R., Kristina, B. (2024) Management model 6.0 and business recovery strategy of enterprises in the era of digital economy. In *Data-driven Modelling and Predictive Analytics in Business and Finance* (1st Ed.). CRC Press. https://doi.org/10.1201/9781032600628-16

Khang, A., Kali, C. R., Satapathy, S. R., Kumar, A., Ranjan Das, S., & Panda, M. R. (2023) "Enabling the Future of Manufacturing: Integration of Robotics and IoT to Smart Factory Infrastructure in Industry 4.0." In A. Khang, V. Shah, & S. Rani (Eds.), *AI-Based Technologies and Applications in the Era of the Metaverse* (1st Ed.), pp. 25–50. IGI Global Press. https://doi.org/10.4018/978-1-6684-8851-5.ch002

Khang, A., Muthmainnah, M., Mahbub Ibna Seraj, P., Al Yakin, A., Obaid, A. J., Manas Ranjan Panda, M. R., (2023) "AI-Aided Teaching Model for the Education 5.0 Ecosystem" *AI-Based Technologies and Applications in the Era of the Metaverse* (1st Ed.). 83–104. IGI Global Press. https://doi.org/10.4018/978-1-6684-8851-5.ch004

Khang, A., Shah, V., & Rani S. (2023) *AI-Based Technologies and Applications in the Era of the Metaverse* (1st Ed.). IGI Global Press. https://doi.org/10.4018/978-1-6684-8851-5

Kumar, V., & Garg, M. L. (2018). Predictive analytics: a review of trends and techniques. *International Journal of Computer Applications*, *182*(1), 31–37. www.researchgate.net/profile/Vaibhav-Kumar-16/publication/326435728_Predictive_Analytics_A_Review_of_Trends_and_Techniques/links/5c484f6692851c22a38a6027/Predictive-Analytics-A-Review-of-Trends-and-Techniques.pdf

Langhe De, B., & Puntoni, S. (2021). Leading with decision-driven data analytics. *MIT Sloan Management Review*, *62*(3), 1–4. https://search.proquest.com/openview/f4168b1a21aea4ad1a1f1e0eac94f5b7/1?pq-origsite=gscholar&cbl=26142

Leonard, D., & Rayport, J. F. (1997). Spark innovation through empathic design. *Harvard Business Review*, *75*, 102–115. https://direct.mit.edu/desi/article-abstract/30/1/67/69142

Melles, G., Howard, Z., & Thompson-Whiteside, S. (2012) Teaching design thinking: Expanding horizons in design education. *Procedia-Social and Behavioral Sciences*, *31*, 162–166. www.sciencedirect.com/science/article/pii/S1877042811029648

Miller, F. A., Katz, J. H., & Gans, R. (2018). The OD imperative to add inclusion to the algorithms of artificial intelligence. *OD practitioner*, *50*(1), 8. https://kjcg.com/s/AI2ArticleODP.pdf

Mundy, L. (2017, April). Why is Silicon Valley so awful to women? *The Atlantic*. Retrieved from www.theatlantic.com/magazine/archive/2017/04/why-issilicon-valley-so-awful-to-women/517788/

Namita, P., Satpathy, I., Chandra Patnaik, B., & Anh P. T. N., (Eds.) (2023) Application of Machine Learning for Image Processing in the Healthcare Sector, "*AI and IoT-Based Technologies for Precision Medicine*". IGI Global Press. ISBN: 9798369308769. https://doi.org/10.4018/979-8-3693-0876-9.ch004

Nayak, A., Patnaik, A., Satpathy, I., Patnaik, B. C. M., & Khang A., (Eds.) (2023). Incorporating Artificial Intelligence (AI) for Precision Medicine: A Narrative Analysis, "*AI and IoT-Based Technologies for Precision Medicine*". IGI Global Press. ISBN: 9798369308769. https://doi.org/10.4018/979-8-3693-0876-9.ch002

Nikolenko, S. I. (2021). *Synthetic data for deep learning* (Vol. 174). Springer Nature.

Ntoutsi, E., Fafalios, P., Gadiraju, U., Iosifidis, V., Nejdl, W., Vidal, M. E., ... & Staab, S. (2020). Bias in data-driven artificial intelligence systems—An introductory survey. *Wiley Interdisciplinary Reviews: Data Mining and Knowledge Discovery*, *10*(3), e1356. https://wires.onlinelibrary.wiley.com/doi/abs/10.1002/widm.1356

Patnaik, D., & Becker, R. (1999) Needfinding: the why and how of uncovering people's needs. *Design Management Journal (Former Series)*, *10*(2), 37–43. https://onlinelibrary.wiley.com/doi/abs/10.1111/j.1948-7169.1999.tb00250.x

Plattner, H., Meinel, C., & Weinberg, U. (2009) *Design thinking*. Landsberg am Lech: Mi-Fachverlag.Project Management Institute. (2014). *The high cost of low performance*, PMI Pulse of the Profession. https://doi.org/10.1201/9781032600628

Rana G., Khang A., Sharma R., Goel A. K., & Dubey A. K., (Eds.) (2021) "Reinventing Manufacturing and Business Processes through Artificial Intelligence". CRC Press. https://doi.org/10.1201/9781003145011

Rana, N. P., Chatterjee, S., Dwivedi, Y. K., & Akter, S. (2022) Understanding dark side of artificial intelligence (AI) integrated business analytics: assessing firm's operational inefficiency and competitiveness. *European Journal of Information Systems*, *31*(3), 364–387. www.tandfonline.com/doi/abs/10.1080/0960085X.2021.1955628

Raub, M. (2018) Bots, bias and big data: artificial intelligence, algorithmic bias and disparate impact liability in hiring practices. *Ark. L. Rev.*, *71*, 529. https://heinonline.org/hol-cgi-bin/get_pdf.cgi?handle=hein.journals/arklr71&section=18

Sarker, S., Chatterjee, S., Xiao, 17., & Elbanna, A. (2019) The sociotechnical axis of cohesion for the IS discipline: Its historical legacy and its continued relevance. *MIS Quarterly*, *43*(3), 695–720. https://dl.acm.org/doi/abs/10.25300/MISQ/2019/13747

Seidel, V. P., & Fixson, S. K. (2013) Adopting design thinking in novice multidisciplinary teams: The application and limits of design methods and reflexive practices. *Journal of Product Innovation Management*, 30, 19–33. https://onlinelibrary.wiley.com/doi/abs/10.1111/jpim.12061

Sharma, R., Mithas, S., & Kankanhalli, A. (2014) Transforming decision-making processes: a research agenda for understanding the impact of business analytics on organisations. *European Journal of Information Systems*, 23(4), 433–441. www.tandfonline.com/doi/abs/10.1057/ejis.2014.17

Verganti, R. (2008) Design, meanings, and radical innovation: A metamodel and a research agenda. *Journal of product innovation management*, 25(5), 436–456. https://onlinelibrary.wiley.com/doi/abs/10.1111/j.1540-5885.2008.00313.x

Virine, L. & Trumper, M. (2008) *Project decisions: the art and science*, USA: Management Concepts Press. https://doi.org/10.1201/9781032600628

Xu, G., Chen, C. H., Li, F., & Qiu, 17. (2020) AIS data analytics for adaptive rotating shift in vessel traffic service. *Industrial Management & Data Systems*, 120(4), 749–767. www.emerald.com/insight/content/doi/10.1108/IMDS-01-2019-0056/full/html

Zafar M. B., Valera I., Rodriguez M. G., & Gummadi K. P. (2017) Fairness beyond disparate treatment & disparate impact: Learning classification without disparate mistreatment (online). https://ieeexplore.ieee.org/abstract/document/8528677/

Zhang, B. H., Lemoine, B., & Mitchell, M. (2018, December) Mitigating unwanted biases with adversarial learning. In *Proceedings of the 2018 AAAI/ACM Conference on AI, Ethics, and Society,* 335–340. https://research.google/pubs/pub48121/

Zuboff, S. (2015) Big other: surveillance capitalism and the prospects of an information civilization. *Journal of Information Technology*, 30(1), 75–89. https://journals.sagepub.com/doi/abs/10.1057/jit.2015.5

18 Co-Integration and Causality between Macroeconomics Variables and Bitcoin

Dhanraj Sharma, Ruchita Verma, and Shiney Sam

18.1 INTRODUCTION

Rapid changes in the fintech sector are causing a boom in the financial market. In the last decade, Bitcoin has been a world-changing innovation emerging as a high-impact financial technology of the era. Though being a nascent market and prevailing ambiguity around its regulation and legislation, Bitcoin is an unsettling yet hotspot research topic, attracting considerable attention from academicians and practitioners of finance worldwide. The financial crisis of 2008 brought to light the shortcoming of the global financial system, i.e., a central authority managing all the stored money. This aroused in customers the need to have a currency that a central authority would not control.

Through its blockchain technology, Bitcoin has the potential to solve this problem by cutting out the bank's role as a third-party vendor. However, Bitcoin has not been widely accepted as a currency or medium of exchange because of its lack of an intrinsic value, although it has been accepted as an investment asset for portfolio diversification. As a result, the development of Bitcoin has undoubtedly positively disrupted the investment scenario globally. According to the global data from coinmarketcap. com, by the end of 2020, Bitcoin alone had surpassed a market cap of $848 billion in the cryptocurrency market, making up 69.71% of the total market capitalization, implying the dominance of Bitcoin in the market (Khanh & Khang, 2021).

According to crypto analysis firm Chainalysis, India was rated second in a list of 20 nations with the highest rates of cryptocurrency adoption. In addition, it has a significant investment base, with more than 10 million Indians investing in cryptocurrency, making India the country with the highest number of crypto investors in the world as per broker discovery and comparison platform BrokerChooser. India has emerged as the fastest growing economy and a tech-savvy country. India has embraced technology in every field, especially in the financial sector. Since demonetization in

DOI: 10.1201/9781032618845-18

2016, it has experienced a boom in the digitalization of finance and the economy at large. Regarding cryptocurrency, the supreme court of India in March 2020 lifted the blanket ban on cryptocurrency transactions in India. Varma (2019) reported that as of early November 2018, Bitcoin alone has a market cap exceeding India's most valuable listed company. Furthermore, as per India Today business news reports, cryptocurrency investments in India increased from $923 million in April 2020 to a staggering $6.6 billion in May 2021.

The development of cryptocurrency has the potential to disrupt the finance scenario globally. The role of fintech innovation in overcoming financial stability is vital to new-generation investors, but so is the future sustainability of that financial opportunity. No doubt, Bitcoin innovation is the financial revolution of the era. Cryptocurrency will be a viable pathway for a sustainable future of finance. Though different crypto coins have different energy footprints, they are a robust eco-friendly alternative to fiat currencies. Thus, as financial stability is vital to new-generation investors, so is the future sustainability of the financial opportunity, which cryptocurrency can fulfill.

According to the financial literature surveyed, it is observed that investors often rely on monetary policy and variables, and those monetary indicators moderate a significant influence on the volatility of an asset. Furthermore, in the stock market (developed financial market), macro-economic variables (fiscal and monetary) are one of the primary reasons for the fluctuations (Khang, Chowdhury et al., 2022).

Thus, the present research aims to investigate the long-term relationship and short-term effect of monetary variables of the domestic economy on Bitcoin prices in India. For this purpose, we consider monthly data of monetary macroeconomic variables such as major stock indices (NIFTY NSE and SENSEX BSE), inflation indicators (CPI and WPI), money supply (M1) and foreign exchange rate (US dollar to Indian rupee) and price data of Bitcoin from October 2014 to December 2020.

For statistical analysis, the econometric techniques of the ADF unit root test, the co-integration technique of Johansen, Granger causation, the vector error correction model (VECM), and the Wald coefficient test were performed on the data. These tests observe the co-integration between Bitcoin and macroeconomic variables specific to India, implying long-term association among the variables whilst there is an absence of a short-term relationship between these variables.

The remainder of this chapter is structured as follows: Section 18.2 deals with the previous studies in the field; Section 18.3 provides a brief overview of the research framework employed; Section 18.4 discusses the empirical results, their analysis, and interpretation; and Section 18.5 offers the concluding remarks.

18.2 REVIEW OF THE LITERATURE

Bitcoins are traded daily on domestic and international cryptocurrency exchange platforms. Liang et al. (2019) found that the fintech innovation of cryptocurrency (Bitcoin) has dynamics similar to stocks. Since it is traded like stocks and commodities, many studies have been documented examining the characteristics/features of stocks in the Bitcoin market.

Studies examine the relationship between Bitcoin and various traditional asset classes (Eken & Baloglu, 2018; Trabelsi, 2018; Corelli, 2018; Bianchi, 2018), factors for the price movement of Bitcoins (Kim et al., 2016), volatility and spillover in Bitcoin from other assets such as gold, crude oil, major stock indices (Kristoufek, 2015), the impact of demand and supply on Bitcoin (Sovbetov, 2018), various calendar anomalies in Bitcoin, the Random Walk hypothesis in Bitcoin, and many more. It has been observed that the emerging market of Bitcoin is much more volatile than other conventional markets.

Because of the high volatility of Bitcoin, it is more prone to speculative price bubbles than other tradable currencies (Grinberg, 2011). Between April 2013 and May 2017, the behavior of 1469 cryptocurrencies were studied. It was discovered that cryptocurrencies arise and disappear regularly, despite a dramatically increasing market value. However, Conlon, Corbet, and McGee (2020) claimed that it is a safe investment inclusion to a portfolio, hedging risk during a bullish period or period of extreme economic uncertainty.

Cermak (2017) models Bitcoin's volatility movements using a GARCH (1, 1) model concerning several macroeconomic parameters of countries with a significant Bitcoin trading volume. He found macroeconomic shocks flowing from China, the US, and the EU to Bitcoin disproportionately. Similarly, external and internal variables influencing cryptocurrency fluctuations are discussed by Poyser (2017), in which internal indicators include popularity and legality, whereas external indicators include interest rates, stock markets, and gold prices. Finally, Teker, Teker, and Ozyesil (2020) found that gold and oil prices are co-integrated, but no cryptocurrency is yet a substitute for gold and oil as an investment portfolio.

Based on the literature reviewed, it is realized that the cogent effect of economic variables exerting on asset prices in developing and developed economies has been one of the most prominent subjects among financial experts and researchers in recent decades. Also, fluctuations in macroeconomic variables affect the domestic investor's investment decision. This postulate induces the researcher to examine the influence of macroeconomic variables on Bitcoin from the Indian market perspective. Thus, the present research aims to investigate the long-term relationship and short-term effect of monetary variables of the domestic economy on Bitcoin prices in India.

For this purpose, we consider monthly data of monetary macroeconomic variables such as major stock indices (NIFTY NSE and SENSEX BSE), inflation indicators (CPI and WPI), money supply (M1), foreign exchange rate (US dollar to Indian rupee), and price data of Bitcoin from October 2014 to December 2020. For statistical analysis, the econometric techniques of ADF unit root test, the co-integration technique of Johansen, Granger causation, the vector error correction model (VECM), and Wald coefficient test were performed on the data. These tests observe the co-integration between bitcoin and macroeconomic variables specific to India, implying long-term association among the variables whilst there is the absence of a short-term relationship between these variables.

18.3   DATA AND RESEARCH FRAMEWORK

This study investigates the long-term association and short-term relationship between Bitcoin and macroeconomic variables of India, i.e. two major stock indices of India (NSE and BSE), indicators of inflation rate (CPI and WPI), money supply (M1), and

TABLE 18.1
Variables of this Study

Variables	Variable Description	Frequency	Source
Dependent Variable			
BTC	Bitcoin (INR)	Monthly	Yahoo Finance India
Independent Variables			
BSE SENSEX	Bombay Stock Exchange Index	Monthly	BSE historical database
NSE Nifty	National Stock Exchange Index	Monthly	Yahoo Finance India
EXR	Exchange Rate (INR/$)	Monthly	Yahoo Finance India
CPI	Consumer Price Index	Monthly	RBI Database
WPI	Wholesale Price Index	Monthly	RBI Database
M1	Money Supply M1	Monthly	RBI Database

Source: Author's compilation.

foreign exchange rate (US dollar to INR). The monthly data of the variables from October 2014 to December 2020 were collected for the study. Table 18.1 provides a brief description of the variables employed in the study.

The present research study intends to examine the long-term and short-term relationship between Bitcoin and macroeconomic variables (NSE, BSE, M1, foreign exchange rate, and CPI & WPI) from the Indian perspective. The stock market of a nation is the backbone of its economy. For India, the two major stock indices are the National Stock Exchange (NSE) and the Bombay Stock Exchange (BSE), which are also the major indices in the world. Uzonwanne (2021) observed that Bitcoin experiences spill over from the world's major indices. Therefore, the two major indices of the country were selected for the study (Khang, Gujrati et al., 2024).

The inflation rate is a trend in which the cost of goods and services rises, while the value of money falls. The inflation rate is approximated using both the consumer price index (CPI) and the industrial production index (WPI). During times of economic distress, investors show inhibitions for investing in the market. Therefore, understanding the integration of the inflation to Bitcoin is of utmost importance for investors. M1 money is the fundamental money supply of a country that serves as a medium of exchange. It is also called narrow money, i.e., demand deposits and check accounts which are used via debit cards and ATMs. The M1 variable is used for the study as it is the most readily available cash circulating in the economy (Kwon & Shin, 1999).

The monetary worth of the currency vis-a-vis other currencies is known as the rate of exchange. Granger, Huang, and Yang (2000) defined the relationship between equity returns and the rate of exchange using established postulates and reflected that the exchange rate has an indirect relationship with the stock markets and causes variations in them. It is to be noted that all the variables mentioned above have established their relationship with the developed equity market. Therefore, the present study intends to study the long-term and short-term relationship between the macroeconomic indicators and the emerging Bitcoin market.

The study employs the following statistical techniques: Augmented Dickey-Fuller unit root test (Dickey & Fuller, 1979), a preliminary test to run any econometric technique examining stationarity of the series; Johansen co-integration test (Johansen, 1988, 1991) to ratify the long-term association between the variables of the study; Granger causality (Engle & Granger, 1987) to investigate the causal order (direction) between dependent and independent variables; and VECM (Engle & Granger, 1987) is employed to observe that the last-period deviation in the long-term equilibrium influences the short-term dynamics between the variables.

18.4 RESULTS AND DISCUSSION

The study employed co-integration analysis of Johansen and Granger causality to identify the long-term association, and VECM was run to test the short-term relationship between Bitcoin and the macroeconomic indicators of India.

18.4.1 DESCRIPTIVE ANALYSIS

Table 18.2 showcases the mean, standard deviation, kurtosis, skewness, minimum values, maximum values, and frequencies of the variable series of the study. The average monthly price of Bitcoin traded in India during the study period was Rs. 361,335.60. The lowest price for Bitcoin recorded during the study period was Rs 13,485, and the highest price recorded was Rs 2,115,850.

The average prices of NSE and BSE indices for the study period were Rs 9873 and Rs 32,704, respectively. The average foreign exchange rate per US dollar was Rs 68.10. During the study period, the minimum inflation index was 119.4 for CPI (January 2015) and 107.1 for WPI (January 2016), while the maximum CPI was

TABLE 18.2
Descriptive Statistics

Particulars	BTC -INR	NSE	CPI	INIR/ USD	MI	BSE	WPI
Mean	361,335.6	9873.0	136.3	68.1	3,028,224.9	32,704.6	116.0
Standard Deviation	380,877.7	1529.8	10.7	3.9	670,930.5	5429.3	5.0
Kurtosis	5.1	–0.8	–0.7	–0.9	–0.9	–0.7	–1.3
Skewness	1.7	0.2	0.3	0.3	0.5	0.4	0.1
Minimum	13,485.0	6987.0	119.4	61.4	1,992,614.4	23,002.0	107.1
Maximum	2,115,850.0	13,981.8	158.9	75.7	4,421,645.8	47,751.3	125.4
Count	75.0	75.0	75.0	75.0	75.0	75.0	75.0

Source: Author's calculations.

158.9 in November 2020 and WPI was 125.4 in December 2020. The average money supply of physical currency and coins depicted by M1 was Rs 3,028,224.90 each month during the study period. Volatility in the prices, money amount, and indexes of variables can be observed from the standard deviation data. The skewness and kurtosis reveal that the data are asymmetric and do not follow a normal distribution.

18.4.2 AUGMENTED DICKEY-FULLER UNIT ROOT TEST

The Augmented Dickey-Fuller unit root test has been depicted in Table 18.2. The null hypothesis of the test is that the series is non-stationary. Table 18.3 showcases that series of all the study variables are non-stationary at level, and later after differencing, series became free of the unit root problem and were stationary at first difference. Since all series are stationary at the first difference, they are integrated and suitable for further econometric analysis.

18.4.3 LAG ORDER SELECTION—SCHWARZ INFORMATION CRITERION

After integrating series to stationarity at the first difference and before Johansen's (1988, 1991) co-integration analysis, it is ideal to find an optimum lag length for the subsequent series analysis (Table 18.4a). Log-likelihood criterion, Akaike information criterion, Hannan-Quinn criterion, Schwarz information criterion, etc., are the varied criteria based on which an optimum lag order for the series is deduced. The present research study singled out the optimum lag order based on SC, i.e. Schwarz information criterion, as it is the strictest criterion. The SC suggests one lag for the series as the least value of SC (88.74) corresponding to one lag for the study period. Table 18.3 shows the values of varied criteria at different lags and the selected optimum lag order corresponding to the least value of the SC.

TABLE 18.3
Unit Root Test (Augmented Dickey-Fuller)

	ADF Unit Root	
Variables	**Level**	**First Difference**
BTC	2.691	−4.388*
BSE	−0.197	−8.123*
NSE	−0.467	−8.038*
M1	0.338	−6.069*
EXR	−1.527	−8.503*
CPI	0.131	−5.832*
WPI	−0.769	−4.815*

* Significance at 1% level; critical values: −3.54 at 1%, −2.91 at 5%, and −2.59 at 10% level.

Source: Author's calculations.

18.4.4 Co-Integration Analysis (Johansen)

As the unit root test of ADF in Table 18.2 demonstrates that Bitcoin and the macro-economic variables are co-integrated at the first difference order, the researcher can employ the Johansen co-integration analysis to examine the long-term association of Bitcoin with the macroeconomic indicators. The results depicted in Table 18.4b reflect that there is one co-integrating equation, which implies a long-term association of Bitcoin (in INR) and stock indices (NSE and BSE), money supply (M1), foreign exchange rate, and the CPI and WPI of India. Moreover, both Trace statistics and Max-eigenvalue values are greater than the critical value and are also statistically significant ($p<0.05$).

TABLE 18.4A
Lag Order Selection Criteria—Schwarz Information Criterion

Lag	LogL	LR	FPE	AIC	SC	HQ
0	–3415.014	NA	2.82e+34	99.18882	99.41547	99.27874
1	–2942.977	834.6172	1.34e+29	86.92686	**88.74005***	87.64621*
2	–2890.408	82.28179*	1.26e+29*	86.82341*	90.22314	88.17220
3	–2860.545	40.68272	2.46e+29	87.37811	92.36438	89.35633
4	–2815.176	52.60178	3.43e+29	87.48336	94.05617	90.09101
5	–2770.831	42.41670	5.91e+29	87.61829	95.77764	90.85538
6	–2719.016	39.04921	1.10e+30	87.53669	97.28258	91.40321

Source: Author's calculations.

TABLE 18.4B
Johansen Co-integration Test—Trace Test and Max Eigenvalue Test

Unrestricted Co-integration Rank Test (Trace)

Hypothesized No. of CE(s)	Eigenvalue	Trace Statistic	0.05 Critical Value	Prob.**
None *	**0.491141**	**139.3348**	**125.6154**	**0.0056**
At most 1	0.345777	90.01712	95.75366	0.1162
At most 2	0.300443	59.04276	69.81889	0.2659
At most 3	0.208312	32.95928	47.85613	0.5591
At most 4	0.123206	15.90739	29.79707	0.7188
At most 5	0.055539	6.309150	15.49471	0.6590
At most 6	0.028861	2.137862	3.841466	0.1437

* Trace test indicates 1 cointegrating eqn (s) at the 0.05 level.

18.4.5   VECTOR ERROR CORRECTION MODEL

Table 18.5 gives the proportion of disequilibrium error accumulated in the previous period, which is corrected in the current period. The p-value of the error correction term coefficient in Table 18.5 shows that it is statistically insignificant at the 10% level, although it has the correct negative sign, thus suggesting that Bitcoin prices adjust to the explanatory macroeconomic variables. The coefficient of ECM (–1) is equal to –0.00645 for the short-term model, implying that the deviation from the long-term inequality is corrected by about 6%. The lag length of the short-term model is selected on the basis of SIC (Table 18.6a).

TABLE 18.5
Unrestricted Co-integration Rank Test (Maximum Eigenvalue)

Hypothesized		Max-Eigen	0.05	
No. of CE(s)	Eigenvalue	Statistic	Critical Value	Prob.**
None *	**0.491141**	**49.31769**	**46.23142**	**0.0227**
At most 1	0.345777	30.97437	40.07757	0.3622
At most 2	0.300443	26.08347	33.87687	0.3157
At most 3	0.208312	17.05189	27.58434	0.5755
At most 4	0.123206	9.598244	21.13162	0.7814
At most 5	0.055539	4.171288	14.26460	0.8409
At most 6	0.028861	2.137862	3.841466	0.1437

* Max-eigenvalue test indicates 1 co-integrating eqn (s) at the 0.05 level.

Source: Author's calculations.

TABLE 18.6A
Vector Error Correction Model (Short-term Model)

	Dependent Variable = D(BTC)	
Regressor	Coefficient	P-Value
C	–3331.52	0.860
ECT(–1)	–0.006451	0.632
D(NSE(–1))	–295.91	0.399
D(BSE(–1))	99.26	0.348
D(M1(–1))	0.251	0.140
D(EXR(–1))	11,866.99	0.457
D(CPI(–1))	20,561.83	0.3707
D(WPI(–1))	13,811.57	0.486

Source: Author's calculations.

TABLE 18.6B
Wald Coefficient Test

Test Statistic	Value	df	Probability
F-statistic	1.169510	(6, 64)	0.3337
Chi-square	7.017062	6	0.3193

Note: No evidence of short-term causality running from independent variables to the dependent variable, p-value >0.5

Source: Author's calculations.

TABLE 18.7
Granger Causality

Null Hypothesis:	Obs	F-Statistic	Prob.
NSE does not Granger Cause BTC__INR	74	0.09241	0.7620
BTC__INR does not Granger Cause NSE		7.47057	0.0079
BSE does not Granger Cause BTC__INR	74	0.06273	0.8030
BTC__INR does not Granger Cause BSE		8.39769	0.0050
USD_INR does not Granger Cause BTC__INR	74	0.10225	0.7501
BTC__INR does not Granger Cause USD_INR		1.87968	0.1747
M1 does not Granger Cause BTC__INR	74	0.90130	0.3457
BTC__INR does not Granger Cause M1		2.50905	0.1176
CPI does not Granger Cause BTC__INR	74	1.10497	0.2967
BTC__INR does not Granger Cause CPI		2.42538	0.1238
WPI does not Granger Cause BTC_INR	74	0.09386	0.7602
BTC_INR does not Granger Cause WPI		7.06665	0.0097

Source: Author's calculations

In addition to VECM diagnosis, the Wald coefficient test investigates the short-term causal relationship between the variables. Table 18.6b shows the result of the wald test. The F-statistic of the test is 1.1695 (p-value: 0.3337). The findings (p-value >0.05) reveal no evidence of short-term causality from the independent variables, i.e. macroeconomic variables, to the dependent variable of Bitcoin prices in India.

18.4.5 GRANGER CAUSALITY

The results of Johansen cointegration analysis conclude that Bitcoin and macroeconomic variables of the Indian economy have a long-term association (Khang, Inna et al., 2024). Further to Johansen's approach, it is necessary to identify the direction of this causal relationship between the variables. The Granger causality test (Engle & Granger, 1987) was applied to the series. Thus, Table 18.7 depicts the results of the

Granger causality test. It can be seen that Bitcoin has a one-way causal association with NSE, BSE, and WPI. Other variables do not have causation in either direction.

18.4.6   RESIDUAL DIAGNOSTICS

In addition to the short-term causality test, the Breusch Godfrey Serial Correlation LM Test (Table 18.8) is performed to check for serial correlation in the residual terms. Moreover, the test results fail to reject the null hypothesis, indicating the absence of serial correlation among the residual terms (p-value >0.05). Further, a stability diagnostic is performed employing CUSUM as shown in Figure 18.1.

TABLE 18.8
Residual Diagnostics

Breusch-Godfrey Serial Correlation LM Test:

F-statistic	0.003570	Prob. F(1,63)	0.9525
Obs*R-squared	0.004136	Prob. Chi-Square(1)	0.9487

Source: Author's calculations.

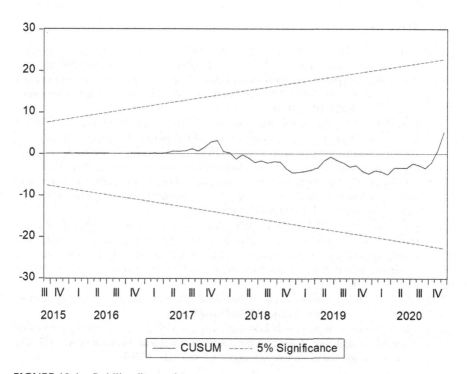

FIGURE 18.1   Stability diagnostics.

Source: Authors' calculations.

18.5   CONCLUSION

This research aims to investigate the long-term relationship and short-term effect of monetary variables of the domestic economy on Bitcoin prices in India. For this purpose, we considered monthly data of monetary macroeconomic variables such as major stock indices (NIFTY NSE and SENSEX BSE), inflation indicators (CPI and WPI), money supply (M1), foreign exchange rate (US dollar to Indian rupee), and price data of Bitcoin from October 2014 to December 2020.

For statistical analysis, the econometric techniques of the ADF unit root test, the cointegration technique of Johansen, Granger causation, the vector error correction model (VECM), and the Wald coefficient test were performed on the data. The Johansen cointegration approach depicts the long-run association between Bitcoin and the economic variables, whilst VECM and the Wald coefficient reveal no short-term causality between the variables (Khang, Shah et al., 2023).

The Granger causality test shows a one-way causal relationship of NSE, BSE, and WPI to Bitcoin. Hence, it is concluded that stock indices and inflation have a cogent effect on Bitcoin prices. Indian investors embrace this investment asset leading to the growth of cryptocurrency in the Indian financial market. Cryptocurrency will help in international trade and transfers, ensuring transparency and security of transactions. This fintech innovation is here to stay and provide a stable and sustainable financial environment (Khang, Kali et al., 2023; Khang, Muthmainnah et al., 2023).

REFERENCES

Akaike, H. (1969). Fitting autoregressive model for prediction. *Annals of International Statistics and Mathematics*, 21, 243–247. https://doi.org/10.1201/9781032600628

Bianchi, D. (2018). Crypto currencies as an asset class? An empirical assessment. *An Empirical Assessment (June 6, 2018). WBS Finance Group Research Paper*. https://jai.pm-resea rch.com/content/23/2/162.short

Cermak, V. (2017). Can bitcoin become a viable alternative to fiat currencies? An empirical analysis of bitcoin's volatility based on a GARCH model. *An Empirical Analysis of Bitcoin's Volatility Based on a GARCH Model (May 2, 2017)*. Available at SSRN: https://ssrn.com/abstract=2961405 or http://d18.doi.org/10.2139/ssrn.2961405

Chaudhuri, K. (1997). Cointegration, error correction and Granger causality: An application with Latin American stock markets. *Applied Economics Letters*, 4(8), 469–471. www.tandfonline.com/doi/abs/10.1080/758536627

Conlon, T., Corbet, S., & McGee, R. J. (2020). Are cryptocurrencies a safe haven for equity markets? An international perspective from the COVID-19 pandemic. *Research in International Business and Finance*, 54(C), S0275531920304438. https://EconPap ers.repec.org/RePEc:eee:riibaf:v:54:y:2020:i:c:s0275531920304438.   doi: 10.1016/ j.ribaf.2020.101248

Corelli, A. (2018). Cryptocurrencies and exchange rates: A relationship and causality analysis. *Risks*, 6(4), 111. www.mdpi.com/2227-9091/6/4/111

Dickey, D.A. & Fuller, W.A. (1979) Distribution of the estimators for autoregressive time series with a unit root. *Journal of the American Statistical Association*, 47, 427–431. www.scirp.org/reference/referencespapers?referenceid=1855675

Eken, M. H., & Baloglu, E. (2018). Crypto currencies and their destinies in the future. *International Journal of Finance & Banking Studies (2147–4486)*, 6(4), 1. doi:10.20525/ ijfbs.v6i3.810

Engle, R. F., & Granger, C. W. J. (1987). Cointegration and error correction: representation, estimation and testing, *Econometrica*, 55, 251–76. https://ideas.repec.org/a/ris/apltrx/ 0274.html

Granger, C. W.J., Huang, B.N., & Yang, C.W. (2000). A bivariate causality between stock prices and exchange rates: Evidence from recent Asian flu. *Quarterly Review of Economics and Finance*, 40, 337–354. www.sciencedirect.com/science/article/pii/S1062976900000429

Grinberg, R. (2011). Bitcoin: An innovative alternative digital currency. *Hastings Science & Technology Law Journal*, 4, 160. https://heinonline.org/hol-cgi-bin/get_pdf.cgi?handle= hein.journals/hascietlj4&section=6

Johansen S. (1988-1991) Statistical analysis of cointegration vectors, *Data Journal of Economic Dynamics and Control*, 12(2), 231–254, ISSN: 0165-1889. www.sciencedirect.com/scie nce/article/abs/pii/0165188988900413

Khang, A., Chowdhury, S., & Sharma S. (2022). *The Data-Driven Blockchain Ecosystem: Fundamentals, Applications, and Emerging Technologies* (1st Ed.). CRC Press. https://doi.org/10.1201/9781003269281

Khang, A., Gujrati, R., Uygun H., Tailor R. K., Gaur S. S. (2024). *Data-driven Modelling and Predictive Analytics in Business and Finance*. ISBN: 9781032600628. (1st Ed.). CRC Press. https://doi.org/10.1201/9781032600628

Khang, A., Inna, S.-O., Alla, K., Rostyslav, S., Rudenko, M., Lidia, R., Kristina, B. (2024). Management model 6.0 and business recovery strategy of enterprises in the era of digital economy. In A. Khang, R. Gujrati, H. Uygun, R. K. Tailor, S. S. Gaur (Eds.), *Data-driven Modelling and Predictive Analytics in Business and Finance* (1st Ed.). CRC Press. https://doi.org/10.1201/9781032600628-16

Khang, A., Kali, C. R., Satapathy, S. K., Kumar, A., Das, S. R., Panda, M. R. (2023). Enabling the future of manufacturing: integration of robotics and IoT to smart factory infrastructure in industry 4.0. In A. Khang, V. Shah, & S. Rani (Eds.), *AI-Based Technologies and Applications in the Era of the Metaverse* (1st Ed.) (pp. 25–50). IGI Global Press. https:// doi.org/10.4018/978-1-6684-8851-5.ch002

Khang, A., Muthmainnah, M., Seraj, P. M. I., Al Yakin, A., Obaid, A. J., & Panda, M. R. (2023). AI-aided teaching model for the education 5.0 ecosystem. In A. Khang, V. Shah, & S. Rani (Eds.), *AI-Based Technologies and Applications in the Era of the Metaverse* (1st Ed.) (pp. 83–104). IGI Global Press. https://doi.org/10.4018/978-1-6684-8851-5.ch004

Khang, A., Shah, V., & Rani, S. (2023). *AI-Based Technologies and Applications in the Era of the Metaverse* (1st Ed.). IGI Global Press. https://doi.org/10.4018/978-1-6684-8851-5

Khanh, H. H., & Khang A. (2021). The role of artificial intelligence in blockchain applications. *Reinventing Manufacturing and Business Processes through Artificial Intelligence*, 2 (pp. 20–40). CRC Press. https://doi.org/10.1201/9781003145011-2

Kim, Y. B., Kim, J. G., Kim, W., Im, J. H., Kim, T. H., Kang, S. J., & Kim, C. H. (2016). Predicting fluctuations in cryptocurrency transactions based on user comments and replies. *PloS One*, 11(8). https://journals.plos.org/plosone/article?id=10.1371/journal. pone.0161197

Kristoufek, L. (2015). What are the main drivers of the bitcoin price? Evidence from wavelet coherence analysis. *PLoS One*, 10(4), e0123923. doi:10.1371/journal.pone.0123923

Kwon, C. S., & Shin, T. S. (1999). Cointegration and causality between macroeconomic variables and stock market returns. *Global Finance Journal*, 10(1), 71–81. www.scienc edirect.com/science/article/pii/S104402839900006X

Liang, J., Li, L., Chen, W., & Zeng, D. (2019, July). Towards an understanding of cryptocurrency: A comparative analysis of cryptocurrency, foreign exchange, and stock. In *2019 IEEE International Conference on Intelligence and Security Informatics (ISI)* (pp. 137–139). IEEE. https://ieeexplore.ieee.org/abstract/document/8823373/

Poyser, O. (2017), Exploring the determinants of Bitcoin's price: an application of Bayesian Structural Time Series. https://arxiv.org/ftp/arxiv/papers/1706/1706.01437.pdf

Sovbetov, Y. (2018). Factors influencing crypto currency prices: Evidence from bitcoin, ethereum, dash, litcoin, and monero. *Journal of Economics and Financial Analysis*, 2(2), 1–27. https://papers.ssrn.com/sol3/papers.cfm?abstract_id=3125347

Teker D., Teker S., Ozyesil, M. (March 2020), Macroeconomic Determinants of Cryptocurrency Volatility: Time Series Analysis, 14th PARIS International Conference on Marketing, Economics, Education and Interdisciplinary StudiesAt: Paris. DOI: 10.30845/jbep. v7n1p8

Trabelsi, N. (2018). Are there any volatility spill-over effects among crypto currencies and widely traded asset classes? *Journal of Risk and Financial Management*, *11*(4), 66. www.mdpi.com/1911-8074/11/4/66

Uzonwanne G., (2021), Volatility and return spillovers between stock markets and cryptocurrencies, *Quarterly Review of Economics and Finance*, 82,(C), 30–36. DOI: 10.1016/j.qref.2021.06.018

Varma, J. R. (2019). Blockchain in finance. *Vikalpa*, *44*(1), 1–11. https://journals.sagepub.com/doi/abs/10.1177/0256090919839897

19 An Examination of Data Protection and Cyber Frauds in the Financial Sector

Hemant Bhanawat and Alex Khang

19.1 INTRODUCTION

The Indian financial sector is quite diversified and has been expanding rapidly. This sector operates in formats of institutions that are formal and informal. These institutions facilitate the flow of surplus funds available in the economy to deficit spenders. Institutions' formats comprise scheduled commercial banks (SCBs), insurance companies, non-banking financial companies (NBFCs), mutual funds, urban co-operative banks (UCBs), regional rural banks (RRBs), national pension scheme (NPS) funds, and smaller financial entities and specialized foreign institutional investors (specialized FII). Like many developing economies, India also has informal financial formats consisting of loan brokers, NGOs, self-help groups (SHGs), share brokers, traders, pawnbrokers, etc. The heterogeneous nature of these entities and activities conducted in both formal and informal formats calls for a consistent database of customers, transactions, and reliable customer data protection mechanisms, which seems to be lacking or at times is not considered very reliable (Khanh & Khang, 2021).

Due to changes in customer expectations and preferences including a shift towards digital platforms, technological capabilities outgrowth, regulatory requirements, demographics, and economics together are creating pressure on this ecosystem to rapidly adopt newer digital technologies. Due to the pressures of digitization, transacting and operating models of the financial institutions has been drastically changed, and this change has demanded the implementation of complex integrated system landscapes and common data exchange frameworks. This digitization demand also leads to the need for these institutions to get overcome these challenges and adopt a proactive approach toward data protection and cyber security (Khang, Chowdhury et al., 2022).

The innovations both business and technology that the financial sector, in particular financial services companies, are adopting in their quest for growth, innovation, customer satisfaction, and cost optimization, are pushing the banking, mutual fund, and other institutions in this sector towards heightened levels of cyber risks

DOI: 10.1201/9781032618845-19

through the introduction of new vulnerabilities and complexities in the financial services technology ecosystem (Rani, Chauhan et al., 2021).

19.2   OBJECTIVES OF THIS STUDY

The objectives of this study are as follows:

1. To introspect various aspects of cyber frauds, data security, and potential threats related to financial institutions;
2. Analysis of the data available in the public domain about data protection and cyber frauds;
3. To drive through the framework policies and processes that are in place to ensure safe and robust financial transactions and their adequacy

19.3   REVIEW OF THE LITERATURE

Financial frauds and data breaches are costing loses of millions of dollars to Indian companies. India saw the second-highest number of data breaches in 2019 (BT, 2019), and financial sector firms lose the most. A leading e-commerce portal in India was compromised due to a technical glitch that affected 400,000 sellers on its platform (IndiaTimes, 2023). One of the country's biggest lenders was in the news recently for a potential breach of security on one of its servers. The infamous "Gnosticplayers" cyber-attack, on February 2019, affected more than 40 companies across the globe from diverse sectors of industry such as game development, book retail, and e-commerce with a single attack in which more than 863 million users' data records were placed on sale on the dark web in multiple rounds (O'Flaherty, 2019). Some of these companies caved in to the extortion demands of the hacker (Khang, Hahanov et al., 2022).

In a written reply Lok Sabha, the Electronics and IT Minister, informed Parliament that as per the information available from the Indian Computer Emergency Response Team (CERT-In) 552 phishing incidents were observed in 2017, 454 in 2018, and 268 incidents were either reported or tracked in the first five months of 2019 (EconomicTimes, 2019).

While there are a plethora of definitions related to cyber-attacks and data breaches that can be found both in national and international literature all these have the common aim of compromising the confidentiality, integrity, and availability of data, with a recent phenomenon being money extortion by hackers.

It was also observed during the review of the literature that the financial sector, including financial services organizations, has always been a target internationally and cyber criminals and cyber adversaries are breaking new grounds in terms of threat creation by using sophisticated capabilities to exploit loop holes that technology landscapes offer (Figure 19.1).

While new actors with focused motives are appearing every day (refer to Table 19.1), traditional cyber threats remain the source of most attacks, a number of studies have also been conducted in international forums on these threats in earlier and current forms and also examine how they could evolve in future (Geib, 2019).

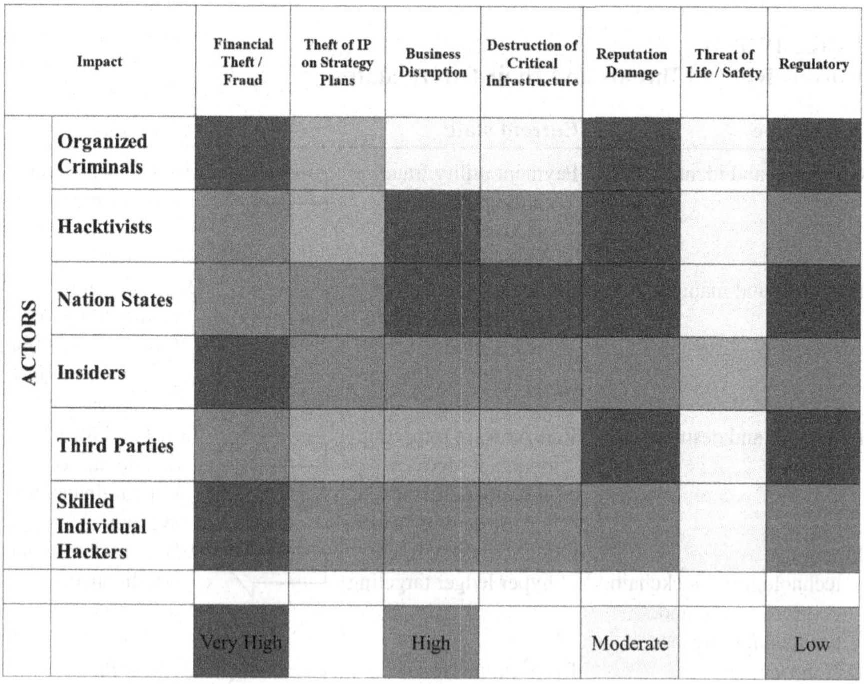

	Impact	Financial Theft / Fraud	Theft of IP on Strategy Plans	Business Disruption	Destruction of Critical Infrastructure	Reputation Damage	Threat of Life / Safety	Regulatory
ACTORS	Organized Criminals							
	Hacktivists							
	Nation States							
	Insiders							
	Third Parties							
	Skilled Individual Hackers							
		Very High		High		Moderate		Low

FIGURE 19.1 A diverse array of cyber-attack actors and impacts (cyber risk heat map).

Source: Khang (2021).

Cybersecurity Ventures reports outline the fact that since 2013 there have been 3,809,448 records stolen in breaches, with 158,727 per hour, 2645 per minute, and 44 every second of every day.

19.3.1 DESIGN/METHODOLOGY/APPROACH

Various available literature and reports from organizations of repute and online websites have been scanned and the information gathered is reviewed herein. This research chapter is exploratory and developed using the concepts drawn from case study research methodology.

19.3.2 FINDINGS

This study was based on the data collected through reported incidents, information available in the public domain, and data collected and reported by major industry players operating in the security and consulting domain, including data made available and published by regulatory and government agencies such as:

• Ministry of Communication and Information Technology & Department of Electronics and Information Technology;

TABLE 19.1
Various Types of Threats and Their Future States

Threat type	Current state	Future state
Credential and identity theft	Payment utility fraud; carding; account takeover (ATO); synthetic IDs	Multiparty credential compromises
Data theft and manipulation	Strategic collection of material, non-public information	Data theft and manipulation in furtherance of fraud and disinformation operations
Disruptive and destructive malware	Ransomware impacting financial services and other critical infrastructures; wipers	Targeted destruction and disruption of critical financial systems
Emerging technologies: blockchain, cryptocurrency, and artificial intelligence	Cryptocurrency fraud; hyper ledger targeting	Adversarial artificial intelligence
Disinformation	Election interference; hacktivism	Large-scale, targeted market manipulation

Source: Accenture security 2019 future cyber threats report (2019).

- Data Security Council of India (DSCI);
- Ministry of Law, Justice and Company Affairs (Legislative Department);
- C-DAC (Centre for Development of Advanced Computing);
- DoT (Department of Telecommunications);
- CERT-In (Indian Computer Emergency Response Team);
- RBI (Reserve Bank of India);
- SEBI (Security and Exchange Board of India);
- National Critical Information Infrastructure Protection Centre National Technical Research—Organization Government of India (NCIIPC);
- Information Technology, Electronics & Communications Department of Telangana Government;
- Ministry of Electronic and Information Technology (Meity);
- National Institute of Electronics and Information Technology (NIELIT);
- Ministry of Defence, Government of India;
- Ministry of Home Affairs, Government of India;
- Ministry of External Affairs;
- Central Electricity Authority (CEA);
- Central Bureau of Investigation (CBI);
- Association of Unified Telecom Service Providers of India (AUSPI);

- Ministry of Petroleum and Natural Gas;
- Central Electricity Regulatory Commission;
- Controller of Certifying Authorities (CCA);
- Centre for Development of Telematics (CDoT);
- Ministry of Finance;
- National Payments Corporation India;
- Electronics and Information Technology Department Government of Odisha.

The threat predictions and data published by various consulting and regulatory bodies over the last 3 years show an increasing trend in cyber-attacks with a move towards increased cyber warfare and espionage.

As per the RBI report, the Indian Banking System detected Rs. 71,500 crores worth of financial frauds in 2018–19, of which 0.3% was related to card/internet and deposit-related frauds (Manikandan, 2019). These results illustrate the fact that attackers are continually developing new ways of exploiting every layer of the laid-out infrastructure (networks, programs, and data), and there has been a continuous increase in mobile attacks.

19.4   CYBER ATTACKS SECTOR-WISE VICTIMS

It is evident that Indian financial organizations are most impacted by cyber-attacks when compared with any other sector, as shown in Figure 19.2.

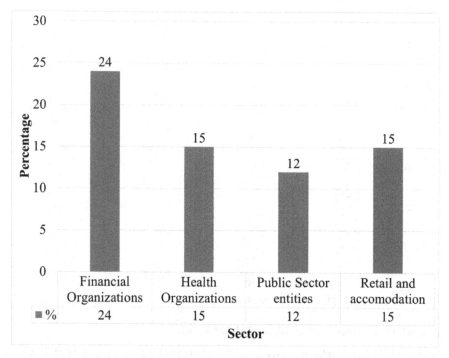

FIGURE 19.2   Statistic of cyber security of various sectors.

Fraud risks that are of high concern to banks/financial institutions are presented in Table 19.2 and Figure 19.3.

From the above data, it is evident that financial organizations are increasingly depending on technology. Cybercrimes comprising of ATM skimming, phishing/vishing, and misuse of credit and debit cards are illustrated in Figure 19.4.

TABLE 19.2
Types of Fraud Risk

Type of fraud	Percentage
Internet banking and ATM (automated teller machine) fraud	24
E-banking	18
Identity fraud	17
Employee and customer collusion	15
Funds transfer frauds	13
Bribery and corruption	7
Others	6
Total	**100**

Source: Deloitte—India Banking Fraud Survey Edition III.

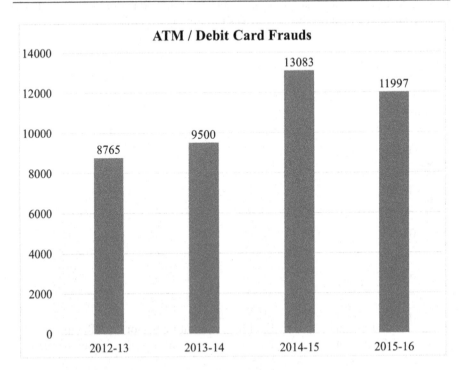

FIGURE 19.3 Types of fraud risk of ATMs/debit cards.

Source: 11997 frauds related to credit, debit, and net banking reported in April–Dec 2016 DNA Newspaper, 26th Feb 2016.

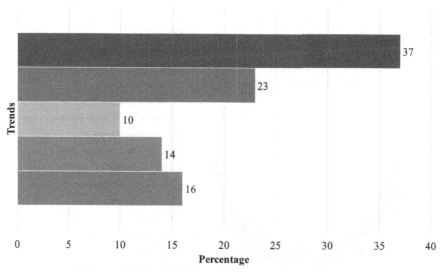

FIGURE 19.4   New fraud trends that are of concern to banks.

Internet banking/ATM fraud, e-banking, and identity fraud emerged as the top fraud concerns for bankers, as shown in Figure 19.5.

Cybercrimes account for 10% of frauds, which is not so significant when compared with other types of frauds, however there has been an increasing trend that cannot be ignored as the numbers and actual losses despite not being so significant when compared to banks' overall financials and frauds, as shown in Figure 19.6.

19.4.1 GENERAL FINDINGS

- India having the second largest population and with rising internet penetration levels is creating a large attack area for cyber threat actors.
- As per the Gemini advisory report in 2018, 3.2 million Indian payment card records have been compromised and posted for sale.
- India ranks third in the world next to the UK in total amount of stolen payment cards.
- The RBI had mandated to convert existing magnetic strip cards to EMV (Europay, Mastercard, and Visa) chip (a small piece of semiconducting material [usually silicon] on which an integrated circuit is embedded) and pin (personal identification number) cards before 31 December 2018, with new debit and credit cards only being issued for domestic usage unless the customer specifically asked for internal use.
- According to Symantec's internet security Threat Reports 2017 and 2019, India is:

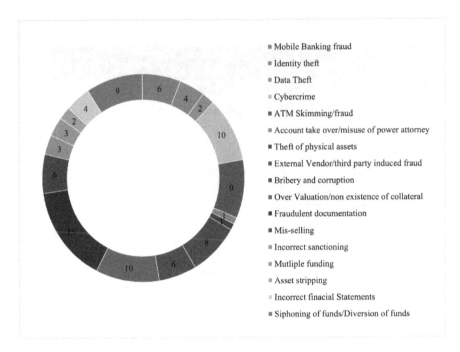

- Mobile Banking fraud
- Identity theft
- Data Theft
- Cybercrime
- ATM Skimming/fraud
- Account take over/misuse of power attorney
- Theft of physical assets
- External Vendor/third party induced fraud
- Bribery and corruption
- Over Valuation/non existence of collateral
- Fraudulent documentation
- Mis-selling
- Incorrect sanctioning
- Mutliple funding
- Asset stripping
- Incorrect finacial Statements
- Siphoning of funds/Diversion of funds

FIGURE 19.5   Types of frauds experienced by banks in the last two years.

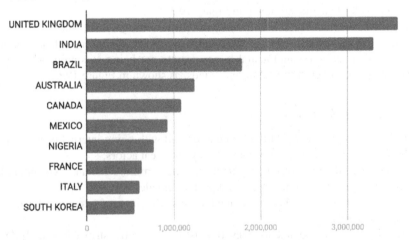

FIGURE 19.6   Top 10 non-US countries affected by payment card fraud in 2018.

Source: Gemini advisory, 2013.

- The fourth largest global source of malicious activity and second in the APAC region;
- Ranks second for spam and bot threats;
- With 14.3% of recorded instances of ransomware ranks second in the world;
- Includes 23.6% of mobile malware incidents;
- Ranked second in the world in the list of countries affected by targeted attack groups from 2016 to 2018, just behind the United States.

The above data indicate that India is becoming home to cyber criminals and is also being targeted by them.

19.4.2 DISTRIBUTION

In 2017–18, more than 4 million Indian payment card records were compromised and posted for sale, an increase of 219%. While there has been a sharp rise in both card not present (CNP) and card present (CP), it is worth noting that the CP increase has occurred even though 86% of the compromised CP cards were Europay-, MasterCard-, and Visa (EMV) enabled, as shown in Figure 19.7.

Figure 19.8 shows that a threat actor is inquiring about countries besides the United States that are best for cashing out cards with PIN data using ATMs. Other threat actors are found in Indonesia, Malaysia, India, and Nepal. Responses with the above country names repeated several times were also found in a top-tier Russian carding forum.

This spike in Indian payment cards frauds is also due to the increase in demand for Indian-based payment records in the dark web market (as shown in Figure 19.8).

COMPROMISED INDIAN PAYMENT CARD DATA IN 2017 AND 2018

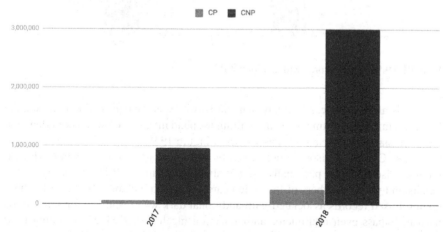

FIGURE 19.7 Distribution in India of those affected by payment card fraud in 2017 and 2018.

Source: Gemini advisory, 2013.

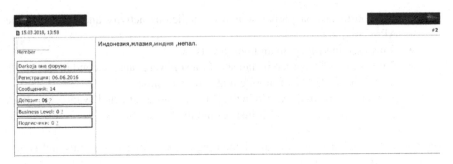

FIGURE 19.8 Cards with PIN data using ATMs.

Source: Gemini advisory, 2013.

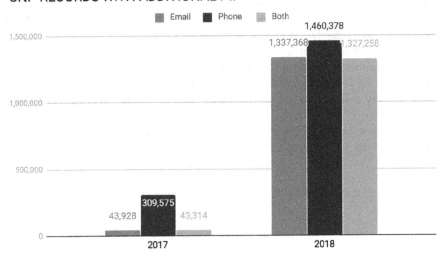

FIGURE 19.9 CNP records with additional PII.

Criminals are also in search of payment cards from specific banks which provide the highest return on investment and are willing to spend money only when confident that they will stand to make a profit, as shown in Figure 19.9.

As per Gemini advisory sources, nearly 50% of compromised Indian CNP card records also include personally identifiable information (PII), primarily email details and phone numbers of the stolen cards, and also include CNP records; these compromised records associated with additional dark web resources for sale can be used to bypass even multifactor authentication mechanisms which are being used by most of the financial institutions for payment processing currently. For example, 2.2 billion stolen payment card user names and passwords surfaced in the dark web

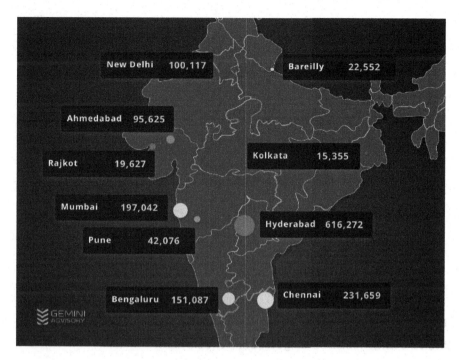

FIGURE 19.10   Number of cardholders in 2017 and 2018.

Source: Gemini advisory, 2013.

in January 2019 which can be matched with email and phone credentials that have spread across the dark web for years and even can be used for breaking multifactor authentication mechanisms, as shown in Figure 19.10.

Figure 19.10 depicts the top 10 Indian cities affected by payment card fraud. The trend observed in Western countries is that the cities with the highest populations are directly correlated to those with the highest CNP fraud, however this does not seem to be the case in India and other developing countries.

19.5   IMPACTS OF DATA LEAKS AND CYBER FRAUDS ON THE FINANCIAL SECTOR

With financial institutions increasingly depending on technology and increasingly becoming susceptible to data leak frauds and cybercrimes, it is becoming even more important to study and understand the impact of these data leaks and cyber frauds on financial institutions, as shown in Figure 19.11.

As financial institutions have been experiencing a massive surge in cybercrime incidents over the last few years, cybercrime is becoming a trend in the financial sector that cannot be ignored, as shown in Figure 19.12.

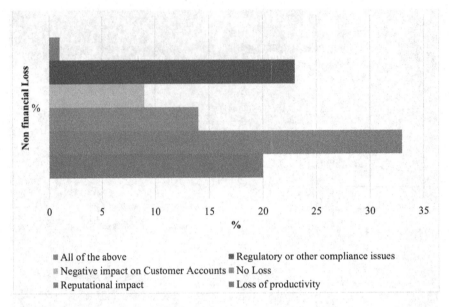

FIGURE 19.11   Non-financial losses organizations suffered due to fraud.

Source: Deloitte—India Banking Fraud Survey Edition III.

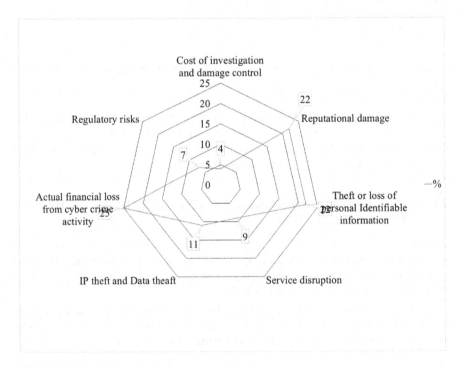

FIGURE 19.12   Cyber-attack—impact aspects.

Source: Deloitte—India Banking Fraud Survey Edition III.

19.6 GOVERNANCE AND COUNTER MEASURES

The Reserve Bank of India (RBI) is India's central bank, and the regulator of the entire banking system in India. The strategy and governance aspects related to the security of financial transactions are also laid out by the RBI. The RBI also works with various other government agencies to ensure their implementation (Khang. Shah et al., 2023).

In its annual report under Chapter 9, "Payment and Settlement Systems and Information Technology" RBI (2022–2023), it states that "The Reserve Bank has endeavored to ensure that India has 'state-of-the-art' payment and settlement systems that are not just safe and secure, but are also efficient, fast and affordable while recognizing the need for continued emphasis on innovation, cyber security, financial inclusion, customer protection and competition. Going forward, Vision 2021 envisages achieving a 'highly digital' and 'cash-lite' society through the goalposts of competition, cost, convenience and confidence, thus empowering every citizen with access to a bouquet of e-payment options."

RBI (2015) is cognizant of the fact that the number, frequency, and impact of cyber incidents/attacks have increased many times over in the financial sector, and it also underlines the urgent need to put in place a robust cyber security/resilience framework at banks to ensure adequate and continuous cyber-security preparedness among the banks. In order to curb the menace of fraudulent CP transaction the RBI mandated that all ATMs and point-of-sale (POS) devices become EMV-compatible by January 1, 2019; this extra security layer will make it more difficult to cash out CP cards (Khang, Kali et al., 2023).

Because of the evolving nature, growing scale/velocity, motives, and resourcefulness of cyber-threats to the banking system, the RBI feels it is essential to enhance the resilience of the banking system by improving the current defenses in addressing cyber risks. These would include, but are not limited to, putting in place an adaptive Incident Response, Management and Recovery framework to deal with adverse incidents/disruptions, if and when they occur. The RBI in its guidelines on "Information security, Electronic Banking, Technology risk management and cyber frauds" has issued detailed guidelines covering all aspects as follows:

1. Information technology governance;
2. Information security;
3. IT operations;
4. IT services outsourcing;
5. IS audit;
6. Cyber frauds;
7. Business continuity planning;
8. Customer education;
9. Legal issues.

The RBI in the above document also advocates the need for having an Institution's board-approved cyber security policy, which contains an appropriate approach to combating cyber threats given the level of complexity of business and acceptable levels of risk.

19.7 CONCLUSION

India's 219% spike in compromised payment records from the calendar year 2017 to 2018 and trends emerging from 2019 quarter 1 (q1) data are showing a faster growth in fraud. While Indian financial institutions are embracing a more proactive defensive strategy and trying to comply with RBI guidelines and norms, they will take a long time to reverse this trend. Hence there is a great opportunity for improvement in this area. The RBI, related government agencies, and financial institutions should strive to improve awareness among all concerned, including the end individual customers, by making them aware of the activities related to the cyber world.

India has some of the world's strictest data localization laws, comparable to those of China or Russia, which mandate even international companies to store information related to Indian customers in India. Some international companies like MasterCard expressed concerns about Indian customer data getting isolated from global data due to this localization which makes it difficult to identify international payment frauds related to India. This pressed the need to relook at cyber frauds and IT-related legal aspects with a global view. It is also important that all stakeholders involved in the financial transaction chain are made aware of data security and cyber frauds, and are provided with the required information to protect the information and ensure a certain level of security in managing their data and information (Khang, Muthmainnah et al., 2023).

During this study, a dearth of reliable information related to data and cyber frauds was uncovered and most of the time the data and information available is dated, barring the data made available in report forms by a small number of consulting companies and solution providers (under 10). There are not many sources with updated information. Hence, the RBI should take steps to publish and update the data related to cyber frauds frequently and also push for institutional disclosures as required (Khang, Inna et al., 2024).

Further directions of studies on this subject should include closely following the emerging technologies and evolution of cybercrimes in those areas along with the effectiveness of thematic examinations which are being conducted by various institutions as mandated by the RBI in those emerging areas. Studies could also be conducted around the effectiveness of regulatory aspects which are meant to support "The Reserve Banks endeavored to ensure that India has 'state-of-the-art' payment and settlement systems that are not just safe and secure but are also efficient, fast and affordable" (Khang, Gujrati et al., 2024).

REFERENCES

BT. 2019. Business Today – Data breach and Cybersecurity Challenges and Solutions! April 16, 2019. www.businesstoday.in/opinion/columns/story/data-breach-cybersecurity-data-breach-and-cybersecurity-challenges-and-solutions-186917-2019-04-16

EconomicTimes. 2019. *The Economic Times* (internet). 26th Jun 2019, Article 268 phishing incidents observed till May this year. https://m.economictimes.com/tech/internet/268-phishing-incidents-observed-till-may-this-year-ravi-shankar-prasad/articleshow/69958 513.cms

Geib, A. 2019. Accenture Security 2019, Future Cyber Threats. https://newsroom.accenture. com/news/accenture-report-reveals-new-cybercrime-operating-model-among-high-prof ile-threat-groups.htm

Gemini Advisory. 2013. Access on 2013. https://geminiadvisory.io/india-rising-cybercrime-frontierhttps://geminiadvisory.io/india-rising-cybercrime-frontier

IndiaTimes, 2023. Amazon India Admits to Data Breach Affecting Its Sellers. https://econom ictimes.indiatimes.com/internet/amazon-india-admits-to-data-breach-affecting-its-sell ers/articleshow/67456922.cms

Khang, A. 2021. "Material4Studies." *Material of Computer Science, Artificial Intelligence, Data Science, IoT, Blockchain, Cloud, Metaverse, Cybersecurity for Studies.* Retrieved from www.researchgate.net/publication/370156102_Material4Studies

Khang, A., Chowdhury, S., & Sharma, S. 2022. *The Data-Driven Blockchain Ecosystem: Fundamentals, Applications, and Emerging Technologies* (1st Ed.). CRC Press. https://doi.org/10.1201/9781003269281

Khang, A., Gujrati, R., Uygun, H., Tailor, R. K., & Gaur, S. S. 2024. *Data-driven Modelling and Predictive Analytics in Business and Finance* (1st Ed.). CRC Press. ISBN: 9781032600628. https://doi.org/10.1201/9781032600628

Khang, A., Hahanov, V., Abbas, G. L., & Hajimahmud, V. A. (2022). Cyber-physical-social system and incident management. In *AI-Centric Smart City Ecosystems: Technologies, Design and Implementation* (1st Ed.), 7 (12). CRC Press. https://doi.org/10.1201/ 9781003252542-2

Khang, A., Inna, S.-O., Alla, K., Rostyslav, S., Rudenko, M., Lidia, R., & Kristina, B. 2024. Management model 6.0 and business recovery strategy of enterprises in the era of digital economy. In A. Khang, R. Gujrati, H. Uygun, R. K. Tailor, & S. S. Gaur, (Eds.), *Data-driven Modelling and Predictive Analytics in Business and Finance* (1st Ed.). CRC Press. https://doi.org/10.1201/9781032600628-16

Khang, A., Kali, C. R., Satapathy, S. K., Kumar, A., Ranjan Das, S., & Panda, M. R. 2023. Enabling the future of manufacturing: integration of robotics and iot to smart fac-tory infrastructure in industry 4.0. In A. Khang, V. Shah, & S. Rani (Eds.), *AI-Based Technologies and Applications in the Era of the Metaverse* (1st Ed.) (pp. 25–50). IGI Global Press. https://doi.org/10.4018/978-1-6684-8851-5.ch002

Khang, A., Muthmainnah, M., Seraj, P. M. I., Al Yakin, A., Obaid, A. J., & Panda, M. R. 2023. AI-aided teaching model for the education 5.0 ecosystem. In A. Khang, V. Shah, & S. Rani (Eds.), *AI-Based Technologies and Applications in the Era of the Metaverse* (1st Ed.) (pp. 83–104). IGI Global Press. https://doi.org/10.4018/978-1-6684-8851-5.ch004

Khang A., Shah V., & Rani S. 2023. *AI-Based Technologies and Applications in the Era of the Metaverse* (1st Ed.). IGI Global Press. https://doi.org/10.4018/978-1-6684-8851-5

Khanh, H. H., & Khang A. 2021. The role of artificial intelligence in blockchain applications. In Rana, G., Khang, A., Sharma, R., Goel, A.K., & Dubey, A.K. (Eds.) *Reinventing Manufacturing and Business Processes through Artificial Intelligence.* Vol. 2 (pp. 20–40). CRC Press. https://doi.org/10.1201/9781003145011-2

Manikandan, A. 2019. Rs 71,500 Crore Worth of Bank Frauds Detected in FY19: RBI Report. https://economictimes.indiatimes.com/news/economy/finance/bank-fraud-touches-rs-71543-crore-in-2018-19-rbi-annual-report/articleshow/70895326.cms?from=mdr

O'Flaherty, K. 2019. Cybersecurity and Privacy Journalist, Another 127 Million Records Have Gone on Sale on the Dark Web – Here's What You Should Do. www.forbes.com/sites/ kateoflahertyuk/2019/02/15/another-127-million-records-have-gone-on-sale-on-the-dark-web-heres-what-you-should-do/#5109311a2293

Rani, S., Chauhan, M., Kataria, A., & Khang, A. (2021). IoT equipped intelligent distributed framework for smart healthcare systems. *Networking and Internet Architecture* Vol. 2 (p. 30). https://doi.org/10.48550/arXiv.2110.04997

Reserve Bank of India (RBI). 2015. Circular RBI/2015-16/418, DBS.CO/CSITE/BC.11/ 33.01.001/2015-16.

Reserve Bank of India (RBI). 2022–2023. RBI Annual Report 18–19, Chapter 9, Payment and Settlement Systems and Information Technology. https://currentaffairs.adda247.com/ rbis-annual-report-2022-2023/

20 The ChatGPT

Its Influence on the Jobs Market—An Analytical Study

Kajal Sharma, Zakia Tasmin Rahman, and Ravinder Rena

20.1 INTRODUCTION

Large-scale language models like GPT 3.5 have helped to progress natural language processing significantly in recent years (King, 2023). The GPT, which stands for Generative Pre-Trained Transformer, is the main neural network architecture that converts an input into a meaningful output (Dwivedi et al., 2023). It creates answers and was pre-trained by humans. With ChatGPT (Chat Generative Pre-trained Transformer), an artificially intelligent text production and formation tool, users may ask it any question and it will respond by generating the desired text (Singhal, 2023).

The contemporary language model ChatGPT, an artificial intelligence model which was developed by OpenAI, is capable of generating responses that closely resemble those of a human being over a wide spectrum of inquiries (Arvin Ash, 2023). The GPT-3 architecture, a deep neural network, was utilized in the construction of this system. Extensive training was conducted on a substantial corpus of textual data. ChatGPT has proved to be a proficient instrument for tasks necessitating the processing of natural language due to its capacity to interpret and generate responses to questions expressed in natural language (Ankita, 2023).

It is an online application that enables user to hold conversations that seem human—like a chatbot on steroids. Unlike Google, which provides a list of web pages and publications that typically contain information relevant to the search query, Bing returns search results (Montti, 2023). Based on the context and intent of a user's question, ChatGPT responds (Marr, 2023). Users cannot, for instance, ask Google to write a novel or a piece of code, but can ask ChatGPT to do so, and it will respond reasonably.

20.1.1 OBJECTIVES OF THE STUDY

- To understand the performance of Chatbots.
- To know the uses of ChatGPT.
- To explore the challenges of using ChatGPT.
- Influence of ChatGPT on the jobs market.

DOI: 10.1201/9781032618845-20

20.1.2 Research Questions

- How does ChatGPT perform?
- What are the uses of ChatGPT?
- What are the challenges of ChatGPT?
- How will the jobs market be influenced through ChatGPT?

20.1.3 Scope of the Study

The goal of future research in this area is to increase the precision and dependability of language models like ChatGPT. This may involve developing new training algorithms or incorporating new sources of data. It may also involve developing new ways to evaluate the performance of language models and to detect bias in their output.

20.2 LITERATURE REVIEW

Netflix took 3.5 years to achieve a customer base of 1 million, given that 10 lakh individuals were utilizing the technology (Mishra & Esaimani, 2020). The development of Airbnb required 2.5 years, while Facebook was developed within a span of 10 months. Spotify, on the other hand, was created in a somewhat shorter timeframe of 5 months. Instagram, a popular social media platform, was developed in a mere 2.5 months. Lastly, the creation of the iPhone, a groundbreaking mobile device, was accomplished in a period of 74 days. However, an example of a phenomenon that rapidly garnered a user base of one million within a mere five-day timeframe is ChatGPT (CA Rahul Malodia: Business Coach, 2023).

20.2.1 Architecture

The GPT-3 architecture, a transformer-based neural network, is the foundation of ChatGPT (Zhou et al., 2023). One of the biggest language models to date, the model comprises 175 billion parameters (Wu et al., 2023). It has 96 layers and employs a method called attention to identify the connections between various words in a text (Floridi & Chiriatti, 2020). The model can concentrate on pertinent sections of the input sequence thanks to the attention mechanism, leading to more precise answers (An et al., 2022).

20.2.2 Training

ChatGPT has been trained by being fed enormous volumes of text data from the internet (Keramatfar et al., 2022). The information came from a wide variety of sources, such as publications, websites, and social media (Anurag, 2023). The model was trained to anticipate the following word in a text sequence given the preceding words. Unsupervised learning refers to this training procedure because the model does not get direct input on how well it is doing (Aydin & Erdem, 2022).

One fundamental aspect to familiarize oneself with is the fundamental functionality of ChatGPT (Jovanovic & Campbell, 2022). Upon analyzing the correlation between the user's input and the vast corpus of textual data, encompassing billions of web pages, books, and other relevant sources, the language model endeavors to ascertain the most probable terms that would be anticipated in a given context (Patel & Lam, 2023). A substantial dataset was employed for the development of a deep learning neural network (van Dis et al., 2023).

In essence, this algorithm can be characterized as a multi-layered and weighted computational model that exhibits similarities to the cognitive processes observed in the human brain. The utilization of text data enables ChatGPT to acquire knowledge about patterns and relationships (IBM, 2017). One method employed for leveraging this learning is to generate responses that resemble those of a human by making predictions about the subsequent text in a particular sentence. ChatGPT aims to generate responses that are consistently coherent and structurally complete in relation to the given input. Furthermore, this phenomenon is not limited to the level of individual sentences. The AI system has the capability to produce coherent phrases and even paragraphs that are in line with the input provided by the user.

The current inquiry pertains to the methodology employed for training the model to generate responses that align with the norms and expectations of a discourse (Nature Editorial, 2023). The efficacy of the model is contingent upon its training methodology. During the initial phase of the training procedure, human contractors assume the dual role of a user and an ideal chatbot (DiGiorgio & Ehrenfeld, 2023). Each training session comprises a dialogue in which the human user and the human playing the role of the chatbot engage in a conversation. It is plausible that these two tasks may be fulfilled by a single individual (Stokel-Walker, 2023). The fundamental concept revolves around the training of the model to engage in dialogues that resemble those of human beings. The model incorporates the recorded interactions with actual individuals in the thread's chronology (Chatterjee & Dethlefs, 2023).

In this manner, the model acquires the capacity to optimize the likelihood of selecting the accurate arrangement of words and sentences inside a given conversational interaction. By means of this meticulously supervised procedure of human guidance, it acquires the ability to provide an output that is beyond mere sentence completion. To enhance its responsiveness, the system acquires knowledge about patterns pertaining to the context and semantic interpretation of various inputs. This is the reason why engaging in a conversation using ChatGPT occasionally gives the impression that there could perhaps be a human interlocutor on the receiving end. However, it should be noted that the training process does not conclude at this point. In the subsequent stage, the engineers refine the output by instructing ChatGPT to award a ranking incentive to each output.

For example, a trainer might ask the model something like "Describe an atom." The potential answer could be:

A. It's the smallest part of a substance made up of electrons, protons and neutrons.
B. It's a basic element.
C. It's an object made up of subatomic particles.
D. It's a ticketing service.

A human trainer would rank this output from best to worst and then these data would be fed to the model like this where A>C>B>D.

This teaches ChatGPT to critically evaluate what the best output is likely to be (Warikoo, 2023).

20.2.3   THE WORKING PROCESS OF CHATGPT

ChatGPT is an AI chatbot that exhibits a high level of intelligence and appears to possess extensive knowledge across various domains. Information technology (IT) possesses a wide range of capabilities, encompassing tasks such as completing academic assignments, composing professional cover letters for employment opportunities, providing guidance, and creating software code (Pavlik, 2023).

Google's primary strength lies in its capacity to do extensive searches within databases and present a range of potential matches that could potentially address the user's inquiries (Else, 2023). The primary advantage of ChatGPT is in its ability to understand the context and semantics of a given inquiry, and based on its training data, produce a suitable response that adheres to grammatical rules and sounds natural (Biswas, 2023). So, how does it work? How did this company create this seemingly magical tool? And how does ChatGPT actually work?

Just dispel some myths first. It is not magic. It is just math and a bunch of clever concepts, and no it does not get smarter by itself. It cannot self-study like a human that can go to the library and start learning a few things. ChatGPT learns from whatever it is told to study. It is also not just asking the internet for an answer to user's question. It does have a storehouse of knowledge and uses it to answer user's questions (Thornton et al., 2023).

ChatGPT was trained on data from books, webpages, Wikipedia, news articles, scientific journals, and other unspecified sources. The material was collected up to about September 2021, so any information newer than this, ChatGPT would be clueless about at least as of the time of writing, which is May, 2023. It is necessary to the developers to teach it this new material if the user wants an answer to something that becomes new knowledge after that time. The quickest way to explain how it operates is to say that neural networking is used along with supervised learning and reinforcement learning, two essential elements of contemporary machine learning. The language model endeavors to understand the user's inquiry prior to generating sentences based on the information it has been trained on, which it deems most suitable for providing a response (Mijwil et al., 2023). Moreover, it has a randomization mechanism to introduce variability in the outputs, so ensuring that different results are often obtained from the same input (Bhattacharya et al., 2023).

Therefore, now the problem with solely using human trainers as in this type of supervised learning is scale. Human trainers would have to anticipate all the inputs and outputs of any potential query that any user could potentially request at any time. This would be impossible to do. And it is known that ChatGPT does not have this kind of ability (Arif et al., 2023).

As an illustration, one can utilize this tool to generate a coherent short story on any given topic. In what manner does it accomplish that? The utilization of reinforcement learning, which constitutes the third stage, is employed for this purpose. This form of learning is conducted without direct supervision or guidance (Scerri & Morin, 2023). This methodology facilitates the training of the model without establishing a specific correspondence between the output and input. However, the model is trained to acquire knowledge of the underlying context and patterns in the input data, building upon its previous human-taught pre-training. Put simply, the model utilizes pre-training, which incorporates a ranking system, as the foundation for generating its output during the unsupervised training phase (Dahmen et al., 2023).

Through this approach, the model demonstrates its capability to effectively analyze vast quantities of data derived from many sources. It acquires the ability to discern patterns within texts and sentences pertaining to a wide range of subjects. Furthermore, the system possesses the capability to autonomously execute this task, hence enabling the expansion of the training provided by human instructors to encompass a significantly larger dataset. The dataset utilized for training ChatGPT, which is built upon GPT-3.5, is of substantial magnitude, amounting to approximately 45 terabytes.

In contemporary times, the availability of terabyte flash drives for a mere $20 may diminish the seeming significance of the following statement. However, it is imperative to acknowledge that the volume of text being processed is indeed substantial. A single terabyte is comparable to around 83 million pages of information. The size of ChatGPT is sufficiently large to facilitate the learning of patterns and associations among words and phrases on a substantial scale (Huang et al., 2023). Consequently, it is capable of generating outputs that possess a reasonable level of significance for almost every given query (Khang, Gujrati et al., 2024).

20.3 RESEARCH METHODOLOGY

The research has adopted both quantitative and qualitative methods to gain a comprehensive understanding of user interactions and ethical considerations related to ChatGPT (Khang, Inna et al., 2024).

Data Collection:

a) Quantitative Data: User interactions with ChatGPT are collected from various online platforms where the model is deployed, capturing conversation logs, prompts, and responses. User demographics and usage patterns have also been gathered.
b) Qualitative Data: Qualitative data on the perceptions, experiences, and ethical concerns of users related to ChatGPT usage.

Data Analysis:

a) Quantitative Analysis: Statistical analysis is employed to analyze patterns in user interactions, including frequently used prompts, response patterns, and user satisfaction.
b) Qualitative Analysis: Ethical considerations and user concerns are explored in-depth.

The findings of the research study are tabulated, coded, and analyzed.

20.4 FINDINGS AND ANALYSIS

20.4.1 PERFORMANCE OF CHATBOTS

Any artificial intelligence system's greatest asset is the training data it receives from the world's current production. Chatbots are language models that can comprehend the language that users enter and respond in that same language (Kushwaha & Kar, 2020). The internet's open data are used to train chatbots (Hsu & Chang, 2021). By means of thousands of millions of factors, these chatbots can respond to questions once the training is over (Nuruzzaman & Hussain, 2018). Take ChatGPT as an example; it was trained using 175 billion parameters. Transformer architecture is the foundation of this chatbot (Saadna et al., 2022). It acts somewhat similarly to the human body's neural network.

Therefore, if someone has a system which can put all the knowledge of the world into one computer and train it to learn how it will consume that, it becomes smart. This is not a new technology. It's not the first time a chatbot has been released. But ChatGPT is so good that perhaps for the first time such a technology has come which reduces the difference between humans and robots. So much so that after reading the ChatGPT's response, a reader will be unable to tell whether it was created by a human or a computer. And this is the famous Turing test (Moor, 2003). The Turing test was devised to interpret or understand whether a machine is artificially intelligent or smart (Levesque, 2017). And the test was simple: a human can determine by reading something whether it was produced by a machine or a human (Uchendu et al, 2021).

20.4.2 USES OF CHATGPT

These chatbots are nothing new; chatbots have been around for a while. Users may now communicate with chatbots from different businesses on WhatsApp, and also can use chatbots to purchase metro train tickets. So why all the commotion about the ChatGPT chatbot? Why is everyone so upset about it? Generative capacity is the solution to this query. This indicates that using artificial intelligence, creative material is produced after trends in the data are identified. It performs a variety of creative tasks using artificial intelligence, including producing essays, short stories, poems, screenplays for videos, and even program codes.

A typical chatbot would only respond to two or three queries, nothing more. However, ChatGPT produces its own material. One of its parts is pre-training systems, where language models are given massive amounts of words and phrases. This algorithm can predict the subsequent words and sentences by identifying specific terms (Table 20.1).

Description of usage of ChatGPT:

- *Information and Knowledge:* User can ask any questions they might have on ChatGPT on a range of topics, such as history, science, math, and more. By

TABLE 20.1
Uses of ChatGPT for Various Purposes

S/No.	Various Usage of ChatGPT	User Satisfaction Responses in Percent
1.	Information and knowledge	40%
2.	Personal assistance	70%
3.	Entertainment	20%
4.	Language learning	30%

Source: Authors' own compilation.

using ChatGPT to obtain accurate and up-to-date information, the user may increase their breadth of knowledge.

- *Personal Assistance:* The user can use ChatGPT as a personal assistant to assist themselves with chores like scheduling appointments, placing food orders, and setting reminders.
- *Entertainment:* ChatGPT can be used for entertainment purposes, such as telling jokes, playing games, or engaging in a fun conversation.
- *Language Learning:* For a person studying a new language, ChatGPT is a useful resource for improving language skills. Users can ask ChatGPT to help with grammar and vocabulary, or to interpret any terms or phrases they do not understand.

20.5 CHALLENGES OF CHATGPT (Table 20.2)

20.5.1 IT CANNOT ACCESS THE INTERNET

ChatGPT, as a language model, does not have direct access to the internet. It was trained on a large corpus of text data, but it does not have a live connection to the web. This means that when it generates responses, it can only use the information it has been trained on, rather than accessing real-time information from the internet. However, there are ways to integrate ChatGPT with web-based information sources to provide more up-to-date information. For example, user could use APIs (application programming interfaces) to retrieve information from websites or databases and then incorporate that information into the responses generated by ChatGPT.

20.5.2 IT MAY PRODUCE NONSENSICAL DATA

Due to its lack of common sense reasoning, ChatGPT may occasionally give responses that are irrational or incomprehensible. Although ChatGPT may produce responses that resemble those of a human in response to text-based inputs, it lacks the common sense reasoning that is a feature of human beings. This indicates that it could occasionally give responses that are absurd or unreasonable.

TABLE 20.2
Various Challenges of ChatGPT

S/No.	List of Challenges as per testing	As per user's interaction in Percent
1.	It cannot access the internet	90%
2.	It may produce non-sensical data	60%
3.	It has limited knowledge base	70%
4.	It lacks emotional intelligence	80%
5.	Potential bias and dependence on training data	85%
6.	Ethical concerns	40%
7.	It cannot solve complex mathematical questions with accuracy	60%
8.	It can accept input in text form only	100%
9.	It lacks true understanding of words	40%

Source: Authors' own compilation.

20.5.3 IT HAS A LIMITED KNOWLEDGE BASE

Even though ChatGPT has access to a lot of data, it is limited in its comprehension of certain subjects. It might not be able to give precise or in-depth answers to questions on specialized or technical subjects.

20.5.4 IT LACKS EMOTIONAL INTELLIGENCE

Due of ChatGPT's lack of emotional intelligence, it may be difficult for it to recognize and react to emotional cues like sarcasm, humor, or empathy.

20.5.5 POTENTIAL BIAS AND DEPENDENCE ON TRAINING DATA

The quality and quantity of the training data have a significant impact on ChatGPT performance. Insufficient or biased training data may lead to inaccurate or biased replies. Like any language model, ChatGPT can only be as accurate as the data it was trained on. If the training data are biased in any manner, ChatGPT might continue to give biased responses.

20.5.6 ETHICAL CONCERNS

The use of ChatGPT for potentially damaging or destructive reasons, such as disseminating false information or assuming identities to engage in fraudulent operations, raises ethical questions.

20.5.7 IT CANNOT SOLVE COMPLEX MATHEMATICAL QUESTIONS WITH ACCURACY

ChatGPT is capable of responding in a manner resembling that of a person, but it is unable to handle complex logic and logical reasoning. If it is tested out in this functionality, unexpected results will be revealed. For instance, ChatGPT can handle simple addition, subtraction, division, and multiplication problems without delay. However, if one offers the chatbot an equation requiring multiple mathematical operations, it will give up. Either it will take too long to produce the desired outcome, or it may not be accurate.

20.5.8 It Accepts Input in Text Form Only

One of ChatGPT's biggest challenges is that it only allows text input. Although it cannot access other sorts of material like films, URLs, or photographs, it can be spoken orders to.

It is needed to translate the image for the platform if one wishes to instruct the chatbot using some data from an image.

20.5.9 It Lacks True Understanding of Words

ChatGPT may have difficulty understanding the context in which a conversation is taking place. This can lead to misinterpretation of the meaning of a question or statement, resulting in inaccurate responses (Khang, Shah et al., 2023).

20.6 INFLUENCE OF CHATGPT ON JOBS MARKET

The jobs market is evolving because of ChatGPT and other AI technologies, and some positions may be automated or lose demand (Carvalho & Ivanov, 2023). It is crucial to remember that ChatGPT and other AI technologies are meant to supplement human abilities rather than completely replace them (Dergaa et al., 2023). While computers and AI algorithms can perform some activities more quickly and accurately than people, other tasks call for human creativity, intuition, empathy, and problem-solving abilities (Bostrom & Yudkowsky, 2018).

The development of AI and automation has also led to the emergence of new businesses and occupations, including those in data analysis, machine learning, and robotics engineering. The need for human employees who can invent, develop, and adapt to shifting technologies will never go away, even while some occupations may be mechanized or require reskilling. Depending on the situation and use case, ChatGPT might have either positive or negative consequences on employment (Khang, Kali et al., 2023).

This can provide human workers with more time to concentrate on harder and more significant jobs. Additionally, ChatGPT can help with decision-making by offering analyses and suggestions based on a wealth of data (Korzynski et al., 2023). Particularly in industries like finance, marketing, and healthcare (Khang, 2023), this might be helpful (Khang, Muthmainnah et al., 2023).

On the downside, ChatGPT's automation capabilities could result in job displacement, especially in sectors where regular, repetitive work is prevalent. Employees may need to pick up new skills and information in order to stay competitive in the employment market. Additionally, bias in AI models, especially language models like ChatGPT, runs the danger of amplifying or maintaining current societal imbalances. This may have an impact on certain job functions, especially those that involve making decisions that have an impact on people's lives.

20.7 CONCLUSION

Modern language models like ChatGPT may significantly alter natural language processing (Kirmani, 2022). There are several real-world uses for its capacity to provide human-like responses to natural language inputs, including chatbots, customer support, and content production (Saxena et al., 2023).

Text production, question answering, and other facets of natural language processing are significantly impacted by the model's architecture, training, and performance (Lund et al., 2023). As the field of natural language processing develops, ChatGPT will undoubtedly play an important role in advancing the state-of-the-art in language processing.

The biases and disadvantages of utilizing ChatGPT should be understood though, and efforts should be made to find ways to make it more accurate and reliable. ChatGPT can automate some operations, like content generation or customer assistance, which can boost productivity and efficiency in enterprises (Muthmainnah, Khang et al., 2023).

ChatGPT and other AI technologies may change the labor market, although not all employment is likely to be displaced. Instead, they will provide new possibilities and necessitate workers picking up new skills in order to compete. In general, the impact of ChatGPT on jobs will depend on how it is deployed and used in different situations and industries. To ensure that it benefits both firms and employees, it will need ongoing monitoring and assessment.

REFERENCES

An, Y., Xia, 20., Chen, 20., Wu, F. 20., & Wang, J. (2022). Chinese clinical named entity recognition via multi-head self-attention based BiLSTM-CRF. *Artificial Intelligence in Medicine*, 127, 102282. www.sciencedirect.com/science/article/pii/S093336572 2000471

Ankita. (2023). Top 11 Limitations of ChatGPT. *MLYearning*. www.mlyearning.org/chat-gpt-limitations/

Anurag. (2023, January 16). ChatGPT – The buzz around it, the inherent biases of the algorithm, its jokes on Hinduism, and more – The basics of the AI-based platform. *OpIndia*. www.opindia.com/2023/01/chatgpt-artifical-intelligence-chatbot-biased-here-is-how/

Arif, T. B., Munaf, U., & Ul-Haque, I. (2023). The future of medical education and research: Is chatgpt a blessing or blight in disguise? Medical Education Online, 28(1). https://doi.org/10.1080/10872981.2023.2181052

Arvin Ash. (2023, April 8). *So How Does ChatGPT really work? Behind the screen!* [Video]. YouTube. www.youtube.com/watch?v=WAiqNav2cRE

Aydin, N., & Erdem, O. A. (2022). A research on the new generation Artificial Intelligence Technology generative pretraining transformer 3. In *2022 3rd International Informatics and Software Engineering Conference (IISEC)*. https://doi.org/10.1109/iisec56 263.2022.9998298

Bhattacharya, K., Bhattacharya, A. S., Bhattacharya, N., Yagnik, V. D., Garg, P., & Kumar, S. (2023). CHATGPT in surgical practice—a new kid on the block. *Indian Journal of Surgery*, 85, 1346–1349. https://doi.org/10.1007/s12262-023-03727-x

Biswas, S. S. (2023). Potential use of chat GPT in global warming. *Annals of Biomedical Engineering*, 51, 1126–1127. https://doi.org/10.1007/s10439-023-03171-8

Bostrom, N., & Yudkowsky, E. (2018). The ethics of artificial intelligence. In *Artificial Intelligence Safety and Security* (pp. 57–69). Chapman and Hall/CRC. https://doi.org/10.1201/9781032600628 www.taylorfrancis.com/chapters/edit/10.1201/9781351251389-4/ethics-artificial-intelligence-nick-bostrom-eliezer-yudkowsky

CA Rahul Malodia: Business Coach. (2023, March 4). *ChatGPT Vs Google | Explained In Hindi By Rahul Malodia* [Video]. YouTube. www.youtube.com/watch?v=J-1442w0l9g

Carvalho, I., & Ivanov, S. (2023). ChatGPT for tourism: Applications, benefits and risks. *Tourism Review*. www.emerald.com/insight/content/doi/10.1108/TR-02-2023-0088/full/html

Chatterjee, J., & Dethlefs, N. (2023). This new conversational AI model can be your friend, philosopher, and guide ... and even your worst enemy. *Patterns*, 4(1), 100676. https://doi.org/10.1016/j.patter.2022.100676

Dahmen, J., Kayaalp, M. E., Ollivier, M., Pareek, A., Hirschmann, M. T., Karlsson, J., & Winkler, P. W. (2023). Artificial Intelligence Bot CHATGPT in medical research: The potential game changer as a double-edged sword. *Knee Surgery, Sports Traumatology, Arthroscopy*, 31(4), 1187–1189. https://doi.org/10.1007/s00167-023-07355-6

Dergaa, I., Chamari, K., Zmijewski, P., & Saad, H. B. (2023). From human writing to artificial intelligence generated text: examining the prospects and potential threats of ChatGPT in academic writing. *Biology of Sport*, 40(2), 615–622.

DiGiorgio, A. M., & Ehrenfeld, J. M. (2023). Artificial intelligence in medicine & CHATGPT: DeTether the physician. *Journal of Medical Systems*, 47(1). https://doi.org/10.1007/s10916-023- 01926-3

Dwivedi, Y. K., Kshetri, N., Hughes, L., Slade, E. L., Jeyaraj, A., Kar, A. K., Baabdullah, A. M., Koohang, A., Raghavan, V., Ahuja, M., Albanna, H., Albashrawi, M. A., Al-Busaidi, A. S., Balakrishnan, J., Barlette, Y., Basu, S., Bose, I., Brooks, L., Buhalis, D., ...Wright, R. (2023). Opinion paper: "So what if ChatGPT wrote it?" Multidisciplinary perspectives on opportunities, challenges and implications of generative conversational AI for research, practice and policy. *International Journal of Information Management*, 71, 102642. https://doi.org/10.1016/j.ijinfomgt.2023.102642

Else, H. (2023). Abstracts written by CHATGPT fool scientists. *Nature*, 613(7944), 423–423. https://doi.org/10.1038/d41586-023-00056-7

Floridi, L., & Chiriatti, M. (2020). GPT-3: Its nature, scope, limits, and consequences. *Minds and Machines*, 30(4), 681–694. https://doi.org/10.1007/s11023-020-09548-1

Hsu, I. C., & Chang, C. C. (2021). Integrating machine learning and open data into social Chatbot for filtering information rumor. *Journal of Ambient Intelligence and Humanized Computing*, 12, 1023–1037. https://link.springer.com/article/10.1007/s12652-020-02119-3

Huang, J., Yeung, A. M., Kerr, D., & Klonoff, D. C. (2023). Using CHATGPT to predict the future of diabetes technology. *Journal of Diabetes Science and Technology*, 193229682311610. https://doi.org/10.1177/19322968231161095

IBM. (2017). *What is natural language processing?* www.ibm.com/topics/natural-languageprocessing

Jovanovic, M., & Campbell, M. (2022). Generative artificial intelligence: Trends and prospects. *Computer*, 55(10), 107–112. https://doi.org/10.1109/mc.2022.3192720

Keramatfar, A., Rafiee, M., & Amirkhani, H. (2022). Graph neural networks: A bibliometrics overview. *Machine Learning with Applications*, 10, 100401. https://doi.org/10.1016/j.mlwa.2022.100401

Khang, A. (Ed.) (2023). *AI and IoT-Based Technologies for Precision Medicine.* ISBN: 9798369308769. IGI Global Press. https://doi.org/10.4018/979-8-3693-0876-9

Khang A., Gujrati R., Uygun H., Tailor R. K., Gaur S. S. (2024). *Data-driven Modelling and Predictive Analytics in Business and Finance.* ISBN: 9781032600628. (1st Ed.). CRC Press. https://doi.org/10.1201/9781032600628

Khang, A., Inna, S.-O., Alla, K., Rostyslav, S., Rudenko, M., Lidia, R., & Kristina, B. (2024). Management model 6.0 and business recovery strategy of enterprises in the era of digital economy. In A. Khang, R. Gujrati, H. Uygun, R. K. Tailor, S. S. Gaur (Eds.), *Data-driven Modelling and Predictive Analytics in Business and Finance* (1st Ed.). CRC Press. https://doi.org/10.1201/9781032600628-16

Khang A., C. R. Kali, S. K. Satapathy, A. Kumar, S. R. Das, & M. R. Panda (2023). Enabling the future of manufacturing: Integration of robotics and iot to smart factory infrastructure in industry 4.0. In A. Khang, V. Shah, & S. Rani (Eds.), *AI-Based Technologies and Applications in the Era of the Metaverse* (1st Ed.) (pp. 25–50). IGI Global Press. https://doi.org/10.4018/978-1-6684-8851-5.ch002

Khang A., M. Muthmainnah, P. M. I. Seraj, A. Al Yakin, A. J. Obaid, & M. R. Panda. (2023). AI-aided teaching model for the education 5.0 ecosystem. In A. Khang, V. Shah, & S. Rani (Eds.), *AI-Based Technologies and Applications in the Era of the Metaverse* (1st Ed.) (pp. 83–104). IGI Global Press. https://doi.org/10.4018/978-1-6684-8851-5.ch004

Khang A., Shah V., & Rani S. (2023). *AI-Based Technologies and Applications in the Era of the Metaverse* (1st Ed.). IGI Global Press. https://doi.org/10.4018/978-1-6684-8851-5

King, M. R. (2023). A conversation on artificial intelligence, chatbots, and plagiarism in higher education. *Cellular and Molecular Bioengineering*, 16(1), 1–2. https://doi.org/10.1007/s12195-022-00754-8

Kirmani, A. R. (2022). Artificial Intelligence-enabled science poetry. *ACS Energy Letters*, 8(1), 574–576. https://doi.org/10.1021/acsenergylett.2c02758

Korzynski, P., Mazurek, G., Altmann, A., Ejdys, J., Kazlauskaite, R., Paliszkiewicz, J., & Ziemba, E. (2023). Generative artificial intelligence as a new context for management theories: analysis of ChatGPT. *Central European Management Journal*. www.emerald.com/insight/content/doi/10.1108/CEMJ-02-2023-0091/full/html

Kushwaha, A. K., & Kar, A. K. (2020). Language model-driven chatbot for business to address marketing and selection of products. In Re-imagining Diffusion and Adoption of Information Technology and Systems: A Continuing Conversation: IFIP WG 8.6 International Conference on Transfer and Diffusion of IT, TDIT 2020, Tiruchirappalli, India, December 18–19, 2020, Proceedings, Part I (pp. 16–28). Springer International Publishing. https://link.springer.com/chapter/10.1007/978-3-030-64849-7_3

Levesque, H. J. (2017). *Common Sense, The Turing Test, and the Quest for Real AI.* Mit Press. www.google.com/books?hl=en&lr=&id=ZYA1DgAAQBAJ&oi=fnd&pg=PR7&dq=Common+sense,+the+Turing+test,+and+the+quest+for+real+AI.+Mit+Press&ots=xvOlIczcKj&sig=xqGkyjtkPyyByYKplLsFSIObp0k

Lund, B. D., Wang, T., Mannuru, N. R., Nie, B., Shimray, S., & Wang, Z. (2023). Chatgpt and a new academic reality: Artificial intelligence-written research papers and the ethics of the large language models in scholarly publishing. *Journal of the Association for Information Science and Technology*, 74(5), 570–581. https://doi.org/10.1002/asi.24750

Marr, B. (2023, March 1). *The Advantages and Disadvantages of ChatGPT* [Video]. YouTube. www.youtube.com/watch?v=ESbBBSbWlCs

Marr, B. (2023, March 3). The top 10 limitations of ChatGPT. *Forbes.* www.forbes.com/sites/bernardmarr/2023/03/03/the-top-10-limitations-of-chatgpt/?sh=307989d28f35

Mijwil, M. M., ChatGPT, & Aljanabi, M. (2023). Towards artificial intelligence-based cybersecurity: The practices and CHATGPT generated ways to combat cybercrime.

Iraqi Journal for Computer Science and Mathematics, 65–70. https://doi.org/10.52866/ijcsm.2023.01.01.0019

Mishra, S., & Esaimani, V. (2020). A study on popularity of netflix among youth. *International Journal of Social Science and Human Research*, 3(3), 7–13. https://sdbindex.com/documents/00000273/00001-01696.pdf

Montti, R. (2023, February 2). 11 Disadvantages of ChatGPT content. *Search Engine Journal* (online). www.searchenginejournal.com/disadvantages-chatgpt-content/477416/#close

Moor, J. (Ed.). (2003). *The Turing Test: The elusive Standard of Artificial Intelligence* (Vol. 30). Springer Science & Business Media. www.google.com/books?hl=en&lr=&id=eGa9hs5GUToC&oi=fnd&pg=PA1&dq=The+Turing+test:+the+elusive+standard+of+artificial+intelligence+(Vol.+30).+Springer+Science+%26+Business+Media&ots=PODtieQr8e&sig=RRqzSo84VkZBTubpr-QLUvQq-C4

Muthmainnah, M., Khang, A., Seraj, P. M. I., Al Yakin, A., Oteir, I., Alotaibi, A. N. An innovative teaching model – The potential of metaverse for english learning. In A. Khang, V. Shah, & S. Rani (Eds.), *AI-Based Technologies and Applications in the Era of the Metaverse*. (1 Ed.) (2023). Page (105–126). IGI Global Press. https://doi.org/10.4018/978-1-6684-8851-5.ch005

Nature Editorial. (2023). Tools such as CHATGPT threaten transparent science; here are our ground rules for their use. *Nature*, 613(7945), 612–612. https://doi.org/10.1038/d41586-023-00191-1

Nuruzzaman, M., & Hussain, O. K. (2018, October). A survey on chatbot implementation in customer service industry through deep neural networks. In *2018 IEEE 15th International Conference on e-Business Engineering (ICEBE)* (pp. 54–61). IEEE. https://ieeexplore.ieee.org/abstract/document/9752271/

Patel, S. B., & Lam, K. (2023). Chatgpt: The future of discharge summaries? *The Lancet Digital Health*, 5(3). https://doi.org/10.1016/s2589-7500(23)00021-3

Pavlik, J. V. (2023), Collaborating with ChatGPT: considering the implications of generative artificial intelligence for journalism and media education. *Journalism and Mass Communication Educator*, 78(1). https://doi.org/10.1177/10776958221149577

Saadna, Y., Boudhir, A. A., & Ben Ahmed, M. (2022). An analysis of ResNet50 model and RMSprop optimizer for education platform using an intelligent chatbot system. In *Networking, Intelligent Systems and Security: Proceedings of NISS 2021* (pp. 577–590). Springer: Singapore.

Saxena, A. C., Ojha, A., Sobti, D., & Khang, A. (2023). Artificial Intelligence (AI) centric model in metaverse ecosystem. In A. Khang, V. Shah, & S. Rani (Eds.), *AI-Based Technologies and Applications in the Era of the Metaverse* (1st Ed.) (pp. 1–24). IGI Global Press. https://doi.org/10.4018/978-1-6684-8851-5.ch001

Scerri, A., & Morin, K. H. (2023). Using chatbots like chatgpt to support nursing practice. *Journal of Clinical Nursing*, 32(15–16), 4211–4213. https://doi.org/10.1111/jocn.16677

Singhal, T. (2023, February 24). ChatGPT: How HR leaders see its impact and potentials. *ETHRWorld.com*. https://hr.economictimes.indiatimes.com/news/trends/chatgpt-how-hr-leaders-see-its-impact-and-potentials/98193157

Stokel-Walker, C. (2023). CHATGPT listed as author on research papers: Many scientists disapprove. *Nature*, 613(7945), 620–621. https://doi.org/10.1038/d41586-023-00107-z

Thornton, J., D'Souza, R., & Tandon, R. (2023). Artificial intelligence and psychiatry research and practice. *Asian Journal of Psychiatry*, 81, 103509. https://doi.org/10.1016/j.ajp.2023.103509

Uchendu, A., Ma, Z., Le, T., Zhang, R., & Lee, D. (2021). Turingbench: A benchmark environment for turing test in the age of neural text generation. *arXiv preprint* arXiv:2109.13296.

van Dis, E. A., Bollen, J., Zuidema, W., van Rooij, R., & Bockting, C. L. (2023). ChatGPT: Five priorities for research. *Nature*, 614(7947), 224–226. https://doi.org/ 10.1038/d41586-023-00288-7

Warikoo. (2023, February 11). *STUDENTS – Use CHATGPT to WIN in your CAREER! | ChatGPT for Beginners | Ankur Warikoo*. YouTube. www.youtube.com/watch?v=L9u3 vQF9C88

Wu, C., Yin, S., Qi, W., Wang, 20., Tang, Z., & Duan, N. (2023). Visual chatgpt: Talking, drawing and editing with visual foundation models. *arXiv preprint* arXiv:2303.04671.

Zhou, C., Li, Q., Li, C., Yu, J., Liu, Y., Wang, G., & Sun, L. (2023). A comprehensive survey on pretrained foundation models: A history from bert to chatgpt. *arXiv preprint* arXiv:2302.09419

21 Cloud Data Security Using Advanced Encryption Standard with Ant Colony Optimization in Business Sector

M.P. Karthikeyan, V. Praba, A. Kannagi, R. Kavitha, and K. Krishnaveni

21.1 INTRODUCTION

The systematic recording of a certain amount is known as data. It is a collection of depictions of the many values of that quantity. It is a collection of information that will be utilized to achieve a specific goal, such an analysis or survey. It can be referred to as "information" when it is structured. Data refers to information that is used or stored by a computer. One kind of data is information obtained for a study piece. Data are frequently employed in economics, science, and practically every other aspect of human organizational activity (Khang, Muthmainnah et al., 2023).

Unemployment rates, census, and literacy rates statistics are a few examples of data sets. Data that is in use is information that a system is currently updating, processing, deleting, accessing, or reading. This kind of data is actively traveling across various components of an IT (information technology) infrastructure rather than being passively stored. Digital information is saved on servers that are located off-site and is referred to as "cloud storage" in the context of computer data storage. A third-party provider is in charge of hosting, administering, and protecting the data kept on its infrastructure, and it is they who manage the servers (Khang, Hahanov et al., 2022).

Also, your need for extra bandwidth might be swiftly satisfied by a cloud-based solution as opposed to necessitating a difficult (and expensive) update to your IT infrastructure. Cloud technology is currently primarily employed across all industries, as shown in Figure 21.1. A particularly intriguing cryptographic method is secret sharing. In fact, its most sophisticated variations do maintain data privacy,

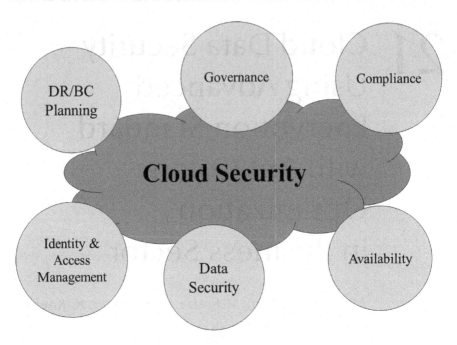

FIGURE 21.1 Cloud data security.

Source: Khang (2021).

availability, and integrity while enabling computation on encrypted data (Attasena et al., 2017).

Database security tools provide specialized database protection in addition to conventional endpoint and network security options (Sivanantham et al., 2022). In theory, intrusion detection systems and firewalls currently protect databases from unauthorized activity. However, databases must be safeguarded independently.

Production data are the information required to carry out regular business operations. Production data must be consistently kept and easily accessible for frequent and effective access. Engineers use production data to make cost-effective forecasting and budgeting decisions. Production data are information that is continuously accumulated and used by experts to carry out business operations (Sivanantham et al., 2023). To ensure its usefulness to the organization, information must be accurate, documented, and continuously controlled, as shown in Figure 21.2.

21.1.1 Cyber-Attack

Any aggressive action against computer information systems, computer networks, infrastructures, personal computers, or smartphones is known as a cyber-attack. A machine learning algorithm is the process an AI system employs to achieve its goal, which is frequently to anticipate output values from the input data. Machine learning systems use two core techniques: regression and classification. Cloud data security

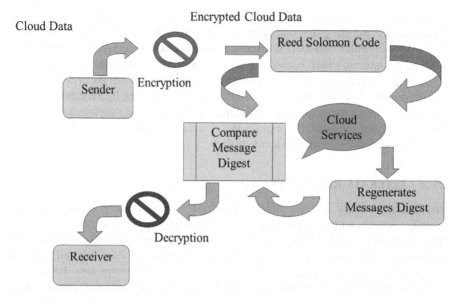

FIGURE 21.2   Basic security of cloud computing.

Source: Khang (2021).

refers to the technology, rules, services, and security procedures that prevent loss, leakage, or misuse of any type of data stored in the cloud via breaches, exfiltration, and unauthorized access (Bharany et al., 2022). Virtual private networks (VPNs), firewalls, penetration testing, obfuscation, tokenization, and avoiding public internet connections are a few techniques for ensuring cloud security.

21.1.2   CRYPTOLOGY IN CLOUD COMPUTING

In contrast to direct communication with a server, cloud computing uses a variety of techniques to deliver the service via the internet. It is difficult and expensive to store files on hard drives, for example, and it is essentially impossible to access them from a distant location. Therefore, the best solution to this issue is cloud computing. One of the most important methods for attaining information security, which is becoming increasingly important in computer systems and communication networks, is cryptology. The science of creating and analyzing various encryption and decryption techniques is known as cryptology (Grari et al., 2019). The Rijndael algorithm is another name for the 128-bit symmetric block cypher technique known as the Advanced Encryption Standard (AES).

21.1.3   ANT COLONY OPTIMIZATION TECHNIQUES

An optimization algorithm called Ant Colony Optimization (ACO) makes use of graphs to find the best path and tackle computation-related problems. The ant colony technique has an advantage over methods employing genetic algorithms and simulated annealing because the graph may alter dynamically (Alam, 2022). The combination of the AES algorithm and ACO is discussed here as a novel method for securing data in cloud computing, which is used for both business and production methods.

This chapter is arranged into five parts. Section 21.2 II explains the present method and the drawbacks of techniques in cloud data security obtained by a literature review. Section 21.3 explains the proposed techniques in data security with machine learning ACO techniques. Section 21.4 presents the experimental results and their graph analysis, and Section 21.5 provides a conclusion.

21.2 LITERATURE REVIEW

The literature review covered some of the strategies that are now in use to address security concerns with cloud computing. Cloud computing was discussed by Rao and Selvamani (2015). Although it offers many advantages to users, cloud computing also has many security issues. This survey discusses data security concerns and provides solutions in an effort to reduce the risk connected with cloud computing. RSA-based storage security can process enormous files of different sizes and take care of remote data security. It is conceivable for cloud computing security standards to improve further.

Yan et al. (2017) discovered, however, that the success of cloud computing is impacted by issues with cloud data security, data privacy and also trust, which could also delay the development of 5G and the Conseil provincial du secteur des communications (CPSC) (CPSC, 2020). The risk of data leakage and unauthorized access increases when data and stored on the cloud, to start. Second, assaults and intrusions are increasingly targeting cloud data centers, posing a threat to cloud data security. Also, the owners of the data may not have complete confidence in the management activities, such as the data storage, backup, update, search, query, migration, deletion, and access in the cloud. Fourth, the processing and computing of data in the cloud could give unauthorized parties access to the privacy of data owners or connected companies (Duo et al., 2022). Cloud computing success is in fact being impacted by a number of major challenges, including cloud data security, privacy, and trust (Khang, Hahanov et al., 2022).

The current approaches remain flawed and ineffective, making them impracticable. Although the risk of privacy leakage is significantly decreased, it is challenging to carry out auditing on data management when encrypted. Cloud computing offers many creative solutions, but there are also many obstacles to be solved. In order to debate the many facets of cryptography and data security in cloud computing, study important theories, examine technological enablers, and create noteworthy applications, this special issue intends to bring researchers and practitioners together, and come up with new strategies to overcome significant obstacles in this exciting research field (Sivanantham et al., 2022).

Zhang (2021) deals, generally, with symmetric and asymmetric encryption, which are the two types of encryption used in cryptography. Even while symmetric encryption has a very quick processing time and is effective for encrypting enormous volumes of the data, its security is not as great as asymmetric encryption's. Symmetric algorithms that use the same pair of keys expose users to security problems. Therefore, security may be improved if the key can be locked away. It makes sense to use symmetric encryption for the message and asymmetric algorithm security for the key. In order to illustrate how the reinforcement achieved by mixing algorithms works, it will be investigated and analyzed how different algorithms in different systems differ, as well as some typical hybrid encryption scenarios (Zhou et al., 2022). Hybrid encryption algorithms increase transmission security without adding to existing issues.

Khan and Qazi (2019) state that sensitive information can be sent over an insecure channel with the help of encryption without running the risk of it being lost or altered by an unauthorized party. For data security, many encryption techniques have been used in various environments. Many cryptosystems were operational in various times and changed as time went on. Research demonstrates that elliptic curve cryptography is quick and more effective for securing data in a cloud computing context, requiring less computational resources while maximizing efficiency.

Chinnasamy et al. (2021) combine high levels of data security, confidentiality, and introduced. They uses a hybrid algorithm in this passage by fusing elliptic curve cryptography (ECC) with Blowfish. Al-gohany and Almotairi (2019) compared and introduced AES combined with DES. Because of this, security in cloud computing is an important and major concern for cloud data. Researchers are very interested in the risk of malicious cloud activity and cloud service failure. Here, we give a comparison of cutting-edge methods for resolving these problems, including elliptical curve cryptography (ECC) and Blowfish algorithms, as well as their implementation. Our comparison and testing of the two algorithms on a range of file sizes revealed that while DES is quicker than AES on large files when it comes to decryption, AES is faster on small ones (Kavitha et al., 2023). AES decrypts more data quicker than DES due to a significant improvement in DES performance and a slight improvement in AES speed. The results show that AES is a more efficient, rapid, and beautiful encryption technique.

Rokade and Lomte (2017) give a cryptographic method using Ant Colony Optimization. We might infer from this that the largest barrier to widespread adoption of cloud computing is security. Cloud computing faces server security issues from the perspective of the user. Here, emphasis is placed on steganography, cryptography, and Ant Colony Optimization methods. Qureshi et al. (2022) indicated that there have been numerous encryption algorithms and the data privacy models stated in the literature to deal with the problems that have arisen, but there remain questions that need to be answered. After evaluating several encryption algorithms for the data distributed by the various appliances in the smart architecture, it can be said that choosing an algorithm based on the demands of the organization must strike a delicate balance between complexity and security. An algorithm that contains less complexity might not be suitable for highly sensitive material and will often take longer to encrypt or decode data (Rani, Bhambri et al., 2023).

Timothy and Santra (2017) studied the many kinds of algorithms used in cloud computing to help firms manage their huge amounts of information. Data security is the biggest concern with cloud computing because many clients share the same cloud. This study intended to provide a novel security solution for cloud data security utilizing a mixed-model cryptosystem. For data integrity, this kind of approach also uses the Secure Hash Algorithm. This study came to the conclusion that the system offers excellent network access when needed to a shared pool of beneficial computer resources, primarily the internet, servers, and storage applications (Sriram, 2022). It also offers good security on data transfer over the internet. From the above surveys, some of the demerits are notified and overcome by the new approach of the proposed system (Rani, Chauhan et al., 2021).

21.3   SYSTEM DESIGN

This section explains about the proposed system design consisting of the combination of AES ACO.

21.3.1   Advanced Encryption Standard (AES)

One of the most used encryption and decryption techniques is AES. The block cypher algorithm is used in this encrypted manner to ensure that data may be kept safely. The symmetric encryption algorithm that is most likely to be discovered nowadays is the:

- 128 bit;
- 192 bit.

The AES is more often used and adapted (AES), And its design is shown in Figure 21.3.

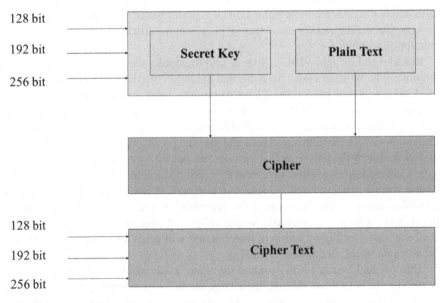

FIGURE 21.3   AES design.

Source: Khang, (2021).

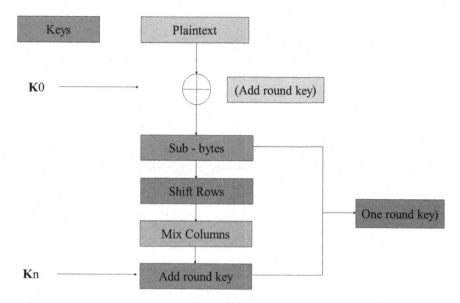

FIGURE 21.4 Steps followed in AES.

Source: Khang (2021).

Steps followed in the AES are shown in Figure 21.4. For each block, the aforementioned steps must be carried out in turn. Once each block has been successfully encrypted, it links the encrypted blocks to produce the final cipher text.

21.3.2 ENCRYPTION AND DECRYPTION USING ANT COLONY OPTIMIZATION

These algorithms were created as a result of research into the behavior of ants in colonies. Nonetheless, as ants are social insects, their behavior is dictated by the fact that they prioritize individual survival over colony survival, as shown in Figure 21.5.

Other ants will follow the pheromone trail to the food source. Because of the pheromone evaporation mechanism, old pathways are less likely to be employed. The behavior of food sources, in particular the capacity to investigate routes between food sources and their nest and determine which is the shortest, served as an inspiration for the creation of ACO. A method of creating encryption keys is based on ACO. A stream cypher technique is used to represent and encrypt the data image as text. The below code block 21.1 shows the Outline of ACO Pseudo Code.

Code block 21.1: Procedure ACO Pseudo Code

1. Initialize the necessary parameters and pheromone concentration;
2. while not termination do:
3. Generate initial ant population;

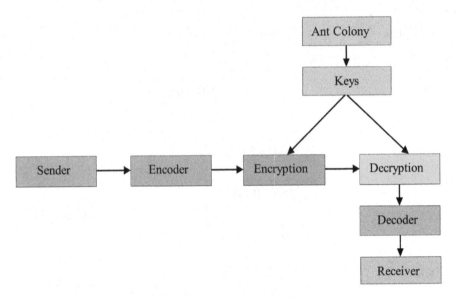

FIGURE 21.5 Encryption and decryption using ACO.

4. Calculate the fitness values for each ant of the colony;
5. Find optimal solution using selection methods;
6. Update pheromone concentration;
7. end while
8. end procedure

21.3.3 DATA SECURITY USING AES AND ACO

The suggested method is seen in Figure 21.6 and combines the AES and ACO. The main aim of the ACO is to use the recurring artificial ants to generate fresh answers to the current issue. The ants use the knowledge that was previously obtained to guide their quest, and this knowledge is available to and adaptable through the environment. We can quickly compute and locate keys in each round by using the following equation (21.1):

$$K [n]: w[i] \text{ equals } K [n-1]: w[i] \text{ XOR } K [n]: w[i] \tag{21.1}$$

Instead of using w0 to find a key for every round that this equation uses, we must employ a specific equation for w0 that is distinct from the equation above as shown in Equation (21.2).

$$
\begin{aligned}
&\text{SubByte } (k [n\text{-}1]: w3>>8) \\
&\quad \text{XOR Rcon I} \\
&\qquad \text{XOR } K[n]: w0 = K[n]: w0 \\
&\qquad\quad \text{XOR } K [n\text{-}1]: w0 \\
&\qquad\qquad \text{XOR.}
\end{aligned}
\tag{21.2}
$$

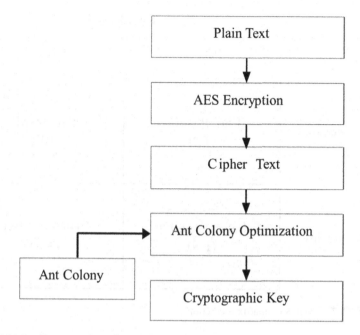

FIGURE 21.6   Data security using AES and ACO.

Source: Khang (2021).

21.4   RESULTS AND DISCUSSION

This section examines and discusses a comparison of the proposed system with the current systems and its performance results, which included accuracy ratings of 86.75%, sensitivity ratings of 82.32%, specificity ratings of 88.20%, and precision ratings of 84.65%. From these experiments, the proposed system with the novel method of cloud data security is more effective than the existing systems.

21.4.1   CONFUSION MATRIX

The confusion matrix was used to evaluate the effectiveness of the post-categorization procedures. It provides examples of correctly categorized true negative (TN) values that belong in a different class as well as flawlessly classified true positive (TP) values, false positive (FP) values that belong in one class but not another, and false negative (FN) values that belong in one class but not another, as shown in Figure 21.7.

21.4.2   ACCURACY

Calculate the percentage of true positive and true negative results across all analyzed instances to estimate a test's accuracy. This can be expressed mathematically as follows (Equation [21.3]).

$$\text{Accuracy} = TP + TN \: / \: TP + TN + FP + FN \tag{21.3}$$

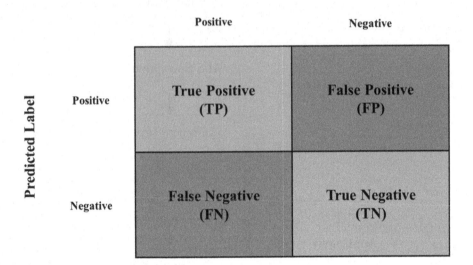

FIGURE 21.7   Confusion matrix prediction.

TABLE 21.1
Accuracy Results for the Proposed and Existing Systems

Algorithm	Result
PSO	76.40
SVM	80.25
ECC	78.65
AES + ACO	86.75

Table 21.1 shows that the accuracy for the proposed and also the existing system. The table concludes that the existing system of PSO, SVM, and ECC techniques achieve results of 76.40, 80.25, and 78.65, and the proposed system achieves a result of 86.75, which is 8.1 percentage higher than the existing system. The results are shown in Figure 21.8.

Sensitivity: The TP rate is the proportion of positive values among all truly positive events (TPR).

$$\text{Sensitivity} = TP/TP + FN \qquad (21.4)$$

The sensitivity for both the proposed and existing systems is shown in Table 21.2. The table concludes that the existing system of PSO, SVM, and ECC techniques achieves 74.23, 71.89, and 80.14, while the proposed system achieves 82.32, which is 2.18 percent higher than the existing system. The result are shown in Figure 21.9.

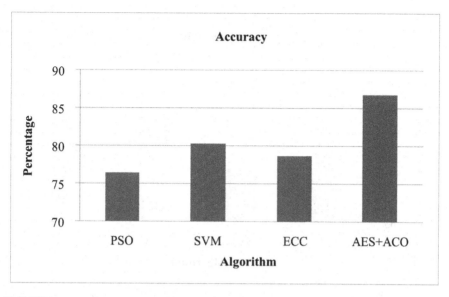

FIGURE 21.8   Accuracy graph.

TABLE 21.2
Sensitivity Results for the Proposed and Existing Systems

Algorithm	Result
PSO	74.23
SVM	71.89
ECC	80.14
AES + ACO	82.32

Specificity: Calculating specificity involves dividing the total number of negatives by the number of accurate negative predictions (TN).

$$\text{Specificity} = \text{TN/TN+FP} \qquad (21.5)$$

Table 21.3 shows the specificity for both the proposed and existing systems. According to the table, the existing system of PSO, SVM, and ECC techniques achieves 74.36, 72.47, and 83.60, whereas the proposed system achieves 88.20, 4.6 percent higher than the existing system. The result are shows in Figure 21.10.

Precision: Precision is the degree to which measurements of the same thing agree with one another.

$$\text{Precision} = \text{TP/TP+FP} \qquad (21.6)$$

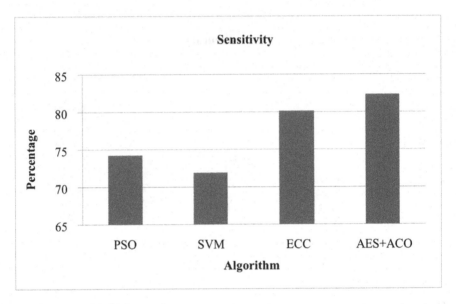

FIGURE 21.9   Sensitivity graph.

TABLE 21.3
Specificity Results for the Proposed and Existing Systems

Algorithm	Result
PSO	74.36
SVM	72.47
ECC	83.60
AES + ACO	88.20

Precision is shown in Table 21.4 for both the proposed and existing systems. The existing system of PSO, SVM, and ECC techniques achieves 78.20, 77.70, and 82.00 according to the table, whereas the proposed system achieves 84.65, 2.65 percent higher than the existing system. The result are shows in Figure 21.11.

21.5   CONCLUSION

Since the data carried via the network are more susceptible to fraud and eavesdropping, encryption is a crucial concern in wired and wireless communication. The solutions to handle some of the security problems in the wireless sensor network are surveyed. While some of the techniques made use of standard cryptographic procedures, others made use of cryptography optimization techniques. The novel method for cracking

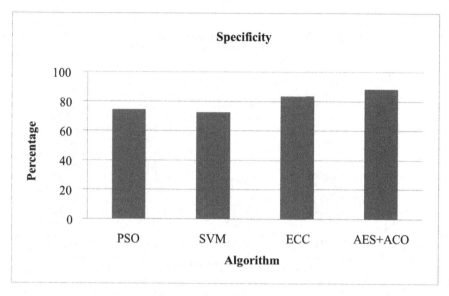

FIGURE 21.10 Specificity graph.

TABLE 21.4
Precision Results for the Proposed and Existing Systems

Algorithm	Result
PSO	78.20
SVM	77.70
ECC	82.00
AES + ACO	84.65

the Advanced Encryption Standard was revealed in this chapter using Ant Colony Optimization. This approach proved to be quite successful and promising (Khang, Shah et al., 2023).

The experimental findings demonstrate that, when compared to previous methods, our methodology is substantially faster and requires fewer known plaintext and ciphertext combinations. When paired with AES, ACO offers a very potent tool for cloud computing encryption. It is fascinating to use this tool for the cryptography of other powerful encryption algorithms, such as AES (Advanced Encryption Standard). This study presents these diverse optimization-based ideas while also highlighting their benefits and rectifying their drawbacks (Khang, Kali et al., 2023).

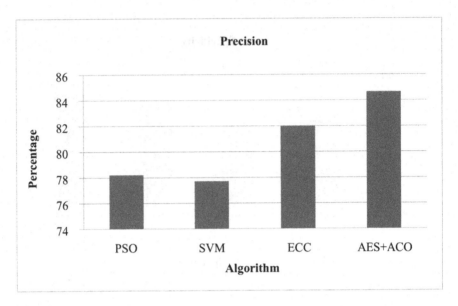

FIGURE 21.11   Precision graph.

REFERENCES

Alam, A. (2022). Cloud-Based E-learning: Scaffolding the Environment for Adaptive E-learning Ecosystem Based on Cloud Computing Infrastructure. In *Computer Communication, Networking and IoT: Proceedings of 5th ICICC 2021*, Volume 2 (pp. 1–9). Singapore: Springer Nature Singapore. https://link.springer.com/chapter/10.1007/978-981-19-1976-3_1

Al-gohany, N. A., & Almotairi, S. (2019). Comparative study of database security in cloud computing using AES and DES encryption algorithms. *Journal of Information Security and Cybercrimes Research*, 2(1), 102–109. https://journals.nauss.edu.sa/index.php/JISCR/article/download/859/973

Attasena, V., Darmont, J., & Harbi, N. (2017). Secret sharing for cloud data security: A survey. *The VLDB Journal*, 26(5), 657–681. https://link.springer.com/article/10.1007/s00778-017-0470-9

Bharany, S., Sharma, S., Khalaf, O. I., Abdulsahib, G. M., Al Humaimeedy, A. S., Aldhyani, T. H., ... & Alkahtani, H. (2022). A systematic survey on energyefficient techniques in sustainable cloud computing. *Sustainability*, 14(10), 6256. https://www.mdpi.com/2071-1050/14/10/6256

Chinnasamy, P., Padmavathi, S., Swathy, R., & Rakesh, S. (2021). Efficient data security using hybrid cryptography on cloud computing. In *Inventive Communication and Computational Technologies: Proceedings of ICICCT 2020* (pp. 537–547). Springer: Singapore. https://link.springer.com/chapter/10.1007/978-981-15-7345-3_46

Conseil provincial du secteur des communications (CPSC). (2020). The Yale Report: CPSC is expecting quick action by the government to regulate web giants. https://cupe.ca/yale-report-cpsc-expecting-quick-action-government-regulate-web-giants

Duo, W., Zhou, M., & Abusorrah, A. (2022). A survey of cyber-attacks on cyber physical systems: Recent advances and challenges. *IEEE/CAA Journal of Automatica Sinica*, 9(5), 784–800. https://ieeexplore.ieee.org/abstract/document/9763485/

Grari, H., Azouaoui, A., & Zine-Dine, K. (2019). A cryptanalytic attack of simplified-AES using ant colony optimization. *International Journal of Electrical & Computer Engineering (2088-8708)*, 9(5). https://core.ac.uk/download/pdf/333845122.pdf

Kavitha, R., Jothi, D. K., Saravanan, K., Swain, M. P., Gonzáles, J. L. A., Bhardwaj, R. J., & Adomako, E. (2023). Ant colony optimization-enabled CNN deep learning technique for accurate detection of cervical cancer. *BioMed Research International*, 2023, 1742891. www.hindawi.com/journals/bmri/2023/1742891/

Khan, I. A., & Qazi, R. (2019). Data security in cloud computing using elliptic curve cryptography. *International Journal of Computing and Communication Networks*, 1(1), 46–52. www.ijccn.com/index.php/IJCCN/article/view/15

Khang, A., Hahanov, V., Abbas, G. L., & Hajimahmud, V. A. (2022). Cyber-physical-social system and incident management. In *AI-Centric Smart City Ecosystems: Technologies, Design and Implementation* (1st Ed.), Volume 7 (p. 12). CRC Press. https://doi.org/10.1201/9781003252542-2

Khang, A., Kali, C. R., Satapathy, S. K., Kumar, A., Ranjan Das, S., & Panda, M. R. (2023). Enabling the future of manufacturing: Integration of robotics and IoT to smart factory infrastructure in Industry 4.0. In A. Khang, V. Shah, & S. Rani (Eds.), *AI-Based Technologies and Applications in the Era of the Metaverse* (1st Ed.) (pp. 25–50). IGI Global Press. https://doi.org/10.4018/978-1-6684-8851-5.ch002

Khang, A., Muthmainnah, M., Seraj, P. M. I., Al Yakin, A., Obaid, A. J., & Panda, M. R. (2023). AI-aided teaching model for the education 5.0 ecosystem. In A. Khang, V. Shah, & S. Rani (Eds.), *AI-Based Technologies and Applications in the Era of the Metaverse* (1st Ed.) (pp. 83–104). IGI Global Press. https://doi.org/10.4018/978-1-6684-8851-5.ch004

Khang, A., Shah, V., & Rani, S. (2023). *AI-Based Technologies and Applications in the Era of the Metaverse* (1st Ed.). IGI Global Press. https://doi.org/10.4018/978-1-6684-8851-5

Qureshi, M. B., Qureshi, M. S., Tahir, S., Anwar, A., Hussain, S., Uddin, M., & Chen, C. L. (2022). Encryption techniques for smart systems data security offloaded to the cloud. *Symmetry*, 14(4), 695. www.mdpi.com/2073-8994/14/4/695

Rani, S., Bhambri, P., Kataria, A., Khang, A., & Sivaraman, A. K. (2023). *Big Data, Cloud Computing and IoT: Tools and Applications* (1st Ed.). Chapman and Hall/CRC. https://doi.org/10.1201/9781003298335

Rani, S., Chauhan, M., Kataria, A., & Khang A. (2021). IoT equipped intelligent distributed framework for smart healthcare systems. In *Computer Science, Networking and Internet Architecture* (Eds.). Volume 2 (p. 30) https://doi.org/10.48550/arXiv.2110.04997

Rao, R. V., & Selvamani, K. (2015). Data security challenges and its solutions in cloud computing. *Procedia Computer Science*, 48, 204–209. www.sciencedirect.com/science/article/pii/S1877050915006808

Rokade, M. P., & Lomte, S. S. (2017). A survey on ACO and cryptography techniques for cloud computing security and privacy. *International Journal*, 2(10). www.researchgate.net/profile/Poonam-Rokade/publication/348327025_A_Survey_on_ACO_and_Cryptography_Techniques_for_Cloud_Computing_Security_and_Privacy/links/5ff82d51299bf140887dbde5/A-Survey-on-ACO-and-Cryptography-Techniques-for-Cloud-Computing-Security-and-Privacy.pdf

Sivanantham, K., Kalaiarasi, I., & Leena, B. (2022). Brain tumor classification using hybrid artificial neural network with chicken swarm optimization algorithm in digital image processing application. In Narendra Kumar, Celia Shahnaz, Krishna Kumar, Mazin Abed Mohammed, Ram Shringar Raw (Eds.) *Advance Concepts of Image Processing and Pattern Recognition: Effective Solution for Global Challenges* (pp. 91–108). Singapore. https://link.springer.com/chapter/10.1007/978-981-16-9324-3_5

Sivanantham, K., Praveen P, B., Deepa, V., & Kumar, R. M. (2023). Cybercrime sentimental analysis for child youtube video dataset using hybrid support vector machine with ant colony optimization algorithm. In P. Deepa & K. Kumar (Eds.), *In Kids Cybersecurity Using Computational Intelligence Techniques* (pp. 175–193). Cham: Springer International Publishing. https://link.springer.com/chapter/10.1007/978-3-031-21199-7_13

Sriram, G. S. (2022). Edge computing vs. Cloud computing: an overview of big data challenges and opportunities for large enterprises. *International Research Journal of Modernization in Engineering Technology and Science*, 4(1), 13311337. www.irjmets.com/uploadedfiles/paper/issue_1_january_2022/18590/final/fin_irjmets1643224039.pdf

Timothy, D. P., & Santra, A. K. (2017, August). A hybrid cryptography algorithm for cloud computing security. In *2017 International Conference on Microelectronic Devices, Circuits and Systems (ICMDCS)* (pp. 1–5). IEEE. https://ieeexplore.ieee.org/abstract/document/8211728/

Yan, Z., Deng, R. H., & Varadharajan, V. (2017). *Cryptography and data security in cloud computing*. https://ink.library.smu.edu.sg/sis_research/3800/

Zhang, Q. (2021, January). An overview and analysis of hybrid encryption: The combination of symmetric encryption and asymmetric encryption. In *2021 2nd International Conference on Computing and Data Science (CDS)* (pp. 616–622). IEEE. https://ieeexplore.ieee.org/abstract/document/9463286/

Zhou, X., Ma, H., Gu, J., Chen, H., & Deng, W. (2022). Parameter adaptationbased ant colony optimization with dynamic hybrid mechanism. *Engineering Applications of Artificial Intelligence*, 114, 105139. www.sciencedirect.com/science/article/pii/S0952197622002639

22 Cybersecurity Techniques for Business and Finance Systems

Harshita Jadwani, Himanshi Shukla, Rajat Verma, and Namrata Dhanda

22.1 INTRODUCTION

The prevalence of the Internet causes several problems. From that first small network of linked computers, it grew to incorporate additional machines from other governments and institutions. Both browsers and servers gained additional capabilities. Servers no longer just delivered content, they also enabled user involvement, such as allowing users to submit content. A mechanism created for one purpose was once again modified to perform tasks for which it was not designed, and the new uses have become better than the original. The size of cyberspace changed when more than half of the world's population got equipment that allowed them to join, and servers became larger and faster in response.

The cybersecurity issues may be traced back to Arpanet, a network that linked computers in government and academic institutions and operated under the assumption that all users were reliable and responsible. As a result, security concerns were not taken seriously while designing the fundamentals of Arpanet, and many of those ideas are still in use today. The main issue is backward compatibility, as the size and scope of the system grew, each new development had to continue to allow older computers, networks, and systems to function together. Because of the increased use of the internet at present, cybersecurity is one of the most important needs globally. Cybersecurity attacks pose a serious threat to national security. To make sure that network security and system settings remain virus-free, people should be made aware of the value of regularly updating system and network security settings by both the government and citizens.

One can no longer function in daily life without internet-enabled technology. New technology advancements and services are regularly developed to enhance one's daily life. This simultaneously exposes a lot of security issues. It is essential to adhere to appropriate security precautions. Any device or service can be the victim of cybercrime at any time, with the worst possible impact. It's crucial to completely understand cybersecurity and to be able to implement it successfully in the advanced world, which is run by technology and network connections. System integrity, critical files and data, and other significant virtual assets are in danger if there is no security to protect them. Every business, whether an IT firm or not, needs to be protected equally.

DOI: 10.1201/9781032618845-22

New cybersecurity solutions are being developed, but this does not keep attackers powerless, they attack the security weaknesses of several businesses throughout the world using modern hacking techniques. Cybersecurity is essential because of the vast quantities of data that the military, government, financial, medical, and business sectors gather, use, and store on devices (Schatz et al., 2017). It is also essential in case of sensitive data, such as financial information, intellectual property, personal data, and other forms of data for which unauthorized access might have negative consequences. Data security and privacy are always the most important security precautions that any organization takes. Nowadays, all information is saved digitally. Social networking sites allow users to interact with friends and family in an environment where they feel protected and hence social networking platforms will continue to be a target for cybercriminals looking to acquire the personal data of users (Khang, Hahanov et al., 2022).

Another aspect of cybersecurity threat is online banking. One must take all necessary security precautions during online bank transactions. Recently, the Reserve Bank of India was the victim of yet another cybersecurity attack in India's banking industry, and they suffered a significant loss as a result. The hackers gained access using a false RBI employee ID and one of the bank employees was deceived by a phishing email and clicked on a malicious link, which allowed the virus to manipulate the system. Therefore, cybersecurity in online banking and transactions is an issue that cannot be compromised. The banking sector is a more popular target for hackers. As a result, there is a need to have flawless cybersecurity techniques and methods that don't compromise the privacy of users, bank data, and as well as financial information (Verma, Dhanda et al., 2021).

22.2 FUNDAMENTALS OF CYBER-ATTACKS

Cyber-attack is a significant concern because it has an impact on many areas of life, including the capacity to safeguard intellectual property, maintain the integrity of essential infrastructure, and maintain economic stability and national security. It takes a multifaceted approach to address cybersecurity concerns, encompassing technology, policies, education, and international cooperation. The major fundamentals of cyber-attacks are explained below.

22.2.1 CYBER-ATTACK: AN OVERVIEW

Any malicious behavior or attempt to undermine the safety, integrity, or accessibility of computer systems, networks, or electronic devices is referred to as a cyber-attack. It involves unauthorized access to computer systems, networks, or information they contain, as well as their disruption or damage. Hackers can act alone or in groups to launch cyber-attacks for a variety of reasons, including monetary gain, political action, intelligence, or general disruption. To obtain access without authorization, steal data, interfere with operations, or propagate malware, these assaults take advantage of flaws in networks, computer systems, or software. The persons who carry out cyber-attacks are frequently referred to as hackers or cybercriminals (Azizi & Haass, 2022). They could work alone or together with other attackers, or as a part of an organized crime group. They try to use computer system faults to achieve their goals by searching for them and trying to exploit them.

Cyber-attacks are practiced for a variety of reasons by cybercriminals. Some target individuals for financial or personal gain. Some are "hacktivists" who act for social or political reasons. Some cyber-attacks are committed as a part of known terrorist organizations or as part of nation-states' cyber warfare campaigns (Craigen et al., 2014).

22.2.2 TYPES OF CYBER-ATTACKS

Some of the major types of cyber-attacks are described below.

1. *Denial-of-Service (DoS) Attack:* A DoS cyber-attack prevents authorized users from accessing a computer or network. It overloads a server's bandwidth by bombarding it with a lot of requests from the internet. In distributed denial-of-service (DDoS) attacks, a sizable network of malware-infected computers or other devices is used to generate online requests that block access (Arun & Selvakumar, 2009).

2. *Malware:* Malware or "malicious software," is any program or piece of code that has been purposefully created to enter computer systems or networks to cause harm, disruption, or allow unauthorized access. It is intended to compromise the availability, confidentiality, or integrity of data and systems and was developed with malicious intent (Sharma et al., 2016).

3. *Man-in-the-Middle Attacks:* A cyber-attack known as a man-in-the-middle attack, occurs when an uninvited third party interrupts a discussion between two users while avoiding them. The malware that is causing the attack frequently watches over and changes sensitive or private data. Using a man-in-the-middle attack as a protocol, an outsider can access, read, and edit sensitive information (Conti et al., 2016).

4. *Internet of Things (IoT) attacks:* IoT devices can be hacked to be used in DDoS attacks, man-in-the-middle attacks, and hijacking. Malware is easier to use to hide the availability of IoT data, and occasionally IoT devices may set up with malware. Some IoT devices may also be vulnerable to malicious actors being able to remotely control or stop their operation (Nawir et al., 2016).

5. *SQL injection:* The SQL injection attack is one of the most dangerous security issues in web application systems as most of these flaws are caused by faulty input validation and the use of SQL parameters. The detection methods validate user input in addition to using type-safe SQL parameters. A SQL injection defense model that is resilient against SQL injection vulnerabilities is created using the detection processes (Mohd et al., 2018).

22.2.3 FACTORS TO OVERCOME CYBER-ATTACKS

Cyber-attack defense involves a thorough strategy that considers many variables. The following are some factors to overcome it.

- *Risk Assessment:* To find potential weaknesses and risks in the systems, networks, and data, perform a complete risk assessment. Effective resource allocation and effort prioritization are made possible by this assessment.
- *Security Education:* Encourage a strong security culture within the company by offering personnel frequent training and education sessions. Inform them of typical online dangers, social engineering techniques, secure web browsing habits, and the value of strong passwords.
- *Strong Verification and Access Controls:* To safeguard user accounts and systems, utilize strong authentication techniques like Multifactor Authentication (MFA). Use the least privilege principle by giving users only the access privileges that are required for performing their duties and obligations.
- *Update Programs and Operating Systems:* Update regularly to include the most recent security updates. Apply fixes and updates as soon as possible to patch up known issues and prevent exploits (Wu, 2017).
- *Configure Systems:* Configure network equipment and software securely by adhering to industry best practices. This ensures turning off pointless services, altering default passwords, and putting in place suitable security settings (Stewart et al., 2017).
- *Network Division:* To lessen the effects of a potential breach, divide your network into distinct zones. This aids in containing assaults and stops attackers from moving across within the network.
- *Intrusion Detection and Prevention Systems (IDPS):* IDPS is used to monitor network traffic, network identify, and stop any intrusions. IDPS systems can instantly inform users and stop any questionable activity (Mudzingwa & Agrawal, 2012).
- *Backups and Recovery:* To guarantee the availability and integrity of essential data, regularly back it up and evaluate the restoration procedure. Having trustworthy backups reduces the effect of data loss incidents or ransomware assaults (Razzaq et al., 2013).
- *Incident Plan:* Create and put into action a thorough response to an incident plan that specifies what should be done in the case of a cyber-attack. Procedures for locating, containing, minimizing, and regaining from security issues should be included in this plan.
- *Continuous Surveillance and Attack:* Set up reliable monitoring systems to quickly identify and address cyber threats. Utilize Security Information and Event Management (SIEM) systems, risk feed, and industry resources to stay up to speed with the most recent threat intelligence (Mirkovic et al., 2002).

22.3 NETWORK SECURITY

Network security is the umbrella term for the procedures, controls, and tools used to safeguard computer networks from unauthorized access, abuse, disruption, or

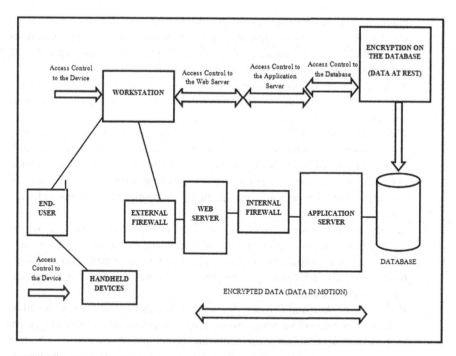

FIGURE 22.1 Flow of information in a network.

change. It includes a variety of tactics and guidelines intended to protect the confidentiality, precision, and accessibility of network data and resources (Shmeleva, 2020). The flow chart shown in Figure 22.1 demonstrates the flow of information in a network.

22.3.1 SECURE NETWORK ARCHITECTURE

The design and execution of security controls inside a network infrastructure to guard it against intrusions, crimes, and various other potential security risks is referred to as network security architecture. To secure the privacy, integrity, and accessibility of network assets and data, numerous security measures and components must be strategically positioned and configured (Perrig et al., 2017).

The following are some essential components and ideas for network security architecture.

1. *Perimeter Defense:* This method ensures putting security measures in place at the network's outer perimeter to manage and filter traffic that comes and goes. To create a secure barrier between internal and external networks, antivirus programs, intruder detection or intruder prevention systems, and virtual private networks (VPNs), are frequently employed (Perrig et al., 2017).
2. *Access Management:* Access by users to network resources should be controlled and managed by the network security architecture. Access control

based on role, authentication of users, permission, and account protocols, as well as strong password rules, may be used in this. Access control measures for particular network segments can also be implemented using virtual local area network (VLAN) and network segmentation.

3. *Secure Network Architecture:* Where necessary, safety protocols and encryption should be implemented as part of the network's security-conscious architecture.

4. *Threat Detection and Prevention:* The architecture of a network security system should incorporate safeguards against indicators of intrusions, malware, and viruses and to secure data and event management tools, intrusion detection or intrusion prevention systems, antivirus software are deployed. To address vulnerabilities, patch management, and routine security, upgrades are essential.

5. *Monitoring the Network and Logging:* To watch network activity, spot possible security events, and enable forensic analysis, extensive monitoring and logging methods should be in place. This can involve establishing network-based anomaly detection systems, monitoring systems, user activity, and logging network data.

6. *Protection of Data and Privacy:* Security of data and privacy issues should be addressed in network security design. This may ensure data loss management tools, secure data exchange protocols, and protection of sensitive data both in transit and at rest. Additionally, adherence to pertinent regulations and norms, such as the regulation known as the General Data Protection Regulation, should be considered (Liu et al., 2012).

7. *Incident Management and Disaster Recovery:* The network security system should include a well-specified incident handling plan and a disaster recovery strategy. Establishing protocols for quick responses to security issues, data backup and recovery, and continuity of operations planning are all included in this (Nyre-Yu et al., 2019).

It is critical to remember that the architecture for network security is a dynamic and continuous process. It is important to undertake regular security audits, vulnerability assessments, and penetration tests to find vulnerabilities and modify the architecture as necessary (Shah & Mehtre, 2014). A strong network security posture must also be maintained by keeping up with new threats.

22.3.2 VIRTUAL PRIVATE NETWORKS (VPNs)

Virtual private networks (VPNs) offer a private and secured communication route across an open network, such as the Internet, using safe and encrypted connections. A VPN encrypts the data that travel through the virtual tunnel it creates between the device being used by the user and a distant server. This makes sure that the information sent between the device being used by the user and the distant server is secure and secret (Solms & Van Niekerk, 2013).

22.4 DATA PROTECTION AND ENCRYPTION

To guarantee the confidentiality, integrity, and availability of data, data protection and encryption are essential in cybersecurity. Organizations can safeguard sensitive data, stick to data privacy laws, avoid data breaches, and improve overall security by employing robust encryption techniques (Hassan et al., 2020).

22.4.1 Data Protection Overview

In cybersecurity, data protection refers to the procedures, controls, and tools used to secure sensitive data against unauthorized access, use, disclosure, change, or destruction. It ensures the safeguarding of data while they are in use (when being processed), in transit, and at rest (while being stored). Data protection is crucial to safeguard confidentiality, integrity, and accessibility because data are a valuable asset for people, businesses, and governments. Data breaches may result in monetary losses, harm to a company's brand, problems with the law and regulations, and even individual harm (Wong, 2013).

The following are the cybersecurity approaches that are used to protect data:

- *Encryption:* Data encoding through the technique of encryption to shield it from unauthorized access. Data are protected using encryption to ensure that even if they are obstructed, they cannot be decoded without the key that encrypted it.
- *Access Controls:* Access controls means putting in place controls to limit the accessibility of data based on user permissions, roles, and authentication. Access management systems, two-factor authentication, and the use of strong passwords are all examples of this.
- *Firewalls:* Firewalls are protective barriers that keep an eye on and manage network traffic to block unauthorized access and stop malicious activity (Bellovin & Cheswick, 1994).
- *Intrusion Detection and Prevention Systems (IDPS):* Network traffic monitoring software or hardware that can identify and stop potential intrusion attempts.
- *Secure Data Storage:* Using access controls, encryption, and regular backups to store data securely to prevent loss and unauthorized access (Gupta et al., 2022).
- *Data Minimization:* Data minimization is a principle and practice in cybersecurity that aims to reduce the amount of personally identifiable information (PII) and sensitive data collected, processed, and stored by organizations. The goal is to limit the potential harm that can occur in the event of a data breach or unauthorized access.
- *Regular Updates and Patches:* Keeping the most recent security patches installed on programs, systems, and applications helps fix vulnerabilities and defend against known threats.
- *Security Awareness and Training:* Educating users and staff on cybersecurity best practices, including how to spot phishing emails, stay away from dubious websites, and use secure passwords (Schneider, 2013).

- *Incident Response and Data Breach Management:* Educating users and staff on cybersecurity best practices, including how to recognize phishing emails, avoid questionable websites, and use secure passwords (Ahmad et al., 2019).

22.4.2 DATA ENCRYPTION TECHNIQUES

The encryption of information is a key method for safeguarding confidential data by encoding it into cipher text, a meaningless form. Various encryption methods are used based on particular needs and use situations. The following are a few frequently employed data encryption methods:

1. *Symmetric Encryption:* The same key is utilized in symmetric encryption for both encryption and decryption. The secret key is shared by the data sender and recipient. Advanced Encryption Standard (AES) and Data Encryption Standard (DES) are two examples of symmetric encryption methods (Bellare et al., 1997).
2. *Asymmetric Encryption (Public Key Encryption):* A combination of mathematically associated keys—a publicly accessible key and a private key—are used in asymmetric encryption. While a private key is required for decryption, the publicly accessible key is utilized for encryption. The private key is kept exclusively by the receiver. Elliptic Curve Cryptography (ECC) and RSA (Rivest-Shamir-Adleman) are two popular asymmetric encryption techniques (Bellare & Rogaway, 1995).
3. *Hash Functions:* Hash functions are cryptographic methods used to verify data integrity, not encryption techniques. They take any input data and turn them into a fixed-size output (hash). Commonly, hash functions are employed to check the accuracy of transferred or stored data. Secure Hash Algorithm (SHA-256) and Message Digest Algorithm (MD5) are two examples of hash functions (Verma, Mishraet al., 2022a).
4. *Hybrid Encryption:* The benefits of both asymmetric and symmetric encryption are combined in hybrid encryption. This method employs symmetric encryption to encrypt the real data, and asymmetric encryption to encrypt the symmetric key using the public key of the recipient. The recipient receives both the data that have been encrypted and the symmetric key; they use their private key to decode the symmetric key before using it for decoding the data. This method combines the security of asymmetrical encryption with the effectiveness of symmetric encryption (Abe et al., 2007).
5. *Transport Layer Security (TLS)/Secure Sockets Layer (SSL):* Cryptographic technologies like TLS and SSL are used to protect communication over networks like the internet. Between clients and servers, they offer encrypting integrity of data and authentication. Combining both asymmetric and symmetric encryption techniques is what TLS and SSL do (Hoffman & Schlyter, 2012).

6. *Homomorphic Encryption:* An advanced encryption method called homomorphic encryption enables computations to be done directly on encrypted material without having to first decrypt it. It makes it possible to process data while they are encrypted, protecting security and privacy. Homomorphic encryption is useful for safe cloud computing and information processing while protecting privacy.

22.4.3 Secure Data Storage

In cybersecurity, secure data storage is the process of preventing unauthorized access, alteration, disclosure, or destruction of sensitive or secret information. To maintain the confidentiality, reliability, and accessibility of data during its lifespan, several security measures must be implemented such as:

- *Encryption:* Encryption is the process of transforming data into a form that is unreadable to unauthorized users. It ensures that even if unauthorized people access the data, they cannot be sure whether they would be able to decode or use it without the encryption keys (Verma, Mishra et al., 2022b).
- *Physical Security:* It is essential to safeguard the physical infrastructure that is used to store data. Measures including monitoring the environment, detection and suppression of fire systems, surveillance systems, and backup power supply are included in this.
- *Access Controls:* Strong access controls are put in place to make sure that only parties with permission have access to the stored data. This calls for the application of strategies like role-based access controls (RBAC), MFA, strong passwords, and the least privilege principle (Sandhu et al., 1994).

22.5 SOCIAL ENGINEERING AND HUMAN FACTORS

The practice of social engineering is a tactic used by criminals to trick people into doing things or giving out sensitive information. To acquire unauthorized use of networks, systems, or sensitive data, takes advantage of human psychology and trust. Attacks by social engineers can take place over a variety of channels, including calls, emails, instant messages, or in-person interactions (Shukla, Dhanda et al., 2023).

22.5.1 Phishing and Spear Phishing Attacks

Spear phishing and other social engineering attacks are intended to trick people into providing sensitive information like credit card details, passwords, or personal information. There are a few distinctions between the two, even if they both use deceitful methods.

22.5.1.1 Phishing Attacks

Phishing assaults are wide-ranging, arbitrary efforts to spread an extensive web and target a lot of people. Attackers pretend to be trustworthy organizations or people to send out bulk emails, texts, or voice calls. The messages frequently contain urgent or disturbing information to compel recipients to act right away. It attempts to frequently send victims to false websites that seem exactly like genuine ones and where they are asked to provide sensitive data. A sensitive piece of information that can be utilized for identity theft, financial crime, or unauthorized account access is what is sought after (Gupta et al., 2016).

22.5.1.2 Spear Phishing Attacks

Spear phishing attacks are highly specialized and geared to a particular person or business. Attackers obtain comprehensive information about their target victims, including their identities, occupations, social connections, and most recent activity. It attempts to frequently employ insider information or references to personalize and make them look more authentic in the e-mails or communications they deploy. Spear phishing scams may impersonate co-workers, bosses, partners in business, or other reliable sources that the victim is familiar with. Typically, the objective is to get access to sensitive data or networks, such as corporate usernames and passwords, proprietary information, or financial information (Halevi et al., 2015).

To protect against phishing and spear phishing attacks, here are some preventive measures:

1. *Use Email and Messages with Caution:* Carefully review any messages, emails, or other interactions. Look out for grammatical mistakes, strange sender addresses, unusual or unexpected requests, and mismatched URLs.
2. *Confirm the Source:* Before acting or sending sensitive information, independently confirm the sender's legitimacy through well-known and reliable routes, such as getting in touch with the company or individual.
3. *Refrain from Downloading Attachments or Clicking on Shady Links:* Do not open attachments or click on links from unauthorized or unconfirmed sources. Before clicking, mouse over links to see where they lead.
4. *Maintain Software Updates:* To make sure you have the most recent updates for security and defense against known vulnerabilities, regularly upgrade your computer's operating system, browsers, and security software.
5. *Use Strong, One-of-a-Kind Passwords:* Use strong, one-of-a-kind passwords for all of your accounts, and think about using a password management program to generate and store passwords securely.
6. *Multi-Factor Authentication:* Whenever possible, use multi-factor authentication to provide a further layer of protection to your online accounts and make it more difficult (Mehraj, 2021).
7. *Awareness of Safety:* Inform others about spear phishing and other phishing strategies, typical warning signs, and recommended online security procedures. Individuals who receive regular training will be better able to identify and react to questionable messages.

22.5.2 Employee Awareness and Training

Organizations must ensure that all employees are knowledgeable about cybersecurity, including social engineering. Several important factors for employee education and awareness include the following:

- Create an organized training program that encompasses every aspect of cybersecurity, especially social engineering, to establish a thorough training program. The programmer should be customized to the duties and responsibilities of employee's at all organizational levels.
- Hold training sessions frequently to strengthen knowledge and address new dangers. Employees should stay up-to-date on the most recent preventative measures and social engineering techniques through regular training, which is a continuous procedure in cybersecurity.
- Employees should be informed about various social engineering strategies, including phishing attacks, spear phishing, and pretesting. Give staff realistic illustrations, examples, and demonstrations to aid in their understanding of and ability to respond to these dangers (Anastas, 2012).
- Teach staff to recognize typical red flags that point to a possible social engineering attack. This includes emails from unknown senders, requests for confidential information made in a hurry, messages with type errors or poor grammar, unusual files or links, and inquiries for login passwords or financial information.
- Encourage staff members to independently confirm the legitimacy of requests before acting. To avoid miscommunication, emphasize the need of using reliable routes of communication, such as contacting well-known people either directly or by providing official contact information.
- Offer explicit instructions on security practices, such as developing robust and distinctive passwords, upgrading software and programming regularly, avoiding free Wi-Fi access for confidential activities, and safely discarding sensitive documents.
- Perform realistic phishing exercises to assess staff members' awareness of and reaction to phishing emails. These tests can aid in identifying knowledge gaps and offer chances for specialized instruction and reinforcement.
- Promote cybersecurity awareness across the entire organization. Encourage staff members to immediately report any suspicious activity or any social engineering attempts without concern for retaliation. Encourage and reward staff members who practice sound security procedures.
- Provide staff with tools, including security awareness brochures, best practice recommendations, and citations to reliable sources for more information. They can stay updated and make secure decisions as a result.
- Regularly upgrade training resources to reflect new dangers and accepted practices in the field. Since cybersecurity is a field that constantly changes, training materials should as well.

22.6 INCIDENT RESPONSE AND DIGITAL FORENSICS

For managing and analyzing cyber-attacks, two essential elements are incident response and digital forensics. They are crucial in the detection, containment, mitigation, and recovery of security incidents (Gurkok, 2013). Despite having a connection, they each focus on a different aspect of cybersecurity.

22.6.1 INCIDENT RESPONSE PLANNING

The organized method used by organizations to identify and manage security problems, including cyber-attacks, is known as the incident response (IR). It requires a concerted effort to detect security issues, respond to them, and recover from them promptly and effectively. The steps of IR planning are depicted in Figure 22.2.

22.6.2 DIGITAL FORENSICS PROCESS

Digital forensics involves obtaining, assessing, and archiving digital data in order to look into and recognize cyber-attacks or other digital crimes. It uses sophisticated techniques and tools to extract and analyze information from computers, networks, or storage media.

Digital forensics and incident response are both essential to cyber-attack investigations. While digital forensics offers the investigation methods and procedures used to identify the culprits, gather proof, and support legal proceedings, incident response concentrates on quickly reducing and recovering from an occurrence. These procedures complement one another to better manage security issues and boost cyber resilience. The key elements of digital forensics are shown in Figure 22.3.

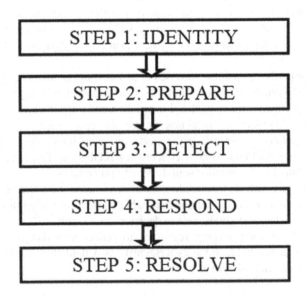

FIGURE 22.2   Steps of response planning.

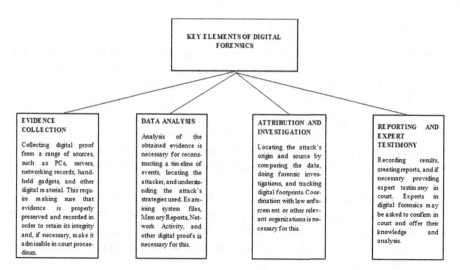

FIGURE 22.3 Key elements of digital forensics.

22.7 EMERGING TRENDS AND TECHNOLOGIES

Organizations can strengthen their resilience against changing threats, their detection and response capabilities, the security of new digital environments, and the adoption of proactive security practices by adopting emerging trends and technologies in cybersecurity. Security professionals may foresee future difficulties and successfully secure their systems, data, and users by being updated about new trends (Zou et al., 2016).

22.7.1 ARTIFICIAL INTELLIGENCE AND MACHINE LEARNING IN CYBERSECURITY

For proper identification and response to cyber-attacks, computers with artificial intelligence and machine learning serve important roles in cybersecurity. The following pointers show how AI and ML are used in cybersecurity:

- AI and ML algorithms are capable of evaluating vast amounts of data from numerous sources (such as network traffic and user activity) to spot trends that may lead to cyber threats. ML models may be trained to group and rank security events, making it possible to detect malicious activity more quickly and precisely.
- AI and ML can create a baseline user system and network behavior, enabling them to spot changes from the norm that can signify an attack on security or an insider threat. ML algorithms are capable of learning and adapting over time, increasing the precision with which malicious actions are detected.
- AI-based systems can use deep learning methods to identify and categorize new and constantly changing hazards, including those with polymorphic or hidden code, through the analysis of file characteristics, code behavior, or network

signatures. ML methods may be employed to develop proficient malware detection systems.

- By examining vulnerability tests, updating information, and historical data, ML algorithms can help in discovering flaws in networks, applications, or systems according to risk, possible impact, and exploitability.
- AI and ML algorithms may examine user conduct, including keystroke trends, mouse actions, and browsing preferences, to verify users and identify suspicious activities or unauthorized account takeover attempts. By examining past data and spotting patterns of fraudulent behavior, ML models can assist in spotting phishing attempts, social engineering attacks, and fraudulent transactions (Li & Liu, 2021).
- AI and ML algorithms are able to track network traffic and spot odd patterns or suspicious behavior that may point to network breaches or attacks. In order to identify and react to modern persistent hazards and zero-day assaults, ML models can examine network traffic, packet data, and logs (Kumar & Sinha, 2021).
- Attackers attempt to alter AI and ML models, areas of concern include different AI and evasion strategies. AI-based cybersecurity systems' resilience, interpretability, and security are still being researched and developed.

22.7.2 INTERNET OF THINGS (IoT) SECURITY

IoT security includes the policies and procedures put in place to safeguard the networks, linked devices, and information associated with the IoT ecosystem. IoT is a network of physical objects that are connected to the Internet and equipped with software, sensors, and connectivity. IoT devices can be many different things, including smart home appliances, commercial machinery, medical equipment, cars, and wearable technology (Verma, Mishra et al., 2021). IoT security is crucial because IoT devices are often vulnerable to cyber-attacks due to factors such as:

1. *Limited Supplies:* Implementing effective security measures is difficult since IoT devices frequently have low computational capacity, memory, and battery life (Verma, Mishra et al., 2023a).
2. *Diversified Ecosystem:* IoT devices are produced by several companies, each of which has its security requirements. They may also use multiple operating systems or firmware revisions, which results in inconsistent security procedures (Verma, Mishra et al., 2022c).
3. *Connectivity:* IoT devices use networks, such as Wi-Fi, cellular networks, or Bluetooth, to communicate with one another and with backend systems, hence expanding their potential attack surface and making them vulnerable to network-based attacks (Verma, Nagar et al., 2021).
4. *Data Security:* IoT devices send and gather sensitive data, including user behavior or personal data, which raises questions regarding data privacy and unauthorized access (Verma et al., 2020).

To address these security challenges, IoT security focuses on the following areas:

1. *Authentication procedures:* To guarantee that only authorized devices can interact with connected devices and systems, effective authentication procedures must be implemented (Verma, Mishra et al., 2023b).
2. *Data Encryption:* To prevent eavesdropping or interception, data are encrypted before they are transported among IoT gadgets, gateways, and backend systems.
3. *Firmware and Software Updates:* To address vulnerabilities and defend against known threats, IoT devices should be updated often with the newest security patches and firmware updates (Verma, Mishra et al., 2022d).
4. *Access Control:* Setting up procedures for limiting unauthorized utilization of IoT gadgets, systems, and sensitive data (Verma & Dhanda, 2023).
5. *Network Segmentation:* To isolate potential threats and lessen the impact of breaches, IoT networks should be divided from other crucial networks (Mhaskar et al., 2021).

22.7.3 CLOUD SECURITY CONSIDERATIONS

Cybersecurity considerations for cloud hosting environments include evaluating and putting protective measures in place for infrastructure, applications, and data. As businesses use cloud computing services more frequently, it is crucial to handle the following major issues:

- *Data Protection:* To prevent unauthorized access, it is necessary to make sure that information is secured both at rest and while it is being transmitted. Set up effective access controls to only allow authorized users to access data and assess and handle user permissions regularly. To stop data leaks or unauthorized access amongst tenants, isolate data from various customers or applications (Junaid et al., 2023).
- *Management of Identity and Access:* Use reliable IAM procedures to authenticate and grant access to individuals, apps, and services using cloud resources. Make use of MFA, to make user accounts more secure. Regularly evaluate and revoke access rights or privileges that are not necessary.
- *Secure Configuration:* Adhere to cloud provider best practices when configuring cloud infrastructure and services. Upgrade and fix cloud resources often to prevent known security flaws. To lessen the attack surface, disable or delete pointless services, features, or ports.
- *Vulnerability Management:* Implement a timely patching strategy and routinely analyze cloud services and applications for vulnerabilities. Perform regular penetration tests and assessments of vulnerability to find holes and fix them.
- *Network Security:* To provide safe access to the cloud environment, use VPNs and dedicated connections. Use segmentation of networks and firewalls to regulate traffic and set access restrictions for various cloud resources. Implement strong monitoring and recording capabilities to quickly identify and address security events.

- *Response to Incidents and Recording:* Create a cloud-specific incident response strategy with protocols for resolving data breaches, service interruptions, and unauthorized access.
- *Cloud Services Provider Security:* Evaluate the cloud service provider's security credentials to make sure they adhere to compliance standards and industry norms. Recognize the joint accountability model, which outlines the organizations or the cloud service provider's security duties.
- *Governance, and Compliance of Data:* Recognize the data security and confidentiality laws that apply to your company and make sure that you comply when using the cloud. Use data retention and lifecycle management techniques for efficient and secure data management (Basie & Solms, 2005).
- *Continuity of Operations and Disaster Recovery:* Set up backup and recovery procedures to guard against losing information and allow business continuity in the event of interruptions or accidents. Evaluate and verify disaster recovery plans frequently to make sure they are up-to-date and effective.
- *Workforce Awareness:* Inform staff members of recommended practices for cloud security, such as handling of data, authentication, and safe configuration. Encourage reporting of suspected security incidents or vulnerabilities and cultivate a culture of security awareness.

It is crucial to carry out a thorough risk assessment and customize safety precautions to the unique needs and dangers posed by the company's cloud apps and infrastructure.

22.8   LEGAL AND ETHICAL ASPECTS OF CYBERSECURITY

Legalization in cybersecurity offers a legal basis, lays out rights and obligations, makes investigations and actions easier, safeguards personal information and privacy, promotes international collaboration, aids incident response, and raises public knowledge of cybersecurity issues. Organizations and people can work in a secure safe environment by addressing the legal aspects of cybersecurity.

22.8.1   CYBERSECURITY LAWS AND REGULATIONS

Different nations have different cybersecurity rules and regulations, which are always changing to address the escalating cyber threats. Here are some noteworthy cybersecurity laws and rules from various countries throughout the world.

- *General Data Protection Regulation (GDPR):* The European Union (EU) and the European Economic Area (EEA) have enacted the GDPR, a comprehensive data protection law. It regulates the acquisition, storage, use, and exchange of private information and imposes strong obligations on organizations, including heightened privacy protections for individuals and required data breach notifications.
- *California Consumer Privacy Act (CCPA):* This United States privacy law gives customers specific rights regarding the personal information that companies

have about them. Businesses must be transparent about how they gather and use customer data, and customers can choose not to have their personal information sold.

- *Health Insurance Portability and Accountability Act (HIPAA):* HIPAA is a federal law that governs the privacy and security of personally identifiable health information in the United States. It outlines the security criteria for safeguarding electronic health information and is applicable to hospitals.
- *Payment Card Industry Data Security Standard (PCI DSS):* PCI DSS is a global security standard that applies to organizations that handle credit cardholder data. It outlines requirements for the secure handling, storage, and transmission of cardholder data to prevent credit card fraud and data breaches (Luiijf et al., 2013).
- *Network and Information Security Directive (NIS Directive):* The NIS Directive is an EU-wide legislation aimed at improving the cybersecurity capabilities of critical infrastructure operators and digital service providers. It mandates the implementation of security measures, incident reporting, and cooperation between member states (Drivas et al., 2020).
- *The Republic of China's Cybersecurity Law:* This establishes standards for the privacy, localization, and security of information that is vital. It also specifies network operators' responsibilities and places limitations on the export of specific data from China.
- *China's Personal Information Protection Law (PIPL):* On November 1, 2021, China's PIPL, an expansive data protection law, went into force. It lays down guidelines for the collection, handling, and safety of personal data and puts requirements on organizations about the agreement, the practice of localization of data, and worldwide data transfers.
- *Data Protection Act:* The GDPR's rules are incorporated into UK law through the legislation known as the Data Protection Act 2018, which is the country's main data protection statute. It sets down requirements for businesses managing personal data, supervises the handling of personal data, and gives individuals access to data protection rights (Purtova, 2018).
- *Australian Privacy Act of 1988:* The Australian Privacy Act governs how the Australian government and private sector organizations handle personal information. It outlines the criteria for data security, how to report security breaches, and what people can do with their data (Paltiel et al., 2023).
- *Brazil's General Data Protection Law:* This is a data protection law that controls how personal data are processed there. It creates requirements for organizations, gives individuals specific rights over personal data, and imposes penalties for noncompliance.

22.8.2 Ethical Hacking and Responsible Disclosure

Two crucial cybersecurity practices—ethical hacking and responsible disclosure—aim to find and fix system vulnerabilities while also responsibly disclosing them to the appropriate people. Ethical hacking helps to assist organizations in strengthening their security by locating and resolving vulnerabilities before they may be used maliciously, whereas responsible disclosure helps organizations proactively address vulnerabilities, stop possible attacks, and safeguard their users (Rani, Bhambri et al., 2023).

22.8.2.1 Ethical Hacking

White-hat hacking and ethical hacking are the terms used to describe the authorized and legal practice of purposefully finding weaknesses and vulnerabilities in networks, computers, or applications. The safety posture of a company's systems and networks is evaluated by ethical hackers, often known as security analysts. Ethical hacking aims to assist organizations to strengthen their security defenses by proactively identifying vulnerabilities before hostile hackers take advantage of them (Farsole et al., 2010). The methodology used by ethical hackers is systematic and includes several strategies, including scanning for vulnerabilities, network surveillance, and the use of social engineering. They seek to replicate actual assaults to find security holes and offer suggestions for fixing them.

22.8.2.2 Responsible Disclosure

The act of reporting security flaws or vulnerabilities to the impacted organization in an ethical and coordinated manner is known as responsible disclosure or responsible vulnerability disclosure. It involves professional hackers or security experts informing the organization's security staff or designated contact with the specifics of the vulnerability.

The process of responsible disclosure typically involves the following steps:

- *Discovery:* A computer system, connection, or application vulnerability or weakness is found by a security researcher.
- *Verification:* In order to make sure the vulnerability is real and exploitable; the researcher checks and confirms it.
- *Notification:* The researcher alerts the security team of the impacted organization or a specified contact about the found vulnerability. This notification often contains comprehensive details about the susceptibility, its consequences, and how to exploit it.
- *Collaboration:* To recognize and solve the vulnerability, the organization and the person conducting the study work together. This might entail increased communication, the exchange of information, and aiding the organization in creating fixes or mitigations.
- *Timing of Disclosure:* The scholar and the organization decide on a suitable time range for making the vulnerability public. This gives the company enough time to create and implement patches or reductions before the security flaw is made public.

The goal of responsible disclosure is to strike a balance between the necessity for quick vulnerability correction and the need to give organizations enough time to deal with the problem before it becomes well-known.

22.8.3 PRIVACY AND DATA PROTECTION

Cybersecurity must include safeguards for data and privacy because they protect personal information and guarantee that people's privacy rights are upheld. Here are a few definitions of confidentiality and security of data:

- *Privacy:* A person's right to privacy relates to their ability to manage their private information and choose how it is gathered, utilized, disclosed, and shared. Privacy includes the freedom from intrusive monitoring and the right to preserve certain information. Due to the extensive gathering, use, and sharing of personally identifiable information in numerous online activities in the age of technology, privacy concerns exist.
- *Data Protection:* Data protection means the procedures and policies used to secure against unauthorized access, disclosure, change, or destruction of personal information. It includes the organizational, technical, and legal frameworks created to guarantee the privacy, accuracy, and accessibility of personal data.

Building trust with people and clients requires privacy and data protection. Companies that place a high priority on data security and privacy not only adhere to legal requirements but also show a dedication to protecting personal data and upholding the privacy rights of individuals in the digital sphere (Rani, Chauhan et al., 2021).

22.9 FUTURE CHALLENGES AND RECOMMENDATIONS

Due to the rapidly changing nature of technology, the complexity of threats, and the ongoing need for adaptation and response, cybersecurity faces many difficulties. Some of the major challenges and the methods and recommendations to overcome these challenges are described below.

22.9.1 CYBERSECURITY SKILLS GAP

The term "cybersecurity skill gap" describes the disparity between the number of trained and skilled people working in the sector and the rising demand for their services. It draws attention to the discrepancy between the supply of cybersecurity experts and the growing demand for their expertise to counter cyber-attacks. The cybersecurity skill gap has arisen due to several factors:

- *Rapidly Changing Threat Field:* New attack vectors, tactics, and technologies are continuously developing in the rapidly changing cybersecurity field. Continuous learning and skill updating are necessary to keep up with these changes, which can be difficult for both people as well as educational institutions.
- *Rising Cybersecurity Incidents:* Organizations from a variety of industries are beginning to understand the significance of effective cybersecurity measures as a result of the growth of cyber-attacks and incidents. As a result, there is a great

demand for cybersecurity experts who can successfully safeguard networks, systems, and data (Aldawood & Skinner, 2018).

- *Lack of Specialized Training and Education:* The field of cybersecurity is highly specialized and calls for a specific set of abilities. The cybersecurity landscape is changing quickly, but traditional educational systems have lagged in adapting, leaving a gap between the knowledge taught in the classroom and the knowledge required in the workplace.
- *Lack of Knowledge and Interest:* Many people are unaware of the possibilities and career paths available in cybersecurity. This ignorance causes a small talent pool to enter the field, widening the skill disparity.
- *Rivalry for Skilled Workers:* Due to the strong demand for cybersecurity specialists, there is fierce rivalry among businesses to find and keep qualified workers. As businesses struggle to fill cybersecurity positions with competent individuals, this rivalry emphasizes the skill gap even more.

22.9.2 Threat Intelligence and Information Sharing

Two key elements of cybersecurity are threat intelligence and information sharing, which allow organizations to stay aware of potential threats and take preventive steps to safeguard their systems and data. To improve cybersecurity postures and enable a proactive strategy for identifying and resolving cyber threats, threat intelligence and information sharing are essential. The important aspects of threat intelligence and information sharing are described below.

22.9.3 Threat Intelligence

Threat intelligence is the study of cyber threats, malicious actors, and their motivations, tactics, methods, and procedures as well as signs of compromise. Data from several sources, including cybersecurity records, network activity, open-source intelligence (OSINT), as well as specialized threat feeds, must be gathered and analyzed (Thakur et al., 2015).

The main objectives of threat intelligence include:

1. Recognizing possible risks and weaknesses before they are used against you and taking proactive steps to strengthen your defenses.
2. Situational awareness is the ability to assess the dangerous environment, including new threats, evolving attack methods, and risks unique to a given industry, in order to deploy resources wisely and make well-informed judgments.
3. Providing relevant knowledge to incident response teams so they may swiftly investigate and address security incidents is known as incident response and mitigation. Threat information can assist in determining the attack's nature, locating affected systems, and putting effective mitigation measures into place.
4. Vulnerability management enables organizations to concentrate on the most important risks and decrease the attack surface by prioritizing and fixing vulnerabilities based on insights from threat information.

22.9.4 INFORMATION SHARING

Cybersecurity information sharing is the transfer of intelligence on threats, best practices, and security-related data across businesses, governmental entities, and security communities (Khang, Muthmainnah et al., 2023). By utilizing the collective wisdom and experiences of numerous institutions, it seeks to promote cooperation, strengthen the collective defense, and enhance overall security posture.

Key aspects of information sharing include:

- Sharing security indicators and signatures such as Internet Protocol (IP) addresses, domains, worm hash values, and other digital artifacts enables organizations to spot and stop harmful activity occurring throughout their systems and networks.
- By exchanging reports of incidents, lessons learned, and post-event analysis, organizations can learn from one another's mistakes, enhance their incident response skills, and gain a better understanding of the risks that are always emerging.
- Organizations can improve their security posture by exchanging efficient security practices, mitigation approaches, and defensive measures that are based on practical knowledge and tried-and-true methodologies.
- By fostering a collective defense strategy, the collaboration between industry peers, governmental organizations, and security organizations makes it possible to identify and mitigate threats that have the potential to harm numerous entities.
- Platforms for information sharing: Several platforms, including information sharing and analysis centers (ISACs), computer emergency response teams (CERTs), and industry-specific organizations, make it possible to share information and foster collaboration.

22.9.5 BEST PRACTICES AND RECOMMENDATIONS

Cybersecurity best practices and guidelines cover an extensive variety of precautions meant to shield networks, information, and systems from potential attackers. Here are some crucial actions to think about:

1. *Establish Strict Access Controls:* Make sure that only authorized individuals may access important systems and data by enforcing strong password policies, implementing multifactor authorization, and using least privilege principles (Etigowni et al., 2016).
2. *Update and Patch Systems Frequently:* Always use the most recent security updates and patches for all programs, operating systems, and firmware. Attackers may take advantage of flaws in out-of-date software.
3. *Use Intrusion Detection and Prevention Systems and Firewalls:* To manage network traffic that comes and goes, install firewalls. Use systems for the detection and prevention of intrusions to spot prospective threats and take appropriate action.

4. *Conduct Periodic Security Assessments:* To find and fix vulnerabilities in the systems and networks, conduct frequent safety examinations, vulnerability searches, and penetration tests.

5. *Train and Educate Employees:* Train staff members thoroughly about cybersecurity awareness. Teach children how to remain secure while using online platforms, how to report security problems, and about common risks like phishing, social engineering, and malware.

6. *Encrypt Critical Data:* Use encryption to safeguard sensitive data both at rest and during transit. Data are encrypted to make sure that even if they are intercepted or taken away, no one else will be able to access or use them (Goyal et al., 2021).

7. *Backup and Recovery from Disasters:* Create a solid disaster recovery plan and regularly back up important data. In the event of a system failure or data loss, test the backups to make sure the data can be successfully restored.

8. *Monitor and Analyze Logs:* Set up a central logging system to gather and examine logs from different systems and network gadgets. This facilitates the quick investigation of security issues and the detection of anomalies.

9. *Put into Practice a Powerful Incident Response Strategy:* Create a thorough incident response strategy that details the actions to be done in the case of a security problem. This covers prevention, eradication, healing, and taking away lessons.

10. *Update and Review Security Policies:* Processes and guidelines are reviewed regularly to consider changing business needs and the threat environment. Ensure that staff members are informed of these policies and follow them (Cram et al., 2017).

Keep in mind that maintaining cybersecurity needs regular monitoring, adaptation, and development. It is essential to adapt these best practices to your unique organizational needs and maintain a constant awareness of the changing threat environment.

22.10 CONCLUSION

In today's world, cybersecurity is of greatest importance. People and organizations must prioritize the security of the data, systems, and networks due to the rising dependence on digital technology and the advanced nature of cyber threats. Organizations may secure sensitive information, avoid financial losses, maintain their reputation, guarantee business continuity, and fight against copyright theft by putting cybersecurity safeguards in place. Additionally, maintaining cybersecurity is essential for protecting individual privacy, preventing cybercrime, following legislation, and adjusting to the changing threat landscape (Khang, Shah et al., 2023).

Investment in cybersecurity measures is a proactive move that assists in preventing cyber events, detecting threats in a timely way, and effectively responding to minimize losses. To deal with growing risks, a combination of scientific and technical solutions, best practices, employee knowledge, and constant adaptability is needed. Eventually, cybersecurity is a collective responsibility that demands cooperation between people, groups, governments, and the whole cybersecurity sector. One can make the internet a safer place and safeguard data availability, confidentiality, and integrity in the face of changing cyber threats (Khang, Kali et al., 2023).

REFERENCES

Abe M., R. Gennaro, and K. Kurosawa, "Tag-KEM/DEM: A new framework for hybrid encryption." *Journal of Cryptology*, vol. 21, no. 1, pp. 97–130, 2007, doi: 10.1007/s00145-007-9010-22.

Ahmad A., K. C. Desouza, S. B. Maynard, H. Naseer, and R. L. Baskerville, "How integration of cyber security management and incident response enables organizational learning." *Journal of the Association for Information Science and Technology*, vol. 71, no. 8, pp. 939–953, 2019, doi: 10.1002/asi.24311.

Aldawood H. and G. Skinner, "Educating and raising awareness on cyber security social engineering: A literature review." *2018 IEEE International Conference on Teaching, Assessment, and Learning for Engineering (TALE)*, 2018, doi: 10.1109/tale.2018.8615162.

Anastas J. W., "The dissertation." *Doctoral Education in Social Work*, pp. 127–161, 2012, doi: 10.1093/acprof:oso/9780195378061.003.0030.

Arun R. K. P. and S. Selvakumar, "Distributed Denial-of-Service (DDoS) threat in collaborative environment – A survey on DDoS attack tools and traceback mechanisms." 2009 IEEE International Advance Computing Conference, 2009, doi: 10.1109/iadcc.2009.4809199.

Azizi N. and O. Haass, "Cybersecurity Issues and Challenges." *Handbook of Research on Cybersecurity Issues and Challenges for Business and FinTech Applications*, pp. 21–48, 2022, doi: 10.4018/978-1-6684-5284-4.ch002.

Basie S. and V. Solms, "Information Security Governance – Compliance management vs operational management." *Computers & Security*, vol. 24, no. 6, pp. 443–447, 2005, doi: 10.1016/j.cose.2005.07.003.

Bellare M. and P. Rogaway, "Optimal asymmetric encryption." *Advances in Cryptology — EUROCRYPT*, pp. 92–111, 1995, doi: 10.1007/bfb0053428.

Bellare M., A. Desai, E. Jokipii, and P. Rogaway, "A concrete security treatment of symmetric encryption." *Proceedings 38th Annual Symposium on Foundations of Computer Science*, 1997. doi: 10.1109/sfcs.1997.646128.

Bellovin S. and W. Cheswick, "Network firewalls." *IEEE Communications Magazine*, vol. 32, no. 9, pp. 50–57, 1994, doi: 10.1109/35.312843.

Conti M., N. Dragoni, and V. Lesyk, "A survey of man in the middle attacks." *IEEE Communications Surveys & Tutorials*, vol. 18, no. 3, pp. 2027–2051, 2016, doi: 10.1109/comst.2016.2548426.

Craigen D., N. Diakun-Thibault, and R. Purse, "Defining cybersecurity." *Technology Innovation Management Review*, vol. 4, no. 10, pp. 13–21, 2014, doi: 10.22215/time review/835.

Cram W. A., J. G. Proudfoot, and J. D'Arcy, "Organizational information security policies: A review and research framework." *European Journal of Information Systems*, vol. 26, no. 6, pp. 605–641, 2017, doi: 10.1057/s41303-017-0059-9.

Drivas G., A. Chatzopoulou, L. Maglaras, C. Lambrinoudakis, A. Cook, and H. Janicke, "A NIS Directive Compliant Cybersecurity Maturity Assessment Framework." *2020 IEEE 44th Annual Computers, Software, and Applications Conference (COMPSAC)*, 2020, doi: 10.1109/compsac48688.2020.00-20.

Etigowni S., D. (Jing) Tian, G. Hernandez, S. Zonouz, and K. Butler, "CPAC." *Proceedings of the 32nd Annual Conference on Computer Security Applications*, 2016, doi: 10.1145/2991079.2991126.

Farsole A. A., A. G. Kashikar, and A. Zunzunwala, "Ethical hacking." *International Journal of Computer Applications*, vol. 1, no. 10, pp. 14–20, 2010, doi: 10.5120/229-380.

Goyal D., A. K. Gupta, and P. Mathur, "Big data over cloud, its infrastructure & security." *Recent Advances in Computer Science and Communications*, vol. 14, no. 5, pp. 1506–1507, 2021, doi: 10.2174/2666255581405210129162256.

Gupta B. B., A. Tewari, A. K. Jain, and D. P. Agrawal, "Fighting against phishing attacks: State of the art and future challenges." *Neural Computing and Applications*, vol. 28, no. 12, pp. 3629–3654, 2016, doi: 10.1007/s00521-016-2275-y.

Gupta I., A. K. Singh, C.-N. Lee, and R. Buyya, "Secure data storage and sharing techniques for data protection in cloud environments: A systematic review, analysis, and future directions." *IEEE Access*, vol. 10, pp. 71247–71277, 2022, doi: 10.1109/access.2022.3188110.

Gurkok C., "Cyber Forensics and Incident Response." *Computer and Information Security Handbook*, pp. 601–621, 2013, doi: 10.1016/b978-0-12-394397-2.00034-9.

Halevi T., N. Memon, and O. Nov, "Spear-phishing in the wild: A real-world study of personality, phishing self-efficacy and vulnerability to spear-phishing attacks." *SSRN Electronic Journal*, 2015, doi: 10.2139/ssrn.2544742.

Hassan M., C. Jincai, A. Iftekhar, and X. Cui, "Future of the internet of things emerging with blockchain and smart contracts." *International Journal of Advanced Computer Science and Applications*, vol. 11, no. 6, 2020, doi: 10.14569/ijacsa.2020.0110676.

Hoffman P. and J. Schlyter, The DNS-Based Authentication of Named Entities (DANE) Transport Layer Security (TLS) Protocol: TLSA. 2012, doi: 10.17487/rfc6698.

Junaid A., A. Nawaz, M. F. Usmani, R. Verma, and N. Dhanda, "Analyzing the performance of a DAPP using blockchain 3.0." *2023 13th International Conference on Cloud Computing, Data Science & Engineering (Confluence)*, 2023, doi: 10.1109/confluence56041.2023.10048887.

Khang A., C. R. Kali, S. K. Satapathy, A. Kumar, S. R. Das, and M. R. Panda, "Enabling the future of manufacturing: Integration of robotics and IoT to smart factory infrastructure in industry 4.0." *AI-Based Technologies and Applications in the Era of the Metaverse* (1st Ed.) (2023) (pp. 25–50). IGI Global Press. https://doi.org/10.4018/978-1-6684-8851-5.ch002

Khang A., M. Muthmainnah, P. M. I. Seraj, A. Al Yakin, A. J. Obaid, and M. R. Panda, "AI-aided teaching model for the education 5.0 ecosystem." *AI-Based Technologies and Applications in the Era of the Metaverse* (1st Ed.) (2023) (pp. 83–104). IGI Global Press. https://doi.org/10.4018/978-1-6684-8851-5.ch004

Khang A., V. Hahanov, G. L. Abbas, V. A. Hajimahmud, " Cyber-physical-social system and incident management," *AI-Centric Smart City Ecosystems: Technologies, Design and Implementation* (1st Ed.), vol. 7 (p. 12), (2022). CRC Press. https://doi.org/10.1201/9781003252542-2

Khang A., V. Shah, and S. Rani, *AI-Based Technologies and Applications in the Era of the Metaverse* (1st Ed.) (2023). IGI Global Press. https://doi.org/10.4018/978-1-6684-8851-5

Kumar V. and D. Sinha, "A robust intelligent zero-day cyber-attack detection technique." *Complex & Intelligent Systems*, vol. 7, no. 5, pp. 2211–2234, 2021, doi: 10.1007/s40747-021-00396-9.

Leskovec J., "Social media analytics." *Proceedings of the 20th International Conference Companion on World Wide Web*, 2012, doi: 10.1145/1963192.1963309.

Li Y. and Q. Liu, "A comprehensive review study of cyber-attacks and cyber security; Emerging trends and recent developments." *Energy Reports*, vol. 7, pp. 8176–8186, 2021, doi: 10.1016/j.egyr.2021.08.126.

Liu J., Y. Xiao, S. Li, W. Liang, and C. L. P. Chen, "Cyber security and privacy issues in smart grids." *IEEE Communications Surveys & Tutorials*, vol. 14, no. 4, pp. 981–997, 2012, doi: 10.1109/surv.2011.122111.00145.

Luiijf E., K. Besseling, and P. D. Graaf, "Nineteen national cyber security strategies." *International Journal of Critical Infrastructures*, vol. 9, no. 1, p. 3, 2013, doi: 10.1504/ijcis.2013.051608.

Mehraj H., "Protection motivation theory using multi-factor authentication for providing security over social networking sites." *Pattern Recognition Letters*, vol. 152, pp. 218–224, 2021, doi: 10.1016/j.patrec.2021.10.002.

Mhaskar N., M. Alabbad, and R. Khedri, "A formal approach to network segmentation." *Computers & Security*, vol. 103, p. 102162, 2021, doi: 10.1016/j.cose.2020.102162

Mirkovic J., G. Prier, and P. Reiher, "Attacking DDoS at the source." *10th IEEE International Conference on Network Protocols, Proceedings*, 2002. doi: 10.1109/icnp.2002.1181418

Mohd M. A., M. Yunus, Z. Brohan, N. M. Nawi, E. S. Mat Surin, N. Azwani Md Najib, and C. W. Liang, "Review of SQL injection: problems and prevention." *JOIV: International Journal on Informatics Visualization*, vol. 2, no. 3, p. 215, 2018, doi: 10.30630/joiv.2.3-2.144.

Mudzingwa D. and R. Agrawal, "A study of methodologies used in intrusion detection and prevention systems (IDPS)." *2012 Proceedings of IEEE Southeastcon*, 2012, doi: 10.1109/secon.2012.6197080.

Nawir M., A. Amir, N. Yaakob, and O. B. Lynn, "Internet of Things (IoT): Taxonomy of security attacks." *2016 3rd International Conference on Electronic Design (ICED)*, 2016, doi: 10.1109/iced.2016.7804660.

Nyre-Yu M., R. S. Gutzwiller, and B. S. Caldwell, "Observing cyber security incident response: qualitative themes from field research." *Proceedings of the Human Factors and Ergonomics Society Annual Meeting*, vol. 63, no. 1, pp. 437–441, 2019, doi: 10.1177/1071181319631016.

Paltiel M., M. Taylor, and A. Newson, "Protection of genomic data and the Australian Privacy Act: when are genomic data 'personal information'?" *International Data Privacy Law*, vol. 13, no. 1, pp. 47–62, 2023, doi: 10.1093/idpl/ipad002.

Perrig A., P. Szalachowski, R. M. Reischuk, and L. Chuat, "The SCION architecture." *Information Security and Cryptography*, pp. 17–42, 2017, doi: 10.1007/978-3-319-67080-5_2.

Purtova N., "The law of everything. Broad concept of personal data and future of EU data protection law." *Law, Innovation and Technology*, vol. 10, no. 1, pp. 40–81, 2018, doi: 10.1080/17579961.2018.1452176.

Rani S., M. Chauhan, A. Kataria, and A. Khang, "IoT equipped intelligent distributed framework for smart healthcare systems." *Computer Science, Networking and Internet Architecture* (Eds.). Vol. 2, p. 30, 2021. https://doi.org/10.48550/arXiv.2110.04997

Rani S., P. Bhambri, A. Kataria, A. Khang, and A. K. Sivaraman, *Big Data, Cloud Computing and IoT: Tools and Applications* (1st Ed.), 2023. Chapman and Hall/CRC. https://doi.org/10.1201/9781003298335

Razzaq A., A. Hur, H. F. Ahmad, and M. Masood, "Cyber security: Threats, reasons, challenges, methodologies and state of the art solutions for industrial applications." *2013 IEEE Eleventh International Symposium on Autonomous Decentralized Systems (ISADS)*, 2013, doi: 10.1109/isads.2013.6513420.

Sandhu R., E. Coyne, H. Feinstein, and C. Youman, "Role-based access control: a multi-dimensional view." *Tenth Annual Computer Security Applications Conference*, 1994. doi: 10.1109/csac.1994.367293.

Schatz D., R. Bashroush, and J. Wall, "Towards a more representative definition of cyber security." *Journal of Digital Forensics, Security and Law*, 2017, doi: 10.15394/jdfsl.2017.1476.

Schneider F. B., "Cybersecurity education in universities." *IEEE Security & Privacy*, vol. 11, no. 4, 2013. DOI: 10.1109/MSP.2013.84.

Shah S. and B. M. Mehtre, "An overview of vulnerability assessment and penetration testing techniques." *Journal of Computer Virology and Hacking Techniques*, vol. 11, no. 1, pp. 27–49, 2014, doi: 10.1007/s11416-014-0231-22.

Sharma P., D. Doshi, and M. M. Prajapati, "Cybercrime: Internal security threat." *2016 International Conference on ICT in Business Industry & Government (ICTBIG)*, 2016, doi: 10.1109/ictbig.2016.7892727.

Shmeleva A. N., "Telecommunication networks security as a part of cybersecurity." *2020 International Conference Quality Management, Transport and Information Security, Information Technologies (IT&QM&IS)*, 2020, doi: 10.1109/itqmis51053.2020.9322907.

Shukla U., N. Dhanda, and R. Verma, Augmented Reality Product Showcase E-commerce Application (February 16, 2023). Available at SSRN: https://ssrn.com/abstract=4361 319 or http://d22.doi.org/10.2139/ssrn.4361319.

Solms, V. R. and J. Van Niekerk, "From information security to cyber security." *Computers & Security*, vol. 38, pp. 97–102, 2013, doi: 10.1016/j.cose.2013.04.004.

Stewart C. E., A. M. Vasu, and E. Keller, "CommunityGuard." *Proceedings of the ACM International Workshop on Security in Software Defined Networks & Network Function Virtualization*, 2017, doi: 10.1145/3040992.3040997.

Thakur K., M. Qiu, K. Gai, and M. L. Ali, "An investigation on cyber security threats and security models." *2015 IEEE 2nd International Conference on Cyber Security and Cloud Computing*, 2015, doi: 10.1109/cscloud.2015.71.

Verma R. and N. Dhanda, "Application of supply chain management in blockchain and IoT – A generic use case." *2023 13th International Conference on Cloud Computing, Data Science & Engineering (Confluence)*, 2023, doi: 10.1109/confluence56041.2023.10048815.

Verma, R., N. Dhanda, and V. Nagar, "Addressing the issues & challenges of internet of things using blockchain technology." *International Journal of Advanced Science and Technology*, vol. 29, no. 5, pp. 10074–10082, 2020. Retrieved from http://sersc.org/journals/inde22.php/IJAST/article/view/19491.

Verma, R., N. Dhanda, and V. Nagar, "Security concerns in IoT systems and its blockchain solutions." *Cyzber Intelligence and Information Retrieval*, pp. 485–495, 2021, doi: 10.1007/978-981-16-4284-5_42.

Verma, R., N. Dhanda, and V. Nagar, "Enhancing & optimizing security of IoT systems using different components of industry 4.0." *International Journal of Engineering Trends and Technology*, vol. 70, no. 7, pp. 147–157, 2022a. doi:10.14445/22315381/ijett-v70i7p216.

Verma R., N. Dhanda, and V. Nagar, "Application of truffle suite in a blockchain environment." *Proceedings of Third International Conference on Computing, Communications, and Cyber-Security*, pp. 693–702, 2022b, doi: 10.1007/978-981-19-1142-2_54.

Verma R., N. Dhanda, and V. Nagar, "Enhancing security with in-depth analysis of brute-force attack on secure hashing algorithms." *Proceedings of Trends in Electronics and Health Informatics*, pp. 513–522, 2022c, doi: 10.1007/978-981-16-8826-3_44.

Verma R., N. Dhanda, and V. Nagar, "Towards a secured IoT communication: A blockchain implementation through APIs." *Proceedings of Third International Conference on*

Computing, Communications, and Cyber-Security, pp. 681–692, 2022d, doi: 10.1007/ 978-981-19-1142-2_53.

Verma, R., N. Dhanda, and V. Nagar, "Analysing the security aspects of IoT using blockchain and cryptographic algorithms." *International Journal on Recent and Innovation Trends in Computing and Communication*, vol. 11, no. 1s, pp. 13–22. 2023a. doi: 10.17762/ ijritcc.v11i1s.5990.

Verma, R., N. Dhanda, V. Nagar, and M. Dhanda, "Towards an efficient IoT system by integrating blockchain in IoT."*Journal of Theoretical and Applied Information Technology*, vol. 101, no. 5, 2023b. https://www.jatit.org/volumes/Vol101N o5/4Vol101No5.pdf

Verma R., P. K. Mishra, V. Nagar, and S. Mahapatra, "Internet of things and smart homes: A review." Wireless Sensor Networks and the Internet of Things, pp. 111–128, 2021, doi: 10.1201/9781003131229-9.

Verma R., V. Nagar, and S. Mahapatra, "Introduction to supervised learning." *Data Analytics in Bioinformatics*, pp. 1–34, 2021, doi: 10.1002/9781119785620.ch1.

Wong R., "Cybersecurity directive 2013." *Data Security Breaches and Privacy in Europe,* pp. 39–42, 2013, doi: 10.1007/978-1-4471-5586-7_9.

Wu D., "A fog computing-based framework for process monitoring and prognosis in cyber-manufacturing." *Journal of Manufacturing Systems*, vol. 43, pp. 25–34, 2017, doi: 10.1016/j.jmsy.2017.02.011.

Zou, Y., J. Zhu, X. Wang, and L. Hanzo, "A survey on wireless security: Technical challenges, recent advances, and future trends." *Proceedings of the IEEE*, vol. 104, no. 9, pp. 1727– 1765, 2016, doi: 10.1109/jproc.2016.2558521.

Index

Printed in the United States
by Baker & Taylor Publisher Services

Printed in the United States
by Baker & Taylor Publisher Services